How To Prepare For The

Comprehensive Postal Exam

Test Battery Series 460/470: For Eight Job Positions

How To Prepare For The

Comprehensive Postal Exam

Test Battery Series 460/470: For Eight Job Positions

By

Philip Barkus
Director, Training for Results

Former Director of Training
New York City Housing Authority

All inquiries should be addressed to:
Philip Barkus
c/o Barron's Educational Series, Inc.
250 Wireless Boulevard
Hauppauge, New York 11788

Library of Congress Cataloging-in-Publication Data

Barkus, Philip.
Barron's how to prepare for the comprehensive U.S. Postal Service examination / by Philip Barkus.
p. cm.
ISBN 0-8120-9397-6
1. Postal service—United States—Examinations, questions, etc. I. Title.
HE6499.B288 1995
383'.1'076—dc20 95-18410
CIP

PRINTED IN THE UNITED STATES OF AMERICA
3456 100 698765

CONTENTS

Learning the Special Techniques

Test Yourself

OVERVIEW

Introduction

WHAT THIS BOOK IS ALL ABOUT

This book has its origin in a series of exam preparation courses attended by several thousand candidates for the most recent Postal Service tests. The courses taught these men and women techniques for taking the test that were based on years of successful test preparation experience. Special research was done to develop the best methods for taking this examination. The end result—success on the actual test—has been the final and best way known to show the value of these methods and the course.

Now, all of this knowledge has been combined with *personal* experiences taking the new U.S. Postal Service Test Battery Series 460/470. This *one* test is used to fill *all* these eight entry-level positions: Postal Clerk, city/rural Carrier, Machine Distribution Clerk, Mail Handler, Mail Processor, Mark-Up Clerk, and Flat-Sorting Machine Operator. The new exam selects portions of the separate exams formerly given for these titles. They are: Address Checking, Memory for Addresses, Number Series, and Following Oral Directions.

Accordingly, this one book combines all of the invaluable test strategies and techniques, drills, self-study exercises, practice tests, and visual aids formerly contained in separate books.

Use this book at home to help you pass—and *pass high*—when you take your examination. It will provide practical information on the following:

- How and when to apply.
- Eligibility requirements.
- Why and what you should study.
- What the U.S. Postal Service Battery Test Series 460/470* is like.
- Complete test-taking strategies and techniques.
- How to study and to apply what you've learned.

The format is simple. First, you will be given a clear description of the application and testing procedures. Sample questions will show you exactly what the real test consists of. Then you will take a Diagnostic Practice Test modeled after the actual examination to help you evaluate your present strengths and weaknesses. The strategies and techniques used to score high on these questions will be clearly explained, step by step. Throughout the book, you will be working on timed practice drills and examinations that show how to apply these techniques under realistic test conditions. Throughout your work, you will follow a diagnostic system whereby you can keep track of your progress. If you study and practice the way this book directs, you will master the kinds of questions that appear on the real test.

Moreover, you will find that the abilities you develop as you use this book are transferable to your job in the Postal Service and to your everyday life. Improving your reading ability, memory, and listening skills will help you become a better worker because these abilities, for which the examination tests, are directly related to learning and performing various Postal Service jobs.

---

* Throughout the remainder of this book, instead of using this rather long title, the test will be referred to merely as Test 460/470 or the new postal exam.

In addition, becoming a faster, more accurate reader, acquiring a better memory, and becoming a good listener are assets that can enlarge the personal, educational, and social aspects of your life.

DO I REALLY NEED TO STUDY?

In the 12 months ended in 1992, over 500,000 persons nationwide applied to take various Postal Service examinations. The vast majority were candidates for the most popular jobs, such as Postal Clerk-Carrier. To get an idea of how strong the competition was, just picture these figures: 8,000 people applied for a Postal Clerk-Carrier examination in St. Louis, Missouri where there were only 50 job openings; 39,000 signed up in Chicago for the Mail Handler exam—but there were only 300 jobs available.

More recent figures seem to show that the competition is increasing. In the fall of 1993, over 300,000 persons applied to take the new Postal Test 460/470 in just three of New York City's five boroughs. To date, approximately 500 jobs have been filled from the resulting lists.

There are similar statistics throughout the country. Why? These Postal Service jobs are extremely attractive in terms of salary, working conditions, and other job benefits. (The *starting* salary of a full-time, regular letter carrier, for instance, is now over $24,000). Undoubtedly, the size of these turnouts is also a reflection of the most recent recession and persistently high levels of unemployment in many parts of the country. Regardless of the times, a job with the Postal Service, particularly since its reorganization in 1971, is quite a good one. It offers a career opportunity with fringe benefits that match or exceed those in many other private agencies and the public sector. In Chapter 1 you will be given specific information on salaries, benefits, and the job itself.

Right now, the most important point to consider about the above statistics is the probable size of your competition on the next test, and the best way to meet it. Obviously, not everyone who applies and passes will be appointed because the number of vacancies is limited. Those who pass will be considered for a job appointment in accordance with their score placements, and those of the competition. The higher your test score, the higher your standing on the placement list and the better your chance for early appointment. Even *one* extra point can boost you hundreds of places on the job appointment list. This, of course, means hard, cold (and welcome) money to you.

Numerous studies and firsthand experience show that those who prepare for this test have a tremendous advantage over those who take the test cold. This book will help you gain that advantage.

Another, perhaps more vivid, way to answer the question, "Do I really need to study?" comes from the author's personal experience taking many Postal Service exams.

I make it a point to meet and talk firsthand with several test takers, both before and after the test. Most people appear nervous and anxious about taking the test but, all in all, the mood is upbeat. Most of them confess that they have prepared for it very little, if at all. They say they've heard that the questions just call for "common sense." There is tension in the air but at the same time a lot of chatter and laughter.

But after the test, the picture is quite different. Many people register shock, disappointment, and amazement over the rigorousness of the exam. The general mood is subdued; there is very little of the laughter and chatter there was before. Some are openly downcast about their performance and their prospects for getting called for a job.

HOW TO USE THIS BOOK

Chapter 1 includes important background information on eligibility and application for the test. Be sure to review the test description and do the sample questions.

You will then be ready to take the Diagnostic Practice Test in **Chapter 2**. Your results on this test will help you to see where your present strengths and weaknesses lie. Record these results on the Personal Progress Record Cards and on the special Diagnostic Charts that accompany each chapter. With these in hand, you can effectively plan your study program and evaluate your progress as you go along.

Chapters 3 through 8 are designed to help you to develop the four basic skills that these examinations have tested for. The test strategies and techniques presented in these chapters are related specifically to the kind of questions you will face. Each method is fully explained and illustrated.

If you wish, you may proceed to the appropriate part of each practice test in Chapters 9 through 14 immediately after reading the corresponding chapters above. Many readers prefer to complete each practice test as a whole. It really doesn't matter which way you work, but, whatever method you select, allow some time between practice tests for reviewing and drilling.

The final section of this book, **Chapters 9 through 14**, is composed of six complete practice tests, each containing questions on Address Checking, Number Series, Memory for Addresses, and Following Oral Directions. As you complete each chapter, enter the results in the Diagnostic Charts within the chapter and the Personal Progress Record on pages 430–431. Note any special areas of weakness and reread the appropriate sections in Chapters 3 through 8. Do additional drilling as necessary before proceeding with the next practice test.

Note that the drills, as well as the practice tests, may be taken several times. The Personal Progress Record has space to record scores for three trials. You should see progress as you continue practicing. Be sure to read the important guidelines and summaries that appear in Chapter 8 and at the beginning of Chapter 11 before you take Practice Tests 1 and 3.

It is recommended that you begin your study program *now*. You cannot be certain when the test registration will open, and when it does, you may have only a few weeks' notice. The *skills and techniques you learn now will not be lost over the passage of time*. Then, when you are given the exact test date, a brief rereading of the text and the summaries on pages 221 to 225 will bring you back to peak performance.

THE NEW TEST FORMAT

Part	Description	Number of Questions	Time Allowed
A	Address Checking	95	6 minutes
B	Memory for Addresses	88	5 minutes
C	Number Series	24	20 minutes
D	Following Oral Directions	30	25 minutes

This time allowance is for the time spent on the *rated* part of the test. You can, however, expect to spend approximately 2½ hours in the examination room. See Chapter 1, page 6 for complete details.

Chapter 1

Application and Testing Procedures

HOW AND WHEN TO APPLY

Your first step is to keep informed of Postal Service job opportunities so that you don't miss taking the next examination that is offered. Often, local radio stations, job referral centers, and government personnel offices publicize forthcoming exams. However, the best way to be certain about postal job opportunities is to visit your local post office or local Federal Job Information Center to find out if it is accepting applications. If so, you will be given the proper application form to fill out. At the same time, you should read the official test announcement, which contains specific, current information on such things as the test-filing period (*which may last only one week*), eligibility requirements, salary, job location, job duties, and the tests you must pass in order to be appointed.

If your local post office is not accepting applications at this time, don't give up. Examinations are not held at the same time for the same job titles for all post offices in a region—especially when it is densely populated. Rather, tests are scheduled to meet the staffing needs of *local* post offices in a particular postal area or "sector." This means that the tests you are interested in may very well be due soon for a post office not too far away. What you should decide on at this point is how anxious you are to get into the Postal Service and how far from home you are willing to travel. Then, check the Post Office Directory at your local post office, and list the postal centers you would consider. Visit them personally. Try to speak to the most knowledgeable persons, such as the postmaster, his assistant, or someone in the personnel department. Get as much information as you can on the tests you are interested in, especially when they were last held and when the next ones are due. Keep track of these visits and follow up on them frequently. You don't want to miss out when registration finally opens up! Exams under the traditional system are usually scheduled *only once every two or three years.*

At some post offices, a different registration system called OPTEX (Open Testing Exam System) is used. Under this system, the filing period is much longer than in the traditional system described above. Registration may be open many weeks; sometimes it stays open indefinitely. The applications that come in during this time are put in a computer file. Then, based on anticipated hiring needs, a percentage of these applications is randomly selected by the computer to be scheduled for examination. The good news about this system is that, although fewer names are called, exams are held more frequently. If you are lucky, your name will be selected early in the process and you won't have to wait for years to take the test. On the other hand, the luck of the draw may leave your application untouched for a long time.

When you visit the various post offices ask about which system is used. If it is OPTEX, find out how long your name will be held in the pool of applicants.

ANSWERS TO FREQUENTLY ASKED QUESTIONS ABOUT ELIGIBILITY FOR THE TEST BATTERY 460/470

Here are some highlights summarized from the most recent official test announcement and other official sources that answer the most frequently asked questions about applying for the Test 460/470:

What are the educational and experience qualifications?
No experience is required; no minimum education is required.

Must I be a U.S. citizen?
You must be a U.S. citizen, or owe allegiance to the United States, or have been granted permanent resident alien status in the United States.

Are there any residence requirements?
There are no residence requirements.

How old must I be to be appointed?
The general minimum age for positions in the Postal Service is 18 at the time of appointment. For high school graduates or persons certified by local school authorities as having terminated formal education for adequate reasons, the minimum age is 16. Applicants who are less than 18 years of age, who are high school graduates, and who have not terminated formal education may participate in the examination if they will reach the age of 18 within two years from the date of examination. There is no maximum age limit.

Are there any physical requirements?
You must be physically able to perform the duties of the position. Physical, medical, and vision examinations are required before appointment as well as a urinalysis to detect drug use.

How is salary determined?
Salary is determined from collective bargaining agreements. (At the time of publication, those appointed as part-time, flexible-schedule clerks will start at a salary of $12.54 per hour with a maximum of $17.72 per hour, including cost of living adjustments, after eight years. Such employees are converted to Regular Status according to seniority and openings, at an annual salary range of between $23,400 and $33,470 including COLA [Cost of Living Adjustment].)

Are there any special requirements for carrier positions?
City and rural carrier applicants must have a valid state driver's license and are required to have a safe driving record. You must also pass a special Postal Service road test before appointment.

How are job vacancies filled?
The examination will be used to establish a register of eligibles or to expand the current register of eligibles from which future vacancies will be filled. Separate registers are prepared according to the different job categories.

Are there any special provisions for veterans?
Absolutely. Once they have passed the test, qualified veterans are eligible to have points added to their basic rating. Depending on your veteran status, you may receive 5 or even 10 points extra; however, you must attain the passing score of 70 before these extra points will be added. Disabled veterans who qualify may also receive absolute priority in hiring. Certain family members of such veterans may also be entitled to these benefits. A reminder: To secure these benefits, you must claim them on your application.

Are there any other policies that govern employment?
If you pass the written and physical tests, you will be required to complete a comprehensive employment application and attend a personal interview. The Postal Service utilizes these means to further assess your suitability for the job in terms of character, qualifications, and employment record. See the Appendix pages 426–429 for a facsimile of the official Employment Application PS 2591.)

You will find two more important policy statements in the official test announcement and on the employment application:

1. The U.S. Postal Service is an Equal Opportunity Employer.
2. THE LAW (39 U.S. CODE 1002) PROHIBITS POLITICAL AND CERTAIN OTHER RECOMMENDATIONS FOR APPOINTMENTS, PROMOTIONS, ASSIGNMENTS, TRANSFERS, OR DESIGNATIONS OF PERSONS IN THE POSTAL SERVICE. Statements relating solely to character and residence are permitted, but every other kind of statement or recommendation is prohibited unless it is either requested by the Postal Service and consists solely of an evaluation of the work performance, ability, aptitude, and general qualifications of an individual or is requested by a government representative investigating the individual's loyalty, suitability, and character. Anyone who requests or solicits a prohibited statement or recommendation is subject to disqualification from the Postal Service, and anyone in the Postal Service who accepts such a statement may be suspended from office.

What kind of a test is this?
Test 460/470 is a written, multiple-choice test designed to test aptitude for learning and performing the duties of these positions. It has four parts described and illustrated on pages 6 to 13. Everyone must achieve a minimum score of 70.

The official test announcement will contain current information on all the topics discussed above. Make sure to read it when it comes out.

How many times may I take this test?
You may take a test for a specific title, e.g., Postal Clerk, more than once, provided you are not retaking the same test used to establish a register at a particular postal installation. Otherwise it is advised that you take as many tests for as many titles as you feel you are eligible for. It is to your advantage to get a place on as many different registers as possible.

FILING THE APPLICATION

Once you have read the official test announcement and have received the application card, be very careful to fill it out legibly, accurately, and completely. Otherwise, it may be rejected. Then return the card *within the time period specified in the announcement.* (It is recommended that you hand it in personally.) You must file your application on time in order to receive your admission card. Without the admission card, you will not be allowed to take the test.

A facsimile of the front of the application form, which consists of two parts—the application card and the admission card—appears below:

APPLICATION CARD

Name *(Last, First, Middle Initial)*	
Address *(House/Apt. No. & Street)*	
City, State, ZIP Code	
Birthdate *(Month, Date, Year)*	**Do Not Write In This Space**
Telephone Number	Today's Date
Title of Examination	
Post Office Applied For	

PS Form 2479-A, April 1983

ADMISSION CARD

Title of Examination		Social Security No.
Date of Birth	Today's Date	Post Office Applied For

If you have performed active duty in the Armed Forces of the United States and were separated under honorable conditions indicate periods of service

From *(Mo., Day, Yr.)* ______ to *(Mo., Day, Yr.)* ______

DO YOU CLAIM VETERAN PREFERENCE? NO YES IF YES, BASED ON

☐ (1) Active duty in the Armed Forces of the U.S. during World War I or the period December 7, 1941, through July 1, 1955 (2) More than 180 consecutive days of active duty (other than for training) in the Armed Forces of the U.S. any part of which occurred between Jan. 31, 1955 and Oct. 14, 1976, or (3) Award of a campaign badge or service medal

☐ Your status as (1) a disabled veteran or a veteran who was awarded the purple heart for wounds or injuries received in action, (2) a veteran's widow who has not remarried, (3) the wife of an ex serviceman who has a service connected disability which disqualifies him for civil service appointment, or (4) the widowed, divorced or separated mother of an ex-service son or daughter who died in action or who is totally and permanently disabled

Print or Type Your Name and Address	Name *(First, Middle, Last)*
	Address *(House, Apt. No. & Street)*
	City, State, ZIP Code *(ZIP Code must be included)*

PS Form 2479-B, April 1983

The admission card will be returned to you later, advising you when and where to report for the test.

With it will come a packet of information specifying what you must bring with you on test day.

BEFORE THE TEST—REMINDERS

- Get a good night's rest. Wake up in time to eat a sensible breakfast.
- Wear comfortable clothes. Include a sweater or light jacket that can be added or removed according to room temperature.

- Gather your supplies. Do not forget to bring your admission card, the Sample Answer Sheet (see below), two properly prepared #2 lead pencils (see page 73) with erasers, and personal identification bearing your picture or description. The identification will be checked, and a fingerprint or signature specimen may be required.
- Come early. If you are not certain about how to get to the test location or how long the trip will take, check these things out as soon as you get your admission card. If you have to rush into the test, worried and out of breath, you will not be in the best condition to take the examination. If you come late, you will not be admitted.
- By coming early, you have a better chance to select a good seat. Pick one where you can see and hear the person conducting the test. Avoid seats where you'll be subject to hot radiators, drafts, or street noise. Stay away from people who might disturb you: loud talkers, coughers, and restless people who drum their fingers or pencils on the table.
- If you're having a problem of any kind, raise your hand and ask one of the monitors to help you. They are there for that purpose. They are supposed to make sure that everyone has a chance to take the test fairly under the best possible conditions.
- *Carefully* complete the Sample Answer Sheet that you will receive along with your admission card. In the exam room, there will be only 15 minutes to copy your work from the Sample Answer Sheet to the Official Answer Sheet. You will not have enough time in the exam room to gather information and dates you may not remember, such as veteran status, Social Security, and disability.

It is particularly important for you to have decided on which post offices you want to work in and on what jobs you want most. (In the packet of information you receive will be a list of post offices—"installations"—and the types of jobs available at each.) *Once you make your choices, you cannot later change them.* Now is the time to take the advice given you on page 1. Visit the locations listed, check on convenience of travel from your home, find out, if you can, how many openings exist at each of those you're interested in. Most of all, decide on the kind of work you'd like best, i.e., carrier, clerk, mail handler, and so on.

In any case, exercise your full choice. (You probably will be given several to pick from.) It is advised that you include post offices that have openings in several titles. That way you may be considered for as many as eight different positions (see page 58 on scoring) and your prospects for an early appointment will be increased.

The test you take will be used to fill the available job positions. Be aware, however, that not all positions are available at every location. The Postal Service will provide you with additional information before you take the exam, specifying which positions exist in the post offices that will use the area register.

WHAT IT'S LIKE AT THE TEST—SOME THINGS TO REMEMBER

When you receive your admission card, it will be accompanied by a few sample questions like the ones you will take on the test. These are useful. Later, you will see what these questions look like. First, to complete the picture of what the testing procedure is like, the following describes what you may experience during the test itself as well as what happens afterward.

On the day of the test, you will be one of a group of other test candidates assembled in a room. The exact number of test takers will depend on many things. The staffing needs of the post offices that are to be served by the exam and the employment situation in the area are two important deciding factors. Often, these tests are held in large public places, such as halls and schools, so that all those who want to take the examination can be accommodated. You may, therefore, find yourself to be one of 300 to 400 persons seated in small groups around tables placed throughout the room. Your identification and admission cards will be checked by Postal Service employees who act as test monitors. The monitor in charge of administering the test will direct you in filling out a form containing questions on your job preference, veteran's status, date of birth, and so on. You must indicate your answers by darkening the boxes on the form. (This is similar to the way you will indicate your answers on the test. In Chapters 2, 9, 10, 11, 12, 13, and 14, you will see and use this kind of answer sheet.) The monitor will also explain the test procedure fully and will emphasize that the various parts of the test are carefully timed. Follow these directions exactly. If you are not sure of something, ask for clarification. *The monitors are extremely strict. It is emphasized repeatedly that failure to follow any directive given by an examiner may be grounds for disqualification.*

The test and the completion of related forms will require approximately 2½ hours.

THE TEST ITSELF—SAMPLE QUESTIONS

As the official announcement indicates, this Postal Service examination is definitely job related. You will be able to see how true this is when you go over some of the sample questions recently sent to test applicants.

Part A—Address Checking

In Part A you will have to decide whether two addresses are alike or different. This kind of question is included in the test because every member of the Postal Service staff is responsible for seeing that each piece of mail arrives at the right destination as quickly as possible. If addresses are misread, delays in delivery will result. In spite of various new developments in sorting and handling the mail that use electronic and computerized devices, the human element is crucial in providing fast and efficient service. Here are the instructions and the sample questions that go with them.

Questions

If the two addresses are alike in every way, darken space Ⓐ for the question. If the two addresses are different in any way, darken space Ⓓ for the question. Mark your answers to these questions in the grids provided.

1.	2134 S 20th St	2134 S 20th St	1 ⒶⒹ
2.	4608 N Warnock St	4806 N Warnock St	2 ⒶⒹ
3.	1202 W Girard Dr	1202 W Girard Rd	3 ⒶⒹ
4.	Chappaqua NY 10514	Chappaqua NY 10514	4 ⒶⒹ
5.	2207 Markland Ave	2207 Markham Ave	5 ⒶⒹ

Answers

1. **A** 2. **D** 3. **D** 4. **A** 5. **D**

The questions seem easy, but the test itself is not. At least, it's not easy if you want to score higher than your many competitors. In the latest test, candidates were given *95* pairs of addresses to compare in *6* minutes.

To pass with high scores, test takers had to work as fast and accurately as possible. They knew that every extra point they made meant they would be that much higher on the list for job appointment. When a list has thousands of names, *one* extra point will make a difference of *hundreds* of places on the list. Also, when there are a limited number of job openings, list position can mean the difference between getting a job or "dying" on the list. That is why merely passing is not good enough. In the next chapters, you will learn exactly what to do to earn those extra points.

Part B—Memory for Addresses

The majority of postal clerks work behind the scenes sorting and distributing mail. They must be able to remember sorting schemes by which mail is organized for delivery. Carriers need to have good memories too. One of a carrier's responsibilities is to arrange mail according to the delivery route he or she will follow on a particular day. For this reason carriers must be able to learn and remember the streets and building addresses on their routes. Now you know why memory questions appear on this exam. Here are some sample questions and instructions for answering them:

Questions

In this test, you will have to memorize the locations (A, B, C, D, or E) of 25 addresses shown in five boxes below. For example, "Sardis" is in Box C, and 5600–6499 West is in Box A.

Study the locations of the addresses for *5 minutes*. As you study, sound them to yourself. Then cover the boxes and try to answer the questions below. Mark your answer for each question by darkening the space in the grids provided, as was done for questions 1 and 2.

A	B	C	D	E
4700–5599 Table	6800–6999 Table	5600–6499 Table	6500–6799 Table	4400–4699 Table
Belmore	Kelford	Joel	Tatum	Rusken
5600–6499 West	6500–6799 West	6800–6999 West	4400–4699 West	4700–5599 West
Hesper	Musella	Sardis	Porter	Nathan
4400–4699 Blake	5600–6499 Blake	6500–6799 Blake	4700–5599 Blake	6800–6999 Blake

1. Musella	1 Ⓐ ● Ⓒ Ⓓ Ⓔ
2. 4700–5599 Blake	2 Ⓐ Ⓑ Ⓒ ● Ⓔ
3. 4700–5599 Table	3 Ⓐ Ⓑ Ⓒ Ⓓ Ⓔ
4. Tatum	4 Ⓐ Ⓑ Ⓒ Ⓓ Ⓔ
5. 4400–4699 Blake	5 Ⓐ Ⓑ Ⓒ Ⓓ Ⓔ
6. Hesper	6 Ⓐ Ⓑ Ⓒ Ⓓ Ⓔ

7. Kelford 7 Ⓐ Ⓑ Ⓒ Ⓓ Ⓔ
8. Nathan 8 Ⓐ Ⓑ Ⓒ Ⓓ Ⓔ
9. 6500–6799 Blake 9 Ⓐ Ⓑ Ⓒ Ⓓ Ⓔ
10. Joel 10 Ⓐ Ⓑ Ⓒ Ⓓ Ⓔ
11. 4400–4699 Blake 11 Ⓐ Ⓑ Ⓒ Ⓓ Ⓔ
12. 6500–6799 West 12 Ⓐ Ⓑ Ⓒ Ⓓ Ⓔ
13. Porter 13 Ⓐ Ⓑ Ⓒ Ⓓ Ⓔ
14. 5600–6499 Table 14 Ⓐ Ⓑ Ⓒ Ⓓ Ⓔ

Answers

1. **B**
2. **D**
3. **A**
4. **D**
5. **A**
6. **A**
7. **B**
8. **E**
9. **C**
10. **C**
11. **A**
12. **B**
13. **D**
14. **C**

Now imagine a test situation where you are given a total of *5* minutes to answer *88* questions! This is what the memory test will be like. Very few people feel that this test is easy. But don't be like those who immediately give up on the memory part by saying, "Either you've got it or you don't." The implication is that nothing can be done to improve memory performance. This belief is not accurate. There are definite methods, universally recognized, that are used for memory improvement. The most helpful and practical of these methods have been selected and refined for your use on the Memory for Addresses section of the Test 460/470. You will be happily surprised at how good your memorization capabilities really are!

Part C: Number Series

The Number Series part of the test is intended to gauge your aptitude for working with machines. Because you may be working on a letter sorting machine and possibly other kinds of machines, this part of the test is relevant to your job duties.

Questions

For each Number Series question, there is at the left a series of numbers that follows some definite order and at the right five sets of two numbers each. You are to look at the numbers in the series at the left and find out what order they follow. Then decide what the next two numbers in that series would be if the same order were continued. Mark your answers to these questions by darkening the proper space in the grids provided. (To help you get started, the answers and explanations for the first five questions are given directly below each question.)

1. 1 2 3 4 5 6 7 __ __

A) 1 2   B) 5 6   C) 8 9   D) 4 5   E) 7 8

The correct answer is C. The numbers in this series are increasing by 1. If the series were continued for two more numbers, it would read: 1 2 3 4 5 6 7 8 9. Therefore, the correct answer is C) 8 and 9.

2. 15 14 13 12 11 10 9 __ __

A) 2 1 B) 17 16 C) 8 9 D) 8 7 E) 9 8

The correct answer is D. The numbers in this series are decreasing by 1. If the series were continued for two more numbers, it would read: 15 14 13 12 11 10 9 8 7. Therefore, the correct answer is 8 and 7 and you should have darkened D for this question.

3. 20 20 21 21 22 22 23 __ __

A) 23 23 B) 23 24 C) 19 19 D) 22 23 E) 21 22

The correct answer is B. Each number in this series is repeated and then increased by 1. If the series were continued for two or more numbers, it would read: 20 20 21 21 22 22 23 23 24. Therefore, the correct answer is 23 and 24.

4. 17 3 17 4 17 5 17 __ __

A) 6 17 B) 6 7 C) 17 6 D) 5 6 E) 17 7

The correct answer is A. In this series the number 17 is separated by numbers increasing by 1, beginning with the number 3. If the series were continued for two more numbers, it would read: 17 3 17 4 17 5 17 6 17. Therefore, the correct answer is 6 and 17, and you should have darkened A.

5. 1 2 4 5 7 8 10 __ __

A) 11 12 B) 12 14 C) 10 13 D) 12 13 E) 11 13

The correct answer is E. The numbers in this series are increasing first by 1 (plus 1) and then by 2 (plus 2). If the series were continued for two more numbers, it would read: 1 2 4 5 7 8 10 (plus 1) 11 (plus 2) 13. Therefore, the correct answer is 11 and 13, and you should have darkened E.

Questions

Now try sample questions 6 through 10, and mark your answers in the grid provided.

6. 21 21 20 20 19 19 18 __ __

A) 18 18 B) 18 17 C) 17 18 D) 17 17 E) 18 19

6 Ⓐ Ⓑ Ⓒ Ⓓ Ⓔ

7. 1 22 1 23 1 24 1 __ __

A) 26 1 B) 25 26 C) 25 1 D) 1 26 E) 1 25

7 Ⓐ Ⓑ Ⓒ Ⓓ Ⓔ

8. 1 20 3 19 5 18 7 __ __

A) 8 9 B) 8 17 C) 17 10 D) 17 9 E) 9 18

8 Ⓐ Ⓑ Ⓒ Ⓓ Ⓔ

9. 4 7 10 13 16 19 22 __ __
   A) 23 26   B) 25 27   C) 25 25   D) 25 28   E) 24 27

9 Ⓐ Ⓑ Ⓒ Ⓓ Ⓔ

10. 30 2 28 4 26 6 24 __ __
   A) 23 9   B) 26 8   C) 8 9   D) 26 22   E) 8 22

10 Ⓐ Ⓑ Ⓒ Ⓓ Ⓔ

Answers

6. **B**   7. **C**   8. **D**   9. **D**   10. **E**

Part D—Following Oral Directions

This part of the test gauges your ability to understand and carry out spoken instructions *exactly* as they are given to you. On the "real-life" job, your supervisor will frequently give you oral instructions and expect you to listen carefully and to comply swiftly and correctly. You may be sure that your future boss will appreciate it if you are able to get a message straight the first time you hear it, without the need for repetition. This test assesses how well you will be able to measure up to these requirements.

In order to answer the sample items on the next page, here is what you should do:

1. Enlist the help of a friend who will be the "reader." He/she will read aloud a series of directions that you are to follow exactly. The reader will need a watch that displays seconds because the directions must be given at the correct speed.
2. Tear out page 11. This is the worksheet you should have in front of you as you follow the directions for Sample 1 through Sample 5.
3. *Now, hand this entire book to the reader.* Ask him/her to review the section on page 13 headed "*Instructions to the Reader*," which explains exactly how to proceed. When the reader is ready, he/she will begin reading the directions to you. YOU ARE NOT TO READ THESE. If you do, you will lose the benefit of this sample exercise.
4. Listen carefully to the instructions for each sample question. Use the blank answer grid at the bottom of the worksheet for your answers. Darken the appropriate spaces in accordance with the directions the reader gives you.

Worksheet for the Sample Test

Sample 1. 5 ___

Sample 2. 1 6 4 3 7

Sample 3. D B A E C

Sample 4. 8 ___ 5 ___ 2 ___ 9 ___ 10 ___

Sample 5. 7 ___ 6 ___ 1 ___ 12 ___

Answer Grid

1	Ⓐ Ⓑ Ⓒ Ⓓ Ⓔ	10	Ⓐ Ⓑ Ⓒ Ⓓ Ⓔ
2	Ⓐ Ⓑ Ⓒ Ⓓ Ⓔ	11	Ⓐ Ⓑ Ⓒ Ⓓ Ⓔ
3	Ⓐ Ⓑ Ⓒ Ⓓ Ⓔ	12	Ⓐ Ⓑ Ⓒ Ⓓ Ⓔ
4	Ⓐ Ⓑ Ⓒ Ⓓ Ⓔ	13	Ⓐ Ⓑ Ⓒ Ⓓ Ⓔ
5	Ⓐ Ⓑ Ⓒ Ⓓ Ⓔ	14	Ⓐ Ⓑ Ⓒ Ⓓ Ⓔ
6	Ⓐ Ⓑ Ⓒ Ⓓ Ⓔ	15	Ⓐ Ⓑ Ⓒ Ⓓ Ⓔ
7	Ⓐ Ⓑ Ⓒ Ⓓ Ⓔ	16	Ⓐ Ⓑ Ⓒ Ⓓ Ⓔ
8	Ⓐ Ⓑ Ⓒ Ⓓ Ⓔ	17	Ⓐ Ⓑ Ⓒ Ⓓ Ⓔ
9	Ⓐ Ⓑ Ⓒ Ⓓ Ⓔ	18	Ⓐ Ⓑ Ⓒ Ⓓ Ⓔ

✂ Remove by cutting on dotted line.

Instructions to the "Reader"

The directions should be read at about 80 words per minute. Practice reading aloud the material in the box below until you can do it in exactly 1 minute. This will give you a feel for the way you should read the test material.

1-MINUTE PRACTICE

(This is for practice in reading aloud. It is not part of the sample test.)

> Look at line 20 on your worksheet. There are two circles and two boxes of different sizes with numbers in them. If 7 if less than 3 and if 2 is smaller than 4, write a C in the larger circle. Otherwise write B as in *baker* in the smaller box. Now on your answer sheet darken the space for the number-letter combination in the box or circle.

As you read the directions (below) you will see words in parentheses. These words should *not* be read aloud. They are there to tell you how long you should pause at the various spots. You should time the pauses using a watch with a second hand. The instruction "Pause slightly" means that you should stop long enough to take a breath.

Do not repeat any directions.

Directions to be read: You are to follow the instructions that I read to you. I cannot repeat them.

Look at the samples. Sample 1 has a number and a line beside it. (Pause slightly.) On the line write an A. (Pause 2 seconds.) Now, on the answer grid, find number 5 (pause 2 seconds) and darken the space for the letter you just wrote on the line. (Pause 5 seconds.)

Look at Sample 2. (Pause slightly.) Draw a line under the third number. (Pause 2 seconds.) Now, on the answer grid, find the number under which you just drew a line and darken space B as in *baker* for that number. (Pause 5 seconds.)

Look at the letters in Sample 3. (Pause slightly.) Draw a line under the third letter in the line. (Pause 2 seconds.) Now, on the answer grid, find number 9 (pause 2 seconds) and darken the space for the letter under which you drew a line. (Pause 5 seconds.)

Look at the five circles in Sample 4. (Pause slightly.) Each circle has a number and a line in it. Write D as in *dog* on the line in the last circle. (Pause 2 seconds.) Now, on the answer grid, darken the space for the number-letter combination that is in the circle you just wrote in. (Pause 5 seconds.)

Look at Sample 5. (Pause slightly.) There are two circles and two boxes of different sizes with numbers in them. (Pause slightly.) If 4 is more than 2 and if 5 is less than 3, write A in the smaller circle. (Pause slightly.) Otherwise write C in the larger box. (Pause 2 seconds.) Now, on the answer grid, darken the space for the number-letter combination that is in the box or circle you just wrote in. (Pause 5 seconds.)

Now look at the answer grid. (Pause slightly.) You should have darkened spaces 4B, 5A, 9A, 10D, and 12C.

AFTER THE TEST

The answer sheets are sent to a special division of the Postal Service that prepares and rates examinations. After the papers have been scored and the registers (lists) established, you will receive a Notice of Rating by mail in about 8 weeks. (The register is established in the order of the scores on the test, subject to veterans preference. If you request and are entitled to veterans preference, you will receive extra points on your rating.) If you have passed, the Notice of Rating will also indicate on which post office registers your name has been placed and the date on which this was done. These locations are the ones you *should notify in writing* if you: (1) change your address, (2) have any change in your availability, (3) have any inquiries, (4) want to extend your eligibility. This last point is particularly important because it gives you an opportunity to remain on the list for an extra year. Normally, eligibility is good for two years only. However, you may receive an extension of your eligibility for an additional year if you send in a written request. Send your request in 18 months from the date on which your name was placed on the register (unless, of course, you have been appointed in the interim). The maximum length of eligibility is three years.

Keep the Notice of Rating in a safe place—you will need it some day. At some point before you are hired, you will be given a longer, more detailed "Application for Employment" to fill out. Just as for the yellow, short-form Application Card, it is most important that you answer every question legibly, truthfully, and completely. Usually, this Application for Employment is accompanied by a sheet of instructions. In the Appendix, both the application (page 426 to 429) and a typical set of instructions have been reproduced.

It is worthwhile for you to assemble all the information required now, ready to submit when you are asked for it.

WHY APPLY TO THE POSTAL SERVICE?

Background

When you work for the U.S. Postal Service, you will be working for an employer that does things in a big way—this is the world's largest mail system. In the 12 months ending September 30, 1993, it handled over 171 billion pieces of mail. To do that, it employed more than 734,000 people in over 29,000 post offices and 11,000 stations, branches, and other locations. It used a fleet of 150,000 cars and trucks that are part of the $10 billion worth of property and equipment belonging to the Postal Service. A lot of money was spent doing this—more than $40 billion, four fifths of which went to pay for salaries and benefits. If listed in the "Fortune 500," the Postal Service would be the nation's ninth largest corporation.

Like many government organizations, countries, cities, states, and the federal government itself, the Postal Service is now operating at a loss. The 1994 fiscal year budget showed a net loss of $914 million. But it should be noted that the Postal Service pays its own way and does not use tax dollars to shore up the operation. Within the last three years, it has begun an aggressive campaign to build its revenue base and effect economies to reduce and eventually eliminate this deficit.

Best of all, though, is the fact that, for the most part, the Postal Service has kept in the good graces of the public. An independent poll (taken in 1993) taken to evaluate public satisfaction with 12 federal agencies reported that the Postal Service was the most highly rated of all. On the other hand, there has been dissatisfaction with some postal operations and performance. To identify and correct the specific areas needing improvement, the Postal Service has developed a Customer Satisfaction Index, which has been measuring overall customer perception of the Postal Service and providing details to guide corrective actions. Beginning in 1991, an independent research firm began surveying 750,000 customers annually and issuing quarterly reports. The 1994 survey found that 89 percent of U.S. households believe that the postal service they receive is excellent, very good, or good.

Among the programs created in recent years to build revenue, increase productivity, increase customer satisfaction, and reduce costs are these:

1. *Postal Customer Councils*—to identify local customers' needs and develop solutions to problems. Presently 314 councils, composed of 176,000 members, meet nationwide.

2. *Postal Answer Line*—an automated telephone service operating 24 hours a day to provide answers to customers' questions.

3. *Easy Stamps Program*—offers Stamps by Mail, Stamps by Phone, Stamps by ATM, Stamps on Consignment, and Stamps by PRODIGY.

4. *Mobile Post Offices*—provides window service to senior communities and elsewhere.

5. *Services to Business*

   - an "Operation Mail Team" visits individual businesses to study their mailing operations. It makes recommendations on the best mailing and addressing practices, thereby reducing costs and generating greater customer response.

   - entered into a third-party partnership with private companies, such as Time Warner and the Fastnet, to create the nation's first electronic post office.

6. In cooperation with the employee unions, such as the National Association of Letter Carriers (NALC), and the American Postal Workers Union (APWU), the Postal Service will be installing computer chips (ROM) the size of a wristwatch inside mailboxes at 180,000 locations nationwide. These chips will record the time and date of mail pickups.

   A different chip (RAM) will be used to keep track of the actual physical condition of each mailbox.

7. A host of other programs and services have continued and expanded, including the computerized Mail Forwarding System, Improved Express Mail Services, Intel-Post, and Lobby Director Program.

Today the U.S. Postal Service, thanks to its continuing introduction of high-speed equipment and technology, is the most highly automated postal system in the world. Among other recent innovations are a high-speed bar-code-reading scanner than can spot bar codes on large-sized mail such as catalogues, magazines, and large direct-mail envelopes regardless of where the code has been put on the piece of mail, and a machine that can read handwritten addresses—even ones that have been *scribbled!*

This continued growth of automated equipment has meant a tremendous reduction in the cost of processing mail. Automated mail handling is more than ten times faster than manual operations. It costs about $40 to process 1,000 letters by manual sorting and $18 by mechanized equipment, but only $4 by automation. In fiscal year 1993, 58 percent of all letter mail was handled by automated equipment. Overall productivity increased 3.8 percent in fiscal year 1993. Hopefully, these percentages will continue to increase.

The New Look

In addition to the new and enlarged programs described above, the Postal Service, *literally,* will have a new look. Its logo, featuring a dark blue eagle ready for flight, has been given a sleeker, more modern look with its head and beak leaning into the wind. The post office lobbies, nationwide, will be painted and decorated to make them warmer and more inviting. Within the next five years, all post offices will feature a red, white, and blue motif. They will be made more customer friendly with more informative, easy-to-read signs, convenient counters and furniture, and open merchandise displays.

Recently, an important part of the new look has been to stress the efforts and support of its employees. An example of this spirit is Carrier Alert, a joint program by the Postal Service and the National Association of Letter Carriers. Under this program, letter carriers keep alert to indications of problems facing elderly and infirm residents on their routes. They watch for accumulated mail and other signs of distress, and they notify the proper authorities to secure help. The Postal Service widely publicizes the numerous instances where its employees act resourcefully and often heroically through its Postal Achievement Awards. Press releases of such newsworthy events are sent to local newspapers.

Other indications that the Postal Service tries to be responsive to the changing times and needs of society include:

- As a humanitarian gesture, the Postal Service, a few years ago, offered a low-cost "airlift" to send aid packages to the Baltic nations and the Soviet Republics. A 5-pound airlift package cost $17.85 for postage instead of the $40.30 required for regular airmail.
- The Postal Inspection Service has devoted much time and staff to combatting the use of the mail to send drugs such as cocaine, heroin, and LSD. It cooperates with local police and agents of the DEA. The number of drug-related arrests by postal inspectors has increased fourfold from 1987 to 1990.
- In an effort to support literacy throughout the country, local post offices have joined with area elementary schools in a venture called "Wee Deliver." Children perform all the duties of a local post office and in the process learn the reading and writing skills required to address and sort mail. At the end of 1992, there were approximately 10,000 schools participating. (Of course, this program involves a simulation of a post office, designed for school use, and the children do not substitute for regular postal workers in the area.)
- In efforts to reduce environmental problems, the Postal Service, in cooperation with the unions involved, has begun experimenting with the use of electric-powered vehicles.

In 1993, The Smithsonian Institution in Washington, D.C. established a National Postal Museum to add to its other 15 museums and galleries. This was done in recognition of what the Postal Service has done to tie our country together. The museum will include one of the largest and most important philatelic collections in the world.

One of the most important aspects of the Postal Service's new look involves personnel relations, which directly concern you as a future employee. Since reorganization, the

Postal Service has abolished political patronage in selecting postmasters and rural carriers, replacing it with a merit system. Now, candidates for these jobs are evaluated and selected by national and regional management selection boards. In 1971, the service signed a historic agreement with employee unions, the first labor contract in the history of the federal government to be achieved through the collective bargaining process. Negotiations with the four major labor organizations representing the various postal employee groups determine wages and working conditions. Most postal clerks and carriers are members of the American Postal Workers Union and The National Association of Letter Carriers.

All does not run perfectly smoothly, however. The Postal Service, in response to a series of adverse incidents and employee complaints, instituted two major employee opinion surveys. These showed that although the majority of its employees favorably rated the categories of pay, benefits, and job security, they also indicated the need to improve working conditions and employee cooperation, and to recognize quality performance. Recently, Congress released its own study confirming the need for change in the workplace culture.

The Postal Service has recognized the need to improve some work methods and supervisory practices and began by allowing employees to rate their bosses' "people skills." It has revised the training courses that managers and supervisors attend, to focus on incorporating desirable change into its daily operations. It has created a leadership team composed of some of its key officials and the presidents of the seven major unions and employee associations to set up similar local leadership teams to adopt new performance-based pay systems, improve teamwork, and gain cooperation throughout the system.

The good morale of most of its workers showed up most visibly in 1993 when thousands of employees went the extra mile during very tough weather conditions. They delivered through the "Storm of the Century" on the East Coast in March and the "Great Midwest Flood" in the summer months, often overcoming great obstacles to serve their customers.

A summary of some benefits and programs that can affect you as an employee is given below. (Unless otherwise specified, all figures apply to full-time regular employees.)

Benefits*

Work Schedules and Classifications

Postal clerks and carriers are classified as *casual*, *part-time flexible*, *part-time regular*, or *full-time*. Casual workers are not career employees but are hired to help process mail during peak mailing or vacation periods. Part-time flexible workers are career employees who work as the need arises and usually work less than 40 hours per week. Part-time regulars have a set work schedule (for example, 4 hours a day). Full-time employees work a 40-hour week over five days. All new career employees work on a probationary basis for their first 90 days of employment.

As employees build seniority, they may request transfer to more desirable or convenient shifts and locations. In order to be considered for such reassignments when they arise, employees prepare written "bids." The bidder with the most seniority gets the job, provided that he or she meets all other qualifications.

---

* The various salary schedules, leave provisions, and other program descriptions currently in effect may change as new policies are adopted by the Postal Service and as new contracts are negotiated between it and the several unions that represent its employees. We suggest that you inquire, at the time you are being hired, as to the current status of the benefits and programs important to you.

Annual Leave

Annual leave includes leave for vacations, personal and emergency purposes, and so on. The amount of paid leave you receive depends upon length of service (as an employee and in military service).

Length of Service	*Leave Days per Year*
Less than 3 years	13 days
3 to 15 years	20 days
Over 15 years	26 days

Sick Leave

You are permitted 13 days of sick leave per year.

Base Wage Scale (Including COLA)

(effective 2/1/95)

It is likely that you will begin your career as a part-time flexible worker. The hourly rate varies according to title:

	START	MAXIMUM
Postal Clerk, City Mail Carrier, Machine Distribution Clerk Flat-Sorting Machine Operator	$12.54/hr	$17.72/hr
Mail Processor, Mark-Up Clerk, Mail Handler	11.81/hr	17.29/hr

The maximum rate is reached through a series of graded increases over a 12-year period. Of course, you may get appointed as a "regular" after a time at which point your salary will be converted to a different scale.

Currently, the maximum salary for a full-time regular clerk exceeds $34,000 per year.

COLA

COLA stands for Cost of Living Adjustment. These adjustments are pay increases that are based on the Consumer Price Indexes for March and September of each year. If they rise, your pay increases too, according to a special formula.

Special Pay Provisions

1. *Overtime.* This is paid at time-and-a-half your base hourly straight-time rate, after 8 hours in a day, or 40 hours in a week.
2. *Night pay.* A premium of 10 percent of your base hourly rate is paid for work done between 6 P.M. and 6 A.M.

Holidays

Regular employees receive 10 paid holidays a year.

Free Life Insurance

You will receive regular life insurance coverage of $10,000 plus an equivalent amount of accidental death and dismemberment insurance. As your base pay increases, your insurance coverage will rise to a maximum of $60,000.

Retirement

As a new employee, you will automatically be covered by the new Federal Employees Retirement System (FERS). This is one of the most important benefit programs you receive as a federal employee since it is designed to help provide financial security for you and your family on your retirement.

The FERS has three components:

Social Security benefits

Basic benefit plan

Savings plan

Many of its features are "portable" so that, if you leave federal employment, you may still qualify for the benefits. Moreover, PERS is flexible and allows you to choose what is best for your situation. Because of this flexibility and the various retirement options available, it is not feasible to go into detail here regarding the kinds and amounts of benefits you may receive. These benefits depend on many factors such as length of service, earnings, family composition, age at retirement, and the Consumer Price Index.

The Postal Service will help guide you to the various sources you need to answer any questions you have about FERS.

Low-Cost Health Insurance

The Postal Service pays 89 percent of the cost.

Program of Cash Awards for Suggestions

The Postal Service has a sliding scale of awards for employees who suggest improvements in procedures, equipment, scheduling, and so on. Last year, an employee in St. Louis was awarded $35,000 for her idea on eliminating duplicate payments for replacement money orders.

Training and Career Development Programs

The Postal Service places a premium on developing a well-trained and committed career work force. It believes that its investment of time and money to do this is essential to its present good health and to its future success. Now that more and more automated and complex equipment is in use, and changes in technology are increasing, proper training of postal employees is a high priority.

Hand in hand with this concern is the Postal Service's adherence to policies that give its employees the opportunity to advance within the organization.

Some key programs now in effect include:

1. *New Employee Training (NET).*
   This provides training and support over the entire 90 days of an employee's probationary period. Orientation and job skills are taught by local supervisors with the assistance of experienced workers who coach and "break in" new workers.

Within the larger cities, there are designated academies that can accommodate the larger groups of new hirees; e.g., there are two district academies in Brooklyn and Queens given the task of preparing 400 new carriers appointed from the test register cited on page xiv.

2. *Postal Employee Development Centers (PEDCs).*
A national network of over 200 centers helps current workers upgrade their skills and knowledge. These centers play a key part in preparing craft employees to operate and repair automation equipment as it comes on line. A great variety of training courses are developed and offered each year through the PEDCs, which are the principal vehicle for employee development. These programs make it possible for a postal worker to learn new skills and eventually qualify for a career change to a higher skilled, better paying job within the Postal Service.

3. *Advancement to Initial-Level Supervisor.*
About 8,000 postal employees are promoted into supervisory jobs each year. This opportunity is open to all employees with one year of career employment. Interested individuals nominate themselves and are then evaluated by their supervisor. They must also take a test designed to measure their supervisory aptitude. A review panel looks over the nominations and makes its recommendations to the officials responsible for selection.

4. *Technical Training Center (TTC).*
A 29,000-square-foot complex situated in Norman, Oklahoma, trains almost 20,000 employees a year in the maintenance and repair of high-technology systems, equipment, vehicles, and facilities.

5. *Nontechnical Training.*
Courses and workshops to develop management and supervisory skills are held in a center in Chicago, Illinois. Training is offered on conflict resolution, team building, communication skills, and so on. A special fast-track management program is offered to qualified employees.
Both centers also use learning devices such as satellite and audio tele-training networks to reach distant locations. On-site training gives employees all across the country a chance to learn and grow without leaving home.

Diversity Development

In 1992, a diversity development unit was created to ensure that the Postal Service recognizes and appreciates the needs of all members of this culturally diverse society. It serves the needs of the employees and customers of the Postal Service by assisting affirmative action, customer relations, and vendor programs. It helps design and analyze the Employee Opinion Survey and tries to increase the awareness and appreciation for ethnic and cultural diversity both in the postal workplace and among customers.

A profile of the workforce for 1993 shows that Blacks, Hispanics, and other minority groups comprise 38 percent of the workforce. About 33 percent of its employees are women, who now constitute 23 percent of the management and supervisory staff.

Rehabilitation Programs

An Employee Assistance Program (EAP) is in operation that seeks to rehabilitate employees with alcohol- and drug-related problems.

How Much Are These Benefits Worth?

It has been estimated* that for a postal employee earning $29,700 a year, the annual contributions by the U.S. Postal Service toward these benefits can easily be worth $10,000. This figure does not include the value of annual leave and sick leave, which in this case amounts to $1,713.

The Nature of the Work

The test you take will be used to fill the job positions described below. Be aware, however, that not all positions are available at every location. The Postal Service will provide you with additional information before you take the exam, specifying which positions exist in the post offices that will use the area register.

Postal Clerks

Most people are familiar with the post office window clerk who sells stamps and accepts parcel post. Window clerks also weigh packages to determine postage and suitability for mailing. They register, certify, and insure mail, and answer questions about postage rates, mailing restrictions, and other postal matters. Occasionally they may help a customer file a claim for a damaged package.

Most postal clerks, however, are distribution clerks who sort incoming and outgoing mail in workrooms out of public view. Distribution clerks work at local post offices or at large mail-processing facilities. Clerks at local post offices sort local mail for delivery to individual customers. Incoming mail gathered from collection boxes is forwarded to the nearest mail processing center, where clerks sort and prepare the mail for delivery.

Working Conditions

Working conditions for clerks differ according to the work assignment and the type of labor-saving machinery available. In small post offices, clerks may use a hand truck to move mail sacks from one part of the building to another and may sort mail by hand. In large post offices and mail processing centers, chutes and conveyors move the mail, and much of the sorting is done with machines. When they are not operating a letter-sorting machine, clerks are usually on their feet reaching for sacks and trays of mail and placing packages and bundles into sacks and trays. (Some of these may weigh as much as 70 pounds.)

Mail Carriers—City/Rural

Most mail carriers travel planned routes delivering and collecting mail. Carriers start work at the post office early in the morning, where they spend a few hours arranging their mail for delivery and taking care of other details.

A carrier may cover the route on foot, by vehicle, or by a combination of both. Foot carriers use a satchel or cart to deliver their mail. In some areas, a car or small truck is used to deliver mail. Carriers serving residential areas cover their routes only once a day, but some carriers assigned to a business district may make two trips a day. Deliveries are made door-to-door, to curbside or roadside mailboxes, to neighborhood delivery and collection boxes, to office buildings, and to apartment houses which have all the mailboxes located in the lobby

Besides delivering and collecting mail, carriers collect money for postage-due and C.O.D. items and obtain signed receipts for registered, certified, and insured mail. If a

* Taken from *Postal Life*, May–June 1990

customer is not home, the carrier leaves a notice that tells what the item is and where it is being held.

After completing their routes, carriers return to the post office with mail gathered from street collection boxes, homes, and business places. They turn in their delivery receipts and money collected during the day, and separate the letters and large flats they collected for further processing by clerks.

Many city carriers have more specialized duties. Some deliver only parcel post while others collect mail from street boxes and receiving boxes in office buildings. In contrast, rural carriers provide a wide variety of postal services. In addition to delivering and picking up mail, they sell stamps and money orders and accept parcels, letters, and items to be registered, certified, or insured.

All carriers answer customers questions about postal regulations and services, and provide change-of-address cards and other postal forms upon request.

Working Conditions

Most carriers begin work early in the morning, some as early as 4:00 A.M. if they have routes in the business district. Carriers spend most of their time outdoors in all kinds of weather delivering mail. Even those who drive often must walk when making deliveries and must lift sacks of parcel post when loading their vehicles.

The job, however, has its advantages. Carriers who begin work early in the morning are through by early afternoon.

Mail Handler

The mail handler is not as visible to the public as the window clerk in an average post office. However, you can get a glimpse of one if you pass the loading platform at the side or rear of a post office. Part of the mail handlers' job is done here, where these workers load and unload trucks carrying sacks of mail, cartons, and pallets from other cities and from airports. They place the sacks onto carts and wheel them to conveyor belts and sorting tables. There they empty the sacks and separate (cull) the contents into various categories, such as newspapers, books, airmail parcels, and oversized mail. Depending on the post office, mail handlers may also be assigned other tasks, for example, working on stamp cancellation machines or operating addressograph or mimeograph machines. Their duties may also include rewrapping parcels, placing outgoing parcels and packages into pouches, and even operating forklift trucks.

Working Conditions

Like most other vocations, the mail handler job has its advantages and disadvantages. There is no doubt that this job is more strenuous. and dirtier than that of the clerk who sorts mail or sells money orders. Mail handlers have to repeatedly lift up to 70 pounds. Then, too, the mail handler may be exposed to inclement weather while working on a loading platform. In some offices, mail handlers work at night and on weekends.

On the other hand, the mail handler may very well enjoy the fresh air, particularly on nice days. Also, because the mail handler shuttles between various workstations, performing a variety of tasks, the job is less routine and more interesting than that of a letter-sorting machine operator, who does a repetitious job all day long.

Mail Processor

The mail processor title is a relatively new one in the Postal Service. The duties of the job include:

1. Starting and stopping a variety of mail-processing equipment such as bar-code sorters and optical bar-code readers.

2. Clearing jams that do not require hand tools.
3. Sweeping mail from bins, tying it into bundles as necessary, and placing the bundles into trays; pulling out nonprocessible items.
4. Loading mail onto transport units.
5. Performing other job-related tasks.

The mail processor's work is performed in large mail-processing facilities in an industrial environment. These employees are required to stand for long periods of time loading and unloading mail on a variety of automated mail-processing equipment. Mail processors normally work nights and weekends. Although the job does involve standing and lifting, it is not as strenuous as that of the mail handler. For this reason, the pay scale is slightly lower.

Machine Distribution Clerks

Machine distribution clerks, operating electronic letter-sorting machines, quickly scan the addresses on the mail that passes before them. Working at the rate of about one letter per second, they sort letters automatically by entering the proper sorting code on a specially developed keyboard. The machine then drops each letter into the proper slot. Needless to say, the letter-sorting machine clerk must have the ability to read addresses quickly and accurately, and to be able to remember and select the appropriate codes and sorting schemes. Operators are required to maintain an average keying accuracy of 98 percent. When they are not operating a letter-sorting machine, clerks are usually on their feet reaching for sacks and trays of mail and placing packages and bundles into sacks and trays.

Working Conditions

The machine distribution clerk must cope with a certain amount of monotony and noise that is inherent in the job. The environment is more akin to a factory or warehouse than an office, with various pieces of machinery and rolling stock in view.

Individuals must have the willingness to maintain close visual attention for sustained periods and must be able to meet performance standards.

Some of the tedium of the job is overcome by the rotation of tasks and by work breaks. Many of the operators listen to music through headphones while they work. It can be an easy job for the right person. These employees usually work at night and on weekends.

The machine distribution clerk is compensated in other ways, too. He or she is slotted at a higher grade than regular clerks and thereby earns more money. Also, chances for advancement and development may be greater because the Postal Service is increasingly committed to the mechanization of mail processing. Greater employment opportunities can be expected by those willing and able to learn how to operate new and sophisticated equipment.

Flat-Sorting Machine Operator

The flat-sorting machine operator's job is very similar to that of the machine distribution clerk. These employees also operate a machine from memory or by using a zip code. Their machine, however, is called a flat sorter and is used to sort oversized letters, magazines, and so on using a special purpose keypad to distribute these flats at the rate of 45 per minute while maintaining an accuracy rate of 98 percent. They, too, must have an ability to maintain close visual attention for long periods of time. These operators usually work at nights and on weekends.

Mark-Up Clerks

Mark-up clerks work indoors entering change of address data into a computer database. They also process mail and perform other clerical functions. They operate a keyboard in order to process these changes and are therefore expected to have some experience with office machines.

Applicants for mark-up clerk must have good data entry skills and are required to pass a typing test. They may work at night and on weekends.

Job Outlook

In its 1993 Annual Report, the Postal Service noted that it had been able to cut its workforce by 34,000 positions since 1992. It accomplished this without resorting to layoffs but rather by introducing automated equipment and through attrition. It plans to continue this trend, so that by 1996 the workforce will be further reduced by many thousands of positions, bringing the number of employees to the lowest level since 1984. Competition for the fewer number of jobs that remain will become even fiercer.

In spite of these job reductions, however, there will continue to be career opportunities and examinations will be offered by the Postal Service to replace some of the workers who are promoted, who transfer to other occupations, or who retire each year. Openings will arise also as a result of growth in the volume of mail handled by the Postal Service, reflecting the expanding economy, the rising population, and the increased emphasis on marketing and customer service. Openings will be most frequent in areas with rapid population growth. Although the Postal Service's policy of increasing mechanization and automation works to decrease the number of clerks needed to process a given volume of mail, it also results in additional opportunities for clerks who wish to learn how to operate the new machines and to transfer to new opportunities within the Postal Service. Employees who plan to continue or expand their education should be aware that there will be a growing need for computer specialists and for electronics, electrical, and mechanical maintenance technicians as more and more sophisticated equipment is used to process the mail. The job outlook for certain other positions such as mail handler and mail processor should be more stable. There seems to be no way to substitute machines for human beings to do these jobs.

A FINAL WORD

You now have a good picture of most matters connected with the Test 460/470—before, during, and after. You will be able to act in your best interests in regard to applying, job choice, retaining eligibility, obtaining information, and so on. You should also have gained a certain amount of confidence in knowing why and how certain things happen. Now we've come to building the best confidence of all, the confidence you feel when you're thoroughly prepared to do well on the test itself. It is that thorough preparation to which the rest of this book is dedicated.

DIAGNOSING YOUR SKILLS

Answer Sheet—Diagnostic Practice Test

Part A—Address Checking

1 Ⓐ Ⓓ	25 Ⓐ Ⓓ	49 Ⓐ Ⓓ	73 Ⓐ Ⓓ
2 Ⓐ Ⓓ	26 Ⓐ Ⓓ	50 Ⓐ Ⓓ	74 Ⓐ Ⓓ
3 Ⓐ Ⓓ	27 Ⓐ Ⓓ	51 Ⓐ Ⓓ	75 Ⓐ Ⓓ
4 Ⓐ Ⓓ	28 Ⓐ Ⓓ	52 Ⓐ Ⓓ	76 Ⓐ Ⓓ
5 Ⓐ Ⓓ	29 Ⓐ Ⓓ	53 Ⓐ Ⓓ	77 Ⓐ Ⓓ
6 Ⓐ Ⓓ	30 Ⓐ Ⓓ	54 Ⓐ Ⓓ	78 Ⓐ Ⓓ
7 Ⓐ Ⓓ	31 Ⓐ Ⓓ	55 Ⓐ Ⓓ	79 Ⓐ Ⓓ
8 Ⓐ Ⓓ	32 Ⓐ Ⓓ	56 Ⓐ Ⓓ	80 Ⓐ Ⓓ
9 Ⓐ Ⓓ	33 Ⓐ Ⓓ	57 Ⓐ Ⓓ	81 Ⓐ Ⓓ
10 Ⓐ Ⓓ	34 Ⓐ Ⓓ	58 Ⓐ Ⓓ	82 Ⓐ Ⓓ
11 Ⓐ Ⓓ	35 Ⓐ Ⓓ	59 Ⓐ Ⓓ	83 Ⓐ Ⓓ
12 Ⓐ Ⓓ	36 Ⓐ Ⓓ	60 Ⓐ Ⓓ	84 Ⓐ Ⓓ
13 Ⓐ Ⓓ	37 Ⓐ Ⓓ	61 Ⓐ Ⓓ	85 Ⓐ Ⓓ
14 Ⓐ Ⓓ	38 Ⓐ Ⓓ	62 Ⓐ Ⓓ	86 Ⓐ Ⓓ
15 Ⓐ Ⓓ	39 Ⓐ Ⓓ	63 Ⓐ Ⓓ	87 Ⓐ Ⓓ
16 Ⓐ Ⓓ	40 Ⓐ Ⓓ	64 Ⓐ Ⓓ	88 Ⓐ Ⓓ
17 Ⓐ Ⓓ	41 Ⓐ Ⓓ	65 Ⓐ Ⓓ	89 Ⓐ Ⓓ
18 Ⓐ Ⓓ	42 Ⓐ Ⓓ	66 Ⓐ Ⓓ	90 Ⓐ Ⓓ
19 Ⓐ Ⓓ	43 Ⓐ Ⓓ	67 Ⓐ Ⓓ	91 Ⓐ Ⓓ
20 Ⓐ Ⓓ	44 Ⓐ Ⓓ	68 Ⓐ Ⓓ	92 Ⓐ Ⓓ
21 Ⓐ Ⓓ	45 Ⓐ Ⓓ	69 Ⓐ Ⓓ	93 Ⓐ Ⓓ
22 Ⓐ Ⓓ	46 Ⓐ Ⓓ	70 Ⓐ Ⓓ	94 Ⓐ Ⓓ
23 Ⓐ Ⓓ	47 Ⓐ Ⓓ	71 Ⓐ Ⓓ	95 Ⓐ Ⓓ
24 Ⓐ Ⓓ	48 Ⓐ Ⓓ	72 Ⓐ Ⓓ	

✂ Remove by cutting on dotted line.

Part B – Memory for Addresses—List 1

1 ⒶⒷⒸⒹⒺ
2 ⒶⒷⒸⒹⒺ
3 ⒶⒷⒸⒹⒺ
4 ⒶⒷⒸⒹⒺ
5 ⒶⒷⒸⒹⒺ
6 ⒶⒷⒸⒹⒺ
7 ⒶⒷⒸⒹⒺ
8 ⒶⒷⒸⒹⒺ
9 ⒶⒷⒸⒹⒺ
10 ⒶⒷⒸⒹⒺ
11 ⒶⒷⒸⒹⒺ
12 ⒶⒷⒸⒹⒺ
13 ⒶⒷⒸⒹⒺ
14 ⒶⒷⒸⒹⒺ
15 ⒶⒷⒸⒹⒺ
16 ⒶⒷⒸⒹⒺ
17 ⒶⒷⒸⒹⒺ
18 ⒶⒷⒸⒹⒺ
19 ⒶⒷⒸⒹⒺ
20 ⒶⒷⒸⒹⒺ
21 ⒶⒷⒸⒹⒺ
22 ⒶⒷⒸⒹⒺ
23 ⒶⒷⒸⒹⒺ
24 ⒶⒷⒸⒹⒺ
25 ⒶⒷⒸⒹⒺ
26 ⒶⒷⒸⒹⒺ
27 ⒶⒷⒸⒹⒺ
28 ⒶⒷⒸⒹⒺ
29 ⒶⒷⒸⒹⒺ
30 ⒶⒷⒸⒹⒺ
31 ⒶⒷⒸⒹⒺ
32 ⒶⒷⒸⒹⒺ
33 ⒶⒷⒸⒹⒺ
34 ⒶⒷⒸⒹⒺ
35 ⒶⒷⒸⒹⒺ
36 ⒶⒷⒸⒹⒺ
37 ⒶⒷⒸⒹⒺ
38 ⒶⒷⒸⒹⒺ
39 ⒶⒷⒸⒹⒺ
40 ⒶⒷⒸⒹⒺ
41 ⒶⒷⒸⒹⒺ
42 ⒶⒷⒸⒹⒺ
43 ⒶⒷⒸⒹⒺ
44 ⒶⒷⒸⒹⒺ
45 ⒶⒷⒸⒹⒺ
46 ⒶⒷⒸⒹⒺ
47 ⒶⒷⒸⒹⒺ
48 ⒶⒷⒸⒹⒺ
49 ⒶⒷⒸⒹⒺ
50 ⒶⒷⒸⒹⒺ
51 ⒶⒷⒸⒹⒺ
52 ⒶⒷⒸⒹⒺ
53 ⒶⒷⒸⒹⒺ
54 ⒶⒷⒸⒹⒺ
55 ⒶⒷⒸⒹⒺ
56 ⒶⒷⒸⒹⒺ
57 ⒶⒷⒸⒹⒺ
58 ⒶⒷⒸⒹⒺ
59 ⒶⒷⒸⒹⒺ
60 ⒶⒷⒸⒹⒺ
61 ⒶⒷⒸⒹⒺ
62 ⒶⒷⒸⒹⒺ
63 ⒶⒷⒸⒹⒺ
64 ⒶⒷⒸⒹⒺ
65 ⒶⒷⒸⒹⒺ
66 ⒶⒷⒸⒹⒺ
67 ⒶⒷⒸⒹⒺ
68 ⒶⒷⒸⒹⒺ
69 ⒶⒷⒸⒹⒺ
70 ⒶⒷⒸⒹⒺ
71 ⒶⒷⒸⒹⒺ
72 ⒶⒷⒸⒹⒺ
73 ⒶⒷⒸⒹⒺ
74 ⒶⒷⒸⒹⒺ
75 ⒶⒷⒸⒹⒺ
76 ⒶⒷⒸⒹⒺ
77 ⒶⒷⒸⒹⒺ
78 ⒶⒷⒸⒹⒺ
79 ⒶⒷⒸⒹⒺ
80 ⒶⒷⒸⒹⒺ
81 ⒶⒷⒸⒹⒺ
82 ⒶⒷⒸⒹⒺ
83 ⒶⒷⒸⒹⒺ
84 ⒶⒷⒸⒹⒺ
85 ⒶⒷⒸⒹⒺ
86 ⒶⒷⒸⒹⒺ
87 ⒶⒷⒸⒹⒺ
88 ⒶⒷⒸⒹⒺ

Part B – Memory for Addresses—List 2

1 ⒶⒷⒸⒹⒺ
2 ⒶⒷⒸⒹⒺ
3 ⒶⒷⒸⒹⒺ
4 ⒶⒷⒸⒹⒺ
5 ⒶⒷⒸⒹⒺ
6 ⒶⒷⒸⒹⒺ
7 ⒶⒷⒸⒹⒺ
8 ⒶⒷⒸⒹⒺ
9 ⒶⒷⒸⒹⒺ
10 ⒶⒷⒸⒹⒺ
11 ⒶⒷⒸⒹⒺ
12 ⒶⒷⒸⒹⒺ
13 ⒶⒷⒸⒹⒺ
14 ⒶⒷⒸⒹⒺ
15 ⒶⒷⒸⒹⒺ
16 ⒶⒷⒸⒹⒺ
17 ⒶⒷⒸⒹⒺ
18 ⒶⒷⒸⒹⒺ
19 ⒶⒷⒸⒹⒺ
20 ⒶⒷⒸⒹⒺ
21 ⒶⒷⒸⒹⒺ
22 ⒶⒷⒸⒹⒺ
23 ⒶⒷⒸⒹⒺ
24 ⒶⒷⒸⒹⒺ
25 ⒶⒷⒸⒹⒺ
26 ⒶⒷⒸⒹⒺ
27 ⒶⒷⒸⒹⒺ
28 ⒶⒷⒸⒹⒺ
29 ⒶⒷⒸⒹⒺ
30 ⒶⒷⒸⒹⒺ
31 ⒶⒷⒸⒹⒺ
32 ⒶⒷⒸⒹⒺ
33 ⒶⒷⒸⒹⒺ
34 ⒶⒷⒸⒹⒺ
35 ⒶⒷⒸⒹⒺ
36 ⒶⒷⒸⒹⒺ
37 ⒶⒷⒸⒹⒺ
38 ⒶⒷⒸⒹⒺ
39 ⒶⒷⒸⒹⒺ
40 ⒶⒷⒸⒹⒺ
41 ⒶⒷⒸⒹⒺ
42 ⒶⒷⒸⒹⒺ
43 ⒶⒷⒸⒹⒺ
44 ⒶⒷⒸⒹⒺ
45 ⒶⒷⒸⒹⒺ
46 ⒶⒷⒸⒹⒺ
47 ⒶⒷⒸⒹⒺ
48 ⒶⒷⒸⒹⒺ
49 ⒶⒷⒸⒹⒺ
50 ⒶⒷⒸⒹⒺ
51 ⒶⒷⒸⒹⒺ
52 ⒶⒷⒸⒹⒺ
53 ⒶⒷⒸⒹⒺ
54 ⒶⒷⒸⒹⒺ
55 ⒶⒷⒸⒹⒺ
56 ⒶⒷⒸⒹⒺ
57 ⒶⒷⒸⒹⒺ
58 ⒶⒷⒸⒹⒺ
59 ⒶⒷⒸⒹⒺ
60 ⒶⒷⒸⒹⒺ
61 ⒶⒷⒸⒹⒺ
62 ⒶⒷⒸⒹⒺ
63 ⒶⒷⒸⒹⒺ
64 ⒶⒷⒸⒹⒺ
65 ⒶⒷⒸⒹⒺ
66 ⒶⒷⒸⒹⒺ
67 ⒶⒷⒸⒹⒺ
68 ⒶⒷⒸⒹⒺ
69 ⒶⒷⒸⒹⒺ
70 ⒶⒷⒸⒹⒺ
71 ⒶⒷⒸⒹⒺ
72 ⒶⒷⒸⒹⒺ
73 ⒶⒷⒸⒹⒺ
74 ⒶⒷⒸⒹⒺ
75 ⒶⒷⒸⒹⒺ
76 ⒶⒷⒸⒹⒺ
77 ⒶⒷⒸⒹⒺ
78 ⒶⒷⒸⒹⒺ
79 ⒶⒷⒸⒹⒺ
80 ⒶⒷⒸⒹⒺ
81 ⒶⒷⒸⒹⒺ
82 ⒶⒷⒸⒹⒺ
83 ⒶⒷⒸⒹⒺ
84 ⒶⒷⒸⒹⒺ
85 ⒶⒷⒸⒹⒺ
86 ⒶⒷⒸⒹⒺ
87 ⒶⒷⒸⒹⒺ
88 ⒶⒷⒸⒹⒺ

Part B – Memory for Addresses—List 3

1 ⒶⒷⒸⒹⒺ	19 ⒶⒷⒸⒹⒺ	37 ⒶⒷⒸⒹⒺ	55 ⒶⒷⒸⒹⒺ	73 ⒶⒷⒸⒹⒺ
2 ⒶⒷⒸⒹⒺ	20 ⒶⒷⒸⒹⒺ	38 ⒶⒷⒸⒹⒺ	56 ⒶⒷⒸⒹⒺ	74 ⒶⒷⒸⒹⒺ
3 ⒶⒷⒸⒹⒺ	21 ⒶⒷⒸⒹⒺ	39 ⒶⒷⒸⒹⒺ	57 ⒶⒷⒸⒹⒺ	75 ⒶⒷⒸⒹⒺ
4 ⒶⒷⒸⒹⒺ	22 ⒶⒷⒸⒹⒺ	40 ⒶⒷⒸⒹⒺ	58 ⒶⒷⒸⒹⒺ	76 ⒶⒷⒸⒹⒺ
5 ⒶⒷⒸⒹⒺ	23 ⒶⒷⒸⒹⒺ	41 ⒶⒷⒸⒹⒺ	59 ⒶⒷⒸⒹⒺ	77 ⒶⒷⒸⒹⒺ
6 ⒶⒷⒸⒹⒺ	24 ⒶⒷⒸⒹⒺ	42 ⒶⒷⒸⒹⒺ	60 ⒶⒷⒸⒹⒺ	78 ⒶⒷⒸⒹⒺ
7 ⒶⒷⒸⒹⒺ	25 ⒶⒷⒸⒹⒺ	43 ⒶⒷⒸⒹⒺ	61 ⒶⒷⒸⒹⒺ	79 ⒶⒷⒸⒹⒺ
8 ⒶⒷⒸⒹⒺ	26 ⒶⒷⒸⒹⒺ	44 ⒶⒷⒸⒹⒺ	62 ⒶⒷⒸⒹⒺ	80 ⒶⒷⒸⒹⒺ
9 ⒶⒷⒸⒹⒺ	27 ⒶⒷⒸⒹⒺ	45 ⒶⒷⒸⒹⒺ	63 ⒶⒷⒸⒹⒺ	81 ⒶⒷⒸⒹⒺ
10 ⒶⒷⒸⒹⒺ	28 ⒶⒷⒸⒹⒺ	46 ⒶⒷⒸⒹⒺ	64 ⒶⒷⒸⒹⒺ	82 ⒶⒷⒸⒹⒺ
11 ⒶⒷⒸⒹⒺ	29 ⒶⒷⒸⒹⒺ	47 ⒶⒷⒸⒹⒺ	65 ⒶⒷⒸⒹⒺ	83 ⒶⒷⒸⒹⒺ
12 ⒶⒷⒸⒹⒺ	30 ⒶⒷⒸⒹⒺ	48 ⒶⒷⒸⒹⒺ	66 ⒶⒷⒸⒹⒺ	84 ⒶⒷⒸⒹⒺ
13 ⒶⒷⒸⒹⒺ	31 ⒶⒷⒸⒹⒺ	49 ⒶⒷⒸⒹⒺ	67 ⒶⒷⒸⒹⒺ	85 ⒶⒷⒸⒹⒺ
14 ⒶⒷⒸⒹⒺ	32 ⒶⒷⒸⒹⒺ	50 ⒶⒷⒸⒹⒺ	68 ⒶⒷⒸⒹⒺ	86 ⒶⒷⒸⒹⒺ
15 ⒶⒷⒸⒹⒺ	33 ⒶⒷⒸⒹⒺ	51 ⒶⒷⒸⒹⒺ	69 ⒶⒷⒸⒹⒺ	87 ⒶⒷⒸⒹⒺ
16 ⒶⒷⒸⒹⒺ	34 ⒶⒷⒸⒹⒺ	52 ⒶⒷⒸⒹⒺ	70 ⒶⒷⒸⒹⒺ	88 ⒶⒷⒸⒹⒺ
17 ⒶⒷⒸⒹⒺ	35 ⒶⒷⒸⒹⒺ	53 ⒶⒷⒸⒹⒺ	71 ⒶⒷⒸⒹⒺ	
18 ⒶⒷⒸⒹⒺ	36 ⒶⒷⒸⒹⒺ	54 ⒶⒷⒸⒹⒺ	72 ⒶⒷⒸⒹⒺ	

✂ Remove by cutting on dotted line.

Part C – Number Series

1 ⒶⒷⒸⒹⒺ	6 ⒶⒷⒸⒹⒺ	11 ⒶⒷⒸⒹⒺ	16 ⒶⒷⒸⒹⒺ	21 ⒶⒷⒸⒹⒺ
2 ⒶⒷⒸⒹⒺ	7 ⒶⒷⒸⒹⒺ	12 ⒶⒷⒸⒹⒺ	17 ⒶⒷⒸⒹⒺ	22 ⒶⒷⒸⒹⒺ
3 ⒶⒷⒸⒹⒺ	8 ⒶⒷⒸⒹⒺ	13 ⒶⒷⒸⒹⒺ	18 ⒶⒷⒸⒹⒺ	23 ⒶⒷⒸⒹⒺ
4 ⒶⒷⒸⒹⒺ	9 ⒶⒷⒸⒹⒺ	14 ⒶⒷⒸⒹⒺ	19 ⒶⒷⒸⒹⒺ	24 ⒶⒷⒸⒹⒺ
5 ⒶⒷⒸⒹⒺ	10 ⒶⒷⒸⒹⒺ	15 ⒶⒷⒸⒹⒺ	20 ⒶⒷⒸⒹⒺ	

Part D – Following Oral Directions

1 ⒶⒷⒸⒹⒺ	19 ⒶⒷⒸⒹⒺ	37 ⒶⒷⒸⒹⒺ	55 ⒶⒷⒸⒹⒺ	73 ⒶⒷⒸⒹⒺ
2 ⒶⒷⒸⒹⒺ	20 ⒶⒷⒸⒹⒺ	38 ⒶⒷⒸⒹⒺ	56 ⒶⒷⒸⒹⒺ	74 ⒶⒷⒸⒹⒺ
3 ⒶⒷⒸⒹⒺ	21 ⒶⒷⒸⒹⒺ	39 ⒶⒷⒸⒹⒺ	57 ⒶⒷⒸⒹⒺ	75 ⒶⒷⒸⒹⒺ
4 ⒶⒷⒸⒹⒺ	22 ⒶⒷⒸⒹⒺ	40 ⒶⒷⒸⒹⒺ	58 ⒶⒷⒸⒹⒺ	76 ⒶⒷⒸⒹⒺ
5 ⒶⒷⒸⒹⒺ	23 ⒶⒷⒸⒹⒺ	41 ⒶⒷⒸⒹⒺ	59 ⒶⒷⒸⒹⒺ	77 ⒶⒷⒸⒹⒺ
6 ⒶⒷⒸⒹⒺ	24 ⒶⒷⒸⒹⒺ	42 ⒶⒷⒸⒹⒺ	60 ⒶⒷⒸⒹⒺ	78 ⒶⒷⒸⒹⒺ
7 ⒶⒷⒸⒹⒺ	25 ⒶⒷⒸⒹⒺ	43 ⒶⒷⒸⒹⒺ	61 ⒶⒷⒸⒹⒺ	79 ⒶⒷⒸⒹⒺ
8 ⒶⒷⒸⒹⒺ	26 ⒶⒷⒸⒹⒺ	44 ⒶⒷⒸⒹⒺ	62 ⒶⒷⒸⒹⒺ	80 ⒶⒷⒸⒹⒺ
9 ⒶⒷⒸⒹⒺ	27 ⒶⒷⒸⒹⒺ	45 ⒶⒷⒸⒹⒺ	63 ⒶⒷⒸⒹⒺ	81 ⒶⒷⒸⒹⒺ
10 ⒶⒷⒸⒹⒺ	28 ⒶⒷⒸⒹⒺ	46 ⒶⒷⒸⒹⒺ	64 ⒶⒷⒸⒹⒺ	82 ⒶⒷⒸⒹⒺ
11 ⒶⒷⒸⒹⒺ	29 ⒶⒷⒸⒹⒺ	47 ⒶⒷⒸⒹⒺ	65 ⒶⒷⒸⒹⒺ	83 ⒶⒷⒸⒹⒺ
12 ⒶⒷⒸⒹⒺ	30 ⒶⒷⒸⒹⒺ	48 ⒶⒷⒸⒹⒺ	66 ⒶⒷⒸⒹⒺ	84 ⒶⒷⒸⒹⒺ
13 ⒶⒷⒸⒹⒺ	31 ⒶⒷⒸⒹⒺ	49 ⒶⒷⒸⒹⒺ	67 ⒶⒷⒸⒹⒺ	85 ⒶⒷⒸⒹⒺ
14 ⒶⒷⒸⒹⒺ	32 ⒶⒷⒸⒹⒺ	50 ⒶⒷⒸⒹⒺ	68 ⒶⒷⒸⒹⒺ	86 ⒶⒷⒸⒹⒺ
15 ⒶⒷⒸⒹⒺ	33 ⒶⒷⒸⒹⒺ	51 ⒶⒷⒸⒹⒺ	69 ⒶⒷⒸⒹⒺ	87 ⒶⒷⒸⒹⒺ
16 ⒶⒷⒸⒹⒺ	34 ⒶⒷⒸⒹⒺ	52 ⒶⒷⒸⒹⒺ	70 ⒶⒷⒸⒹⒺ	88 ⒶⒷⒸⒹⒺ
17 ⒶⒷⒸⒹⒺ	35 ⒶⒷⒸⒹⒺ	53 ⒶⒷⒸⒹⒺ	71 ⒶⒷⒸⒹⒺ	
18 ⒶⒷⒸⒹⒺ	36 ⒶⒷⒸⒹⒺ	54 ⒶⒷⒸⒹⒺ	72 ⒶⒷⒸⒹⒺ	

Chapter 2

Diagnostic Practice Test

One of the first questions that you may be asking yourself is, What kind of test score could I make right now? Where would I stand in relation to others taking the same test?

To help answer these questions, it is suggested that you take the following Diagnostic Practice Test, which is modeled after actual Postal Service tests. After you have taken the test, you will be shown how to score it and how that score will compare with the scores of typical test candidates. By knowing your present level of achievement and your strengths and weaknesses, you will be able to direct your improvement efforts. You will know exactly *what* and *how much* to study and practice. You will have a starting point against which to measure the progress you make as you go through this book. The satisfaction you get from seeing your score improve is the best motivating force we know.

These test questions and many additional examples will be used to illustrate certain techniques and strategies given in Chapters 3 through 8. Before you begin, read the section below:

TIMING METHODS FOR PRACTICE TESTS AND DRILLS

The best method for timing your practice tests and drills is to have someone else do it for you. In that way, you will be free from the distraction and loss of time involved in looking at a timepiece. Also, you will be less likely to lose your rhythm or your place on the question and answer sheets. (On the actual test, one of the monitors directs all the timing.)

If you cannot get someone to time you, you can minimize the disadvantages of working alone by following some of these suggestions:

1. Use a count down timer that can be preset so that, when the time is up for a particular study or practice period, an alarm sounds or flashes to alert you.
2. Use an ordinary wall clock, with a face large enough for you to see the numerals clearly from your seat. Mount it at eye level, in a position where you can see it without moving your head or searching for it. It must have a sweep second-hand or a continuous digital readout in seconds. Clocks without this feature allow too much margin for error.
3. Use a wristwatch, taking it off your wrist and setting it in front of you before you begin work. It, too, must show the passage of seconds as well as minutes, and have a clear, easy-to-read display.
4. Use a stopwatch or chronometer that can be preset for an exact time period. It ensures extreme accuracy.

5. Use a metronome for the drills and practice tests on address checking. You can develop a rhythm for working that will help you move along at a consistent pace. (See pages 79 to 80.)

6. Do *not* use egg timers or spring-wound kitchen timers. They do not keep time accurately and consistently. Being even a few seconds off can make an appreciable difference in your final score.

DIAGNOSTIC PRACTICE TEST

Part A — Address Checking

Work—6 minutes

In this test you are to decide whether two addresses are alike or different. If the two addresses are *exactly alike in every way*, darken space Ⓐ. If they are *different in any way*, darken space Ⓓ.

Mark your answers on the Answer Sheet for Address Checking at the beginning of this section. Tear it out, put today's date on it, and place it next to the questions.

Use any of the timing methods described in this chapter, page 31 to 32, but remember to allow yourself *exactly 6 minutes* to do as many of the 95 questions as you can. If you finish before the time is up, check your answers.

1.	La Molte Iowa 52045	La Molte Iowa 52045
2.	608 La Calle Bienvenida	607 La Calle Bienvenida
3.	3224 W Winecona Pl	3224 W Winecona Pl
4.	1166 N Beaumont Dr	1166 S Beaumont Dr
5.	729 Lincolnwood Blvd	729 Lincolnwood Blvd
6.	3124 S 71st St	3142 S 71st St
7.	1987 Wellington Ave SW	1987 Wellington Ave SW
8.	7310 Via de los Pisos	7310 Via de los Pinos
9.	225 El Camino Blvd	225 El Camino Ave
10.	Kendall Calif 90551	Kendell Calif 90551
11.	3478 W Cavanaugh Ct	3478 W Cavenaugh Ct
12.	1003 Winchester Rd	1003 Westchester Rd
13.	52626 W Ogelsby Dr	52626 W Ogelsby Dr
14.	7526 Naranganset Pl SW	7526 Naraganset Pl SW
15.	516 Avenida de Las Americas NW	516 Avenida de Las Americas NW
16.	36218 Overhills Dr	36218 Overhills Dr
17.	1928 S Fairfield Ave	1928 S Fairfield St
18.	Byram Conn 10573	Byram Conn 10573
19.	22 Sagnaw Pkwy	22 Saganaw Pkwy
20.	3824 Massasoit St	3824 Massasoit St
21.	Washington DC 20013	Washington DC 20018
22.	565 Greenville Blvd SE	565 Greenview Blvd SE
23.	2764 N Rutherford Pl	2764 N Rutherford Pl
24.	6434 E Pulaski St	6434 E Pulaski Ct

25.	1172 W 83rd Ave	1127 W 83rd Ave
26.	Dayton Okla 73449	Dagton Okla 73449
27.	4598 E Kenilworth Dr	4598 E Kenilworth Dr
28.	1274 Manzana Rd	1274 Manzana Rd
29.	32 Oaklawn Blvd	32 Oakland Blvd
30.	7117 N Burlingham Ave	7117 N Burlingham Ave
31.	3282 E Downington St	3282 E Dunnington St
32.	758 Los Arboles Ave SE	758 Los Arboles Ave SW
33.	Mason City Iowa 50401-4072	Mason City Iowa 50401-4072
34.	4631 Central Ave	4631 Central Ave
35.	2560 Lansford Pl	2560 Lansford St
36.	635 La Calle Mayor	653 La Calle Mayor
37.	3886 Sunrise Ct	3886 Sunrise Ct
38.	1689 N Derwood Dr	1689 N Derwood Dr
39.	1330 Cheverly Ave NE	1330 Cheverly Ave NE
40.	3628 S Zeeland St	3268 S Zeeland St
41.	3429 Hermosa Dr	3429 Hermoso Dr
42.	Sodus NY 14551	Sodus NY 14551
43.	Wideman Ark	Wiseman Ark
44.	121 N Rippon St	121 N Rippon St
45.	8406 La Casa St	8406 La Cosa St
46.	607 S Calaveras Rd	607 S Calaveras Rd
47.	405 Winter Rd NW	405 Winter Rd NW
48.	Findlay Ohio 45840	Findley Ohio 45840
49.	1201 S Court House Rd	1201 S Court House Rd
50.	3226 M St NW	3226 N St NW
51.	2421 Menokin Dr	2421 Menokin Dr
52.	3613 S Taylor Ave	3631 S Taylor Ave
53.	67158 Capston Dr	67158 Capston Dr
54.	3508 Camron Mills Rd	3508 Camron Mills Rd
55.	Chaptico Md	Chaptica Md
56.	7115 Highland Dr	7115 Highland Dr
57.	2924 26th St N	2929 26th St N
58.	1008 Pennsylvania Ave SE	1008 Pennsylvania Ave SW
59.	Jenkinjones W Va	Jenkinjones, W VA
60.	851 Esperanza Blvd	851 Esperanza Blvd

61.	6643 Burlington Pl	6643 Burlingtown Pl
62.	3405 Prospect St	3405 Prospect St
63	321 Tijeras Ave NW	321 Tijeras Ave NW
64.	1100 Cermaken St	1100 Cermaker St
65.	847 Mesa Grande Pl	847 Mesa Grande Ct
66.	5117 E 67th Pl	5171 E 67th Pl
67.	2445 Sangamow Ave SE	2445 Sangamow Ave SE
68.	96753 Wrightwood Ave	96753 Wrightwood Ave
69.	Sparta Ga	Sparta Va
70.	1198 N St NW	1198 M St NW
71.	4423 S Escenaba St	4423 S Escenaba St
72.	6649 Solano Dr	6649 Solana Dr
73.	8751 Elmhurst Blvd	8751 Elmwood Blvd
74.	2674 E Champlain Cir	2764 E Champlain Cir
75.	Skamokawa Wash	Skamohawa Wash
76.	3987 E Westwood Ave	3987 W Westwood Ave
77.	235 Calle de Los Vecinos	235 Calle de Los Vecinos
78.	2270 N Leanington St	2270 N Leanington St
79.	6431 Ingleside St SE	6431 Ingleside St SE
80.	8774 W Winona Pl	8774 E Winona Pl
81.	512 La Vega Dr	512 La Veta Dr
82.	94002 Chappel Ct	94002 Chappel Ct
83.	1226 Odell Blvd NW	1226 Oddell Blvd NW
84.	3465 S Nashville St	3465 N Nashville St
85.	Altro Tex 75923	Altra Tex 75923
86.	57895 E Drexyl Ave	58795 E Drexyl Ave
87.	6337 C St SW	6337 G St SW
88.	7732 Avenida Manana SW	7732 Avenida Manana SW
89.	351 S Berwyn Rd	351 S Berwyn Pl
90.	114 Estancia Ave	141 Estancia Ave
91.	12742 N Deerborn S	12724 N Deerborn St
92.	165 32nd Ave	165 32nd Ave
93.	4279 Sierra Grande Ave NE	4279 Sierra Grande Dr NE
94.	2343 Broadview Ave	2334 Broadview Ave
95.	8625 Armitage Ave NW	8625 Armitage Ave NW

STOP.

If you finish before the time is up, go back and check the questions in this section of the test only.

Part B — Memory for Addresses

In this test you will have five boxes labeled A, B, C, D, and E. Each box contains five addresses. Three of the five are groups of street addresses, such as 2100–2799 Mall, 4800–4999 Cliff, and 1900–2299 Laurel; and two are names of places. The addresses are different in each box.

There will be several opportunities to study the addresses and the boxes they are in. You will also be given three tests of 88 questions each, and the task of deciding where each address belongs. In some cases, you will have the list *and* the boxes in front of you at the same time; in others you will not. List 1 and List 2 are for warm-up practice. List 3 is the real one that will be scored.

Make sure you understand the format by examining the pretest samples below.

Pretest Samples

A	B	C	D	E
2100–2799 Mall	3900–4399 Mall	4400–4599 Mall	3400–3899 Mall	2800–3399 Mall
Ceres	Cedar	Niles	Cicero	Delhi
4800–4999 Cliff	4000–4299 Cliff	3300–3999 Cliff	4500–4799 Cliff	4300–4499 Cliff
Natoma	Foster	Dexter	Pearl	Magnet
1900–2299 Laurel	2300–2999 Laurel	3200–3799 Laurel	3000–3199 Laurel	1500–1899 Laurel

Questions

Questions 1 through 7 show the way the questions look. You have to decide in which lettered box (A, B, C, D, or E) the address belongs and then mark your answer by darkening the appropriate space in the answer grid.

1. 3300–3999 Cliff — 1 Ⓐ Ⓑ Ⓒ Ⓓ Ⓔ
2. Natoma — 2 Ⓐ Ⓑ Ⓒ Ⓓ Ⓔ
3. Foster — 3 Ⓐ Ⓑ Ⓒ Ⓓ Ⓔ
4. 1500–1899 Laurel — 4 Ⓐ Ⓑ Ⓒ Ⓓ Ⓔ
5. 3900–4399 Mall — 5 Ⓐ Ⓑ Ⓒ Ⓓ Ⓔ
6. Pearl — 6 Ⓐ Ⓑ Ⓒ Ⓓ Ⓔ
7. 3200–3799 Laurel — 7 Ⓐ Ⓑ Ⓒ Ⓓ Ⓔ

Answers

1. **C** 2. **A** 3. **B** 4. **E** 5. **B** 6. **D** 7. **C**

Now that you know what to do, you can begin Part B of the Diagnostic Test. To get the most out of it and the other six practice tests in this book, follow the directions and timing *exactly.* Follow each phase of Part B of this Diagnostic Test, page by page, until you've completed List 3. It is modeled on the way the Postal Service actually conducts its tests.

Turn to the next page to begin.

Study—3 minutes

You will be given 3 minutes to spend memorizing the addresses in the boxes. *They are exactly the same ones that will be used for all three tests.* Try to memorize as many as you can. When the 3 minutes are up, turn to the next page and read the instructions for *List 1*.

A	B	C	D	E
2100–2799 Mall	3900–4399 Mall	4400–4599 Mall	3400–3899 Mall	2800–3399 Mall
Ceres	Cedar	Niles	Cicero	Delhi
4800–4999 Cliff	4000–4299 Cliff	3300–3999 Cliff	4500–4799 Cliff	4300–4499 Cliff
Natoma	Foster	Dexter	Pearl	Magnet
1900–2299 Laurel	2300–2999 Laurel	3200–3799 Laurel	3000–3199 Laurel	1500–1899 Laurel

List 1

Work—3 minutes

Tear out the Answer Sheet for Memory for Addresses for List 1. For each question, mark the answer sheet to show the letter of the box in which the address belongs. Try to remember the locations of as many addresses as you can. *You will now have 3 minutes to complete List 1.* If you are not sure of an answer, you should guess.

A	B	C	D	E
2100–2799 Mall	3900–4399 Mall	4400–4599 Mall	3400–3899 Mall	2800–3399 Mall
Ceres	Cedar	Niles	Cicero	Delhi
4800–4999 Cliff	4000–4299 Cliff	3300–3999 Cliff	4500–4799 Cliff	4300–4499 Cliff
Natoma	Foster	Dexter	Pearl	Magnet
1900–2299 Laurel	2300–2999 Laurel	3200–3799 Laurel	3000–3199 Laurel	1500–1899 Laurel

1. Magnet
2. Niles
3. 3400–3899 Mall
4. 1900–2299 Laurel
5. Cicero
6. Dexter
7. 2300–2999 Laurel
8. 3300–3999 Cliff
9. 3200–3799 Laurel
10. 2100–2799 Mall
11. Pearl
12. 3200–3799 Laurel
13. Ceres
14. 4500–4799 Cliff
15. 3900–4399 Mall
16. Delhi
17. 4300–4499 Cliff
18. 3000–3199 Laurel
19. Ceres
20. Foster
21. Natoma
22. 4400–4599 Mall
23. Cedar
24. 2300–2999 Laurel
25. 1500–1899 Laurel
26. 4000–4299 Cliff
27. Dexter
28. Magnet
29. 3300–3999 Cliff
30. 3400–3899 Mall
31. Niles
32. 2100–2799 Mall
33. 1900–2299 Laurel
34. Cedar
35. Pearl
36. 2800–3399 Mall
37. 4800–4999 Cliff
38. 3900–4399 Mall
39. Foster
40. 3000–3199 Laurel
41. Ceres
42. Niles
43. 3400–3899 Mall
44. Delhi

45. 2300–2999 Laurel
46. 4500–4799 Cliff
47. Dexter
48. Magnet
49. 3300–3999 Cliff
50. Cicero
51. 4300–4499 Cliff
52. 3900–4399 Mall
53. Natoma
54. 3200–3799 Laurel
55. Pearl
56. 4000–4299 Cliff
57. 4500–4799 Cliff
58. 2100–2799 Mall
59. Foster
60. 4400–4599 Mall
61. 4800–4999 Cliff
62. Ceres
63. 2800–3399 Mall
64. 1500–1899 Laurel
65. Natoma
66. 3000–3199 Laurel
67. 4000–4299 Cliff
68. Niles
69. 2300–2999 Laurel
70. Magnet
71. Delhi
72. 4400–4599 Mall
73. Cicero
74. Cedar
75. 2800–3399 Mall
76. 1900–2299 Laurel
77. Dexter
78. Pearl
79. 4300–4499 Cliff
80. 3900–4399 Mall
81. Foster
82. 4800–4999 Cliff
83. Delhi
84. Ceres
85. 1500–1899 Laurel
86. Natoma
87. 2800–3399 Mall
88. Niles

STOP.
If you finish before the time is up, go back and check the questions in this section of the test only.

List 2

Work—3 minutes

Do these questions *without* looking back at the boxes. For each question, mark your answer on the Answer Sheet for List 2. If you are not sure of an answer, guess.

1. Cedar
2. 4300–4499 Cliff
3. 4400–4599 Mall
4. Natoma
5. 2300–2999 Laurel
6. 4500–4799 Cliff
7. Ceres
8. 3400–3899 Mall
9. Delhi
10. Dexter
11. 1900–2299 Laurel
12. 3300–3999 Cliff
13. Cicero
14. 4000–4299 Cliff
15. 2100–2799 Mall
16. Foster
17. Magnet
18. Ceres
19. 2800–3399 Mall
20. 3200–3799 Laurel
21. 4300–4499 Cliff
22. Pearl
23. 3900–4399 Mall
24. Natoma
25. 4800–4999 Cliff
26. 1500–1899 Laurel
27. Cedar
28. 4400–4599 Mall
29. 4500–4799 Cliff
30. Dexter
31. 3000–3199 Laurel
32. Niles
33. Delhi
34. 3900–4399 Mall
35. Cicero
36. Dexter
37. 4800–4999 Cliff
38. 2300–2999 Laurel
39. 2100–2799 Mall
40. 3300–3999 Cliff
41. 3400–3899 Mall
42. 4300–4499 Cliff
43. Ceres
44. Foster

45. Magnet
46. 3200–3799 Laurel
47. Pearl
48. 1500– 1899 Laurel
49. 4500–4799 Cliff
50. 1900–2299 Laurel
51. Niles
52. 3300–3999 Cliff
53. 2800–3399 Mall
54. Cicero
55. Delhi

56. 4000–4299 Cliff
57. Dexter
58. Magnet
59. 3000–3199 Laurel
60. 3900–4399 Mall
61. Natoma
62. 3000–3199 Laurel
63. 4300–4499 Cliff
64. Cedar
65. 4400–4599 Mall
66. 1500–1899 Laurel
67. 4800–4999 Cliff
68. Delhi
69. Pearl
70. 2300–2999 Laurel
71. 4500–4799 Cliff
72. Niles
73. 4000–4299 Cliff
74. 3400–3899 Mall
75. 1900–2299 Laurel
76. 2800–3399 Mall
77. Ceres

78. Magnet
79. Cicero
80. 3200–3799 Laurel
81. 3000–3199 Laurel
82. 3900–4399 Mall
83. Natoma
84. 3300–3999 Cliff
85. 3400–3899 Mall
86. Foster
87. 2100–2799 Mall
88. 4300–4499 Cliff

STOP.
If you finish before the time is up, go back and check the questions in this section of the test only.

List 3

Study—5 minutes

You are now about to take the test using List 3. *(This is the test that counts!)*

Turn back to page 38 and study the boxes again. *You have 5 minutes to restudy the addresses.* When the time is up, tear out the Answer Sheet for List 3. Use it for the test.

Work—5 minutes

For each question, mark the Answer Sheet to show the letter of the box in which the address belongs. You have exactly 5 minutes to do the test. During these 5 minutes, *do not* turn to any other page.

1. Foster
2. Ceres
3. 4300–4499 Cliff
4. 3400–3899 Mall
5. 3300–3999 Cliff
6. Magnet
7. 2300–2999 Laurel
8. 4800–4999 Cliff
9. Dexter
10. Cicero
11. 3900–4399 Mall
12. Delhi
13. Niles
14. 3000–3199 Laurel
15. Dexter
16. 4500–4799 Cliff
17. 4400–4599 Mall
18. Cedar
19. 1500–1899 Laurel
20. 4800–4999 Cliff
21. Natoma
22. 3900–4399 Mall
23. Pearl
24. 4300–4499 Cliff
25. 3200–3799 Laurel
26. 2800–3399 Mall
27. Ceres
28. Magnet
29. Foster
30. 2100–2799 Mall
31. 4000–4299 Cliff
32. Cicero
33. 3300–3999 Cliff
34. 1900–2299 Laurel
35. Dexter
36. Delhi
37. 3400–3899 Mall
38. Ceres
39. 4500–4799 Cliff
40. 2300–2999 Laurel
41. Natoma
42. 4400–4599 Mall
43. 4300–4599 Cliff
44. Cedar

45. 4300–4499 Cliff
46. 2100–2799 Mall
47. Foster
48. 3400–3899 Mall
49. 3300–3999 Cliff
50. Natoma
51. 3900–4399 Mall
52. 3000–3199 Laurel
53. 3200–3799 Laurel
54. Cicero
55. Magnet
56. Ceres
57. 2800–3399 Mall
58. 1900–2299 Laurel
59. 3400–3899 Mall
60. 4000–4299 Cliff
61. Niles
62. 4500–4799 Cliff
63. 2300–2999 Laurel
64. Pearl
65. Delhi
66. 4800–4999 Cliff
67. 1500–1899 Laurel
68. 4400–4599 Mall
69. Cedar
70. 4300–4499 Cliff
71. 3000–3199 Laurel
72. Natoma
73. 3900–4399 Mall
74. 3000–3199 Laurel
75. Magnet
76. Dexter
77. 4000–4299 Cliff
78. Delhi
79. Cicero
80. 2800–3399 Mall
81. 3300–3999 Cliff
82. Niles
83. 1900–2299 Laurel
84. 4500–4799 Cliff
85. 1500–1899 Laurel
86. Pearl
87. 3200–3799 Laurel
88. Magnet

STOP.

If you finish before the time is up, go back and check the questions in this section of the test only.

Part C — Number Series

Work—20 minutes

For each Number Series question, there is at the left, a series of numbers that follows some definite order, and below each, five sets of two numbers each. You are to look at the numbers in the series at the left and find out what order they follow. Then decide what the next two numbers in that series would be if the same order were continued. Mark your choice of answers on the Answer Sheet for Number Series at the beginning of this section. Tear it out, put today's date on it, and place it next to the questions.

You have 20 minutes to complete this part of the test. If you finish before the time is up, check your answers. The correct answers and answer explanations are given at the end of the test on pages 56 and 57.

Questions

1. 12 10 15 13 18 16 21 __ __
   A) 19 24 B) 17 19 C) 19 20 D) 26 24 E) 21 23

2. 8 11 14 10 13 16 12 __ __
   A) 15 14 B) 15 11 C) 14 16 D) 11 8 E) 15 18

3. 15 16 17 15 16 17 15 __ __
   A) 15 16 B)16 17 C) 16 15 D) 17 15 E) 15 17

4. 3 4 6 9 13 18 24 __ __
   A) 30 37 B) 31 38 C) 32 40 D) 29 35 E) 31 39

5. 7 7 8 9 9 10 11 __ __
   A) 11 12 B) 12 13 C) 13 13 D) 11 11 E) 10 11

6. 10 6 6 10 7 7 10 __ __
   A) 10 10 B) 8 10 C) 10 8 D) 8 8 E) 8 9

7. 18 9 17 10 16 11 15 __ __
   A) 13 14 B) 14 13 C) 12 14 D) 14 12 E) 12 13

8. 7 8 16 9 10 15 11 __ __
   A) 14 10 B) 13 12 C) 13 14 D) 15 13 E) 12 14

9. 4 9 8 13 12 17 16 __ __
   A) 18 19 B) 20 21 C) 21 19 D) 21 20 E) 18 21

10. 1 2 2 4 4 8 8 16 __ __
A) 16 16 B) 16 32 C) 32 18 D) 12 32 E) 20 36

11. 6 9 10 7 11 12 8 __ __
A) 9 10 B) 9 13 C) 16 14 D) 13 14 E) 14 15

12. 7 5 3 9 7 5 11 __ __
A) 13 12 B) 7 5 C) 9 7 D) 13 7 E) 9 9

13. 7 9 18 10 12 18 13 __ __
A) 18 14 B) 15 18 C) 14 15 D) 15 14 E) 14 18

14. 40 10 39 12 37 14 34 16 __ __
A) 18 33 B) 28 20 C) 30 18 D) 29 18 E) 16 31

15. 7 9 12 14 17 19 22 __ __
A) 25 27 B) 23 24 C) 23 25 D) 24 27 E) 26 27

16. 3 23 5 25 7 27 9 __ __
A) 10 11 B) 27 29 C) 29 11 D) 11 28 E) 28 10

17. 18 17 16 14 13 12 10 __ __
A) 9 8 B) 6 7 C) 8 6 D) 8 7 E) 10 9

18. 13 12 18 13 13 19 13 14 __ __
A) 15 20 B) 17 13 C) 19 23 D) 13 18 E) 20 13

19. 28 27 25 24 22 21 19 __ __
A) 18 16 B) 17 16 C) 18 17 D) 17 15 E) 20 18

20. 2 2 4 6 6 8 10 __ __
A) 12 12 B) 12 14 C) 10 10 D) 10 8 E) 10 12

21. 2 7 3 8 4 9 5 __ __
A) 6 7 B) 10 6 C) 6 10 D) 10 11 E) 5 10

22. 1 4 5 9 14 23 37 __ __
A) 52 67 B) 63 17 C) 60 97 D) 73 105 E) 49 84

23. 3 5 7 7 4 6 8 8 5 7 9 __ __

A) 9 6 B) 6 6 C) 6 9 D) 10 8 E) 8 10

24. 15 26 24 16 21 19 17 16 14 18 __ __

A) 17 15 B) 11 9 C) 15 14 D) 17 16 E) 11 10

STOP.

If you finish before the time is up, go back and check the questions in this section of the test only.

Part D — Following Oral Directions

This part of the test gauges your ability to understand and carry out spoken directions *exactly* as they are given to you.

In order to prepare to take Part D of the test, follow the steps below:

1. Enlist the help of a friend (the "reader") whose job it will be to read aloud a series of directions that you are to follow *exactly.* The reader will need a watch that displays seconds, because the directions must be read at the correct speed.
2. Tear out pages 49 and 50. These are the worksheets you should have in front of you as you listen to the directions given by the reader, who will tell you to do certain things with the items on each line on the worksheets.
3. Tear out the Answer Sheet for Following Oral Directions on page 29, and insert today's date. You will darken the appropriate spaces in accordance with the directions given by the reader.
4. *Now hand this entire book to the reader.* Ask him/her to review the section on page 51 headed "Instructions to the Reader." It explains exactly how the reader is to proceed.

When you and the reader are ready to start this part of the Diagnostic Practice Test, he/she will begin reading to you the section marked "Directions." YOU ARE NOT TO READ THESE AT ANY TIME BEFORE OR DURING THE TEST. If you do, you will lose the benefit of this part of the Diagnostic Practice Test.

Diagnostic Practice Test—Worksheet 1

Part D—Following Oral Directions

1. 13 23 2 19 6

2. E B D E C A B

3. [30 ___] [18 ___] [5 ___] [14 ___] [7 ___]

4. (26 ___) (16 ___) (23 ___) (22 ___) (27 ___)

5. [3 ___] [14 ___] [8 ___] [18 ___]

6. 12 ___ 5 ___ 22 ___

7. (4 ___) (1 ___) (6 ___) (7 ___) (19 ___)

8. 26 ___ 9 ___

9. 17 23 11 18 20 32 25 10 9

10. 16 30 13 25 10 14 23 26 19

11. (9:12 ___ A) (9:28 ___ B) (9:24 ___ C) (9:11 ___ D) (9:32 ___ E)

✂ Remove by cutting on dotted line.

Diagnostic Practice Test—Worksheet 2

Part D—Following Oral Directions

12. 17 ___ | 10 ___ | 26 ___ | 8 ___ | 25 ___

13. ___ A | ___ B | ___ C | ___ D | ___ E

14. 3 ___ | 10 ___ | 20 ___ | 32 ___

15. 2 ___ | 31 ___ | 29 ___ | ABLE | EASY | DESK

16. X X O X O O O X O X X O X X

17. 22 ___ | 3 ___ | 21 ___ | 28 ___

18. 21 ___ | 8 ___ | 29 ___ | 31 ___

19. 3 DETROIT HARTFORD ___ | 26 ST. LOUIS CLEVELAND ___

Instructions to the "Reader"

These directions should be read at about 80 words per minute. You should practice reading the material in the box until you can do it in exactly 1 minute. This will give you a feel for the way you should read the test material.

1-MINUTE PRACTICE

> Look at line 17 on your worksheet. There are two circles and two boxes of different sizes with numbers in them. If 7 is less than 3 and if 2 is smaller than 4, write C in the larger circle. Otherwise write B as in *baker* in the smaller box. Now, on your answer sheet darken the space for the number-letter combination in the box or circle.

You should read the entire test aloud before you read it to the person taking the test, in order to acquaint yourself with the procedure and the desired rate of reading.

Read slowly, but at a natural pace. In other words, do not space the words so that there are unnaturally long pauses between them. The instruction "Pause slightly" indicates only enough time to take a breath. The other instructions for pauses give the recommended length for each. If possible, use a watch with a second hand.

All the material that follows, except the words in parentheses, is to be read aloud. Now start reading the directions. *Do not repeat any of the directions.*

Directions: In this test, I will read instructions to you. You are to mark your worksheets according to the instructions that I read. After each set of instructions, I'll give you time to record your answers on your answer sheet.

Try to understand the instructions as I read them; I cannot repeat them. Do not ask any questions from now on.

If, when you go to darken a space for a number, you find that you have already darkened another space for that number, either (1) erase the first mark and darken the space for your new choice, or (2) let the first mark stay and do not darken any other space. When you finish, you should have no more than one space darkened for each number.

Turn to Worksheet 1.

Look at line 1 on your worksheet. (Pause slightly.) Draw a line under the fourth number in the line. (Pause 2 seconds.) Now, on your answer sheet, find the number under which you just drew the line and darken space A for that number. (Pause 5 seconds.)

Look at the letters in line 2 on your worksheet again. (Pause slightly.) Now draw two lines under the third letter in the line. (Pause 2 seconds.) Now, on your answer sheet, find number 21 (pause 2 seconds) and darken the space for the letter under which you drew two lines. (Pause 5 seconds.)

Look at line 3 on your worksheet. (Pause slightly.) Write an E in the last box. (Pause 2 seconds.) Now, on your answer sheet, find the number in that box and darken space E for that number. (Pause 5 seconds.)

Look at line 3 again. (Pause slightly.) Write an A in the first box. (Pause 2 seconds.) Now, on your answer sheet, find the number in that box and darken space A for that number. (Pause 5 seconds.)

Look at line 4. The number in each circle is the number of packages in a mail sack. In the circle for the sack holding the largest number of packages, write a B as in *baker.* (Pause 2 seconds.) Now, on your answer sheet, darken the space for the number-letter combination that is in the circle you just wrote in. (Pause 5 seconds.)

Look at line 4 again. In the circle for the sack holding the smallest number of packages, write an E. (Pause 2 seconds.) Now, on your answer sheet, darken the space for the number-letter combination that is in the circle you just wrote in. (Pause 5 seconds.)

Look at the drawings on line 5 on your worksheet. The four boxes are trucks for carrying mail. (Pause slightly.) The truck with the highest number is to be loaded first. Write B as in *baker* on the line beside the highest number. (Pause 2 seconds.) Now, on your answer sheet, darken the space for the number-letter combination that is in the box you just wrote in. (Pause 5 seconds.)

Look at line 6 on your worksheet. (Pause slightly.) Next to the middle number write the letter D as in *dog.* (Pause 2 seconds.) Now, on your answer sheet, find the number beside which you wrote and darken space D as in *dog* for that number. (Pause 5 seconds.)

Look at the five circles on line 7 on your worksheet. (Pause slightly.) Write B as in *baker* on the blank in the second circle. (Pause 2 seconds.) Now, on your answer sheet, darken the space for the number-letter combination that is in the circle you just wrote in. (Pause 5 seconds.)

Look at line 7 again. (Pause slightly.) Write C on the blank in the third circle on line 7. (Pause 2 seconds.) Now, on your answer sheet, darken the space for the number-letter combination that is in the circle you just wrote in. (Pause 5 seconds.)

Look at line 8 on your worksheet. (Pause slightly.) Write A on the line next to the right-hand number. (Pause 2 seconds.) Now, on your answer sheet, find the number beside which you wrote, and darken space A. (Pause 5 seconds.)

Look at line 9 on your worksheet. (Pause slightly.) Draw a line under every number that is more than 20 but less than 30. (Pause 12 seconds.) Now, on your answer sheet, for each number that you drew a line under, darken space C. (Pause 25 seconds.)

Look at line 10 in your worksheet. (Pause slightly.) Draw a line under every number that is more than 5 but less than 15. (Pause 10 seconds.) Now, on your answer sheet, for each number you drew a line under, darken space D as in *dog.* (Pause 25 seconds.)

Look at line 11 on your worksheet. (Pause slightly.) In each circle there is a time when the mail must leave. In the circle for the latest time, write on the line the last two figures of the time. (Pause 5 seconds.) Now, on your answer sheet, darken the space for the number-letter combination that is in the circle you just wrote in. (Pause 5 seconds.)

Now turn to Worksheet 2.

Look at the five boxes in line 12 on your worksheet. (Pause slightly.) If 6 is less than 3, put an E in the fourth box. (Pause slightly.) If 6 is not less than 3, put a B as in *baker* in the first box. (Pause 5 seconds.) Now, on your answer sheet, darken the space for the number-letter combination that is in the box you just wrote in. (Pause 5 seconds.)

Now look at line 13 in your test booklet. (Pause slightly.) There are 5 circles. Each circle has a letter. (Pause slightly.) In the second circle, write the answer to this question: Which of the following numbers is smallest: 32, 11, 22, 31, 16? (Pause 5 seconds.) Now, on your answer sheet, darken the space for the number-letter combination that is in the circle you just wrote in. (Pause 5 seconds.)

In the third circle on the same line, write 28. (Pause 2 seconds.) Now, on your answer sheet, darken the space for the number-letter combination that is in the circle you just wrote in. (Pause 5 seconds.)

In the fourth circle do nothing. In the fifth circle write the answer to this question: How many months are there in a year? (Pause 2 seconds.) Now, on your answer sheet, darken the space for the number-letter combination that is in the circle you just wrote in. (Pause 5 seconds.)

Look at line 14 on your worksheet. (Pause slightly.) There are two circles and two boxes of different sizes with numbers in them. (Pause slightly.) If 2 is smaller than 4 and if 7 is less than 3, write A in the larger circle. (Pause slightly.) Otherwise write B as in *baker* in the smaller box. (Pause 2 seconds.) Now, on your answer sheet, darken the space for the number-letter combination that is in the box or circle you just wrote in. (Pause 5 seconds.)

Look at the boxes and words in line 15 on your worksheet. (Pause slightly.) Write the second letter of the first word in the third box. (Pause 2 seconds.) Write the first letter of the second word in the first box. (Pause 2 seconds.) Write the first letter of the third word in the second box. (Pause 2 seconds.) Now, on your answer sheet, darken the spaces for the number-letter combinations that are in the three boxes you just wrote in. (Pause 10 seconds.)

Look at line 16 on your worksheet. (Pause slightly.) Draw a line under every "O" in the line. (Pause 5 seconds.) Count the number of lines that you have drawn, subtract 2, and write that number at the end of the line. (Pause 5 seconds.) Now, on your answer sheet, find that number and darken space D as in *dog* for that number. (Pause 5 seconds.)

Look at line 17 on your worksheet. (Pause slightly.) If the number in the left-hand circle is smaller than the number in the right-hand circle, add 2 to the number in the left-hand circle, and change the number in that circle to this number. (Pause 8 seconds.) Then write B as in *baker* next to the new number. (Pause slightly.) Otherwise write E next to the number in the smaller box. (Pause 3 seconds.) Then, on your answer sheet, darken the space for the number-letter combination that is in the box or circle you just wrote in. (Pause 5 seconds.)

Look at line 18 on your worksheet. (Pause slightly.) If in a year January comes before February, write A in the box with the smallest number. (Pause slightly.) If it does not, write C in the box with the largest number. (Pause 3 seconds.) Now, on your answer sheet, darken the space for the number-letter combination that is in the box you just wrote in. (Pause 5 seconds.)

Look at line 19 on your worksheet. (Pause slightly.) Mail for Detroit and Hartford is to be put in box 3. (Pause slightly.) Mail for Cleveland and St. Louis is to be put in box 26. (Pause slightly.) Write C in the box in which you put mail for St. Louis. Now, on your answer sheet, darken the space for the number-letter combination that is in the box you just wrote in. (Pause 5 seconds.)

END OF EXAMINATION.
If you finish before the time is up, go back and check the questions in this section of the test only.

ANSWER KEY

Part A—Address Checking

1. **A**	11. **D**	21. **D**	31. **D**	41. **D**	51. **A**	61. **A**	71. **A**	81. **D**	91. **D**
2. **D**	12. **D**	22. **D**	32. **D**	42. **A**	52. **D**	62. **A**	72. **D**	82. **A**	92. **A**
3. **A**	13. **A**	23. **A**	33. **A**	43. **D**	53. **A**	63. **A**	73. **D**	83. **D**	93. **D**
4. **D**	14. **D**	24. **D**	34. **A**	44. **A**	54. **A**	64. **D**	74. **D**	84. **D**	94. **D**
5. **A**	15. **A**	25. **D**	35. **D**	45. **D**	55. **D**	65. **D**	75. **D**	85. **D**	95. **A**
6. **D**	16. **A**	26. **D**	36. **D**	46. **A**	56. **A**	66. **D**	76. **D**	86. **D**	
7. **A**	17. **D**	27. **A**	37. **A**	47. **A**	57. **D**	67. **A**	77. **A**	87. **D**	
8. **D**	18. **A**	28. **A**	38. **A**	48. **D**	58. **A**	68. **A**	78. **A**	88. **A**	
9. **D**	19. **D**	29. **D**	39. **A**	49. **A**	59. **D**	69. **D**	79. **A**	89. **D**	
10. **D**	20. **A**	30. **A**	40. **D**	50. **D**	60. **A**	70. **D**	80. **D**	90. **D**	

Part B—Memory for Addresses

List 1

1. **E**	10. **A**	19. **A**	28. **E**	37. **A**	46. **D**	55. **D**	64. **E**	73. **D**	82. **A**
2. **C**	11. **D**	20. **B**	29. **C**	38. **B**	47. **C**	56. **B**	65. **A**	74. **B**	83. **E**
3. **D**	12. **C**	21. **A**	30. **D**	39. **B**	48. **E**	57. **D**	66. **D**	75. **E**	84. **A**
4. **A**	13. **A**	22. **C**	31. **C**	40. **D**	49. **C**	58. **A**	67. **B**	76. **A**	85. **E**
5. **D**	14. **D**	23. **B**	32. **A**	41. **A**	50. **D**	59. **B**	68. **C**	77. **C**	86. **A**
6. **C**	15. **B**	24. **B**	33. **A**	42. **C**	51. **E**	60. **C**	69. **B**	78. **D**	87. **E**
7. **B**	16. **E**	25. **E**	34. **B**	43. **D**	52. **B**	61. **A**	70. **E**	79. **E**	88. **C**
8. **C**	17. **E**	26. **B**	35. **D**	44. **E**	53. **A**	62. **A**	71. **E**	80. **B**	
9. **C**	18. **D**	27. **C**	36. **E**	45. **B**	54. **C**	63. **E**	72. **C**	81. **B**	

List 2

1. **B**	10. **C**	19. **E**	28. **C**	37. **A**	46. **C**	55. **E**	64. **B**	73. **B**	82. **B**
2. **E**	11. **A**	20. **C**	29. **D**	38. **B**	47. **D**	56. **B**	65. **C**	74. **D**	83. **A**
3. **C**	12. **C**	21. **E**	30. **C**	39. **A**	48. **E**	57. **C**	66. **E**	75. **A**	84. **C**
4. **A**	13. **D**	22. **D**	31. **D**	40. **C**	49. **D**	58. **E**	67. **A**	76. **E**	85. **D**
5. **B**	14. **B**	23. **B**	32. **C**	41. **D**	50. **A**	59. **D**	68. **E**	77. **A**	86. **B**
6. **D**	15. **A**	24. **A**	33. **E**	42. **E**	51. **C**	60. **B**	69. **D**	78. **E**	87. **A**
7. **A**	16. **B**	25. **A**	34. **B**	43. **A**	52. **C**	61. **A**	70. **B**	79. **D**	88. **E**
8. **D**	17. **E**	26. **E**	35. **D**	44. **B**	53. **E**	62. **D**	71. **D**	80. **C**	
9. **E**	18. **A**	27. **B**	36. **C**	45. **E**	54. **D**	63. **E**	72. **C**	81. **D**	

List 3

1. **B**	10. **D**	19. **E**	28. **E**	37. **D**	46. **A**	55. **E**	64. **D**	73. **B**	82. **C**
2. **A**	11. **B**	20. **A**	29. **B**	38. **A**	47. **B**	56. **A**	65. **E**	74. **D**	83. **A**
3. **E**	12. **E**	21. **A**	30. **A**	39. **D**	48. **D**	57. **E**	66. **A**	75. **E**	84. **D**
4. **D**	13. **C**	22. **B**	31. **B**	40. **B**	49. **C**	58. **A**	67. **E**	76. **C**	85. **E**
5. **C**	14. **D**	23. **D**	32. **D**	41. **A**	50. **A**	59. **D**	68. **C**	77. **B**	86. **D**
6. **E**	15. **C**	24. **E**	33. **C**	42. **C**	51. **B**	60. **B**	69. **B**	78. **E**	87. **C**
7. **B**	16. **D**	25. **C**	34. **A**	43. **E**	52. **D**	61. **C**	70. **E**	79. **D**	88. **E**
8. **A**	17. **C**	26. **E**	35. **C**	44. **B**	53. **C**	62. **D**	71. **D**	80. **E**	
9. **C**	18. **B**	27. **A**	36. **E**	45. **E**	54. **D**	63. **B**	72. **A**	81. **C**	

Part C—Number Series

1. **A**	4. **E**	7. **C**	10. **B**	13. **B**	16. **C**	19. **A**	22. **C**
2. **E**	5. **A**	8. **E**	11. **D**	14. **C**	17. **A**	20. **E**	23. **A**
3. **B**	6. **D**	9. **D**	12. **C**	15. **D**	18. **E**	21. **B**	24. **B**

Part D—Following Oral Directions

1. **B**	5. **D**	9. **A**	13. **D**	17. **B**	21. **D**	25. **C**	29. **B**
2. **E**	6. **C**	10. **D**	14. **D**	18. **B**	22. *	26. **C**	30. **A**
3. *	7. **E**	11. **B**	15. **C**	19. **A**	23. **C**	27. **B**	31. **D**
4. **D**	8. **A**	12. **E**	16. **E**	20. **B**	24. **B**	28. **C**	32. **E**

* Note: No answers were called for in answer places 3 and 22.

ANSWER EXPLANATIONS FOR PART C— NUMBER SERIES

1. **A** A loop diagram clearly shows the rule for this series

   −2 +5 −2 +5 −2 +5 −2 +5

   12 10 15 13 18 16 21...*19 24*

2. **E** The rule for progressing from one number to the next is a little more complex, but again, the loop diagram will make it clear

   +3 +3 −4 +3 +3 −4 +3 +3

   8 11 14 10 13 16 12...*15 18*

3. **B** This series is simply a repetition of three numbers: 15 16 17
4. **E** The difference between each number keeps increasing by 1.

   +1 +2 +3 +4 +5 +6 +7 +8

   3 4 6 9 13 18 24...*31 39*

5. **A** In this series the numbers are increasing by 1, with every second number being repeated before it increases.
6. **D** This time you have the number 10 interrupting a sequence of numbers that go up by 1 after each has been repeated. (This rule is not easy to understand if it is *stated* or *written*. That is why it is strongly urged to use diagrams and other techniques you'll read about in Chapter 6.) Look at how readily the pattern shows up when properly diagrammed:

   +0 +1 +0 +1 +0

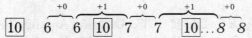

   [10] 6 6 [10] 7 7 [10]...*8 8*

7. **C** The rule for this series is easy to follow if you consider it to be composed of two alternating series

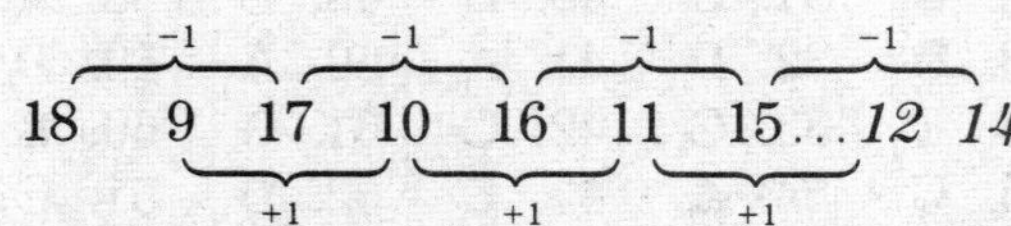

   One series begins with 18 and decreases by *1*. The other begins with 9 and increases by 1.

8. **E** This is another example of alternating series, one going up by 1, the other going down by 1. In this case however, the series that is increasing continues for two numbers before it is interrupted by the other.

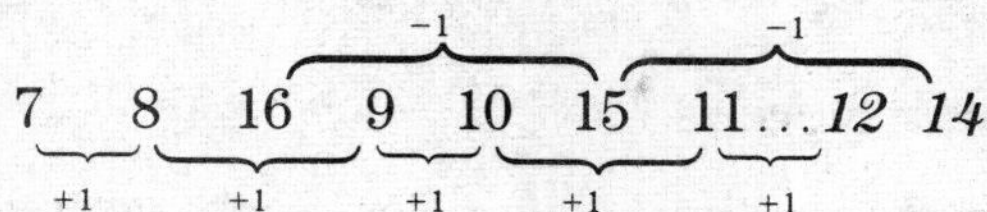

Most of the foregoing examples were diagrammed as well as explained to help you get started. The examples on the next page will not be diagrammed. You may do that now or after you've read Chapter 6.

9. **D** The rule here is +5, –l; +5, –l; etc.
10. **B** In this series multiplication by 2 is used to connect the numbers. After each multiplication the new number is repeated once and then the process continues.
11. **D** This series of numbers can be considered to be composed of *three* alternating series—one increasing by +1; two increasing by +2. If you wish, you can see them connected one to the other by this rule: +3, +1, –3; +4, +1, –4; . . . *+5, +1*
12. **C** This series follows the rule: –2, –2, +6.
13. **B** Basically, this is a series that increases according to this rule: +2, +1; +2, +1; . . . It is interrupted after every two numbers by the number 18.
14. **C** Here again are two alternating series. One decreases by ever increasing amounts –1, –2, –3 . . . etc. The other increases by +2.
15. **D** The rule is: +2, +3; +2, +3 . . .
16. **C** There are two alternating series here: one increases by +2. The alternate series also increases by +2
17. **A** This series follows the rule: –1, –1, –2; –1, –1, –2, etc.
18. **E** This series can be quite confusing until you realize that the number 13 interrupts the series by appearing every *third* number. With that fact accounted for, we have a series that follows the rule: +6, –5; +6, –5 . . .
19. **A** The series follows the pattern: –1, –2; –1, –2 . . .
20. **E** In this series the numbers are increasing by 2. Every other number is repeated before it increases.
21. **B** You can view this as two alternating series, each of which increases by +l. If you wish, you may connect them by the rule: +5, – 4; +5, – 4; +5, – 4 . . .
22. **C** Each number is obtained by adding together the two preceding numbers; that is, 1 + 4 = 5; 4 + 5 = 9; 5 + 9 = 14; 9 + 14 = 23; 14 + 23 = 37; 23 + 37; = *60*; 37 + 60 = *97*
23. **A** These numbers follow a complex set of rules. They may be viewed either as groups of 3 number "mini-series"—that is, 3 5 7; 4 6 8; 5 7 9, each of which increases by +2. Or they may be seen as three alternating series. In either case, the last number of the group is repeated once. In Chapter 6 you will see how to diagram and identify this series either way.
24. **B** This too is made of two alternating series: one is increasing by + l (see 15 . . . 16 . . . 17 . . .); the other follows the rule –2, –3; –2, –3 (see 26 . . . 24 . . . 21 . . . 19 . . .) and is interrupted after every two numbers by one member of the first series.

EVALUATING YOUR PROGRESS*

Part A—Address Checking

Computing Your Score

Check your answers against the Answer Key. Score yourself by using this formula:

Number right
− Number wrong

YOUR SCORE

For example, if you completed 52 questions and got 8 wrong,

Number right	=	44
− Number wrong	=	− 8
Your score	=	36

Notice that you do *not* figure in the questions that you did not answer.

Guidelines

How good is the score you just made?

52 or higher .... Good

Between 32 and 52 .... Fair

Below 32 .... You need to improve.

These are commonly accepted figures. However, you should not be satisfied with anything *less* than 52. In training many people to prepare for this test, it has been shown that most serious test candidates who use the preparation program described in this book (Chapter 3 covers Address Checking) will be able to raise their score to the upper sixties, seventies, or eighties.

Personal Progress Record

One of the most satisfying things that can happen while you are working toward a goal is to see signs of progress. The improvement you make on Address Checking can readily be seen by examining the scores you make on the practice tests and exercises in this book. You can keep track of your growing skill on the Personal Progress Record, furnished for your use on page 430.

The following is a sample of this Personal Progress Record to familiarize you with it. The entries on this sample are based on the example above.

Furthermore, even though you take one test, your final score will vary depending on the title. For example, your rating on the Mail Handler register may very well be different

* Please note that the scores you obtain by following the computation instructions for the various parts of this test are "raw" scores. The Postal Service combines and converts the raw scores for the various parts of the test into a scaled score obtained by using special conversion formulas that are kept confidential. This scaled score (plus any veteran's credits to which you are entitled) forms the basis for your final rating and your standing on the list. This final rating will be sent to you after the tests have been marked.

from your rating on the Postal Clerk-Carrier register. Apparently, the relative rating given to each part of the test varies according to title. This is another argument for taking as many tests in as many titles as possible, as suggested on page 3.

You are encouraged to calculate your raw scores because they furnish a realistic and convenient way for you to keep track of your relative performance and progress as you work your way through this book.

PERSONAL PROGRESS RECORD—SAMPLE

ADDRESS CHECKING												
Initial Tests								Repeated Tests			
Date	Test	Number Completed	Number Correct	–	Number Wrong	=	Score	Date	Score	Date	Score
5/15	Diagnostic Practice Test	52	44	–	8	=	36				
5/16	Practice Test 1	64	54	–	10	=	44				
5/18	Practice Test 2	66	57	–	9	=	48				
5/20	Practice Test 3	70	60	–	10	=	50				
	Practice Test 4			–		=					
	Practice Test 5			–		=					
	Practice Test 6			–		=					

Now turn to page 430 In the table entitled “Personal Progress Record–Address Checking,” make the proper entries on the line for the Diagnostic Practice Test you just took. This table will help you record your progress as you take additional practice tests.

Part B—Memory for Addresses

Computing Your Score

Check the answers on your answer sheet against the Answer Key. Calculate your score by using these four steps:

1. Enter the name of answers you got right .... ______
2. Enter the number of answers you got wrong... ______
3. Divide the number wrong by 4 (or multiply by ¼) .... – ______
4. Subtract Line 3 from Line 1 .... YOUR SCORE = ______

Follow this example to make sure that you have figured your score correctly. Assume that you have completed 32 questions, of which you got 24 right and 8 wrong.

Line 1 . . . Number right. 24
Line 2 . . . Number wrong. 8
Line 3 . . . ¼ of line 2 = ¼ × 8. . . . –2
Line 4 . . . 24 – 2 YOUR SCORE = 22

Notice that, just as for Address Checking, questions that are not answered are *not* taken into account.

Guidelines

How good is the score you just made?

44 or more .... Good

26 to 43................. Fair

25 or less .... You need to improve.

If your score on this test was low, don't be discouraged. *Just about everyone who takes this memory test "cold" has the same experience.* Yet, most persons go on to make a vast improvement in their score after they have studied Chapters 4 and 5. If you are like the average person, and are willing to invest a little time in study and practice, you can confidently set your sights on a mark well above 44. In fact, scores of 70 and above are attainable by those who prepare thoroughly.

Personal Progress Record

Turn to page 430. Use the table entitled "Personal Progress—Memory for Addresses" to keep a permanent record of your scores on List 3 of the practice tests. A sample is printed below to familiarize you with it. The entries are based on the preceding example:

PERSONAL PROGRESS RECORD—SAMPLE

MEMORY FOR ADDRESSES												
Initial Tests									Repeated Tests			
Date	Test	Number Completed	Number Correct *A*	Number Wrong	× ¼ =		Points off *B*	Score (*A* − *B*)	Date	Score	Date	Score
5/15	Diagnostic Practice Test	32	24	8	× ¼	=	2	22				
5/16	Practice Test 1	46	38	8	× ¼	=	2	36				
5/18	Practice Test 2	58	52	6	× ¼	=	1½	50½				
5/20	Practice Test 3	64	60	4	× ¼	=	1	59				
	Practice Test 4				× ¼	=						
	Practice Test 5				× ¼	=						
	Practice Test 6				× ¼	=						

Make the proper entries on the record on page 430 for the Diagnostic Practice Test that you just took. You should be pleasantly surprised at how much higher your next entry on this table will be.

Part C—Number Series

Computing Your Score

Check the answers on your Answer Sheet against the Answer Key. Calculate your score by adding up the number of correct answers you have. You *do not* lose any credit for wrong answers or for questions you don't answer. For example, on a test having 24 questions, if you had 5 correct, 3 incorrect, and omitted 16, your score would be 5.

Guidelines

How good is the score you just made?

17 or higher . . . . Good

Between 12 and 16 . . . . Fair

Below 12. . . . . You need to improve

Once you have mastered the techniques explained in this book, you should routinely be scoring 20 to 24 correct.

Personal Progress Record

One of the most satisfying things that can happen while you are working toward a goal is to see signs of progress. The improvement you make by studying and practicing can readily be seen by examining the scores you make on the practice tests and exercises in this book. You can keep track of your increasing skill on the Personal Progress Record, furnished for your use on page 431.

The following is a sample of this Personal Progress Record to familiarize you with it. The entries on this sample are based on the example above.

PERSONAL PROGRESS RECORD—SAMPLE

NUMBER SERIES							
Initial Tests				Repeated Tests			
Date	Test	Number Completed	Number Correct (Your Score)	Date	Score	Date	Score
5/15	Diagnostic Practice Test	8	5				
5/16	Practice Test 1	15	11				
5/18	Practice Test 2	17	15				
5/20	Practice Test 3	20	19				
	Practice Test 4						
	Practice Test 5						
	Practice Test 6						

Now turn to page 431. Look at the table entitled "Personal Progress Record— Number Series." Make the proper entries on the line for the Diagnostic Practice Test you just took. This table will help you record your progress as you take additional practice tests.

Part D—Following Oral Directions

Computing Your Score

Check your answers against the Answer Key. Calculate your score by adding up the number of correct answers you have. You do *not* lose any credit for wrong answers or for questions you don't answer. For example, on a test having 30 questions, if you had 17 correct and 6 incorrect, and omitted 7, your score would be 17.

Guidelines

How good is the score you just made?

28 or higher . . . . Good

Between 24 and 27 . . . . Fair

Below 24. . . . . You need to improve.

Once you have mastered the techniques explained in this book (Chapter 7 covers Following Oral Directions), you should routinely score 28 to 30 correct.

Personal Progress Record

Now turn to page 431. In the table entitled "Personal Progress Record—Following Oral Directions," make the proper entries on the line for the Diagnostic Practice Test you just took. This table will help you record your progress as you take additional practice tests. A sample is printed below to familiarize you with it. The first entry is based on the preceding example.

PERSONAL PROGRESS RECORD—SAMPLE

FOLLOWING ORAL DIRECTIONS							
Initial Tests				Repeated Tests			
Date	Test	Number Completed	Number Correct (Your Score)	Date	Score	Date	Score
5/15	Diagnostic Practice Test	23	17				
5/16	Practice Test 1	23	19				
5/18	Practice Test 2	27	25				
5/20	Practice Test 3	29	28				
	Practice Test 4						
	Practice Test 5						
	Practice Test 6						

How Addresses May Differ

Now that you have completed the Diagnostic Practice Test and checked your answers, you can see that the differences between address pairs fall into four main categories.

1. Number Differences. In a street address or a zip code number, numbers may be:

a. *Transposed.*

635 La Calle Mayor *versus* 653 La Calle Mayor

b. *Changed.*

Washington DC 20013 *versus* Washington DC 20018

c. *Omitted.*

10476 Eastern Avenue *versus* 1047 Eastern Avenue

2. Directional Differences. These can occur *before* or *after* the street name.

1166 N Beaumont Dr *versus* 1166 S Beaumont Dr

758 Los Arboles Ave SE *versus* 758 Los Arboles Ave SW

3. Abbreviation Differences

a. *Streets, Drives, Avenues, etc.*

2560 Lansford Pl *versus* 2560 Lansford St

6434 E Pulaski St *versus* 6434 E Pulaski Ct

b. *States.*

These abbreviations are particularly important now that the new two-letter abbreviations of state names are replacing many of the longer, easy-to-distinguish ones. For example, the *Postal Service Directory* abbreviates California as CA, *not* CAL or CALIF. The abbreviation for Minnesota is MN, *not* MINN. Because many states now have two-letter abbreviations beginning or ending with the same letter, there is a greater chance to overlook the differences if they appear on the test. For example:

Sparta GA *versus* Sparta VA

Shreveport LA *versus* Shreveport IA

Portland OR *versus* Portland OH

(A complete list of the two-letter state abbreviations, with which you may practice, appears on page 423.)

4. Spelling Differences

a. *Single letters may be added, transposed, or changed.*

22 Sagnaw Pkwy *versus* 22 Saganaw Pkwy

3302 W Avalon Rd *versus* 3302 W Alavon Rd

8406 La Casa St *versus* 8406 La Cosa St

b. *Small groups of letters may be changed.*

3282 E Downington St *versus* 3282 Dunnington St

565 Greenville Blvd SE *versus* 565 Greenview Blvd SE

(Very often these are groups that look or sound somewhat alike. A brief list of such groups is given in the table on page 85.)

DIAGNOSTIC CHARTS

The following charts will help pinpoint your weaknesses by making it easy for you to determine what particular type of question in each part of the test is most difficult for you.

Part A—Address Checking

Type of Difference	"D" Questions	Number of "D" Questions Wrong		
		Trial 1	Trial 2	Trial 3
Numbers: transposed	6, 25, 36, 40, 52, 66, 74, 86, 90, 91, 94			
changed	2, 21, 57			
omitted				
Directions	4, 32, 58, 76, 80, 84			
Abbreviations: streets, roads, avenues, etc.	9, 17, 24, 35, 65, 70, 89, 93			
states	69			
Spelling: single letters	8, 10, 11, 19, 26, 41, 43 45, 48, 50, 55, 64, 72, 75 81, 83, 85, 87			
groups of letters	12, 22, 29, 31, 61, 73			
Total number of All Types	53			
	Use the columns on the right to enter the question numbers of "A" items you marked "D."			

This chart will help you to pinpoint the kinds of errors you made on the Practice Test. Use it as directed below after you have taken and marked the test.

The first column on the left, "Type of Difference," contains the categories whereby addresses may differ (see page 63 to 64). On the same line across, the second column gives the numbers of the questions that fall within each category. In the third column, you are to enter the numbers of any "A" questions you answered as "D." Do not include questions that you did not do. Checking the addresses you got wrong may reveal a problem on which you will want to work.

After you have made all the entries, you will be able to see the areas in which you need to improve. Then turn to the appropriate parts of Chapter 3: Address Checking—How to Improve Your Score, read them, and practice the drills that can help. For example, if you find you have been making too many errors picking out number differences, read page 88 and do Drills 18 through 21. If you have a problem with single letters because of reversals like *b* and *d*, or if you have been overlooking the differences between *a*, *e*, and *o*, read page 85. Examine the table and work on Drills 10 and 11 if the problem persists.

Remember that this chart is designed for diagnostic purposes and guidance on further practice. It has been drawn so that you can enter the results each time you retake a practice test. In this way you will be able to see how you are progressing. It is not necessary to record your scores here. That is best done by using the Personal Progress Record Card.

Part B—Memory for Addresses

Kind of Address		Number of Questions	Number Wrong		
			Trial 1	Trial 2	Trial 3
Direct:					
	List 1	40			
	List 2	36			
	List 3	37			
Numbered:					
	List 1	48			
	List 2	52			
	List 3	51			

The purpose of this chart is to help you evaluate your performance on the two kinds of memory questions that appear in the Diagnostic Practice Test—the questions on the direct (name) addresses and the questions on the numbered addresses. Use the chart as directed below after you have taken and marked the entire test.

The first column on the left, "Kind of Address," is divided by category into "Direct Address" versus "Numbered Address." The second column gives the number of questions in each category on List 1, List 2, and List 3. Use the third column to enter the total number of questions in each category that you answered incorrectly. There is room for you to make additional entries if you take the Diagnostic Practice Test more than once.

At a glance, you will be able to see which area you need to concentrate on and how well you are progressing as you take repeat trials. Use Chapter 4 and the drills in it to improve your memory for the direct addresses. Use Chapter 5 for the numbered addresses.

Remember to use the Personal Progress Record Card (Memory for Addresses) on page 430 to keep track of your actual scores as you keep studying and practicing.

Part C—Number Series and Part D—Following Oral Directions

Because of the nature of the questions in these tests, Diagnostic Charts for them have not been provided. If you find that you made many errors on these tests, study the techniques suggested in Chapters 6 and 7.

LEARNING THE SPECIAL TECHNIQUES

Chapter 3

Address Checking—How to Improve Your Score

TEST STRATEGY

Before specific ways to increase speed and accuracy are considered, test strategy should be discussed. One definition of strategy is "a plan, method, or series of maneuvers for obtaining a specific goal or result." You can see the importance of effective strategy everywhere. Effective strategy makes the difference between champions and also-rans in every field of human endeavor—from fighting a war to managing a baseball team. The reason why great big-league managers earn so much is that they have been known to take teams that ranked in fifth or sixth place under former managers and mold them into league champions. How? By using ways to make the most of the team's ability. Using *your* ability to the best advantage is what effective test strategy is all about. This is what we will now discuss.

Don't Go for 100 Percent

On the Address Checking test, your goal is, of course, to get the highest score you can. It is to your advantage to work as quickly and accurately as possible since the test score is based on the number of wrong answers as well as the number of right answers. The problem for most of us is that the faster we work, the more errors we make. But everyone is different in his or her speed and skills. Therefore, each of us has to know what combination of speed and accuracy will yield the best results. Practice, including trial and error, will determine the correct combination for *you*. To illustrate these ideas, here are a couple of examples:

> Joe Smith is preparing to take a U.S. Postal Service examination. He decides to work very carefully, as he did in school, and to avoid any errors. After taking the test, his results on the Address Checking part show that he completed 32 questions and got only 2 wrong. If he were graded the way he used to be in school, he would have a score of 94 percent!

But that's not the way this test is actually scored. Joe's true score (see page 58 will be calculated by the formula you saw before:

30 Right
− 2 Wrong
______
28 = Joe Smith's Score

This score is definitely too low according to the criteria on page 58.

A few years later, Joe has another opportunity to take a similar Postal Service examination. This time he prepares for it, and he rethinks his test strategy. He decides to push on a bit faster, even though he is not sure whether he can be as accurate as before.

Here is what happened:

He answered 44 questions and got 5 wrong.
His percentage score = 88 percent, quite a drop; *but* . . .
his actual test score = 34 (39 – 5).

Joe's new strategy paid off—he raised his score from 28 (below par) to 34 (fair) even though he got more than twice as many wrong!

Don't Guess Wildly

This discussion of test strategy wouldn't be complete without discussing the matter of guessing. After all, why not raise the number of possible right answers by making sure you've answered all 95 questions even if you have to guess blindly at the last 20 or 30? Guessing is *not* advisable if you consider the odds involved. You have a 50-50 chance on each question. If you guess, you will probably get as many wrong as you get right. The net result is zero—nothing gained. You might even be unlucky and get more wrong than right. In that case, you would be penalized because each wrong answer would deduct a point from your score. You would also stand to lose time better spent working at your usual pace, which you *know* would net you a few extra points.

Because everyone is different, you, the reader, will need to work out your individual test strategy on this and other parts of the test. You will learn how fast you can proceed while still maintaining reasonable accuracy. If you study and practice the techniques described in the following pages, you will increase speed and accuracy and keep raising your score. Use the Personal Progress Record on page 430 to help you see what your optimum speed is to yield the best score.

As was mentioned before, it is within the realm of possibility to score in the high eighties or above on this section of the test. The wonderful thing about this program is that *you are in charge* of your progress—you can go as fast and as far as your ability and persistence allow.

Don't Do More Than You Have To

Remember that the test directions specify, "If they [the two addresses] are *different in any way,* darken space D." This means that, just as soon as you have found a *single* difference between the addresses in a pair, you should immediately mark answer D. There is no point to checking the address any further. You are just wasting time you could be using to answer the next question. (For more on double-checking, see pages 77 and 78.)

TECHNIQUES FOR INCREASING YOUR ADDRESS CHECKING SKILLS

In any activity requiring skill, whether bowling, chess, or typing, the key to success is knowing the correct techniques and then practicing them. A good example of what proper technique and training can accomplish is seen in the advances that have been made in track and field sports.

Barely 50 years ago, a world record of 4 minutes and 6.2 seconds for the one-mile run was set by the "Flying Swede," Gunder Haegg. Running experts at that time were sure it would never be broken. The 4-minute mile wasn't even on the horizon. But things have certainly changed. Recently, 7 out of 11 runners competing in a one-mile race broke the once-invincible 4-minute barrier! What happened to explain this phenomenal performance? For one thing, the sport was scientifically studied to learn more about running techniques and training methods. Everything was scrutinized, including length of stride, recovery time, track shoe design, pacing, diet, and the psychology of running. Anything and everything, no matter how minute, was considered, as long as it led to faster time. Then, too, increased interest and participation in running led athletes to start their careers and training at an earlier age. Athletes trained longer and harder. Sports medicine used scientific methods to establish the best training regimens. You can see how the two factors—correct technique and diligent practice (see page 140) have paid dividends.

Correct technique and diligent practice are also the basis for this book. Every technique that can help you raise your score has been carefully considered and explained. Learn and practice each of them. Remember: when you raise your speed record, you get that much closer to a job appointment.

(Incidentally, the present world record is 3 minutes and 44.39 seconds, and no one talks about limits too much any more.)

Use Both Hands Properly

When you take the Postal Service test, you will find that the questions are printed on a separate page from the answer sheet (as has been done in this book). Nevertheless, many candidates lose time by not using their hands correctly. The most common error is to leave one or both hands idle and out of position while reading each address line. When the candidates have decided on Ⓐ or Ⓓ, they then have to bring their pencils up to the correct line on the answer sheet. Valuable fractions of a second are lost performing this movement. Sometimes the test taker loses his or her place on the question sheet or on the answer sheet. This wastes more time and may even result in putting an answer on the wrong line, a mistake that could lead to disaster. Every succeeding answer will then appear on the wrong line.

The remedy is simply to *keep both hands in the correct position relative to the question and answer sheets.* Assuming you are right-handed,* you should keep your left hand on the question sheet as a guide, slowly moving it down for each question. Or else, use a second pencil as a guide across each line. Your right hand, holding the pencil, should be

---

* *Note for left-handed test takers:* The illustrations show a right-handed test taker. If you are left-handed, you will, of course, be placing the answer sheet on your left and the question page on the right. Be prepared, however, for the possibility that, on the Postal Service exam, the question page and the answer sheet may be bound together in a booklet *with the answer sheet on the right.* With a little practice ahead of time, you should be able to use your right hand to fill in the spaces just as speedily as your left.

poised on the corresponding question number on the answer sheet. Keep both hands working together in this way as you take the test.

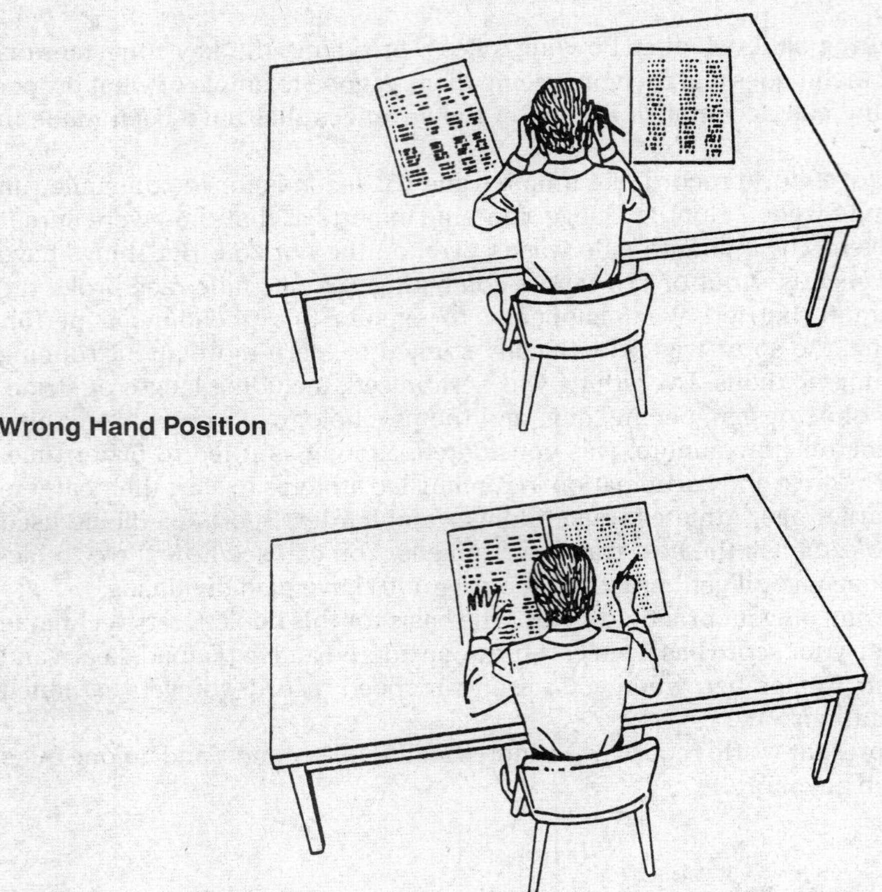

Wrong Hand Position

Correct Hand Position

Make Your Mark Neatly and Clearly

The instructions you receive at the time of the official test will include directions on how to fill out the answer sheet. Make sure you follow these directions, but be careful that you don't misinterpret them and do what is unnecessary and time-wasteful.

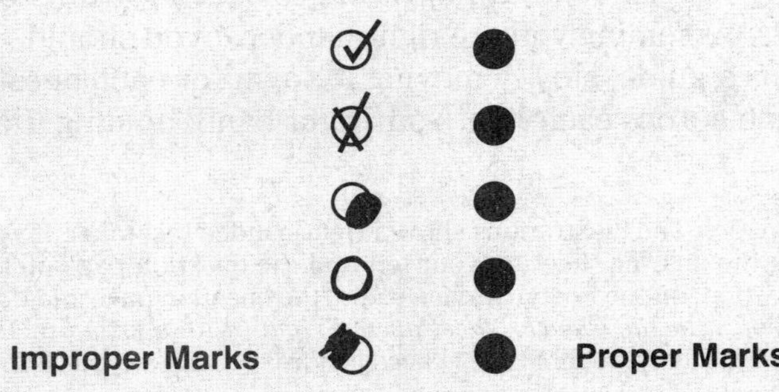

In referring to the way you are supposed to mark the answer sheet, you are instructed to darken completely the answer space that you have selected. You must keep your mark neat and stay within the circle.

On the other hand, some test candidates spend as much time carefully outlining and darkening the spaces as they did in examining the question and in deciding on the answer! This test is *not* an artistic competition. Don't waste time! You could be completing perhaps 50 to 100 percent more questions using the time wasted making beautiful marks.

Preparing Your Pencil

Prepare your pencil point so that the tip is angled, flat, and shaped like an oval about ⅛ inch long. An easy way to do this is by holding a regularly sharpened pencil point at a 45° angle to a piece of scrap paper and rubbing it back and forth until you get the desired size and shape. Your goal is to be able to darken an answer space with *one* circular rotation of your pencil instead of the half-dozen or more rotations you may have been making. (See pages 82 to 84 for practice in marking answers clearly and quickly.)

Prepare three or four pencils, with erasers, to take to the examination room. Incidentally, when you buy your pencils, tell the clerk at the store what they will be used for; they are supposed to leave a very dark mark without smearing. If the examiners require you to use pencils that they supply, all is not lost. You can readily prepare the points right there and then, using the method described above.

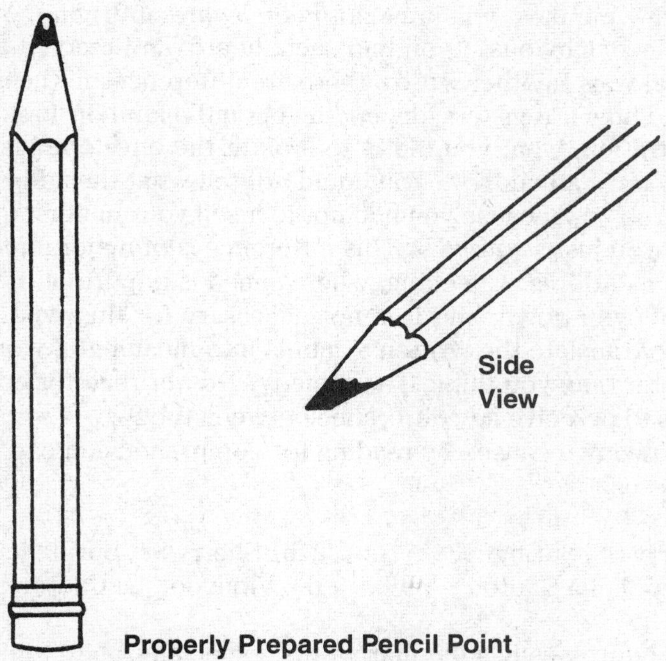

Properly Prepared Pencil Point

More Tips on Marking Your Answers

- *Remember that only one answer is allowed per question.* The machine that "reads" your answer sheet will mark you wrong if it picks up more than one answer.
- *Keep erasing to a minimum,* especially when speed is absolutely essential (Address Checking). You will probably lose more points than you gain if you stop to reexam-

ine a question, erase the previous answer, and enter a new one. (Read the paragraphs on guessing in the Test Strategy sections at the beginning of Chapters 3 and 4.)

- *Know when erasing is advisable;* if you notice smudges and extraneous pencil marks near the answer spaces; if you have blackened two answer spaces for one question; after you've completed all the questions in one part of the test and you are reviewing your answers to earlier questions. (You can speed up this review process by placing a check mark in the question booklet next to each question you aren't sure of.)
- *If you must erase an answer, do so completely.* The machine may read smudges and incomplete erasures as second answers.
- *Don't write words or anything else on the answer sheet.* The machine understands nothing but blackened spaces.

Use a Different Kind of "Reading"

Notice that this test is called "Address Checking." *Checking* is not the same as ordinary reading. For example, you can check a letter to see whether it has a return address without reading the address if it's there. Similarly, you can quickly check a "Help Wanted" column to see if there are any job openings for "receptionists" or "engineers" without reading the details in the ads. Did you ever have the experience of driving a car and suddenly realizing that, for a few minutes, you have not been aware of driving? Yet the car and you were still in one piece. Obviously, you had seen, heard, and reacted to the traffic about you, but in a special way. In other words, there are differences in the amount and quality of what you see and how it registers, depending upon the kind of "looking" you are doing.

In the first illustration, what you did is to look at the envelope just long enough and hard enough to *perceive* an address. You could not tell what the address was in terms of name, number, and so on, because you had not focused your understanding on it. You did not really *read* it—you just *scanned* it. This difference is of major importance to you in a test situation such as Address Checking, where speed is important. Reading for comprehension would slow you down, and it is not necessary for this type of test. Your brain would need time to translate the written symbols into meaningful words. You would not be able to read faster than you think. The remedy? Do *not* read for comprehension. Just scan the addresses to perceive any difference between the two.

To see how a slowdown caused by reading for comprehension can occur, check these two pairs of addresses:

2461 Cherry St., Springfield	2461 Sherry St., Springfield	Ⓐ Ⓓ
195 Vloovook, La Canton	195 Vloovool, La Canton	Ⓐ Ⓓ

The first pair of addresses has familiar words, especially Cherry and Sherry. If you let yourself visualize Cherry as a bunch of fruit and Sherry as a bottle of wine, you have attached meaning to these words. The momentary mental pause for recognition slowed you down. Your job was only to see that <u>C</u>herry was different from <u>S</u>herry and to mark choice Ⓓ.

When you looked at the second pair, you may have fallen into *two* time-consuming traps. First, you may have allowed yourself to reflect momentarily on that weird, unusual name—Vloovook. Maybe you tried to connect it to something or someplace you have heard of . . . Eskimos, perhaps?

Second, you may have sounded it out. Whether you whispered it aloud or to yourself, you lost time. Sounding it out lowered your speed of perception to that of your oral reading speed, which is far slower than your silent speed. Many people who read this way are largely unaware that they do so. To make sure that you are not moving your lips or subvocalizing, conduct this simple test. As you read, put your fingers gently alongside your lips and throat. You will feel a slight muscle movement or vibration if you are vocalizing. The cure lies first in becoming aware of the habit. Then, you must keep trying to let your brain register what your eyes see, in an instantaneous flash of recognition. Keep your lips still. Don't even think about how the words sound. Try keeping a pencil clenched between your teeth when you do the practice exercises in this book or whenever you read anything.

To summarize, your task is to compare Vloovook with Vloovool and to notice the difference between *k* and *l*. You must be able to perceive distinctions in shape,* spacing, and position, whether in letters, numbers, or names, as quickly as you can. That's all! Many test takers prepare themselves mentally for address checking by imagining that their eyes are picking up images the way a camera or an optical scanner does. It may seem silly, but for the purpose of this test, say to yourself, "*I am a camera.*"

Use the exercises on pages 86 through 89 to develop your perceptual speed and accuracy. Here's one to try right now: Quickly read the sentence below, keeping track of the number of "t's" you see.

Two trees on the left and one shrub standing in between are attractive.

Now count the *t's* in the sentence *one time*—don't go back to check. Write the number here _____. The answer is nine *t's*. Did you get it right?

Widen Your Eye Span

To see how this important technique can help, imagine that you are timing two test candidates, Tom and Barbara, as they check these addresses on their test:

1462 Church Av Eaton Ill	1462 Church Av Eaton Ind

Results: Both candidates correctly selected choice Ⓓ.

Tom took a total of 6 seconds to come up with the answer; Barbara took only 4 seconds.

Although both of them got the right answer, Barbara worked 50 percent faster than Tom. At that rate, she could answer 75 questions in the same time it would take Tom to do 50! Her test score would then be in the upper ranks, whereas Tom's would be far, far behind.

* NOTE: Certain letters and letter combinations may cause perceptual problems. For example, the letters *b* and *d* are often mistaken for each other by people who reverse them. Reversal can occur vertically with the letters *m* and *w*. Errors may occur with words or parts of words, for example, "was" versus "saw." Some people are more prone to these difficulties than others. If you find you have this kind of problem, spend extra time practicing the letters and words that cause you trouble. Use the table "Some Common Perception Errors Made in Reading" page 85, which has a sampling of commonly confused letters, groups of letters, and words.

One of the factors working in Barbara's favor may have been her wider eye span, that is, her ability to perceive more at a glance than Tom could. To understand what eye span, or *span of perception*, really means, it is necessary to examine how the eye works.

The eyes are controlled by six tiny muscles as they move along a line of print. This eye movement is not smooth; it is more like a series of jumps and stops. It is during these stops, called *fixations*, that one actually perceives words. The units of type (numbers, letters, and spaces) the eyes pick up at each stop is called *eye span*. The wider your eye span, the faster you can go. To illustrate, note how Barbara and Tom each read the line below:

BARBARA

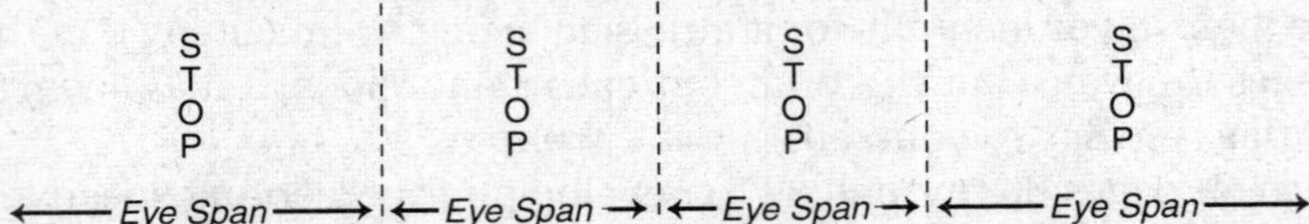

Notice that when Barbara reads this sentence, she stops four times. At each stop or fixation, her eye has spanned an average of three words.

Tom has not developed his eye span sufficiently. He reads the same line this way:

TOM

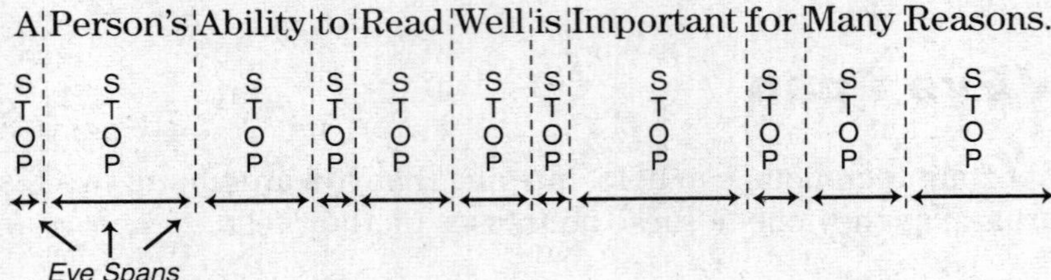

Tom has stopped for a fixation on every word. His average eye span is only *one* word. The result? He has read the line far slower than Barbara.

Word-by-word reading, with its greater number of fixations, slows a reader down dramatically. (On page 75 it was noted that "sounding out" words can be another reason for reading words in a sentence one at a time.) What makes matters worse is that many people who read this way are unaware of it. Now that it has been established that Tom is one of these people, compare the way Tom and Barbara read the address on page 77: In the samples that follow, dots (•) have been used to indicate points above which the eye focuses at each fixation; a solid line underscores the width of the eye span. Eye span width is measured by counting the units of type, including the spaces between words, in each fixation.

TOM

1462 Church Av Eaton Ill — 1462 Church Av Eaton Ind

Number of fixations = 5 per side.
Average eye span = 5 type units.

BARBARA

1462 Church Av Eaton Ill — 1462 Church Av Eaton Ind

Number of fixations = 3 per side.
Average eye span = 8 type units.

These diagrams clearly show the reason why Barbara is going 50 percent faster than Tom. But even Barbara's performance can be improved! It is possible to see each side in two, or in even in *one*, fixation if you train yourself to widen your eye span. You can learn to use your peripheral vision to widen your perception span to its maximum by using the exercises given on pages 98 through 103. As your eyes become able to grasp larger and larger "bunches" of each address at a time, your checking speed will increase.

There is still another benefit that comes with increased eye span. You save extra time because your eyes move back and forth fewer times as you compare the two addresses. If Barbara's eye movements could be seen as they sweep back and forth between the left- and right-hand columns, their path would look like this:

BARBARA

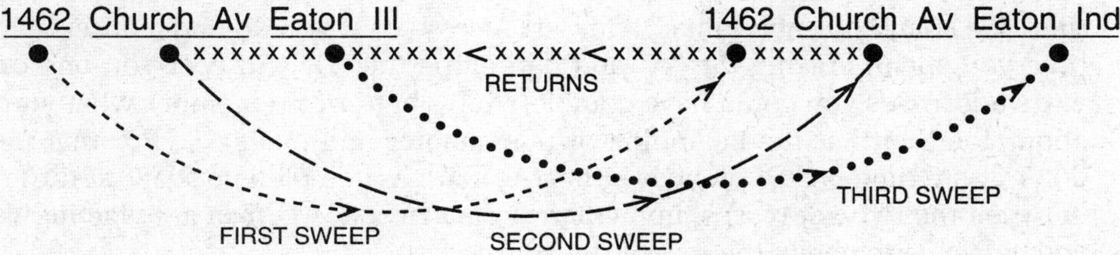

(The loops have been exaggerated to make the diagram clearer.)

Barbara made three "eye sweeps" going from the left side to the right side (plus the returns). She compared the "eyeful" gathered during each fixation on the left with the corresponding part of the address on the right. If Tom worked the same way, he would need more time because his eyes would have to make five sweeps (one for each fixation).

There is still room for improvement! Barbara could work even faster if she checked the entire address on the left side and then compared the mental images of the three fixations with the corresponding parts of the address line on the right.

Don't Go Back—Don't Regress

One day, a student who had just begun one of our exam preparation classes took the Address Checking portion of the Diagnostic Practice Test and scored only 15. When it was asked if he would describe any special difficulty he was having, he shamefacedly said, "I really feel awful about my score. If anything, I should have come out higher than most. After all, I work for a printer as a proofreader!" He was asked a few more questions about his job, and the reason for his troubles became clear. He had formed a tendency, reinforced by years of proofreading, to scrutinize all printed matter with the utmost care so that absolutely no errors appeared in the magazines his firm published. He developed into a perfectionist as far as catching errors in his on-the-job reading matter. Sad to say, he carried these proofreading habits over to *everything* he read, including the addresses on the Postal Service test. As a result, his test score was drastically low. On pages 69 through 70 test strategy was discussed and the reasons why absolute perfectionism is *not* a good idea. The proofreader's case makes the point perfectly. Others whose occupations may lead them into the same problem include stenographer-typists, file clerks, and accountants.

If you find yourself rereading work or pausing over an item in an address for too long a time, you can end the habit by (1) rereading the explanation on test strategy and (2) pushing yourself ahead to greater and greater speeds by using the special exercises at the end of this chapter.

There are still other reasons for regression:

1. Some adults carry over habits formed in school when they read and studied for exams. When people are reading difficult material that they must remember and understand thoroughly, they naturally read at a slower pace. There is often a need to reread and reflect until the material sinks in. Obviously, address checking involves a completely different kind of reading. So why not change your reading style to fit the task at hand?

2. Many people regress because they feel they have missed something, and they must look back to make sure they didn't. This is especially true for some people after they have chosen "A" for a particular address. They feel a need to check the address for a difference they may have missed. *Don't do it!* You'll be doubling the time you spend on each "alike" address. Also, even if you do find a difference, the time you spend erasing the "A" and darkening the "D" will cost you one or two extra addresses you could have completed. It's better to remember what you read about Joe Smith at the beginning of this chapter and push on. (For that matter, don't waste time on "D" choices either. As soon as you pick up the *first* difference between the two addresses, immediately darken space D. You are wasting time if you continue to check the rest of the address.)

3. Most people don't concentrate effectively. They daydream or let outside thoughts enter their consciousness. At that point, their work suffers. They may slow up. They may *really* miss seeing words. How can you learn to concentrate better? The secret is to focus your attention and not allow internal or external distractions to intrude. Become a machine! Pretend nothing can stop you—that you're an electronic scanning device passing over a succession of word and number images. (See Chapter 4 for more on putting yourself into the proper mental state.)

   Regardless of the reason, you can stop yourself from regressing. Each time you catch yourself ready to look back—force yourself to go on! Psych yourself into believing that you are really not going to miss much or make many errors, if you keep on going. To help you build that kind of confidence, special exercises have been provided that are aimed at overcoming regression. Turn to page 104 of this chapter for directions.

Work Rhythmically

As you do the practice tests and drills in this book, you should carefully time yourself. Soon you will get the feel of how fast you are going without looking at a clock. You will know when you are going at a pace that balances speed and accuracy for best results. Learn to feel that pace in your bones. Translate it into a rhythm, as your eyes sweep from one address to the other. If you keep the rhythm without letting regression or distractions get the better of you, you will *consistently* complete a certain number of lines in a given time. (This is one of the reasons why you are advised against stopping to erase in order to change an answer.)

To help you visualize how to go about finding, feeling, and using rhythm on the test, another illustration can be used. Assume that Tom becomes able to check an address in two fixations. He now needs only two eye sweeps to complete a typical address like this:

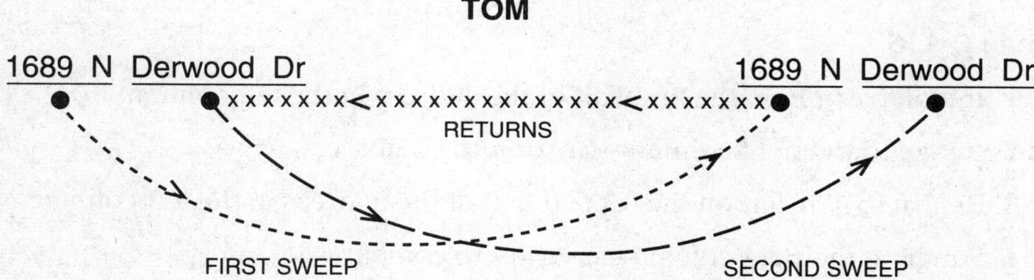

(The loops have been exaggerated to make the diagram clearer.)

Furthermore, assume that he has learned how to work at a rhythmic pace.

Tom then takes another practice test, completes 70 of the 95 questions, and gets 10 percent of his answers wrong. His score is: 63 right − 7 wrong = 56. Rhythm cannot be discussed without mentioning time, so calculate how long it took him to do *one* line. Divide 6 minutes (360 seconds) by 70. This works out to approximately 5 seconds per line (including the time needed for Tom to mark down his answer and move to the next line).

Because Tom has been practicing, he can really feel what a 5-second period is like. It is as though he has a mental metronome keeping time for him. His brain, eye movements, and hands all work together at the right rhythm to drive him along at the rate of 5 seconds per line.

How about you? Do you know what a 5-second period of time feels like? Or a 4-second period of time? Try this experiment:

Assume you are working to reach a 4-second-per-line speed. First, practice getting the feel of 4 seconds and the right rhythm by counting off 4 seconds as you look at a sweep second watch face. Do that several times. Then, chant out loud a few times " 1 - 2 - 3 - 4," etc. Now, chant mentally. When you think you've got the feel of a 4-second time period, check the addresses below. Fit your movements into that 4-second time slot. Establish the right rhythm. Try to move smoothly.

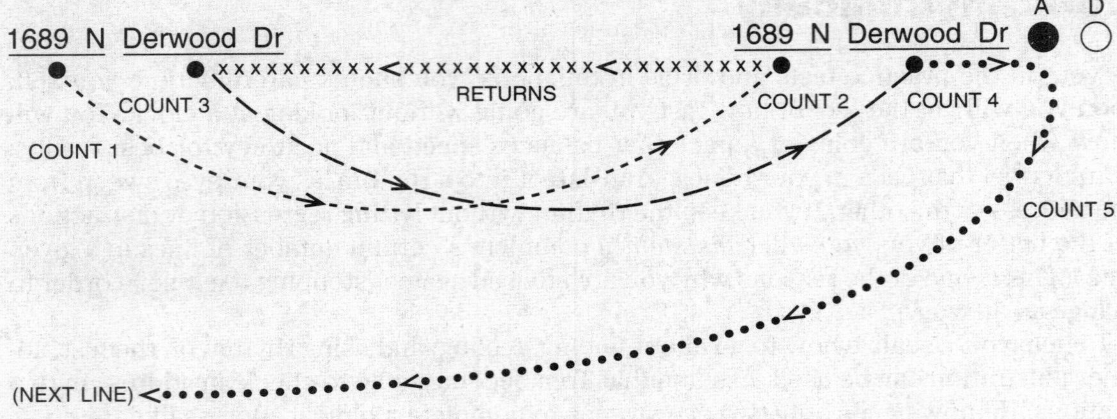

(The loops have been exaggerated to make the diagram clearer.)

Rhythmic Cycle

Count 1 Initial *fixation* on the first half of the address in the left column.

Count 2 *Sweep* to the right column—*fixation* to compare.

Count 3 Return to *fixation* on the second half of the address in the left column.

Count 4 *Sweep* to the right column—*fixation* to compare.

Count 5 Mark answer and *sweep* to the next line.

Repeat this cycle a few times. This experiment was intended only to illustrate the technique of working in rhythm. The 4-second cycle is probably too fast for you . . . *now*. Only you will be able to feel what is right for you at this stage. Experiment with the various practice tests in this book.

SPECIAL EXERCISES FOR BUILDING ADDRESS CHECKING SKILLS

You now have the "tools." You have learned the strategies and techniques that make a high score possible. Now you must be certain that you can apply them at test time. That means practice.

This section contains various exercises and drills. They will help you to eliminate any bad habits that you may have and to build the address checking skills you need. Work on them as needed. As you practice, remember that your progress may not be steady. Dramatic improvements are often followed by plateaus, times when your scores level off for a while. Sometimes there are even dips. These variations are perfectly natural and occur in all skills training. Just keep on practicing in the sure knowledge that your scores must rise. (Remember that 4-minute mile!)

Note that an Answer Key may be found on pages 110 to 111. In order to check your progress, since you may wish to take a number of exercises more than once, refer to the Drill Record Charts on pages 432 to 433 to record your scores.

Increasing Speed in Marking Answers

Drills 1–9

Use pages 82 through 84 to develop speed. There are nine answer drills with 95 answer lines in each. Four of the drills are laid out horizontally; five are laid out vertically. On the test, the answer sheets may be laid out either way. Prepare your pencil properly. Darken *one* space on each line, either box A or D. Pick boxes at random; it doesn't matter which you select. The idea is to practice making the entries cleanly and quickly. Time yourself. Practice until you can make 95 entries in one minute.

Answer Sheet—Drills 1–9

Drill 1

1 Ⓐ Ⓓ 2 Ⓐ Ⓓ 3 Ⓐ Ⓓ 4 Ⓐ Ⓓ 5 Ⓐ Ⓓ 6 Ⓐ Ⓓ 7 Ⓐ Ⓓ 8 Ⓐ Ⓓ 9 Ⓐ Ⓓ
10 Ⓐ Ⓓ 11 Ⓐ Ⓓ 12 Ⓐ Ⓓ 13 Ⓐ Ⓓ 14 Ⓐ Ⓓ 15 Ⓐ Ⓓ 16 Ⓐ Ⓓ 17 Ⓐ Ⓓ 18 Ⓐ Ⓓ
19 Ⓐ Ⓓ 20 Ⓐ Ⓓ 21 Ⓐ Ⓓ 22 Ⓐ Ⓓ 23 Ⓐ Ⓓ 24 Ⓐ Ⓓ 25 Ⓐ Ⓓ 26 Ⓐ Ⓓ 27 Ⓐ Ⓓ
28 Ⓐ Ⓓ 29 Ⓐ Ⓓ 30 Ⓐ Ⓓ 31 Ⓐ Ⓓ 32 Ⓐ Ⓓ 33 Ⓐ Ⓓ 34 Ⓐ Ⓓ 35 Ⓐ Ⓓ 36 Ⓐ Ⓓ
37 Ⓐ Ⓓ 38 Ⓐ Ⓓ 39 Ⓐ Ⓓ 40 Ⓐ Ⓓ 41 Ⓐ Ⓓ 42 Ⓐ Ⓓ 43 Ⓐ Ⓓ 44 Ⓐ Ⓓ 45 Ⓐ Ⓓ
46 Ⓐ Ⓓ 47 Ⓐ Ⓓ 48 Ⓐ Ⓓ 49 Ⓐ Ⓓ 50 Ⓐ Ⓓ 51 Ⓐ Ⓓ 52 Ⓐ Ⓓ 53 Ⓐ Ⓓ 54 Ⓐ Ⓓ
55 Ⓐ Ⓓ 56 Ⓐ Ⓓ 57 Ⓐ Ⓓ 58 Ⓐ Ⓓ 59 Ⓐ Ⓓ 60 Ⓐ Ⓓ 61 Ⓐ Ⓓ 62 Ⓐ Ⓓ 63 Ⓐ Ⓓ
64 Ⓐ Ⓓ 65 Ⓐ Ⓓ 66 Ⓐ Ⓓ 67 Ⓐ Ⓓ 68 Ⓐ Ⓓ 69 Ⓐ Ⓓ 70 Ⓐ Ⓓ 71 Ⓐ Ⓓ 72 Ⓐ Ⓓ
73 Ⓐ Ⓓ 74 Ⓐ Ⓓ 75 Ⓐ Ⓓ 76 Ⓐ Ⓓ 77 Ⓐ Ⓓ 78 Ⓐ Ⓓ 79 Ⓐ Ⓓ 80 Ⓐ Ⓓ 81 Ⓐ Ⓓ
82 Ⓐ Ⓓ 83 Ⓐ Ⓓ 84 Ⓐ Ⓓ 85 Ⓐ Ⓓ 86 Ⓐ Ⓓ 87 Ⓐ Ⓓ 88 Ⓐ Ⓓ 89 Ⓐ Ⓓ 90 Ⓐ Ⓓ
91 Ⓐ Ⓓ 92 Ⓐ Ⓓ 93 Ⓐ Ⓓ 94 Ⓐ Ⓓ 95 Ⓐ Ⓓ

Drill 2

1 Ⓐ Ⓓ 2 Ⓐ Ⓓ 3 Ⓐ Ⓓ 4 Ⓐ Ⓓ 5 Ⓐ Ⓓ 6 Ⓐ Ⓓ 7 Ⓐ Ⓓ 8 Ⓐ Ⓓ 9 Ⓐ Ⓓ
10 Ⓐ Ⓓ 11 Ⓐ Ⓓ 12 Ⓐ Ⓓ 13 Ⓐ Ⓓ 14 Ⓐ Ⓓ 15 Ⓐ Ⓓ 16 Ⓐ Ⓓ 17 Ⓐ Ⓓ 18 Ⓐ Ⓓ
19 Ⓐ Ⓓ 20 Ⓐ Ⓓ 21 Ⓐ Ⓓ 22 Ⓐ Ⓓ 23 Ⓐ Ⓓ 24 Ⓐ Ⓓ 25 Ⓐ Ⓓ 26 Ⓐ Ⓓ 27 Ⓐ Ⓓ
28 Ⓐ Ⓓ 29 Ⓐ Ⓓ 30 Ⓐ Ⓓ 31 Ⓐ Ⓓ 32 Ⓐ Ⓓ 33 Ⓐ Ⓓ 34 Ⓐ Ⓓ 35 Ⓐ Ⓓ 36 Ⓐ Ⓓ
37 Ⓐ Ⓓ 38 Ⓐ Ⓓ 39 Ⓐ Ⓓ 40 Ⓐ Ⓓ 41 Ⓐ Ⓓ 42 Ⓐ Ⓓ 43 Ⓐ Ⓓ 44 Ⓐ Ⓓ 45 Ⓐ Ⓓ
46 Ⓐ Ⓓ 47 Ⓐ Ⓓ 48 Ⓐ Ⓓ 49 Ⓐ Ⓓ 50 Ⓐ Ⓓ 51 Ⓐ Ⓓ 52 Ⓐ Ⓓ 53 Ⓐ Ⓓ 54 Ⓐ Ⓓ
55 Ⓐ Ⓓ 56 Ⓐ Ⓓ 57 Ⓐ Ⓓ 58 Ⓐ Ⓓ 59 Ⓐ Ⓓ 60 Ⓐ Ⓓ 61 Ⓐ Ⓓ 62 Ⓐ Ⓓ 63 Ⓐ Ⓓ
64 Ⓐ Ⓓ 65 Ⓐ Ⓓ 66 Ⓐ Ⓓ 67 Ⓐ Ⓓ 68 Ⓐ Ⓓ 69 Ⓐ Ⓓ 70 Ⓐ Ⓓ 71 Ⓐ Ⓓ 72 Ⓐ Ⓓ
73 Ⓐ Ⓓ 74 Ⓐ Ⓓ 75 Ⓐ Ⓓ 76 Ⓐ Ⓓ 77 Ⓐ Ⓓ 78 Ⓐ Ⓓ 79 Ⓐ Ⓓ 80 Ⓐ Ⓓ 81 Ⓐ Ⓓ
82 Ⓐ Ⓓ 83 Ⓐ Ⓓ 84 Ⓐ Ⓓ 85 Ⓐ Ⓓ 86 Ⓐ Ⓓ 87 Ⓐ Ⓓ 88 Ⓐ Ⓓ 89 Ⓐ Ⓓ 90 Ⓐ Ⓓ
91 Ⓐ Ⓓ 92 Ⓐ Ⓓ 93 Ⓐ Ⓓ 94 Ⓐ Ⓓ 95 Ⓐ Ⓓ

Drill 3

1 Ⓐ Ⓓ 2 Ⓐ Ⓓ 3 Ⓐ Ⓓ 4 Ⓐ Ⓓ 5 Ⓐ Ⓓ 6 Ⓐ Ⓓ 7 Ⓐ Ⓓ 8 Ⓐ Ⓓ 9 Ⓐ Ⓓ
10 Ⓐ Ⓓ 11 Ⓐ Ⓓ 12 Ⓐ Ⓓ 13 Ⓐ Ⓓ 14 Ⓐ Ⓓ 15 Ⓐ Ⓓ 16 Ⓐ Ⓓ 17 Ⓐ Ⓓ 18 Ⓐ Ⓓ
19 Ⓐ Ⓓ 20 Ⓐ Ⓓ 21 Ⓐ Ⓓ 22 Ⓐ Ⓓ 23 Ⓐ Ⓓ 24 Ⓐ Ⓓ 25 Ⓐ Ⓓ 26 Ⓐ Ⓓ 27 Ⓐ Ⓓ
28 Ⓐ Ⓓ 29 Ⓐ Ⓓ 30 Ⓐ Ⓓ 31 Ⓐ Ⓓ 32 Ⓐ Ⓓ 33 Ⓐ Ⓓ 34 Ⓐ Ⓓ 35 Ⓐ Ⓓ 36 Ⓐ Ⓓ
37 Ⓐ Ⓓ 38 Ⓐ Ⓓ 39 Ⓐ Ⓓ 40 Ⓐ Ⓓ 41 Ⓐ Ⓓ 42 Ⓐ Ⓓ 43 Ⓐ Ⓓ 44 Ⓐ Ⓓ 45 Ⓐ Ⓓ
46 Ⓐ Ⓓ 47 Ⓐ Ⓓ 48 Ⓐ Ⓓ 49 Ⓐ Ⓓ 50 Ⓐ Ⓓ 51 Ⓐ Ⓓ 52 Ⓐ Ⓓ 53 Ⓐ Ⓓ 54 Ⓐ Ⓓ
55 Ⓐ Ⓓ 56 Ⓐ Ⓓ 57 Ⓐ Ⓓ 58 Ⓐ Ⓓ 59 Ⓐ Ⓓ 60 Ⓐ Ⓓ 61 Ⓐ Ⓓ 62 Ⓐ Ⓓ 63 Ⓐ Ⓓ
64 Ⓐ Ⓓ 65 Ⓐ Ⓓ 66 Ⓐ Ⓓ 67 Ⓐ Ⓓ 68 Ⓐ Ⓓ 69 Ⓐ Ⓓ 70 Ⓐ Ⓓ 71 Ⓐ Ⓓ 72 Ⓐ Ⓓ
73 Ⓐ Ⓓ 74 Ⓐ Ⓓ 75 Ⓐ Ⓓ 76 Ⓐ Ⓓ 77 Ⓐ Ⓓ 78 Ⓐ Ⓓ 79 Ⓐ Ⓓ 80 Ⓐ Ⓓ 81 Ⓐ Ⓓ
82 Ⓐ Ⓓ 83 Ⓐ Ⓓ 84 Ⓐ Ⓓ 85 Ⓐ Ⓓ 86 Ⓐ Ⓓ 87 Ⓐ Ⓓ 88 Ⓐ Ⓓ 89 Ⓐ Ⓓ 90 Ⓐ Ⓓ
91 Ⓐ Ⓓ 92 Ⓐ Ⓓ 93 Ⓐ Ⓓ 94 Ⓐ Ⓓ 95 Ⓐ Ⓓ

Drill 4

1 Ⓐ Ⓓ 2 Ⓐ Ⓓ 3 Ⓐ Ⓓ 4 Ⓐ Ⓓ 5 Ⓐ Ⓓ 6 Ⓐ Ⓓ 7 Ⓐ Ⓓ 8 Ⓐ Ⓓ 9 Ⓐ Ⓓ
10 Ⓐ Ⓓ 11 Ⓐ Ⓓ 12 Ⓐ Ⓓ 13 Ⓐ Ⓓ 14 Ⓐ Ⓓ 15 Ⓐ Ⓓ 16 Ⓐ Ⓓ 17 Ⓐ Ⓓ 18 Ⓐ Ⓓ
19 Ⓐ Ⓓ 20 Ⓐ Ⓓ 21 Ⓐ Ⓓ 22 Ⓐ Ⓓ 23 Ⓐ Ⓓ 24 Ⓐ Ⓓ 25 Ⓐ Ⓓ 26 Ⓐ Ⓓ 27 Ⓐ Ⓓ
28 Ⓐ Ⓓ 29 Ⓐ Ⓓ 30 Ⓐ Ⓓ 31 Ⓐ Ⓓ 32 Ⓐ Ⓓ 33 Ⓐ Ⓓ 34 Ⓐ Ⓓ 35 Ⓐ Ⓓ 36 Ⓐ Ⓓ
37 Ⓐ Ⓓ 38 Ⓐ Ⓓ 39 Ⓐ Ⓓ 40 Ⓐ Ⓓ 41 Ⓐ Ⓓ 42 Ⓐ Ⓓ 43 Ⓐ Ⓓ 44 Ⓐ Ⓓ 45 Ⓐ Ⓓ
46 Ⓐ Ⓓ 47 Ⓐ Ⓓ 48 Ⓐ Ⓓ 49 Ⓐ Ⓓ 50 Ⓐ Ⓓ 51 Ⓐ Ⓓ 52 Ⓐ Ⓓ 53 Ⓐ Ⓓ 54 Ⓐ Ⓓ
55 Ⓐ Ⓓ 56 Ⓐ Ⓓ 57 Ⓐ Ⓓ 58 Ⓐ Ⓓ 59 Ⓐ Ⓓ 60 Ⓐ Ⓓ 61 Ⓐ Ⓓ 62 Ⓐ Ⓓ 63 Ⓐ Ⓓ
64 Ⓐ Ⓓ 65 Ⓐ Ⓓ 66 Ⓐ Ⓓ 67 Ⓐ Ⓓ 68 Ⓐ Ⓓ 69 Ⓐ Ⓓ 70 Ⓐ Ⓓ 71 Ⓐ Ⓓ 72 Ⓐ Ⓓ
73 Ⓐ Ⓓ 74 Ⓐ Ⓓ 75 Ⓐ Ⓓ 76 Ⓐ Ⓓ 77 Ⓐ Ⓓ 78 Ⓐ Ⓓ 79 Ⓐ Ⓓ 80 Ⓐ Ⓓ 81 Ⓐ Ⓓ
82 Ⓐ Ⓓ 83 Ⓐ Ⓓ 84 Ⓐ Ⓓ 85 Ⓐ Ⓓ 86 Ⓐ Ⓓ 87 Ⓐ Ⓓ 88 Ⓐ Ⓓ 89 Ⓐ Ⓓ 90 Ⓐ Ⓓ
91 Ⓐ Ⓓ 92 Ⓐ Ⓓ 93 Ⓐ Ⓓ 94 Ⓐ Ⓓ 95 Ⓐ Ⓓ

Drill 5

1	ⒶⒹ	49	ⒶⒹ
2	ⒶⒹ	50	ⒶⒹ
3	ⒶⒹ	51	ⒶⒹ
4	ⒶⒹ	52	ⒶⒹ
5	ⒶⒹ	53	ⒶⒹ
6	ⒶⒹ	54	ⒶⒹ
7	ⒶⒹ	55	ⒶⒹ
8	ⒶⒹ	56	ⒶⒹ
9	ⒶⒹ	57	ⒶⒹ
10	ⒶⒹ	58	ⒶⒹ
11	ⒶⒹ	59	ⒶⒹ
12	ⒶⒹ	60	ⒶⒹ
13	ⒶⒹ	61	ⒶⒹ
14	ⒶⒹ	62	ⒶⒹ
15	ⒶⒹ	63	ⒶⒹ
16	ⒶⒹ	64	ⒶⒹ
17	ⒶⒹ	65	ⒶⒹ
18	ⒶⒹ	66	ⒶⒹ
19	ⒶⒹ	67	ⒶⒹ
20	ⒶⒹ	68	ⒶⒹ
21	ⒶⒹ	69	ⒶⒹ
22	ⒶⒹ	70	ⒶⒹ
23	ⒶⒹ	71	ⒶⒹ
24	ⒶⒹ	72	ⒶⒹ
25	ⒶⒹ	73	ⒶⒹ
26	ⒶⒹ	74	ⒶⒹ
27	ⒶⒹ	75	ⒶⒹ
28	ⒶⒹ	76	ⒶⒹ
29	ⒶⒹ	77	ⒶⒹ
30	ⒶⒹ	78	ⒶⒹ
31	ⒶⒹ	79	ⒶⒹ
32	ⒶⒹ	80	ⒶⒹ
33	ⒶⒹ	81	ⒶⒹ
34	ⒶⒹ	82	ⒶⒹ
35	ⒶⒹ	83	ⒶⒹ
36	ⒶⒹ	84	ⒶⒹ
37	ⒶⒹ	85	ⒶⒹ
38	ⒶⒹ	86	ⒶⒹ
39	ⒶⒹ	87	ⒶⒹ
40	ⒶⒹ	88	ⒶⒹ
41	ⒶⒹ	89	ⒶⒹ
42	ⒶⒹ	90	ⒶⒹ
43	ⒶⒹ	91	ⒶⒹ
44	ⒶⒹ	92	ⒶⒹ
45	ⒶⒹ	93	ⒶⒹ
46	ⒶⒹ	94	ⒶⒹ
47	ⒶⒹ	95	ⒶⒹ
48	ⒶⒹ		

Drill 6

1	ⒶⒹ	49	ⒶⒹ
2	ⒶⒹ	50	ⒶⒹ
3	ⒶⒹ	51	ⒶⒹ
4	ⒶⒹ	52	ⒶⒹ
5	ⒶⒹ	53	ⒶⒹ
6	ⒶⒹ	54	ⒶⒹ
7	ⒶⒹ	55	ⒶⒹ
8	ⒶⒹ	56	ⒶⒹ
9	ⒶⒹ	57	ⒶⒹ
10	ⒶⒹ	58	ⒶⒹ
11	ⒶⒹ	59	ⒶⒹ
12	ⒶⒹ	60	ⒶⒹ
13	ⒶⒹ	61	ⒶⒹ
14	ⒶⒹ	62	ⒶⒹ
15	ⒶⒹ	63	ⒶⒹ
16	ⒶⒹ	64	ⒶⒹ
17	ⒶⒹ	65	ⒶⒹ
18	ⒶⒹ	66	ⒶⒹ
19	ⒶⒹ	67	ⒶⒹ
20	ⒶⒹ	68	ⒶⒹ
21	ⒶⒹ	69	ⒶⒹ
22	ⒶⒹ	70	ⒶⒹ
23	ⒶⒹ	71	ⒶⒹ
24	ⒶⒹ	72	ⒶⒹ
25	ⒶⒹ	73	ⒶⒹ
26	ⒶⒹ	74	ⒶⒹ
27	ⒶⒹ	75	ⒶⒹ
28	ⒶⒹ	76	ⒶⒹ
29	ⒶⒹ	77	ⒶⒹ
30	ⒶⒹ	78	ⒶⒹ
31	ⒶⒹ	79	ⒶⒹ
32	ⒶⒹ	80	ⒶⒹ
33	ⒶⒹ	81	ⒶⒹ
34	ⒶⒹ	82	ⒶⒹ
35	ⒶⒹ	83	ⒶⒹ
36	ⒶⒹ	84	ⒶⒹ
37	ⒶⒹ	85	ⒶⒹ
38	ⒶⒹ	86	ⒶⒹ
39	ⒶⒹ	87	ⒶⒹ
40	ⒶⒹ	88	ⒶⒹ
41	ⒶⒹ	89	ⒶⒹ
42	ⒶⒹ	90	ⒶⒹ
43	ⒶⒹ	91	ⒶⒹ
44	ⒶⒹ	92	ⒶⒹ
45	ⒶⒹ	93	ⒶⒹ
46	ⒶⒹ	94	ⒶⒹ
47	ⒶⒹ	95	ⒶⒹ
48	ⒶⒹ		

Drill 7

1	ⒶⒹ	49	ⒶⒹ
2	ⒶⒹ	50	ⒶⒹ
3	ⒶⒹ	51	ⒶⒹ
4	ⒶⒹ	52	ⒶⒹ
5	ⒶⒹ	53	ⒶⒹ
6	ⒶⒹ	54	ⒶⒹ
7	ⒶⒹ	55	ⒶⒹ
8	ⒶⒹ	56	ⒶⒹ
9	ⒶⒹ	57	ⒶⒹ
10	ⒶⒹ	58	ⒶⒹ
11	ⒶⒹ	59	ⒶⒹ
12	ⒶⒹ	60	ⒶⒹ
13	ⒶⒹ	61	ⒶⒹ
14	ⒶⒹ	62	ⒶⒹ
15	ⒶⒹ	63	ⒶⒹ
16	ⒶⒹ	64	ⒶⒹ
17	ⒶⒹ	65	ⒶⒹ
18	ⒶⒹ	66	ⒶⒹ
19	ⒶⒹ	67	ⒶⒹ
20	ⒶⒹ	68	ⒶⒹ
21	ⒶⒹ	69	ⒶⒹ
22	ⒶⒹ	70	ⒶⒹ
23	ⒶⒹ	71	ⒶⒹ
24	ⒶⒹ	72	ⒶⒹ
25	ⒶⒹ	73	ⒶⒹ
26	ⒶⒹ	74	ⒶⒹ
27	ⒶⒹ	75	ⒶⒹ
28	ⒶⒹ	76	ⒶⒹ
29	ⒶⒹ	77	ⒶⒹ
30	ⒶⒹ	78	ⒶⒹ
31	ⒶⒹ	79	ⒶⒹ
32	ⒶⒹ	80	ⒶⒹ
33	ⒶⒹ	81	ⒶⒹ
34	ⒶⒹ	82	ⒶⒹ
35	ⒶⒹ	83	ⒶⒹ
36	ⒶⒹ	84	ⒶⒹ
37	ⒶⒹ	85	ⒶⒹ
38	ⒶⒹ	86	ⒶⒹ
39	ⒶⒹ	87	ⒶⒹ
40	ⒶⒹ	88	ⒶⒹ
41	ⒶⒹ	89	ⒶⒹ
42	ⒶⒹ	90	ⒶⒹ
43	ⒶⒹ	91	ⒶⒹ
44	ⒶⒹ	92	ⒶⒹ
45	ⒶⒹ	93	ⒶⒹ
46	ⒶⒹ	94	ⒶⒹ
47	ⒶⒹ	95	ⒶⒹ
48	ⒶⒹ		

Drill 8

1	ⒶⒹ	49	ⒶⒹ
2	ⒶⒹ	50	ⒶⒹ
3	ⒶⒹ	51	ⒶⒹ
4	ⒶⒹ	52	ⒶⒹ
5	ⒶⒹ	53	ⒶⒹ
6	ⒶⒹ	54	ⒶⒹ
7	ⒶⒹ	55	ⒶⒹ
8	ⒶⒹ	56	ⒶⒹ
9	ⒶⒹ	57	ⒶⒹ
10	ⒶⒹ	58	ⒶⒹ
11	ⒶⒹ	59	ⒶⒹ
12	ⒶⒹ	60	ⒶⒹ
13	ⒶⒹ	61	ⒶⒹ
14	ⒶⒹ	62	ⒶⒹ
15	ⒶⒹ	63	ⒶⒹ
16	ⒶⒹ	64	ⒶⒹ
17	ⒶⒹ	65	ⒶⒹ
18	ⒶⒹ	66	ⒶⒹ
19	ⒶⒹ	67	ⒶⒹ
20	ⒶⒹ	68	ⒶⒹ
21	ⒶⒹ	69	ⒶⒹ
22	ⒶⒹ	70	ⒶⒹ
23	ⒶⒹ	71	ⒶⒹ
24	ⒶⒹ	72	ⒶⒹ
25	ⒶⒹ	73	ⒶⒹ
26	ⒶⒹ	74	ⒶⒹ
27	ⒶⒹ	75	ⒶⒹ
28	ⒶⒹ	76	ⒶⒹ
29	ⒶⒹ	77	ⒶⒹ
30	ⒶⒹ	78	ⒶⒹ
31	ⒶⒹ	79	ⒶⒹ
32	ⒶⒹ	80	ⒶⒹ
33	ⒶⒹ	81	ⒶⒹ
34	ⒶⒹ	82	ⒶⒹ
35	ⒶⒹ	83	ⒶⒹ
36	ⒶⒹ	84	ⒶⒹ
37	ⒶⒹ	85	ⒶⒹ
38	ⒶⒹ	86	ⒶⒹ
39	ⒶⒹ	87	ⒶⒹ
40	ⒶⒹ	88	ⒶⒹ
41	ⒶⒹ	89	ⒶⒹ
42	ⒶⒹ	90	ⒶⒹ
43	ⒶⒹ	91	ⒶⒹ
44	ⒶⒹ	92	ⒶⒹ
45	ⒶⒹ	93	ⒶⒹ
46	ⒶⒹ	94	ⒶⒹ
47	ⒶⒹ	95	ⒶⒹ
48	ⒶⒹ		

Drill 9

1	ⒶⒹ	49	ⒶⒹ
2	ⒶⒹ	50	ⒶⒹ
3	ⒶⒹ	51	ⒶⒹ
4	ⒶⒹ	52	ⒶⒹ
5	ⒶⒹ	53	ⒶⒹ
6	ⒶⒹ	54	ⒶⒹ
7	ⒶⒹ	55	ⒶⒹ
8	ⒶⒹ	56	ⒶⒹ
9	ⒶⒹ	57	ⒶⒹ
10	ⒶⒹ	58	ⒶⒹ
11	ⒶⒹ	59	ⒶⒹ
12	ⒶⒹ	60	ⒶⒹ
13	ⒶⒹ	61	ⒶⒹ
14	ⒶⒹ	62	ⒶⒹ
15	ⒶⒹ	63	ⒶⒹ
16	ⒶⒹ	64	ⒶⒹ
17	ⒶⒹ	65	ⒶⒹ
18	ⒶⒹ	66	ⒶⒹ
19	ⒶⒹ	67	ⒶⒹ
20	ⒶⒹ	68	ⒶⒹ
21	ⒶⒹ	69	ⒶⒹ
22	ⒶⒹ	70	ⒶⒹ
23	ⒶⒹ	71	ⒶⒹ
24	ⒶⒹ	72	ⒶⒹ
25	ⒶⒹ	73	ⒶⒹ
26	ⒶⒹ	74	ⒶⒹ
27	ⒶⒹ	75	ⒶⒹ
28	ⒶⒹ	76	ⒶⒹ
29	ⒶⒹ	77	ⒶⒹ
30	ⒶⒹ	78	ⒶⒹ
31	ⒶⒹ	79	ⒶⒹ
32	ⒶⒹ	80	ⒶⒹ
33	ⒶⒹ	81	ⒶⒹ
34	ⒶⒹ	82	ⒶⒹ
35	ⒶⒹ	83	ⒶⒹ
36	ⒶⒹ	84	ⒶⒹ
37	ⒶⒹ	85	ⒶⒹ
38	ⒶⒹ	86	ⒶⒹ
39	ⒶⒹ	87	ⒶⒹ
40	ⒶⒹ	88	ⒶⒹ
41	ⒶⒹ	89	ⒶⒹ
42	ⒶⒹ	90	ⒶⒹ
43	ⒶⒹ	91	ⒶⒹ
44	ⒶⒹ	92	ⒶⒹ
45	ⒶⒹ	93	ⒶⒹ
46	ⒶⒹ	94	ⒶⒹ
47	ⒶⒹ	95	ⒶⒹ
48	ⒶⒹ		

Overcoming Reversal Errors

Drills 10–12

The following table shows errors made when individual letters, groups of letters, or entire words are somehow reversed, or otherwise changed, in our perception. Check the questions you had wrong on the Address Checking portion of the Diagnostic Practice Test. Pick out any errors showing this kind of mistake.

SOME COMMON PERCEPTION ERRORS MADE IN READING

Letters	Letter Groups	Words
b–d	ton–town	on–no
p–d	ville–view	top–pot
q–d	lawn–land	cite–ten
p–q	man–mon	never–ever
u–n	la–al	not–ton
u–v	le–el	pat–tap
n–m	ry–rey	saw–was
m–w	berg–burg	own–won
a–e	mont–mount	mar–arm
a–o	ham–heim	mint–tin

The three drills explained below may be used to remedy this situation. It is assumed, for the sake of illustration, that you are confusing *b* and *d*.

Drill 10

Write the letters *b* and *d* side by side.

b–d

1. _____ 3. _____ 5. _____ 7. _____ 9. _____
2. _____ 4. _____ 6. _____ 8. _____ 10. _____

Reverse their order and write them again.

d–b

1. _____ 3. _____ 5. _____ 7. _____ 9. _____
2. _____ 4. _____ 6. _____ 8. _____ 10. _____

Immediately after you write each pair, look away and picture the letters mentally. Write each pair ten times at each drill. Do this with other reversals with which you are having a problem.

Drill 11

On one side of a 3" × 5" card, write the letter *b* about one inch high. Write *d* on the other side. You have just made a flash card. Have a friend (or do it yourself) flash one side before you for the briefest instant. Call out what you see. Jot it down. Either side should be flashed at random. Each drill need last only 1 or 2 minutes. Do this with other reversals with which you are having a problem.

Drill 12

Take 3 seconds to check the line below to see how many *b*'s there are. Now check it for the number of *d*'s. Jot down the figures (the answer is at the end of this chapter).

b b d b d d d b d d

Number of *b*'s	Number of *d*'s
_____	_____

You or a friend can prepare similar lines consisting of the letters or groups of letters causing difficulty. Make certain that the number of items on each line varies. Drill several different lines each time.

Developing Speed and Accuracy With Names

Directions for Drills 13 through 17

A word or name is presented in Column 1. This word is not always a real one. Look at it once and then compare it to the words in Column 2. As your eyes sweep along these words, pick out the ones that are *exactly* the same as the one in Column 1. In the answer column, jot down the number of times you saw the original word repeated.

Example

Column 1	Column 2	Answers
heater	heaten heated heater beater heater heated	2

Do the following drills. The answer column has a space for you to repeat each drill three times. (Cover the column of answers you have already done so they do not influence you.) Keep a record in the space at the bottom of the answer column of the time (in seconds) and the number of correct answers. The object is to build required speed and accuracy. Do at least one drill a day. The answers to these drills are on page 110. Mark your progress on the Drill Record Chart on page 432.

Drill 13

Column 1	Column 2	Answers Trials 3	2	1
1. Hobart	Habart Hobard Habort Hobart Habort Hobart Habart			
2. Mainly	Mainley Mainly Manley Mairly Manly Mainly			
3. Pinelawn	Pinalawn Pinlawn Pinelaun Pineland			
4. Wood	Wood Wode Wood Wood Mood Woode			
5. Purton	Purtem Purdom Pumtom Partom Purdam			
6. Dumont	Dumont Dumomt Dumount Dummon Dumuumt Dumont			
7. Clover	Clover Claver Clovar Glover Clever			
8. Dunville	Duval Dunville Deville Duville Duvalle			
9. Logan	Logan Logan Locan Logan Locan Logam			
10. Mounte	Momte Montey Mounty Monte Mounte Mounty			
	Number Right			
	Time			

Drill 14

Column 1	Column 2	Answers Trials 3	2	1
1. Hammond	Hammon Hammand Hammont Hammon Hamnond			
2. Iceburg	Iceberg Iceburg Iceburg Iceberg Iceburg			
3. Forge	Force Farce Fogge Forge			
4. Minnow	Minnow Minnow Minmow Nimmow Minow Minnou			
5. Fieldson	Fielson Feldson Fekdson Fiestone Fellson			
6. Never	Nevem Nevel Levem Ever Evers			
7. Pomona	Ponoma Panoma Pomona Pomana Ponoma			
8. Lafayette	Lafayette Lafayitte Lafayete Lefayette Lafayute			
9. Hanger	Hunger Hanker Hancer Hangar Hangar			
10. Sierra	Seirra Siera Sierra Aerra Sierra Sierra			
	Number Right			
	Time			

Drill 15

Column 1	Column 2	Answers Trials 3	2	1
1. Soundport	Soundpoint Soomdport Somdport Southport Southpert			
2. Eggnog	Eccnog Eccnoc Eggnog Eggnag Egnog Egmog			
3. Fullawn	Fulland Fullamn Fulawn Fillawn			
4. Windfall	Wimdfall Wimdfall Windfall Windfall Windfall			
5. Jaspar	Jasper Jaspar Jasper Jaspar Jasquar Jasdar			
6. Yucca	Yucco Yucce Yucca Yucca Yugga Yucca			
7. Germantown	Germentown Germanton Germanton Germentown Germantown			
8. Levine	Lavine Levine Lewine Lavine Levin Lavine			
9. La Jolie	La Jolia Le Jolie La Jalie La Jolie La Jolee			
10. Crescent	Cressent Crescent Crescent Crescant Crescent Crescent			
	Number Right			
	Time			

Drill 16

Column 1	Column 2	Answers Trials 3	2	1
1. Narrowsburg	Narrowsberg Narowsburg Narromburg Narrowsberg			
2. Trenton	Trenton Trentin Trenton Trentan Trenton Trenton			
3. Vinton	Windon Vintom Vindon Vanton Winton Vimton			
4. Alberta	Elberta Alberta Alperta Alberta Elberta Alburto			
5. Sawridge	Sawbridge Sawridge Sawridge Samridge			
6. Zanocca	Zanocca Zannocca Zanoca Zamocca Zawocca			
7. Boca Raton	Boca Raton Baca Raton Boca Ratan Bocca Raton			
8. Realsboro	Reelsboro Realboro Realborough Realsboro Realsboro			
9. Catnap	Catnip Gatnap Catmap Catnap Catnip Catnap			
10. Kaspar	Kaspar Kaspar Kastar Kasper Kaspar Kasdar Kasper			
	Number Right			
	Time			

Drill 17

Column 1	Column 2	Answers Trials 3	2	1
1. Fishkill	Fishkill Dishkill Fisskill Fishkill Fishkill			
2. Ankava	Ankava Ankara Ankaqe Ankare Ankara Emkara Ankara			
3. Ellville	Ellvile Ellvalle Elville Ellview Elville Ellville			
4. Shepherd	Shepherd Shepherd Sheepherd Shepard Shepherd Shephard			
5. Seminary	Seminary Seminary Suminary Seminary Seminary			
6. Wallaby	Wallaby Wallbye Wallabey Wallaby Wallaby Wallaby			
7. Palmtry	Palmtree Palmitry Palmtry Palmtrey Palmtry Palmtry			
8. Overview	Overview Ovarview Ovarview Overville			
9. Lansdale	Lawnsdale Lansdale Landale Landsdale Lamdale			
10. Rottal	Rottal Rottel Rottal Rottel Rattal Rattle			
	Number Right			
	Time			

Developing Speed and Accuracy With Numbers

Directions for Drills 18 through 21

A number is printed in Column 1. Look at it once and then compare it to the numbers in Column 2. As your eyes sweep along these numbers pick out the ones that are *exactly* the same as the one in Column 1. In the answer column jot down the number of times you saw the original number repeated.

Example

Column 1	Column 2	Answers
11240	11240 12140 12104 11240 11240 21240 11204	3

Do the four drills on these pages. The answer column has a space for you to repeat each drill three times. (Cover the column of answers you have already done so they do not influence you.) Keep a record in the space at the bottom of the answer column of the time (in seconds) and the number of correct answers. The object is speed and accuracy. Do one drill a day. See page 110 for the answers.

Drill 18

Column 1	Column 2	Answers Trials 3	2	1
1. 142	142 142 241 214 124 142 412 142			
2. 361	316 361 361 631 613 136 361 316 316			
3. 519	591 591 159 519 159 519			
4. 890	890 980 890 809 809 980 890 890			
5. 378	387 738 873 378 378			
6. 233	323 332 233 323 233 233 323 233 323			
7. 980	980 980 890 980 890 908 908			
8. 442	424 442 244 424 442 424 442 442 442			
9. 257	527 527 257 257 275 275 257 257			
10. 693	693 639 643 639 693 396 963 963			
	Number Right			
	Time			

Drill 19

Column 1	Column 2	Answers: Trials 3	2	1
1. 2280	2280 2230 2820 2208 2280 2276			
2. 8193	8913 8913 8193 8182 8139			
3. 7455	7455 7545 7455 7455 7454			
4. 1010	1010 1100 1100 1010 1010 1100 1001			
5. 9648	9648 9643 9648 9468 9968 9648			
6. 1412	1412 1412 1421 1241 1421 1412 1412 1421 1422			
7. 3359	3359 3859 3395 3395 3359 3395 3395			
8. 7276	7276 7277 7267 7262 7276 7726 7276			
9. 1340	1304 1390 1840 1304 1304 1304 1034			
10. 2645	2645 2645 2645 2645 2644 2645 2645 2645			
	Number Right			
	Time			

Drill 20

Column 1	Column 2	Answers: Trials 3	2	1
1. 46342	46342 46324 46224 46342 46324 46342 43642			
2. 96114	96141 91614 96114 96141 96114			
3. 97423	79423 97432 97243 97433 97723 94732			
4. 59340	59304 59344 59840 95840 95340 95430			
5. 39045	30945 39044 39045 39054 39045 39044			
6. 42566	42566 42565 45266 46256 42666 42555			
7. 28683	28683 28688 28683 23683 23683 23688 28683			
8. 98337	97833 98373 98387 98337 68337 98333 98331			
9. 04567	04567 04568 04561 40516 4061 04576 04596			
10. 70634	70634 70634 70634 79634 70684 70674			
	Number Right			
	Time			

Drill 21

Column 1	Column 2	Answers: Trials 3	2	1
1. 50401	54010 50901 50401 50410 50410 50410 50140			
2. 28013	28031 82013 28113 28018 28310			
3. 90551	95051 90551 90515 90551 99551 90515 90551			
4. 52045	52045 52545 25452 50245 52095			
5. 75923	79523 75923 75923 75924 75932 75932			
6. 10458	14058 10458 10458 10485 10458 10458 10458 10458			
7. 11762	17162 11726 17162 11726 11762 11762			
8. 41097	41097 41097 40197 41097 41079 41094 41097			
9. 23819	32819 23819 28819 28819 23819 28819 28819			
10. 55710	57510 55710 55701 55701 55710 55107 55017 55017			
	Number Right			
	Time			

Increasing Eye Span

Directions for Drills 22–29

Here are several methods to increase eye span. All of them work, but for the sake of variety you may wish to alternate their use from day to day.

Method A: The Pyramid

Twenty-five addresses and parts of addresses are printed on separate lines on pages 91 and 92. They form a pyramid as the lines get successively wider toward the bottom of the page. Try to read each line with one fixation at its midpoint. The midpoint is indicated by a dot immediately above the line. Use your peripheral vision to make out the letters or numbers at the beginning and end of each line. Do not shift or slide your eyes. With practice you will be able to grasp (perceive) larger and larger pieces of each address. The width of each line is measured by the number of type units it includes: letters, numbers, and spaces in between. That number is printed near the right margin. Drill daily until you can span at least 15 units at one fixation. This span will enable you to check half of any address that you are likely to encounter on the test. Eventually, you can develop your eye span to take in a *long* address (22–25 type units) at one fixation.

Two full-scale drills are on the next two pages. Before you work on them, try this little drill. Do it before each of your practice sessions.

•
I

•
am

•
sure

•
to see

•
increases

•
in my span

•
if I practice

•
keeping my eyes

•
focused on the spot

•
at the middle of the line

Drill 22

	Type Units
• St	2
• 929	3
• Bank	4
• 02446	5
• Westom	6
• Captree	7
• 91 Fifth	8
• 364 Birch	9
• 1278 Apple	10
• Cedar Mount	11
• 820 W Fourth	12
• Grand View CA	13
• W Palm Springs	14
• Brookline 02108	15
• 2203 West End Ave	16
• 3491 Draper Dr SE	17
• Wailand Tenn 37886	18
• 4102 Georgia Ave NW	19
• 2293 Montgomery Lane	20
• 1904 John Marshall Dr	21
• 5 West End Av NY 10062	22
• 1401 Eastern Blvd Bklyn	23
• 6 Columbia Heights Rd La	24
• 93 Missouri St Tenn 47121	25

Drill 23

	Type Units
46	2
NYC	3
Ohio	4
37142	5
Oak St	6
W Drive	7
276 Pear	8
El Centro	9
Paducah KY	10
394 E Apple	11
10 Orange Dr	12
Beaverkill NY	13
1004 Pitkim Av	14
795 N Jefferson	15
2 Brentwood Lane	16
Creelling Av W VA	17
98 S 132 Dr Joliet	18
4 Haring Zemba Kans	19
West Philadelphia PA	20
Jameville Calif 96114	21
5504 Caroline St Miami	22
Small Point Maine 04567	23
East Falmouth Mass 02536	24
158 St Massapequa Park NY	25

Method B: Using the Eye Span Selector

Two Eye Span Selectors are printed on page 95. These Selectors have been designed to help you gradually develop a greater eye span. Together, the Selectors have 14 slot windows ranging in size from 4 to 32 type units. The greater the number of type units, the wider the eye span you will need to see them all at one fixation. The middle slots on both cards, which are 32 type units wide, enable you to see even the longest address at one glance. Use the Selectors to check the address pairs in Drills 24 through 29.

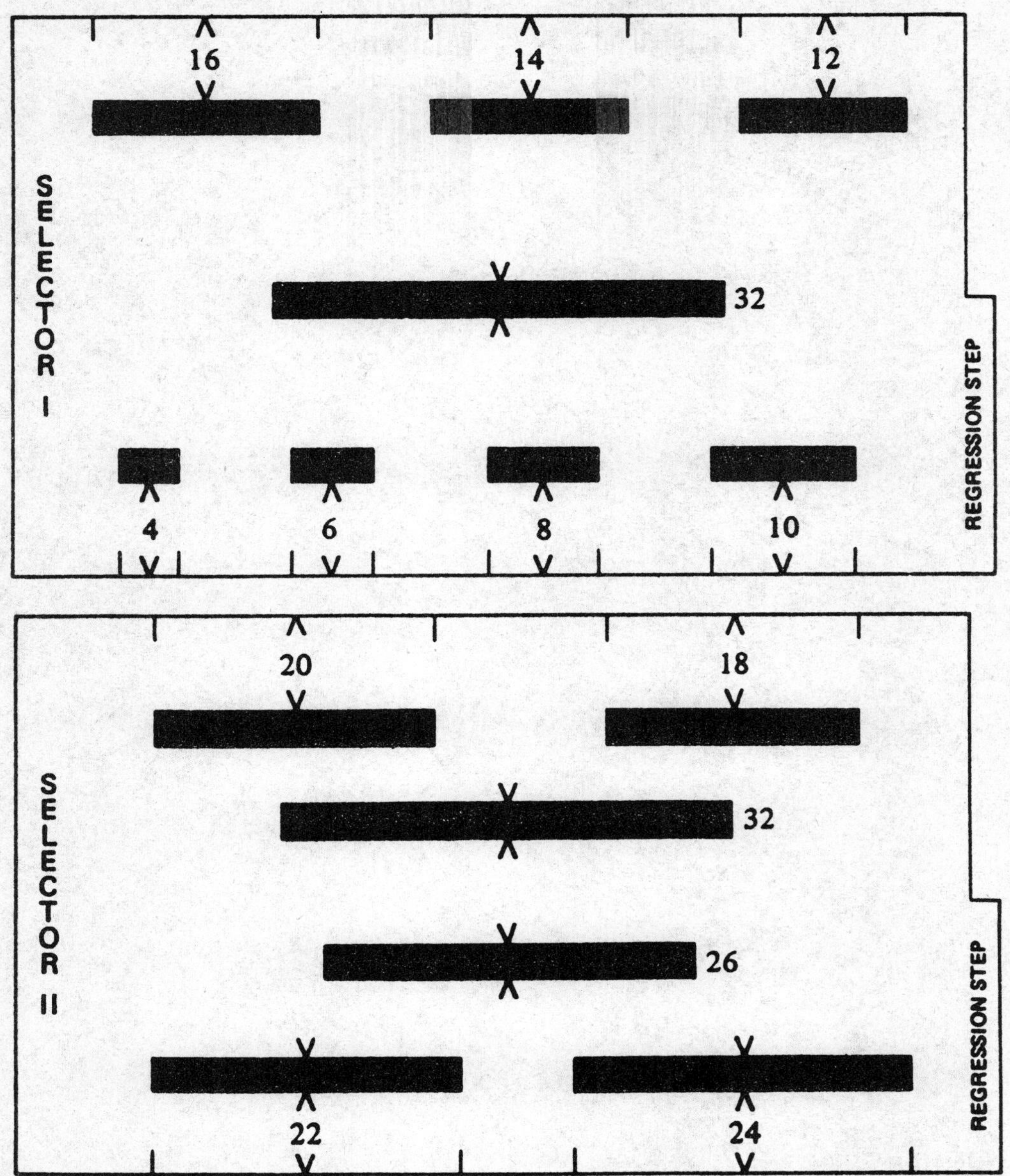
16
14
12
SELECTOR I
32
REGRESSION STEP
4
6
8
10
20
18
SELECTOR II
32
26
REGRESSION STEP
22
24

How to Use the Eye Span Selector in the Following Drills

1. Cut out both Selectors. Trace the outline of each selector onto cardboard, and then cut the cardboard to the same size. Tape each Selector to a separate piece of cardboard to provide a firm backing. Now cut out each slot window.
2. Select a slot window that just about matches your present eye span, or is even a trifle wider.
3. Place the window over the first address line so that the beginning of the address and the left edge of the slot line up.
4. You should now see part of the address framed in the slot. Notice that a small arrow indicates the middle of the slot.
5. Quickly scan the part of the address you see. Use your peripheral vision to see the beginning and ending letters or numbers. Remember: your task is to compare whatever you see with the line below.
6. Make the comparison of the address either by (a) moving the Selector back and forth from the top line to the one below until you have scanned the entire address, or (b) moving the Selector horizontally along each part of the entire address and then checking what you saw against each part of the line below.
7. In either case, write in your answer choice, A (alike) or D (different), in the spaces available. (Cover the column of answers you have already completed so that they do not influence you on your second and third trials.)
8. If you wish, you may use the "guidelines" scribed along the top and bottom edges of the Selectors. The space between each pair of lines corresponds exactly in width to the slot adjoining it. The center of each width is indicated by an arrow. The "guidelines" may be used for exactly the same purpose as the window slots. Which method you use is strictly a matter of preference. Incidentally, the Selectors may be used for practice when you are reading *any* printed matter—your favorite newspaper, magazine, or book.
9. The important thing is to keep drilling until you've mastered a certain width. Then move on to the next larger size. Keep increasing the size of the slots until you reach one that brings you consistently good results. You will, therefore, progress from Selector I to Selector II.
10. Do away with the Selector as soon as you can. It is only a tool designed to help develop new habits. At every opportunity drill for awhile *without* it. Soon, you will find your new skills are a natural part of the way you read.

Drill 24

To complete this exercise, follow the directions for using the Eye Span Selector on page 97.

	Answers		
Trials	3	2	1
1. Mobile Al 36608 Mobile Al 36608			
2. 399 Powell Av NE 399 Powell Av NW			
3. 6241 Daly Rd 6242 Dely Rd			
4. 19 Washington Av SW 19 Washington Av SW			
5. Cambridge Springs PA 16043 Cambridge Springs PA 16043			
6. 200 Peter Smith W 300 Peter Smith W			
7. 2762 Airport S Acres 2762 Airport S Acres			
8. 12 W Normandy Dr 12 W Normandy Dr			
9. 3204 Princess Court Ln E 3204 Princess Court Ln W			
10. Bethleyville PA 15314 Bethleyview PA 15314			
11. 4902 Briarcliff Cir NE 4902 Briarcliff Cir SE			
12. 143 Park Av S 103 Park Av S			
13. 7671 Claremont Av N 7671 Claremont Rd N			
14. 634 Rocky Fork Blvd SW 643 Rocky Fork Blvd SW			
15. Ridgedale Drive Columbus OH Ridgefield Drive Columbus OH			
16. 1943 S Overhill Rd 1943 S Overdale Rd			
17. 4001 Harvard Av E 4010 Harvard Av E			
18. 123 Bellefontaine Dr 223 Bellefontaine Dr			
19. 561 E 145 St 561 E 145 Ct			
20. 1466 S Findlay Av 1466 S Findly Av			
Number Right			
Time			

Drill 25

To complete this exercise, follow the directions for using the Eye Span Selector on page 97.

	Answers		
Trials	3	2	1
1. 54631 Amagansett Court NW 54631 Amagansitt Court NW			
2. Sumter GA 31709 Sumtre GA 31709			
3. 8732 E Farmers Dr 8732 E Farmers Dr			
4. Morrisville VT 05657 Morristown VT 05657			
5. 1015 El Rancho Way West 1015 Le Rancho Way West			
6. 13 Long Lake Dr SE 13 Long Lake Dr SE			
7. 87–34 84 Av Howard Beach 87–34 84 Av Howard Beach			
8. 2204 Jibstav Ct SE 2024 Jibstay Ct SE			
9. Berkeley West Va 25420 Barkeley West Va 25420			
10. 4114 W Momongalia St 4114 W Momomgalia St			
11. 1032 Aldus St Bx 10485 1032 Aldus St Bx 10485			
12. 243 1st Av Paterson 234 1st Av Paterson			
13. 10 Alexander Hamilton Pkwy 10 Alexander Hamilton Pkwy			
14. 14013 NW Knollwood Ct 14013 NW Knollwood Ct			
15. Vermilion La 70510 Vermilion La 70510			
16. 98 N Winding Way Rd 89 N Winding Way Rd			
17. 2401 Sterling Terrace E 2401 Sterling Terrace W			
18. Saint James La 70052 Saint James La 70052			
19. 4910 Queens Blvd SW 4910 Queens Blvd NW			
20. Massapequa Park NY 11762 Massapequa Park NJ 11762			
Number Right			
Time			

Drill 26

To complete this exercise, follow the directions for using the Eye Span Selector on page 97.

	Answers		
Trials	3	2	1
1. 1401 Apricale Ln 1401 Apricale Pl			
2. 2894 Cremona Ave E 2984 Cremona Ave E			
3. 6401 Downdale Pl W 6401 Downdale Pl W			
4. 4561 Griffing Blvd 4561 Griffith Blvd			
5. 1095 S Westlawn Rd 1095 S Westlawn Rd			
6. 3798 NW 62nd Pl 3798 NE 62nd Pl			
7. Naples FL 33940 Naples FL 33940			
8. 17094 Rosemond Ct S 17094 Rosemond Ct S			
9. 676 Willow Point Ter 676 Willow Point Pkwy			
10. 8281 Van Born Ct 8181 Van Boren Ct			
11. 3938 E Parkingham St 3938 E Parkingham St			
12. Bethesda MD 21046 Bethesda ME 21046			
13. 1601 E 224 Rd 1601 E 229 Rd			
14. 6204 Dahlonega Dr SE 6204 Dahlonega Dr NE			
15. Rockford IL 61108 Rockport IL 61108			
16. 4409 Stanton Lane S 4490 Stanton Lane S			
17. 9118 Kettering Rd W 9118 Kettering Rd W			
18. 4532 N Sterling Way 4532 N Starling Way			
19. 2004 E Stonehedge Ter 2004 E Stonehedge Ter			
20. 6571 N Salisbury Blvd 6571 N Salisburg Blvd			
Number Right			
Time			

Drill 27

To complete this exercise, follow the directions for using the Eye Span Selector on page 97.

	Answers		
Trials	3	2	1
1. 6789 Rutherglen Ave S 6798 Rutherglen Ave S			
2. 7307 Sunnymeade Path 7037 Synnymeade Path			
3. 2781 E Rapadan Ln 2781 E Ramadan Ln			
4. 3898 N 14th Ave 3898 N 14th Ave			
5. Huntsville AL 35805 Huntsville AR 35805			
6. 3803 W Abercorn St 3803 W Abercorn St			
7. 4947 Braxfield Dr NE 4947 Braxfield Dr NE			
8. 6412 N Parkchester Blvd 6419 N Parkchester Blvd			
9. 1681 Quincy Ct S 1681 Quince Ct S			
10. 17094 Highway North Ext 17094 Highway North Ext			
11. Jackson MI 49203 Jackson ME 49203			
12. 1514 Grand Gorge Pkwy 1514 Grand Groge Pkwy			
13. 252 S Andrea Rd 252 S Angrea Rd			
14. 7603 S Garahime Ave 7603 S Garaheim Ave			
15. 8124 E Hickory Dr 8124 E Hickory Dr			
16. Camino CA 95709 Camina CA 95709			
17. 2504 S 114th Pl 2504 S 114th Pl			
18. 5288 Riverview Walk SW 5288 Riverview Walk SW			
19. 50 Buena Vista Trailer Ct 50 Buena Vista Trailer Ct			
20. Jeffersonville NY 12748 Jeffersonville NY 12747			
Number Right			
Time			

Drill 28

To complete this exercise, follow the directions for using the Eye Span Selector on page 97.

	Answers		
Trials	3	2	1
1. 9664 W Oahu Ave 9664 W Oahu Ave			
2. 7793 S Glastonbury Ave 7793 S Glastonbury Ave			
3. Burbank CA 91505 Burbank CO 91505			
4. 6167 E 217th Ter 6167 E 216th Ter			
5. 1514 Sewickley Way SE 1514 Sweickley Way SE			
6. 29418 W Main St 29418 W Main St			
7. 3712 E Jewell Ave 3712 E Jewett Ave			
8. 6036 W Yolande St 6036 W Yolande Ct			
9. Scottsdale AZ 85257 Scottsdale AZ 85257			
10. Rhoadesville VA 22542 Rhoadesville VA 22542			
11. 7453 E Athlone Ave 7453 E Athbone Ave			
12. 3816 McCollough Ct NW 3816 McCullough Ct NW			
13. Marengo IN 47140 Marango IN 47140			
14. 1614 S 161st Pl 1614 S 161st Pl			
15. 1705 Forest Isle Ct W 1705 Forest Isle Ct W			
16. 8067 N Trimbach Ln 8067 N Trimback Ln			
17. 4134 Nottingham Park Pl 4143 Nottingham Park Pl			
18. Woodbridge VA Woodridge VA			
19. 6491 S Burntwood Cir 6491 N Burntwood Cir			
20. 4849 Summitville View Walk 4849 Summitville View Walk			
Number Right			
Time			

Drill 29

To complete this exercise, follow the directions for using the Eye Span Selector on page 97.

	Answers		
Trials	3	2	1
1. 4198 109th Ave NE 4198 109th Ave NE			
2. 5771 S Newell St 5771 S Nevell St			
3. Glendale AZ 85304 Glendale AZ 85304			
4. 7061 S 20th Cir 7061 S 20th Ct			
5. 1352 Johanna Ave SW 1352 Johanna Ave SE			
6. 20739 Back River Neck Rd 20739 Back River Neck Rd			
7. 86 Fair Meadows Pl 86 Fair Meadows Pl			
8. 1440 W Platten Dr 1440 W Platte Dr			
9. 282 McDuffie Ln S 282 MacDuffie Ln S			
10. 5753 Oakcrest Pl 5735 Oakcrest Pl			
11. 9367 E Pohick Ln 9367 E Potick Ln			
12. 135 San Carlos Ct 135 San Carlas Ct			
13. 2031 Spotted Jack Loop 2031 Spotted Jack Loop			
14. 8043 Shasta Blvd S 8043 Shanta Blvd S			
15. Port Neches TX 77651 Port Neches TX 77651			
16. 6457 N Penelope Cir 6457 N Penelope Cir			
17. 89 S Mescolero Dr 89 S Mescolera Dr			
18. 4172 E Compere Blvd 4171 E Compere Blvd			
19. 100 La Salle Ridge Rd 100 La Salle Ridge Rd			
20. 5307 W 104th St 5307 W 104th St			
Number Right			
Time			

Preventing Regression

Drills 30 and 31

There are several methods to use to help break yourself of the habit of rereading an address.

1. Use the top edge of the Eye Span Selector or of any small index card to block off each line after you have checked it. In that way you won't be able to look back even if you want to. Keep moving the card down the page, line by line, as rapidly as you can. This method may be used with any of the practice tests or drills in this book.

2. You may find that you are looking back at *parts* of an address instead of moving ahead to scan the rest of the line. The Eye Span Selector has a simple, yet effective design feature to help overcome that practice. Use it to check the addresses on the next drills. (See the figures below and on the next page on "Using the Selector for Regressions" and the instructions that follow.)

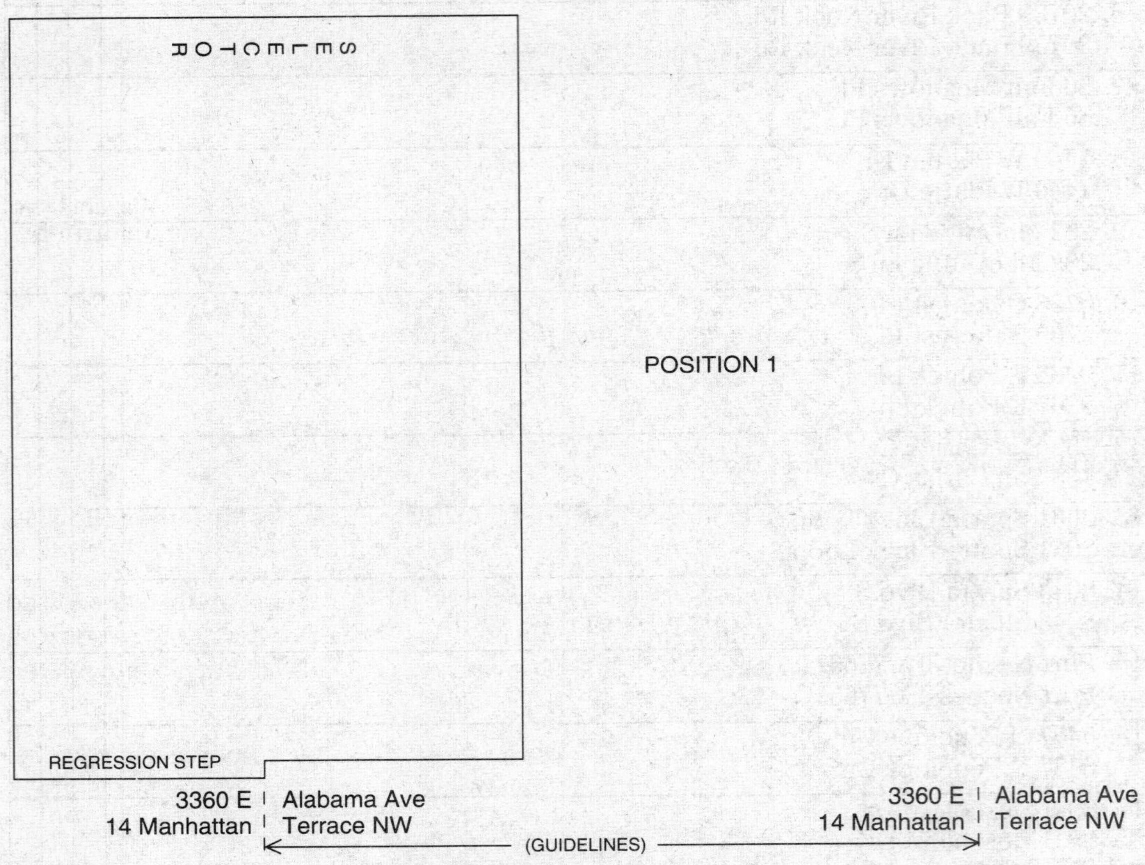

Using the Selector for Regressions

(position 2 on next page)

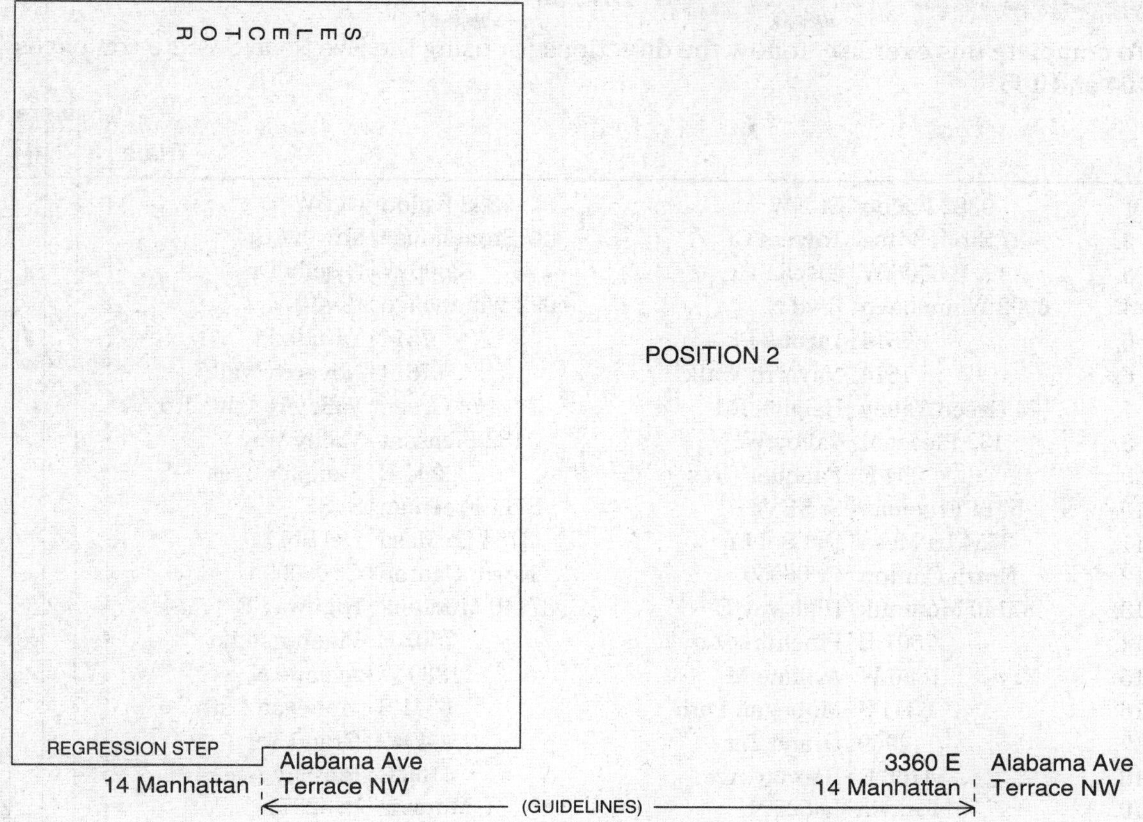

Using the Selector for Regressions

How to Use the Selector to Prevent Regression in the Following Drills

Assuming that you will be checking each address using two fixations, use the following procedure.

1. Hold the Selector *above the first line of addresses* on the page. Line up the edge of the little "STEP" with the dotted guide line (see Position 1). Scan the left half of the address in Column 1. Compare it with the left half of the address in Column 2 while moving the Selector down one line to Position 2.
2. Scan the *remaining portion of the address* in Column 1 and compare it to the remaining portion in Column 2. Now write your answer as to whether the items are A (alike) or D (different).
3. The Selector is now in the correct position for you to begin checking the *next line.* Now repeat steps 1 and 2 above.

Drill 30

To complete this exercise, follow the directions for using the Eye Span Selector on pages 104 and 105.

					Answers Trials 3	2	1
1.	9382 Ivaloo	Ct NW	9382 Ivaloo	Ct SW			
2.	437 Stonehorse	Towers Ct	437 Stonehouse	Towers Ct			
3.	3606 W	Gisella Dr	3606 W	Gisella Dr			
4.	5992 Winnebago	Blvd N	5992 Winnebago	Blvd N			
5.	7514	Yaruba Pl	7514	Yaruda Pl			
6.	7614	Navarro Walk	7614	Navarro Walk			
7.	74 Green Valley	Heights Rd	74 Green	Valley Heights Rd			
8.	132 Pleasant	Valley Way	132 Pleasant	Valley Way			
9.	204 E	Fauquer Cres	204 E	Fauquer Cres			
10.	5711 Freeman	St SE	5711 Freeman	St SE			
11.	3754 La Mesa	Del Sol Ln	3754 La Mesa	Del Sol Ln			
12.	North Canton	Ct 06059	North Canton	Ct 06059			
13.	87140 Montauk	Highway E	87140 Montauk	Highway E			
14.	7501 E	Pinehurst Ln	7501 E	Pinehorse Ln			
15.	1830 W	Avenue M	1830 W	Avenue N			
16.	6341 S	Mohegan Path	6341 S	Mohegan Path			
17.	4949	Grand Ter	4949	Grand Ter			
18.	4166 E	Barclay Ave	4166 E	Barclay Ave			
19.	Moravia	Ia 52571	Moravia	Ia 52571			
20.	19914	Southold Pkwy	19914	Southold Pkwy			
21.	9405 Val	de Mere Ave	9405 Val	de Mere Ave			
22.	2114 Eckhart	Hill Ct	2114 Eckhard	Hill Ct			
23.	4308 S	Trumbull Ave	4308 N	Trumbull Ave			
24.	583 Natrona	Ave W	583 Natrona	Ave W			
25.	314	Virgilina Cir	314	Virgilina Cir			
26.	8784 S	Oscalosa St	8874 S	Oscalosa St			
27.	Boscobel	WI	Boscobel	WI			
28.	5171 Shady	Point Canal Rd	5117 Schady	Point Canal Rd			
29.	3347 E	207 St	3347 E	270 St			
30.	Westfield	NJ 07066	Westfield	NJ 07006			
31.	2741	Vaughan Ave	2741	Vaughan Ave			
32.	4189 S	Montserrado Pl	4189 S	Montserrato Pl			
33.	6004 El	Florencia Ave	6004 El	Florencia Ave			
34.	2834	E Bentwood	2834 E	Brentwood Ct			
35.	80–17	150th Dr	80–17	160th Dr			
36.	5076 Nottingham	Ln E	5076 Nottingham	Ln E			
37.	West	Falmouth MA	West	Falmouth ME			
38.	1012 Saint	Mihiel Ave	1012 Saint	Mihiel Ave			
39.	6499 El	Campo Grande Ave	6499 El	Campo Grande Ave			
40.	Sarcoxie	MO 64862	Sarcoxie	MO 64852			
41.	Nassawadox	VA 23413	Nassawadox	VA 23143			
42.	4908 Decoty	Blvd N	4908 Degoty	Blvd N			
43.	109 E	148th Pl	109 E	148th Pl			
44.	Woodbine	MD 21797	Woodbone	MD 21797			

45.	2457 N	Guerida St	2457 N	Guerita Pl			
46.	1156 Seneca	Trl W	1156 Seneca	Trl W			
47.	8756 Rosemond	Path NE	8756 Rosemond	Path NW			
48.	3847 W	Woodbridge Cir	3847 W	Woodbridge Cir			
49.	1423 Luddington	Rd NW	1423 Luddingtown	Rd NW			
50.	968	Deepdene Rd	968	Deepdene Rd			
51.	6943	Merchant Blvd	6943	Merchant Blvd			
52.	3617 S	Chimney Rock Ln	3617 S	Chimney Rock Ln			
53.	27045	Rockview Rd	27045	Rockview Rd			
54.	9450	Remsen Ave	9540	Remsen Ave			
55.	6257 Villalobos	Park Cir	6257 Villalobos	Park Cir			
56.	947	Petaluma Blvd	947	Petalumo Blvd			
57.	6061	Okendorfer Ct	6061	0kendorfer Ct			
58.	1843	Janof Pl	1843	Janof Pl			
59.	8108	Helsley Ave	8108	Hemsley Ave			
60.	2843 Tappahonnock	Blvd SE	2834 Tappahonnock	Blvd SE			
				Number Right			
				Time			

Drill 31

To complete this exercise, follow the directions for using the Eye Span Selector on pages 104 and 105.

				Answers Trials	3	2	1
1.	1913 Via	Las Cumbres	1913 Via	Las Combres			
2.	3731	Temescal Ter	3731	Tenescal Ter			
3.	8108	Rutland Dr	8108	Rutland Dr			
4.	6761	Powhattan Ln	6761	Powhattan Ln			
5.	324 S	Miramar St	324 S	Mirimar St			
6.	1534 S	112 Pl	1534 E	112 Pl			
7.	9413 S	Blazewood Pl	9413 S	Blakewood Pl			
8.	Holladay	Vt 84117	Holliday	Vt 84117			
9.	200 E	Angelucci Way	200 E	Andelucci Way			
10.	734 Quantico	Ave S	734 Quantico	Ave S			
11.	7748 Quesada	Path S	7748 Quesada	Path S			
12.	7008 Yuerba	Buena Rd	7008 Yuerba	Buena Rd			
13.	6281 Point	Loma Ct NE	6281 Point	Loma Ct NE			
14.	Arlington Heights	IL 60004	Arlington Heights	IL 60004			
15.	3650	Baccus Ct	3650	Baccus Ct			
16.	5936	Frobisher Cir	5936	Frobisher Cir			
17.	2870 Stockton	Pl E	2870 Stockton	Pl E			
18.	4473	Viewbridge Pl	4473	Viewridge Pl			
19.	17 Kandace	Villa Ln	17 Kandace	Villa Pl			
20.	West Ossipee	NH 03890	West Ossipee	NH 03890			
21.	17981	Ashford Ave	17931	Ashford Ave			
22.	647 West	Portal St	647 West	Portol St			
23.	7200 Hempstead	Cir S	7200 Hempstead	Cir S			
24.	8483	Isleta Ave	8483	Isleta Cir			

25.	Vestaburg	PA 15368	Vestaburg	PA 15368			
26.	6011 N	Gabarda Rd	6011 S	Gabarda Rd			
27.	2587 Leicester	Way NW	2587 Leicester	Way SW			
28.	17045 Kelloch	Ave NE	17405 Kelloch	Ave NE			
29.	1617 Alta	Vista Way	1617 Alta	Vista Way			
30.	4025	Urbano Dr	4025	Urbano Dr			
31.	Kenosha	WI 53142	Kenosha	WI 53132			
32.	9724 Junipero	Serra Blvd	9724 Jupitero	Serra Blvd			
33.	8293 N	Idora Ave	8293 N	Idopa Ave			
34.	8039 S	Revelstoke Ter	8039 S	Bevelstore Ter			
35.	5732 O'Farrell	St SE	5732 O'Farrell	St SE			
36.	7012 W	Hamerton Ave	7012 W	Hammerton Ave			
37.	4712 Fratessa	Ct S	4712 Fratessa	Ct S			
38.	2751	Triton Blvd	2751	Triton Blvd			
39.	Sturdivant	MO 64782	Sturdivant	MO 63782			
40.	9658 South	Van Ness Ave	9658 South	Van Ness Ave			
41.	Alvaton	KY 42122	Alvaton	KS 42122			
42.	481 Bernal	Heights Blvd	481 Bernal	Heights Blvd			
43.	Cecilton	MD 21913	Cecilton	MD 21913			
44.	Wynantkill	NY 12198	Wynantrill	NY 12198			
45.	5908 W	Wayland Ave	5908 W	Wayland Ave			
46.	4360 New	Salem Ter	4360 New	Salem Ter			
47.	4289	Cale Nobleza	4289	Cale Nobleza			
48.	5527	El Mirasol	5572 El	Mirasol Pl			
49.	6349 Grand	View Ter	6349 Grand	View Trl			
50.	9112	Jocatal St	9112	Jocatal St			
51.	Yacima	WA 98902	Yakima	WA 98902			
52.	3712 Upshur	St W	3712 Upshur	St E			
53.	3597	Mariposa St	3597	Mariposo St			
54.	5051	Orleck Pl	5015	Orleck Pl			
55.	2580 W	234 Dr	2580 W	234 Dr			
56.	4745 Nob	Hill Cir	4745 Knob	Hill Cir			
57.	9401	Sabina Rd	9401	Sabrina Rd			
58.	85 Zircon	Ln SW	85 Zircon	Ln SW			
59.	5053	Zagala Ln	5053	Zacala Ln			
60.	3089 E	Codman Pl	3089 E	Cadman Pl			
				Number Right			
				Time			

Miscellaneous Drills

There are opportunities all around you for practicing address checking skills. When walking down the street, quickly scan license plates, street signs, and posters. Look away and attempt to repeat them. Try to read the quickly moving screen credits shown on television and in the movies. Practice using the Eye Span Selector or index card on the books, newspapers, and magazines you normally read. Use wider and wider slots to increase your eye span.

Also, have a friend help you play the following game. Your friend should checkmark, at random, a few names, telephone numbers, or addresses on different pages of an old phone book or catalog, making notes of the page numbers. You are to turn to each of these pages, scan the checkmarked item as fast as you can, and jot it down immediately. Then compare it with the book to see how accurate you are.

Or, have someone (or do it yourself) prepare 3" x 5" flash cards (see page 85), with the same address on either side. Make some exactly the same—Ⓐ, and others different—Ⓓ. After you have a stack of 20 or more cards, shuffle them and flash each side of each card before your eyes as quickly as you can. See how well you pick out the Ⓐ's and Ⓓ's.

The possibilities for practice are endless. Just use your imagination.

ANSWER KEY FOR DRILLS

Drills 1–11, not applicable

Drill 12, page 86

4 *b*'s
6 *d*'s

Drill 13, page 86

1. **2**	2. **2**	3. **0**	4. **3**	5. **0**	6. **2**	7. **1**	8. **1**	9. **3**	10. **1**

Drill 14, page 87

1. **0**	2. **3**	3. **1**	4. **2**	5. **0**	6. **0**	7. **1**	8. **1**	9. **0**	10. **3**

Drill 15, page 87

1. **0**	2. **1**	3. **0**	4. **3**	5. **2**	6. **3**	7. **1**	8. **1**	9. **1**	10. **4**

Drill 16, page 87

1. **0**	2. **4**	3. **0**	4. **2**	5. **2**	6. **1**	7. **1**	8. **2**	9. **2**	10. **3**

Drill 17, page 88

1. **3**	2. **1**	3. **1**	4. **3**	5. **4**	6. **4**	7. **3**	8. **1**	9. **1**	10. **2**

Drill 18, page 88

1. **4**	2. **3**	3. **2**	4. **4**	5. **2**	6. **4**	7. **3**	8. **5**	9. **4**	10. **2**

Drill 19, page 89

1. **2**	2. **1**	3. **3**	4. **3**	5. **3**	6. **4**	7. **2**	8. **3**	9. **0**	10. **7**

Drill 20, page 89

1. **3**	2. **2**	3. **0**	4. **0**	5. **2**	6. **1**	7. **3**	8. **1**	9. **1**	10. **3**

Drill 21, page 89

1. **1**	2. **0**	3. **3**	4. **1**	5. **2**	6. **6**	7. **2**	8. **4**	9. **2**	10. **2**

Drills 22–23, not applicable

Drill 24, page 98

1. **A**	3. **D**	5. **A**	7. **A**	9. **D**	11. **D**	13. **D**	15. **D**	17. **D**	19. **D**
2. **D**	4. **A**	6. **D**	8. **A**	10. **D**	12. **D**	14. **D**	16. **D**	18. **D**	20. **D**

Drill 25, page 99

1. **D**	3. **A**	5. **D**	7. **A**	9. **D**	11. **A**	13. **A**	15. **A**	17. **D**	19. **D**
2. **D**	4. **D**	6. **A**	8. **D**	10. **D**	12. **D**	14. **A**	16. **D**	18. **A**	20. **D**

Drill 26, page 100

1. **D** 3. **A** 5. **A** 7. **A** 9. **D** 11. **A** 13. **D** 15. **D** 17. **A** 19. **A**

2. **D** 4. **D** 6. **D** 8. **A** 10. **D** 12. **D** 14. **D** 16. **D** 18. **D** 20. **D**

Drill 27, page 101

1. **D** 3. **D** 5. **D** 7. **A** 9. **D** 11. **D** 13. **D** 15. **A** 17. **A** 19. **A**

2. **D** 4. **A** 6. **A** 8. **D** 10. **A** 12. **D** 14. **D** 16. **D** 18. **A** 20. **D**

Drill 28, page 102

1. **A** 3. **D** 5. **D** 7. **D** 9. **A** 11. **D** 13. **D** 15. **A** 17. **D** 19. **D**

2. **A** 4. **D** 6. **A** 8. **D** 10. **A** 12. **D** 14. **A** 16. **D** 18. **D** 20. **A**

Drill 29, page 103

1. **A** 3. **A** 5. **D** 7. **A** 9. **D** 11. **D** 13. **A** 15. **A** 17. **D** 19. **A**

2. **D** 4. **D** 6. **A** 8. **D** 10. **D** 12. **D** 14. **D** 16. **A** 18. **D** 20. **A**

Drill 30, page 106

1. **D** 7. **A** 13. **A** 19. **A** 25. **A** 31. **A** 37. **D** 43. **A** 49. **D** 55. **A**

2. **D** 8. **A** 14. **D** 20. **A** 26. **D** 32. **D** 38. **A** 44. **D** 50. **A** 56. **D**

3. **A** 9. **A** 15. **D** 21. **A** 27. **A** 33. **A** 39. **A** 45. **D** 51. **A** 57. **A**

4. **A** 10. **A** 16. **A** 22. **D** 28. **D** 34. **D** 40. **D** 46. **A** 52. **A** 58. **A**

5. **D** 11. **A** 17. **A** 23. **D** 29. **D** 35. **D** 41. **D** 47. **D** 53. **A** 59. **D**

6. **A** 12. **A** 18. **A** 24. **A** 30. **D** 36. **A** 42. **D** 48. **A** 54. **D** 60. **D**

Drill 31, page 107

1. **D** 7. **D** 13. **A** 19. **D** 25. **A** 31. **D** 37. **A** 43. **A** 49. **D** 55. **A**

2. **D** 8. **D** 14. **A** 20. **A** 26. **D** 32. **D** 38. **A** 44. **D** 50. **A** 56. **D**

3. **A** 9. **D** 15. **A** 21. **D** 27. **D** 33. **D** 39. **D** 45. **A** 51. **D** 57. **D**

4. **A** 10. **A** 16. **A** 22. **D** 28. **D** 34. **D** 40. **A** 46. **A** 52. **D** 58. **A**

5. **D** 11. **A** 17. **A** 23. **A** 29. **A** 35. **A** 41. **D** 47. **A** 53. **D** 59. **D**

6. **D** 12. **A** 18. **D** 24. **D** 30. **A** 36. **D** 42. **A** 48. **D** 54. **D** 60. **D**

Chapter 4

Memory for *Direct* (Name) Addresses—How to Improve Your Score

TEST STRATEGY

You have seen how important good test strategy is in taking the Address Checking part of the Test 460/470. You will be even more impressed by what an effective strategy can mean to your score on the Memory for Addresses part. Three major suggestions should be considered.

Use Some Practice Time for Studying

On the actual test, after you have completed Part A, you will be given a preliminary period of time to review the test directions for Part B and to do some sample questions. The purpose is to make certain that the test takers understand what the exam is all about—what is wanted, and where and how the answers should be indicated. *But you already know all of that.* The Diagnostic Practice Test you took used the same format that has appeared on prior examinations. Furthermore, if there should be any change in the type of question or in the format, you will know about it ahead of time. (All test candidates receive, before the test, a description of the test and several sample questions.) So why spend time rereading the same directions and doing samples? *Instead, use this time to memorize the addresses in the boxes.*

After reviewing the directions and the pre-test sample questions (see p. 36), you will be given several trial tests, preceded by brief study periods. On some of these tests you must answer the questions from memory. But for the other trial tests, the boxes with the addresses will be in view as you answer the questions. You may then proceed to answer the questions from memory in the regular way. On the other hand, you may decide to spend the allotted time *studying* the addresses in the boxes instead. It is believed, for most people, time is better spent studying the boxes rather than answering the pre-test sample questions or the questions on List 1 and List 2. It is true that there is a benefit in answering the warm-up questions by memory and then discovering what you don't know. On the other hand, comparatively little *new* learning takes place. The majority of students report far better results by spending almost all the available time studying and remembering the addresses.

In the past, the time *designated* for study totaled 8 minutes. A test candidate who followed the suggestions above and took advantage of all the time *available* for study might easily have doubled that amount. In this book, an effort has been made to be conservative by estimating that a total of 14 minutes will be available for study. Rather than being overly optimistic, it is better to be trained and ready to meet stricter standards. In any case, you will have a distinct advantage over your competitors! (See pages 222 to 223 for a step-by-step approach to handling the memory part of the exam.)

Eliminate the Last Box

If you master the memory techniques explained in the following pages, you won't need to employ this second strategy. It is believed that, with practice, you will be able to remember all 25 items. But if you have difficulty, consider skipping Box E either entirely or in part and concentrating on Boxes A, B, C, and D. *Then, when you take the test, you can mark Box E for any name that you don't recognize. And you'll be correct!*

Guess If You're Not Sure

What if you come across an address that you are not sure about? Should you guess? *The answer is YES.* Mathematically, even for a completely blind guess, you won't lose anything if you guess. Here's why. For each question, there are five choices, Box A, B, C, D, and E. Since one of these five has to be correct, you have one chance out of five (20 percent) of getting the correct answer, even if you guess. For example, if you took a test that had 100 questions and you guessed the answers to all of them, you would be likely to answer 20 correctly (20 percent of 100) and get the other 80 wrong. For *any* number of questions the odds are still the same. See how this fact affects your actual score: assume you guessed the answers to five of the memory questions instead of leaving them blank. If you got only what the odds dictated, you would end up with one answer correct and four wrong.

Calculations:	Number right.	1
	Number wrong 4	
	$\frac{1}{4} \times 4$	−1
	YOUR SCORE = 1 − 1 =	0

In this case, you have not lost anything, but you have not gained anything either.

However, you won't be making a *completely* blind guess on most questions you are not sure of. More likely, you will have a glimmer of recognition and will be unsure as to which one of two or three boxes to choose. If you then guess at one of them, you are going to come out ahead in the long run. The odds are such that when you are guessing at one out of two or three choices, you will get enough questions right to more than make up for the ones you get wrong.

To summarize, you now know three vital test strategies. Decide how to use them after you have studied Chapters 4 and 5 and after you have gained some experience doing the practice tests.

IMPROVING YOUR MEMORY

Science has yet to discover exactly how the human brain works. It knows enough to tell us that the brain is an awesomely complex structure that makes the most advanced computer look crude. It is also known that it has enormous untapped potential. One commonly cited bit of knowledge has it that the average person uses only about 10 percent of his or her ten billion brain cells. A person who could tap the unused powers of the mind might be able to accomplish wondrous things. Studies that have been made of individuals with just such extraordinary mental abilities bear out this supposition.

One famous case that was extensively documented is that of Mr. S. He was an obscure Russian who had a fantastic memory. He was able to memorize a list of 18 six-digit numbers in 3 minutes. He retained it so well that he could repeat the list in any order, even reciting each number in reverse! Amazingly, he was able to repeat these feats years later, even though he had not seen the list in the interim! Extraordinary displays of memory also are given by professional entertainers, the so-called memory experts who can recall the names and addresses of dozens of members of an audience they have never met before. In addition, you may have heard stories about famous generals, hostesses, and politicians who never forget a name or a place.

Intensive studies of people with "super memories" have helped psychologists understand how those with ordinary memories may improve them. The methods outlined below are based on such studies and on *demonstrated improvements* made by students who have used these methods to prepare for the Postal Service exam.

The study plan that was used for these students will be followed now as you look at various memory techniques. First, the techniques applicable to remembering the names of "direct" (name) addresses will be reviewed. In the next chapter, techniques to remember "numbered" addresses will be studied. It is strongly recommended that you begin your memory improvement program with the *direct* addresses. Experience shows that the techniques for remembering direct addresses will bring you quick, encouraging results. The confidence you gain will help when you undertake the more difficult task of remembering numbered addresses.

TECHNIQUES FOR REMEMBERING DIRECT ADDRESSES

Association and Imagery

If you are like most people, you will find it easier to remember names than numbers because a name brings forth a meaningful association with something familiar. It may remind you of a place, a thing, or a word you know about. Even better, the address name may bring a vivid picture to mind. For example, take the word *ice.* As soon as you see or hear this word, you may form an association with the word *cream* or *snow.* You may also associate *ice* with ideas or feelings such as *cold* or *chilly.* In your mind's eye, the image of an *iceberg* or an *ice cube* may form without conscious effort.

When you see a name that carries a meaningful association and presents an image, the name will probably stick in your memory. Two key memorization techniques to use, therefore, are *association* and *imagery.* Here is an illustration of the power and practicality of these techniques applied to the Memory of Addresses portion of the Diagnostic Practice Test. (For the sake of clarity, only direct addresses have been reproduced.)

A	B	C	D	E
Ceres Natoma	Cedar Foster	Niles Dexter	Cicero Pearl	Dehli Magnet

In Box A, *Ceres* looks and sounds like . . . sure, like *Cereal* or *Series*. You may also have associated Ceres with something out of a myth (Ceres happens to be the name of the ancient Roman goddess of agriculture). What about *Natoma?* It looks like the word *atom*. Remember what was discussed about associations and images? If you can form a single picture associating both names, they will stay in your memory even better. Can you picture a bowl of breakfast cereal (Ceres) with little atoms (Natoma) floating about in it? It may seem absurd, but in a way that's the point! Authorities on memory techniques say that the more vivid, colorful, and startling the image is, the better you'll remember it.

Nevertheless, you are not done yet. How about Box A? After all, on the test you are required to remember in which box each address belongs. A useful technique to employ now is to make up a little picture story to link either or both addresses to Box A. It can be weird or silly, as long as it helps to connect the box with the names. Let's assume, for example, that an *Apple* stands for *Box A*. Now the associations are complete. You have got a mental picture of little Apples (Box A) and Atoms (Natoma) floating in a bowl of Cereal (Ceres). You will never forget that.

What if you made a quick association between Ceres and Series? That brings to mind the World Series with its two opposing leagues, the *A*merican (Box *A*) and *N*ational (*N*atoma). **Remember,** the association you make does not have to fit and spell exactly right. As long as *you* make the connection, that's all that counts. You might even have imagined an *A*ce (Box *A*) pitching in the World Series (Ceres) for the *N*ational (*N*atoma) League. This image is vivid, and forms a good association among the two words and Box A. *You won't forget it on the test.*

Actually, Box A illustrates one of the more difficult associations you will have to make because the names Ceres and Natoma are offbeat. If you now feel confident of your ability to remember them, you will find remembering Box B even easier. Start associating the names in the box.

> Cedar brings to mind . . . a tree, a storage chest, wood, shingles, and so on.
>
> Foster brings to mind . . . a forest, a baby, the actor Foster Brooks, and so on.

That's it!

> . . . see the Cedar (Cedar) tree standing in the Forest (Foster),
>
> . . . see a Foster (Foster) baby, in her cradle, hanging from a Cedar (Cedar) tree.

How about the connection to *Box B?*

> . . . Make the tree a *B*lue Cedar (which is a common type).
>
> If you like, hang a hundred *B*ananas on it or a *B*eehive
>
> . . . See Foster Baby *B*urping.

As you have seen, the *sound* and the *appearance* of words are especially helpful when you encounter address names such as Ceres and Natoma that do not yield good associations based on meaning.

Another technique also uses sound and appearance as aids in remembering address names in their boxes. You construct an artificial word starting with the box letter and add whatever parts of both address names you need to make the new word stick. To illustrate, for Box A you could have made "A-CER-NA." See it and sound it in your mind as one word: ACERNA. Similarly, the names in Box E could yield "E-DEH-MA" or EDEHMA. Each of these words has a pleasing, catchy lilt and would work very well to bring together, in one word, everything you need to remember. Try this method for Box D. Check on page 135 for an answer.

How about Box C? Now that you have a whole kit of memory tools at your disposal, you should have very little trouble remembering the names in Box C. Start making associations for the names in the box:

> *Niles brings to mind* . . . river, Cleopatra, Egypt.
>
> *Niles sounds like* . . . nails.
>
> *Dexter means* . . . on the right side, a boy's name.
>
> *Dexter sounds and looks like* . . . dexterity, dextrose (sugar), dexedrine.
>
> *Box C sounds like* . . . sea, see.

Undoubtedly, you may have your own associations that haven't been listed here. In any case, you now can quite readily put together some unforgettable picture-stories:

*C*leopatra (*Box C*) rowed her barge with *dexterity* (*Dexter*) down the *Nile.*

*C*leopatra ate a box of *dextrose* sugar candy (*Dexter*) while riding down the *Nile* to the *sea* (*Box C*)

Dexter said, My goodness, just *see* (*Box C*) how long your *nails* (*Niles*) are!

And so it goes. The possibilities for imagery and extended associations are great in Box C. Although everyone may use a slightly different approach, everyone *can* make helpful associations. Practice these techniques on the tests in this book, letting your imagination run free. Start now by trying your hand with the names in Boxes D and E.

The "Loci" Technique

Mr. S., the Russian with the fabulous memory, partially explained it by telling about a system of "places" he used. (*Loci* is a Greek word meaning "places.") He said that he remembered long lists of objects by mentally putting each object in a particular place that was familiar to him. By remembering the place, he could "see" the object. For example, if Mr. S. were given a list of objects to remember, such as a hat, cane, dog, and violin, he would assign each of them to a particular place in a certain scene.

A scene that he sometimes used was a street near his home. He knew every inch of it because he walked it daily. To remember the list of objects, he would merely imagine himself walking down the street. On his imaginary walk, he would place the *hat* on a lamp post, lean the *cane* against the side of a shop, see the *dog* near a tree across the road, and put the *violin* in a pawnshop window. He could recall each object by mentally retracing his path down the street. So, when he saw the tree, he would see the dog, too! Each of the other objects on his list was recalled in the same way.

Performers, politicians, students, and others from all walks of life have been using the loci system, or a variation of it, down through the ages. It will work for you, too, provided you do two things:

1. Decide on your personal systems of places, or loci. Each system will need at least five objects or features.

2. Become so familiar with your loci that you can immediately "see" every one of these places.

You might choose a street on the way to work, your shop or office, a room in your house. The objects can range from your kitchen shelf to your desk drawer. Make the scene as detailed as you wish. The more "places" it has in it, the more items you will be able to remember.

Using the Loci Technique on the Test

The system or scene that you set up needs to have only five places, each one corresponding to one of the five boxes—A, B, C, D, and E. For example, a good system to use is the layout of rooms in your home. One student followed the room layout in her house like this:

A	B	C	D	E
Kitchen	Bathroom	Dining Room	Living Room	Workroom

In her mind's eye she was able to build the following pictures, using the boxes on page 115 as a basis.

BOX A—KITCHEN

I'm sitting in my kitchen eating a bowl of Cereal (*Ceres*) with little Atoms (*Natoma*) floating in it.

Note that she did not have to think of an association with Box A (such as Apple) because Box A is the kitchen.

BOX B—BATHROOM

I'm giving my *Foster* baby a bath and rubbing his Chest (*Cedar*) with soap.

If you like her system, see if you can use it to remember the addresses in Boxes C, D, and E. Do it now—the more you practice the art of imagery, the faster you will learn to do it. If you prefer to use your own system of places, remember to use the guidelines above.

Reduction Coding

Reduction coding, the third memory technique, has become the favorite of many students. It means that you cut down, or *reduce*, the amount you have to remember and then put what remains into a special, easy-to-remember form. Here are some simple examples:

Example

We can remember the order in which the colors of the rainbow appear (**r**ed, **o**range, **y**ellow, **g**reen, **b**lue, **i**ndigo, **v**iolet) by using their initials, ROYGBIV.

Example

If you want to remember the names of the Great Lakes, just remember the word HOMES:

Huron
Ontario
Michigan
Erie
Superior

In each case, *one* word replaces many words.

The third example is a word frequently used by those preparing for a test to select managers. (That might be you after you enter the Postal Service.)

Example

The word is POSDCORB, and it stands for the seven basic duties of every manager:

Planning
Organizing
Staffing
Directing
C } ordinating
O
Reporting
Budgeting

Seven different words made into one! Although POSDCORB, as a word, doesn't mean anything, it can be *sounded out* and seen in the mind's eye very easily. In this way, it will be remembered far longer and better than by drilling on the original seven.

You can see how this method works on another sample test question.

A	B	C	D	E
1800–2299 Peach	2400–2999 Peach	1200–1799 Peach	3000–3699 Peach	2300–2399 Peach
Frechett	Stokes	Hyberg	Graybar	Lorry
3100–3299 Kerry	4500–4999 Kerry	3600–4499 Kerry	3300–3599 Kerry	5000–5899 Kerry
Benson	Yalta	Island	Otiak	Upville
1500–1999 Martin	2000–2199 Martin	2700–3499 Martin	4100–4499 Martin	3500–4099 Martin

To remember the ten direct (name) addresses in these boxes by using *reduction coding*, you have your choice of four approaches.

Method A—Work Horizontally Across the Five Boxes

MAKE AN *IMAGE*.
Use the first letter of each of the five direct addresses in the second row, going from left to right, to set up your first new word.

FSHGL . . . See it in your mind's eye.
Make an image.

Do the same thing with the five direct addresses in the fourth row.

BYIOU . . . See it in your mind's eye.
Make an image.

***SOUND* OUT THE WORD.**
If your mind can retain the special sound or quality of the new "word" even though it has no meaning, then you have the battle more than half won. You will now have a fine substitute for the five original words *in the same order* in which they appear in each of the five boxes. Thereafter, whenever you see the address name Lorry, you will associate it with the last box —E, because the *l* sound comes last in the word FSHGL. Likewise, you can use the sound of FSHGL to correctly place each of the words on line 2 of each of the boxes: *F*rechett, *S*tokes, *H*yberg, *G*raybar, and *L*orry. You will be able to mentally see each of these words in its correct order.

You now have two of your senses working for you—sound and sight. You will have no need to attempt any of the usual memorization and repetitious drilling which yield far less satisfying results.

USE THE *MEANING*, IF ANY, OF THE NEW WORD.
Although it was pointed out that the new word need not have any meaning, sometimes it does. Instead, it may be associated with a word that does mean something. (It need not be an English word. A word in Spanish, German, Hindi, or any other language you know will do.) Once you have attached a meaning to the word, remembering it will become still easier.

Now go back to FSHGL. What do these five letters sound like when you try to pronounce them? Of course! The words sounds like FISH GILL, the breathing agent of a fish. I don't think there is any chance that you will easily forget the vivid picture associated with this word. Once this picture flashes into your awareness (which should take only a brief second), you can work confidently on the rest of the addresses in the five boxes.

What about the five remaining direct addresses on the fourth line? They formed your second new word—BYIOU. Suppose you now use these two new words to see how well you can employ the methods we've just discussed.

Drill 1

Below are 20 addresses contained in the five sample boxes on page 118. Study only the direct name addresses and their locations in these five boxes for *1 minute*, using the two new words FSHGL and BYIOU. Then, from memory, enter the correct box location (A–E) for each. (You may wish to do this exercise more than once.)

Answers — Trials	3	2	1
1. Frechett			
2. Lorry			
3. Benson			
4. Stokes			
5. Island			
6. Otiak			
7. Graybar			
8. Lorry			
9. Yalta			
10. Benson			

Answers — Trials	3	2	1
11. Hyberg			
12. Stokes			
13. Otiak			
14. Upville			
15. Frechett			
16. Otiak			
17. Island			
18. Lorry			
19. Graybar			
20. Hyberg			
Number Right			
Time			

Did you use BYIOU successfully? Did you sound it? It has a musical, easy-to-remember sound. You probably noticed immediately that BYIOU sounds exactly like the word *bayou* (as in the song "Blue Bayou"). Does it have any meaning? Indeed it does: it is a body of water, an arm of a lake or river. Now you have formed a vivid, mental image. With the triple combination of *sound*, *meaning*, and *imagery* that BYIOU conjures up, you cannot help but remember those five addresses.

MAKE UP A *STORY*.
Use the five letters as the initial letters of a five-word story, slogan, or phrase—the more vivid and breezy, the better.

Example

FSHGL — Feel So Happy Go Lucky.
Few Sleepy Heads Get Lively.
Father Saw His Green Lawn.

Example

BYIOU — Buy Yourself! IOU.
Bananas are Yellow, Inside, Outside and Underneath.
Baby is Young and Innocent, not Old and Ugly.

The trick is to be able to create the story freely and quickly. With a little practice, you can develop the knack. When you have it, you can remember any five-letter combination even if you cannot sound it (Step 2) or find any meaning (Step 3).

Method B—Work Vertically Within Each Box

For a variety of reasons that will be discussed later, you may decide to memorize all the addresses within each of the boxes A, B, C, D, and E, separately. If so, you may still employ reduction coding.

MAKE AN *IMAGE*.
Select the first letter of each of the two addresses in each box plus the letter above the box itself.

Example

For Box A, you would select the letters *A*, *F* and *B*. For Box B, select letters *B*, *S* and *Y*.

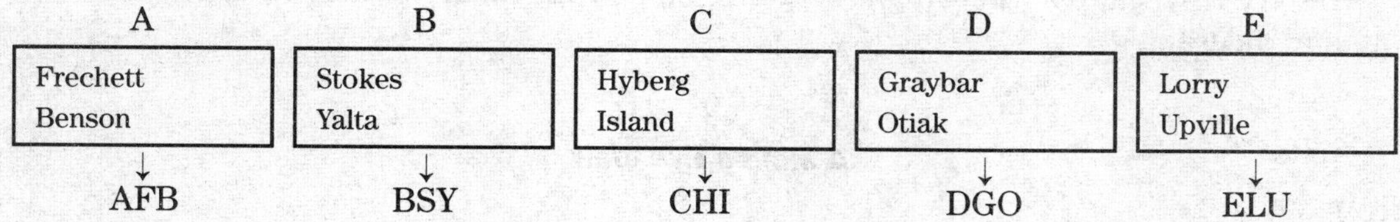

SOUND OUT THE WORD.
You don't get anything too useful with AFB, but you get immediate results with Box B. When you sound BSY you get—BUSY! Notice that the *B* in "Busy" immediately gives you the box location.

USE THE *MEANING*, IF ANY, OF THE NEW WORD.
When using associations was discussed, it was said that many of the best associations are strictly personal and exist only for you. This means that one of the three-letter words may be an abbreviation of a person, place, or thing with which only *you* are familiar. If so, you will immediately make the association and store it for future use. For example, in Box A, AFB might be the initials of your best friend, Alfred Frederick Bates, or, in military terms, Air Force Base. In Box C, CHI might be the letters of your old fraternity, or the City of Chicago, where you once lived.

But go further. You will learn how to use the three-letter combinations in other ways, if Steps 2 and 3 don't produce immediate results.

***MOVE* THE LETTERS AROUND.**
If the three letters do not produce a meaningful sound or word, play mental Scrabble. For instance, move just one letter of DGO and you've got DOG, man's best friend; DOG has the key letter *D*, which gives you the box location on which you peg the *O* and *G*. These letters stand, of course, for OTIAK and GRAYBAR. A problem arises only when you are given five boxes that contain two or more addresses with the same first letter. This problem, however, can be readily solved by Method C (see next page).

Drill 2

Transpose the initial letters of the direct addresses in Boxes A and C on page 121. In each case you will be able to come up with meaningful words.

1. Box A ______________________________

2. Box C ______________________________

MAKE UP A *STORY*.
Use exactly the same technique as explained on page 120. You will find this step even easier because your story needs only three words instead of five.

Method C—Combine the Horizontal and Vertical Methods

Sometimes you may wish to combine Methods A and B. In our sample question you may have felt very confident about remembering BYIOU, but not about FSHGL (Method A). You might then use a few of the three-letter words developed in Method B to reinforce your memory for the remaining addresses.

Now try to visualize what might be going on in your mind's eye by drawing a simple "mental diagram."

A Mind's Eye View

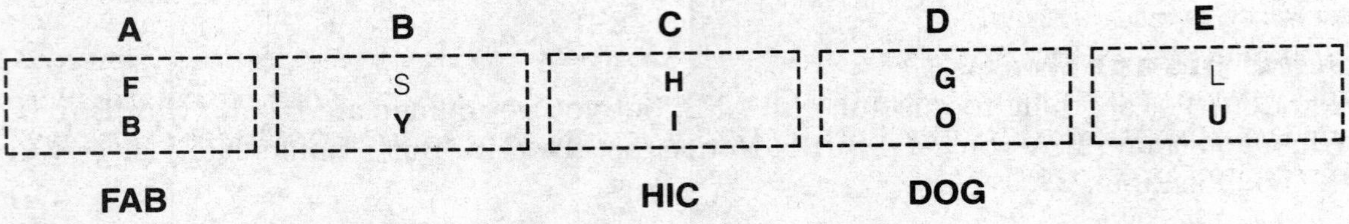

A	B	C	D	E
F	S	H	G	L
B	Y	I	O	U
FAB		HIC	DOG	

Here, the three-letter words, FAB, HIC, and DOG plus the word BYIOU stand out clearly. They give you eight of the ten direct addresses without any of the ordinary rote memorization on your part. They also give you cues on the two missing address names. By memorizing only *one* of them, you can ensure knowing all ten well enough to attain a perfect score!

EIDETIC (PHOTOGRAPHIC) MEMORY

You can form mental pictures that you are able to review whenever you want to remember something. Methods A, B, and C all employ this ability to some extent.

There are a few people who have "picture taking" ability far beyond the capabilities of most. They can reproduce a mental picture they have taken in such great detail that it is as though they literally were looking at a photograph. They can even see the picture in color and keep it stored for a long time.

Needless to say, those who were born with eidetic memories have an enormous advantage on this test. For the rest, although you cannot hope to develop photographic memories, you can learn, through practice, to intensify and retain longer the mental pictures you make.

In any case, you now have an arsenal of techniques that eliminate the need for special or hard-to-achieve powers. You can use them on some of the practice tests or wait until you have read Chapter 5, which will teach you how to deal with numbered addresses.

SPECIAL EXERCISES FOR BUILDING MEMORY FOR *DIRECT* ADDRESSES

Warm-up Drills

Do Drills 3 through 6 to get the feel of associating words and images freely and quickly. They are fun to do and you can do them by yourself or, if you prefer, with a friend.

Directions for Drills 3 through 6

Each drill consists of a list of 20 names. Cover the list with your hand or a piece of paper so that you can uncover one name at a time as you move down the list. If a friend is helping you, just hand the friend the list and ask him or her to call out each name when you are ready to begin.

As soon as you hear or see the name, call out the images and the words that come into your mind. Be free and spontaneous. Don't be concerned or embarrassed if your associations seem weird or foolish. The thing that *is* important is that the images come to you quickly and naturally. That is why there is no answer key to these drills. The only right answers are what *you* supply.

Take no more than 8 to 10 seconds per name on the average. In succeeding drills you will become able to make associations more rapidly. If you blank out on a particular name, skip over it and continue the drill until you complete all 20 names. These drills may be repeated as often as you like.

Drill 3

	Answers		
Trials	3	2	1
1. Avalon			
2. Hudson			
3. Linden			
4. Valley			
5. Illinois			
6. Oppenheim			
7. Jethro			
8. Inchon			
9. Dresden			
10. Charlotte			

	Answers		
Trials	3	2	1
11. Plummer			
12. Updike			
13. Rillmont			
14. Oleander			
15. Brighton			
16. Marcy			
17. Nugent			
18. Youngsville			
19. Xenon			
20. Chester			
Number Right			
Time			

Drill 4

	Answers		
Trials	3	2	1
1. Stanton			
2. Milltown			
3. Vesper			
4. Appleby			
5. Yaphank			
6. Nippon			
7. Fashion			
8. Blyden			
9. Carrington			
10. Zestal			

	Answers		
Trials	3	2	1
11. Foster			
12. Kramer			
13. Delancey			
14. Mercy			
15. Hartley			
16. Bloomingdale			
17. Eldridge			
18. Quail			
19. Teton			
20. Jersey			
Number Right			
Time			

Drill 5

	Answers		
Trials	3	2	1
1. Clarabelle			
2. Zweig			
3. Epsom			
4. Neversink			
5. Rashid			
6. Udam			
7. President			
8. Finster			
9. Xerxes			
10. Amstel			

	Answers		
Trials	3	2	1
11. Esther			
12. Lionel			
13. Shaverly			
14. Beirut			
15. Masters			
16. Disney			
17. Kingston			
18. Orange			
19. Dopel			
20. Gattling			
Number Right			
Time			

Drill 6

	Answers		
Trials	3	2	1
1. Lesley			
2. Chester			
3. Heron			
4. Quentin			
5. Gurnsey			
6. Ostreich			
7. Johnson			
8. Vermont			
9. Farmington			
10. Tuscan			

	Answers		
Trials	3	2	1
11. Kramden			
12. Partridge			
13. Toronto			
14. Fairchild			
15. Zoltan			
16. Huntington			
17. Spooner			
18. Greenberg			
19. Pontiac			
20. Ibis			
Number Right			
Time			

Using Association and Imagery

The next two drills (7 and 8) will be especially helpful to those who intend to rely primarily on forming associations and images to remember the direct name addresses. (Numbered addresses have been left out for the sake of clarity.) For a full discussion on this method, see pages 110 to 114.

Here are some guidelines.

1. As you examine each address name, make your associations and *see* the images each brings forth.

2. Associate the images in each box with their corresponding box letter (A, B, C, D, or E) by means of a mental picture story.

3. Drill on the names that you were not able to incorporate in your picture stories.

Drill 7

Study the ten address names and memorize in which box (A, B, C, D, or E) each belongs. *Take exactly 5 minutes to study these names and their locations.* When the study time is over, cover the boxes and answer as many of the 40 questions as you can in *2 minutes.* For each question, mark the answer space next to it to show the letter of the box in which the address belongs. (Cover the column of answers you have already completed so that they do not influence you on your second and third trials.)

A	B	C	D	E
Green Ryan	Robin Valley	Walnut Broad	Kingston Gemma	Burns Field

Trials	3	2	1
1. Green			
2. Walnut			
3. Kingston			
4. Broad			
5. Gemma			
6. Valley			
7. Walnut			
8. Field			
9. Broad			
10. Robin			
11. Ryan			
12. Burns			
13. Valley			
14. Green			

Trials	3	2	1
15. Walnut			
16. Robin			
17. Field			
18. Burns			
19. Broad			
20. Kingston			
21. Walnut			
22. Field			
23. Kingston			
24. Robin			
25. Burns			
26. Green			
27. Ryan			
28. Gemma			

Trials	3	2	1
29. Valley			
30. Burns			
31. Walnut			
32. Valley			
33. Robin			
34. Ryan			
35. Broad			
36. Green			
37. Burns			
38. Valley			
39. Ryan			
40. Field			
Number Right			
Time			

Drill 8

Study the ten address names and memorize in which box (A, B, C, D, or E) each belongs. *Take exactly 5 minutes to study these names and their locations.* When the study time is over, cover the boxes and answer as many of the 40 questions as you can in *2 minutes.* For each question, mark the answer space next to it to show the letter of the box in which the address belongs. (Cover the column of answers you have already completed so that they do not influence you on your second and third trials.)

A	B	C	D	E
Marx Pointe	Akron Wheeler	Eggers Limon	Drive Pitcher	Stake House

	Answers Trials 3	2	1
1. Limon			
2. Pointe			
3. House			
4. Marx			
5. Pitcher			
6. Akron			
7. Limon			
8. Eggers			
9. House			
10. Wheeler			
11. Pitcher			
12. Pointe			
13. Stake			
14. Akron			

	Answers Trials 3	2	1
15. House			
16. Drive			
17. Wheeler			
18. Limon			
19. Stake			
20. Marx			
21. Akron			
22. Eggers			
23. Pointe			
24. Drive			
25. Stake			
26. House			
27. Wheeler			
28. Marx			

	Answers Trials 3	2	1
29. Drive			
30. Pointe			
31. Eggers			
32. Pitcher			
33. Drive			
34. Stake			
35. Limon			
36. Wheeler			
37. Pitcher			
38. Eggers			
39. Marx			
40. Akron			
Number Right			
Time			

Using the Loci System

You may have decided that you like the loci system,* in conjunction with associations and imagery, for remembering direct name addresses. If so, do Drills 9 and 10 with these guidelines in mind:

1. Make sure that your loci system is at your command. You should be able to visualize instantly which box each place in your system represents.

* NOTE: Those who are not using the loci system, but are relying on regular associations, may use these drills in the same way as for Drills 7 and 8.

2. Form your association with the two direct names in each box in the regular way to come up with a vivid object picture for each name.

3. Place each of these object pictures in the place representing the box in your system. Make up a little story or slogan if it helps to strengthen the association.

Drill 9

Study the ten address names and memorize in which box (A, B, C, D, or E) each belongs. *Take exactly 5 minutes to study these names and their locations.* When the study time is over, cover the boxes and answer as many of the 40 questions as you can in *2 minutes.* For each question, mark the answer space next to it to show the letter of the box in which the address belongs. (Cover the column of answers you have already completed so that they do not influence you on your second and third trials.)

A	B	C	D	E
Carpenter Brazil	Young Stork	Beach Button	Wrigley Parson	Firestone Marshall

Answers

Trials	3	2	1
1. Brazil			
2. Wrigley			
3. Stork			
4. Parson			
5. Young			
6. Carpenter			
7. Firestone			
8. Beach			
9. Stork			
10. Brazil			
11. Button			
12. Marshall			
13. Wrigley			
14. Parson			

Answers

Trials	3	2	1
15. Marshall			
16. Carpenter			
17. Firestone			
18. Beach			
19. Marshall			
20. Young			
21. Parson			
22. Brazil			
23. Young			
24. Beach			
25. Stork			
26. Firestone			
27. Button			
28. Wrigley			

Answers

Trials	3	2	1
29. Young			
30. Carpenter			
31. Button			
32. Parson			
33. Marshall			
34. Wrigley			
35. Button			
36. Carpenter			
37. Firestone			
38. Brazil			
39. Beach			
40. Stork			
Number Right			
Time			

Drill 10

Study the ten address names and memorize in which box (A, B, C, D, or E) each belongs. *Take exactly 5 minutes to study these names and their locations.* When the study time is over, cover the boxes and answer as many of the 40 questions as you can in *2 minutes.* For each question, mark the answer space next to it to show the letter of the box in which the address belongs. (Cover the column of answers you have already completed so that they do not influence you on your second and third trials.)

A	B	C	D	E
Dahlia Table	Street Kane	Irons Oldham	Vista Summer	Nestle Clocks

Answers

Trials	3	2	1
1. Nestle			
2. Oldham			
3. Table			
4. Street			
5. Irons			
6. Kane			
7. Clocks			
8. Summer			
9. Dahlia			
10. Oldham			
11. Summer			
12. Irons			
13. Vista			
14. Table			

Answers

Trials	3	2	1
15. Summer			
16. Kane			
17. Nestle			
18. Clocks			
19. Summer			
20. Vista			
21. Street			
22. Irons			
23. Kane			
24. Nestle			
25. Dahlia			
26. Street			
27. Vista			
28. Oldham			

Answers

Trials	3	2	1
29. Clocks			
30. Street			
31. Dahlia			
32. Nestle			
33. Vista			
34. Table			
35. Dahlia			
36. Irons			
37. Oldham			
38. Clocks			
39. Kane			
40. Table			
Number Right			
Time			

Using Reduction Coding (Method A)

Drills 11 and 12 give you an opportunity to practice the reduction coding system for memorizing direct name addresses (see pages 119 to 120 for the complete discussion). Below is a summary of the steps to follow if you are going to use *horizontal* coding (Method A).

1. Use the first letter of each of the five name addresses on the top row to make a five-letter word. Visualize it.

2. Sound the word mentally. Is it catchy and easy to remember?

3. Does the word have any meaning or evoke a picture?

4. Make up a little story or slogan using the five letters. (Step 4 is optional. You need not use it if you are able to remember the new "word" after completing Steps 1 to 3.)
5. Repeat Steps 1 to 4 for the second row of five direct name addresses.

Drill 11

Study the ten address names and memorize in which box (A, B, C, D, or E) each belongs. *Take exactly 5 minutes to study these names and their locations.* When the study time is over, cover the boxes and answer as many of the 40 questions as you can in *2 minutes.* For each question, mark the answer space next to it to show the letter of the box in which the address belongs. (Cover the column of answers you have already completed so that they do not influence you on your second and third trials.)

A	B	C	D	E
Tyrone Samson	Richter Wiley	Kersey Marble	Sharon Omar	Elvis Faile

Answers Trials	3	2	1
1. Kersey			
2. Faile			
3. Elvis			
4. Sharon			
5. Tyrone			
6. Kearsey			
7. Richter			
8. Samson			
9. Faile			
10. Wiley			
11. Marble			
12. Omar			
13. Sharon			
14. Richter			

Answers Trials	3	2	1
15. Elvis			
16. Tyrone			
17. Samson			
18. Faile			
19. Marble			
20. Wiley			
21. Omar			
22. Tyrone			
23. Elvis			
24. Sharon			
25. Kearsey			
26. Richter			
27. Samson			
28. Faile			

Answers Trials	3	2	1
29. Tyrone			
30. Omar			
31. Wiley			
32. Elvis			
33. Marble			
34. Kearsey			
35. Wiley			
36. Sharon			
37. Faile			
38. Samson			
39. Omar			
40. Richter			
Number Right			
Time			

Using Reduction Coding (Method B)

In this method, you employ the same basic idea as for Method A except that you memorize the *individual* box letters as you memorize the addresses in each. Here is a summary of the steps.

1. For each individual box (A, B, C, D, and E), use the first letter of each of the two direct name addresses and the box letter itself to make up a three-letter word.
2. Sound the "word" mentally. Is it catchy and easy to remember?
3. Does the "word" have any meaning or evoke a picture?
4. Transpose the letters if it helps produce a better "word."
5. Make up a little story or slogan using the three letters. (Step 5 is optional. You need not use it if you are able to remember the new "word" after completing Step 4.)
6. Repeat Steps 1 to 5 for each box in turn.

Drill 12

Study the ten address names and memorize in which box (A, B, C, D, or E) each belongs. *Take exactly 5 minutes to study these names and their locations.* When the study time is over, cover the boxes and answer as many of the 40 questions as you can in *2 minutes*. For each question, mark the answer space next to it to show the letter of the box in which the address belongs. (Cover the column of answers you have already completed so that they do not influence you on your second and third trials.)

A	B	C	D	E
Queens Wright	Oshkosh Gully	Branch Sykes	Yucca Newark	Leeds Ishtar

Answers

Trials	3	2	1
1. Gully			
2. Wright			
3. Sykes			
4. Newark			
5. Queens			
6. Oshkosh			
7. Branch			
8. Ishtar			
9. Leeds			
10. Branch			
11. Sykes			
12. Yucca			
13. Leeds			
14. Wright			

Answers

Trials	3	2	1
15. Sykes			
16. Newark			
17. Queens			
18. Branch			
19. Oshkosh			
20. Gully			
21. Wright			
22. Gully			
23. Yucca			
24. Sykes			
25. Queens			
26. Oshkosh			
27. Branch			
28. Oshkosh			

Answers

Trials	3	2	1
29. Gully			
30. Sykes			
31. Newark			
32. Yucca			
33. Queens			
34. Ishtar			
35. Oshkosh			
36. Ishtar			
37. Yucca			
38. Sykes			
39 Newark			
40. Ishtar			
Number Right			
Time			

Making Up Stories and Slogans

A little story or slogan that connects the address names with each other and with the box letters can be very useful for strengthening associations, particularly if you use reduction coding and want to make sure of some hard-to-remember initials (read pages 120 to 121 for a complete discussion). Here are some brief guidelines to follow.

Your task is to use five initials (Method A) or three initials (Method B) to make up the words forming a brief story or slogan. For example, if you had to deal with the initials FSTAB, you might come up with "Five Sailors Took A Boat" or "Feed Salami To A Baby." Three letters such as CTB could stand for "Cock-eyed Teddy Bears" or "Chocolate Tastes Best." Anything goes. The more humorous, colorful, and vivid the story/slogan is, the better.

Do Drills 13 to 22 to develop your facility and speed. In each of Drills 13 to 17, there are five 3-letter combinations; in each of Drills 18 to 22, two 5-letter combinations. Each drill, therefore, contains the equivalent of ten direct name addresses, the same as on the regular test.

Directions for Drills 13 through 22

Take 5 minutes to study each drill. Make up your story/slogan as you examine each group of three or five letters. When the 5 minutes are up, cover the letter groups and jot down the initials, *in the same order as originally given*, on the answer line for that group. *Take 30 seconds to do this.* (Cover the column of answers you have already completed so that they do not influence you on your second and third trials.)

Drill 13

	Answers		
Trials	**3**	**2**	**1**
1. NDG			
2. FAR			
3. PTL			
4. ZUG			
5. OMY			
Number Right			
Time			

Drill 14

	Answers		
Trials	**3**	**2**	**1**
1. HXP			
2. YEC			
3. DUM			
4. JYO			
5. BLT			
Number Right			
Time			

Drill 15

	Answers		
Trials	**3**	**2**	**1**
1. TEC			
2. FCH			
3. MRS			
4. IRL			
5. LMA			
Number Right			
Time			

Drill 16

	Answers		
Trials	**3**	**2**	**1**
1. GAJ			
2. NPD			
3. WNG			
4. CIO			
5. UPI			
Number Right			
Time			

Drill 17

	Answers		
Trials	3	2	1
1. EKU			
2. LIZ			
3. CEO			
4. HFC			
5. MPQ			
Number Right			
Time			

Drill 18

	Answers		
Trials	3	2	1
1. YRADB			
2. GLUCR			
Number Right			
Time			

Drill 19

	Answers		
Trials	3	2	1
1. ICZTS			
2. ALFHO			
Number Right			
Time			

Drill 20

	Answers		
Trials	3	2	1
1. JWLAH			
2. PWACR			
Number Right			
Time			

Drill 21

	Answers		
Trials	3	2	1
1. EGUNX			
2. MVSGT			
Number Right			
Time			

Drill 22

	Answers		
Trials	3	2	1
1. DKHMP			
2. IMFYA			
Number Right			
Time			

ANSWER KEY FOR DRILLS

Drill 1, page 120

1. **A**	3. **A**	5. **C**	7. **D**	9. **B**	11. **C**	13. **D**	15. **A**	17. **C**	19. **D**
2. **E**	4. **B**	6. **D**	8. **E**	10. **A**	12. **B**	14. **E**	16. **D**	18. **E**	20. **C**

Drill 2, page 122

1. Box *A* plus *F* and *B* gives—*FAB*, the laundry detergent.
2. Box *C* plus *H* and *I* gives—*CHI*, slang for CHICAGO.
   —*HIC*, as in HICCUP.

Drills 3–6, not applicable

Drill 7, page 126

1. **A**	5. **D**	9. **C**	13. **B**	17. **E**	21. **C**	25. **E**	29. **B**	33. **B**	37. **E**
2. **C**	6. **B**	10. **B**	14. **A**	18. **E**	22. **E**	26. **A**	30. **E**	34. **A**	38. **B**
3. **D**	7. **C**	11. **A**	15. **C**	19. **C**	23. **D**	27. **A**	31. **C**	35. **C**	39. **A**
4. **C**	8. **E**	12. **E**	16. **B**	20. **D**	24. **B**	28. **D**	32. **B**	36. **A**	40. **E**

Drill 8, page 127

1. **C**	5. **D**	9. **E**	13. **E**	17. **B**	21. **B**	25. **E**	29. **D**	33. **D**	37. **D**
2. **A**	6. **B**	10. **B**	14. **B**	18. **C**	22. **C**	26. **E**	30. **A**	34. **E**	38. **C**
3. **E**	7. **C**	11. **D**	15. **E**	19. **E**	23. **A**	27. **B**	31. **C**	35. **C**	39. **A**
4. **A**	8. **C**	12. **A**	16. **D**	20. **A**	24. **D**	28. **A**	32. **D**	36. **B**	40. **B**

Drill 9, page 128

1. **A**	5. **B**	9. **B**	13. **D**	17. **E**	21. **D**	25. **A**	29. **B**	33. **E**	37. **E**
2. **D**	6. **A**	10. **A**	14. **D**	18. **C**	22. **A**	26. **E**	30. **A**	34. **D**	38. **A**
3. **B**	7. **E**	11. **C**	15. **E**	19. **E**	23. **B**	27. **C**	31. **C**	35. **C**	39. **C**
4. **D**	8. **C**	12. **E**	16. **A**	20. **B**	24. **C**	28. **D**	32. **D**	36. **A**	40. **B**

Drill 10, page 129

1. **E**	5. **C**	9. **A**	13. **D**	17. **E**	21. **B**	25. **A**	29. **E**	33. **D**	37. **C**
2. **C**	6. **B**	10. **C**	14. **A**	18. **E**	22. **C**	26. **B**	30. **B**	34. **A**	38. **E**
3. **A**	7. **E**	11. **D**	15. **D**	19. **D**	23. **B**	27. **D**	31. **A**	35. **A**	39. **B**
4. **B**	8. **D**	12. **C**	16. **B**	20. **D**	24. **E**	28. **C**	32. **E**	36. **C**	40. **A**

Drill 11, page 130

1. **C**	5. **A**	9. **E**	13. **D**	17. **A**	21. **D**	25. **C**	29. **A**	33. **C**	37. **E**
2. **E**	6. **C**	10. **B**	14. **B**	18. **E**	22. **A**	26. **B**	30. **E**	34. **C**	38. **A**
3. **E**	7. **B**	11. **C**	15. **E**	19. **C**	23. **E**	27. **A**	31. **B**	35. **B**	39. **D**
4. **D**	8. **A**	12. **D**	16. **A**	20. **B**	24. **D**	28. **E**	32. **C**	36. **D**	40. **B**

Drill 12, page 131

1. **B**	5. **A**	9. **E**	13. **E**	17. **A**	21. **A**	25. **A**	29. **B**	33. **A**	37. **D**
2. **A**	6. **B**	10. **B**	14. **A**	18. **C**	22. **B**	26. **B**	30. **C**	34. **E**	38. **C**
3. **C**	7. **C**	11. **C**	15. **C**	19. **B**	23. **D**	27. **C**	31. **D**	35. **B**	39. **D**
4. **D**	8. **E**	12. **D**	16. **D**	20. **A**	24. **C**	28. **B**	32. **D**	36. **E**	40. **E**

Drills 13–22, not applicable

Exercise from page 116, using appearance and sound to remember the Box D addresses: To remember Box D, combine D-CI-PEL to give the word DCIPEL, which looks and *sounds* like *disciple* and *decibel!*

Chapter 5

Memory for *Numbered* Addresses—How to Improve Your Score

If you have been studying and practicing as recommended, you should feel quite good about what you have accomplished. You probably are able to remember all of the direct (name) addresses in the practice tests without trouble. If you can, you must still do more to earn a respectable score. (If 40 percent of the 88 questions are direct names, and you get all of them right, your score will be 32.) Don't be satisfied with that! By pushing on and learning how to remember the numbered addresses, your score will easily rise to the sixties, seventies, and beyond.

In this chapter, solutions will be given to the problems most test takers have in remembering the numbered addresses.

TEST STRATEGY

In addition to the three memory strategies described in Chapter 4, pages 112 through 113, there is another strategy applicable only to the numbered addresses, which we will call "reduce the number."

Reduce the Number

The sample boxes in the Diagnostic Practice Test can serve as an illustration of this. (For the sake of clarity, only the numbered addresses have been reproduced.)

A	B	C	D	E
2100–2799 Mall 4800–4999 Cliff 1900–2299 Laurel	3900–4399 Mall 4000–4299 Cliff 2300–2999 Laurel	4400–4599 Mall 3300–3999 Cliff 3200–3799 Laurel	3400–3899 Mall 4500–4799 Cliff 3000–3199 Laurel	2800–3399 Mall 4300–4499 Cliff 1500–1899 Laurel

Original Numbered Addresses

You can reduce all of the above to a far simpler and easier-to-remember form. The boxes illustrate how few items you actually need to remember.

A	B	C	D	E
21 48 19	39 40 23	44 33 32	34 45 30	28 43 15

Simplified Numbered Addresses

Now See Why

1. *The addresses on each horizontal line follow each other in consecutive order.* This can be seen for the "Mall" line when the five addresses are rearranged:

A	E	D	B	C
2100–2799	2800–3399	3400–3899	3900–4399	4400–4599

Where one address ends, the other begins. For example, Box A covers 2100–2799 Mall; Box E begins with 2800. There are no gaps. Therefore, the last half of the address, 2799, need not be remembered. All addresses beginning with 2100 Mall must be in Box A.

2. *The questions on the text are always about the same ranges of numbers.* For example, there are no questions about single numbers in the middle of a range of numbers, such as 2345 Mall or 2697 Mall. Neither are there questions about other ranges, such as 2200–2400 Mall. You need focus only on the numbers shown, such as 2100 Mall.

3. *The last two digits of every address number are either "00" or "99."* So, why bother remembering them? It is easier to keep 21 in mind than 2100.

To sum up: Each of the address ranges is fully represented by the first two digits. Why take on the task of memorizing eight? Using this simple technique, the alert test candidate can reduce the original total of 30 four-digit numbers to 15 two-digit numbers!

An additional way to make the test easier involves the names—Mall, Cliff, Laurel. You may not have to remember them at all. That's because the two-digit numbers themselves pinpoint the box. You don't need to remember the name Laurel to place the 23 in Box B except in the event that 23 is used to start *another* address on the Cliff or Mall lines.

What would you do then? When you reach the end of this chapter, you'll find a full discussion on how to remember and place duplicate numbers.

Drill 1

Answer the questions below to get the feel of this discussion. Look only at the first two digits in each address to determine whether it would be found in Box A, B, C, D, or E of the set of boxes on page 136. (You may wish to do this exercise more than once.)

		Answers		
	Trials	3	2	1
1.	3400–3899 Mall			
2.	1900–2299 Laurel			
3.	3300–3999 Cliff			
4.	2300–2999 Laurel			
5.	2800–3399 Mall			
Number Right				
Time				

TECHNIQUES FOR REMEMBERING NUMBERED ADDRESSES

There are two principal techniques to choose from in preparing for the memory part of the posted exam: *visualization* and *association.* Both will be described fully in this chapter.

The Visualization Technique

Chunk the Number

Example

Try this experiment. Get a pencil and a blank sheet of paper. Next, study line 1 below for 5 seconds. Then look away and write, in order, the numbers you saw.

Line 1: 7 4 3 0 1 9 4 1 1 8 6 5

That was not easy. Try it once more, using line 2 below. Study the line for 5 seconds, look away, and write the numbers from memory.

Line 2: 7430 1941 1865

It was much easier to do the second time, wasn't it? Although the numbers were identical, the fact that they were organized into "chunks" made all the difference. Here is why.

The way the mind works, most people, unless they have trained themselves, cannot retain more than seven or eight pieces of information presented separately. The way the numbers were displayed on line 1, you were required to remember *12* separate items. On line 2, the same numbers were gathered into chunks of four numbers each. Each of these chunks, believe it or not, is as difficult (or easy) to remember as just *one* of the original digits. In effect, a chunk counts as a single piece of information. This is particularly true when the chunks have a meaningful association. In the example above, most people will associate 1941 with Pearl Harbor, and 1865 with the end of the Civil War or President Lincoln's assassination. The chunking technique will make it far easier to remember the numbers in the boxes. Chunk them like this:

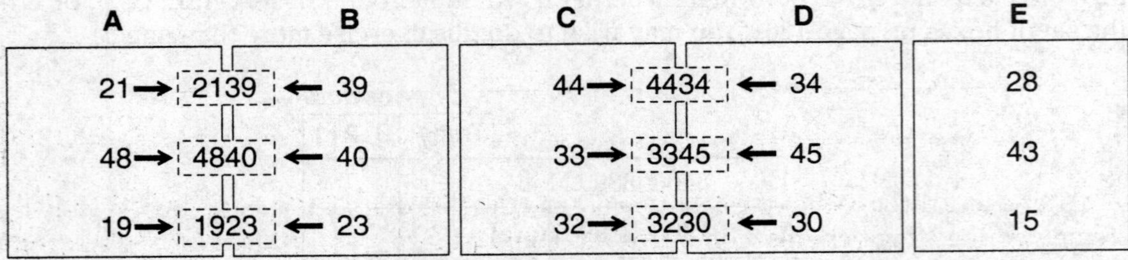

At this point, the original job of remembering 30 four-digit numbers has been cut down to remembering 6! This assumes that you are omitting Box E in accordance with "Eliminate the Last Box," the strategy discussed on page 113.

Now, use your powers of visualization. Help your memory by forming a mental screen like the one above, on which you see each four-number chunk in its place, alongside the same street. In that way, you will be able to identify in which box each part belongs. For example, when you picture 2139 between Box A and Box B on the top line (Mall) in the figure, you are automatically putting 21 in Box A and 39 in Box B. Similarly, see how 4434 can be used for Box C and Box D.

Chunking across each line in this way also has another advantage. It guarantees that you will get the right box for this address: 2800–3399 Mall—if you visualize "chunks" 2139 and 4434 "floating" on the top line of your screen (the "Mall" line). The only possible answer to an unfamiliar numbered address with "Mall" in it, *has* to be Box E.

Drill 2

Project the image below on your mental screen. It shows only what is necessary to score a perfect mark on these numbered addresses. Study it for 5 minutes.

2139	4434	28	MALL
4840	3345	43	CLIFF
1923	3230	15	LAUREL

Now cover the above boxes from view and write as many chunks as you can remember in the empty numbered boxes below. After writing each chunk, split it into 2 two-digit numbers and place each on the appropriate line below the boxes. Also enter the (3) numbers belonging in Box E.

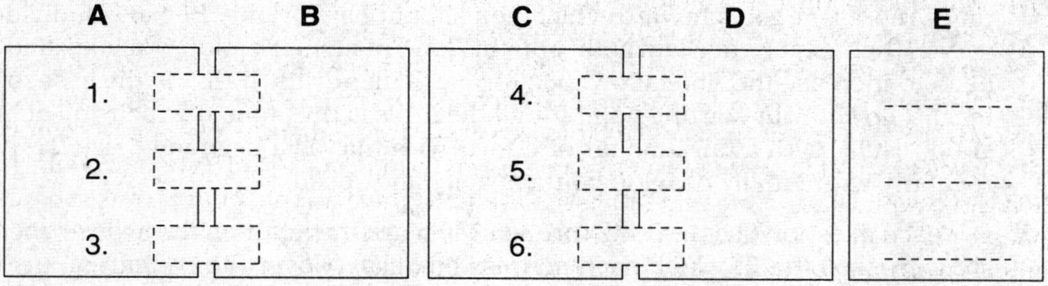

A	B	C	D	E
1.		4.		______
2.		5.		______
3.		6.		______

	A	B		C	D	E
1.	______	— ______	4.	______	— ______	______
2.	______	— ______	5.	______	— ______	______
3.	______	— ______	6.	______	— ______	______

After using these techniques for some of the drills and practice tests, you may find that remembering 4-digit chunks comes easy to you. You may want to attempt a 6-digit chunk by combining the 3 numbers in Box E. If you are successful, there will now be only *7* separate items to remember; i.e., the (6) 4-digit chunks from Boxes A, B, C, and D, plus (1) 6-digit chunk from Box E!

In the example, Box E's numbers, written as one chunk, become 284315. *Of course, you must remember them in that order because their position determines the street name each belongs to.* (Some students are good at remembering telephone numbers and write the new number as E28-4315.)

Additional Drills Using Chunking

Drills 3 through 12 will help you to develop your ability to organize and remember four-digit number chunks (see pages 138 to 139 for a full discussion and explanation). The two-digit numbers from which the chunks are to be formed have been printed in four adjoining columns marked A, B, C, and D. The numbers representing addresses in Box E have been omitted at this point. The space between the four columns is about the same as would be between the numbers if they were in boxes. (The direct name addresses have been omitted for clarity.)

These drills proceed in stages, increasing from one line to three and thereby from two chunks to six. Each line has a street name alongside it similar to the way the questions are displayed on the test. These names are essential, of course, when there are duplicate numbers among the addresses. (Only a few of the drills in this section have such duplicates.) After you have read "Dealing With Duplicates" at the end of this chapter, you will have an opportunity to do Drills 13 to 28, which will have more and more duplicate addresses and which will include Box E addresses as well.

Directions for Drills 3 through 12

1. For each horizontal street line, combine mentally the numbers in Columns A and B on page 141 so that they become a single four-digit number. Do the same with the numbers in Columns C and D.
2. Visualize each chunk as though it were in its place between two boxes. (See the diagram on page 138.)
3. Study the numbers, using the time posted above each group as a guide. These times represent goals toward which you should be working. Because individuals vary in their experience and ability on this kind of memorization, you may find you need to increase the time allowance for particular drills. If that is the case, by all means, do so. Your starting point for all the drills is the point at which you achieve good results with a fair amount of effort. With that as a beginning, use the drills regularly to gradually develop your capacity and speed.
4. For each question on pages 142 through 146 mark the letter on the answer sheet to show the column in which each address belongs. (Cover the column of answers you have already completed so that they do not influence you on your second and third trials.) Work at a reasonable speed, gradually increasing it between trials.

Don't be discouraged if you have difficulty with these drills at first. Most people do. On the other hand, you may discover you have unsuspected capabilities. The results of a recent study on the effects of training and practice reveal that ordinary people may often achieve astounding feats. To illustrate, the standard view repeated in almost every psychology textbook, is that the ordinary limit on short-term memory is for seven or so bits of information—the length of a phone number. But in a stunning demonstration of the power of *sheer practice* to break barriers in the mind's ability to handle information . . . college students have been taught to listen to a list of as many as *102* digits and then recite it correctly. After 50 hours of *practice* with differing sets of random digits, four students were able to remember up to *20* digits after a *single hearing. One student . . . not especially talented in mathematics, was able to remember 102 digits!*

Studies of chess masters, virtuoso musicians, and star athletes show that relentless *training* routines allow them to break through ordinary limits in memory and physiology, and so perform at levels that had been thought impossible.

The old joke—"How do you get to Carnegie Hall? Practice, practice, practice" is getting a scientific spin.

Drills 3 and 4—1 minute each

Drill No.	Street Name	A	B	C	D	Street Name
3.	Grand	31	42	35	49	Grand
4.	Locke	17	24	32	38	Locke

Drills 5 and 6—3 minutes each

Drill No.	Street Name	A	B	C	D	Street Name
5.	Viceroy	36	12	19	52	Viceroy
	Main	73	65	—	—	Main
6.	Tinton	21	13	26	30	Tinton
	Prince	60	66	—	—	Prince

Drills 7 and 8—5 minutes each

Drill No.	Street Name	A	B	C	D	Street Name
7.	Wendall	11	23	27	15	Wendall
	Cross	43	50	32	39	Cross
8.	Bride	72	80	63	69	Bride
	Elder	34	47	41	58	Elder

Drills 9 and 10—8 minutes each

Drill No.	Street Name	A	B	C	D	Street Name
9.	Delar	56	65	73	78	Delar
	Fleet	19	29	23	37	Fleet
	Hardy	40	37	—	—	Hardy
10.	Railroad	21	10	14	25	Railroad
	Vine	31	15	18	21	Vine
	Nestle	54	40	—	—	Nestle

Drills 11 and 12—9 minutes each

Drill No.	Street Name	A	B	C	D	Street Name
11.	Blue	66	58	73	61	Blue
	Glover	45	52	61	70	Glover
	Park	34	41	53	58	Park
12.	New	65	71	79	84	New
	School	68	57	55	65	School
	Oxford	18	29	26	14	Oxford

Drill 3

Answers

Trials	3	2	1
1. 31 Grand			
2. 42 Grand			
3. 35 Grand			
4. 49 Grand			
5. 31 Grand			
6. 42 Grand			
7. 49 Grand			
8. 35 Grand			
9. 35 Grand			
10. 42 Grand			
11. 31 Grand			
12. 35 Grand			
13. 49 Grand			
14. 31 Grand			
15. 35 Grand			
16. 42 Grand			

Answers

Trials	3	2	1
17. 31 Grand			
18. 42 Grand			
19. 35 Grand			
20. 49 Grand			
21. 35 Grand			
22. 49 Grand			
23. 42 Grand			
24. 31 Grand			
25. 35 Grand			
26. 31 Grand			
27. 35 Grand			
28. 42 Grand			
29. 49 Grand			
30. 42 Grand			
31. 31 Grand			
32. 49 Grand			

Answers

Trials	3	2	1
33. 35 Grand			
34. 42 Grand			
35. 31 Grand			
36. 42 Grand			
37. 49 Grand			
38. 35 Grand			
39. 42 Grand			
40. 31 Grand			
41. 49 Grand			
42. 35 Grand			
43. 49 Grand			
44. 31 Grand			
Number Right			
Time			

Drill 4

Answers

Trials	3	2	1
1. 17 Locke			
2. 24 Locke			
3. 32 Locke			
4. 38 Locke			
5. 32 Locke			
6. 24 Locke			
7. 17 Locke			
8. 38 Locke			
9. 24 Locke			
10. 17 Locke			
11. 32 Locke			
12. 38 Locke			
13. 32 Locke			
14. 24 Locke			
15. 17 Locke			
16. 24 Locke			

Answers

Trials	3	2	1
17. 32 Locke			
18. 38 Locke			
19. 32 Locke			
20. 24 Locke			
21. 38 Locke			
22. 24 Locke			
23. 17 Locke			
24. 24 Locke			
25. 38 Locke			
26. 32 Locke			
27. 17 Locke			
28. 17 Locke			
29. 38 Locke			
30. 32 Locke			
31. 24 Locke			
32. 38 Locke			

Answers

Trials	3	2	1
33. 17 Locke			
34. 17 Locke			
35. 24 Locke			
36. 38 Locke			
37. 32 Locke			
38. 24 Locke			
39. 17 Locke			
40. 32 Locke			
41. 24 Locke			
42. 38 Locke			
43. 24 Locke			
44. 32 Locke			
Number Right			
Time			

Drill 5

Answers	3	2	1
1. 36 Viceroy			
2. 12 Viceroy			
3. 73 Main			
4. 65 Main			
5. 52 Viceroy			
6. 65 Main			
7. 19 Viceroy			
8. 73 Main			
9. 65 Main			
10. 12 Viceroy			
11. 19 Viceroy			
12. 52 Viceroy			
13. 65 Main			
14. 73 Main			
15. 65 Main			
16. 36 Viceroy			

Answers	3	2	1
17. 12 Viceroy			
18. 73 Main			
19. 19 Viceroy			
20. 65 Main			
21. 52 Viceroy			
22. 73 Main			
23. 19 Viceroy			
24. 52 Viceroy			
25. 65 Main			
26. 73 Main			
27. 52 Viceroy			
28. 65 Main			
29. 12 Viceroy			
30. 36 Viceroy			
31. 73 Main			
32. 19 Viceroy			

Answers	3	2	1
33. 52 Viceroy			
34. 73 Main			
35. 36 Viceroy			
36. 12 Viceroy			
37. 73 Main			
38. 65 Main			
39. 12 Viceroy			
40. 12 Viceroy			
41. 73 Main			
42. 65 Main			
43. 36 Viceroy			
44. 12 Viceroy			
Number Right			
Time			

Drill 6

Answers	3	2	1
1. 26 Tinton			
2. 30 Tinton			
3. 21 Tinton			
4. 13 Tinton			
5. 60 Prince			
6. 66 Prince			
7. 26 Tinton			
8. 30 Tinton			
9. 66 Prince			
10. 21 Tinton			
11. 13 Tinton			
12. 60 Prince			
13. 60 Prince			
14. 13 Tinton			
15. 26 Tinton			
16. 21 Tinton			

Answers	3	2	1
17. 66 Prince			
18. 13 Tinton			
19. 26 Tinton			
20. 21 Tinton			
21. 30 Tinton			
22. 66 Prince			
23. 60 Prince			
24. 13 Tinton			
25. 26 Tinton			
26. 21 Tinton			
27. 30 Tinton			
28. 60 Prince			
29. 26 Tinton			
30. 30 Tinton			
31. 60 Prince			
32. 60 Prince			

Answers	3	2	1
33. 21 Tinton			
34. 13 Tinton			
35. 66 Prince			
36. 26 Tinton			
37. 13 Tinton			
38. 21 Tinton			
39. 60 Prince			
40. 30 Tinton			
41. 66 Prince			
42. 21 Tinton			
43. 13 Tinton			
44. 26 Tinton			
Number Right			
Time			

Drill 7

	Answers Trials 3	2	1
1. 11 Wendall			
2. 23 Wendall			
3. 43 Cross			
4. 50 Cross			
5. 32 Cross			
6. 27 Wendall			
7. 15 Wendall			
8. 39 Cross			
9. 23 Wendall			
10. 15 Wendall			
11. 50 Cross			
12. 27 Wendall			
13. 15 Wendall			
14. 11 Wendall			
15. 43 Cross			
16. 50 Cross			

	Answers Trials 3	2	1
17. 32 Cross			
18. 27 Wendall			
19. 15 Wendall			
20. 23 Wendall			
21. 39 Cross			
22. 11 Wendall			
23. 23 Wendall			
24. 32 Cross			
25. 50 Cross			
26. 27 Wendall			
27. 23 Wendall			
28. 43 Cross			
29. 50 Cross			
30. 39 Cross			
31. 32 Cross			
32. 27 Wendall			

	Answers Trials 3	2	1
33. 15 Wendall			
34. 32 Cross			
35. 39 Cross			
36. 11 Wendall			
37. 23 Wendall			
38. 50 Cross			
39. 32 Cross			
40. 23 Wendall			
41. 27 Wendall			
42. 15 Wendall			
43. 43 Cross			
44. 50 Cross			
Number Right			
Time			

Drill 8

	Answers Trials 3	2	1
1. 41 Elder			
2. 58 Elder			
3. 72 Bride			
4. 80 Bride			
5. 63 Bride			
6. 69 Bride			
7. 34 Elder			
8. 47 Elder			
9. 47 Elder			
10. 63 Bride			
11. 69 Bride			
12. 80 Bride			
13. 58 Elder			
14. 41 Elder			
15. 58 Elder			
16. 34 Elder			

	Answers Trials 3	2	1
17. 47 Elder			
18. 80 Bride			
19. 69 Bride			
20. 34 Elder			
21. 47 Elder			
22. 63 Bride			
23. 69 Bride			
24. 80 Bride			
25. 72 Bride			
26. 41 Elder			
27. 58 Elder			
28. 69 Bride			
29. 34 Elder			
30. 63 Bride			
31. 41 Elder			
32. 72 Bride			

	Answers Trials 3	2	1
33. 69 Bride			
34. 34 Elder			
35. 80 Bride			
36. 72 Bride			
37. 80 Bride			
38. 41 Elder			
39. 47 Elder			
40. 63 Bride			
41. 69 Bride			
42. 34 Elder			
43. 47 Elder			
44. 80 Bride			
Number Right			
Time			

Drill 9

	Answers: Trials 3	2	1
1. 23 Fleet			
2. 37 Fleet			
3. 40 Hardy			
4. 37 Hardy			
5. 56 Delar			
6. 65 Delar			
7. 23 Fleet			
8. 19 Fleet			
9. 19 Fleet			
10. 29 Fleet			
11. 73 Delar			
12. 40 Hardy			
13. 37 Hardy			
14. 65 Delar			
15. 73 Delar			
16. 37 Fleet			

	Answers: Trials 3	2	1
17. 23 Fleet			
18. 37 Fleet			
19. 40 Hardy			
20. 37 Hardy			
21. 73 Delar			
22. 78 Delar			
23. 29 Fleet			
24. 37 Fleet			
25. 56 Delar			
26. 73 Delar			
27. 78 Delar			
28. 19 Fleet			
29. 23 Fleet			
30. 37 Fleet			
31. 37 Hardy			
32. 56 Delar			

	Answers: Trials 3	2	1
33. 65 Delar			
34. 40 Hardy			
35. 78 Delar			
36. 37 Fleet			
37. 19 Fleet			
38. 29 Fleet			
39. 23 Fleet			
40. 73 Delar			
41. 78 Delar			
42. 37 Fleet			
43. 19 Fleet			
44. 78 Delar			
Number Right			
Time			

Drill 10

	Answers: Trials 3	2	1
1. 18 Vine			
2. 21 Vine			
3. 54 Nestle			
4. 40 Nestle			
5. 21 Railroad			
6. 10 Railroad			
7. 31 Vine			
8. 15 Vine			
9. 21 Railroad			
10. 10 Railroad			
11. 14 Railroad			
12. 25 Railroad			
13. 40 Nestle			
14. 10 Railroad			
15. 18 Vine			
16. 15 Vine			

	Answers: Trials 3	2	1
17. 46 Nestle			
18. 14 Railroad			
19. 25 Railroad			
20. 21 Railroad			
21. 31 Vine			
22. 54 Nestle			
23. 18 Vine			
24. 21 Vine			
25. 15 Vine			
26. 25 Railroad			
27. 10 Railroad			
28. 18 Vine			
29. 21 Vine			
30. 54 Nestle			
31. 15 Vine			
32. 14 Railroad			

	Answers: Trials 3	2	1
33. 25 Railroad			
34. 10 Railroad			
35. 15 Vine			
36. 40 Nestle			
37. 21 Vine			
38. 21 Railroad			
39. 10 Railroad			
40. 18 Vine			
41. 21 Vine			
42. 54 Nestle			
43. 40 Nestle			
44. 31 Vine			
Number Right			
Time			

Drill 11

Answers Trials	3	2	1
1. 66 Blue			
2. 58 Blue			
3. 61 Glover			
4. 70 Glover			
5. 34 Park			
6. 41 Park			
7. 45 Glover			
8. 52 Glover			
9. 61 Glover			
10. 58 Blue			
11. 61 Blue			
12. 34 Park			
13. 45 Glover			
14. 61 Blue			
15. 73 Blue			
16. 61 Blue			

Answers Trials	3	2	1
17. 58 Park			
18. 53 Park			
19. 45 Glover			
20. 61 Glover			
21. 61 Blue			
22. 58 Blue			
23. 60 Blue			
24. 58 Blue			
25. 53 Park			
26. 41 Park			
27. 61 Glover			
28. 52 Glover			
29. 66 Blue			
30. 58 Blue			
31. 70 Glover			
32. 66 Blue			

Answers Trials	3	2	1
33. 58 Blue			
34. 41 Park			
35. 34 Park			
36. 52 Glover			
37. 61 Blue			
38. 53 Park			
39. 66 Blue			
40. 58 Park			
41. 34 Park			
42. 41 Park			
43. 45 Glover			
44. 52 Glover			
Number Right			
Time			

Drill 12

Answers Trials	3	2	1
1. 65 School			
2. 18 Oxford			
3. 29 Oxford			
4. 68 School			
5. 65 New			
6. 71 New			
7. 26 Oxford			
8. 14 Oxford			
9. 55 School			
10. 65 School			
11. 71 New			
12. 18 Oxford			
13. 29 Oxford			
14. 57 School			
15. 55 School			
16. 65 School			

Answers Trials	3	2	1
17. 79 New			
18. 71 New			
19. 68 School			
20. 57 School			
21. 18 Oxford			
22. 29 Oxford			
23. 14 Oxford			
24. 26 Oxford			
25. 79 New			
26. 84 New			
27. 68 School			
28. 71 New			
29. 29 Oxford			
30. 18 Oxford			
31. 65 New			
32. 71 New			

Answers Trials	3	2	1
33. 65 School			
34. 55 School			
35. 68 School			
36. 57 School			
37. 26 Oxford			
38. 14 Oxford			
39. 65 New			
40. 79 New			
41. 84 New			
42. 51 School			
43. 65 New			
44. 71 New			
Number Right			
Time			

Hopefully, you found yourself among those capable of remembering 5 or 6 "chunks," and placing the individual addresses in the correct boxes. If so, it is suggested that you proceed directly to do the drills 13 through 27 based on the addresses on pages 159 and 160. These drills progress in difficulty by involving all five boxes and by including more and more duplicate numbers.

Those who attain high scores may very well decide to move directly on to the Memory for Addresses parts of Practice Tests 1 through 6 using the visualization skills they've perfected.

After doing these tests, you may be in a position to make the important decision as to the memory approach most suitable for you on the real test. If you have done well using visualization, you can approach the real test with confidence of attaining a perfect or nearly perfect score. But unless you are certain, read on. The association techniques furnish *another* road to a perfect score.

The Associations Technique

Using associations to remember the address names was discussed in Chapter 4. It works quickly and easily with many of the names: *Pearl*—Bailey, necklace; *Magnet*—pull, iron; *Cedar*—tree, chest, red; *Niles*—river, Cleopatra.

Numbers may be remembered in the same way.

Now See Why

There Are Numbers That Hold Immediate Associations for Almost Everyone.

With four digits

1492—Columbus, Discovery of America

1776—Declaration of Independence, Revolutionary War

1865—Lincoln assassinated, Civil War ends

1914—World War I starts

1929—Crash of stock market

1941—Pearl Harbor attacked

1945—World War II ends

1963—John F. Kennedy assassinated

With two digits

10—Commandments

12—Dozen eggs, midnight, lunch, noon, disciples

13—Bad luck, bar mitzvah

16—Sweet sixteen

21—Adulthood

25—Christmas

40—Thieves, life begins at

(Only illustrations of two-digit and four-digit numbers are shown because these are the kinds of numbers you need to remember for the test.)

Now see the figure below.

A		B	C		D	E
21 →	2139	← 39	44 →	4434	← 34	28
48 →	4840	← 40	33 →	3345	← 45	43
19 →	1923	← 23	32 →	3230	← 30	15

Note the number 2139. Imagine 21 as an *A*dult in Box A. What was the name of the famous comedian who always claimed he was 39 years old? Right—*B*enny in Box B.

Note the number 4840. What do you associate with 40? That's when life *B*egins (Box B).

Some Numbers Hold Personal Associations.

The chances are that most people can make an immediate connection with all or part of some of the following items.

address—	home, business, friend	*license plate number—*	________________
age—	yours, spouse, child	*anniversary—*	wedding, job, retirement
telephone number—	home, job, friend	*birthdate—*	yours, loved ones'
Social Security number—	________________	*credit card number—*	________________

Study for a moment the chunks and the two-digit numbers on the preceding page. Does anything connect for you? Does anyone you know have a *b*irthday (Box B) in one of the years whose number is in Box B (put a 19- in front of the number, of course)? Does your home or business *a*ddress (Box A) begin or end with 21, 48, or 19? Do you wear an undergarment sized 40B, 32C, or 34D? If any of these possibilities applies to you, then you are in luck. Keep track of these and all other numbers that have strong personal associations for you. (See page 149.)

Associate Numbers With Your "Loci"

The "loci" technique doesn't work as well with numbers as it does with direct names. Nevertheless, you may find a few good "fits" between some numbers and their boxes. Using the place system on page 117, one might see a phonograph in the living room (Box D) playing old 45 and 78 rpm records while a stack of 33 rpm LPs are sitting on a table in the dining room (Box C).

Make Up a Story

Chapter 4 mentioned briefly the technique of combining address name associations in a box with each other, and with the letter of the box itself (see pages 115 and 116). The idea was to make up a picture-story that would make these names and their images vivid and easy to remember. This technique is even more important when it comes to remembering numbers. Your memory needs as much reinforcement as you can give it.

Everyone can take advantage of this method, but a lot depends on how extensively you have built your list of two-digit number-word associations. To make this clear, here are two examples based on the boxes from the Diagnostic Practice Test (see page 36).

> *For Box C:* The *c*rooks (*Box C*) used a *.32 c*aliber pistol and a *.44 c*aliber rifle to rob us of *33* silver *c*oins.
>
> *For Box D:* The *d*raftsmen (*Box D*) used a *d*rawing tool with a *45 d*egree and a *30 d*egree angle to *d*esign a *d*esk *34* inches *d*eep.

As you can see, the method really works. If you like it, you'll need to prepare thoroughly. Start off by working on Drill 13 on page 159.

Your Personal Master List

See the list of numbers from 10 to 99 below. Next to each, write the word, name, or idea that immediately comes to mind.

Example

10—Bowling

11—Seven Eleven food stores

12—Months in a year

13—Baker's dozen

If nothing comes to mind for a particular number, examine some of the numbers in your life (see pages 147 and 148 for suggestions). See if any of these numbers, or any part of them, evokes a word or name. Extend your list every day by ten numbers until you reach item 99. The more complete your list is, the better the odds are in your favor of making a quick number-word association on the test. Remember—these associations do not have to ring a bell with anyone else except you.

10. ____________________
11. ____________________
12. ____________________
13. ____________________
14. ____________________
15. ____________________
16. ____________________
17. ____________________
18. ____________________
19. ____________________
20. ____________________
21. ____________________
22. ____________________
23. ____________________
24. ____________________
25. ____________________
26. ____________________
27. ____________________
28. ____________________
29. ____________________
30. ____________________
31. ____________________
32. ____________________
33. ____________________
34. ____________________
35. ____________________
36. ____________________
37. ____________________
38. ____________________
39. ____________________
40. ____________________
41. ____________________
42. ____________________
43. ____________________
44. ____________________
45. ____________________

46. ____________
47. ____________
48. ____________
49. ____________
50. ____________
51. ____________
52. ____________
53. ____________
54. ____________
55. ____________
56. ____________
57. ____________
58. ____________
59. ____________
60. ____________
61. ____________
62. ____________
63. ____________
64. ____________
65. ____________
66. ____________
67. ____________
68. ____________
69. ____________
70. ____________
71. ____________
72. ____________
73. ____________
74. ____________
75. ____________
76. ____________
77. ____________
78. ____________
79. ____________
80. ____________
81. ____________
82. ____________
83. ____________
84. ____________
85. ____________
86. ____________
87. ____________
88. ____________
89. ____________
90. ____________
91. ____________
92. ____________
93. ____________
94. ____________
95. ____________
96. ____________
97. ____________
98. ____________
99. ____________

Use Phonetics and the Number Tree

If you worked at it, and were fortunate enough, by now you have one or more entries next to many of the 90 numbers in Drill 13. On the other hand, you undoubtedly have some gaps in your list and need words to fill them in. There is a method that uses the *sounds* of words (phonetics) for that purpose. It is one of several such systems used to strengthen memory (you have already seen phonetics at work when you learned about imagery [page 114] and reduction coding [page 118]).

A Number-Language System

This is a system used to translate numbers into sounds, and then sounds into words. As you have seen, once you can replace numbers with words, you have made memorizing numbered addresses far easier. Here is how the system works:

1. *The Number Tree*—numbers into sounds (See illustration below.)
   Each number, from 0 to 9, stands in a column that forms the center or "trunk" of the tree. The left side of the tree has branches that give the *beginning sound* of each number. The right side of the tree has branches that show the way each number *sounds when it ends.* For example, say the number 1 out loud. When you pronounce it, it sounds like WON or WUN (depending on your accent). The beginning sound is "w"; the ending is "on" or "un." You can see them on the top left and right branches. Similarly, the number 2 has a "t" sound to begin, and an "o͞o" sound at

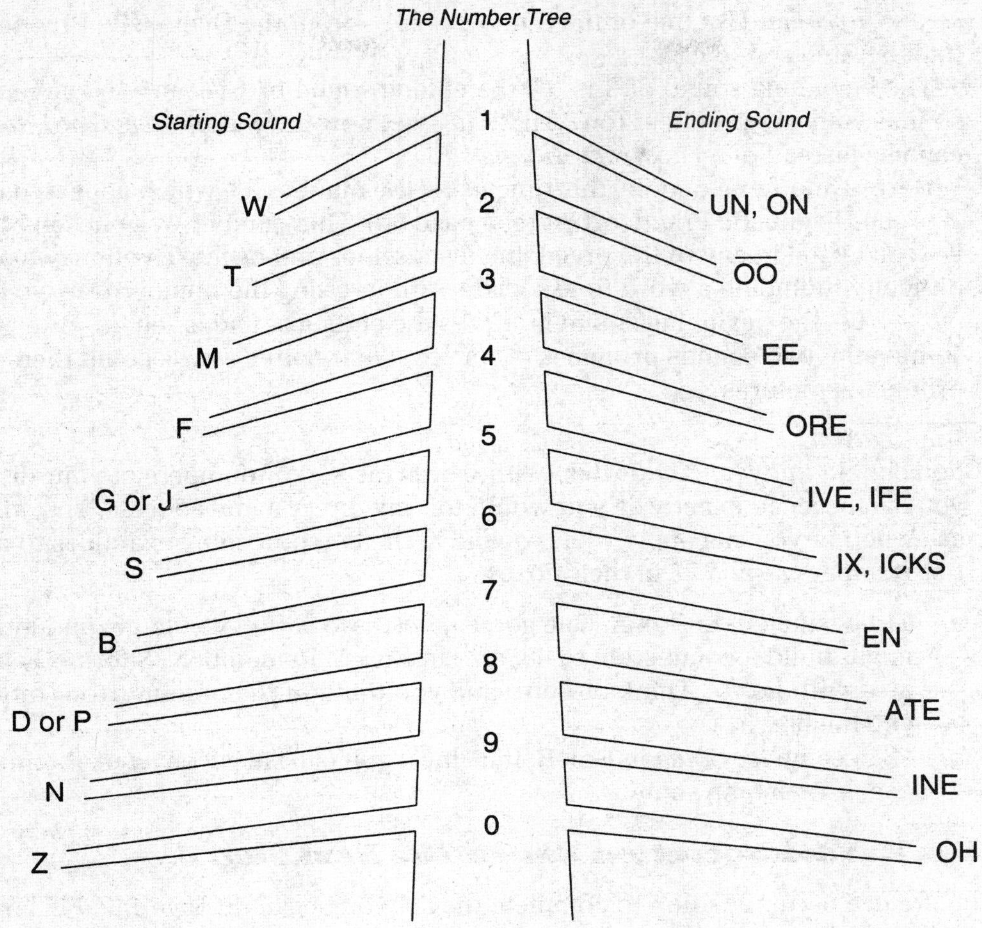

the end. As you look down the number tree, say each of the words aloud. Notice the beginning and ending sounds that compare them to the branches of the number tree, which has the phonetic breakdown for each number 0 through 9. (There are only four exceptions to this method: the beginning sounds of 3, 5, 7, and 8. These are the only parts of the number tree that you will have to memorize. Everything else follows the way you naturally pronounce the numbers.*)

2. *Sounds into Words*
The job now is to convert the two-digit address numbers into meaningful words. The *number tree* will enable you to do that since all two-digit addresses must use some combination of the numbers 0 through 9. *The way to proceed is to join the beginning sound of the first number in the address to the ending sound of the*

---

* These exceptions were made to avoid confusion between similar sounds or to provide a more useful beginning sound.
3. "m" will help build better words than "th"
5. "g" or j avoids confusion with the "f" that is used for "four"
7. "b" avoids confusion with the "s" that is used for "six"
8. "p" was chosen because "eight" (ate) doesn't have the "hard" sound useful in beginning many words.

Zero does not usually appear at the first digit among the addresses. If you should be given a number like 04, use the "Z" sound shown on the number tree. Think of it as an accented version of "s" and it becomes most useful. The address, (04) connects to "zore" (sore); (03) becomes zee (see), and so on.

second number. Use one of the numbers—21—from the Diagnostic Practice Test to illustrate:

The beginning sound of 2 is "t"; the ending sound of 1 is "un" or "on." Join the sounds, and you produce "ton." That's it—you now have a *concrete word, ton,* you can use instead of an *abstract number, 21.*

Here is another example, this time using the number 23, which appeared in Box B of the Diagnostic Practice Test (see page 36). This number was chosen because it wasn't used in any of the preceding discussions and because you may have had difficulty in finding a word to associate with it. Using the number tree, you have:

2—the beginning sound is "t"; 3—the ending sound is "ee."

Joining the two sounds produces *tee* or *tea.* What better words could there be for producing pictures?

3. *Application*
You should know all about this. With words instead of numbers at your disposal, you can proceed exactly as you would for any direct name address. You will now see whether you can apply what you did in the two preceding examples to memorize numbers 21 and 23 in their boxes.

a. 21 became *ton* in Box A. One good, quick association would be *a*mount. (This might build a connection to 48, also in Box A. Remember *48* formerly associated with Lotto? Think of Lotto and you think of the *a*mount (ton) of money you might win.)
b. 23 became *tee* or *tea* in Box B. Imagine a golf *b*all sitting on a tee. Picture a tea *b*ag, a T-*b*ar, and so on.

Number-Word Association Chart: The Next Step

Now you are in a better position to complete the list you began on page 149. Fill any gaps with words developed by using the number tree.

If you prefer, you can prepare another very useful chart (see page 153) that enables you to be even more thorough and systematic in building your number-name list. Here are some important points to keep in mind in connection with this chart.

- It is going to be *your* chart containing words useful to *you.* No one has to approve it or even understand the associations you make. Everyone has a different background and a different life experience. One person's list will probably be very different from another's.

- The best associations are the ones that come quickly and naturally. Often these come from your personal history. The most important data of your life may mean absolutely nothing to others. For example if you got married on November 28, 1967, the numbers *11 - 28 - 67* on your chart should have words like *a*nniversary, *b*ride, *c*eremony next to them. Your spouse's name should be there, too. If it begins with A, B, C, D, or E, so much the better.

- Even though the list is personal, others can help you build it. Perhaps you have a friend who is knowledgeable and willing to help you recall dates you learned in school, or in your reading, that you have not thought about in a long time—for example, 17*76*, 17*89*, 18*12*, 19*14*. You can match the important person or event with the date, thereby gaining additional useful associations. Similarly, your wife, parents, or an old friend can assist you in recalling important numbers in your own life: graduation dates, old addresses, the number of your public school (P.S. 28), and so on.

- It is perfectly acceptable to enter *more than one word* for any particular number—in fact, it is desirable. You will have that much more opportunity to produce images to fit different boxes. If you come up with *more than one number* that you associate with a particular word, that is also good. Just make sure that you reinforce the association between the word and the particular number you need to recall.
- If you have a choice of several words to use for a particular number, choose the one that produces the most vivid, colorful, action-filled image. Concrete nouns like *bee* and *gun* are the most effective in building picture-stories. You can see this clearly in the case of number *19*. The words produced by using the Number Tree are *wine* and *whine*. Although *whine* can be used successfully to build a connection to the boxes, *wine* is even better (see illustrations on page 155).
- If the only word you can develop for a particular number is an unfamiliar or abstract one, you must drill it until the association comes easily. Make sure that you fully understand the word's meaning and its proper use in a sentence. This is necessary if you are going to be able to incorporate it in a "picture story."

SAMPLE NUMBER-WORD ASSOCIATION CHART FOR NUMBERS 10–19

Number	Number Tree Words	Common Associations	Personal Associations	Number
10	WOE	Commandments, decimal system, bowling pins		10
11	WON	Veterans Day, football team		11
12	WOO	Disciples, Lincoln's birthday, dozen eggs		12
13	WEE	Baker's dozen		13
14	WAR WORE	Valentine's Day Civil Rights amendment		14
15	WIFE	Tennis, Martin Luther King, Jr.'s birthday		15
16	WICKS	Sweet sixteen, pint (16 ounces)		16
17	WHEN	Magazine		17
18	WEIGHT WAIT	Vote, army		18
19	WINE WHINE	Women's suffrage amendment		19

This is a sample of the kind of chart used to build and remember number-word associations. The format of this chart and its headings may be used as is or with any changes you desire.

The entries under "common associations" are the author's. You probably have others.

There are no entries for "personal associations" because such entries would be the author's and would mean nothing to you. It is most important that you fill in as many of yours as you can.

- Use the sounds associated with the numbers on the number tree in a *consistent* way. Unless you do so, you will have difficulty translating the number *into* a word, and even more in *reconstructing* a number *from* a word.
- Remember that you increase the odds in your favor of scoring high on the memory test each time you add another good number-word association to your chart. Try to produce some word for every number.

A Little More Insurance

At this point, you have everything you need to remember the numbers in addresses for a perfect score. You have a wide choice of association techniques to make the numbers more memorable. The illustrations and examples on the preceding pages have also shown you how to locate the numbers in their proper boxes.

Sometimes the associated word itself is used, for example, 21—*A*dult—Box A. In other cases, we employed a simple picture story—"The *c*rooks (*Box C*) used a *.32 c*aliber pistol . . ." to connect the numbers to their box.

If you have prepared a good number-word chart, stories and images will make it very simple to connect any number with any box. For example, if the number 21 (Adult), instead of being in Box A, were in one of the other four boxes, how would you have made the connection? You should have had no problem. Here's how:

21—Adult—*A*dult—Box A

21—Adult—*B*ig—Box B

21—Adult—*C*onsent, *C*ontrol—Box C

21—Adult—*D*ad, *D*evelop—Box D

21—Adult—*E*lder, *E*nd—Box E

For that matter, if the number 21 brought you even quicker associations with the word *big* or *blackjack* than it did with *adult*, you could have made these connections:

For *Big*	For *Blackjack*
21—Big—*A*pple, *A*pe, *A*dult—Box A	21—Blackjack—*A*ce—Box A
21—Big—*B*ig, *B*ang—Box B	21—Blackjack—*B*uy, *B*low—Box B
21—Big—*C*heese, *C*reep—Box C	21—Blackjack—*C*ards, *C*ut—Box C
21—Big—*D*addy, *D*eal—Box D	21—Blackjack—*D*raw—Box D
21—Big—*E*normous—Box E	21—Blackjack—*E*nough—Box E

All that was done was to use simple and natural *extended associations* stemming from the original number-word associations between 21 and *a*dult, *b*ig, and *b*lackjack.

See whether you can do the same thing with two of the word associations that were developed, using the number tree, for number 19—*wine, whine*. Some of the possible choices are shown on page 155.

If you do not want to rely entirely on your ability to work these extended associations at test time (the moment of truth), or if you are determined to do everything possible to insure a perfect score, then you should consider preparing the extended association *beforehand. In other words, you would do for every number from 10 through 99 what was done for number 21.* You will end up with a ready-made match connecting the original number—the original associated word—with a set of five words, each keyed to a particular box.

It is not difficult to do this, but it will take some time. Here are some guidelines to follow:

1. If you originally associated more than one word with a number (look back at your number-word chart), select the *best one* to be the original associated word. As you know, the best one is usually the most concrete and visual one. Words like *ham*, *cow*, *tree*, *worm*, fit the bill. Such words are the easiest to *extend* to yield additional associations.
2. In turn, try to select the four or five new *keyed* words so that each of them is concrete and as visual as possible. It is easier to visualize *eggs* than *eager.*
3. Prepare a chart specifically for the 90 key sets. (Use the examples for number 21 on page 154 and for 19 on this page as models.
4. Practice.

Number	Original Association	Extended (Keyed) Association	Box
19	Wine	*A*lcohol, *A*roma	A
	Wine	*B*ottle, *B*ar, *B*urgundy	B
	Wine	*C*ocktail, *C*ellar, *C*hablis	C
	Wine	*D*rink, *D*regs	D
	Wine	*E*lbow (bend it), *E*njoy	E
19	Whine	*A*ngry, *A*nnoy	A
	Whine	*B*other, *B*rat	B
	Whine	*C*omplain	C
	Whine	*D*emand, *D*rone	D
	Whine	*E*ngine	E

Dealing With Duplicate Numbers

At the beginning of this chapter (page 136), the possibility was raised of the number (23) appearing in more than one box. The new postal exams show that this is more than a possibility; it's certain enough so that you must be prepared. Previous tests have had as many as two or three duplicate numbers. The sample, issued by the U.S. Postal Service, reproduced on page 7, displays 15 different street addresses, with the same range of numbers appearing three times, each attached to a street name on a different line. This means that one can no long rely solely on the association between *one number and one particular box.* On page 152, (23) was used to illustrate a good solid connection between the number and its box that would enable you to remember it early on: (*23*) became *tea* or *tee* in Box *B.* Two vivid associations arose immediately; i.e., *Tea-Bag* and *T-Ball.* There was no need to remember that (23) appeared on the Laurel line. Now things are different.

What would you do if 23 appeared three times, as illustrated below? (For clarity, only the "2300" addresses are shown.)

Figure 5.1

A	B	C	D	E
	2300–2999 Laurel	2300–3999 Cliff	2300–3899 Mall	

To resolve this problem, what has been studied thus far on association will be combined with several additional memory hints. Figures 5.2 and 5.3 will illustrate how it's done.

Once again (23)'s image as *tea* or *tee* makes for good associations: In Box C, you get (23) *tea C*up; in Box D, you see (23) *tee-D*ivot. But how do you distinguish between the 23 in Box B, the 23 in Box C and the 23 in Box D, when all you are given on the test is 2300–2999 Laurel, Cliff, or Mall? The answer is, with great difficulty!

Figure 5.2

2300–2999 Laurel, becomes . . . . . . *23*00 + Laurel in Box B
Association converts to . . . . . . Tea + *Laurel* Leaves, *Bush* in *B*ag or *B*otanical garden
Result . . . . *Tea Leaves* in a *B*ag — *Answer B!*
or . . . . *Tea Bush* in a *B*otanical garden — *Answer B!*
If you wished, you could
have used *Sounds* . . . . *23*00 + Laurel in Box B
Sound . . . . *T* + *L* + B
Combining Sounds—Result . . T + L or *Teal* (Blue) + *B* (Blue) — *Answer B*

2300–2999 Cliff, becomes . . . . *23*00 + Cliff in Box C
Converts to . . . . *Tea* + *C*liff in C
Combining Sounds . . . . *Tea* + *K* in C = Teak *C*abinet — *Answer C*
or
If you wished, you could . . . . . *23*00 + Cliff in Box C
have used associations . . . . *Tea* + *Cup* in a *C*abinet — *Answer C*

2300–2999 Mall, becomes . . . . *23*00 + *M*all in Box D
Converts to . . . . Tea + *Mall + D*
Combining Sounds to . . . . *Team* —*D*odgers— — *Answer D*
or . . . . *Teem* (rain) + *D*(drip)— — *Answer D*

No doubt you could have made your own connections as well! Now use these ideas with a numbered address as it appeared in the U.S. Postal Service Sample (see page 7). The number (47), which does *not* immediately yield as good an image or association as did (23), has been selected on purpose.

The three duplicate street addresses by themselves appear in Figures 5.2, 5.3, and 5.4.

Following the procedure described above, first try to associate (47) with an image or a meaning. Probably you can't unless (47) connects with something personal like your age, home address, Social Security number, a memorable date, and so on. If you don't come up with a quick connection, then use the number tree on page 151 to convert (47) to "fen." What is a fen? It's a bog, swamp, marsh, or Chinese coin. Given choices like these, it is usually best to pick the shortest word. It lends itself more easily to sound combinations. Now try the *4700–5599* address using *bog.* (Note, you can switch to "fen" or marsh if it *works better for you,* but you must never forget the association with *47!*)

Figure 5.3

4700–5599 Table, becomes .... *4700* + Table in Box A
bog + T + A
Combining sounds .... Bog-T-A or *BOGATA* ...... *Answer A*
(Capital of Colombia)

"BOG-T-A" becomes *Bogota* (the capital of Colombia) when you pronounce the word and letters together as one word. Whenever you have adjoining consonants like the "g" and "T," the missing vowel sound automatically comes forth. This fact is the basis for many of the associations you may need to make in the test.

Very often, a real word is produced, and that is so much the better. But it really doesn't matter that much if you didn't recognize "Bogota" for what it is. The word has a distinctive *sound* you will hear and retain in your memory.

Figure 5.4

4700–5599 West, becomes........ *4700* + West in Box E
Converts to................ *Bog* + W + E
Combining sounds .... BogWE* .... *Answer E*
or, using an alternate .... Swamp + W + E
associating initials........... S— W— E
(3 points of the compass)

You might very well have used Box E's position and initial at the *E*nd. . . . See a *Bog* at the *West End* (of your ranch).

Figure 5.5

4700–5599 Blake, becomes....... *4700* + Blake in Box D
Using associations .... Bog + Black + Dark .... Answer D

In this case, many memory techniques were used: the *number tree* to convert (47) to Bog, the *sound* and *appearance* of Blake to derive Black, and finally the *initial* D, which rounds out the *image of a dark swamp.*

These illustrations employ almost every associative memory technique useful in dealing with duplicate numbered addresses: substituting words or images for numbers; using the numbers tree to convert numbers to words; using the sounds of words, and their appearance; and reducing names to initials. The end result is a unique, powerful tool to help the test taker. A step-by-step summary of the methods to use on the test follows.

---

* "Bogwe" doesn't mean anything but it has a good sound that leads directly to Box E. If you saw that "Bogwe" could easily become "Bogweed," you'd be using sound and appearance to form a good image. But, you'd also be running the risk of deciding that *D* was the correct box since "Bogweed" ends in a "d." Please remember that Step 3 of the procedure directs you to combine the box letter with the number and the street. *This is usually best accomplished as was seen in the various examples by using the box letter at the beginning or end of the new word or image.*

The Five Step Process

STEP 1. Scan the numbered addresses to see in which boxes and lines the *duplicate* number addresses appear. *Addresses whose numbers are not duplicated* may be remembered in the usual way, i.e., just connect the numbers to the box letters as explained on pages 148 to 155. There is no need to take the street name into account, which obviously makes matters easier.

STEP 2. If you can, establish an association between the duplicated number and some specific image. Use the list of personal associations you developed in drill 13 on pages 149 to 150. They will be particularly helpful at this time.

STEP 3. If Step 2 does not yield a useful word or image, immediately convert the number to a word by using the number tree, e.g., (23) to tea. If *this* new word has no *meaning* for you, be prepared to use its *sound* or the sound of its *initial* letter.

STEP 4. Connect the word, image or sound you obtained for this number with its adjoining street *name* or with the *initial* of the street name, or with the *appearance* of the street name.

Example 1: (23) Tea + Laurel (leaves) → tea leaves
Example 2: (23) Tea + Mall → Team
Example 3: (47) Bog + Blake (Black) → Black bog

Look at the combination or connection. Does it *mean* anything?

Sound out the combination—Does it *mean* anything? Is the sound memorable?

Step 4 is vital. It separates and places the duplicate numbers, each according to its adjoining street name. Only then can one connect the original number to its proper box.

STEP 5. Associate the result of Step 4 with its box letter.

Tea Leaves in a *B*ag	Box B
Team → *D*odgers	Box D
Black Bog → *D*ark	Box D

Remember this five-step process. With practice, you will actually be able to read the answers as they arise in association, from the very numbers, words and boxes in each question.

DEVELOP YOUR IMAGINATION. WITH PRACTICE YOU WILL EASILY BE ABLE TO ATTAIN A PERFECT SCORE!

Now that you've learned the many powerful devices that may be used, it is advisable to practice and refine your memory techniques. Then you will be better able to decide on the approach or combination of approaches that works best for you.

DRILLS 13 Through 27

Drills 13 through 26 are displayed like Drills 3 through 12 and are to be used in much the same way. There are three important differences between the two sets.

1. Drills 13 through 26 display all five boxes, including Box E.
2. These drills contain an ever increasing number of duplicates.

3. They are designed to be answered using any or all memory tools explained in Chapters 4 and 5, not just chunking.

Directions for Drills 13 Through 27

- Study the addresses using the method(s) of your choice to remember them. Use the time indicated above each drill as a guide.
- When the study time is up, turn to the Answer Sheet. Enter the box letter for as many of the addresses as you can. Work for a reasonable amount of time but don't worry about speed as yet. Note the elapsed time to keep track of your progress. The answer sheets allow for three trials but allow a couple of weeks to pass before repeating them.

Drills 13 Through 15—1 minute each

Drill No.	Street Name	A	B	C	D	E	Street Name
13	West	25	18	21	14	12	West
14	Mark	49	51	57	42	64	Mark
15	Larue	12	19	27	17	31	Larue

Drills 16 Through 18—3 minutes each

Drill No.	Street Name	A	B	C	D	E	Street Name
16	Ohio	38	32	16	26	41	Ohio
	Peach	41	39	—	—	—	Peach
17	Merry	57	55	61	69	51	Merry
	Pinto	12	20	—	—	—	Pinto
18	Laurel	97	91	83	85	71	Laurel
	Billings	71	68	—	—	—	Billings

Drills 19 Through 21—5 minutes each

Drill No.	Street Name	A	B	C	D	E	Street Name
19	East	30	26	43	21	34	East
	Quince	17	34	22	27	13	Quince
20	Clarol	21	28	37	45	19	Clarol
	Apple	19	11	21	25	30	Apple
21	Ridell	36	42	33	50	52	Ridell
	Maple	50	64	45	36	39	Maple

Drills 22 and 23—8 minutes each

Drill No.	Street Name	A	B	C	D	E	Street Name
22	Niger	37	42	48	31	53	Niger
	Violet	15	18	29	37	24	Violet
	Delray	55	42	67	—	—	Delray
23	Oxford	80	77	90	93	85	Oxford
	Klein	63	85	60	74	53	Klein
	Star	85	47	70	—	—	Star

Drills 24 Through 27—9 minutes each

Drill No.	Street Name	A	B	C	D	E	Street Name
24	Palov	16	37	11	47	58	Palov
	Unit	53	74	68	58	64	Unit
	Vermont	58	83	62	74	—	Vermont
25	Fleet	39	16	23	44	10	Fleet
	Chase	40	23	39	46	19	Chase
	Ash	62	72	34	39	54	Ash
26	Race	58	73	49	54	33	Race
	Poplar	73	41	33	60	53	Poplar
	Eric	33	43	67	46	73	Eric
27	Centra	58	69	32	50	41	Centra
	Tremont	57	70	77	42	32	Tremont
	Mill	51	57	42	74	63	Mill

Drill 13

	Answers Trials 3	2	1
1. 12 West			
2. 25 West			
3. 14 West			
4. 25 West			
5. 18 West			
6. 21 West			
7. 18 West			
8. 12 West			
9. 25 West			
10. 21 West			
11. 18 West			
12. 12 West			
13. 14 West			
14. 25 West			
15. 18 West			
16. 12 West			

	Answers Trials 3	2	1
17. 14 West			
18. 21 West			
19. 18 West			
20. 25 West			
21. 18 West			
22. 14 West			
23. 12 West			
24. 21 West			
25. 25 West			
26. 18 West			
27. 14 West			
28. 21 West			
29. 18 West			
30. 25 West			
31. 12 West			
32. 14 West			

	Answers Trials 3	2	1
33. 21 West			
34. 21 West			
35. 18 West			
36. 12 West			
37. 25 West			
38. 18 West			
39. 12 West			
40. 21 West			
41. 14 West			
42. 18 West			
43. 21 West			
44. 25 West			
Number Right			
Time			

Drill 14

	Answers Trials 3	2	1
1. 49 Mark			
2. 51 Mark			
3. 57 Mark			
4. 42 Mark			
5. 64 Mark			
6. 51 Mark			
7. 49 Mark			
8. 42 Mark			
9. 64 Mark			
10. 57 Mark			
11. 42 Mark			
12. 49 Mark			
13. 51 Mark			
14. 57 Mark			
15. 64 Mark			
16. 51 Mark			

	Answers Trials 3	2	1
17. 57 Mark			
18. 64 Mark			
19. 49 Mark			
20. 64 Mark			
21. 51 Mark			
22. 57 Mark			
23. 49 Mark			
24. 51 Mark			
25. 57 Mark			
26. 42 Mark			
27. 51 Mark			
28. 49 Mark			
29. 64 Mark			
30. 42 Mark			
31. 64 Mark			
32. 51 Mark			

	Answers Trials 3	2	1
33. 57 Mark			
34. 49 Mark			
35. 64 Mark			
36. 42 Mark			
37. 57 Mark			
38. 49 Mark			
39. 57 Mark			
40. 51 Mark			
41. 42 Mark			
42. 49 Mark			
43. 51 Mark			
44. 57 Mark			
Number Right			
Time			

Drill 15

Answers — Trials	3	2	1
1. 27 Larue			
2. 17 Larue			
3. 12 Larue			
4. 19 Larue			
5. 31 Larue			
6. 12 Larue			
7. 19 Larue			
8. 31 Larue			
9. 17 Larue			
10. 27 Larue			
11. 31 Larue			
12. 19 Larue			
13. 27 Larue			
14. 17 Larue			
15. 12 Larue			
16. 27 Larue			

Answers — Trials	3	2	1
17. 17 Larue			
18. 31 Larue			
19. 27 Larue			
20. 17 Larue			
21. 12 Larue			
22. 31 Larue			
23. 19 Larue			
24. 12 Larue			
25. 27 Larue			
26. 17 Larue			
27. 31 Larue			
28. 12 Larue			
29. 19 Larue			
30. 31 Larue			
31. 17 Larue			
32. 27 Larue			

Answers — Trials	3	2	1
33. 19 Larue			
34. 12 Larue			
35. 19 Larue			
36. 27 Larue			
37. 31 Larue			
38. 12 Larue			
39. 12 Larue			
40. 17 Larue			
41. 27 Larue			
42. 17 Larue			
43. 12 Larue			
44. 19 Larue			
Number Right			
Time			

Drill 16

Answers — Trials	3	2	1
1. 16 Ohio			
2. 26 Ohio			
3. 41 Peach			
4. 39 Peach			
5. 38 Ohio			
6. 32 Ohio			
7. 39 Peach			
8. 16 Ohio			
9. 41 Peach			
10. 26 Ohio			
11. 32 Ohio			
12. 38 Ohio			
13. 41 Ohio			
14. 32 Ohio			
15. 38 Ohio			
16. 32 Ohio			

Answers — Trials	3	2	1
17. 41 Ohio			
18. 39 Peach			
19. 16 Ohio			
20. 26 Ohio			
21. 38 Ohio			
22. 39 Peach			
23. 41 Ohio			
24. 41 Peach			
25. 16 Ohio			
26. 26 Ohio			
27. 38 Ohio			
28. 32 Ohio			
29. 41 Peach			
30. 39 Peach			
31. 26 Ohio			
32. 41 Peach			

Answers — Trials	3	2	1
33. 32 Ohio			
34. 38 Ohio			
35. 41 Peach			
36. 16 Ohio			
37. 26 Ohio			
38. 32 Ohio			
39. 39 Peach			
40. 38 Ohio			
41. 41 Ohio			
42. 38 Ohio			
43. 32 Ohio			
44. 41 Ohio			
Number Right			
Time			

Drill 17

Answers Trials	3	2	1
1. 57 Merry			
2. 55 Merry			
3. 61 Merry			
4. 19 Merry			
5. 12 Pinto			
6. 20 Pinto			
7. 51 Merry			
8. 55 Merry			
9. 20 Pinto			
10. 12 Pinto			
11. 19 Merry			
12. 61 Merry			
13. 51 Merry			
14. 20 Pinto			
15. 12 Pinto			
16. 51 Merry			

Answers Trials	3	2	1
17. 19 Merry			
18. 61 Merry			
19. 55 Merry			
20. 57 Merry			
21. 55 Merry			
22. 12 Pinto			
23. 20 Pinto			
24. 61 Merry			
25. 69 Merry			
26. 51 Merry			
27. 51 Merry			
28. 12 Pinto			
29. 20 Pinto			
30. 55 Merry			
31. 61 Merry			
32. 19 Merry			

Answers Trials	3	2	1
33. 51 Merry			
34. 20 Pinto			
35. 57 Merry			
36. 12 Pinto			
37. 61 Merry			
38. 69 Merry			
39. 57 Merry			
40. 57 Merry			
41. 55 Merry			
42. 61 Merry			
43. 19 Merry			
44. 51 Merry			
Number Right			
Time			

Drill 18

Answers Trials	3	2	1
1. 71 Billings			
2. 68 Billings			
3. 97 Laurel			
4. 91 Laurel			
5. 83 Laurel			
6. 85 Laurel			
7. 71 Laurel			
8. 71 Billings			
9. 68 Billings			
10. 85 Laurel			
11. 83 Laurel			
12. 91 Laurel			
13. 97 Laurel			
14. 71 Laurel			
15. 68 Billings			
16. 97 Laurel			

Answers Trials	3	2	1
17. 91 Laurel			
18. 71 Laurel			
19. 83 Laurel			
20. 85 Laurel			
21. 71 Laurel			
22. 91 Laurel			
23. 83 Laurel			
24. 85 Laurel			
25. 71 Billings			
26. 97 Laurel			
27. 91 Laurel			
28. 71 Laurel			
29. 68 Billings			
30. 85 Laurel			
31. 71 Billings			
32. 68 Billings			

Answers Trials	3	2	1
33. 83 Laurel			
34. 97 Laurel			
35. 91 Laurel			
36. 83 Laurel			
37. 85 Laurel			
38. 71 Billings			
39. 71 Laurel			
40. 68 Billings			
41. 97 Laurel			
42. 91 Laurel			
43. 71 Laurel			
44. 71 Billings			
Number Right			
Time			

Drill 19

Answers Trials	3	2	1
1. 17 Quince			
2. 34 Quince			
3. 43 East			
4. 21 East			
5. 22 Quince			
6. 27 Quince			
7. 34 East			
8. 13 Quince			
9. 30 East			
10. 26 East			
11. 17 Quince			
12. 34 Quince			
13. 43 East			
14. 21 East			
15. 34 East			
16. 26 East			

Answers Trials	3	2	1
17. 30 East			
18. 13 Quince			
19. 27 Quince			
20. 22 Quince			
21. 17 Quince			
22. 34 East			
23. 43 East			
24. 21 East			
25. 30 East			
26. 26 East			
27. 22 Quince			
28. 27 Quince			
29. 13 Quince			
30. 34 East			
31. 21 East			
32. 30 East			

Answers Trials	3	2	1
33. 17 Quince			
34. 22 Quince			
35. 13 Quince			
36. 34 East			
37. 43 East			
38. 34 Quince			
39. 21 East			
40. 34 Quince			
41. 26 East			
42. 22 Quince			
43. 43 East			
44. 34 East			
Number Right			
Time			

Drill 20

Answers Trials	3	2	1
1. 21 Clarol			
2. 28 Clarol			
3. 37 Clarol			
4. 45 Clarol			
5. 19 Clarol			
6. 11 Apple			
7. 21 Apple			
8. 25 Apple			
9. 19 Apple			
10. 30 Apple			
11. 21 Clarol			
12. 25 Apple			
13. 21 Clarol			
14. 28 Clarol			
15. 37 Clarol			
16. 21 Apple			

Answers Trials	3	2	1
17. 19 Apple			
18. 11 Apple			
19. 30 Apple			
20. 19 Clarol			
21. 45 Clarol			
22. 37 Clarol			
23. 21 Clarol			
24. 28 Clarol			
25. 21 Apple			
26. 25 Apple			
27. 30 Apple			
28. 11 Apple			
29. 19 Apple			
30. 11 Apple			
31. 21 Clarol			
32. 28 Clarol			

Answers Trials	3	2	1
33. 19 Clarol			
34. 30 Apple			
35. 37 Clarol			
36. 45 Clarol			
37. 21 Apple			
38. 25 Apple			
39. 28 Clarol			
40. 21 Clarol			
41. 11 Apple			
42. 19 Apple			
43. 30 Apple			
44. 19 Clarol			
Number Right			
Time			

Drill 21

Answers	Trials 3	2	1
1. 36 Ridell			
2. 42 Ridell			
3. 50 Maple			
4. 64 Maple			
5. 33 Ridell			
6. 50 Ridell			
7. 36 Maple			
8. 39 Maple			
9. 45 Maple			
10. 36 Maple			
11. 36 Ridell			
12. 42 Ridell			
13. 52 Ridell			
14. 39 Ridell			
15. 45 Maple			
16. 36 Maple			

Answers	Trials 3	2	1
17. 64 Maple			
18. 42 Ridell			
19. 33 Ridell			
20. 36 Ridell			
21. 39 Maple			
22. 33 Ridell			
23. 50 Ridell			
24. 52 Ridell			
25. 39 Maple			
26. 64 Maple			
27. 50 Maple			
28. 36 Ridell			
29. 39 Maple			
30. 36 Ridell			
31. 42 Ridell			
32. 52 Ridell			

Answers	Trials 3	2	1
33. 39 Ridell			
34. 50 Maple			
35. 64 Maple			
36. 33 Ridell			
37. 50 Ridell			
38. 45 Maple			
39. 50 Maple			
40. 36 Ridell			
41. 36 Maple			
42. 33 Ridell			
43. 50 Ridell			
44. 50 Maple			
Number Right			
Time			

Drill 22

Answers	Trials 3	2	1
1. 15 Violet			
2. 18 Violet			
3. 29 Violet			
4. 37 Violet			
5. 55 Delray			
6. 42 Delray			
7. 48 Niger			
8. 31 Niger			
9. 37 Niger			
10. 42 Niger			
11. 24 Violet			
12. 53 Niger			
13. 29 Violet			
14. 37 Violet			
15. 24 Violet			
16. 53 Niger			

Answers	Trials 3	2	1
17. 42 Niger			
18. 37 Niger			
19. 18 Violet			
20. 15 Violet			
21. 55 Delray			
22. 42 Delray			
23. 48 Niger			
24. 31 Niger			
25. 53 Niger			
26. 24 Violet			
27. 37 Violet			
28. 42 Niger			
29. 24 Violet			
30. 48 Niger			
31. 31 Niger			
32. 53 Niger			

Answers	Trials 3	2	1
33. 24 Violet			
34. 55 Delray			
35. 42 Delray			
36. 42 Niger			
37. 37 Niger			
38. 29 Violet			
39. 37 Violet			
40. 53 Niger			
41. 67 Delray			
42. 24 Violet			
43. 48 Niger			
44. 31 Niger			
Number Right			
Time			

Drill 23

Answers	Trials 3	2	1
1. 80 Oxford			
2. 77 Oxford			
3. 63 Klein			
4. 85 Klein			
5. 85 Star			
6. 47 Star			
7. 90 Oxford			
8. 93 Oxford			
9. 85 Oxford			
10. 53 Klein			
11. 60 Klein			
12. 74 Klein			
13. 70 Star			
14. 85 Star			
15. 47 Star			
16. 85 Oxford			

Answers	Trials 3	2	1
17. 53 Klein			
18. 63 Klein			
19. 85 Klein			
20. 80 Oxford			
21. 77 Oxford			
22. 60 Klein			
23. 74 Klein			
24. 90 Oxford			
25. 93 Oxford			
26. 70 Star			
27. 93 Oxford			
28. 90 Oxford			
29. 85 Klein			
30. 63 Klein			
31. 80 Oxford			
32. 77 Oxford			

Answers	Trials 3	2	1
33. 85 Star			
34. 47 Star			
35. 63 Klein			
36. 85 Klein			
37. 60 Klein			
38. 74 Klein			
39. 85 Oxford			
40. 53 Oxford			
41. 63 Klein			
42. 85 Klein			
43. 85 Star			
44. 47 Star			
Number Right			
Time			

Drill 24

Answers	Trials 3	2	1
1. 16 Palov			
2. 37 Palov			
3. 68 Unit			
4. 64 Unit			
5. 47 Palov			
6. 11 Palov			
7. 58 Unit			
8. 53 Unit			
9. 83 Vermont			
10. 58 Vermont			
11. 74 Unit			
12. 58 Palov			
13. 62 Vermont			
14. 47 Palov			
15. 11 Palov			
16. 16 Palov			

Answers	Trials 3	2	1
17. 37 Palov			
18. 58 Unit			
19. 53 Unit			
20. 68 Unit			
21. 66 Unit			
22. 74 Unit			
23. 58 Palov			
24. 83 Vermont			
25. 58 Vermont			
26. 62 Vermont			
27. 16 Palov			
28. 37 Palov			
29. 58 Unit			
30. 53 Unit			
31. 11 Palov			
32. 47 Palov			

Answers	Trials 3	2	1
33. 16 Palov			
34. 37 Palov			
35. 68 Unit			
36. 64 Unit			
37. 74 Unit			
38. 58 Palov			
39. 62 Vermont			
40. 68 Unit			
41. 64 Unit			
42. 62 Vermont			
43. 58 Vermont			
44. 74 Vermont			
Number Right			
Time			

Drill 25

	Answers Trials 3	2	1
1. 62 Ash			
2. 72 Ash			
3. 39 Chase			
4. 46 Chase			
5. 39 Fleet			
6. 16 Fleet			
7. 40 Chase			
8. 23 Chase			
9. 10 Fleet			
10. 19 Chase			
11. 54 Ash			
12. 34 Ash			
13. 72 Ash			
14. 62 Ash			
15. 40 Chase			
16. 23 Chase			

	Answers Trials 3	2	1
17. 23 Fleet			
18. 44 Fleet			
19. 10 Fleet			
20. 23 Fleet			
21. 44 Fleet			
22. 54 Ash			
23. 19 Chase			
24. 10 Fleet			
25. 62 Ash			
26. 72 Ash			
27. 39 Chase			
28. 46 Chase			
29. 16 Fleet			
30. 39 Chase			
31. 34 Ash			
32. 39 Ash			

	Answers Trials 3	2	1
33. 54 Ash			
34. 40 Chase			
35. 23 Chase			
36. 39 Chase			
37. 46 Chase			
38. 23 Fleet			
39. 44 Fleet			
40. 39 Fleet			
41. 16 Fleet			
42. 16 Fleet			
43. 19 Chase			
44. 54 Ash			
Number Right			
Time			

Drill 26

	Answers Trials 3	2	1
1. 58 Race			
2. 73 Race			
3. 33 Race			
4. 60 Race			
5. 33 Race			
6. 53 Poplar			
7. 73 Eric			
8. 33 Eric			
9. 43 Eric			
10. 73 Poplar			
11. 41 Poplar			
12. 67 Eric			
13. 46 Eric			
14. 53 Poplar			
15. 73 Eric			
16. 49 Race			

	Answers Trials 3	2	1
17. 54 Race			
18. 33 Poplar			
19. 60 Poplar			
20. 33 Eric			
21. 43 Eric			
22. 58 Race			
23. 73 Race			
24. 33 Race			
25. 53 Poplar			
26. 73 Eric			
27. 73 Poplar			
28. 41 Poplar			
29. 33 Poplar			
30. 60 Poplar			
31. 53 Poplar			
32. 67 Eric			

	Answers Trials 3	2	1
33. 46 Eric			
34. 43 Eric			
35. 73 Eric			
36. 33 Race			
37. 53 Poplar			
38. 73 Eric			
39. 49 Race			
40. 54 Race			
41. 67 Eric			
42. 46 Eric			
43. 73 Poplar			
44. 41 Poplar			
Number Right			
Time			

Drill 27

Trials	Answers 3	2	1
1. 58 Centra			
2. 69 Centra			
3. 41 Centra			
4. 32 Tremont			
5. 63 Mill			
6. 51 Mill			
7. 57 Mill			
8. 77 Tremont			
9. 42 Tremont			
10. 42 Mill			
11. 74 Mill			
12. 32 Centra			
13. 50 Centra			
14. 41 Centra			
15. 32 Tremont			
16. 63 Mill			

Trials	Answers 3	2	1
17. 51 Mill			
18. 57 Mill			
19. 77 Tremont			
20. 42 Tremont			
21. 57 Tremont			
22. 70 Tremont			
23. 32 Centra			
24. 50 Centra			
25. 58 Centra			
26. 69 Centra			
27. 42 Mill			
28. 74 Mill			
29. 63 Mill			
30. 41 Centra			
31. 32 Tremont			
32. 63 Mill			

Trials	Answers 3	2	1
33. 77 Tremont			
34. 42 Tremont			
35. 57 Mill			
36. 70 Tremont			
37. 32 Centra			
38. 50 Centra			
39. 58 Centra			
40. 69 Centra			
41. 42 Mill			
42. 74 Mill			
43. 41 Centra			
44. 32 Tremont			
Number Right			
Time			

ANSWER KEY FOR DRILLS

Drill 1, page 137

1. **D** 2. **A** 3. **C** 4. **B** 5. **E**

Drill 2, not applicable

Drill 3, page 142

1. **A** 6. **B** 11. **A** 16. **B** 21. **C** 25. **C** 29. **D** 33. **C** 37. **D** 41. **D**

2. **B** 7. **D** 12. **C** 17. **A** 22. **D** 26. **A** 30. **B** 34. **B** 38. **C** 42. **C**

3. **C** 8. **C** 13. **D** 18. **B** 23. **B** 27. **C** 31. **A** 35. **A** 39. **B** 43. **D**

4. **D** 9. **C** 14. **A** 19. **C** 24. **A** 28. **B** 32. **D** 36. **B** 40. **A** 44. **A**

5. **A** 10. **B** 15. **C** 20. **D**

Drill 4, page 142

1. **A** 6. **B** 11. **C** 16. **B** 21. **D** 25. **D** 29. **D** 33. **A** 37. **C** 41. **B**

2. **B** 7. **A** 12. **D** 17. **C** 22. **B** 26. **C** 30. **C** 34. **A** 38. **B** 42. **D**

3. **C** 8. **D** 13. **C** 18. **D** 23. **A** 27. **A** 31. **B** 35. **B** 39. **A** 43. **B**

4. **D** 9. **C** 14. **B** 19. **C** 24. **B** 28. **A** 32. **D** 36. **D** 40. **C** 44. **C**

5. **C** 10. **A** 15. **A** 20. **B**

Drill 5, page 143

1. **A** 6. **B** 11. **C** 16. **A** 21. **D** 25. **B** 29. **B** 33. **D** 37. **A** 41. **A**

2. **B** 7. **C** 12. **D** 17. **B** 22. **A** 26. **A** 30. **A** 34. **A** 38. **B** 42. **B**

3. **A** 8. **A** 13. **B** 18. **A** 23. **C** 27. **D** 31. **A** 35. **A** 39. **B** 43. **A**

4. **B** 9. **B** 14. **A** 19. **C** 24. **D** 28. **B** 32. **C** 36. **B** 40. **B** 44. **B**

5. **D** 10. **B** 15. **B** 20. **B**

Drill 6, page 143

1. **C** 6. **B** 11. **B** 16. **A** 21. **D** 25. **C** 29. **C** 33. **A** 37. **B** 41. **B**

2. **D** 7. **C** 12. **A** 17. **B** 22. **B** 26. **A** 30. **D** 34. **B** 38. **A** 42. **A**

3. **A** 8. **D** 13. **A** 18. **B** 23. **A** 27. **D** 31. **A** 35. **B** 39. **A** 43. **B**

4. **B** 9. **B** 14. **B** 19. **C** 24. **B** 28. **B** 32. **A** 36. **C** 40. **D** 44. **C**

5. **A** 10. **A** 15. **C** 20. **A**

Drill 7, page 144

1. **A** 6. **C** 11. **C** 16. **B** 21. **D** 25. **B** 29. **B** 33. **D** 37. **B** 41. **C**

2. **B** 7. **D** 12. **C** 17. **C** 22. **A** 26. **C** 30. **D** 34. **C** 38. **B** 42. **D**

3. **A** 8. **D** 13. **D** 18. **C** 23. **B** 27. **B** 31. **C** 35. **D** 39. **C** 43. **A**

4. **B** 9. **B** 14. **A** 19. **D** 24. **C** 28. **A** 32. **C** 36. **A** 40. **B** 44. **B**

5. **C** 10. **D** 15. **A** 20. **B**

Drill 8, page 144

1. **C** 6. **D** 11. **D** 16. **A** 21. **B** 25. **A** 29. **A** 33. **D** 37. **B** 41. **D**

2. **D** 7. **A** 12. **B** 17. **B** 22. **C** 26. **C** 30. **D** 34. **A** 38. **C** 42. **A**

3. **A** 8. **B** 13. **D** 18. **B** 23. **D** 27. **D** 31. **C** 35. **B** 39. **B** 43. **B**

4. **B** 9. **B** 14. **C** 19. **D** 24. **B** 28. **D** 32. **A** 36. **A** 40. **C** 44. **B**

5. **C** 10. **C** 15. **D** 20. **A**

Drill 9, page 145

1. **C** 6. **B** 11. **C** 16. **D** 21. **C** 25. **A** 29. **C** 33. **B** 37. **A** 41. **D**
2. **D** 7. **C** 12. **A** 17. **C** 22. **D** 26. **C** 30. **D** 34. **A** 38. **B** 42. **D**
3. **A** 8. **A** 13. **B** 18. **D** 23. **B** 27. **D** 31. **B** 35. **D** 39. **C** 43. **A**
4. **B** 9. **A** 14. **B** 19. **A** 24. **D** 28. **A** 32. **A** 36. **D** 40. **C** 44. **D**
5. **A** 10. **B** 15. **C** 20. **B**

Drill 10, page 145

1. **C** 6. **B** 11. **C** 16. **B** 21. **A** 25. **B** 29. **D** 33. **D** 37. **D** 41. **D**
2. **E** 7. **A** 12. **D** 17. **B** 22. **A** 26. **D** 30. **A** 34. **B** 38. **A** 42. **B**
3. **A** 8. **B** 13. **B** 18. **C** 23. **C** 27. **B** 31. **B** 35. **B** 39. **B** 43. **A**
4. **B** 9. **A** 14. **B** 19. **D** 24. **D** 28. **C** 32. **C** 36. **B** 40. **C** 44. **A**
5. **A** 10. **B** 15. **C** 20. **A**

Drill 11, page 146

1. **A** 6. **B** 11. **D** 16. **D** 21. **D** 25. **C** 29. **A** 33. **B** 37. **D** 41. **A**
2. **B** 7. **A** 12. **A** 17. **E** 22. **B** 26. **B** 30. **B** 34. **B** 38. **C** 42. **B**
3. **C** 8. **B** 13. **A** 18. **C** 23. **A** 27. **C** 31. **D** 35. **A** 39. **A** 43. **A**
4. **D** 9. **C** 14. **A** 19. **A** 24. **B** 28. **B** 32. **A** 36. **B** 40. **E** 44. **B**
5. **A** 10. **B** 15. **C** 20. **C**

Drill 12, page 146

1. **C** 6. **B** 11. **B** 16. **D** 21. **A** 25. **C** 29. **B** 33. **D** 37. **C** 41. **D**
2. **A** 7. **C** 12. **A** 17. **C** 22. **B** 26. **D** 30. **A** 34. **C** 38. **D** 42. **B**
3. **B** 8. **D** 13. **B** 18. **B** 23. **D** 27. **A** 31. **A** 35. **A** 39. **A** 43. **A**
4. **B** 9. **C** 14. **B** 19. **A** 24. **C** 28. **B** 32. **B** 36. **B** 40. **C** 44. **B**
5. **A** 10. **D** 15. **C** 20. **B**

Drill 13, page 161

1. **E** 6. **C** 11. **B** 16. **E** 21. **B** 25. **A** 29. **B** 33. **C** 37. **A** 41. **D**
2. **A** 7. **D** 12. **E** 17. **D** 22. **D** 26. **B** 30. **A** 34. **C** 38. **B** 42. **B**
3. **D** 8. **E** 13. **D** 18. **C** 23. **E** 27. **D** 31. **E** 35. **B** 39. **E** 43. **C**
4. **A** 9. **A** 14. **A** 19. **B** 24. **C** 28. **C** 32. **D** 36. **E** 40. **C** 44. **A**
5. **B** 10. **C** 15. **B** 20. **A**

Drill 14, page 161

1. **A** 6. **B** 11. **D** 16. **B** 21. **B** 25. **C** 29. **E** 33. **C** 37. **C** 41. **D**
2. **B** 7. **A** 12. **A** 17. **C** 22. **C** 26. **D** 30. **D** 34. **A** 38. **A** 42. **A**
3. **C** 8. **D** 13. **B** 18. **E** 23. **A** 27. **B** 31. **E** 35. **E** 39. **C** 43. **B**
4. **D** 9. **E** 14. **C** 19. **A** 24. **B** 28. **A** 32. **B** 36. **D** 40. **B** 44. **C**
5. **E** 10. **C** 15. **E** 20. **E**

Drill 15, page 162

1. **C** 6. **A** 11. **E** 16. **C** 21. **A** 25. **C** 29. **B** 33. **B** 37. **E** 41. **C**
2. **D** 7. **B** 12. **B** 17. **D** 22. **E** 26. **D** 30. **E** 34. **A** 38. **A** 42. **D**
3. **A** 8. **E** 13. **C** 18. **E** 23. **B** 27. **E** 31. **D** 35. **B** 39. **A** 43. **A**
4. **B** 9. **D** 14. **D** 19. **C** 24. **A** 28. **A** 32. **C** 36. **C** 40. **D** 44. **B**
5. **E** 10. **C** 15. **A** 20. **D**

Drill 16, page 162

1. C 6. B 11. B 16. B 21. A 25. C 29. A 33. B 37. D 41. E
2. D 7. B 12. A 17. E 22. B 26. D 30. B 34. A 38. B 42. A
3. A 8. C 13. E 18. B 23. E 27. A 31. D 35. A 39. B 43. B
4. B 9. A 14. B 19. C 24. A 28. B 32. A 36. C 40. A 44. E
5. A 10. D 15. A 20. D

Drill 17, page 163

1. A 6. B 11. D 16. E 21. B 25. D 29. B 33. E 37. C 41. B
2. B 7. E 12. C 17. D 22. A 26. E 30. B 34. B 38. D 42. C
3. C 8. B 13. E 18. C 23. B 27. E 31. C 35. A 39. E 43. D
4. D 9. B 14. B 19. B 24. C 28. A 32. D 36. A 40. A 44. E
5. A 10. A 15. A 20. A

Drill 18, page 163

1. A 6. D 11. C 16. A 21. E 25. A 29. B 33. C 37. D 41. A
2. A 7. E 12. B 17. B 22. B 26. A 30. D 34. A 38. A 42. B
3. A 8. A 13. A 18. E 23. C 27. A 31. A 35. B 39. E 43. E
4. B 9. B 14. E 19. C 24. D 28. E 32. B 36. C 40. B 44. A
5. C 10. D 15. B 20. D

Drill 19, page 164

1. A 6. D 11. A 16. B 21. A 25. A 29. E 33. A 37. C 41. B
2. B 7. E 12. B 17. A 22. E 26. B 30. B 34. C 38. B 42. C
3. C 8. E 13. C 18. E 23. C 27. C 31. D 35. E 39. D 43. C
4. D 9. A 14. D 19. D 24. D 28. D 32. A 36. B 40. B 44. B
5. C 10. B 15. E 20. C

Drill 20, page 164

1. A 6. B 11. A 16. C 21. D 25. C 29. A 33. A 37. C 41. B
2. B 7. C 12. D 17. A 22. C 26. D 30. B 34. E 38. D 42. A
3. C 8. D 13. A 18. B 23. A 27. E 31. A 35. C 39. B 43. E
4. D 9. A 14. B 19. E 24. B 28. B 32. B 36. D 40. A 44. E
5. E 10. E 15. C 20. E

Drill 21, page 165

1. A 6. D 11. D 16. D 21. E 25. E 29. E 33. E 37. D 41. D
2. B 7. D 12. B 17. B 22. C 26. B 30. A 34. A 38. C 42. C
3. A 8. E 13. E 18. B 23. D 27. A 31. B 35. B 39. A 43. D
4. B 9. C 14. E 19. C 24. E 28. A 32. E 36. C 40. A 44. A
5. C 10. A 15. C 20. D

Drill 22, page 165

1. A 6. B 11. E 16. E 21. A 25. E 29. E 33. E 37. A 41. C
2. B 7. C 12. E 17. B 22. B 26. E 30. C 34. A 38. C 42. E
3. C 8. D 13. C 18. A 23. C 27. D 31. D 35. B 39. D 43. C
4. D 9. A 14. D 19. B 24. D 28. B 32. E 36. B 40. E 44. D
5. A 10. B 15. E 20. A

Drill 23, page 166

1. **A** 6. **B** 11. **C** 16. **E** 21. **B** 25. **D** 29. **B** 33. **B** 37. **C** 41. **A**
2. **B** 7. **C** 12. **D** 17. **E** 22. **C** 26. **C** 30. **A** 34. **B** 38. **D** 42. **B**
3. **A** 8. **D** 13. **C** 18. **A** 23. **D** 27. **D** 31. **A** 35. **A** 39. **E** 43. **A**
4. **B** 9. **E** 14. **A** 19. **B** 24. **C** 28. **C** 32. **B** 36. **B** 40. **E** 44. **B**
5. **A** 10. **E** 15. **B** 20. **A**

Drill 24, page 166

1. **A** 6. **C** 11. **B** 16. **A** 21. **E** 25. **A** 29. **D** 33. **A** 37. **B** 41. **E**
2. **B** 7. **D** 12. **E** 17. **B** 22. **B** 26. **C** 30. **A** 34. **B** 38. **E** 42. **C**
3. **C** 8. **A** 13. **C** 18. **D** 23. **E** 27. **A** 31. **C** 35. **C** 39. **C** 43. **A**
4. **E** 9. **B** 14. **D** 19. **A** 24. **B** 28. **B** 32. **D** 36. **E** 40. **C** 44. **D**
5. **D** 10. **A** 15. **C** 20. **C**

Drill 25, page 167

1. **A** 6. **B** 11. **E** 16. **B** 21. **D** 25. **A** 29. **B** 33. **E** 37. **D** 41. **B**
2. **B** 7. **A** 12. **C** 17. **C** 22. **E** 26. **B** 30. **C** 34. **A** 38. **C** 42. **B**
3. **C** 8. **B** 13. **B** 18. **D** 23. **E** 27. **C** 31. **C** 35. **B** 39. **D** 43. **E**
4. **D** 9. **E** 14. **A** 19. **E** 24. **E** 28. **D** 32. **D** 36. **C** 40. **A** 44. **E**
5. **A** 10. **E** 15. **A** 20. **C**

Drill 26, page 167

1. **A** 6. **E** 11. **B** 16. **C** 21. **B** 25. **E** 29. **C** 33. **D** 37. **E** 41. **C**
2. **B** 7. **E** 12. **C** 17. **D** 22. **A** 26. **E** 30. **D** 34. **B** 38. **E** 42. **D**
3. **E** 8. **A** 13. **D** 18. **C** 23. **B** 27. **A** 31. **E** 35. **A** 39. **C** 43. **A**
4. **D** 9. **B** 14. **E** 19. **D** 24. **E** 28. **B** 32. **C** 36. **E** 40. **D** 44. **B**
5. **E** 10. **A** 15. **E** 20. **A**

Drill 27, page 168

1. **A** 6. **A** 11. **D** 16. **E** 21. **A** 25. **A** 29. **E** 33. **C** 37. **C** 41. **C**
2. **B** 7. **B** 12. **C** 17. **A** 22. **B** 26. **B** 30. **E** 34. **D** 38. **D** 42. **D**
3. **E** 8. **C** 13. **D** 18. **B** 23. **C** 27. **C** 31. **E** 35. **B** 39. **A** 43. **E**
4. **E** 9. **D** 14. **E** 19. **C** 24. **D** 28. **D** 32. **E** 36. **B** 40. **B** 44. **E**
5. **E** 10. **C** 15. **E** 20. **D**

Chapter 6

Number Series—How To Improve Your Score

TEST STRATEGY

Go in Turn

Start at question 1 and answer each question in turn. Don't be tempted to look for the easy ones to do first. You'll probably be able to do most of them without any problem. If you do get stuck and you are uncertain about the answer to a question *after a reasonable try* (see below), leave the answer space blank and move on to the next question. Be sure that you answer the new question in its correct number space.

Use Time Wisely

Without rushing, you should be able to complete all 24 questions in the 20 minutes allotted. But you can't afford to spend too long on any one question. After you've completed a few timed practice tests, you'll know how to pace yourself. Bring a watch, just for insurance.

Guess

You won't have much need for guessing if you've mastered the techniques for doing number series questions. Every once in a while, however, you may get stumped by some unusual or complex series. These are the ones alluded to above, and these are the ones you will want to return to after you've gone through all the other questions. If you have timed yourself properly, you will have a few minutes to give these a last try. If you still can't figure out the answer, then by all means, guess! Put in some answer. You are not penalized for guessing—so do it. You have nothing to lose and an extra point to gain.

NATURE OF THIS PART OF THE EXAM

It is safe to say that most people taking the postal service test for the first time have never seen number series questions before. It is also true, unfortunately, that most people are afraid of math tests. The combination of inexperience and fear is a potent one that severely penalizes those who take this test unprepared. By the same token, you, who should be fully prepared after reading this book, have a golden opportunity to outstrip your competition.

First, to allay any fears you may have about the mathematical skill you need, *only the simplest arithmetic applications of addition, subtraction, multiplication and division are involved.* You are *not* taking a *math* test. This test is designed to measure your ability to *see patterns* (more about that later).

Another comforting thing to know about number series questions is that they are very fair to the test taker. The rules for answering them are exact and easily understood. There is only one right answer and that answer can immediately be checked out. If you find you have made an error, you will have time to change your answer.

That brings you to another plus concerning the number series part (Part C) of the test. You will not have to work at the great speed required for the address checking, questions (Part A) or memory questions (Part B). All these factors put together mean that you have a real chance for a perfect score if you absorb the techniques that follow.

The basis for all the techniques you will learn is a full understanding of the directions you are supposed to follow. So, therefore, re-read these official directions—very carefully.

"For each Number Series question there is at the left a series of numbers which follow some definite order and at the right five sets of two numbers each. You are to look at the numbers in the series at the left and find out what order they follow. Then decide what the next two numbers in that series would be if the same order were continued." There are four key phrases in these directions:

1) . . . "a series of numbers which follow some definite order. . ." In other words, they are connected in some way. They just didn't pop up at random. The person who prepared the series did so according to some *definite rule* or *pattern* that determines how you go from one number to the next. The illustrations below show three number series and the pattern each follows.

Series A: 1 2 3 4 5 6 7 - - -

Pattern: as you proceed from left to right, you *add 1* to each number to get the next number in the series. That is, 1 plus 1 = 2, 2 plus 1 = 3, 3 plus 1 = 4, and so on.

Series B: 21 20 19 18 17 16 15 - - -

Pattern: as you proceed from left to right, you *subtract 1* from each number to get the next number in the series.

Series C: 2 4 8 16 32 64 - - -

Pattern: as you proceed from left to right you multiply each number by two to get the next number in the series. That is, $2 \times 2 = 4$, $4 \times 2 = 8$, $8 \times 2 = 16$, and so on.

2) ". . . look at the numbers - - -" Sometimes you will be able to identify the pattern in a simple series such as examples A and B above, just by looking at it. But to find the order in a more complex series such as series D, below, you will probably need the help of some special techniques. For now, try to find its pattern just by looking at it. (For the answer, see paragraph 4 below).

Series D: 1 8 8 5 12 12 9 16
Pattern: ?

3) ". . . find the order - - -" There are many possible patterns for number series questions. You will learn to recognize more and more of them as you answer the questions in this book. Learning the techniques for finding patterns will make it easy to pick out new ones that you've never seen before. Here is an example of a pattern you have already seen even though, at first, it looks new:

Series E: 5 10 15 20 25 30 35 - - -

Pattern: You get from one number to the next in the series by *addition*, exactly as you did in Series A. The only difference is that you add 5 each time instead of 1. What happens is, 5 plus 5 = 10, 10 plus 5 = 15, 15 plus 5 = 20, and so on.

4) ". . . what the next two numbers are - - -" This is the easiest part of all. Once you have figured out the rule, it is mostly a matter of using ordinary arithmetic to find the next two numbers, *that is—in simple series!*

Here are the next two numbers for the series completed above:

Series A—	1	2	3	4	5	6	7	8	9		(keep adding 1)
Series B—	21	20	19	18	17	16	15	14	13		(keep subtracting 1)
Series C—	2	4	8	16	32	64	128	256			(keep multiplying by 2)
Series D—	1	8	8	5	12	12	9	16	16	13	*
Series E—	5	10	15	20	25	30	35	40	45		(keep adding 5)

* This pattern cannot be explained just by a simple progression of additions or subtractions. It is one of the more complex types for which you will want the techniques explained in the next section.

TECHNIQUES FOR ANSWERING NUMBER SERIES QUESTIONS

In this section, you will learn to use a technique for answering number series questions. With it you will be able to troubleshoot a question and uncover the pattern governing the numbers. You have already seen some techniques used to explain the answers to a few of the Number Series questions in the Diagnostic Test. Because the loop technique is so important, you should take a closer look at it.

The **loop diagram** helps you to *see the connections among the numbers.* On this page there is an enlarged illustration of a typical number series question with a loop diagram and labels. Instead of your trying to keep the number connections in your mind, the loops actually form a visual record that shows which numbers follow each other to make a pattern. Sometimes, the pattern is easy to grasp and remember. In the illustration, for example, where there is a direct connection between one number and the next, you draw the loops as shown. That's easy. *But,* if the connections are *not* direct, and are supposed to skip every second or third number (as in examples 7 and 8 from the Diagnostic Test), then the pattern becomes very difficult to visualize and remember. This is where the loops are *indispensable* if you want to be sure that you are *not skipping* any number and that your pattern is *consistent* and that you will be picking out the next two numbers in the *correct order.* A very common error committed by test takers is for them to select an answer with the two correct numbers—but, *in the wrong order.* (See example 7—Choice D is incorrect because it has *14 12* instead of *12 14.*)

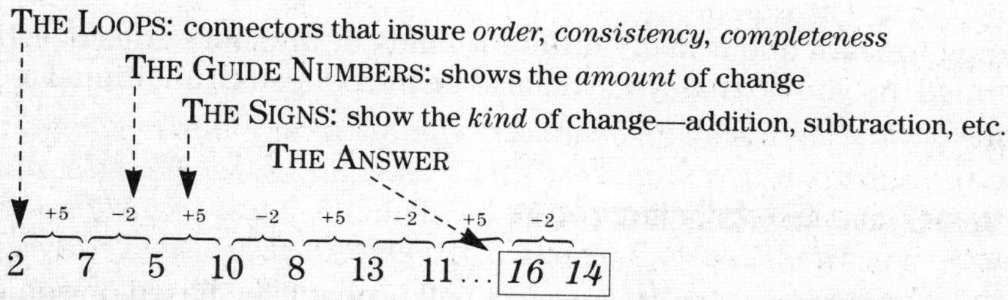

The pattern immediately comes into view: "You proceed from one number to the next by first adding 5, and then subtracting 2."

The Guide Numbers

These are the numbers you put in to show by *how much* one number differs from the other. For many number series questions such as the example in the illustration you go from one number to another by adding or subtracting. It is suggested that the first thing you do when you begin answering a question is to test it out to see if there is a pattern of addition or subtraction. Get the difference between each number and the next. Write it down above the center of the loop as shown. That way you can't forget it. It's just another piece of insurance to help you find a *consistent* pattern. In the series: 2 4 6 8 10 12 14, it is easy to see and remember that the difference between one number and the next is always +2. But in a more complex series like Example 2 of the Diagnostic Test, the pattern of +3, +3, −4, repeated, would be most difficult to keep in mind without writing down the guide numbers above the loops.

The Signs

You have seen from various examples that sometimes the numbers in a series go up, sometimes down, and sometimes they alternate, like in the illustrated example. Unless you put a + or a − in front of each guide number, you may become hopelessly confused (it's like zigging, when you should have zagged).

Now you can appreciate the beauty and the value of the loop diagram. It allows you to *see* the pattern clearly and unmistakably. If you have used the diagram correctly, you will *know* it when you are right. You could even *hear* the pattern if you were to chant it to yourself.

This is why it is said that number series questions are fair. Now, all you have to do is to be careful about applying the techniques and you are on your way to scoring 100 percent on this test.

Applying the Loop

There are two other factors involved in using the loop diagram that can affect your mark on number series questions. One is your ability to add, subtract, multiply and divide simple numbers. The other involves your ability to draw the loops accurately when you connect the numbers. Two tables are provided at the back of this chapter to help you review and check your arithmetic. One is for addition and subtraction; the other is for multiplication and division. There is also a series of drills on arithmetic and on drawing loops. (Please note that you are allowed to mark the loops, guide numbers, and so on *on your exam booklet*, but make these notations lightly, and in pencil. You may have to change something as you test the series to see what pattern fits. Do *not*, however, make any extraneous marks on your *answer sheet*).

TYPES OF NUMBER SERIES QUESTIONS

Now you are going to learn about many different kinds of number series questions and how they are formed. As you do that, you will also be introduced to additional techniques for solving them.

Addition and/or Subtraction

Most of the number series questions on your test will probably be based on some pattern involving addition and/or subtraction. What you have already learned about the loop diagram is sufficient to solve all of them. Here are some of the major types:

A Constant Adder or Subtractor

Example 1

$$\underbrace{2\quad 4}_{+2}\ \underbrace{\quad 6}_{+2}\ \underbrace{\quad 8}_{+2}\ \underbrace{\quad 10}_{+2}\ldots$$

This is the simplest type. The guide number is +2 and never changes as you go from one number to the next.

Alternating Adders and/or Subtractors

Example 2

$$2 \overset{+3}{\frown} 5 \overset{+1}{\frown} 6 \overset{+3}{\frown} 9 \overset{+1}{\frown} 10 \overset{+3}{\frown} 13\ldots$$

The guide numbers alternate between +3 and +1 as you go from one number to the next.

Example 3

$$6 \overset{+6}{\frown} 12 \overset{-2}{\frown} 10 \overset{+6}{\frown} 16 \overset{-2}{\frown} 14 \overset{+6}{\frown} 20\ldots$$

This is exactly the same type as in Example 2 except you alternately *add* 6 and *subtract* 2.

"Complex" Rules

Example 4

$$8 \overset{-2}{\frown} 6 \overset{-2}{\frown} 4 \overset{+6}{\frown} 10 \overset{-2}{\frown} 8 \overset{-2}{\frown} 6 \overset{+6}{\frown} 12\ldots$$

This pattern goes in a cycle of three operations: −2, −2, +6 and then repeats the cycle −2, −2, +6, and so on. You can see it at a glance at the loop diagram.

The Variable Adder and/or Subtractor

Example 5

$$4 \overset{+1}{\frown} 5 \overset{+2}{\frown} 7 \overset{+3}{\frown} 10 \overset{+4}{\frown} 14 \overset{+5}{\frown} 19\ldots$$

Here, the guide number is ever changing. It keeps increasing by 1 as you advance in the series.

Example 6

$$73 \overset{-18}{\frown} 55 \overset{-15}{\frown} 40 \overset{-12}{\frown} 28 \overset{-9}{\frown} 19\ldots$$

There are two ways of describing this pattern. First, you may readily notice that the difference keeps decreasing by 3 as you go from one number to the next. Second, you may see that each guide number is a multiple of $\underline{3}$. That is, 18 is $\underline{6} \times 3$; 15 is $\underline{5} \times 3$; 12 is $\underline{4} \times 3$; etc.

Repeating Elements

Sometimes an addition/subtraction series will include certain numbers as part of its pattern that cannot be accounted for by addition or subtraction. These questions usually fall into three categories:

1. Repetitions Using Series Numbers.

Example 7

+2 +2 +2

10 10 12 12 14 14 16...

Here, the numbers progress by adding 2. But, after each addition, the new number is repeated. Although Example 7 is fairly simple, other repetitions are not. It is suggested you add the following techniques to use with the loop diagram.

- connect the repetitions with a loop and use the *guide number "0,"* or the *guide letter "R."*

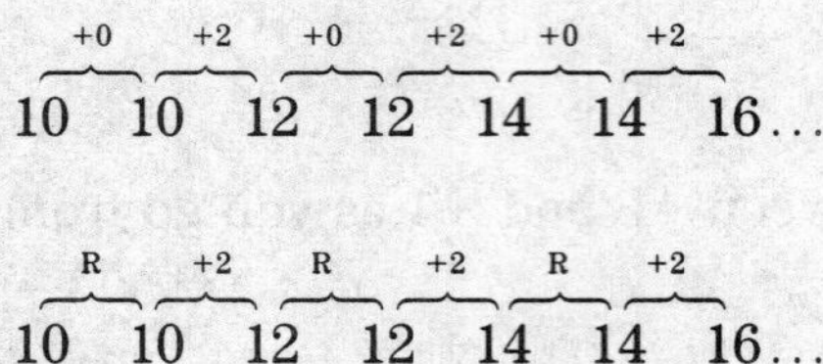

Either way, a consistent pattern is established that is easily seen and continued.

- Join the repetitions by *underlining* or *blocking* them.

+2 +2 +2

10 10 12 12 14 14 16...

+2 +2

10 10 | 12 12 | 14 14 | 16...

2. Repetition of an Arbitrary Number

Occasionally, a number that is entirely unrelated by addition, subtraction, or anything else is introduced at regular intervals in the series. The result can be quite confusing.

Example 8 3 4 11 5 6 11 7...

Here the number 11 is inserted after every second number in the series. The series itself follows a simple +1 pattern.

3. Repetitions Using Both Series and Arbitrary Numbers

All sorts of even more complex patterns can be established in this way.

Example 9

+0 +1 +0 +1

3 4 4 3 5 5 3 6...

Another technique to use when you want to test the pattern to see if repetition is involved is to *softly chant* the number series. You can pick up the rhythm that occurs when numbers repeat themselves.

Drill 1

It would be a good idea if you checked yourself now to see how well you understand the Addition/Subtraction series. See if you can continue the series for two more numbers in each of Examples 1 through 9 discussed above. The answers are given on page 200.

Drill 2

Do questions 1 through 8 below for more practice answering number series questions in the category of addition/subtraction. The answers and explanations are given at the end of this chapter on page 200.

1. 10 13 17 20 24 27 31 __ __
   A) 37 34 B) 33 35 C) 35 38 D) 34 38 E) 35 37

2. 11 5 13 7 15 9 17 __ __
   A) 11 19 B) 9 17 C) 23 15 D) 19 11 E) 12 20

3. 6 6 10 12 12 16 18 __ __
   A) 22 24 B) 24 20 C) 20 22 D) 18 24 E) 18 22

4. 37 32 29 28 23 20 19 __ __
   A) 13 10 B) 15 16 C) 18 13 D) 16 15 E) 14 11

5. 8 8 10 14 20 28 38 __ __
   A) 52 66 B) 54 64 C) 48 66 D) 50 64 E) 50 70

6. 41 41 40 42 42 41 43 __ __
   A) 43 44 B) 42 43 C) 43 42 D) 45 46 E) 42 44

7. 7 9 10 11 13 10 15 __ __
   A) 17 19 B) 17 10 C) 18 20 D) 10 18 E) 11 18

8. 4 5 6 6 7 8 8 9 __ __
   A) 9 10 B) 9 9 C) 9 11 D) 10 10 E) 10 11

Multiplication and/or Division

As mentioned previously, your first step in doing a number series question is to examine it for addition, subtraction, and repetition. If that doesn't work, one of the next things to do is to quickly check to see if multiplication and/or division was used to connect the numbers. Although this type appears less frequently than addition/subtraction series, it is worth knowing about since a few such questions probably will appear and thereby affect your score.

The loop diagram and the other techniques described for addition/subtraction apply here just as well but with two modifications. The *signs* you use in front of the guide number will be $\times$ for multiplication, and $\div$ for division. The other change concerns the way you determine the guide number(s). Examples 1 and 2 that follow will explain the methods.

A. A Constant Multiplier

Example 1 1 2 4 8 16 32 . . .

Just by inspection, you can see that each number in the series is far greater than the one before it. That means multiplication (×) may be involved. The next step is to determine what the guide number is. You do that by taking any number in the series (usually the second) and dividing it by the preceding number. In this example, this is 2 ÷ 1 = 2. 2 is the guide number provided it checks out. You do this by using it to go from one number to the next as follows: $1 \times \underline{2} = 2$; $2 \times \underline{2} = 4$; $4 \times \underline{2} = 8$; $8 \times \underline{2} = 16$; $6 \times \underline{2} = 32$. The pattern is now established as × 2, × 2, × 2, etc., which you can then enter on the loop diagram.

$$\overbrace{1 \quad 2}^{\times 2}\!\!\overbrace{\quad 4}^{\times 2}\!\!\overbrace{\quad 8}^{\times 2}\!\!\overbrace{\quad 16}^{\times 2}\!\!\overbrace{\quad 32}^{\times 2} \ldots$$

Example 2 800 400 200 100 50 . . .

By inspection, you can see that each of the numbers decreases greatly. That means that division (÷) is a possibility. The guide number is determined by dividing the first number by the second. Thus, 800 ÷ 400 = 2, which is the guide number, *if it checks out.* (Another way of finding the guide number is by asking yourself—"400 times ? = 800"; *Answer* $400 \times \underline{2} = 800$). In any case, you then should check out 2, to see if it really is the guide number, by using it to divide each number in turn: $800 \div \underline{2} = 400$; $400 \div \underline{2} = 200$; $200 \div \underline{2} = 100$; $100 \div \underline{2} = 50$. It fits, and the problem is solved.

$$\overbrace{800 \quad 400}^{\div 2}\!\!\overbrace{\quad 200}^{\div 2}\!\!\overbrace{\quad 100}^{\div 2}\!\!\overbrace{\quad 50}^{\div 2} \ldots$$

B. Alternating Multipliers and/or Divisors

Example 3

$$\overbrace{1 \quad 3}^{\times 3}\!\!\overbrace{\quad 6}^{\times 2}\!\!\overbrace{\quad 18}^{\times 3}\!\!\overbrace{\quad 36}^{\times 2}\!\!\overbrace{\quad 108}^{\times 3} \ldots$$

The rule for this series is to alternately multiply by 3, then by 2, then by 3, and so on.

Example 4 1 4 2 8 4 16 8

The numbers in this kind of series do not steadily increase *or* decrease as the series progresses. They *alternately* increase and decrease, which means that you must find one guide number for multiplying and one for dividing. In this example, we find the multiplier and the divisor in the same way as we did in Examples 1 and 2 in Section A above.

For the Multiplier: 4 ÷ 1 = 4. The guide number is written as × 4.

For the Divisor: (In this series the second and the third numbers are examined since this is where the first decrease occurs.) Thus, you have: 4 ÷ 2 = 2. The guide number is written as ÷ 2. Drawing in the loops completes the pattern for this question.

$$\overbrace{1 \quad 4}^{\times 4}\!\!\overbrace{\quad 2}^{\div 2}\!\!\overbrace{\quad 8}^{\times 4}\!\!\overbrace{\quad 4}^{\div 2}\!\!\overbrace{\quad 16}^{\times 4}\!\!\overbrace{\quad 8}^{\div 2} \ldots$$

C. Complex Rules

Example 5

$$\overset{\times 2}{2\quad 4}\quad \overset{\times 3}{\ }\quad 12 \quad \overset{\div 2}{\ } 6 \quad \overset{\times 2}{\ } 12 \quad \overset{\times 3}{\ } 36 \quad \overset{\div 2}{\ } 18\ldots$$

This pattern follows a cycle of three operations: ×2, ×3, ÷2; ×2, ×3, ÷2; and so on. The method of finding each guide number and its sign is the same as in Examples 1 and 2.

D. The Variable Multiplier and/or Divisor

Example 6

$$2 \overset{\times 1}{\ } 2 \overset{\times 2}{\ } 4 \overset{\times 3}{\ } 12 \overset{\times 4}{\ } 48\ldots$$

The multiplier keeps increasing by 1 as you progress in the series.

Repeating Numbers Included in Multiplication/Division Series

You have seen numbers that are repeated and used to form part of the pattern in the Addition/Subtraction number series. They are used in the Multiplication/Division series as well. Such numbers, whether they come from the numbers in the series itself, whether they are totally unrelated to the series, or whether some combination is used, make the pattern more complex. Any of them, however, can be identified by using the methods shown on pages 175 to 176.

Example 7

$$1 \overset{\times 3}{\ } 3 \overset{R}{\ } 3 \overset{\times 3}{\ } 9 \overset{R}{\ } 9 \overset{\times 3}{\ } 27 \overset{R}{\ } 27\ldots$$

This series follows a pattern of × 3, repeat (R); × 3, repeat. . .

Multiplication/Division Combined With Addition/Subtraction

These combinations are among the most complex number series you might ever encounter. Nevertheless, if you use the methods already presented, you will be able to handle them. Just be extra careful about entering the guide numbers and the signs. The signs are particularly important because it is easy to confuse a + for an ×. You are in for a lot of trouble if you multiply when you should have added. This is why it is suggested that you work on the drills at the end of the chapter, especially if your entries are not as clear as they should be.

Example 8 14 10 20 16 32 28 . . .

If you start out as usually suggested, you will first check for addition/subtraction. In this series, you will find that every second number in it is 4 less than the one before it, i.e., $14 - 10 = 4$; $20 - 16 = 4$; etc. But you still must find a rule that decides how you go from 10 to 20 and from 16 to 32. Arithmetic differences do not work here, but multiplication does, i.e., $10 \times 2 = 20$; $16 \times 2 = 32$. When you combine these two rules, using the loop diagram, you arrive at a consistent pattern that accounts for every number in the series. It looks like this:

$$14 \overset{-4}{\ } 10 \overset{\times 2}{\ } 20 \overset{-4}{\ } 16 \overset{\times 2}{\ } 32 \overset{-4}{\ } 28$$

There are other combinations with even more complex rules, some of which involve repeating numbers as well. You have all the ammunition you need to solve them.

Drill 3

Continue the series in each of Examples 1 through 8 on the previous pages for two more numbers. The answers are given on page 200.

Drill 4

Do questions 1 through 8 below to practice answering number series questions in the category of multiplication/division. The answers and explanations are given at the end of this chapter on page 200.

1. 8 8 10 20 20 22 44 __ __
   A) 44 46 B) 44 88 C) 46 48 D) 46 46 E) 88 90

2. 1 2 2 4 4 4 8 8 __ __
   A) 8 12 B) 8 8 C) 8 16 D) 16 8 E) 12 12

3. 2 12 6 36 18 108 __ __
   A) 218 1296 B) 54 108 C) 216 27 D) 54 324 E) 216 36

4. 2 1 2 7 6 12 17 __ __
   A) 34 33 B) 32 31 C) 16 32 D) 22 44 E) 18 36

5. 11 12 7 11 14 9 11 18 __ __
   A) 36 13 B) 23 11 C) 16 36 D) 15 21 E) 13 11

6. 1 200 2 100 4 50 8 __ __
   A) 12 16 B) 16 25 C) 12 25 D) 40 16 E) 25 16

7. 9 6 3 12 9 6 24 __ __
   A) 21 72 B) 72 69 C) 12 48 D) 21 18 E) 18 36

8. 2 8 3 12 4 16 __ __
   A) 6 18 B) 5 20 C) 8 24 D) 24 8 E) 6 24

Alternating Series

Sometimes, the easiest way to see the pattern in a number series question is to look for *two* separate series whose numbers *alternate* with each other.

Example 1

−36 +34 −31 +29 −26 +24

40 4 38 7 36 10 34...

It is perfectly possible to use a loop diagram in the usual way (see page 182) to pick out the pattern and continue the series. But it isn't easy when you are dealing with a series like Example 1. (Before you read on, try to figure out the next two numbers.) If you found it a bit difficult or if you didn't get the correct answer—(13 32)—it isn't surprising. You have to do some mental gymnastics and possibly use a pencil and paper to get the answer.

A much easier, quicker, and safer method to use in this case is shown below:

−2 −2 −2 −2

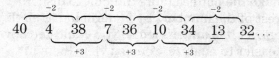

40 4 38 7 36 10 34 <u>13</u> <u>32</u>...

+3 +3 +3

Many series lend themselves to this approach including some you have already worked on in this book. (See Example 7 on the Diagnostic Test; Example 2, on page 177; and Examples 3 and 4 on page 180). In these cases, it really doesn't matter which approach you take as long as you feel comfortable with it and as long as it works for you. In other cases (like Example 1, above), using the alternating series approach is far superior and very often, indispensable. Typical examples of such cases follow. As you go along, you will learn some additional techniques.

Example 2

A −3 −4 −3 −4 −3 A

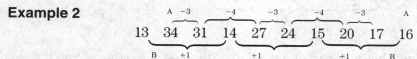

13 34 31 14 27 24 15 20 17 16

B +1 +1 +1 B

This is an example of two alternating series, both of the addition/subtraction type. The series labeled "A" follows the rule: −3, −4; −3, −4, etc. The other series, labeled "B" keeps increasing by +1. In Example 1 above, each number in both series alternates one-for-one with the other. In this example, the numbers in series "B" appear after every *two* numbers of series A.

In order to keep track of this rather complex pattern, it is suggested that you do something to differentiate between the two sets of loops. In the example the letters A and B were used. Some students prefer to make one set of loops with solid lines; the other with dashed lines. Do what is best for you.

Example 3

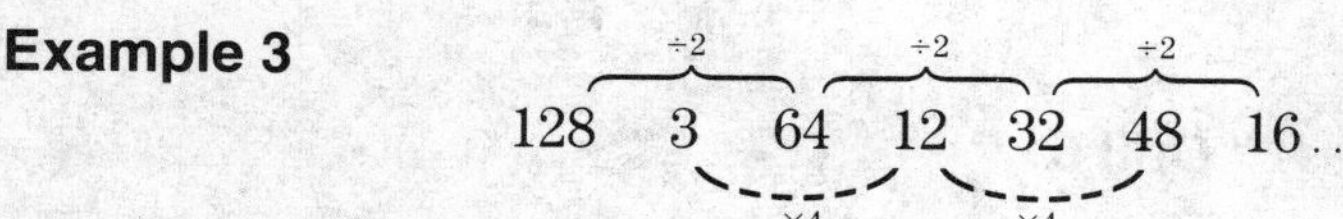

Here is an example of a multiplication series alternating number-for-number with a division series. The first decreases by following the rule of ÷2, ÷2, ÷2, etc. The other increases by ×4, ×4, ×4, and so on. This question would be impossible to answer if you didn't look for alternating series. (This time, a dashed loop was used to point up the difference between the two series.)

Example 4

+2

+2 +1 +1 +2 +1 +1

18 20 | 1 2 3 | 22 24 | 4 5 6 |

A B A B

+1

These might be called alternating "mini-series." One mini-series, A, increases by +2 and continues for two numbers before being interrupted by the other mini-series B, which increases by +1 and comes in bunches of three. If you should encounter a question like this where you believe there are alternating mini-series, try putting in light vertical lines (see above) to partition one group from the other. The lines highlight each group (A and B) and make it easy to keep track of their alternations.

Example 5 15 19 27 15 20 28 15 21 29...

This series contains a repeating number, 15, which is entirely unrelated to the other numbers. It just serves to make the pattern more difficult to discern. Once you have spotted it, separate it from the rest of the numbers by underlining it, circling it, or using a partition line as in Example 4 above. It is underlined so you could see how it works. Now, the remaining numbers are far easier to analyze. You can view them in two ways:

A) Following a +8, −7; rule:

+8 −7 +8 −7 +8

15 19 27 15 20 28 15 21 29

or,

B) As two alternating series, each following a +1 rule:

+1 +1

15 19 27 15 20 28 15 21 29

+1 +1

Once again, it is stressed that you can choose any of the methods above. You'll know what suits you best after you have done some of the practice exercises and drills.

Example 6

A +3 R +3 R +3 R

7 1 10 10 2 13 13 4 16 16 8...

B ×2 ×2 ×2

Once again, there is a repeater that makes the series more difficult. In this example, you have two alternating series. One increases by 3, and repeats the number before adding 3 again (see Series A). Series B is one that follows the rule of multiplying by 2.

Drill 5

Continue the series for two more numbers in each of Examples 1 through 6 above. The answers are given on page 201.

Drill 6

Do questions 1 through 8 below, to practice answering number series questions in the category of Alternating Series. The answers and explanations are given at the end of this chapter on page 201.

1. 4 37 9 35 14 33 19 __ __

   A) 28 24 B) 24 31 C) 31 24 D) 24 28 E) 31 17

2. 1 2 3 4 6 8 4 5 6 10 __ __

   A) 11 12 B) 12 13 C) 7 8 D) 12 14 E) 10 7

3. 6 18 23 12 21 23 18 24 23 __ __
   A) 25 24 B) 27 33 C) 26 27 D) 24 25 E) 24 27

4. 64 64 34 32 32 42 16 16 50 __ __
   A) 50 12 B) 8 50 C) 58 8 D) 12 52 E) 8 8

5. 16 29 21 28 26 26 31 23 __ __
   A) 22 35 B) 23 36 C) 36 19 D) 21 28 E) 27 34

6. 31 1 27 3 23 9 19 __ __
   A) 12 17 B) 15 24 C) 27 15 D) 16 27 E) 15 27

7. 40 42 38 40 36 38 34 __ __
   A) 34 36 B) 30 34 C) 32 34 D) 38 36 E) 36 32

8. 21 8 19 11 18 14 16 17 15 __ __
   A) 13 20 B) 11 18 C) 16 17 D) 14 19 E) 20 13

Cycles/Repetitions/Combinations

You have already seen numbers repeat themselves as part of the pattern of many number series. Sometimes, the pattern of a series is based more on repeating, cycling or combining numbers than on arithmetic rules. In the section that follows, you will see examples of such series and learn the techniques of answering them.

Example 1 64 13 87 | 64 13 87 | 64...

This is a series that uses a sequence of three unrelated numbers and keeps recycling them. If you take a quick look at the series as a whole, you will easily pick up the pattern. Using *partition* lines as shown above is a quick and easy way of proving you are right and helping you continue the series. You may encounter series of this kind that use sequences of 2 or 4 numbers. It makes no difference. The principle is the same.

Example 2 9 10 11 14 9 10 11 14 9...

This series is formed by *recycling* the numbers 9 10 11. It is similar to the sequence in Example 1, except that the number 14 appears between each cycle. Incidentally, you could use an arithmetic rule +1, +1, 14; repeat +1, +1, 14; and so on . . . but it is easier to use the numbers themselves in sequence.

Example 3 2 3 4 5 4 3 2 3...

This series *ascends* from 2 to 5 and then *descends* in *reverse* order. Then the cycle repeats.

Example 4 1 2 12 3 4 34 5...

This example shows how number *combinations* (or placement) may be used to form series. Here, every third number is formed by combining the previous *two* and writing them as *one* number, i.e., 1→2 becomes 12; 3→4 becomes 34.

Example 5 1 1 2 1 2 3 1 2 3 4...

Here, although you could find an arithmetic rule, it is much easier to see this series as a series of sequences, each increasing in length by one number. Once again, drawing partition lines makes the rule stand out clearly:

1 | 1 2 | 1 2 3 | 1 2 3 4 |...

The technique of softly *chanting* the numbers to yourself, which was mentioned before, is another way you can "see" the pattern.

Example 6

+10 +10

30 31 32 | 40 41 42 | 50...

You could see this as three alternating series, or as successive *cycles* of three number sequences each beginning with a number ten higher than the one before it. Each sequence follows a +1 rule.

Example 7 1 2 2 3 3 3 4 4...

In this series, the number of *repetitions* is *directly related* to the number itself—for example, number 2 is repeated *twice*; number 3 is repeated *three* times, etc.

Example 8 68 86 82 28 24 42...

Part of the rule governing this series depends upon *reversals of numbers.* For example, 68 and 86 use the same numbers but in reverse order. Each succeeding pair does the same thing. The rule for connecting the pairs is to subtract 4. When you draw the loop diagram, the full pattern shows up more clearly:

−4 −4

| 68 86 | | 82 28 | | 24 42 | ...

As you have already learned, any series can be made more complex by inserting an extraneous number into it at regular intervals. With the use of the various devices we have introduced, however, such as partitions, underlining, and so on, you should be able to fit them into the pattern.

Drill 7

Continue the series for two more numbers in each of Examples 1 through 8 above. The answers are on page 202.

Drill 8

Do questions 1 through 8 below to practice answering number series questions in the category of Cycles/Repetitions/Combinations. The answers and explanations are at the end of this chapter on pages 201 to 202.

1. 47 46 45 44 43 44 45 __ __
   A) 47 48 B) 46 45 C) 46 44 D) 45 47 E) 46 47

2. 29 74 61 19 29 74 61 __ __
   A) 29 19 B) 54 41 C) 51 74 D) 19 29 E) 49 29

3. 8 7 9 7 6 8 6 5 __ __
   A) 4 3 B) 7 8 C) 7 5 D) 8 9 E) 7 7

4. 24 26 28 14 34 36 38 14 __ __
   A) 40 44 B) 44 14 C) 14 40 D) 44 46 E) 46 48

5. 38 3 8 49 4 9 60 __ __
   A) 71 5 B) 5 10 C) 7 9 D) 6 0 E) 10 71

6. 15 16 17 17 18 19 20 20 __ __
   A) 20 21 B) 22 21 C) 21 22 D) 22 23 E) 21 21

7. 30 50 70 30 50 70 30 __ __
   A) 50 70 B) 40 50 C) 50 60 D) 30 50 E) 70 50

8. 51 52 53 52 53 54 53 __ __
   A) 56 55 B) 54 55 C) 55 55 D) 53 55 E) 55 56

Miscellaneous

This is the fifth and last category of number series questions. It includes series based on other kinds of rules. Some of these types have appeared on prior Number Series tests; others have not. Since it is in your interest to be fully prepared, the following have been assembled for you to study.

Example 1 $1 + 4 \overset{=}{+} 5 \overset{+}{=} 9 \overset{=}{+} 14 \overset{+}{=} 23 = 37 \ldots$

Each number in this series, beginning with 5, is obtained by adding together the two numbers preceding it: 1 + 4 = 5; 4 + 5 = 9; 5 + 9 = 14; and so on. One way of diagramming this series is shown above.

Example 2 3 2 6 3 3 9 3 4 12 3...

Like Example 1 above, this series uses the numbers in the series itself to progress. Here the rule is to *multiply* the first two numbers in the series to get the third in a trio, i.e., $3 \times \mathit{2} = 6$; $3 \times \mathit{3} = 9$; $3 \times \mathit{4} = 12$. You will notice that for each new trio, you multiply *3* by an ever-increasing number.

Example 3 1 4 9 16 25 36...

Each number in this series is the *square* of consecutive numbers starting with number 1. (You square a number by multiplying it by itself.) Thus, $1 \times 1 = \mathit{1}$; $2 \times 2 = \mathit{4}$; $3 \times 3 = \mathit{9}$; $4 \times 4 = \mathit{16}$; and so on.

Example 4 $\frac{1}{2}$ $\frac{1}{3}$ $\frac{1}{4}$ $\frac{1}{5}$ $\frac{1}{6}$ $\frac{1}{7}$...

You may have forgotten how to work with fractions but that really doesn't matter. It was mentioned at the very beginning of this chapter that you are not taking a math test. You are being tested on your ability to see the pattern existing in a progression of numbers. In this example, all you need is to detect that the bottom number (the denominator) of each fraction keeps increasing by 1. It is that simple.

Example 5 10^{14} 10^{13} 10^{12} 10^{11} 10^{10} 10^{9} 10^{8}...

The moral behind this series is the same as for Example 4. You do not have to know that the little numbers are called exponents or what they do, just as long as you see that in each successive number they decrease by 1.

Example 6 +2 +2 −4 +2 +2 −4 +2...

In this series, each number has a sign before it. The numbers themselves follow a repetitive sequence of three and, of course, carry their signs with them.

Drill 9

Continue the series for two more numbers in each of Examples 1 through 6 above. The answers are on page 202.

Drill 10

Do questions 1 through 8 below to practice answering number series questions in the Miscellaneous category. The answers and explanations are given at the end of this chapter on page 202.

1. 81 9 64 8 49 7 36 __ __

   A) 25 6 B) 6 36 C) 5 25 D) 6 25 E) 25 16

2. $9\frac{1}{9}$ $10\frac{2}{10}$ $11\frac{3}{11}$ $12\frac{4}{12}$ $13\frac{5}{13}$ $14\frac{6}{14}$

   A) $14\frac{7}{16}$ $15\frac{5}{15}$ B) $15\frac{7}{14}$ $16\frac{8}{16}$ C) $15\frac{7}{15}$ $14\frac{8}{16}$

   D) $15\frac{7}{15}$ $16\frac{8}{16}$ E) $16\frac{7}{16}$ $17\frac{8}{17}$

3. 2 2 4 3 3 9 4 4 16 __ __

A) 16 16 B) 16 4 C) 5 5 D) 5 17 E) 5 25

4. −1 +2 −3 −1 +2 −3 −1 +2 __ __

A) +3 −1 B) −3 +2 C) +3 −2 D) −2 −3 E) −3 −1

5. .1 1.1 1.01 11.01 11.001 111.001 __ __

A) 111.001 1111.001 B) 111.0100 111.00001 C) 101.001 111.001

D) 110.001 1110.0001 E) 111.0001 1111.0001

6. 89 55 34 21 13 8 __ __

A) 7 6 B) 5 6 C) 5 3 D) 9 4 E) 7 5

7. 3 8 63 80 99 __ __

A) 109 142 B) 119 153 C) 120 143 D) 109 150 E) 131 165

8. 5 6 8 12 20 36 __ __

A) 48 66 B) 68 132 C) 44 70 D) 56 88 E) 49 81

SPECIAL EXERCISES FOR BUILDING NUMBER SERIES SKILLS

You now have the tools. You have learned the strategies and techniques that make a high score possible. Now you must be certain that you can apply them at test time. That means practice.

Addition/Subtraction Review

You may have found by now that you are a little rusty on the arithmetic required for Number Series, even though it is very basic. This can show up in two ways. First, you may find that as you do a series and look for differences between numbers, your guide numbers keep changing, not in accordance with any rule, but because you are making errors. Second, you may be taking too long on each calculation. In either case, you are wasting time, and even worse, getting confused, and thereby having difficulty seeing the pattern.

If this is the case with you,* your problem can be easily remedied. Read and follow the following directions for improving your arithmetic.

The table below gives you a convenient way to review and drill on adding and subtracting numbers between 1 and 10.

Scale A / Scale B	1	2	3	4	5	6	7	8	9	10
1	2	3	4	5	6	7	8	9	10	11
2	3	4	5	6	7	8	9	10	11	12
3	4	5	6	7	8	9	10	11	12	13
4	5	6	7	8	9	10	11	12	13	14
5	6	7	8	9	10	11	12	13	14	15
6	7	8	9	10	11	12	13	14	15	16
7	8	9	10	11	12	13	14	15	16	17
8	9	10	11	12	13	14	15	16	17	18
9	10	11	12	13	14	15	16	17	18	19
10	11	12	13	14	15	16	17	18	19	20

To Add

As an example, assume you wanted to check the answer to adding 9 + 8. Find the number 9 on either of the two scales of numbers on the outside of the table. If you used the horizontal scale (labeled the "A" scale), your next step is to find the other number—8—on the vertical "B" scale. The answer 17 is obtained in a moment, by following the vertical column under the 9 until it intersects with the horizontal row alongside the 8. (See Figure 6.1)

* If you have no difficulty with the arithmetic in the number series, skip directly to page 195.

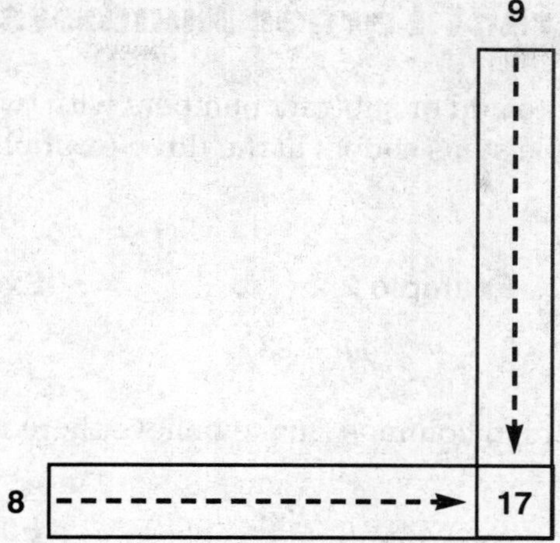

Figure 6.1 Adding: 9 + 8

To Subtract

As an example, if you were checking 16−7, you would locate the number 7 on either the A or the B scale. If you used the vertical scale, B, then you would follow the row alongside number 7 until you reached the number 16. Then, all you do is follow the vertical column from 16 up until it reaches the A scale. It shows the answer—9. (See Figure 6.2)

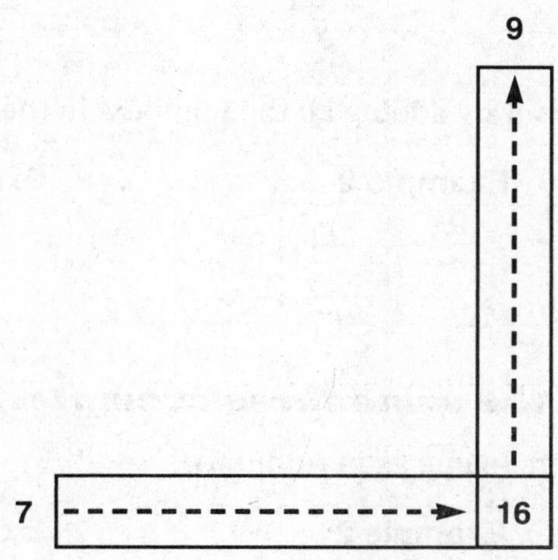

Figure 6.2 Subtracting: 16 − 7

Drills

With the table, you can drill by yourself or with the help of a friend.

For Addition: Pick any number from Scale A and any other number from Scale B. Without looking at the table and without using a paper and pencil, add the two and call out the answer.

For Subtraction: Pick out any number in the table itself and any other number on either scale. Then calculate the difference.

If necessary, check your answer against the table. Your aim is to perform each calculation mentally and with reasonable speed.

To Add and Subtract Larger Numbers

Occasionally, you may have to add or subtract numbers with two digits. You can easily do this by following a few simple steps shown in the three examples below.

To Add

Example 1	Example 2	Example 3

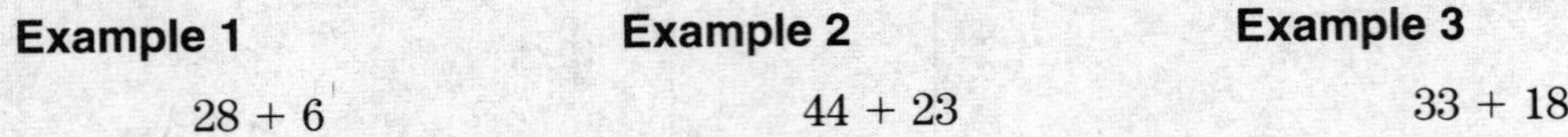

Example 1	Example 2	Example 3
28 + 6	44 + 23	33 + 18

Step 1 Line up the numbers in columns (make believe there is an imaginary line on the right).

Example 1	Example 2	Example 3
28 + 6	44 +23	33 +18

Step 2 Mentally, add the two numbers in the farthest column on the right and enter the answer in the same columns on the bottom. If the answer has two digits, carry the first one into the next column (see the small circled numbers).

Example 1	Example 2	Example 3
28 +①6 4	44 +23 7	33 +①18 1

Step 3: Complete the answer by adding all the numbers in the left-hand column.

Example 1	Example 2	Example 3
28 +①6 34	44 +23 67	33 +①18 51

To Subtract (Using the same three examples):

Step 1 Line up the numbers (same as in Addition)

Example 1	Example 2	Example 3
28 − 6	44 −23	33 −18

Step 2 Mentally, subtract the two numbers in the farthest column on the right

Example 1	Example 2	Example 3
8−6=2	4−3=1	13−8=5

and enter the answer on the bottom of the same column. In cases like Example 3 where the first number—3—is smaller than the second—8, a 1 has been placed in front of the 3 making it 13. When you do that you have to make up for it by putting 1 in the second column (see next page).

Example 1	Example 2	Example 3
28	44	33
− 6	−23	−①18
2	1	5

Step 3 Complete the answer by subtracting the bottom numbers from the top ones.

Example 1	Example 2	Example 3
28	44	33
− 6	−23	−①18
22	21	15

Note—Example 3, you must add both bottom numbers before subtracting, i.e., 1 + 1 = 2; 3 − 2 = 1.

Drills

If you wish to practice adding and subtracting two-digit numbers, work on Examples 1 through 60. The answers are given on page 203. Try to do as many of these questions as you can without rewriting them. You will lose time if you do; on the real test you can't afford the time. Just call out your answer if you are drilling with a friend or jot down the answer in the space provided.

Addition

Answers — Trials	3	2	1
1. 28 + 4 =			
2. 15 + 6 =			
3. 23 + 9 =			
4. 48 + 16 =			
5. 52 + 8 =			
6. 19 + 8 =			
7. 27 + 8 =			
8. 31 + 10 =			
9. 81 + 6 =			
10. 77 + 19 =			
11. 15 + 23 =			
12. 11 + 3 =			
13. 33 + 49 =			
14. 91 + 13 =			
15. 12 + 3 =			

Answers — Trials	3	2	1
16. 44 + 5 =			
17. 47 + 22 =			
18. 17 + 4 =			
19. 46 + 6 =			
20. 18 + 9 =			
21. 21 + 12 =			
22. 38 + 19 =			
23. 14 + 7 =			
24. 35 + 7 =			
25. 52 + 6 =			
26. 19 + 2 =			
27. 39 + 4 =			
28. 16 + 9 =			
29. 10 + 10 =			
30. 41 + 3 =			
Number Right			
Time			

Subtraction

	Answers		
Trials	3	2	1
31. 12 − 3 =			
32. 34 − 2 =			
33. 16 − 9 =			
34. 38 − 7 =			
35. 49 − 9 =			
36. 27 − 8 =			
37. 14 − 6 =			
38. 58 − 2 =			
39. 71 − 14 =			
40. 44 − 8 =			
41. 12 − 9 =			
42. 38 − 5 =			
43. 86 − 8 =			
44. 19 − 9 =			
45. 14 − 8 =			

	Answers		
Trials	3	2	1
46. 63 − 7 =			
47. 78 − 14 =			
48. 50 − 16 =			
49. 37 − 16 =			
50. 48 − 12 =			
51. 21 − 5 =			
52. 57 − 7 =			
53. 24 − 6 =			
54. 78 − 8 =			
55. 36 − 6 =			
56. 42 − 4 =			
57. 33 − 3 =			
58. 11 − 8 =			
59. 15 − 7 =			
60. 26 − 7 =			
Number Right			
Time			

Multiplication/Division Review

Scale A	Scale B 1	2	3	4	5	6	7	8	9	10
1		2	3	4	5	6	7	8	9	10
2		4	6	8	10	12	14	16	18	20
3		6	9	12	15	18	21	24	27	30
4		8	12	16	20	24	28	32	36	40
5		10	15	20	25	30	35	40	45	50
6		12	18	24	30	36	42	48	54	60
7		14	21	28	35	42	49	56	63	70
8		16	24	32	40	48	56	64	72	80
9		18	27	36	45	54	63	72	81	90
10		20	30	40	50	60	70	80	90	100

The table above will be helpful to those wishing to check their multiplication and division. There are relatively few questions of this type on most Number Series tests and those that do appear are of the simplest kind, involving multipliers and divisors like 2, 3, or 4. Just to be safe, however, it is suggested that you check the table and drill on any products or quotients you may have forgotten. The two illustrations below the table show how to check multiplication and division examples. (Figures 6.3 and 6.4).

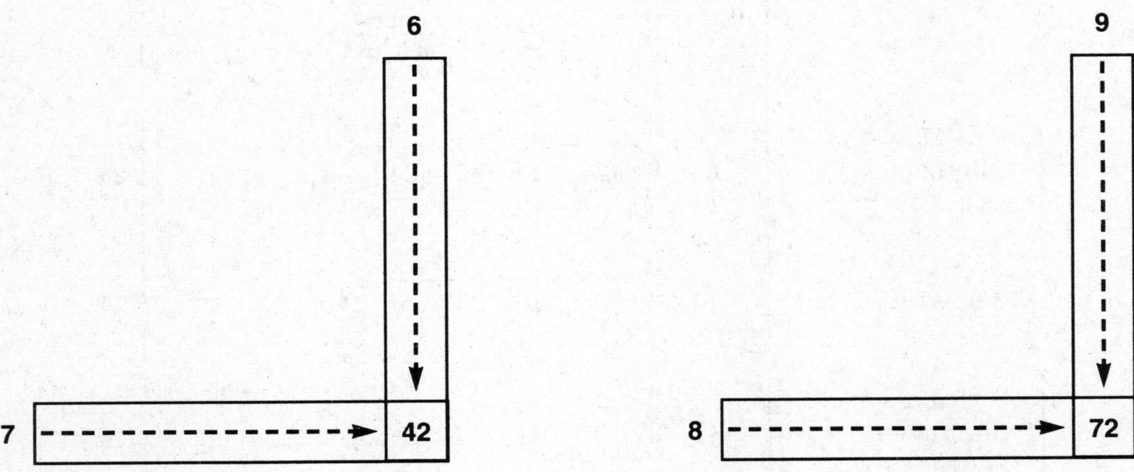

Figure 6.3 Multiplying: 6 × 7 = 42

Figure 6.4 Dividing: 72 ÷ 9 = 8

Drills Using the Loop Diagram

This series of drills is designed to give you practice on the arithmetical and mechanical operations used in making a loop diagram. They will help you avoid making careless errors on the real test. Common errors test takers make include: losing track of which numbers to connect, errors in arithmetic, writing guide numbers that do not do the job because they are too small, too large, or illegible; losing track of the proper sequence in the case of complex or alternating series.

In these drills you will be given the rule that series is to follow, together with the first sequence of numbers needed to illustrate the rule. It is your job to write in the *next six numbers* in the series according to this rule. Use connecting loops and guide numbers to do this. Check the *last two* numbers in the series you developed against the key answers given in the column on the far right side of the page. The first six questions have been worked out to illustrate what you should do.

DRILL—LOOP DIAGRAMS

No.	Rule	Number Series	Answer
1.	+4; . . .	+4 +4 +4 +4 +4 +4 5 9 13 17 21 25 29	25 29
2.	−1, +2; . . .	−1 +2 −1 +2 −1 +2 3 2 4 3 5 4 6	4 6
3.	Series A −5; . . . Alternates Series B +8; . . .	−5 −5 −5 45 5 40 13 35 21 30 29. . . . . +8 +8 +8	30 29
4.	×3, −2; . . .	×3 −2 ×3 −2 ×3 −2 2 6 4 12 10 30 28	30 28
5.	+2, +5; . . . Alternates 24	+2 +5 +2 +5 6 8 [24] 13 15 [24] 20	24 20
6.	+6, −1,R; . . .	+6 −1 R +6 −1 R 14 20 19 19 25 24 24.	24 24
7.	Series A +1; . . . Alternates Series B +4; . . .	A +1 12 27 13 31 __ __ __ __ __ __ B +4	16 43
8.	+3; . . .	+3 32 35 __ __ __ __ __ __	50 53
9.	−2, −3; . . .	−2 −3 29 27 24 __ __ __ __ __ __	12 9

No.	Rule	Number Series	Answer
10.	Series A ×3; . . . Alternates Series B −4; . . .	1 47 3 43 (A ×3; B −4) ___ ___ ___ ___	81 31
11.	−8, R; . . .	36 28 28 (−8, R) ___ ___ ___ ___	4 4
12.	Series A −1; . . . Alternates Series B R, −1; . . .	20 41 41 19 40 (−1; R, −1) ___ ___ ___ ___	17 38
13.	21, 22, 23; . . .	21 22 23 | 21 ___ ___ ___ ___	23 21
14.	−2, +3, −4, R; . . .	25 23 26 22 22 (−2, +3, −4, R) ___ ___ ___ ___	17 20
15.	−3, −3,R; . . .	30 30 27 27 (−3, −3, R) ___ ___ ___ ___	15 15
16.	R, R, +2; . . .	9 9 9 11 (R, R, +2) ___ ___ ___ ___	13 15
17.	×2, −1, R; . . .	8 16 15 15 (×2, −1, R) ___ ___ ___ ___	57 57
18.	Series A +10; . . . Alternates Series B −5; . . .	10 45 20 40 (A +10; B −5) ___ ___ ___ ___	50 25
19.	17, 18, 19; . . .	17 18 19 | ___ ___ ___ ___	18 19
20.	Series A −2; . . . Alternates Series B +5; . . .	22 1 20 6 (A −2; B +5) ___ ___ ___ ___	14 21
21.	Series A −3; . . . Alternates 19	47 [19] 44 (A −3) ___ ___ ___ ___	19 35
22.	Series A ×4; . . . Alternates Series B +3; . . .	1 19 4 22 (A ×4; B +3) ___ ___ ___ ___	256 31

No.	Rule	Number Series	Answer
23.	+1, R, R, −2; . . .	10 11 11 11 9 __ __ __ __ __	9 9
24.	−9, R; . . .	65 56 56 __ __ __ __ __	29 29
25.	×2, ×3, ÷2; . . .	3 6 18 9 __ __ __ __ __	162 81
26.	Mini-Series A +1, +1; . . . Alternates Series B +2, +2; . . .	1 2 3 | 2 4 6 | 4 __ __ __ __ __	12 7
27.	Series A ×5; . . . Alternates Series B −6; . . .	2 49 10 43 __ __ __ __ __	1250 25
28.	Series A +1; . . . Alternates Series B −2, −3; . . .	14 27 25 15 22 __ __ __ __ __	17 12
29.	11 Alternates Series A +6; . . . and Series B −2; . . .	11 4 57 11 10 55 __ __ __ __ __	22 51
30.	−10, −9, −8, etc.; . . .	71 61 52 44 37 __ __ __ __ __	16 15
31.	Series A −2; . . . Alternates Series B +7; . . .	50 48 1 8 15 46 __ __ __ __ __	42 40
32.	Series A +1; . . . Alternates 32	24 25 26 32 27 __ __ __ __ __	31 32
33.	+3, ×2, −4, R; . . .	3 6 12 8 8 __ __ __ __ __	21 42
34.	−1, R, +2, R; . . .	6 5 5 7 7 __ __ __ __ __	7 7
35.	−3, +9; . . .	4 1 10 __ __ __ __ __	19 28

No.	Rule	Number Series	Answer
36.	+5, R, +5; . . .	10 15 15 20 (+5, R, +5) ___ ___ ___ ___	35 40

Symbols

; . . . shows a rule is complete

R Tells you to repeat the previous number

[2] the number in the box is periodically repeated

ANSWERS AND EXPLANATIONS FOR NUMBER SERIES EXERCISES

Addition and/or Subtraction

Drill 1 page 178

1. **12 14**	3. **18 24**	5. **25 32**	7. **16 18**	9. **6 3**
2. **14 17**	4. **10 8**	6. **13 10**	8. **8 11**	

Drill 2 page 179

1. **D** The rule is: + 3, + 4, +3, + 4; and so on.
2. **A** You may see this series in two ways. First, as following the pattern: − 6, + 8, − 6, + 8; and so on. Second, you may view it as two alternating series, each increasing by 2.
3. **E** A more complex rule applies here, easily seen using a loop diagram:

   R +4 +2 R +4 +2 R +4

   6 6 10 12 12 16 18... 18 22

   You might also see the entire series as composed of two alternating series, one of which repeats each of its numbers. (For practice, diagram it that way.)
4. **E** The rule here is: − 5, − 3, − 1; − 5, − 3, − 1; and so on.
5. **D** The "adder" for the series is variable. Its keeps increasing by + 2. Your guide numbers should be: 0, + 2, + 4, + 6, + 8, + 10. Continuing the series: 38 + 12 = 50; 50 + 14 = 64.
6. **C** This series is another one that follows a complex rule. Here, beginning with the first number, 41, it is: repeat the number, − 1, + 2; repeat the number, − 1, + 2; and so on.
7. **B** This is a simple + 2 series, with the number 10 inserted after every two of its numbers.
8. **D** This series follows the rule: + 1, + 1, repeat the number; + 1, + 1, repeat the number. You might also see it as a progression of three-number mini-series, each beginning 2 higher than the previous one:

   4 5 6 | 6 7 8 | 8 9 10 | 10 and so on.

Multiplication/Division

Drill 3 page 182

1. **64 128**	3. **216 648**	5. **36 108**	7. **81 81**
2. **25 12½**	4. **32 16**	6. **240 1440**	8. **56 52**

Drill 4 page 182

1. **A** This series follows a complex rule that includes repetition, addition, and multiplication. The loop diagram shows it clearly:

   R +2 ×2 R +2 ×2 R +2

   8 8 10 20 20 22 44... 44 46

2. **B** This is a × 2 series that repeats each new term the same number of times as its positions in the series, e.g., 2 appears *twice*, 4 appears *three* times (it's in *third* place). Therefore 8, which is in *fourth* place, appears *four* times.
3. **D** The pattern here is: × 6, ÷ 2; × 6, ÷ 2; and so on. If you prefer, you may view it as two alternating series, each following a × 3 rule.
4. **C** Here is another complex series. It combines subtraction, multiplication and addition. The rule is: − 1, × 2, + 5; − 1, × 2, + 5; and so on.
5. **E** This series follows a pattern of × 2, − 5, × 2, − 5; and so on. It is made difficult to see because an arbitrary number, 11, is inserted as every third number in the series.
6. **E** There are two alternating series here. The first one increases by successive multiplications by 2. The other decreases by successive divisions by 2.
7. **D** The complex rule for this series is: − 3, − 3, × 4; − 3, − 3, × 4; and so on.
8. **B** Each pair of numbers beginning with 2 8 is connected by × 4, i.e. 2 × 4 = 8; 3 × 4 = 12. The first number in each successive pair increases by 1. You can also consider the pattern as composed of two alternating series—one following a + 1 rule, and the other following a + 4 rule.

Alternating Series

Drill 5 page 184

1. **16 30**
2. **13 10**
3. **192 8**
4. **26 28**
5. **15 22**
6. **19 19**

Drill 6 page 184

1. **C** There are two alternating series here, one of which increases by a + 5 rule; the other decreases by a − 2 rule.
2. **D** There are two alternating series here, each of which continues for three numbers, after which it is interrupted by the other. One increases by + 1; the other by + 2. In effect, each group of three numbers is a "mini-series." Partitions and guide numbers make it easier to see.

+2 +2 +2 +2 +2

1 2 3 | 4 6 8 | 4 5 6 | 10 12 14

+1 +1 +1

3. **E** This series of numbers is formed by two alternating series and the arbitrary number 23. Without a loop diagram like the one shown, such a complex pattern is extremely difficult to pick up.

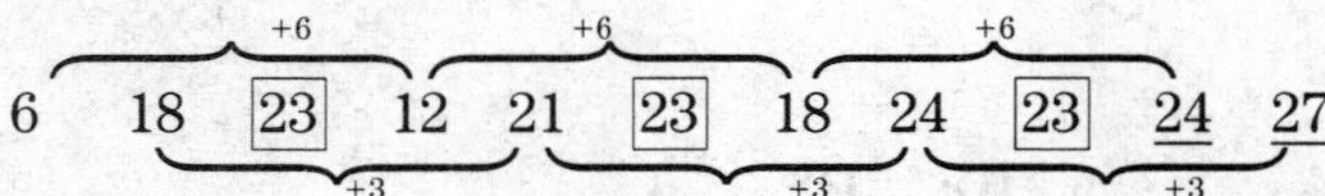

4. **E** Here, one series decreases by dividing by 2. This series repeats each of its numbers. The alternating series follows a + 8 rule.
5. **C** One of the two alternating series contained in this progression increases steadily by adding 5. The other has *variable* "subtractors" starting with − 1 and continuously increasing to − 2, − 3, − 4, and so on.
6. **C** Two alternating series are present here. One follows a × 3 rule. The other decreases by a − 4 rule.
7. **E** Here is a comparatively easy one. Both alternating series decrease, each by − 2.

8. **E** In this pair of alternating series, one of them *steadily* increases by adding 3. The other series alternates its subtractors according to a − 2, − 1; − 2, − 1; pattern.

Cycles/Repetitions/Combinations

Drill 7 page 186

1. **13 87**	3. **4 5**	5. **1 2**	7. **4 4**
2. **10 11**	4. **6 56**	6. **51 52**	8. **38 83**

Drill 8 page 187

1. **E** This series of numbers *descends* from 47 to 43 and then *ascends* using the same numbers in reverse order.
2. **D** This is a sequence of four unrelated numbers (29 74 61 19) that keeps repeating itself.
3. **C** Here you have a succession of three-number "mini-series" each of whose numbers is one less than the corresponding number in the preceding series. You could also see this progression as made up of three alternating series, each following a − 1 rule. (For practice, try diagramming it that way.)
4. **D** Again, you find "mini-series." This time, each group of numbers starts 10 higher than the one before. Within each "mini-series," the numbers follow a + 2 rule. The arbitrary number 14 separates one mini-series from the next.
5. **D** Each two-digit number, starting with 38, is followed by the two numbers that combined to form it. Thus, 38 breaks down into 3 and 8, 49 into 4 and 9, and so on. The rule for going from one two-digit number to the next is to add 11.
6. **C** Each of the four-member mini-series (like 15, 16, 17, 17) that makes up the progression follows a + 1 rule and repeats the last number. Each mini-series begins three numbers higher than the last series began.
7. **A** The sequence: 30 50 70 keeps recycling.
8. **B** If you draw a partition between each group of three numbers it becomes easy to see that each group begins and ends one number higher than in the preceding group. This pattern can also be revealed by softly chanting the numbers in groups of three.

51 52 53 | 52 53 54 | 53 <u>54</u> <u>55</u>

+1 +1

Miscellaneous

Drill 9 page 188

1. **60 97**	3. **49 64**	5. $\mathbf{10^7}$ $\mathbf{10^6}$
2. **5 15**	4. **1/8 1/9**	6. **+2 −4**

Drill 10 page 188 to 189

1. **D** This is a series based on the *square* of numbers from 9 on down. The first number 81 is the square of 9, which follows it in the series. The third number 64 is the square of 8, which follows it, and so on.
2. **D** You do not need to understand fractions to do this question. You do have to see that each fraction has *three* parts: the whole number at the beginning 9, 10, 11, and so

on. These increase by 1 for each successive fraction. Then there is the number at the top of the fraction (numerator) and the number at the bottom (denominator) each of which follows the simple rule of + 1. If you're careful to track each one of those three numbers, you'll get the answer.

3. **C** This series illustrates the case where a series uses its own numbers to progress. This process works like this: $\underline{2} \times \underline{2} = 4$; $\underline{3} \times \underline{3} = 9$; and so on. For each group of three numbers, the multipliers increase by 1.
4. **E** The sequence $-1, +2, -3$ keeps repeating. This series may look unusual because each number is preceded by a *sign*, but the idea of finding a pattern is the same.
5. **E** This series is difficult to keep track of because each number is so long. The pattern is a simple one nevertheless. As you proceed from left to right, you alternately add a 1 to the left of the decimal point and a 0 to the right of the decimal point.
6. **C** Like the series in example 3, this one uses its own numbers to progress. The rule is: subtract each number from its preceding number to get the number next in the series, e.g., $\underline{89} - \underline{55} = 34$; $55 - 34 = 21$; $34 - 21 = 13$; and so on.
7. **C** Again, squares are involved in a series. This time, each number in the series is the square of a number, -1. Starting with 4 (which is the square of 2) $- 1 = 3$; 9 (square of 3) $- 1 = 8$; and so on.
8. **B** Unless you have seen one of this type of series before, you would find it most difficult. A *double* operation ($-2, \times 2$) is performed to arrive at each number. Starting with the number 5 we have $5 - 2 \times 2 = \underline{6}$; $6 - 2 \times 2 = \underline{8}$; $8 - 2 \times 2 = \underline{12}$ and so on.

Drills pages 193 to 194

1. **32**	7. **35**	13. **82**	19. **52**	25. **58**	31. **9**	37. **8**	43. **78**	49. **21**	55. **30**
2. **21**	8. **41**	14. **104**	20. **27**	26. **21**	32. **32**	38. **56**	44. **10**	50. **36**	56. **38**
3. **32**	9. **87**	15. **15**	21. **33**	27. **43**	33. **7**	39. **57**	45. **6**	51. **16**	57. **30**
4. **64**	10. **96**	16. **49**	22. **57**	28. **25**	34. **31**	40. **36**	46. **56**	52. **50**	58. **3**
5. **60**	11. **38**	17. **69**	23. **21**	29. **20**	35. **40**	41. **3**	47. **64**	53. **18**	59. **8**
6. **27**	12. **14**	18. **21**	24. **42**	30. **44**	36. **19**	42. **33**	48. **34**	54. **70**	60. **19**

Chapter 7

Following Oral Directions—How to Improve Your Score

NATURE OF THE TEST

This may seem like an easy test. After all, everyone has had to listen to someone giving orders, instructions, or advice. Whether your spouse, your boss, or your doctor does the talking, each of them expects you to be able to listen. Most probably *hear*, but how good are people at *listening?* Do you always understand what others tell you, and are you willing to take the actions they propose? On this test you had better prepare yourself to do both.

Other demands are made upon you in this test. As you've probably discovered after doing the sample questions in Chapter 1 and the Diagnostic Practice Test, the test instructions themselves may be difficult to follow at first. Ninety percent of students reported they had a problem concerning *where* to mark their answers because the questions and answers do not follow each other in the normal order. If you don't understand these points *exactly*, you are a "dead duck" on this exam.

On top of all this, you will find yourself in a highly competitive situation when you take the new Postal Service examination. You want the job, and you must score high to get it. This means that you have to overcome a certain amount of natural nervousness and tension.

Therefore it's important, just as for every other part of the test, that you learn every possible technique to achieve your maximum performance.

TEST STRATEGY

Almost everything about Part D of the test is different from the other parts. The test strategies and techniques discussed below take these differences into account.

Sit Close to the Examiner

Every word the examiner says is important. You will not be able to follow the directions unless you can hear them. Therefore, if you have a hearing problem, come early and request a seat close to the examiner or a loudspeaker.

Guess Cautiously

Ordinarily, guessing would be fine on a test like this. You are not penalized for wrong answers (as you are in Address Checking). If you don't make *any* choice, you earn nothing for that question. Therefore you have a point to gain and nothing to lose by guessing, *provided you observe one very important precaution. You must not end up with more than one letter space darkened for each number on your answer sheet.* If you do, you will lose all credit for your answers on that number. (At the time of your test, check this point with the oral and written instructions given by the test examiner.)

Go for 100 Percent

The standards for a "good" mark are very high (see guidelines for Part D on page 62). Strive for perfection in the way you listen and carry out the directions. The examiner will speak at a normal pace, and you need not feel time conscious or rushed. You will not have to sacrifice accuracy for speed. Your strategy is simple: you know you can make a perfect score, so go for it!

TECHNIQUES FOR INCREASING YOUR ABILITY TO FOLLOW ORAL DIRECTIONS

Become a Good Listener

Becoming a good listener is the most important part of your test preparation. It also happens to be one of the most useful skills you can acquire, since it affects every area of your life—how well you learn new things on the job or in school, how adept you are in dealing with others, how well you carry on your affairs in business, how much you get out of a play, TV program, or movie, and so on. Whole books have been written on the subject, but for your purposes you will consider some basic highlights, as they relate to this exam.

CULTIVATE AN ACCEPTING ATTITUDE.
It is important to understand that no one is trying to trick you. You need to feel confident about accepting the directions the examiner gives you without delay or hesitation. The test is fair, even though some of the directions you receive will be unfamiliar and even seem silly. For example, on the Diagnostic Practice Test the directions for line 17 began, "If the number in the left-hand circle is smaller than the number in the right-hand circle, add 2 to the number in the left-hand circle, and change the number in that circle to this number. Then write B as in *baker* next to the new number. Otherwise . . . ." Whoever gets directions like that? Certainly mail handlers on the job don't. The purpose of this test is to assess your ability and willingness to follow directions *exactly;* it is not a test of your judgment. Therefore, for the purposes of this test, make believe you're a soldier or a robot. Listen with an open mind. Do whatever you're told.

FREE YOURSELF FROM ALL PHYSICAL AND MENTAL TENSION.
Get yourself into the most relaxed and receptive state possible. You want to be calm, yet alert. If you know any effective relaxation or meditation techniques, use them. (See page 210 for a sample exercise.) Sometimes, merely stretching, taking a few slow, deep breaths, or closing your eyes for a few moments will do the trick. Make sure you work on the sample questions the examiner will give preceding the actual test. They will help you get into the proper mood.

AVOID ANY PHYSICAL DISTRACTIONS.
Wear comfortable clothing. Eat an adequate meal before you leave home so that you are not hungry or thirsty during the test.

Respond Properly

REMEMBER THAT EVERY NEW SET OF DIRECTIONS BEGINS WITH THE SAME WORDS, "LOOK AT THE LINE . . . ," OR A SLIGHT VARIATION.
The *way you look* at the line can help you later on. For example, on the Diagnostic Practice Test the instructions for line 15 began, "Look at the boxes and words in line 15 . . . ." The examiner then paused slightly and continued, "Write the second letter of the first word in the third box . . . ."

2___	31__	29__	ABLE	EASY	DESK

Listeners who had *looked properly* at line 15 during the pause would at least have picked up a picture of three boxes, each containing a number, followed by three short words. They would have been able to go directly to the word *able*, pick out the letter *B*, and place it next to 29, more quickly and smoothly than those who didn't look at line 15 in the *right* way.

Looking properly means more than an idle glance. It means getting an overall view of the *key* elements on a line and their positions relative to one another. In the example, listeners who had looked properly at line 15 knew immediately where the *first word* and the *third box* were. They didn't have to orient themselves as the instructions were being given. When you look at a line, therefore, try to take in as many of the following aspects as you can:

What the items are—circles, boxes, letters, numbers, crosses, and so on.

What differences in size exist—are some items smaller than others?

You probably will not be able to pick up any more details, but if you have the time, focus on characteristics such as these: the largest item, the smallest, how many of each, and their relative positions.

ACTIVELY RESPOND TO THE DIRECTIONS AS THEY ARE GIVEN.
Use the directions for line 13 of the Diagnostic Practice Test as an example. The examiner read, "In the second circle [you should immediately put your finger on the second circle], write the answer to this question: Which of the following numbers is smallest: 32, 11, 22, 31, 16?" As these numbers were read, you could (unless otherwise directed) be jotting them down in the margin of your worksheet. Why commit them to memory?

Here is another example, taken from line 5. While the examiner was reading, "The truck with the highest number is to be loaded first," you should be placing your finger on the last box, which contains the number 18.

WATCH OUT FOR THE TWO-PART, "IF . . . OTHERWISE" TYPE OF QUESTION.
In the preceding item, it was suggested that you respond actively. That doesn't mean you should stop listening and anticipate the answer. For this type of question many test takers make the error of selecting an answer *before* they've heard the *entire* question. The directions for line 14 of the Diagnostic Practice Test will illustrate.

"Look at line 14 on your worksheet. There are two circles and two boxes of different sizes with numbers in them. If 2 is smaller than 4 and if 7 is less than 3, write A in the larger circle." *Many test takers stopped listening after hearing "4."* If they had kept listening, they would have heard ". . . *and* if 7 is less than 3 . . . ," a statement that is, of course, untrue. The key word is *and*, which means that *both* parts of the condition must be true. Otherwise the *entire* choice is wrong. Remember this principle for this test and for any other civil service multiple-choice test you take.

The correct action to take for line 14 is given after the word *Otherwise:* "write B as in *baker* in the smaller box." The correct answer is 20B.

KEEP PACE.

If you miss part of the instructions for a line, continue listening to the remainder anyhow. The question may have several parts, some of which you may still be able to answer based on what you did pick up. The most important thing is to keep pace with the examiner as he/she continues to read the subsequent directions. Do not dwell on what you have missed.

Mark Your Answer in the Right Place

Previously, it was mentioned that many test takers became confused about where to enter their answers. This problem arises because, on most exams, you are directed to enter the answers to questions 1, 2, and so on, in spaces or boxes, or on lines, on an answer sheet, that are correspondingly marked Answer 1, Answer 2, and so on. For example, on the Address Checking part of this examination, you are told to darken the space for your answer, A or D, for question 1 on the line marked 1 on the answer sheet, and similarly for the answers to questions 2, 3, and so on.

Not so on this test. Do not try to match up questions and answers in that way. The Following Oral Directions part uses a system whereby you are given a worksheet or question booklet and a separate answer sheet. The lines on the worksheet are called line 1, line 2, and so on, or just 1, 2, and so on. The questions are *based* on the lines, but the *answer numbers* do not necessarily correspond to the *line numbers.* For example, on the Diagnostic Practice Test, the directions for line 1 were to draw a line under the fourth number on the line. That number was 19. You were then told to find the same number (19) on your answer sheet and darken space A. The final result, 19A, on your answer sheet bears no relationship to the fact that it is the answer to the first question. Unfortunately, many test takers darken space A on line 1 of their answer sheet because this line corresponds numerically to the first question they answer.

Another new feature you may expect is to have two, three, or even more questions based on a single line. Line 4 of the Diagnostic Test illustrates this. You were directed to place a B in the circle for the sack holding the largest number of packages. That sack contained a 27. Then you were told to darken your answer sheet space for the number-letter combination in that circle, which, of course, was 27B. Later, you were told to look at line 4 again, and this time to put an E in the circle for the sack with the smallest number of packages. The resulting number-letter combination was 16E on your answer sheet.

Be prepared, therefore, to skip around on your answer sheet, which may contain anywhere from 32 to 88 spaces. *Do not* forget, however, that, when you have entered all your answers, you should not have more than *one* space darkened for any *one* line on the answer sheet.

ADDITIONAL TIPS AND TECHNIQUES

Various questions from the Diagnostic Practice Test will illustrate some more helpful ideas.

Count From Left to Right

When you are told to "draw a line under the fourth number on the line" (see directions for line 1), you are to begin counting from the *left end of the line:*

13 23 2 19 6

Starting with the number 13, proceed until you reach the count of four. That brings you to the correct number, 19. If you had started counting from the right side of the line, you would have ended at 23, which is absolutely wrong.

Many questions on the test required you to count off a certain number of numbers, letters, circles, boxes, and so on, in the same way. Others asked you to select the *first* or the *last* item on a line. The rule is the same—begin counting from the left. (The only exception would occur if the test examiner specifically directed you to proceed from the right side. This can happen. That's why it is so important for you to really listen!)

Persons with an English-speaking background find it natural to read from left to right. Other test candidates, such as those speaking the Hebrew language, may be used to reading from right to left. The latter group needs to be particularly careful on this type of question.

Watch Out for the "More Than and Less Than" Direction

This type of direction seems to appear at least once or twice on each of these examinations. Many test takers have trouble with it. Lines 9 and 10 of the Diagnostic Practice Test can be used to show the proper way of handling these directions.

The directions for line 9 were as follows: "Draw a line under every number that is more than 20 but less than 30."

17 23 11 18 20 32 25 10 9

You should have underlined only numbers 23 and 25. Many test takers get this question wrong because they underline number 20 as well. They violate the directions, which specifically state "*more* than 20." The rule for this kind of question is simple: exclude whatever numbers are given as *limits.*

For line 10 you were directed to "Draw a line under every number that is more than 5 but less than 15."

16 30 13 25 10 14 23 26 19

Following the rule above, you would exclude 5 and 15 (neither of which appeared, anyhow) and underline only numbers 13, 10, and 14.

Screen Out "Extra" Information

Line 5 of the Diagnostic Practice Test contained superfluous information. The fact that the four boxes are trucks for carrying mail is not needed to answer the question. The boxes might as well have been crates containing herrings. Harm is done only if you let the extra information distract you. Remember: good listening includes the skill to screen out irrelevant materials and select what is really important.

Learn to Handle the Complex, Multiple-Part Direction

Line 17 of the Diagnostic Practice Test is different because its directions require you to do several things in less time than most of the other lines do. There is no need to feel rushed, however; this line seems more difficult than it really is, particularly if you haven't practiced as yet.

Here is a breakdown of the directions to show what you should be doing as the examiner is reading. Additionally, it will help you review some of the techniques you've already covered.

Examiner	*You*
"Look at line 17 . . ."	*Really look!* Notice two circles and two boxes of different size.
"If . . ."	*Go on alert!* A yes or no decision is coming.
"the number in the left-hand circle is smaller than the number in the right-hand circle . . ."	*Make an instant comparison:* 22 versus 28. The *decision* is yes (place one finger on each circle if you wish).
"add 2 to the number in the left-hand circle . . ."	*Mentally add* 22 + 2 = 24.
"change the number in that circle to this number."	*Change:* (~~22~~— 24)
"Then write B as in *baker* next to the new number."	*Write:* (~~22~~— 24B)

Some Key Words to Listen For

all	every	none
and	first	only
but	if	otherwise
different	last	same
each	less	

The words above frequently are heard in this exam. Any one of them can radically change what the correct answer should be. Stay on the alert! (See the Appendix, Checklist 1, page 438, for additional important words.)

TWO IMPORTANT CHECKLISTS

In order to follow the directions for any line, you must be prepared in three ways. First, you must *understand the meanings* of all the words you hear. Second, you have to be able to *perform the actions* called for. Finally, you should *possess certain general knowledge*, such as the number of items that make up a dozen. You should be prepared in these three ways so well that you can respond to the directions without the slightest hesitation. There isn't time enough during the test to sit and wonder what the directions mean.

To help you on these three areas, three special checklists have been compiled, which appear on pages 438 to 439 in the Appendix. At the end of this chapter (page 217) there are suggestions for further practice.

EXERCISES FOR RELAXING, LOOKING, AND LISTENING

Relaxing

Undoubtedly, you have your own favorite way to relax. It may be reading a book, playing ball, watching TV, or playing cards. There is nothing wrong with any of these, except that you can't use them to relax yourself immediately before or during a test. The relaxation exercise described below can be done just about anytime, anywhere.

1. Sit comfortably in your seat. Rest your arms on a desk or table, and close your eyes.
2. Inhale slowly. As you do, count to yourself: "1, 2, 3, 4." At the count of 4, say to yourself a word or nonsense sound such as *peace, rest, calm, om.* Keep that word or sound in your mind as you gently exhale. The idea of counting and using the word or sound is to help your mind (and nervous system) free itself from all thoughts and the tensions they cause.
3. Relax the muscles in your face, neck, shoulders, and arms. As you breathe gently, *visualize* these muscles progressively relaxing. A good way to help the process is to run your fingertips down your face from time to time. You will actually feel the muscles soften and smooth out.
4. Don't concentrate or strain as you are doing this exercise. If a thought or a worry about the test or anything else enters your mind, just let it drift away. Let the breaths you take, and the counting, gently wash the thought away. Keep in mind a picture of your muscles relaxing and losing their tension. A feeling of peace will take its place.
5. Keep in mind that 2 to 5 minutes should be all you need to achieve the desired state of awareness. Experienced practitioners of this method report that they can put themselves into this relaxed state in 30 seconds to 1 minute. You *do not* want to get sleepy. Remember: the effect you are after is calm, yet alert consciousness.
6. If you believe that this relaxation approach can help you, start practicing it now. Doing it twice a day for about 20 minutes at a time is recommended.

Although the chief purpose of presenting this relaxation exercise has been to help you on the test, you should know that it can also help in other ways. Studies have shown that it can produce a wide range of benefits, including lowered blood pressure, control of heart rate, and improved academic performance.

Looking

Look and Respond

The following exercises are designed to make you more effective as a "looker." One of the techniques given earlier (see page 206) suggested that test takers take full advantage of the slight pause the examiner usually allows after saying, "Look at line. . . ."

It is recommended that you secure the help of a friend when you practice these exercises. You will get a better practice session, and find it more interesting as well. You can, however, work alone and still benefit.

DIRECTIONS

Look at the figures on pages 213 and 215. They show various symbols, shapes, numbers, letters, and words similar to the items that appear on Part D of the new Postal Service examination. Paste each sheet on a piece of cardboard or some other stiff and fairly durable material (e.g., a piece of light plastic or linoleum). Then cut the sheet along the dotted line, and you will have a "deck" of 54 cards for each figure set. Mark the back of each card with an arrow, ↑, to indicate the top edge.

IF YOU ARE PRACTICING ALONE

1. Place the "cards" face down on a table, and shuffle them by moving them about for a moment or two.
2. Then select two or three cards, and align them with the arrows facing upward. *Now, look away as you turn over each card.*
3. When all the cards are right side up, allow yourself 2 seconds to scan the line of cards.
4. Immediately thereafter, look away and copy on a piece of paper whatever you remember seeing on the cards. Remember: you want to see how much registered in your mind about the shape and position of each item and what, if anything, it contained.

IF YOU ARE PRACTICING WITH A FRIEND

1. Have your friend do all the shuffling and selection of cards. *Do not look on.*
2. Instruct your friend to say, when he/she has finished setting up a line of cards, "Now look at the line."
3. Begin scanning the line as soon as you hear your friend say "now," and continue for 2 seconds.
4. Then, without looking at the line, tell your friend as much as you remember about the items on the line.
5. Continue following whatever directions your friend gives you concerning the items on the line. Your friend may wish to make up the directions as he/she is looking at the line. It is better, however, if your friend prepares them ahead of time, just after setting up the line. The directions can be modeled after those in the diagnostic and practice tests. Most of the symbols in Figure Set I were purposely left blank so your friend can insert letters, numbers, or anything else he/she wishes to select as part of the instructions. With a little imagination and practice, your friend will easily be able to make up the directions. (See the example on the next page.)

Example

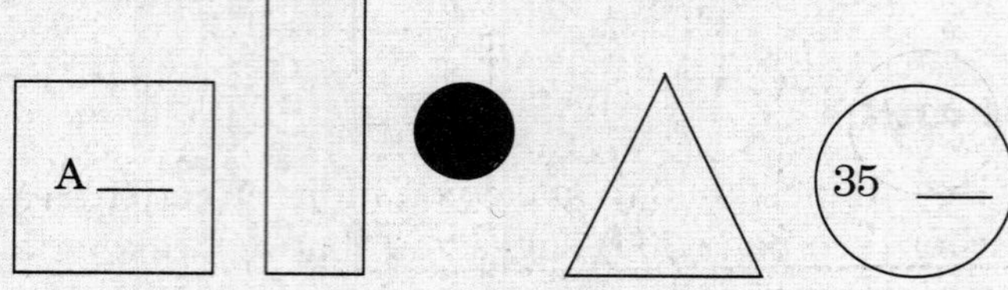

Directions: "Now look at the line. (Pause slightly.) There is a number in the circle at the right-hand end of the line. Subtract 4 from that number. (Pause slightly.) Place the new number on the line next to the letter in the box at the left end of the line. (Pause 2 seconds.) Now darken the space for the number-letter combination that is in the box you just wrote in." (Pause 5 seconds.) *Answer:* 35A

✂ Remove by cutting on dotted line.

16 ___			B ___		
39 ___			E ___		
43 ___			A ___		
18 ___			C ___		
75 ___			D ___		
66 ___					
	6 ___				
	3 ___				
	8 ___				

1	2	3	4	5	6
7	8	9	10	11	12
32	33	45	46	57	58
69	70	71	83	84	97
A	B	C	D	E	F
G	H	I	J	K	L
M	N	P	R	S	T
DESK	MILK	PEACH	STILL	SHOE	CAR
ELSE	READ	TABLE	STAIR	FIVE	NUT

✂ Remove by cutting on dotted line.

FURTHER SUGGESTIONS FOR PRACTICE

- As you keep practicing and improving, increase the number of items on a line. There can be as many as ten separate items on a line, although the average line should have no more than five or six. Remember that a line *may* contain only one or two items.
- If you discover that you have difficulty in following certain kinds of directions, such as those involving counting or arithmetic, ask your friend to include more of these types of directions.
- Although most of the time you can write your answers on a piece of scrap paper, occasionally practice entering answers the way you will on the actual test. For this purpose, use the answer sheets provided on page 219. Make photocopies if you need more. (The answer sheet you will be given on the actual test may contain only 32 or as many as 88 lines. Answer sheets with 88 lines have been supplied here to allow you to practice making entries in widely separated spaces.)
- Note that literally thousands of lines and directions can be constructed from the 108 cards that have been supplied. Use them to supplement the practice tests and to drill on areas of weakness. The "deck" of cards may be coated with a thin layer of spray-on lacquer or shellac. Once coated, they can be written on and erased many times without damaging the surface.

Listening

You can practice listening skills every day of your life. Whenever and wherever you hear human speech, there is the opportunity to practice. A brief summary of some important ideas on listening is given below. Look it over before you take each practice test. You might want to read it to yourself before you do a relaxation exercise. Incorporate its ideas into the calm and alert state of mind you are seeking to achieve.

Acceptance:

- This is a fair, not a trick, test.
- My job is to do exactly what I'm told.
- I can easily make a perfect score.

Attention:

- After the test has begun, nothing in the world exists except the examiner's voice and the worksheet.
- Outside noises or distractions and internal thoughts cannot interfere. I will let them flow through me and drift away.

Reaction:

- My mind will remain free, calm, and alert.
- I will not anticipate the examiner's words.
- I will use my fingers and my eyes to respond to the directions as I hear them.

Answer Sheets for Practice Exercises on Looking

✂ Remove by cutting on dotted line.

Exercise 1

1 ⒶⒷⒸⒹⒺ	19 ⒶⒷⒸⒹⒺ	37 ⒶⒷⒸⒹⒺ	55 ⒶⒷⒸⒹⒺ	73 ⒶⒷⒸⒹⒺ
2 ⒶⒷⒸⒹⒺ	20 ⒶⒷⒸⒹⒺ	38 ⒶⒷⒸⒹⒺ	56 ⒶⒷⒸⒹⒺ	74 ⒶⒷⒸⒹⒺ
3 ⒶⒷⒸⒹⒺ	21 ⒶⒷⒸⒹⒺ	39 ⒶⒷⒸⒹⒺ	57 ⒶⒷⒸⒹⒺ	75 ⒶⒷⒸⒹⒺ
4 ⒶⒷⒸⒹⒺ	22 ⒶⒷⒸⒹⒺ	40 ⒶⒷⒸⒹⒺ	58 ⒶⒷⒸⒹⒺ	76 ⒶⒷⒸⒹⒺ
5 ⒶⒷⒸⒹⒺ	23 ⒶⒷⒸⒹⒺ	41 ⒶⒷⒸⒹⒺ	59 ⒶⒷⒸⒹⒺ	77 ⒶⒷⒸⒹⒺ
6 ⒶⒷⒸⒹⒺ	24 ⒶⒷⒸⒹⒺ	42 ⒶⒷⒸⒹⒺ	60 ⒶⒷⒸⒹⒺ	78 ⒶⒷⒸⒹⒺ
7 ⒶⒷⒸⒹⒺ	25 ⒶⒷⒸⒹⒺ	43 ⒶⒷⒸⒹⒺ	61 ⒶⒷⒸⒹⒺ	79 ⒶⒷⒸⒹⒺ
8 ⒶⒷⒸⒹⒺ	26 ⒶⒷⒸⒹⒺ	44 ⒶⒷⒸⒹⒺ	62 ⒶⒷⒸⒹⒺ	80 ⒶⒷⒸⒹⒺ
9 ⒶⒷⒸⒹⒺ	27 ⒶⒷⒸⒹⒺ	45 ⒶⒷⒸⒹⒺ	63 ⒶⒷⒸⒹⒺ	81 ⒶⒷⒸⒹⒺ
10 ⒶⒷⒸⒹⒺ	28 ⒶⒷⒸⒹⒺ	46 ⒶⒷⒸⒹⒺ	64 ⒶⒷⒸⒹⒺ	82 ⒶⒷⒸⒹⒺ
11 ⒶⒷⒸⒹⒺ	29 ⒶⒷⒸⒹⒺ	47 ⒶⒷⒸⒹⒺ	65 ⒶⒷⒸⒹⒺ	83 ⒶⒷⒸⒹⒺ
12 ⒶⒷⒸⒹⒺ	30 ⒶⒷⒸⒹⒺ	48 ⒶⒷⒸⒹⒺ	66 ⒶⒷⒸⒹⒺ	84 ⒶⒷⒸⒹⒺ
13 ⒶⒷⒸⒹⒺ	31 ⒶⒷⒸⒹⒺ	49 ⒶⒷⒸⒹⒺ	67 ⒶⒷⒸⒹⒺ	85 ⒶⒷⒸⒹⒺ
14 ⒶⒷⒸⒹⒺ	32 ⒶⒷⒸⒹⒺ	50 ⒶⒷⒸⒹⒺ	68 ⒶⒷⒸⒹⒺ	86 ⒶⒷⒸⒹⒺ
15 ⒶⒷⒸⒹⒺ	33 ⒶⒷⒸⒹⒺ	51 ⒶⒷⒸⒹⒺ	69 ⒶⒷⒸⒹⒺ	87 ⒶⒷⒸⒹⒺ
16 ⒶⒷⒸⒹⒺ	34 ⒶⒷⒸⒹⒺ	52 ⒶⒷⒸⒹⒺ	70 ⒶⒷⒸⒹⒺ	88 ⒶⒷⒸⒹⒺ
17 ⒶⒷⒸⒹⒺ	35 ⒶⒷⒸⒹⒺ	53 ⒶⒷⒸⒹⒺ	71 ⒶⒷⒸⒹⒺ	
18 ⒶⒷⒸⒹⒺ	36 ⒶⒷⒸⒹⒺ	54 ⒶⒷⒸⒹⒺ	72 ⒶⒷⒸⒹⒺ	

Exercise 2

1 ⒶⒷⒸⒹⒺ	19 ⒶⒷⒸⒹⒺ	37 ⒶⒷⒸⒹⒺ	55 ⒶⒷⒸⒹⒺ	73 ⒶⒷⒸⒹⒺ
2 ⒶⒷⒸⒹⒺ	20 ⒶⒷⒸⒹⒺ	38 ⒶⒷⒸⒹⒺ	56 ⒶⒷⒸⒹⒺ	74 ⒶⒷⒸⒹⒺ
3 ⒶⒷⒸⒹⒺ	21 ⒶⒷⒸⒹⒺ	39 ⒶⒷⒸⒹⒺ	57 ⒶⒷⒸⒹⒺ	75 ⒶⒷⒸⒹⒺ
4 ⒶⒷⒸⒹⒺ	22 ⒶⒷⒸⒹⒺ	40 ⒶⒷⒸⒹⒺ	58 ⒶⒷⒸⒹⒺ	76 ⒶⒷⒸⒹⒺ
5 ⒶⒷⒸⒹⒺ	23 ⒶⒷⒸⒹⒺ	41 ⒶⒷⒸⒹⒺ	59 ⒶⒷⒸⒹⒺ	77 ⒶⒷⒸⒹⒺ
6 ⒶⒷⒸⒹⒺ	24 ⒶⒷⒸⒹⒺ	42 ⒶⒷⒸⒹⒺ	60 ⒶⒷⒸⒹⒺ	78 ⒶⒷⒸⒹⒺ
7 ⒶⒷⒸⒹⒺ	25 ⒶⒷⒸⒹⒺ	43 ⒶⒷⒸⒹⒺ	61 ⒶⒷⒸⒹⒺ	79 ⒶⒷⒸⒹⒺ
8 ⒶⒷⒸⒹⒺ	26 ⒶⒷⒸⒹⒺ	44 ⒶⒷⒸⒹⒺ	62 ⒶⒷⒸⒹⒺ	80 ⒶⒷⒸⒹⒺ
9 ⒶⒷⒸⒹⒺ	27 ⒶⒷⒸⒹⒺ	45 ⒶⒷⒸⒹⒺ	63 ⒶⒷⒸⒹⒺ	81 ⒶⒷⒸⒹⒺ
10 ⒶⒷⒸⒹⒺ	28 ⒶⒷⒸⒹⒺ	46 ⒶⒷⒸⒹⒺ	64 ⒶⒷⒸⒹⒺ	82 ⒶⒷⒸⒹⒺ
11 ⒶⒷⒸⒹⒺ	29 ⒶⒷⒸⒹⒺ	47 ⒶⒷⒸⒹⒺ	65 ⒶⒷⒸⒹⒺ	83 ⒶⒷⒸⒹⒺ
12 ⒶⒷⒸⒹⒺ	30 ⒶⒷⒸⒹⒺ	48 ⒶⒷⒸⒹⒺ	66 ⒶⒷⒸⒹⒺ	84 ⒶⒷⒸⒹⒺ
13 ⒶⒷⒸⒹⒺ	31 ⒶⒷⒸⒹⒺ	49 ⒶⒷⒸⒹⒺ	67 ⒶⒷⒸⒹⒺ	85 ⒶⒷⒸⒹⒺ
14 ⒶⒷⒸⒹⒺ	32 ⒶⒷⒸⒹⒺ	50 ⒶⒷⒸⒹⒺ	68 ⒶⒷⒸⒹⒺ	86 ⒶⒷⒸⒹⒺ
15 ⒶⒷⒸⒹⒺ	33 ⒶⒷⒸⒹⒺ	51 ⒶⒷⒸⒹⒺ	69 ⒶⒷⒸⒹⒺ	87 ⒶⒷⒸⒹⒺ
16 ⒶⒷⒸⒹⒺ	34 ⒶⒷⒸⒹⒺ	52 ⒶⒷⒸⒹⒺ	70 ⒶⒷⒸⒹⒺ	88 ⒶⒷⒸⒹⒺ
17 ⒶⒷⒸⒹⒺ	35 ⒶⒷⒸⒹⒺ	53 ⒶⒷⒸⒹⒺ	71 ⒶⒷⒸⒹⒺ	
18 ⒶⒷⒸⒹⒺ	36 ⒶⒷⒸⒹⒺ	54 ⒶⒷⒸⒹⒺ	72 ⒶⒷⒸⒹⒺ	

Chapter 8

Putting It All Together

Before you take the practice tests in Chapters 9 through 14, it is suggested that you read this brief chapter. It summarizes key information on the four parts of the Test Battery 460/470 that you can review quickly and conveniently. Examine it periodically, especially a day or two before you take the actual examination. Read it now, before you take Practice Test 1.

A REVIEW OF TEST STRATEGIES AND TECHNIQUES

Address Checking

1. *Work out the optimum balance for you.* Find *your* best combination of speed and accuracy.
2. *Don't go for 100 percent.* Percentages do not count. It is okay to make some errors. Your final score—number right minus number wrong—is what counts.
3. *Do not guess wildly.* Your score will suffer in the long run.
4. *Use your hands properly.* Do not lose time or your place because of wasted motions.
5. *Prepare the point of your pencil.* Shape it to a flat, oval form.
6. *Make your mark properly.* Make it neat, dark, and *fast*—but *don't* seek perfection.
7. *Do not read for comprehension.* Your job is to perceive differences between addresses, not to study and interpret them.
8. *Do not sound out addresses.* This will waste time. No one is listening, anyway.
9. *Do not regress.* Don't reread addresses. Make your choice, and go on to the next question.
10. *Widen your eye span.* If you see more at a glance, your checking speed will increase. Never read word for word.
11. *Work with rhythm.* Maintain a smooth, even pace. You will get more done.
12. *Practice, practice, practice.*

Memory for Addresses—Final Study Plans

Up until now, the discussion on memory has separated questions on direct name addresses from questions on numbered addresses. This was done to help you become thoroughly familiar with the special techniques for each and with the techniques common to both. Now, you can put together everything you have learned so that you will achieve the highest possible score on the real test, where you must handle both direct name and numbered addresses. Consider these factors:

1. *How to divide your study time between the direct and numbered addresses on Part B?* If you, like most people, find it easier to memorize the direct name addresses, it is suggested that you start out by allocating one third of your study time (about 5 minutes) to the direct names, and two thirds of your study time (about 9 minutes) to the numbers. (It is estimated that a *total* of 14 minutes may be used for studying.)

   During the exam, if there should be *any other brief intervals between* the various exercises on Part B, use this extra time to study. Even if you don't have the boxes before you, use the time to review your imagery and associations, especially for the addresses you were weak on. See the boxes in your mind's eye, once more. Keep the memories alive.

2. *What method to use for memorization?* Use any of the memorization methods, or combination of methods, that work best for you. See the list of these methods on pages 223 to 224 for a quick review. As you do more of the practice tests, you will be in a good position to make a final decision on how to proceed on the real test. **Make this decision by the time you complete all of the practice tests in this book and, definitely, *before* you take the actual exam.** For example, if you have been getting good scores on the practice tests by the use of reduction coding, stick to it. For memorizing numbers, you may be doing very well remembering number associations. Others will have found they are good at chunking and should immediately use that technique on the test.

3. *How much to go for?* After sufficient practice, you will know more or less what your memory achievement level is. For example, you will know whether or not you can remember five or six chunks of numbers. If you find that you have no problem with six, then you have to decide whether to concentrate on those six and use visualization to remember Box E, *or* to go for all seven chunks. Keep in mind that a *perfect* score is attainable.

4. *How to make the best use of test time?* It is recommended that you take each question in order, and answer each to the best of your ability. Some people feel that they might do better on Part B by answering all of the direct names first, and then going back to work on the numbers. Do this *only* if you cannot remember any numbers at all. This is extremely unlikely. Even if you can remember only a few numbered addresses, answer every question in turn, guessing when you must. Chapters 3 and 4 contain detailed discussions about guessing on each part of the examination.

   The timing and directions for taking Practice Tests 1 through 6 are exactly the same as those for the Diagnostic Practice Test. These directions are reprinted at the beginning of each part of each test.

5. *How much time will I actually have for memorization?* As noted previously for the new exam, the time *designated* for study is 8 minutes. Test candidates who fol-

low the given suggestions and take all the time *available* for study, can increase that to 14 minutes and more. For example: Use the 3 minutes or so allotted to the pretest sample to study the addresses. In the past, they were identical to the boxes on the real test. Work on the direct (name) addresses only. If the direct names for the real test turn out to differ, nothing has been lost. But if they *are* the same, you will have gained extra time to study the more difficult numbered addresses—that is a tremendous advantage! Do not study the numbered addresses in the pre-test sample. That could lead to confusion later on when you take the real exam.

Memory Checklists

Direct Addresses

1. *Use association and imagery.* Attach a vivid, colorful, or active image to the address, and it comes alive and is easier to remember—for example, Grand with Canyon, Crescent with Moon, Carpenter with Swinging a Hammer.

2. *Make up a new word.* Start it with the letter of a box. Add whatever parts of the two address names in that box are needed to give the new "word" a distinctive sound or look. Remember ACERNA (see page 116).

3. *Use loci.* Decide on a familiar setting and imagine each of the five boxes—A, B, C, D, and E—to be parts of that scene. For example, the setting could be your office, with Box A standing for your desk; Box B, for the filing cabinet; Box C for the window; and so on. Assume that, on a test the actual address names in Box A were Gruyer and French. The picture you could come up with could show a big, smelly piece of cheese (Gruyer) between two slices of bread (French) lying on top of your desk—Box A.

4. *Apply reduction coding.* NATO is easier to remember than *North Atlantic Treaty Organization.* The acronyms CEO, FBI, and UNICEF are other examples of how lengthy words and phrases may be easily remembered by using their initials to form a new word. On the test you can use this principle to remember each box individually with its two direct name addresses. For example, if Box B has Newton and Fresco, reduce this to BNF. The same idea is employed if you take five names on a line that includes all the boxes.

   Check the sound. The new word may have a distinctive sound, like "BUZ" or "CRUMP."

   Check for meaning. The new word may mean something, as does the one formed by the initials of these five address names:

   GANTT RAMAPO OTIS WEST SHORE

   Make up a story/slogan. Use the initials to make up a story or slogan. For example, if the five letters are TRMAB you could think of The Red Monkey Ate Bananas. The three initials above, BNF, might be used for the slogan "broiled, not fried."

5. *Eliminate the last box.* If you have memorized all the address names in four out of the five boxes, you know automatically that an unfamiliar address belongs in the fifth box.

6. *Guess.* You have more to gain than to lose. Enter an answer for every question.

7. *Practice, practice, practice.*

Numbered Addresses

(All references are to the addresses on page 136.)

1. *Reduce numbers.* 2100–2799 Mall can be replaced by 21.
2. *Chunking numbers.* Combine two adjoining (reduced) numbers such as 21 in box A and 39 in Box B to get 2139. Do the same for the numbers in Box C and D.
3. *Visualize* the chunks on the *same horizontal street line;* e.g., Mall. Do the same for all three lines. *Use your mental screen.*
4. *If you are able*—remember one 6-digit chunk for the reduced numbers in Box E. Otherwise, *visualize* Box E with its numbers and street name, separately.
5. *Make associations to the box letters:* use stories, images, sounds, and so on.
6. *Prepare a number-word chart.* Use the *number tree* and associations of all kinds to build your *personal* list of words to associate with each number from 10 through 99.
7. *Dealing with Duplicate Numbers*
   a. Review the five-step procedure on page 158. This is the key technique to use for combining the *street number* with the *street name* with the *box letter.*
   b. *Use every tool*—images, meanings, sounds, initials, appearances, placement, and so on *in any way that works for you.*
8. *Use your imagination.* This is the magic cement that helps to combine all your associations as need be. You can develop it by practicing.

Number Series

1. *Find the Pattern.* There is *always* a definite rule to be found in every number series question. It must account for every number. If it doesn't, look for a new rule.
2. *Use a Loop Diagram*—a most useful tool for identifying and applying the rule.
   a. The loops are connections that ensure order, consistency, and completeness.
   b. The guide numbers show the amount of change.
   c. The signs show the kind of change—addition, subtraction, multiplication, and so on.
   d. *The answer*—make sure your numbers are in the correct order.
3. *Softly chant the numbers to yourself.* Sometimes this leads directly to the next two numbers.
4. *Types of Number Series.* The most common types are a) addition/subtraction, b) alternating series, c) cycles, repetitions, and combinations, and d) multiplication/division.
5. *Check It Out.* You will know it when you've found the rule. If you're not sure, you can always check it.

FOLLOWING ORAL DIRECTIONS

1. *Go for 100 percent.* The standard for a good mark on this test is very high. There is no reason why you cannot achieve a perfect score.
2. *Guess intelligently.* If you must, guess rather than miss a question altogether. Just make sure that you do not end up with two answers on the same line.
3. *Sit where you can easily hear the examiner's voice.*
4. *Become a good listener.* Accept the examiner's directions exactly as heard. Free yourself of physical and mental tension. Avoid physical distractions like uncomfortable clothing and hunger pangs.
5. *Look properly.* Get an overall view of *what kind* of items are on a line and any *differences* in size or shape among them.
6. *Actively respond.* Direct your eyes and your fingers to the proper items as they are mentioned.
7. *Keep pace.* If you should miss *part* of the instructions, keep listening to the *remainder.* You may be able to score on another part of the question.
8. *Watch out for the two-part "if . . . otherwise" question.* Don't anticipate the answer.
9. *Mark your answers in the spaces specified by the directions.* Remember that the lines on the worksheet, and the questions based on them, do *not* necessarily correspond to the numbered lines on the answer sheet.
10. Be alert to "key" words (see the lists on pages 209 and 438 to 439).
11. *Periodically, review pages 207 to 208 for some additional tips and techniques.*

Chec
vith

TEST YOURSELF

In Chapters 9 through 14 there are six increasingly difficult complete practice tests. Each chapter also contains an answer key and information on how to compute your scores, record your personal progress, and diagnose your particular weak areas.*

The 460/470 Test Battery has four parts: Part A—Address Checking, with 95 questions; Part B—Memory for Addresses, with 88 questions; Part C—Number Series, with 24 questions; and Part D—Following Oral Directions, with 30 questions.

Suggestions for the Practice Sessions

- When you sit down to take these practice tests, select a time and place where there will be no interruptions or distractions.
- Work on a clean, well-lighted desk or table.
- Time yourself or get a friend to help you. (See page 31.)
- Tear out the appropriate answer sheet, and position it in accordance with the sketch on page 72.

---

* Before doing any of the practice tests, you may wish to make copies of the answer sheets that are at the beginning of each test. That way you will be able to retake these tests for additional practice as you see fit.

Answer Sheet—Practice Test 1

Part A—Address Checking

1 ⒶⒹ
2 ⒶⒹ
3 ⒶⒹ
4 ⒶⒹ
5 ⒶⒹ
6 ⒶⒹ
7 ⒶⒹ
8 ⒶⒹ
9 ⒶⒹ
10 ⒶⒹ
11 ⒶⒹ
12 ⒶⒹ
13 ⒶⒹ
14 ⒶⒹ
15 ⒶⒹ
16 ⒶⒹ
17 ⒶⒹ
18 ⒶⒹ
19 ⒶⒹ
20 ⒶⒹ
21 ⒶⒹ
22 ⒶⒹ
23 ⒶⒹ
24 ⒶⒹ
25 ⒶⒹ
26 ⒶⒹ
27 ⒶⒹ
28 ⒶⒹ
29 ⒶⒹ
30 ⒶⒹ
31 ⒶⒹ
32 ⒶⒹ
33 ⒶⒹ
34 ⒶⒹ
35 ⒶⒹ
36 ⒶⒹ
37 ⒶⒹ
38 ⒶⒹ
39 ⒶⒹ
40 ⒶⒹ
41 ⒶⒹ
42 ⒶⒹ
43 ⒶⒹ
44 ⒶⒹ
45 ⒶⒹ
46 ⒶⒹ
47 ⒶⒹ
48 ⒶⒹ
49 ⒶⒹ
50 ⒶⒹ
51 ⒶⒹ
52 ⒶⒹ
53 ⒶⒹ
54 ⒶⒹ
55 ⒶⒹ
56 ⒶⒹ
57 ⒶⒹ
58 ⒶⒹ
59 ⒶⒹ
60 ⒶⒹ
61 ⒶⒹ
62 ⒶⒹ
63 ⒶⒹ
64 ⒶⒹ
65 ⒶⒹ
66 ⒶⒹ
67 ⒶⒹ
68 ⒶⒹ
69 ⒶⒹ
70 ⒶⒹ
71 ⒶⒹ
72 ⒶⒹ
73 ⒶⒹ
74 ⒶⒹ
75 ⒶⒹ
76 ⒶⒹ
77 ⒶⒹ
78 ⒶⒹ
79 ⒶⒹ
80 ⒶⒹ
81 ⒶⒹ
82 ⒶⒹ
83 ⒶⒹ
84 ⒶⒹ
85 ⒶⒹ
86 ⒶⒹ
87 ⒶⒹ
88 ⒶⒹ
89 ⒶⒹ
90 ⒶⒹ
91 ⒶⒹ
92 ⒶⒹ
93 ⒶⒹ
94 ⒶⒹ
95 ⒶⒹ

✂ Remove by cutting on dotted line.

Part B—Memory for Addresses—List 1

1 ⒶⒷⒸⒹⒺ	19 ⒶⒷⒸⒹⒺ	37 ⒶⒷⒸⒹⒺ	55 ⒶⒷⒸⒹⒺ	73 ⒶⒷⒸⒹⒺ
2 ⒶⒷⒸⒹⒺ	20 ⒶⒷⒸⒹⒺ	38 ⒶⒷⒸⒹⒺ	56 ⒶⒷⒸⒹⒺ	74 ⒶⒷⒸⒹⒺ
3 ⒶⒷⒸⒹⒺ	21 ⒶⒷⒸⒹⒺ	39 ⒶⒷⒸⒹⒺ	57 ⒶⒷⒸⒹⒺ	75 ⒶⒷⒸⒹⒺ
4 ⒶⒷⒸⒹⒺ	22 ⒶⒷⒸⒹⒺ	40 ⒶⒷⒸⒹⒺ	58 ⒶⒷⒸⒹⒺ	76 ⒶⒷⒸⒹⒺ
5 ⒶⒷⒸⒹⒺ	23 ⒶⒷⒸⒹⒺ	41 ⒶⒷⒸⒹⒺ	59 ⒶⒷⒸⒹⒺ	77 ⒶⒷⒸⒹⒺ
6 ⒶⒷⒸⒹⒺ	24 ⒶⒷⒸⒹⒺ	42 ⒶⒷⒸⒹⒺ	60 ⒶⒷⒸⒹⒺ	78 ⒶⒷⒸⒹⒺ
7 ⒶⒷⒸⒹⒺ	25 ⒶⒷⒸⒹⒺ	43 ⒶⒷⒸⒹⒺ	61 ⒶⒷⒸⒹⒺ	79 ⒶⒷⒸⒹⒺ
8 ⒶⒷⒸⒹⒺ	26 ⒶⒷⒸⒹⒺ	44 ⒶⒷⒸⒹⒺ	62 ⒶⒷⒸⒹⒺ	80 ⒶⒷⒸⒹⒺ
9 ⒶⒷⒸⒹⒺ	27 ⒶⒷⒸⒹⒺ	45 ⒶⒷⒸⒹⒺ	63 ⒶⒷⒸⒹⒺ	81 ⒶⒷⒸⒹⒺ
10 ⒶⒷⒸⒹⒺ	28 ⒶⒷⒸⒹⒺ	46 ⒶⒷⒸⒹⒺ	64 ⒶⒷⒸⒹⒺ	82 ⒶⒷⒸⒹⒺ
11 ⒶⒷⒸⒹⒺ	29 ⒶⒷⒸⒹⒺ	47 ⒶⒷⒸⒹⒺ	65 ⒶⒷⒸⒹⒺ	83 ⒶⒷⒸⒹⒺ
12 ⒶⒷⒸⒹⒺ	30 ⒶⒷⒸⒹⒺ	48 ⒶⒷⒸⒹⒺ	66 ⒶⒷⒸⒹⒺ	84 ⒶⒷⒸⒹⒺ
13 ⒶⒷⒸⒹⒺ	31 ⒶⒷⒸⒹⒺ	49 ⒶⒷⒸⒹⒺ	67 ⒶⒷⒸⒹⒺ	85 ⒶⒷⒸⒹⒺ
14 ⒶⒷⒸⒹⒺ	32 ⒶⒷⒸⒹⒺ	50 ⒶⒷⒸⒹⒺ	68 ⒶⒷⒸⒹⒺ	86 ⒶⒷⒸⒹⒺ
15 ⒶⒷⒸⒹⒺ	33 ⒶⒷⒸⒹⒺ	51 ⒶⒷⒸⒹⒺ	69 ⒶⒷⒸⒹⒺ	87 ⒶⒷⒸⒹⒺ
16 ⒶⒷⒸⒹⒺ	34 ⒶⒷⒸⒹⒺ	52 ⒶⒷⒸⒹⒺ	70 ⒶⒷⒸⒹⒺ	88 ⒶⒷⒸⒹⒺ
17 ⒶⒷⒸⒹⒺ	35 ⒶⒷⒸⒹⒺ	53 ⒶⒷⒸⒹⒺ	71 ⒶⒷⒸⒹⒺ	
18 ⒶⒷⒸⒹⒺ	36 ⒶⒷⒸⒹⒺ	54 ⒶⒷⒸⒹⒺ	72 ⒶⒷⒸⒹⒺ	

Part B—Memory for Addresses—List 2

1 ⒶⒷⒸⒹⒺ	19 ⒶⒷⒸⒹⒺ	37 ⒶⒷⒸⒹⒺ	55 ⒶⒷⒸⒹⒺ	73 ⒶⒷⒸⒹⒺ
2 ⒶⒷⒸⒹⒺ	20 ⒶⒷⒸⒹⒺ	38 ⒶⒷⒸⒹⒺ	56 ⒶⒷⒸⒹⒺ	74 ⒶⒷⒸⒹⒺ
3 ⒶⒷⒸⒹⒺ	21 ⒶⒷⒸⒹⒺ	39 ⒶⒷⒸⒹⒺ	57 ⒶⒷⒸⒹⒺ	75 ⒶⒷⒸⒹⒺ
4 ⒶⒷⒸⒹⒺ	22 ⒶⒷⒸⒹⒺ	40 ⒶⒷⒸⒹⒺ	58 ⒶⒷⒸⒹⒺ	76 ⒶⒷⒸⒹⒺ
5 ⒶⒷⒸⒹⒺ	23 ⒶⒷⒸⒹⒺ	41 ⒶⒷⒸⒹⒺ	59 ⒶⒷⒸⒹⒺ	77 ⒶⒷⒸⒹⒺ
6 ⒶⒷⒸⒹⒺ	24 ⒶⒷⒸⒹⒺ	42 ⒶⒷⒸⒹⒺ	60 ⒶⒷⒸⒹⒺ	78 ⒶⒷⒸⒹⒺ
7 ⒶⒷⒸⒹⒺ	25 ⒶⒷⒸⒹⒺ	43 ⒶⒷⒸⒹⒺ	61 ⒶⒷⒸⒹⒺ	79 ⒶⒷⒸⒹⒺ
8 ⒶⒷⒸⒹⒺ	26 ⒶⒷⒸⒹⒺ	44 ⒶⒷⒸⒹⒺ	62 ⒶⒷⒸⒹⒺ	80 ⒶⒷⒸⒹⒺ
9 ⒶⒷⒸⒹⒺ	27 ⒶⒷⒸⒹⒺ	45 ⒶⒷⒸⒹⒺ	63 ⒶⒷⒸⒹⒺ	81 ⒶⒷⒸⒹⒺ
10 ⒶⒷⒸⒹⒺ	28 ⒶⒷⒸⒹⒺ	46 ⒶⒷⒸⒹⒺ	64 ⒶⒷⒸⒹⒺ	82 ⒶⒷⒸⒹⒺ
11 ⒶⒷⒸⒹⒺ	29 ⒶⒷⒸⒹⒺ	47 ⒶⒷⒸⒹⒺ	65 ⒶⒷⒸⒹⒺ	83 ⒶⒷⒸⒹⒺ
12 ⒶⒷⒸⒹⒺ	30 ⒶⒷⒸⒹⒺ	48 ⒶⒷⒸⒹⒺ	66 ⒶⒷⒸⒹⒺ	84 ⒶⒷⒸⒹⒺ
13 ⒶⒷⒸⒹⒺ	31 ⒶⒷⒸⒹⒺ	49 ⒶⒷⒸⒹⒺ	67 ⒶⒷⒸⒹⒺ	85 ⒶⒷⒸⒹⒺ
14 ⒶⒷⒸⒹⒺ	32 ⒶⒷⒸⒹⒺ	50 ⒶⒷⒸⒹⒺ	68 ⒶⒷⒸⒹⒺ	86 ⒶⒷⒸⒹⒺ
15 ⒶⒷⒸⒹⒺ	33 ⒶⒷⒸⒹⒺ	51 ⒶⒷⒸⒹⒺ	69 ⒶⒷⒸⒹⒺ	87 ⒶⒷⒸⒹⒺ
16 ⒶⒷⒸⒹⒺ	34 ⒶⒷⒸⒹⒺ	52 ⒶⒷⒸⒹⒺ	70 ⒶⒷⒸⒹⒺ	88 ⒶⒷⒸⒹⒺ
17 ⒶⒷⒸⒹⒺ	35 ⒶⒷⒸⒹⒺ	53 ⒶⒷⒸⒹⒺ	71 ⒶⒷⒸⒹⒺ	
18 ⒶⒷⒸⒹⒺ	36 ⒶⒷⒸⒹⒺ	54 ⒶⒷⒸⒹⒺ	72 ⒶⒷⒸⒹⒺ	

Part B—Memory for Addresses—List 3

1 ⒶⒷⒸⒹⒺ	19 ⒶⒷⒸⒹⒺ	37 ⒶⒷⒸⒹⒺ	55 ⒶⒷⒸⒹⒺ	73 ⒶⒷⒸⒹⒺ
2 ⒶⒷⒸⒹⒺ	20 ⒶⒷⒸⒹⒺ	38 ⒶⒷⒸⒹⒺ	56 ⒶⒷⒸⒹⒺ	74 ⒶⒷⒸⒹⒺ
3 ⒶⒷⒸⒹⒺ	21 ⒶⒷⒸⒹⒺ	39 ⒶⒷⒸⒹⒺ	57 ⒶⒷⒸⒹⒺ	75 ⒶⒷⒸⒹⒺ
4 ⒶⒷⒸⒹⒺ	22 ⒶⒷⒸⒹⒺ	40 ⒶⒷⒸⒹⒺ	58 ⒶⒷⒸⒹⒺ	76 ⒶⒷⒸⒹⒺ
5 ⒶⒷⒸⒹⒺ	23 ⒶⒷⒸⒹⒺ	41 ⒶⒷⒸⒹⒺ	59 ⒶⒷⒸⒹⒺ	77 ⒶⒷⒸⒹⒺ
6 ⒶⒷⒸⒹⒺ	24 ⒶⒷⒸⒹⒺ	42 ⒶⒷⒸⒹⒺ	60 ⒶⒷⒸⒹⒺ	78 ⒶⒷⒸⒹⒺ
7 ⒶⒷⒸⒹⒺ	25 ⒶⒷⒸⒹⒺ	43 ⒶⒷⒸⒹⒺ	61 ⒶⒷⒸⒹⒺ	79 ⒶⒷⒸⒹⒺ
8 ⒶⒷⒸⒹⒺ	26 ⒶⒷⒸⒹⒺ	44 ⒶⒷⒸⒹⒺ	62 ⒶⒷⒸⒹⒺ	80 ⒶⒷⒸⒹⒺ
9 ⒶⒷⒸⒹⒺ	27 ⒶⒷⒸⒹⒺ	45 ⒶⒷⒸⒹⒺ	63 ⒶⒷⒸⒹⒺ	81 ⒶⒷⒸⒹⒺ
10 ⒶⒷⒸⒹⒺ	28 ⒶⒷⒸⒹⒺ	46 ⒶⒷⒸⒹⒺ	64 ⒶⒷⒸⒹⒺ	82 ⒶⒷⒸⒹⒺ
11 ⒶⒷⒸⒹⒺ	29 ⒶⒷⒸⒹⒺ	47 ⒶⒷⒸⒹⒺ	65 ⒶⒷⒸⒹⒺ	83 ⒶⒷⒸⒹⒺ
12 ⒶⒷⒸⒹⒺ	30 ⒶⒷⒸⒹⒺ	48 ⒶⒷⒸⒹⒺ	66 ⒶⒷⒸⒹⒺ	84 ⒶⒷⒸⒹⒺ
13 ⒶⒷⒸⒹⒺ	31 ⒶⒷⒸⒹⒺ	49 ⒶⒷⒸⒹⒺ	67 ⒶⒷⒸⒹⒺ	85 ⒶⒷⒸⒹⒺ
14 ⒶⒷⒸⒹⒺ	32 ⒶⒷⒸⒹⒺ	50 ⒶⒷⒸⒹⒺ	68 ⒶⒷⒸⒹⒺ	86 ⒶⒷⒸⒹⒺ
15 ⒶⒷⒸⒹⒺ	33 ⒶⒷⒸⒹⒺ	51 ⒶⒷⒸⒹⒺ	69 ⒶⒷⒸⒹⒺ	87 ⒶⒷⒸⒹⒺ
16 ⒶⒷⒸⒹⒺ	34 ⒶⒷⒸⒹⒺ	52 ⒶⒷⒸⒹⒺ	70 ⒶⒷⒸⒹⒺ	88 ⒶⒷⒸⒹⒺ
17 ⒶⒷⒸⒹⒺ	35 ⒶⒷⒸⒹⒺ	53 ⒶⒷⒸⒹⒺ	71 ⒶⒷⒸⒹⒺ	
18 ⒶⒷⒸⒹⒺ	36 ⒶⒷⒸⒹⒺ	54 ⒶⒷⒸⒹⒺ	72 ⒶⒷⒸⒹⒺ	

✂ Remove by cutting on dotted line.

Part C—Number Series

1 ⒶⒷⒸⒹⒺ	6 ⒶⒷⒸⒹⒺ	11 ⒶⒷⒸⒹⒺ	16 ⒶⒷⒸⒹⒺ	21 ⒶⒷⒸⒹⒺ
2 ⒶⒷⒸⒹⒺ	7 ⒶⒷⒸⒹⒺ	12 ⒶⒷⒸⒹⒺ	17 ⒶⒷⒸⒹⒺ	22 ⒶⒷⒸⒹⒺ
3 ⒶⒷⒸⒹⒺ	8 ⒶⒷⒸⒹⒺ	13 ⒶⒷⒸⒹⒺ	18 ⒶⒷⒸⒹⒺ	23 ⒶⒷⒸⒹⒺ
4 ⒶⒷⒸⒹⒺ	9 ⒶⒷⒸⒹⒺ	14 ⒶⒷⒸⒹⒺ	19 ⒶⒷⒸⒹⒺ	24 ⒶⒷⒸⒹⒺ
5 ⒶⒷⒸⒹⒺ	10 ⒶⒷⒸⒹⒺ	15 ⒶⒷⒸⒹⒺ	20 ⒶⒷⒸⒹⒺ	

Part D—Following Oral Directions

1 ⒶⒷⒸⒹⒺ	19 ⒶⒷⒸⒹⒺ	37 ⒶⒷⒸⒹⒺ	55 ⒶⒷⒸⒹⒺ	73 ⒶⒷⒸⒹⒺ
2 ⒶⒷⒸⒹⒺ	20 ⒶⒷⒸⒹⒺ	38 ⒶⒷⒸⒹⒺ	56 ⒶⒷⒸⒹⒺ	74 ⒶⒷⒸⒹⒺ
3 ⒶⒷⒸⒹⒺ	21 ⒶⒷⒸⒹⒺ	39 ⒶⒷⒸⒹⒺ	57 ⒶⒷⒸⒹⒺ	75 ⒶⒷⒸⒹⒺ
4 ⒶⒷⒸⒹⒺ	22 ⒶⒷⒸⒹⒺ	40 ⒶⒷⒸⒹⒺ	58 ⒶⒷⒸⒹⒺ	76 ⒶⒷⒸⒹⒺ
5 ⒶⒷⒸⒹⒺ	23 ⒶⒷⒸⒹⒺ	41 ⒶⒷⒸⒹⒺ	59 ⒶⒷⒸⒹⒺ	77 ⒶⒷⒸⒹⒺ
6 ⒶⒷⒸⒹⒺ	24 ⒶⒷⒸⒹⒺ	42 ⒶⒷⒸⒹⒺ	60 ⒶⒷⒸⒹⒺ	78 ⒶⒷⒸⒹⒺ
7 ⒶⒷⒸⒹⒺ	25 ⒶⒷⒸⒹⒺ	43 ⒶⒷⒸⒹⒺ	61 ⒶⒷⒸⒹⒺ	79 ⒶⒷⒸⒹⒺ
8 ⒶⒷⒸⒹⒺ	26 ⒶⒷⒸⒹⒺ	44 ⒶⒷⒸⒹⒺ	62 ⒶⒷⒸⒹⒺ	80 ⒶⒷⒸⒹⒺ
9 ⒶⒷⒸⒹⒺ	27 ⒶⒷⒸⒹⒺ	45 ⒶⒷⒸⒹⒺ	63 ⒶⒷⒸⒹⒺ	81 ⒶⒷⒸⒹⒺ
10 ⒶⒷⒸⒹⒺ	28 ⒶⒷⒸⒹⒺ	46 ⒶⒷⒸⒹⒺ	64 ⒶⒷⒸⒹⒺ	82 ⒶⒷⒸⒹⒺ
11 ⒶⒷⒸⒹⒺ	29 ⒶⒷⒸⒹⒺ	47 ⒶⒷⒸⒹⒺ	65 ⒶⒷⒸⒹⒺ	83 ⒶⒷⒸⒹⒺ
12 ⒶⒷⒸⒹⒺ	30 ⒶⒷⒸⒹⒺ	48 ⒶⒷⒸⒹⒺ	66 ⒶⒷⒸⒹⒺ	84 ⒶⒷⒸⒹⒺ
13 ⒶⒷⒸⒹⒺ	31 ⒶⒷⒸⒹⒺ	49 ⒶⒷⒸⒹⒺ	67 ⒶⒷⒸⒹⒺ	85 ⒶⒷⒸⒹⒺ
14 ⒶⒷⒸⒹⒺ	32 ⒶⒷⒸⒹⒺ	50 ⒶⒷⒸⒹⒺ	68 ⒶⒷⒸⒹⒺ	86 ⒶⒷⒸⒹⒺ
15 ⒶⒷⒸⒹⒺ	33 ⒶⒷⒸⒹⒺ	51 ⒶⒷⒸⒹⒺ	69 ⒶⒷⒸⒹⒺ	87 ⒶⒷⒸⒹⒺ
16 ⒶⒷⒸⒹⒺ	34 ⒶⒷⒸⒹⒺ	52 ⒶⒷⒸⒹⒺ	70 ⒶⒷⒸⒹⒺ	88 ⒶⒷⒸⒹⒺ
17 ⒶⒷⒸⒹⒺ	35 ⒶⒷⒸⒹⒺ	53 ⒶⒷⒸⒹⒺ	71 ⒶⒷⒸⒹⒺ	
18 ⒶⒷⒸⒹⒺ	36 ⒶⒷⒸⒹⒺ	54 ⒶⒷⒸⒹⒺ	72 ⒶⒷⒸⒹⒺ	

Chapter 9

Practice Test 1

Part A — ADDRESS CHECKING

Work — 6 minutes

In this part of the test, you are to decide whether two addresses are alike or different. If the two addresses are *exactly alike in every way*, darken space Ⓐ. If they are *different in any way*, darken space Ⓓ.

Mark your answers on the Answer Sheet on page 229. Tear it out, put today's date on it, and place it next to the questions.

Allow yourself exactly 6 minutes to do as many of the 95 questions as you can. If you finish before the time is up, check your answers.

1.	303 S Wellington Ave	303 S Wellington Ave
2.	1553 Kreutzinger Ln E	1553 Kreutzinger Ln S
3.	4601 N Palmetto Ct	4601 N Palmetto Ct
4.	8701 Holokahana Ln W	8701 Holokahana Ln W
5.	7489 Ella St	7489 Ello St
6.	3123 Ivy Pky NE	3123 Ivy Pky NW
7.	139 Hammock Rd	139 Hammond Rd
8.	2216 N Dubuque Ave	2216 N Dubuque Ave
9.	6398 Greenleaf Ave	6398 Greenleaf St
10.	6319 Loch Lomond Trl	3619 Loch Lomond Trl
11.	57 Oakwood Trail South Dr	57 Oakwood Trail South Dr
12.	842 18th Pl SE	842 19th St SE
13.	7164 Malabar Dr NE	7164 Malabar Dr NE
14.	10 Quincy Dr	10 Quincy Rd
15.	4010 Narcissus Ave SW	4010 Narccissus Ave SW
16.	735 Delmar Ct SE	735 Denar Ct SE
17.	McKeesport PA 15132	MacKeesport PA 15132
18.	9767 Jonquil Ter	9767 Jonquil Ter
19.	1184 E Casteel Ct	1184 W Casteel Ct
20.	8305 Iglehart Ct	8305 Iglehert Ct
21.	9545 Buckwalter Rd NW	9545 Buckwalter Rd NW
22.	Duluth MN 55812	Duluth MN 58512
23.	7449 E 220 St	4749 E 220 St
24.	64 North Point Cir Dr	64 North Point Cir Dr

25.	1804 Gills Mill Ct	1804 Gills Mill Ct
26.	2123 Cregier Ave	2123 Cregeir Ave
27.	3327 Campbell Rd	3327 Campbell Rd
28.	1764 Pamakani Pl NE	1764 Pamakani Pl NE
29.	119 E Guerad Dr	119 W Guerad Dr
30.	1189 6th St NE	1189 6th Pl NE
31.	Hardee FL 33834	Hardee FL 33834
32.	4999 Whippoorwill Ct SE	4999 Whippoorwill Ct SE
33.	5 Keswick Dr NW	5 Keswick Dr NW
34.	2665 Ida St	2665 Ida St
35.	984 S York St	984 S York Pl
36.	5450 Sawgrass Rd	5450 Sawgrass Rd
37.	8282 Gardiner Rock Ln	8282 Garpiner Rock Ln
38.	6612 Conover Ave SW	6612 Connover Ave SW
39.	96 Willow St	96 Willow St
40.	3622 S Stanley St	3622 S Stanley Ct
41.	2066 W. Lockerbie Dr	2066 W Lockerdie Dr
42.	1187 W Brompton Ave	1178 W Brompton Ave
43.	5405 Xavier St	5540 Xavier St
44.	Aaronsburg PA	Aaronsburg PA
45.	1121 Acom Dr	1121 Agom Dr
46.	2704 Kingsbury Rd	2704 Kingsbury Rd
47.	403 American Blvd SW	403 Amerigan Blvd SW
48.	4071 Cartwright Blvd	4017 Cartwright Blvd
49.	4621 Jackson Ave	4612 Jackson Ave
50.	7218 Queensbridge Commons Ct	7218 Queensbridge Commons Ct
51.	9225 Shelbyville Rd N	9225 Shelbyville Rd N
52.	Grande Ronde OR	Grande Ronde OH
53.	3773 Valley Brook Dr	3773 Valley Brood Dr
54.	8118 Fairfield Pl	8118 Fairfield Pl
55.	Owyhee NV	Omyhee NV
56.	San Mateo CA 94020	San Mateo CA 94020
57.	998 N Alta Vista Ter	998 N Alta Viste Ter
58.	5606 Fournoy St	5606 Fournoy St
59.	Pawtucket RI 02941	Pawtucket RI 02941
60.	High Point NC 27609	High Point NC 27609

61.	4232 Yale Rd	4232 Yale Rd
62.	1152 East Hickory Landing Way	1152 East Hickory Landing Way
63.	4045 Twin Willow Dr	4045 Twin Willow Dr
64.	3894 W Diversey Blvd	3894 E Diversey Blvd
65.	Elyria OH 44039	Elyrio OH 44039
66.	4003 Johnathan St.	4003 Jonathan St
67.	217 Intervale Rd	217 Interile Rd
68.	865 S 3rd St	865 S 3rd St
69.	83 Rue Le Ray	83 Rue La Ray
70.	Shreveport LA 71109	Shreveport LA 71109
71.	7368 Eggleston Ave S	7368 Eggleston Ave S
72.	6069 El Paso Blvd	6069 El Peso Blvd
73.	9002 Fortingale Dr	9002 Fortindale Dr
74.	5992 N Upland Ave	5992 N Udland Ave
75.	82 East Handy Dr NW	82 West Handy Dr NW
76.	9623 Fort Rapadan Heights Ln	9623 Fort Ramadan Heights Ln
77.	655 E Vermillion Ave	655 E Vermillion Ave
78.	943 Gaspar Cir E	943 Gaspar Cir E
79.	2909 Pennsylvania Ave	2909 Pennsylvania Ave
80.	1021 S Port O'Manaco Ter	1021 S Port O'Manaco Ter
81.	198 Gideons Dr SW	198 Gideons Dr SW
82.	6745 E 92nd St	6745 E 92nd St
83.	989 S Poplar St	989 N Poplar St
84.	7820 Hamilton St	7820 Hamilton St
85.	7004 Flintridge Sq S	7004 Flintridge Sq S
86.	7589 Wrightwood Ave W	7589 Wrightwood Ave W
87.	Union Traction Blvd IN	Union Traction Blvd IN
88.	1698 Railroad Ave	1689 Railroad Ave
89.	2204 Youngs Ridge Ct	2204 Youngs Ridge Ct
90.	5924 S Breeze Ln	5924 S Breeze Ln
91.	240 Halcyon Dr	240 Halcyon Dr
92.	Orocovis Pr	Ocorovis Pr
93.	489 W 5th St	489 W 5th St
94.	6231 Martin Luther King Dr	6213 Martin Luther King Dr
95.	3676 E Edmunds Ave	3786 E Edmunds Ave

STOP

If you finish before the time is up, go back and check the questions in this section of the test only.

PART B — MEMORY FOR ADDRESSES

In this part of the test, you will have five boxes labeled A, B, C, D, and E. Each box contains five addresses. Three of the five are groups of street addresses, such as 2300–2999 Reade, 3600–4299 Stone, and 3800–4399 Back; and two are names of places. The addresses are different in each box.

There will be several opportunities to study the addresses and the boxes they are in. You will also be given three tests of 88 questions each, and the task of deciding where each address belongs. In some cases, you will have the list *and* the boxes in front of you at the same time; in others you will not. List 1 and List 2 are for warm-up practice. List 3 is the real one that will be scored.

Make sure you understand the format by examining the pretest samples below.

Pretest Samples

A	B	C	D	E
2300–2999 Reade	1900–2299 Reade	3000–4099 Reade	4100–4399 Reade	4400–5199 Reade
Barley	Lymon	Hillary	Olive	Graves
4300–4699 Stone	2600–3599 Stone	3600–4299 Stone	5000–5499 Stone	4700–4999 Stone
Young	Erasmus	Trinity	Newton	Iris
5000–6299 Back	2300–3799 Back	4400–4999 Back	3800–4399 Back	6300–6799 Back

Questions 1 through 7 show the way the questions look. You have to decide in which lettered box (A, B, C, D, or E) the address belongs and then mark your answer by darkening the appropriate space in the answer grid.

1. 3600–4299 Stone — 1 Ⓐ Ⓑ Ⓒ Ⓓ Ⓔ
2. Young — 2 Ⓐ Ⓑ Ⓒ Ⓓ Ⓔ
3. Erasmus — 3 Ⓐ Ⓑ Ⓒ Ⓓ Ⓔ
4. 4400–5199 Reade — 4 Ⓐ Ⓑ Ⓒ Ⓓ Ⓔ
5. 3800–4399 Back — 5 Ⓐ Ⓑ Ⓒ Ⓓ Ⓔ
6. Olive — 6 Ⓐ Ⓑ Ⓒ Ⓓ Ⓔ
7. 4300–4699 Stone — 7 Ⓐ Ⓑ Ⓒ Ⓓ Ⓔ

Answers

1. **C** 2. **A** 3. **B** 4. **E** 5. **D** 6. **D** 7. **A**

Now that you know what to do, you may begin Part B of Practice Test 1. To get the most out of it and the other five practice tests in this book, follow the directions and timing *exactly*. Follow each phase of Part B of the test, page by page, until you've completed List 3. It is modeled on the way the Postal Service actually conducts its tests.

Turn to the next page to begin.

Study — 3 minutes

You will be given 3 minutes to spend memorizing the addresses in the boxes. *They are exactly the same ones that will be used for all three tests.* Try to memorize as many as you can. When the 3 minutes are up, turn to page 238 and read the instructions for *List 1*.

A	B	C	D	E
2300–2999 Reade	1900–2299 Reade	3000–4099 Reade	4100–4399 Reade	4400–5199 Reade
Barley	Lymon	Hillary	Olive	Graves
4300–4699 Stone	2600–3599 Stone	3600–4299 Stone	5000–5499 Stone	4700–4999 Stone
Young	Erasmus	Trinity	Newton	Iris
5000–6299 Back	2300–3799 Back	4400–4999 Back	3800–4399 Back	6300–6799 Back

List 1

Work — 3 minutes

Tear out the Answer Sheet for List 1. For each question, mark the Answer Sheet on page 230 to show the letter of the box in which the address belongs. Try to remember the locations of as many addresses as you can. *You will now have 3 minutes to complete List 1.* If you are not sure of an answer, you should guess.

A	B	C	D	E
2300–2999 Reade	1900–2299 Reade	3000–4099 Reade	4100–4399 Reade	4400–5199 Reade
Barley	Lymon	Hillary	Olive	Graves
4300–4699 Stone	2600–3599 Stone	3600–4299 Stone	5000–5499 Stone	4700–4999 Stone
Young	Erasmus	Trinity	Newton	Iris
5000–6299 Back	2300–3799 Back	4400–4999 Back	3800–4399 Back	6300–6799 Back

1. 3000–4099 Reade
2. Young
3. Lymon
4. 1900–2299 Reade
5. Hillary
6. 2300–2999 Reade
7. 5000–6299 Back
8. Olive
9. 6300–6799 Back
10. Young
11. Trinity
12. 4100–4399 Reade
13. 4400–4999 Back
14. 2600–3599 Stone
15. Iris
16. 3800–4399 Back
17. Graves
18. Newton
19. 2300–3799 Back
20. Olive
21. Trinity
22. 4700–4999 Stone
23. Erasmus
24. 4400–5199 Reade
25. Barley
26. 4300–4699 Stone
27. 3600–4299 Stone
28. 5000–6299 Back
29. Barley
30. Lymon
31. 4100–4399 Reade
32. Lymon
33. 3600–4299 Stone
34. Olive
35. Barley
36. Erasmus
37. 5000–5499 Stone
38. Trinity
39. 5000–5499 Stone
40. Trinity
41. 4400–5199 Reade
42. Erasmus
43. 2300–2999 Reade
44. 2300–3799 Back

45. 3800–4399 Back
46. 5000–5499 Stone
47. Hillary
48. 4400–5199 Reade
49. Iris
50. 4300–4699 Stone
51. Graves
52. 2600–3599 Stone
53. Young
54. Trinity
55. 4100–4399 Reade
56. Barley
57. 4700–4999 Stone
58. Hillary
59. 4300–4699 Stone
60. 1900–2299 Reade
61. 5000–6299 Back
62. Iris
63. 2600–3599 Stone
64. Lymon
65. Erasmus
66. Iris
67. 4700–4999 Stone
68. 4400–4999 Back
69. Olive
70. Graves
71. 2300–3799 Back
72. 3600–4299 Stone
73. Young
74. 2300–2999 Reade
75. Olive
76. Newton
77. 6300–6799 Back
78. Newton
79. Young
80. 1900–2299 Reade
81. Hillary
82. 3000–4099 Reade
83. Newton
84. 4400–4999 Back
85. 3800–4399 Back
86. 6300–6799 Back
87. Graves
88. 3000–4099 Reade

STOP.
If you finish before the time is up, go back and check the questions in this section of the test only.

List 2

Work — 3 minutes

Do these questions *without* looking back at the boxes. For each question, mark your answer on the Answer Sheet for List 2 on page 230. If you are not sure of an answer, you should guess.

1. 2300–3799 Back
2. 2300–2999 Reade
3. Erasmus
4. 4400–5199 Reade
5. Trinity
6. 5000–5499 Stone
7. Trinity
8. 5000–5499 Stone
9. Erasmus
10. Barley
11. Olive
12. 3600–4299 Stone
13. Lymon
14. 4100–4399 Reade
15. Lymon
16. Barley
17. 5000–6299 Back
18. 3600–4299 Stone
19. 4300–4699 Stone
20. Barley
21. 4400–5199 Reade
22. Erasmus
23. 4700–4999 Stone
24. Trinity
25. Olive
26. 2300–3799 Back
27. Newton
28. Graves
29. 3800–4399 Back
30. Iris
31. 2600–3599 Stone
32. 4400–4999 Back
33. 4100–4399 Reade
34. Trinity
35. Young
36. 6300–6799 Back
37. Olive
38. 5000–6299 Back
39. 2300–2999 Reade
40. Hillary
41. 1900–2299 Reade
42. Lymon
43. Young
44. 3000–4099 Reade

45. 3000–4099 Reade
46. Graves
47. 6300–6799 Back
48. 3800–4399 Back
49. 4400–4999 Back
50. Newton
51. 3000–4099 Reade
52. Hillary
53. 1900–2299 Reade
54. Young
55. 1900–2299 Reade
56. 6300–6799 Back
57. Newton
58. Olive
59. 2300–2999 Reade
60. Young
61. 3600–4299 Stone
62. 2300–3799 Back
63. Graves
64. Olive
65. 4400–4999 Back
66. 4700–4999 Stone
67. Iris
68. Erasmus
69. Lymon
70. 2600–3599 Stone
71. Iris
72. 5000–6299 Back
73. 1900–2299 Reade
74. 4300–4699 Stone
75. Hillary
76. 4700–4999 Stone
77. Barley
78. 4100–4399 Reade
79. Trinity
80. Young
81. 2600–3599 Stone
82. Graves
83. 4300–4699 Stone
84. Iris
85. 4400–5199 Reade
86. Hillary
87. 5000–5499 Stone
88. 3800–4399 Back

STOP.
If you finish before the time is up, go back and check the questions in this section of the test only.

List 3

Study — 5 minutes

You are now about to take the test using List 3. *(This is the test that counts!)*

Turn back to page 237 and study the boxes again. *You have 5 minutes to restudy the addresses.*

Work — 5 minutes

For each question, mark the Answer Sheet on page 231 to show the letter of the box in which the address belongs. You have *exactly 5 minutes* to do the test. During these 5 minutes, *do not* turn to any other page.

1. Trinity
2. 5000–5499 Stone
3. Young
4. Trinity
5. 4100–4399 Reade
6. Barley
7. 4400–4999 Back
8. Olive
9. Graves
10. 2300–3799 Back
11. 3600–4299 Stone
12. Erasmus
13. 4700–4999 Stone
14. Young
15. Lymon
16. 1900–2299 Reade
17. 4300–4699 Stone
18. Graves
19. Hillary
20. 5000–6299 Back
21. Iris
22. 1900–2299 Reade
23. Hillary
24. 5000–6299 Back
25. Barley
26. Lymon
27. 2600–3599 Stone
28. 2300–2999 Reade
29. Trinity
30. 6300–6799 Back
31. Newton
32. Hillary
33. Lymon
34. Erasmus
35. Iris
36. 4700–4999 Stone
37. 4400–5199 Reade
38. Olive
39. Erasmus
40. 2300–2999 Reade
41. 6300–6799 Back
42. Graves
43. 2600–3599 Stone
44. 6300–6799 Back

45. Iris
46. Hillary
47. 3000–4099 Reade
48. 4400–5199 Reade
49. Barley
50. Young
51. Trinity
52. Graves
53. 2600–3599 Stone
54. Newton
55. 2300–3799 Back
56. 3800–4399 Back
57. Trinity
58. 1900–2299 Reade
59. Newton
60. 4400–4999 Back
61. 3800–4399 Back
62. 4700–4999 Stone
63. Olive
64. Newton
65. 3000–4099 Reade
66. Iris
67. 2300–3799 Back
68. Olive
69. 3600–4299 Stone
70. Olive
71. 5000–5499 Stone
72. 4300–4699 Stone
73. Young
74. 4100–4399 Reade
75. 4400–4999 Back
76. Erasmus
77. 3600–4299 Stone
78. 3000–4099 Reade
79. Barley
80. Erasmus
81. 5000–6299 Back
82. 3000–4099 Reade
83. Young
84. 2300–2999 Reade
85. 4100–4399 Reade
86. Lymon
87. 3800–4399 Back
88. 5000–5499 Stone

STOP.
If you finish before the time is up, go back and check the questions in this section of the test only.

Part C — NUMBER SERIES

Work — 20 minutes

For each Number Series question, there is a series of numbers that follow some definite order, and below each are five sets of two numbers each. You are to look at the numbers in the series and find out what order they follow. Then decide what the next two numbers in that series would be if the same order were continued. Mark your answers on the Answer Sheet for Number Series on page 231.

You have 20 minutes to complete this part of the test. If you finish before the time is up, check your answers. The answers and explanations are on pages 254 to 255.

1. 6 9 12 15 18 21 24 __ __
   A) 26 28 B) 27 30 C) 28 31 D) 28 32 E) 27 31

2. 34 33 33 32 32 31 31 __ __
   A) 31 30 B) 30 30 C) 31 29 D) 31 31 E) 29 29

3. 10 12 14 17 19 21 24 __ __
   A) 25 27 B) 26 30 C) 27 29 D) 26 28 E) 26 29

4. 6 13 8 16 10 19 12 __ __
   A) 14 20 B) 15 21 C) 23 16 D) 15 17 E) 22 14

5. 1 2 2 4 4 8 8 __ __
   A) 16 10 B) 10 16 C) 18 16 D) 10 10 E) 16 16

6. 9 15 11 9 15 11 9 __ __
   A) 11 15 B) 11 9 C) 15 9 D) 15 11 E) 9 15

7. 13 16 14 17 15 18 16 __ __
   A) 19 17 B) 20 18 C) 17 19 D) 20 19 E) 20 17

8. 3 11 11 11 19 19 19 __ __
   A) 27 36 B) 27 35 C) 27 27 D) 19 27 E) 26 28

9. 32 34 37 41 46 52 __ __
   A) 59 67 B) 58 64 C) 60 68 D) 59 66 E) 58 65

10. 36 35 35 31 30 30 26 __ __
    A) 26 25 B) 25 25 C) 26 24 D) 25 21 E) 25 26

11. 18 54 19 52 20 50 21 __ __
    A) 22 48 B) 48 22 C) 52 20 D) 48 23 E) 49 20

12. 5 7 9 6 9 12 7 __ __
A) 10 13 B) 9 8 C) 9 10 D) 9 11 E) 11 13

13. 4 16 9 21 14 26 19 __ __
A) 24 31 B) 21 27 C) 25 32 D) 28 32 E) 31 24

14. 6 12 8 16 12 24 20 __ __
A) 22 26 B) 30 18 C) 44 32 D) 36 38 E) 40 36

15. 53 49 45 41 37 33 29 __ __
A) 26 22 B) 29 26 C) 25 21 D) 28 24 E) 25 22

16. 27 24 22 12 19 17 12 __ __
A) 14 12 B) 10 15 C) 12 16 D) 15 12 E) 11 12

17. 7 18 18 8 16 16 9 __ __
A) 10 14 B) 14 12 C) 14 14 D) 10 12 E) 14 10

18. 17 20 21 14 17 20 21 14 __ __
A) 20 21 B) 17 14 C) 15 21 D) 21 14 E) 17 20

19. 31 36 41 41 46 51 __ __
A) 56 51 B) 51 56 C) 51 51 D) 56 56 E) 56 61

20. 15 21 19 18 24 22 21 __ __
A) 27 25 B) 22 26 C) 20 26 D) 19 25 E) 23 19

21. 2 3 5 8 13 21 34 __ __
A) 42 57 B) 48 63 C) 55 89 D) 65 109 E) 49 65

22. 8 9 7 10 11 8 12 13 9 __ __
A) 10 11 B) 11 12 C) 14 15 D) 13 10 E) 14 16

23. 12 7 14 9 16 11 18 __ __
A) 19 20 B) 12 17 C) 13 20 D) 18 23 E) 14 21

24. 44 6 41 12 38 18 35 __ __
A) 33 19 B) 24 32 C) 20 33 D) 32 24 E) 22 28

STOP.
If you finish before the time is up, go back and check the questions in this part of the test only.

PART D — FOLLOWING ORAL DIRECTIONS

This part of the test gauges your ability to understand and carry out spoken directions *exactly* as they are given to you.

In order to prepare to take Part D of the test, follow the steps below:

1. Enlist the help of a friend who will be the "reader." It will be his or her job to read aloud a series of directions that you are to follow *exactly*. The reader will need a watch that displays seconds, because the directions must be read at the correct speed.

2. Tear out pages 251 and 252. These are the worksheets you should have in front of you as you listen to the directions given by the reader, who will tell you to do certain things with the items on each line on the worksheets.

3. Use the Answer Sheet for Following Oral Directions on page 231 and insert today's date. You will darken the appropriate spaces in accordance with the directions given by the reader.

4. *Now hand this entire book to the reader.* Ask him/her to review the section below headed "Instructions to the Reader." It explains exactly how the reader is to proceed.

When you and the reader are ready to start this part of Practice Test 1, he/she will begin reading to you the section marked "Directions." YOU ARE NOT TO READ THESE AT ANY TIME BEFORE OR DURING THE TEST. If you do, you will lose the benefit of this part of the practice test.

Instructions to the "Reader"

These instructions should be read at about 80 words per minute. You should practice reading the material in the box until you can do it in exactly 1 minute. This will give you a feel for the way you should read the test material.

1-MINUTE PRACTICE

> Look at line 20 on your worksheet. There are two circles and two boxes of different sizes with numbers in them. If 7 is less than 3 and if 2 is smaller than 4, write C in the larger circle. Otherwise write B as in *baker* in the smaller box. Now on your answer sheet, darken the space for the number-letter combination in the box or circle.

You should read the entire test aloud before you read it to the person taking the test, in order to acquaint yourself with the procedure and the desired rate of reading.

Read slowly, but at a natural pace. In other words, do not space the words so that there are unnaturally long pauses between them. the instruction "Pause slightly" indicates only enough time to take a breath. The other instructions for pauses give the recommended length for each. If possible, use a watch with a second hand.

All the material that follows, except the words in parentheses, is to be read aloud. Now start reading the directions. *Do not repeat any of the directions.*

Directions: In this test, I will read instructions to you.

You are to mark your worksheets according to the instructions that I read to you. After each set of instructions, I'll give you time to record your answers on your answer sheet.

Try to understand the instructions as I read them; I cannot repeat them. Do not ask any questions from now on.

If, when you go to darken a space for a number, you find that you have already darkened another space for that number, either (1) erase the first mark and darken the space for your new choice, or (2) let the first mark stay and do not darken any other space. When you finish, you should have no more than one space darkened for each number.

Turn to Worksheet 1.

Look at line 1 on your worksheet. (Pause slightly.) Draw a line under the fourth letter in the line. (Pause 2 seconds.) Now, on your answer sheet, find number 21, and darken the space for the letter under which you drew the line. (Pause 5 seconds.)

Look at the numbers on line 2 on your worksheet. (Pause slightly.) Draw three lines under the last number in the line. (Pause 2 seconds.) Now, on your answer sheet, find the number under which you just drew three lines and darken space C for that number. (Pause 5 seconds.)

Look at line 3 on your worksheet. (Pause slightly.) The number in each circle represents a day of the month. In the circle containing the latest day in the month, write the letter C. (Pause 2 seconds.) Now, on your answer sheet, darken the space for the number-letter combination that is in the circle you just wrote in. (Pause 5 seconds.)

Look at line 3 again. (Pause slightly.) In the circle containing the earliest date, write the letter E. (Pause 2 seconds.) Now, on your answer sheet, darken the space for the number-letter combination that is in the circle you just wrote in. (Pause 5 seconds.)

Now look at the five boxes in line 4 on your worksheet. (Pause slightly.) Write the letter B as in *baker* in the middle box. (Pause 2 seconds.) Now, on your answer sheet, darken the space for the number-letter combination that is in the box you just wrote in. (Pause 5 seconds.)

Look at line 5. (Pause slightly.) Next to the first number write the letter A. (Pause 2 seconds.) Now, on your answer sheet, find the line for the number beside which you just wrote and darken space A. (Pause 5 seconds.)

Now look at line 6 on your worksheet. (Pause slightly.) In the second box, write the answer to this question: How many pennies are there in a dime? (Pause 2 seconds.) Now, on your answer sheet, darken the space for the number-letter combination that is in the box you just wrote in. (Pause 5 seconds.)

Look at line 6 again. (Pause slightly.) In the fourth box, write the answer to this question: How many minutes are there in 1 hour? (Pause 2 seconds.) Now, on your answer sheet, darken the space for the number-letter combination that is in the box you just wrote in. (Pause 5 seconds.)

Look at the four circles in line 7 on your worksheet. (Pause slightly.) Each circle has a number inside it. If the largest number is in the smallest circle, write the letter C in the largest circle. (Pause slightly.) Otherwise, write A in the smallest circle. (Pause 2 seconds.)

Look at line 7 again. (Pause slightly.) Write the letter B as in *baker* in the third circle. (Pause 2 seconds.) Now, on your answer sheet, darken the spaces for the number-letter combinations that are in the circles you just wrote in. (Pause 10 seconds.)

Look at line 8 on your worksheet. (Pause slightly.) Draw a line under every number that is more than 25 but less than 35. (Pause 12 seconds.) Now, on your answer sheet, for every number that you drew a line under, darken space A. (Pause 25 seconds.)

Look at line 9 on your worksheet. (Pause slightly.) Put a circle around any letter that is among the first five letters in the alphabet. (Pause 10 seconds.) Now, on your answer sheet, find number 52 and darken the space for any letter around which you drew a circle. (Pause 15 seconds.)

Look at the figures in line 10 on your worksheet. (Pause slightly.) Each figure has a number inside it. Write the letter D as in *dog* inside any figure that does not have four sides. (Pause 5 seconds.) Now, on your answer sheet, darken the space for each of the number-letter combinations that are in the figures you just wrote in. (Pause 8 seconds.)

Look at line 11 on your worksheet. The number in each circle is the number of parcels in a mail sack. In the circle for the sack holding the largest number of parcels, write A. (Pause 2 seconds.) Now, on your answer sheet, darken the space for the number-letter combination that is in the circle you just wrote in. (Pause 5 seconds.)

Look at line 11 again. In the circle for the sack holding the smallest number of parcels, write C. (Pause 2 seconds.) Now, on your answer sheet, darken the space for the number-letter combination that is in the circle you just wrote in. (Pause 5 seconds.)

Now turn to Worksheet 2. (Pause 5 seconds.)

Look at the five boxes on line 12 on your worksheet. (Pause slightly.) If 9 is less than 5, write B as in *baker* on the line under the number in the second box. (Pause slightly.) If 9 is not less than 5, write C on the line under the number in the fifth box. (Pause 5 seconds.) Now, on your answer sheet, darken the space for the number-letter combination that is in the box you just wrote in. (Pause 5 seconds.)

Look at line 13 on your worksheet. (Pause slightly.) There are two circles and two triangles of different sizes with numbers in them. (Pause slightly.) If 7 is more than 2 and 5 is less than 3, write E in the larger triangle. (Pause 2 seconds.) Otherwise, write D as in *dog* in the smaller circle. (Pause 2 seconds.) Now, on your answer sheet, darken the space for the number-letter combination that is in the triangle or circle you just wrote in. (Pause 5 seconds.)

Look at line 14 on your worksheet. (Pause slightly.) Draw a line under every "X" in the line. (Pause 5 seconds.) Count the number of lines that you have drawn, add 5, and write that number at the end of the line. (Pause 5 seconds.) Now, on your answer sheet, find that number and darken space E. (Pause 5 seconds.)

Look at the circles and the words in line 15 on your worksheet. (Pause slightly.) Write the first letter of the second word in the third circle. (Pause 2 seconds.) Write the second letter of the first word in the second circle. (Pause 2 seconds.) Write the fourth letter of the third word in the first circle. (Pause 2 seconds.) Now, on your answer sheet, darken the spaces for the number-letter combinations that are in the three circles you just wrote in. (Pause 20 seconds.)

Look at line 16 on your worksheet. (Pause slightly.) On the line next to the right-hand letter, write the answer to this question: How many feet are there in a yard? (Pause 2 seconds.) Now, on your answer sheet, darken the space for the number-letter combination you have just written. (Pause 5 seconds.)

Look at line 17 on your worksheet. (Pause slightly.) In each circle there is a time when mail is dispatched. In the circle for the latest time, write on the line the last two figures of the time. (Pause 5 seconds.) Now, on your answer sheet, darken the space for the number-letter combination that is in the circle you just wrote in. (Pause 5 seconds.)

Look at line 17 again. (Pause slightly.) In the circle for the earliest time, write on the line the last two figures of the time. (Pause 5 seconds.) Now, on your answer sheet, darken the space for the number-letter combination that is in the circle you just wrote in. (Pause 5 seconds.)

Look at line 18 on your worksheet. (Pause slightly.) Mail for Akron and Canton is to be put in box 40. (Pause slightly.) Mail for St. Louis and Philby is to be put in box 70. (Pause slightly.) Write B as in *baker* in the box in which you put mail for Akron. Now, on your answer sheet, darken the space for the number-letter combination that is in the box you just wrote in. (Pause 5 seconds.)

Look at line 19 on your worksheet. (Pause slightly.) There are two circles and two boxes of different sizes with numbers in them. (Pause slightly.) Subtract 4 from the number in the larger box, and change the number in that box to this number. (Pause 6 seconds.) Then write A next to the new number. (Pause slightly.) In the smaller circle, do nothing. In the larger circle, write the letter C. (Pause 2 seconds.) Now, on your answer sheet, darken the spaces for the number-letter combinations that are in the boxes and circles you just wrote in. (Pause 20 seconds.)

END OF EXAMINATION.
If you finish before the time is up, go back and check the questions in this section of the test only.

Practice Test 1—Worksheet 1

Part D—Following Oral Directions

1. E C B A E D

2. 16 9 41 10 28 9 38

3. 28 ___ 4 ___ 19 ___ 12 ___ 29 ___

4. 6 ___ 12 ___ 8 ___ 15 ___ 18 ___

5. 39 ___ 10 ___ 4 ___ 9 ___

6. A ___ B ___ C ___ D ___ E ___

7. 14 ___ 32 ___ 45 ___ 63 ___

8. 35 32 20 34 22 56 27

9. F S E H N T J O

10. 63 ___ 20 ___ 74 ___ 36 ___

11. 59 ___ 66 ___ 84 ___ 82 ___ 77 ___

✂ Remove by cutting on dotted line.

Practice Test 1—Worksheet 2

Part D—Following Oral Directions

12. 51 ___ 33 ___ 17 ___ 43 ___ 87 ___

13. 7 ___ 41 ___ 63 ___ 56 ___

14. X O O X X O X X X O O X ___

15. 28 ___ 69 ___ 78 ___ PEACH APPLE HIDE

16. ___ C ___ E

17. 4:31 ___ A 2:55 ___ B 3:59 ___ C 5:11 ___ D 4:48 ___ E

18. 40 CANTON AKRON 70 ST. LOUIS PHILBY

19. 48 ___ 49 ___ 66 ___ 71 ___

ANSWER KEY

Part A—Address Checking

1. **A**	11. **A**	21. **A**	31. **A**	41. **D**	51. **A**	61. **A**	71. **A**	81. **A**	91. **A**
2. **D**	12. **D**	22. **D**	32. **A**	42. **D**	52. **D**	62. **A**	72. **D**	82. **D**	92. **D**
3. **A**	13. **A**	23. **D**	33. **A**	43. **D**	53. **D**	63. **A**	73. **D**	83. **D**	93. **A**
4. **A**	14. **D**	24. **A**	34. **A**	44. **A**	54. **A**	64. **D**	74. **D**	84. **A**	94. **D**
5. **D**	15. **D**	25. **A**	35. **D**	45. **D**	55. **D**	65. **D**	75. **D**	85. **A**	95. **D**
6. **D**	16. **D**	26. **D**	36. **A**	46. **A**	56. **A**	66. **D**	76. **D**	86. **A**	
7. **D**	17. **D**	27. **A**	37. **D**	47. **D**	57. **D**	67. **D**	77. **A**	87. **A**	
8. **A**	18. **A**	28. **A**	38. **D**	48. **D**	58. **A**	68. **A**	78. **A**	88. **D**	
9. **D**	19. **D**	29. **D**	39. **A**	49. **D**	59. **D**	69. **D**	79. **A**	89. **A**	
10. **D**	20. **D**	30. **D**	40. **D**	50. **A**	60. **A**	70. **A**	80. **A**	90. **A**	

Part B—Memory for Addresses

List 1

1. **C**	10. **A**	19. **B**	28. **A**	37. **D**	46. **D**	55. **D**	64. **B**	73. **A**	82. **C**
2. **A**	11. **C**	20. **D**	29. **A**	38. **C**	47. **C**	56. **A**	65. **B**	74. **A**	83. **D**
3. **B**	12. **D**	21. **C**	30. **B**	39. **D**	48. **E**	57. **E**	66. **E**	75. **D**	84. **C**
4. **B**	13. **C**	22. **E**	31. **D**	40. **C**	49. **E**	58. **C**	67. **E**	76. **D**	85. **D**
5. **C**	14. **B**	23. **B**	32. **B**	41. **E**	50. **A**	59. **A**	68. **C**	77. **E**	86. **E**
6. **A**	15. **E**	24. **E**	33. **C**	42. **B**	51. **E**	60. **B**	69. **D**	78. **D**	87. **E**
7. **A**	16. **D**	25. **A**	34. **D**	43. **A**	52. **B**	61. **A**	70. **E**	79. **A**	88. **C**
8. **D**	17. **E**	26. **A**	35. **A**	44. **B**	53. **A**	62. **E**	71. **B**	80. **B**	
9. **E**	18. **D**	27. **C**	36. **E**	45. **D**	54. **C**	63. **B**	72. **C**	81. **C**	

List 2

1. **B**	10. **A**	19. **A**	28. **E**	37. **D**	46. **E**	55. **B**	64. **D**	73. **B**	82. **E**
2. **A**	11. **D**	20. **A**	29. **D**	38. **A**	47. **E**	56. **E**	65. **C**	74. **A**	83. **A**
3. **B**	12. **C**	21. **E**	30. **E**	39. **A**	48. **D**	57. **D**	66. **E**	75. **C**	84. **E**
4. **E**	13. **B**	22. **B**	31. **B**	40. **C**	49. **C**	58. **D**	67. **E**	76. **E**	85. **E**
5. **C**	14. **D**	23. **E**	32. **C**	41. **B**	50. **D**	59. **A**	68. **B**	77. **A**	86. **C**
6. **D**	15. **B**	24. **C**	33. **D**	42. **B**	51. **C**	60. **A**	69. **B**	78. **D**	87. **D**
7. **C**	16. **A**	25. **D**	34. **C**	43. **A**	52. **C**	61. **C**	70. **B**	79. **C**	88. **D**
8. **D**	17. **A**	26. **B**	35. **A**	44. **C**	53. **B**	62. **B**	71. **E**	80. **A**	
9. **B**	18. **C**	27. **D**	36. **E**	45. **C**	54. **A**	63. **E**	72. **A**	81. **B**	

List 3

1. **C**	10. **B**	19. **C**	28. **A**	37. **E**	46. **C**	55. **B**	64. **D**	73. **A**	82. **C**
2. **D**	11. **C**	20. **A**	29. **C**	38. **D**	47. **E**	56. **D**	65. **C**	74. **D**	83. **A**
3. **A**	12. **B**	21. **E**	30. **D**	39. **B**	48. **E**	57. **C**	66. **E**	75. **C**	84. **A**
4. **C**	13. **E**	22. **B**	31. **C**	40. **A**	49. **A**	58. **A**	67. **B**	76. **B**	85. **D**
5. **D**	14. **A**	23. **C**	32. **B**	41. **E**	50. **A**	59. **D**	68. **D**	77. **C**	86. **B**
6. **A**	15. **B**	24. **A**	33. **B**	42. **E**	51. **C**	60. **C**	69. **C**	78. **C**	87. **D**
7. **C**	16. **B**	25. **A**	34. **E**	43. **B**	52. **E**	61. **D**	70. **D**	79. **A**	88. **D**
8. **D**	17. **A**	26. **B**	35. **E**	44. **E**	53. **B**	62. **E**	71. **D**	80. **B**	
9. **E**	18. **E**	27. **A**	36. **E**	45. **E**	54. **D**	63. **D**	72. **A**	81. **A**	

Part C—Number Series

1. **B**	4. **E**	7. **A**	10. **B**	13. **E**	16. **A**	19. **B**	22. **C**
2. **B**	5. **E**	8. **C**	11. **B**	14. **E**	17. **C**	20. **A**	23. **C**
3. **D**	6. **D**	9. **A**	12. **D**	15. **C**	18. **E**	21. **C**	24. **B**

Part D—Following Oral Directions

3. **E**	10. **B**	14. **A**	28. **E**	34. **A**	39. **A**	45. **B**	56. **D**	69. **E**	78. **A**
4. **E**	11. **D**	21. **A**	29. **C**	36. **D**	40. **B**	52. **E**	59. **C**	71. **C**	84. **A**
8. **B**	12. **E**	27. **A**	32. **A**	38. **C**	44. **A**	55. **B**	60. **D**	74. **D**	87. **C**

ANSWER EXPLANATIONS FOR PART C—NUMBER SERIES

1. **B** This is a simple + 3 series.
2. **B** The pattern for this series is −1, repeat the number; −1 repeat the number; and so on.
3. **D** This series follows the complex rule: + 2, + 2, + 3; + 2, + 2, + 3; and so on.
4. **E** There are two alternating series here: one that increases by 2; the other that increases by 3.
5. **E** The rule for this series is × 2, repeat the number; × 2, repeat the number; and so on. You can be thrown off at the very beginning if you do not see that 1 × 2 = 2.
6. **D** The sequence 9 15 11 keeps repeating.
7. **A** Here again are two alternating series: one series begins with 13 and increases by 1; the other begins with 16 and increases by 1. If you saw it as following the rule + 3, − 2; + 3, − 2; and so on, you would also get the correct answer.
8. **C** Each number in this series is repeated three times before increasing by 8.
9. **A** The numbers in this series increase according to a *variable* "adder" that keeps increasing by 1. The correct answer is calculated as follows:

   +2 +3 +4 +5 +6 +7 +8

   32 34 37 41 46 52 59 67

10. **B** This series follows the rule: − 1, repeat the number, − 4; − 1, repeat the number, −4. A loop diagram makes this clear instantly.
11. **B** In this pair of alternating series, the series starting with 18 is ascending by + 1. The other series starting with 54 is descending by − 2.

    18 54 19 52 20 50 21 48 22

12. **D** Two alternating "mini-series" are present here, each of which continues for three numbers, after which it is interrupted by the other. One increases by + 2. The other increases by + 3. Each sequence of three numbers begins one higher than the last. Partition lines in a loop diagram show this clearly.

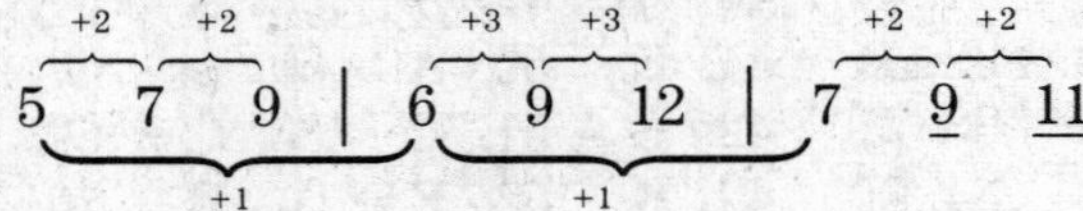

13. **E** Two alternating series make up this group of numbers. Both follow a + 5 rule.

14. **E** Multiplication and subtraction are used to form this series. The numbers follow a × 2, − 4; × 2, − 4; and so on rule.
15. **C** Each number in this series decreases by 4.
16. **A** This can be a difficult pattern to find because the arbitrary number *12* is periodically inserted in the series. The series itself follows a − 3, − 2; − 3, − 2; and so on rule.
17. **C** One of the two alternating series here increases by 1 (7, 8, 9). The other decreases by 2 after each of its numbers has been repeated once (18, 18, 16, 16)
18. **E** A sequence of *four* numbers, 17, 20, 21, 14; keeps recycling.
19. **B** There is a complex rule used here: + 5, + 5, repeat the number; + 5, + 5, repeat the number.
20. **A** Another complex rule underlies this series. It is + 6, − 2, − 1; + 6, − 2, − 1; and so on. Without using a loop diagram, this and the previous example would be most difficult.
21. **C** Here is an example of a series that uses its own numbers to progress itself. Each number in this series, beginning with 5, is obtained by adding together the two numbers preceding it.

    $2 + 3 \underset{+}{=} 5 \overset{+}{=} 8 \underset{+}{=} 13 \overset{+}{=} 21 \underset{+}{=} 34 \overset{+}{=} \underline{55} = \underline{89}$
22. **C** Because the numbers are so close together, it may have been difficult to identify the two alternating series present here. Both follow a simple + 1 rule. One intrudes after every *two* numbers of the other.
23. **C** The pattern this series follows is − 5, + 7; − 5, + 7; and so on. If you wish, you may see this as two alternating series, each increasing by 2.
24. **B** There are two alternating series here. One (starting with 44) decreases by 3; the other (starting with 6) increases by 6.

EVALUATING YOUR PROGRESS*

Part A—Address Checking

Computing Your Score

Check your answers against the Answer Key. Score yourself by using this formula:

Number right
− Number wrong
YOUR SCORE

* Please note that the scores you obtain by following the computation instructions for the various parts of this test are "raw" scores. The Postal Service combines and converts the raw scores for the various parts of the test into a scaled score obtained by using special conversion formulas that are kept confidential. This scaled score (plus any veteran's credits to which you are entitled) forms the basis for your final rating and your standing on the list. This final rating will be sent to you after the tests have been marked.

Furthermore, even though you take one test, your final score will vary depending on the title. For example, your rating on the Mail Handler register may very well be different from your rating on the Postal Clerk-Carrier register. Apparently, the relative rate given to each part of the test varies according to title. This is another argument for taking as many tests in as many titles as possible, as suggested on page 3.

You are encouraged to calculate your raw scores because they furnish a realistic and convenient way for you to keep track of your relative performance and progress as you work your way through this book.

For example, if you completed 52 questions and got 8 wrong,

Number right	=	44
− Number wrong	=	− 8
Your score	=	36

Notice that you do *not* figure in the questions that you did not answer.

Guidelines

How good is the score you just made?

52 or higher . . . . Good
Between 32 and 52 . . . . . . Fair
Below 32 . . . . You need to improve.

These are commonly accepted figures. It is believed, however, that you should not be satisfied with anything *less* than 52. Experience in training many people to prepare for this test shows that most serious test candidates who use the preparation program described in this book (Chapter 3 covers Address Checking) will be able to raise their score to the upper sixties, seventies, or eighties.

Personal Progress Record

One of the most satisfying things that can happen while you are working toward a goal is to see signs of progress. The improvement you make on Address Checking can readily be seen by examining the scores you make on the practice tests and exercises in this book. Keeping track of your growing skill is important, so a Personal Progress Record has been furnished for your use on page 430.

The following is a sample of this Personal Progress Record to familiarize you with it. The entries on this sample are based on the example above.

PERSONAL PROGRESS RECORD—SAMPLE

ADDRESS CHECKING												
Initial Tests									Repeated Tests			
Date	Test	Number Completed	Number Correct	−	Number Wrong	=	Score	Date	Score	Date	Score
5/15	Diagnostic Practice Test	52	44	−	8	=	36				
5/16	Practice Test 1	64	54	−	10	=	44				
5/18	Practice Test 2	66	57	−	9	=	48				
5/20	Practice Test 3	70	60	−	10	=	50				
	Practice Test 4			−		=					
	Practice Test 5			−		=					
	Practice Test 6			−		=					

Now turn to page 430. In the table entitled "Personal Progress Record—Address Checking," make the proper entries on the line for Practice Test 1, which you just took. Review the special techniques in Chapter 3: Address Checking—How to Improve Your Score, before taking Practice Test 2. After taking the additional practice tests, enter the results immediately. Keep this record. It will help you record your progress.

Part B—Memory for Addresses

Computing Your Score

Check the answers on your answer sheet against the Answer Key. Calculate your score by using these four steps:

1. Enter the number of answers you got right .... ______
2. Enter the number of answers you got wrong .... ______
3. Divide the number wrong by 4 (or multiply by ¼) .... − ______
4. Subtract Line 3 from Line 1 .... YOUR SCORE = ______

Follow this example to make sure that you have figured your score correctly. It will be assumed that you completed 32 questions, of which you got 24 right and 8 wrong.

Line 1.......	Number right	24
Line 2.......	Number wrong 8	
Line 3.......	¼ of line 2 = ¼ × 8......	− 2
Line 4.......	24 − 2 .. YOUR SCORE =	22

Notice that, just as for Address Checking, questions that are *not* answered are not taken into account.

Guidelines

How good is the score you just made?

44 or more .... Good
26 to 43................ Fair
25 or less .... You need to improve.

If your score on this test was low, don't be discouraged. Nevertheless, you may wish to review Chapters 4 and 5, which offer special techniques for handling Part B—Memory for Addresses, before taking Practice Test 2.

Personal Progress Record

Turn to page 430. Use the table entitled "Personal Progress—Memory for Addresses" to keep a permanent record of your scores on List 3 of the practice tests. A sample is printed on the next page to familiarize you with it. The first entry is based on the preceding example.

PERSONAL PROGRESS RECORD—SAMPLE

MEMORY FOR ADDRESSES												
Initial Tests									Repeated Tests			
Date	Test	Number Completed	Number Correct A	Number Wrong	× ¼ =		Points off B	Score (A − B)	Date	Score	Date	Score
5/15	Diagnostic Practice Test	32	24	8	× ¼	=	2	22				
5/16	Practice Test 1	46	38	8	× ¼	=	2	36				
5/18	Practice Test 2	58	52	6	× ¼	=	1½	50½				
5/20	Practice Test 3	64	60	4	× ¼	=	1	59				
	Practice Test 4				× ¼	=						
	Practice Test 5				× ¼	=						
	Practice Test 6				× ¼	=						

Part C—Number Series

Computing Your Score

Check the answers on your Answer Sheet against the Answer Key. Calculate your score by adding up the number of correct answers you have. You *do not* lost any credit for wrong answers or for questions you don't answer. For example, on a test having 24 questions, if you had 5 correct, 3 incorrect, and omitted 16, your score would be 5.

Guidelines

How good is the score you just made?

17 or higher . . . . Good
Between 12 and 16 . . . . . . Fair
Below 12 . . . . You need to improve.

Once you have mastered the techniques explained in this book, you should routinely be scoring 20 to 24 correct.

Personal Progress Record

The following is a sample of this Personal Progress Record to familiarize you with it. The entries on this sample are based on the example above.

PERSONAL PROGRESS RECORD—SAMPLE

NUMBER SERIES							
Initial Tests				Repeated Tests			
Date	Test	Number Completed	Number Correct (Your Score)	Date	Score	Date	Score
5/15	Diagnostic Practice Test	8	5				
5/16	Practice Test 1	15	11				
5/18	Practice Test 2	17	15				
5/20	Practice Test 3	20	19				
	Practice Test 4						
	Practice Test 5						
	Practice Test 6						

Now turn to page 431. Look at the table entitled "Personal Progress Record—Number Series." Make the proper entries on the line for the practice test you just took. This table will help you record your progress as you take additional practice tests.

Part D—Following Oral Directions

Computing Your Score

Check your answers against the Answer Key. Calculate your score by adding up the number of correct answers you have. You do *not* lose any credit for wrong answers or for questions you don't answer. For example, on a test having 30 questions, if you had 17 correct and 6 incorrect, and omitted 7, your score would be 17.

Guidelines

How good is the score you just made?

28 or higher . . . . Good
Between 24 and 27 . . . . . . Fair
Below 24 . . . . You need to improve.

Once you have mastered the techniques explained in this book (Chapter 7 covers Following Oral Directions), you should routinely score 28 to 30 correct.

Personal Progress Record

Now turn to page 431. In the table entitled "Personal Progress Record—Following Oral Directions," make the proper entries on the line for the practice test you just took. This table will help you record your progress as you take additional practice tests. A sample is printed on the next page to familiarize you with it. The first entry is based on the preceding example.

PERSONAL PROGRESS RECORD—SAMPLE

FOLLOWING ORAL DIRECTIONS							
Initial Tests				Repeated Tests			
Date	Test	Number Completed	Number Correct (Your Score)	Date	Score	Date	Score
5/15	Diagnostic Practice Test	23	17				
5/16	Practice Test 1	23	19				
5/18	Practice Test 2	27	25				
5/20	Practice Test 3	29	28				
	Practice Test 4						
	Practice Test 5						
	Practice Test 6						

DIAGNOSTIC CHARTS

The following charts will help pinpoint your weaknesses by making it easy for you to determine what particular type of question in each part of the test is most difficult for you.

Part A—Address Checking

Type of Difference	"D" Questions	Number of "D" Questions Wrong		
		Trial 1	Trial 2	Trial 3
Numbers: transposed	10, 22, 23, 42, 48, 49, 88, 94			
changed	12, 43, 95			
omitted	82			
Directions	2, 6, 19, 29, 64, 83			
Abbreviations: streets, roads, avenues, etc.	9, 14, 30, 35, 40			
states	52			
Spelling: single letters	5, 15, 17, 20, 26, 37, 38, 41, 45, 47, 53, 55, 57, 65, 66, 69, 72, 73, 74, 76			
groups of letters	7, 16, 67, 75, 92			
Total Number of All Types	49			
	Use the columns on the right to enter the question numbers of "A" items you marked "D."			

This chart will help you to pinpoint the kinds of errors you made on Practice Test 1. Use it as directed below after you have taken and marked the test.

The first column on the left, "Type of Difference," contains the categories whereby addresses may differ (see page 63). On the same line across, the second column gives the numbers of the questions that fall within each category. In the third column, you are to enter the numbers of any "A" questions you answered as "D." Do not include questions that you did not do. Checking the addresses you got wrong may reveal a problem on which you will want to work.

After you have made all the entries, you will be able to see the areas in which you need to improve. Then turn to the appropriate parts of Chapter 3: Address Checking—How to Improve Your Score, read them, and practice the drills that can help. For example, if you find you have been making too many errors picking out number differences, read page 88 and do Drills 18 through 21. If you have a problem with single letters because of reversals like *b* and *d*, or if you have been overlooking the differences between *a*, *e*, and *o*, read page 85. Examine the table and work on Drills 10 and 11 if the problem persists.

Remember that this chart is designed for diagnostic purposes and guidance on further practice. It has been drawn so that you can enter the results each time you retake a practice test. In this way you will be able to see how you are progressing. It is not necessary to record your scores here. That is best done by using the Personal Progress Record Card.

Part B—Memory for Addresses

Kind of Address		Number of Questions	Number Wrong		
			Trial 1	Trial 2	Trial 3
Direct:	List 1	43			
	List 2	42			
	List 3	44			
Numbered:	List 1	45			
	List 2	46			
	List 3	44			

The purpose of this chart is to help you evaluate your performance on the two kinds of memory questions that appear in these memory tests—the questions on the direct (name) addresses and the questions on the numbered addresses. Use the chart as directed below after you have taken and marked the entire test.

The first column on the left, "Kind of Address," is divided by category into "Direct Address" versus "Numbered Address." The second column gives the number of questions in each category on List 1, List 2, and List 3. Use the third column to enter the total number of questions in each category that you answered incorrectly. There is room for you to make additional entries if you take the practice test more than once.

At a glance, you will be able to see which area you need to concentrate on and how well you are progressing as you take repeat trials. Use Chapter 4 and the drills in it to improve your memory for the direct addresses. Use Chapter 5 for the numbered addresses.

Remember to use the Personal Progress Record Card (Memory for Addresses) on page 430 to keep track of your actual scores as you keep studying and practicing.

Part C—Number Series and Part D—Following Oral Directions

Because of the nature of the questions in these tests, Diagnostic Charts are not provided for them. If you find that you made many errors on these tests, study the techniques suggested in Chapters 6 and 7.

Answer Sheet—Practice Test 2

Part A – Address Checking

1 Ⓐ Ⓓ	25 Ⓐ Ⓓ	49 Ⓐ Ⓓ	73 Ⓐ Ⓓ
2 Ⓐ Ⓓ	26 Ⓐ Ⓓ	50 Ⓐ Ⓓ	74 Ⓐ Ⓓ
3 Ⓐ Ⓓ	27 Ⓐ Ⓓ	51 Ⓐ Ⓓ	75 Ⓐ Ⓓ
4 Ⓐ Ⓓ	28 Ⓐ Ⓓ	52 Ⓐ Ⓓ	76 Ⓐ Ⓓ
5 Ⓐ Ⓓ	29 Ⓐ Ⓓ	53 Ⓐ Ⓓ	77 Ⓐ Ⓓ
6 Ⓐ Ⓓ	30 Ⓐ Ⓓ	54 Ⓐ Ⓓ	78 Ⓐ Ⓓ
7 Ⓐ Ⓓ	31 Ⓐ Ⓓ	55 Ⓐ Ⓓ	79 Ⓐ Ⓓ
8 Ⓐ Ⓓ	32 Ⓐ Ⓓ	56 Ⓐ Ⓓ	80 Ⓐ Ⓓ
9 Ⓐ Ⓓ	33 Ⓐ Ⓓ	57 Ⓐ Ⓓ	81 Ⓐ Ⓓ
10 Ⓐ Ⓓ	34 Ⓐ Ⓓ	58 Ⓐ Ⓓ	82 Ⓐ Ⓓ
11 Ⓐ Ⓓ	35 Ⓐ Ⓓ	59 Ⓐ Ⓓ	83 Ⓐ Ⓓ
12 Ⓐ Ⓓ	36 Ⓐ Ⓓ	60 Ⓐ Ⓓ	84 Ⓐ Ⓓ
13 Ⓐ Ⓓ	37 Ⓐ Ⓓ	61 Ⓐ Ⓓ	85 Ⓐ Ⓓ
14 Ⓐ Ⓓ	38 Ⓐ Ⓓ	62 Ⓐ Ⓓ	86 Ⓐ Ⓓ
15 Ⓐ Ⓓ	39 Ⓐ Ⓓ	63 Ⓐ Ⓓ	87 Ⓐ Ⓓ
16 Ⓐ Ⓓ	40 Ⓐ Ⓓ	64 Ⓐ Ⓓ	88 Ⓐ Ⓓ
17 Ⓐ Ⓓ	41 Ⓐ Ⓓ	65 Ⓐ Ⓓ	89 Ⓐ Ⓓ
18 Ⓐ Ⓓ	42 Ⓐ Ⓓ	66 Ⓐ Ⓓ	90 Ⓐ Ⓓ
19 Ⓐ Ⓓ	43 Ⓐ Ⓓ	67 Ⓐ Ⓓ	91 Ⓐ Ⓓ
20 Ⓐ Ⓓ	44 Ⓐ Ⓓ	68 Ⓐ Ⓓ	92 Ⓐ Ⓓ
21 Ⓐ Ⓓ	45 Ⓐ Ⓓ	69 Ⓐ Ⓓ	93 Ⓐ Ⓓ
22 Ⓐ Ⓓ	46 Ⓐ Ⓓ	70 Ⓐ Ⓓ	94 Ⓐ Ⓓ
23 Ⓐ Ⓓ	47 Ⓐ Ⓓ	71 Ⓐ Ⓓ	95 Ⓐ Ⓓ
24 Ⓐ Ⓓ	48 Ⓐ Ⓓ	72 Ⓐ Ⓓ	

✂ Remove by cutting on dotted line.

Part B—Memory for Addresses—List 1

1 ⒶⒷⒸⒹⒺ	19 ⒶⒷⒸⒹⒺ	37 ⒶⒷⒸⒹⒺ	55 ⒶⒷⒸⒹⒺ	73 ⒶⒷⒸⒹⒺ
2 ⒶⒷⒸⒹⒺ	20 ⒶⒷⒸⒹⒺ	38 ⒶⒷⒸⒹⒺ	56 ⒶⒷⒸⒹⒺ	74 ⒶⒷⒸⒹⒺ
3 ⒶⒷⒸⒹⒺ	21 ⒶⒷⒸⒹⒺ	39 ⒶⒷⒸⒹⒺ	57 ⒶⒷⒸⒹⒺ	75 ⒶⒷⒸⒹⒺ
4 ⒶⒷⒸⒹⒺ	22 ⒶⒷⒸⒹⒺ	40 ⒶⒷⒸⒹⒺ	58 ⒶⒷⒸⒹⒺ	76 ⒶⒷⒸⒹⒺ
5 ⒶⒷⒸⒹⒺ	23 ⒶⒷⒸⒹⒺ	41 ⒶⒷⒸⒹⒺ	59 ⒶⒷⒸⒹⒺ	77 ⒶⒷⒸⒹⒺ
6 ⒶⒷⒸⒹⒺ	24 ⒶⒷⒸⒹⒺ	42 ⒶⒷⒸⒹⒺ	60 ⒶⒷⒸⒹⒺ	78 ⒶⒷⒸⒹⒺ
7 ⒶⒷⒸⒹⒺ	25 ⒶⒷⒸⒹⒺ	43 ⒶⒷⒸⒹⒺ	61 ⒶⒷⒸⒹⒺ	79 ⒶⒷⒸⒹⒺ
8 ⒶⒷⒸⒹⒺ	26 ⒶⒷⒸⒹⒺ	44 ⒶⒷⒸⒹⒺ	62 ⒶⒷⒸⒹⒺ	80 ⒶⒷⒸⒹⒺ
9 ⒶⒷⒸⒹⒺ	27 ⒶⒷⒸⒹⒺ	45 ⒶⒷⒸⒹⒺ	63 ⒶⒷⒸⒹⒺ	81 ⒶⒷⒸⒹⒺ
10 ⒶⒷⒸⒹⒺ	28 ⒶⒷⒸⒹⒺ	46 ⒶⒷⒸⒹⒺ	64 ⒶⒷⒸⒹⒺ	82 ⒶⒷⒸⒹⒺ
11 ⒶⒷⒸⒹⒺ	29 ⒶⒷⒸⒹⒺ	47 ⒶⒷⒸⒹⒺ	65 ⒶⒷⒸⒹⒺ	83 ⒶⒷⒸⒹⒺ
12 ⒶⒷⒸⒹⒺ	30 ⒶⒷⒸⒹⒺ	48 ⒶⒷⒸⒹⒺ	66 ⒶⒷⒸⒹⒺ	84 ⒶⒷⒸⒹⒺ
13 ⒶⒷⒸⒹⒺ	31 ⒶⒷⒸⒹⒺ	49 ⒶⒷⒸⒹⒺ	67 ⒶⒷⒸⒹⒺ	85 ⒶⒷⒸⒹⒺ
14 ⒶⒷⒸⒹⒺ	32 ⒶⒷⒸⒹⒺ	50 ⒶⒷⒸⒹⒺ	68 ⒶⒷⒸⒹⒺ	86 ⒶⒷⒸⒹⒺ
15 ⒶⒷⒸⒹⒺ	33 ⒶⒷⒸⒹⒺ	51 ⒶⒷⒸⒹⒺ	69 ⒶⒷⒸⒹⒺ	87 ⒶⒷⒸⒹⒺ
16 ⒶⒷⒸⒹⒺ	34 ⒶⒷⒸⒹⒺ	52 ⒶⒷⒸⒹⒺ	70 ⒶⒷⒸⒹⒺ	88 ⒶⒷⒸⒹⒺ
17 ⒶⒷⒸⒹⒺ	35 ⒶⒷⒸⒹⒺ	53 ⒶⒷⒸⒹⒺ	71 ⒶⒷⒸⒹⒺ	
18 ⒶⒷⒸⒹⒺ	36 ⒶⒷⒸⒹⒺ	54 ⒶⒷⒸⒹⒺ	72 ⒶⒷⒸⒹⒺ	

Part B—Memory for Addresses—List 2

1 ⒶⒷⒸⒹⒺ	19 ⒶⒷⒸⒹⒺ	37 ⒶⒷⒸⒹⒺ	55 ⒶⒷⒸⒹⒺ	73 ⒶⒷⒸⒹⒺ
2 ⒶⒷⒸⒹⒺ	20 ⒶⒷⒸⒹⒺ	38 ⒶⒷⒸⒹⒺ	56 ⒶⒷⒸⒹⒺ	74 ⒶⒷⒸⒹⒺ
3 ⒶⒷⒸⒹⒺ	21 ⒶⒷⒸⒹⒺ	39 ⒶⒷⒸⒹⒺ	57 ⒶⒷⒸⒹⒺ	75 ⒶⒷⒸⒹⒺ
4 ⒶⒷⒸⒹⒺ	22 ⒶⒷⒸⒹⒺ	40 ⒶⒷⒸⒹⒺ	58 ⒶⒷⒸⒹⒺ	76 ⒶⒷⒸⒹⒺ
5 ⒶⒷⒸⒹⒺ	23 ⒶⒷⒸⒹⒺ	41 ⒶⒷⒸⒹⒺ	59 ⒶⒷⒸⒹⒺ	77 ⒶⒷⒸⒹⒺ
6 ⒶⒷⒸⒹⒺ	24 ⒶⒷⒸⒹⒺ	42 ⒶⒷⒸⒹⒺ	60 ⒶⒷⒸⒹⒺ	78 ⒶⒷⒸⒹⒺ
7 ⒶⒷⒸⒹⒺ	25 ⒶⒷⒸⒹⒺ	43 ⒶⒷⒸⒹⒺ	61 ⒶⒷⒸⒹⒺ	79 ⒶⒷⒸⒹⒺ
8 ⒶⒷⒸⒹⒺ	26 ⒶⒷⒸⒹⒺ	44 ⒶⒷⒸⒹⒺ	62 ⒶⒷⒸⒹⒺ	80 ⒶⒷⒸⒹⒺ
9 ⒶⒷⒸⒹⒺ	27 ⒶⒷⒸⒹⒺ	45 ⒶⒷⒸⒹⒺ	63 ⒶⒷⒸⒹⒺ	81 ⒶⒷⒸⒹⒺ
10 ⒶⒷⒸⒹⒺ	28 ⒶⒷⒸⒹⒺ	46 ⒶⒷⒸⒹⒺ	64 ⒶⒷⒸⒹⒺ	82 ⒶⒷⒸⒹⒺ
11 ⒶⒷⒸⒹⒺ	29 ⒶⒷⒸⒹⒺ	47 ⒶⒷⒸⒹⒺ	65 ⒶⒷⒸⒹⒺ	83 ⒶⒷⒸⒹⒺ
12 ⒶⒷⒸⒹⒺ	30 ⒶⒷⒸⒹⒺ	48 ⒶⒷⒸⒹⒺ	66 ⒶⒷⒸⒹⒺ	84 ⒶⒷⒸⒹⒺ
13 ⒶⒷⒸⒹⒺ	31 ⒶⒷⒸⒹⒺ	49 ⒶⒷⒸⒹⒺ	67 ⒶⒷⒸⒹⒺ	85 ⒶⒷⒸⒹⒺ
14 ⒶⒷⒸⒹⒺ	32 ⒶⒷⒸⒹⒺ	50 ⒶⒷⒸⒹⒺ	68 ⒶⒷⒸⒹⒺ	86 ⒶⒷⒸⒹⒺ
15 ⒶⒷⒸⒹⒺ	33 ⒶⒷⒸⒹⒺ	51 ⒶⒷⒸⒹⒺ	69 ⒶⒷⒸⒹⒺ	87 ⒶⒷⒸⒹⒺ
16 ⒶⒷⒸⒹⒺ	34 ⒶⒷⒸⒹⒺ	52 ⒶⒷⒸⒹⒺ	70 ⒶⒷⒸⒹⒺ	88 ⒶⒷⒸⒹⒺ
17 ⒶⒷⒸⒹⒺ	35 ⒶⒷⒸⒹⒺ	53 ⒶⒷⒸⒹⒺ	71 ⒶⒷⒸⒹⒺ	
18 ⒶⒷⒸⒹⒺ	36 ⒶⒷⒸⒹⒺ	54 ⒶⒷⒸⒹⒺ	72 ⒶⒷⒸⒹⒺ	

Part B—Memory for Addresses—List 3

1 ⒶⒷⒸⒹⒺ	19 ⒶⒷⒸⒹⒺ	37 ⒶⒷⒸⒹⒺ	55 ⒶⒷⒸⒹⒺ	73 ⒶⒷⒸⒹⒺ
2 ⒶⒷⒸⒹⒺ	20 ⒶⒷⒸⒹⒺ	38 ⒶⒷⒸⒹⒺ	56 ⒶⒷⒸⒹⒺ	74 ⒶⒷⒸⒹⒺ
3 ⒶⒷⒸⒹⒺ	21 ⒶⒷⒸⒹⒺ	39 ⒶⒷⒸⒹⒺ	57 ⒶⒷⒸⒹⒺ	75 ⒶⒷⒸⒹⒺ
4 ⒶⒷⒸⒹⒺ	22 ⒶⒷⒸⒹⒺ	40 ⒶⒷⒸⒹⒺ	58 ⒶⒷⒸⒹⒺ	76 ⒶⒷⒸⒹⒺ
5 ⒶⒷⒸⒹⒺ	23 ⒶⒷⒸⒹⒺ	41 ⒶⒷⒸⒹⒺ	59 ⒶⒷⒸⒹⒺ	77 ⒶⒷⒸⒹⒺ
6 ⒶⒷⒸⒹⒺ	24 ⒶⒷⒸⒹⒺ	42 ⒶⒷⒸⒹⒺ	60 ⒶⒷⒸⒹⒺ	78 ⒶⒷⒸⒹⒺ
7 ⒶⒷⒸⒹⒺ	25 ⒶⒷⒸⒹⒺ	43 ⒶⒷⒸⒹⒺ	61 ⒶⒷⒸⒹⒺ	79 ⒶⒷⒸⒹⒺ
8 ⒶⒷⒸⒹⒺ	26 ⒶⒷⒸⒹⒺ	44 ⒶⒷⒸⒹⒺ	62 ⒶⒷⒸⒹⒺ	80 ⒶⒷⒸⒹⒺ
9 ⒶⒷⒸⒹⒺ	27 ⒶⒷⒸⒹⒺ	45 ⒶⒷⒸⒹⒺ	63 ⒶⒷⒸⒹⒺ	81 ⒶⒷⒸⒹⒺ
10 ⒶⒷⒸⒹⒺ	28 ⒶⒷⒸⒹⒺ	46 ⒶⒷⒸⒹⒺ	64 ⒶⒷⒸⒹⒺ	82 ⒶⒷⒸⒹⒺ
11 ⒶⒷⒸⒹⒺ	29 ⒶⒷⒸⒹⒺ	47 ⒶⒷⒸⒹⒺ	65 ⒶⒷⒸⒹⒺ	83 ⒶⒷⒸⒹⒺ
12 ⒶⒷⒸⒹⒺ	30 ⒶⒷⒸⒹⒺ	48 ⒶⒷⒸⒹⒺ	66 ⒶⒷⒸⒹⒺ	84 ⒶⒷⒸⒹⒺ
13 ⒶⒷⒸⒹⒺ	31 ⒶⒷⒸⒹⒺ	49 ⒶⒷⒸⒹⒺ	67 ⒶⒷⒸⒹⒺ	85 ⒶⒷⒸⒹⒺ
14 ⒶⒷⒸⒹⒺ	32 ⒶⒷⒸⒹⒺ	50 ⒶⒷⒸⒹⒺ	68 ⒶⒷⒸⒹⒺ	86 ⒶⒷⒸⒹⒺ
15 ⒶⒷⒸⒹⒺ	33 ⒶⒷⒸⒹⒺ	51 ⒶⒷⒸⒹⒺ	69 ⒶⒷⒸⒹⒺ	87 ⒶⒷⒸⒹⒺ
16 ⒶⒷⒸⒹⒺ	34 ⒶⒷⒸⒹⒺ	52 ⒶⒷⒸⒹⒺ	70 ⒶⒷⒸⒹⒺ	88 ⒶⒷⒸⒹⒺ
17 ⒶⒷⒸⒹⒺ	35 ⒶⒷⒸⒹⒺ	53 ⒶⒷⒸⒹⒺ	71 ⒶⒷⒸⒹⒺ	
18 ⒶⒷⒸⒹⒺ	36 ⒶⒷⒸⒹⒺ	54 ⒶⒷⒸⒹⒺ	72 ⒶⒷⒸⒹⒺ	

Part C—Number Series

1 ⒶⒷⒸⒹⒺ	6 ⒶⒷⒸⒹⒺ	11 ⒶⒷⒸⒹⒺ	16 ⒶⒷⒸⒹⒺ	21 ⒶⒷⒸⒹⒺ
2 ⒶⒷⒸⒹⒺ	7 ⒶⒷⒸⒹⒺ	12 ⒶⒷⒸⒹⒺ	17 ⒶⒷⒸⒹⒺ	22 ⒶⒷⒸⒹⒺ
3 ⒶⒷⒸⒹⒺ	8 ⒶⒷⒸⒹⒺ	13 ⒶⒷⒸⒹⒺ	18 ⒶⒷⒸⒹⒺ	23 ⒶⒷⒸⒹⒺ
4 ⒶⒷⒸⒹⒺ	9 ⒶⒷⒸⒹⒺ	14 ⒶⒷⒸⒹⒺ	19 ⒶⒷⒸⒹⒺ	24 ⒶⒷⒸⒹⒺ
5 ⒶⒷⒸⒹⒺ	10 ⒶⒷⒸⒹⒺ	15 ⒶⒷⒸⒹⒺ	20 ⒶⒷⒸⒹⒺ	

✂ Remove by cutting on dotted line.

Part D—Following Oral Directions

1 ⒶⒷⒸⒹⒺ	19 ⒶⒷⒸⒹⒺ	37 ⒶⒷⒸⒹⒺ	55 ⒶⒷⒸⒹⒺ	73 ⒶⒷⒸⒹⒺ
2 ⒶⒷⒸⒹⒺ	20 ⒶⒷⒸⒹⒺ	38 ⒶⒷⒸⒹⒺ	56 ⒶⒷⒸⒹⒺ	74 ⒶⒷⒸⒹⒺ
3 ⒶⒷⒸⒹⒺ	21 ⒶⒷⒸⒹⒺ	39 ⒶⒷⒸⒹⒺ	57 ⒶⒷⒸⒹⒺ	75 ⒶⒷⒸⒹⒺ
4 ⒶⒷⒸⒹⒺ	22 ⒶⒷⒸⒹⒺ	40 ⒶⒷⒸⒹⒺ	58 ⒶⒷⒸⒹⒺ	76 ⒶⒷⒸⒹⒺ
5 ⒶⒷⒸⒹⒺ	23 ⒶⒷⒸⒹⒺ	41 ⒶⒷⒸⒹⒺ	59 ⒶⒷⒸⒹⒺ	77 ⒶⒷⒸⒹⒺ
6 ⒶⒷⒸⒹⒺ	24 ⒶⒷⒸⒹⒺ	42 ⒶⒷⒸⒹⒺ	60 ⒶⒷⒸⒹⒺ	78 ⒶⒷⒸⒹⒺ
7 ⒶⒷⒸⒹⒺ	25 ⒶⒷⒸⒹⒺ	43 ⒶⒷⒸⒹⒺ	61 ⒶⒷⒸⒹⒺ	79 ⒶⒷⒸⒹⒺ
8 ⒶⒷⒸⒹⒺ	26 ⒶⒷⒸⒹⒺ	44 ⒶⒷⒸⒹⒺ	62 ⒶⒷⒸⒹⒺ	80 ⒶⒷⒸⒹⒺ
9 ⒶⒷⒸⒹⒺ	27 ⒶⒷⒸⒹⒺ	45 ⒶⒷⒸⒹⒺ	63 ⒶⒷⒸⒹⒺ	81 ⒶⒷⒸⒹⒺ
10 ⒶⒷⒸⒹⒺ	28 ⒶⒷⒸⒹⒺ	46 ⒶⒷⒸⒹⒺ	64 ⒶⒷⒸⒹⒺ	82 ⒶⒷⒸⒹⒺ
11 ⒶⒷⒸⒹⒺ	29 ⒶⒷⒸⒹⒺ	47 ⒶⒷⒸⒹⒺ	65 ⒶⒷⒸⒹⒺ	83 ⒶⒷⒸⒹⒺ
12 ⒶⒷⒸⒹⒺ	30 ⒶⒷⒸⒹⒺ	48 ⒶⒷⒸⒹⒺ	66 ⒶⒷⒸⒹⒺ	84 ⒶⒷⒸⒹⒺ
13 ⒶⒷⒸⒹⒺ	31 ⒶⒷⒸⒹⒺ	49 ⒶⒷⒸⒹⒺ	67 ⒶⒷⒸⒹⒺ	85 ⒶⒷⒸⒹⒺ
14 ⒶⒷⒸⒹⒺ	32 ⒶⒷⒸⒹⒺ	50 ⒶⒷⒸⒹⒺ	68 ⒶⒷⒸⒹⒺ	86 ⒶⒷⒸⒹⒺ
15 ⒶⒷⒸⒹⒺ	33 ⒶⒷⒸⒹⒺ	51 ⒶⒷⒸⒹⒺ	69 ⒶⒷⒸⒹⒺ	87 ⒶⒷⒸⒹⒺ
16 ⒶⒷⒸⒹⒺ	34 ⒶⒷⒸⒹⒺ	52 ⒶⒷⒸⒹⒺ	70 ⒶⒷⒸⒹⒺ	88 ⒶⒷⒸⒹⒺ
17 ⒶⒷⒸⒹⒺ	35 ⒶⒷⒸⒹⒺ	53 ⒶⒷⒸⒹⒺ	71 ⒶⒷⒸⒹⒺ	
18 ⒶⒷⒸⒹⒺ	36 ⒶⒷⒸⒹⒺ	54 ⒶⒷⒸⒹⒺ	72 ⒶⒷⒸⒹⒺ	

Chapter 10

Practice Test 2

Part A — ADDRESS CHECKING

Work — 6 minutes

In this part of the test you are to decide whether two addresses are alike or different. If the two addresses are *exactly alike in every way*, darken space Ⓐ. If they are different in any way, darken space Ⓓ.

Mark your answers on the Answer Sheet on page 263. Tear it out, put today's date on it, and place it next to the questions.

Allow yourself *exactly 6 minutes* to do as many of the 95 questions as you can. If you finish before the time is up, check your answers.

1.	7004 W 214 St	7004 W 241 St
2.	8996 Harthlodge Dr W	8996 Harthlodge Dr W
3.	3064 10th Ave NE	3064 10th Ave SE
4.	9606 Itaska Dr SE	9606 Itaska Dr SE
5.	216 West Anawanda Dr	217 West Anawanda Dr
6.	Evensville TN	Evansville TN
7.	16049 E 229 St	19049 E 229 St
8.	6256 Wachusett Ave	6256 Wachusett St
9.	2884 Cavvy Rd	2884 Cavvy Rd
10.	Toledo OH 44483	Toledo OK 44483
11.	5690 Vespa Ln	5690 Vesda Ln
12.	9777 64th St E	9777 64th Rd E
13.	9412 Ingham Ave W	9412 Ingram Ave W
14.	5209 S Emilie Pl	5209 S Emilie Pl
15.	Provo UT	Provo UT
16.	5851 Marionette Ave	5815 Marionette Ave
17.	Cherry Hill NJ 07013	Cherry Hill NJ 07103
18.	75 Grosvenor Rd	75 Grosvenor Rd
19.	Warren MI	Warren MT
20.	5237 Vandaveer Ave SE	2537 Vandaveer Ave SE
21.	2408 W Bernath Dr	2408 W Bernath Dr
22.	9073 Hacienda Ave E	9078 Hacienda Ave E
23.	6130 Florister Dr N	6130 Florister Dr N
24.	Green Bay WI	Green Bay WI

25.	1316 Jachurst St SE	1316 Jachurst St SE
26.	4893 West Haven Ct	4893 West Haven Ct
27.	7692 Woodbine Ave	7629 Woodbine Ave
28.	383 Armijo Pl SW	383 Armija Pl SW
29.	Farmington GA	Farmington GU
30.	3047 E Charlotte Ave	3047 E Charlotte Ave
31.	3782 SE Kassabian Ave	3782 SE Kassabian Ave
32.	Glendale CA	Glendale CO
33.	1213 Provencher St	1231 Provencher St
34.	2704 S Winchester St	2704 S Westchester St
35.	3764 Disbrow Ct	3763 Disbrow Ct
36.	3006 Le Brun Ln	3006 Le Brun Ln
37.	8034 Hudson River Rd	8034 Hudson River Rd
38.	1981 E Rickman Way	1981 E Rickman Way
39.	9700 Alamosa Dr	9700 Amalosa Dr
40.	6883 E Wyandanch Ave	6883 W Wyandanch Ave
41.	601 Orange Blvd	601 Orange Blvd
42.	5723 Emaline Ave NW	5723 Evaline Ave NW
43.	2867 Kingshighway Blvd N	2867 Kingshighway Blvd N
44.	1390 E Dean St	1390 E Dean St
45.	2417 W Townsend Ave	2417 W Townsend Ter
46.	1103 W Sindelar Rd	1103 W Sindelar Rd
47.	8090 W Zeamer St	8090 W Zoamer St
48.	6083 Oso Grande Ct	6803 Oso Grande Ct
49.	3841 Tanglewood Cir W	3841 Tanglewood Cir W
50.	8004 Quimera Trl SE	8004 Guimera Trl SE
51.	4723 McDougal Dr	4723 McDougal Dr
52.	9170 Worthen Pl	9170 Worthen Pl
53.	7481 Prince Charles Ct	7481 Prince Charles St
54.	Arlington VA	Arlington WA
55.	1401 Abbott Dr	1401 Abbott Dr
56.	152 Nez Perce Lookout	152 Nez Perce Lookout
57.	Homestead FL 33034	Homestead FL 33034
58.	7470 Oakleigh St	7470 Oakland St
59.	94 Quimby Rd E	94 Quimby Rd E
60.	89140 Palmyra Ave	89104 Palmyra Ave

61. 8182 Stream Ct NW	8182 Stream Pl NW
62. 10 Burlington Ave	10 Burlingham Ave
63. Gadsden AL 39503	Gapsdan AL 39503
64. 2647 E Pearsonville Rd	2647 E Pearsonville Rd
65. 6083 Featherstone Dr	6083 Featherstone Dr
66. Wilkes-Barre, PA 17402	Wilkes-Barre, PE 17402
67. 714 Gapsch Ln	714 Gapsch Ln
68. 1033 Remillard Rd	1033 Remillard Rd
69. Pawtucket RI 02861	Pawtucket RI 02851
70. 5148 Nemesia Pl NE	5148 Nemesia Pl NE
71. 1114 S Sycamore St	1114 E Sycamore St
72. 9276 Interpol Blvd NE	9276 Interpol Blvd NE
73. 4342 E Upstone St	4234 E Upstone St
74. 4101 Ludington St	4101 Ludington St
75. 8270 S Homestead Ave	8270 S Homestead Ave
76. 6398 S Oquendo Rd	6398 S Oquendo Rd
77. 141 Aberfeldy Ter	141 Abernathy Ter
78. 505 Fairfax St	505 Fairfax St
79. 3381 Claymont Path	3381 Claymont Path
80. 6814 Havelock Blvd	6814 Havelock Blvd
81. 7 Paso Del Puma NW	7 Paso Del Puma NE
82. Corpus Christi TX 78410	Corpus Christi TX 78410
83. 5504 Wilmore Dr E	5504 Wilmont Dr E
84. Fort Smith AR 72903	Forth Smith AR 72903
85. Los Alamos CA 93440	Los Alamos CA 93440
86. 801 Xenia St	801 Xenia St
87. 8430 Quanta Ln SW	8430 Quanta Ln SW
88. 83 Grass Valley St	83 Green Valley St
89. 4799 SW Eastgate Cir	4789 SW Eastgate Cir
90. 3994 Vista Campo Blvd	3994 Vista Campo Blvd
91. 1809 N 236th Ave	1809 S 236th Ave
92. 2908 Sagamore Ave	2908 Sagamore Ter
93. 2403 Jamestown Way	2403 Jameston Way
94. 462 Los Poblanos Ranch Ln	462 Los Poblanos Ranch Pl
95. 4871 Dadebridge Ct	4871 Dadebridge Ct

STOP.
If you finish before the time is up, go back and check the questions in this section of the test only.

PART B — MEMORY FOR ADDRESSES

In this part of the test you will have five boxes labeled A, B, C, D, and E. Each box contains five addresses. Three of the five are groups of street addresses, such as 8100–8899 Tremont, 6100–6999 Caleb, and 4500–5799 Broad; and two are names of places. The addresses are different in each box.

There will be several opportunities to study the addresses and the boxes they are in. You will also be given three tests of 88 questions each, and the task of deciding where each address belongs. In some cases, you will have the list *and* the boxes in front of you at the same time; in others you will not. List 1 and List 2 are for warm-up practice. List 3 is the real one that will be scored.

Make sure you understand the format by examining the pretest samples below.

Pretest Samples

A	B	C	D	E
7300–7799 Tremont	6900–7299 Tremont	6300–6899 Tremont	7800–8099 Tremont	8100–8899 Tremont
Pierce	Rockport	April	Desert	Zane
5800–6099 Caleb	7000–7299 Caleb	6100–6999 Caleb	7300–7999 Caleb	4900–5799 Caleb
Veil	Indian	Pullman	Crystal	Eva
6300–6899 Broad	7200–7599 Broad	5800–6299 Broad	4500–5799 Broad	6900–7199 Broad

Questions 1 through 7 show the way the questions look. You have to decide in which lettered box (A, B, C, D, or E) the address belongs and then mark your answer by darkening the appropriate space in the answer grid.

1. 5800–6099 Caleb — 1 Ⓐ Ⓑ Ⓒ Ⓓ Ⓔ
2. Indian — 2 Ⓐ Ⓑ Ⓒ Ⓓ Ⓔ
3. Pullman — 3 Ⓐ Ⓑ Ⓒ Ⓓ Ⓔ
4. 8100–8899 Tremont — 4 Ⓐ Ⓑ Ⓒ Ⓓ Ⓔ
5. 7200–7599 Broad — 5 Ⓐ Ⓑ Ⓒ Ⓓ Ⓔ
6. Veil — 6 Ⓐ Ⓑ Ⓒ Ⓓ Ⓔ
7. Desert — 7 Ⓐ Ⓑ Ⓒ Ⓓ Ⓔ

Answers

1. **A** 2. **B** 3. **C** 4. **E** 5. **B** 6. **A** 7. **D**

Now that you know what to do, you may begin Part B of Practice Test 2. To get the most out of it and the remaining four practice tests in this book, follow the directions and timing *exactly*. Follow each phase of Part B of the test, page by page, until you've completed List 3. It is modeled on the way the Postal Service actually conducts its tests.

Turn to the next page to begin.

Study — 3 minutes

You will be given 3 minutes to spend memorizing the addresses in the boxes. *They are exactly the same ones that will be used for all three tests.* Try to memorize as many as you can. When the 3 minutes are up, turn to page 272 and read the instructions for *List 1*.

A	B	C	D	E
7300–7799 Tremont	6900–7299 Tremont	6300–6899 Tremont	7800–8099 Tremont	8100–8899 Tremont
Pierce	Rockport	April	Desert	Zane
5800–6099 Caleb	7000–7299 Caleb	6100–6999 Caleb	7300–7999 Caleb	4900–5799 Caleb
Veil	Indian	Pullman	Crystal	Eva
6300–6899 Broad	7200–7599 Broad	5800–6299 Broad	4500–5799 Broad	6900–7199 Broad

List 1

Work — 3 minutes

Tear out the Answer Sheet for List 1. For each question, mark the Answer Sheet on page 264 to show the letter of the box in which the address belongs. Try to remember the locations of as many addresses as you can. *You will now have 3 minutes to complete List 1.* If you are not sure of an answer, you should guess.

A	B	C	D	E
7300–7799 Tremont	6900–7299 Tremont	6300–6899 Tremont	7800–8099 Tremont	8100–8899 Tremont
Pierce	Rockport	April	Desert	Zane
5800–6099 Caleb	7000–7299 Caleb	6100–6999 Caleb	7300–7999 Caleb	4900–5799 Caleb
Veil	Indian	Pullman	Crystal	Eva
6300–6899 Broad	7200–7599 Broad	5800–6299 Broad	4500–5799 Broad	6900–7199 Broad

1. 6300–6899 Broad
2. 7200–7599 Broad
3. Pierce
4. Rockport
5. 7300–7799 Tremont
6. 8100–8899 Tremont
7. 5800–6699 Caleb
8. Veil
9. April
10. Desert
11. 6900–7299 Tremont
12. Pierce
13. Zane
14. 6300–6899 Tremont
15. Zane
16. 6900–7199 Broad
17. Indian
18. 6300–6899 Broad
19. Pullman
20. Eva
21. Rockport
22. 4900–5799 Caleb
23. Crystal
24. 6900–7199 Broad
25. 7800–8099 Tremont
26. Indian
27. 5800–6299 Broad
28. Eva
29. 7000–7299 Caleb
30. 4500–5799 Broad
31. 7300–7999 Caleb
32. 6100–6999 Caleb
33. Veil
34. 4500–5799 Broad
35. Rockport
36. Pierce
37. 6900–7199 Broad
38. Zane
39. 4900–5799 Caleb
40. 7300–7999 Caleb
41. Crystal
42. 7000–7299 Caleb
43. Veil
44. 5800–6299 Broad

45. Crystal
46. 8100–8899 Tremont
47. Pullman
48. 7800–8099 Tremont
49. 7000–7299 Caleb
50. Pullman
51. April
52. 7300–7999 Caleb
53. Desert
54. 7200–7599 Broad
55. Pierce
56. Eva
57. Zane
58. 7300–7799 Tremont
59. 6900–7199 Broad
60. 5800–6099 Caleb
61. Pierce
62. Desert
63. Crystal
64. 6300–6899 Tremont
65. 6300–6899 Broad
66. 7300–7799 Tremont
67. 4900–5799 Tremont
68. April
69. 7800–8099 Tremont
70. 6300–6899 Tremont
71. 8100–8899 Tremont
72. Rockport
73. Eva
74. 5800–6099 Caleb
75. Indian
76. Pullman
77. Indian
78. April
79. 4500–5799 Broad
80. 6100–6999 Caleb
81. Eva
82. 7200–7599 Broad
83. 6300–6899 Broad
84. Veil
85. Desert
86. 6100–6999 Caleb
87. 5800–6299 Broad
88. Pullman

STOP.
If you finish before the time is up, go back and check the questions in this section of the test only.

List 2

Work — 3 minutes

Do these questions *without* looking back at the boxes. For each question, mark your answer on the Answer Sheet for List 2 on page 264. If you are not sure of an answer, you should guess.

1. 7200–7599 Broad
2. Rockport
3. 8100–8899 Tremont
4. Veil
5. Desert
6. Pierce
7. 6300–6899 Tremont
8. 6900–7199 Broad
9. 6300–6899 Broad
10. Eva
11. 4900–5799 Caleb
12. 6900–7199 Broad
13. Indian
14. Eva
15. 4500–5799 Broad
16. 6100–6999 Caleb
17. 4500–5799 Broad
18. Pierce
19. Zane
20. 7300–7999 Caleb
21. 7000–7299 Caleb
22. 5800–6299 Broad
23. 8100–8899 Tremont
24. 7800–8099 Tremont
25. Pullman
26. 7300–7999 Caleb
27. 7200–7599 Broad
28. Eva
29. 7300–7799 Tremont
30. 5800–6099 Caleb
31. Desert
32. 6300–6899 Tremont
33. 7300–7799 Tremont
34. April
35. 6300–6899 Tremont
36. Rockport
37. 5800–6099 Caleb
38. Pullman
39. April
40. 6100–6999 Caleb
41. 7200–7599 Broad
42. Veil
43. 6100–6999 Caleb
44. Pullman

45. 6300–6899 Broad
46. Pierce
47. 7300–7799 Tremont
48. 5800–6699 Caleb
49. April
50. 6900–7299 Tremont
51. Zane
52. 6100–6999 Caleb
53. Indian
54. Pullman
55. Rockport
56. Crystal
57. 7800–8099 Tremont
58. 5800–6299 Broad
59. 7000–7299 Caleb
60. 7300–7999 Caleb
61. Veil
62. Rockport
63. 6900–7199 Broad
64. 4900–5799 Caleb
65. Crystal
66. Veil
67. Crystal
68. Pullman
69. 7000–7299 Caleb
70. April
71. Desert
72. Pierce
73. Zane
74. 6900–7199 Broad
75. Pierce
76. Crystal
77. 6300–6899 Broad
78. 4900–5799 Caleb
79. 7800–8099 Tremont
80. 8100–8899 Tremont
81. Eva
82. Indian
83. 7000–7299 Caleb
84. 4500–5799 Broad
85. Eva
86. 6300–6899 Broad
87. Desert
88. 5800–6299 Broad

STOP.
If you finish before the time is up, go back and check the questions in this section of the test only.

List 3

Study — 5 minutes

You are now about to take the test using List 3. *(This is the test that counts!)*

Turn back to page 271 and study the boxes again. *You have 5 minutes to restudy the addresses.*

Work — 5 minutes

For each question, mark the Answer Sheet on page 265 to show the letter of the box in which the address belongs. You have *exactly 5 minutes* to do the test. During these 5 minutes, *do not* turn to any other page.

1. 5800–6299 Broad
2. Veil
3. 7000–7299 Caleb
4. Crystal
5. 7300–7999 Caleb
6. 4900–5799 Caleb
7. Zane
8. 6900–7199 Broad
9. Pierce
10. Rockport
11. 4500–5799 Broad
12. Veil
13. 6100–6999 Caleb
14. 7300–7999 Caleb
15. 4500–5799 Broad
16. 7000–7299 Caleb
17. Eva
18. 5800–6299 Broad
19. Indian
20. 7800–8099 Tremont
21. 6900–7199 Broad
22. Crystal
23. 4900–5799 Caleb
24. Rockport
25. Eva
26. Pullman
27. 6300–6899 Broad
28. Indian
29. 6900–7199 Broad
30. Zane
31. 6300–6899 Tremont
32. Zane
33. Pierce
34. 6900–7299 Tremont
35. Desert
36. April
37. Veil
38. 5800–6699 Caleb
39. 8100–8899 Tremont
40. 7300–7799 Tremont
41. Rockport
42. Pierce
43. 7200–7599 Broad
44. 6300–6899 Broad

45. Pullman
46. 5800–6299 Broad
47. 6100–6999 Caleb
48. Desert
49. Veil
50. 6300–6899 Broad
51. 7200–7599 Broad
52. Eva
53. 6100–6999 Caleb
54. 4500–5799 Broad
55. April
56. Indian
57. Pullman
58. 7000–7299 Caleb
59. 5800–6099 Caleb
60. Eva
61. Rockport
62. 8100–8899 Tremont
63. 6300–6899 Tremont
64. 7800–8099 Tremont
65. April
66. 4900–5799 Caleb
67. 7300–7799 Tremont
68. 6300–6899 Broad
69. 6300–6899 Tremont
70. Crystal
71. Desert
72. Pierce
73. 5800–6099 Caleb
74. 6900–7199 Broad
75. 7300–7799 Tremont
76. Zane
77. Eva
78. Pierce
79. 7200–7599 Broad
80. Desert
81. 7300–7999 Caleb
82. April
83. Pullman
84. 7000–7299 Caleb
85. 7800–8099 Tremont
86. Pullman
87. 8100–8899 Tremont
88. Crystal

STOP.
If you finish before the time is up, go back and check the questions in this section of the test only.

PART C — NUMBER SERIES

Work — 20 minutes

For each Number Series question, there is a series of numbers that follow some definite order, and below each are five sets of two numbers each. You are to look at the numbers in the series and find out what order they follow. Then decide what the next two numbers in that series would be if the same order were continued. Mark your answers on the Answer Sheet for Number Series on page 265.

You have 20 minutes to complete this part of the test. If you finish before the time is up, check your answers. The answers and explanations are on pages 286 to 287.

1. 80 70 65 60 50 65 40 __ __
   A) 30 20 B) 55 45 C) 30 65 D) 65 55 E) 65 30

2. 17 14 18 15 19 16 20 __ __
   A) 21 17 B) 18 19 C) 17 15 D) 17 21 E) 19 16

3. 36 37 38 39 38 37 36 __ __
   A) 35 34 B) 36 37 C) 37 38 D) 38 39 E) 35 33

4. 2 2 2 3 6 6 4 12 __ __
   A) 12 5 B) 12 12 C) 5 12 D) 7 14 E) 12 7

5. 28 18 31 21 34 24 37 __ __
   A) 26 36 B) 27 38 C) 38 25 D) 28 38 E) 27 40

6. 41 36 31 26 21 16 11 __ __
   A) 10 5 B) 11 6 C) 6 5 D) 6 1 E) 7 2

7. 6 38 18 31 30 24 42 __ __
   A) 34 48 B) 30 54 C) 17 54 D) 35 36 E) 52 18

8. $\frac{1}{3}$ $\frac{2}{6}$ $\frac{3}{9}$ $\frac{4}{12}$ $\frac{5}{15}$ $\frac{6}{18}$ $\frac{7}{21}$ __ __
   A) $\frac{8}{22}$ $\frac{9}{23}$ B) $\frac{9}{24}$ $\frac{9}{25}$ C) $\frac{9}{24}$ $\frac{10}{26}$ D) $\frac{6}{23}$ $\frac{7}{23}$ E) $\frac{8}{24}$ $\frac{9}{27}$

9. 11 13 8 15 17 12 19 __ __
   A) 20 21 B) 14 21 C) 13 18 D) 23 11 E) 21 16

10. 18 20 21 21 23 24 24 __ __
    A) 25 27 B) 24 25 C) 28 27 D) 26 27 E) 25 26

11. 1 4 2 8 3 12 4 __ __
    A) 5 13 B) 14 5 C) 16 5 D) 8 20 E) 6 18

12. 5 6 3 12 13 10 40 __ __
A) 20 50 B) 39 50 C) 11 8 D) 15 60 E) 41 38

13. 15 12 89 15 12 89 15 __ __
A) 12 89 B) 15 12 C) 89 15 D) 12 15 E) 89 12

14. 11 53 22 42 33 31 44 __ __
A) 30 22 B) 20 55 C) 32 53 D) 29 40 E) 56 36

15. 20 17 8 9 14 11 8 9 8 __ __
A) 5 8 B) 9 9 C) 8 9 D) 10 5 E) 12 4

16. 81 27 27 27 9 9 9 __ __
A) 6 6 B) 3 3 C) 6 3 D) 3 6 E) 3 1

17. 18 14 14 24 12 12 30 __ __
A) 14 36 B) 16 22 C) 10 10 D) 7 15 E) 5 15

18. 13 21 11 19 9 17 7 __ __
A) 15 9 B) 18 8 C) 5 19 D) 7 15 E) 15 5

19. 12 3 10 3 8 3 6 __ __
A) 3 6 B) 4 3 C) 3 3 D) 3 4 E) 2 3

20. 3 4 4 3 3 4 4 __ __
A) 4 3 B) 5 3 C) 3 3 D) 4 4 E) 3 4

21. 18 26 24 19 18 16 20 __ __
A) 21 19 B) 12 10 C) 14 8 D) 10 8 E) 18 10

22. 10 14 12 6 10 8 4 __ __
A) 4 10 B) 6 10 C) 8 6 D) 8 10 E) 4 2

23. 5 6 7 10 8 9 10 9 __ __
A) 10 11 B) 11 10 C) 9 8 D) 11 12 E) 7 10

24. 2 11 11 3 12 12 4 __ __
A) 5 12 B) 13 5 C) 5 13 D) 13 14 E) 13 13

STOP.
If you finish before the time is up, go back and check the questions in this section of the test only.

PART D — FOLLOWING ORAL DIRECTIONS

This part of the test gauges your ability to understand and carry out spoken directions *exactly* as they are given to you.

In order to prepare to take Part D of the test, follow the steps below:

1. Enlist the help of a friend who will be the "reader." It will be his or her job to read aloud a series of directions that you are to follow *exactly*. The reader will need a watch that displays seconds, because the directions must be read at the correct speed.
2. Tear out pages 285 and 286. These are the worksheets you should have in front of you as you listen to the directions given by the reader, who will tell you to do certain things with the items on each line on the worksheets.
3. Use the Answer Sheet for Following Oral Directions on page 285, and insert today's date. You will darken the appropriate spaces in accordance with the directions given by the reader.
4. *Now hand this entire book to the reader.* Ask him/her to review the section below headed "Instructions to the Reader." It explains exactly how the reader is to proceed.

When you and the reader are ready to start this part of Practice Test 2, he/she will begin reading to you the section marked "Directions." YOU ARE NOT TO READ THESE AT ANY TIME BEFORE OR DURING THE TEST. If you do, you will lose the benefit of this part of the practice test.

Instructions to the "Reader"

These instructions should be read at about 80 words per minute. You should practice reading the material in the box until you can do it in exactly 1 minute. This will give you a feel for the way you should read the test material.

1-MINUTE PRACTICE

> Look at line 20 on your worksheet. There are two circles and two boxes of different sizes with numbers in them. If 7 is less than 3 and if 2 is smaller than 4, write C in the larger circle. Otherwise write B as in *baker* in the smaller box. Now, on your answer sheet, darken the space for the number-letter combination in the box or circle.

You should read the entire test aloud before you read it to the person taking the test, in order to acquaint yourself with the procedure and the desired rate of reading.

Read slowly but at a natural pace. In other words, do not space the words so that there are unnaturally long pauses between them. The instruction "Pause slightly" indicates only enough time to take a breath. The other instructions for pauses give the recommended length for each. If possible, use a watch with a second hand.

All the material that follows, except the words in parentheses, is to be read aloud. Now start reading the directions. *Do not repeat any of the directions.*

Directions: In the test, I will read instructions to you. You are to mark your worksheets according to the instructions that I read to you. After each set of instructions, I'll give you time to record your answers on your answer sheet.

Try to understand the instructions as I read them; I cannot repeat them. Do not ask any questions from now on.

If, when you go to darken a space for a number, you find that you have already darkened another space for that number, either (1) erase the first mark and darken the space for your new choice, or (2) let the first mark stay and do not darken any other space. When you finish, you should have no more than one space darkened for each number.

Turn to Worksheet 1.

Look at line 1 on your worksheet. (Pause slightly.) Write A next to the middle number. (Pause 2 seconds.) Now, on your answer sheet, find the number beside which you wrote and darken space A for that number. (Pause 5 seconds.)

Look at line 2 on your worksheet. (Pause slightly.) There are 5 circles. Each circle has a number in it. (Pause slightly.) Write an E in the circle that has the highest number in it. (Pause 2 seconds.) Now, on your answer sheet, darken the space for the number-letter combination that is in the circle you just wrote in. (Pause 5 seconds.)

Look at line 2 again. (Pause slightly.) In the circle with the lowest number write B as in *baker.* (Pause 2 seconds.) Now, on your answer sheet, darken the space for the number-letter combination that is in the circle you just wrote in. (Pause 5 seconds.)

Look at line 3 on your worksheet. (Pause slightly.) There are 5 boxes. Each box has a letter in it. In the fourth box write the answer to this question: Which of the following numbers is largest: 17, 21, 23, 15, 19? (Pause 5 seconds.) Now, on your answer sheet, darken the space for the number-letter combination that is in the box you just wrote in. (Pause 5 seconds.)

In the second box do nothing. In the first box write 46. (Pause 2 seconds.) Now, on your answer sheet, darken the space for the number-letter combination that is in the box you just wrote in. (Pause 5 seconds.)

Look at line 3 again. (Pause slightly.) In the fifth box, write the answer to this question: At what number do the hands of a clock point when it is midnight? (Pause 2 seconds.) Now, on your answer sheet, darken the space for the number-letter combination that is in the box you just wrote in. (Pause 5 seconds.)

Look at line 4 on your worksheet. (Pause slightly.) Draw a line under every number that is more than 25 but less than 35. (Pause 12 seconds.) Now, on your answer sheet, for every number that you drew a line under, darken space C. (Pause 25 seconds.)

Look at line 5 on your worksheet. There are three boxes with letters and words in them. (Pause slightly.) Each box represents a post office in a different area of the city. Post Office E delivers mail in the Westchester Square area, Post Office D delivers mail in the Corley Circle area, and Post Office C delivers mail in the Union Junction area. (Pause slightly.) Write the number 68 on the line inside the box which represents the post office that delivers mail in the Corley Circle area. (Pause 2 seconds.) Now, on your answer sheet, find number 68 and darken the space for the letter that is in the box you just wrote in. (Pause 5 seconds.)

Now look at line 6 on your worksheet. (Pause slightly.) There are four boxes with numbers on them. Each number represents the age of one of the four workers in a local post office. (Pause slightly.) Write B as in *baker* on the line in the box containing the age of the youngest worker in that post office. (Pause 2 seconds.) Now, on your answer sheet, darken the space for the number-letter combination that is in the box you just wrote in. (Pause 5 seconds.)

Look at line 7 on your worksheet. (Pause slightly.) There are five circles on the line. Some of the circles are partially or entirely shaded. (Pause slightly.) Count the number of circles that are partially or entirely shaded, add 3, and write that number in the middle circle. (Pause 2 seconds.) Now, on your answer sheet, darken the space for the number-letter combination that is in the circle you just wrote in.

Look at line 7 again. (Pause slightly.) Count the number of circles that do not have any shading, subtract 1, and write that number in the first circle. (Pause 2 seconds.) Now, on your answer sheet, darken the space for the number-letter combination that is in the circle you just wrote in. (Pause 5 seconds.)

Look at the letters on line 8 on your worksheet. (Pause slightly.) Draw a line under the second letter in the line. (Pause 2 seconds.) Now, on your answer sheet, find number 53 and darken the space for the letter under which you drew a line. (Pause 5 seconds.)

Look at line 8 again. (Pause slightly.) Draw two lines under the sixth letter in the line. (Pause 3 seconds.) Now, on your answer sheet, find number 63 and darken the space for the letter under which you drew two lines. (Pause 5 seconds.)

Look at line 9 on your worksheet. (Pause slightly.) There are two circles and two boxes of different sizes with numbers in them. (Pause slightly.) If 8 is more than 5 and if 7 is less than 4, write E in the larger circle. (Pause slightly.) Otherwise, write D as in *dog* in the smaller box. (Pause 2 seconds.) Now, on your answer sheet, darken the space for the number-letter combination that is in the box or circle you just wrote in. (Pause 5 seconds.)

Look at line 10 on your worksheet. (Pause slightly.) Draw a line under every "O" in the line. (Pause 5 seconds.) Count the number of lines you have drawn, and write that number at the end of the line. (Pause 5 seconds.) Now, write an E next to the number you just wrote. (Pause 2 seconds.) Now, on your answer sheet, darken the space for the number-letter combination you just wrote at the end of the line. (Pause 5 seconds.)

Look at the numbers on line 11 on your worksheet. (Pause slightly.) Draw a circle around every number that is more than 35 but less than 45. (Pause 12 seconds.) Now, on your answer sheet, for each number around which you drew a circle, darken box E. (Pause 25 seconds.)

Now turn to Worksheet 2. (Pause 5 seconds.)

Look at line 12 on your worksheet. (Pause slightly.) There are a number and a letter in each of the five boxes. In the box that has the highest number write on the line the last two figures of that number. (Pause 2 seconds.) Now, on your answer sheet, darken the space for the number-letter combination that is in the box you just wrote in. (Pause 5 seconds.)

Look at line 13 on your worksheet. (Pause slightly.) Each of the boxes and circles has a letter of the alphabet in it. If, in the alphabet, the letter in the small box comes after the letter in the large circle, write 84 on the line in the small circle. (Pause 2 seconds.) Otherwise, write 71 in the large box. (Pause 2 seconds.) Now, on your answer sheet, darken the space for the number-letter combination that is in the circle or box you just wrote in. (Pause 5 seconds.)

Look at the boxes and words on line 14 on your worksheet. (Pause slightly.) Write the second letter of the first word in the third box. (Pause 2 seconds.) Write the first letter of the second word in the first box. (Pause 2 seconds.) Write the fourth letter of the third word in the second box. (Pause 2 seconds.) Now, on your answer sheet, darken the spaces for the number-letter combinations that are in the three boxes you just wrote in. (Pause 25 seconds.)

Look at line 15 on your worksheet. (Pause slightly.) In each circle there is the time when a piece of express mail was received. In the circle for the earliest time, write on the line the last two figures of the time. (Pause 2 seconds.) Now, on your answer sheet, darken the space for the number-letter combination that is in the circle you just wrote in. (Pause 5 seconds.)

Look at line 16. (Pause slightly.) On the line next to the left-hand letter write the answer to this question: how many weeks are there in a year? (Pause 2 seconds.) Now, on your answer sheet, find the number you just wrote and darken the space for the letter you wrote it next to. (Pause 5 seconds.)

Look at the drawing on line 17 on your worksheet. (Pause slightly.) The four boxes are bins used to sort mail. If 6 is smaller than 9, and 7 is more than 5, write C in the lower right-hand bin. Otherwise, write D as in *dog* in the upper left-hand bin. (Pause 2 seconds.) Now, on your answer sheet, darken the space for the number-letter combination that is in the bin you just wrote in. (Pause 5 seconds.)

Now look at line 18 on your worksheet. (Pause slightly.) Each box has a number in it. Write C in any box which has a number that does not have three digits in it. (Pause 2 seconds.) Now, on your answer sheet, darken the space for the number-letter combination in each box you just wrote in. (Pause 5 seconds.)

Look at line 19 on your worksheet. (Pause slightly.) Count the number of A's in the three boxes, add 5, and write that number on the first line to the right of the three boxes. (Pause 2 seconds.) On the line next to that number, write B as in *boy*. (Pause 2 seconds.) Now, on your answer sheet, darken the space for the number-letter combination that is on the two lines you just wrote on. (Pause 5 seconds.)

END OF EXAMINATION.
If you finish before the time is up, go back and check the questions in this section of the test only.

Practice Test 2—Worksheet 1

Part D—Following Oral Directions

1. 68 ___ 13 ___ 37 ___

2. (19 ___) (65 ___) (49 ___) (72 ___) (74 ___)

3. [C ___] [A ___] [E ___] [B ___] [D ___]

4. 29 11 16 33 20 9 15 35 26

5. [E WESTCHESTER SQUARE ___] [D CORLEY CIRCLE ___] [C UNION JUNCTION ___]

6. [41 ___] [62 ___] [47 ___] [53 ___]

7. (___ B) (___ D) (___ A) ( ) (___ E)

8. B C E D E A B E D

9. (57 ___) (18 ___) [39 ___] [13 ___]

10. X O O O X O X X X O O X O X X

11. 44 35 57 38 46 30 40 45

✂ Remove by cutting on dotted line.

Practice Test 2—Worksheet 2

Part D—Following Oral Directions

12. | 285 ___ D | 361 ___ A | 455 ___ C | 371 ___ B | 514 E ___ |

13. | ___ A | ___ C | ___ D | ___ B |

14. | 5 ___ | 17 ___ | 56 ___ | CAMP | BEND | RIPE |

15. | 10:12 ___ E | 10:51 ___ D | 10:11 ___ C | 10:32 ___ B | 10:45 ___ A |

16. ___ B ___ E

17.

78 ___	49 ___
61 ___	82 ___

18. | 741 ___ | 580 ___ | 194 ___ | 692 ___ | 85 ___ | 304 ___ |

19.

A	A	D
D	E	A
A	C	B

ANSWER KEY

Part A—Address Checking

1. D	11. D	21. A	31. A	41. A	51. A	61. D	71. D	81. D	91. D
2. A	12. D	22. D	32. D	42. D	52. A	62. D	72. A	82. A	92. D
3. D	13. D	23. A	33. D	43. A	53. D	63. D	73. D	83. D	93. D
4. A	14. A	24. A	34. D	44. A	54. D	64. A	74. A	84. A	94. D
5. D	15. A	25. A	35. D	45. D	55. A	65. A	75. A	85. A	95. A
6. D	16. D	26. A	36. A	46. A	56. A	66. D	76. A	86. A	
7. D	17. D	27. D	37. A	47. D	57. A	67. A	77. D	87. A	
8. D	18. A	28. D	38. A	48. D	58. D	68. A	78. A	88. D	
9. A	19. D	29. D	39. D	49. A	59. A	69. D	79. A	89. D	
10. D	20. A	30. A	40. D	50. D	60. D	70. A	80. A	90. A	

Part B—Memory for Addresses

List 1

1. A	10. D	19. C	28. E	37. E	46. E	55. A	64. C	73. E	82. B
2. B	11. B	20. E	29. B	38. E	47. C	56. E	65. B	74. A	83. A
3. A	12. A	21. B	30. E	39. E	48. D	57. E	66. A	75. B	84. A
4. B	13. E	22. E	31. D	40. D	49. B	58. A	67. E	76. C	85. D
5. A	14. C	23. D	32. C	41. D	50. C	59. E	68. C	77. B	86. C
6. E	15. E	24. E	33. A	42. B	51. C	60. A	69. D	78. C	87. C
7. A	16. E	25. D	34. D	43. A	52. A	61. A	70. C	79. D	88. C
8. A	17. B	26. B	35. B	44. C	53. D	62. D	71. E	80. C	
9. C	18. E	27. C	36. A	45. D	54. B	63. D	72. B	81. E	

List 2

1. B	10. E	19. E	28. E	37. A	46. A	55. B	64. E	73. E	82. B
2. B	11. E	20. D	29. A	38. C	47. A	56. D	65. D	74. E	83. B
3. E	12. E	21. B	30. A	39. C	48. A	57. D	66. A	75. A	84. D
4. A	13. B	22. A	31. D	40. C	49. C	58. C	67. D	76. D	85. E
5. D	14. E	23. E	32. C	41. B	50. B	59. B	68. C	77. A	86. A
6. A	15. D	24. D	33. A	42. A	51. E	60. D	69. B	78. E	87. D
7. C	16. C	25. C	34. C	43. C	52. C	61. A	70. C	79. D	88. C
8. E	17. D	26. D	35. C	44. C	53. B	62. B	71. D	80. E	
9. A	18. A	27. B	36. B	45. A	54. C	63. E	72. A	81. E	

List 3

1. C	10. B	19. B	28. B	37. A	46. C	55. C	64. D	73. A	82. C
2. A	11. D	20. D	29. E	38. A	47. C	56. B	65. C	74. E	83. C
3. B	12. A	21. E	30. E	39. E	48. D	57. C	66. E	75. A	84. B
4. D	13. C	22. D	31. A	40. A	49. A	58. B	67. A	76. E	85. D
5. D	14. D	23. E	32. E	41. B	50. A	59. A	68. A	77. E	86. C
6. E	15. D	24. B	33. A	42. A	51. B	60. E	69. C	78. A	87. E
7. E	16. B	25. E	34. B	43. B	52. E	61. B	70. D	79. B	88. D
8. E	17. E	26. C	35. D	44. A	53. C	62. E	71. D	80. D	
9. A	18. C	27. A	36. C	45. C	54. D	63. C	72. A	81. D	

Part C—Number Series

1. **C**	4. **A**	7. **C**	10. **D**	13. **A**	16. **B**	19. **D**	22. **C**
2. **D**	5. **E**	8. **E**	11. **C**	14. **B**	17. **C**	20. **C**	23. **D**
3. **C**	6. **D**	9. **E**	12. **E**	15. **A**	18. **E**	21. **D**	24. **E**

Part D—Following Oral Directions

1. **B**	7. **E**	12. **D**	17. **E**	26. **C**	38. **E**	41. **B**	52. **B**	63. **A**	74. **E**
5. **B**	9. **B**	13. **A**	19. **B**	29. **C**	39. **D**	44. **E**	53. **C**	68. **D**	82. **C**
6. **A**	11. **C**	14. **E**	23. **B**	33. **C**	40. **E**	46. **C**	56. **A**	71. **A**	85. **C**

ANSWER EXPLANATIONS FOR PART C—NUMBER SERIES

1. **C** The numbers in this series decrease by 10. <u>65</u> is inserted after every two numbers of the series.
2. **D** This series follows a − 3, + 4; and so on rule.
3. **C** These numbers follow an ascending-descending pattern, from 36 to 39 and back down again; repeating the same cycle again and again.
4. **A** Each group of three numbers, beginning with 2 2 2 may be considered to be a mini-series. Each mini-series begins one number higher than the first number in the preceding series. Each beginning number is multiplied and the result is repeated. The multipliers keep increasing by one. It is a lot easier to see what is happening if you use a loop diagram.

   ×1 R | ×2 R | ×3 R

   2 2 2 | 3 6 6 | 4 12 <u>12</u> | <u>5</u>

   +1 +1 +1

5. **E** Here you have a pair of alternating series, each increasing by 3. If you wish, you could consider these numbers as following a − 10, + 13; rule, but the arithmetic can be a little tricky.
6. **D** This series is absolutely simple compared to the series in Examples 4 and 5 above. It merely follows a − 5 rule.
7. **C** Here again is a case of two alternating series. One ascends by + 12. The other descends by − 7.
8. **E** The top number of each fraction keeps increasing by 1. The bottom number increases by 3.
9. **E** One of these two alternating series follows a + 2 rule. The other one, which increases by 4, appears after every *two* numbers of the first.
10. **D** There is a complex rule that governs these numbers: + 2, + 1, repeat; + 2, + 1, repeat; and so on.
11. **C** You can see this series in two ways. First, as a pair of alternating series, one increasing by 1; the other increasing by 4. Or, you could see each pair of numbers as connected by × 4. For example:

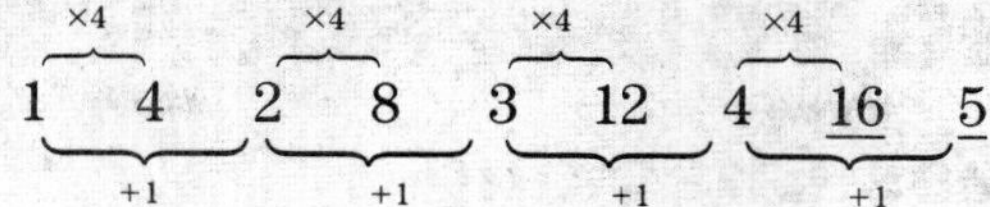

12. **E** A complex rule that includes addition, subtraction and multiplication is at work here: + 1, − 3, × 4; and so on.
13. **A** A sequence of three unrelated numbers: 15, 12, 89 keeps repeating.
14. **B** These are two alternating series. One follows a + 11 rule; the other a − 11 rule.
15. **A** This series appears confusing. It is a − 3 series that continues for two numbers and is then interrupted by the arbitrary numbers, 8 9. This pattern keeps repeating. You have to be extremely careful in selecting the next two numbers.
16. **B** After a number has been *divided* by 3, the answer repeats three times.
17. **C** Here you have two alternating series. One (starting with 18) increases by 6. The other decreases by 2 and repeats the number.
18. **E** You may consider these numbers either as following a + 8, − 10 pattern, or as two alternating series, each following a − 2 rule.
19. **D** The number 3 appears between every two numbers in this − 2 series.
20. **C** Here you have the numbers 3 and 4 continually reversing their order. You might also see a pattern that consists of the sequence 3 4 4 3 continually recycling.
21. **D** There are two alternating series here. The loop diagram shown makes this very difficult question easy to answer.

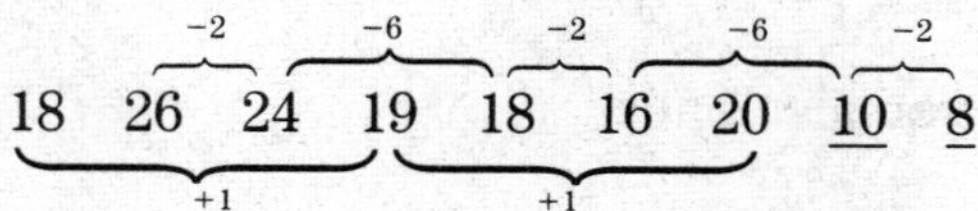

22. **C** The complex rule: + 4, − 2, ÷ 2 connects members of this series. Here, too, a loop diagram is most important.
23. **D** One of the two alternating series in this group of numbers increases by 1. It continues for *three* numbers and is then interrupted by *one* member of a descending series that follows a − 1 rule.
24. **E** Both alternating series follow a + 1 rule. One series repeats each number before being interrupted by a member of the other series.

EVALUATING YOUR PROGRESS*

Part A—Address Checking

Computing Your Score

Check your answers against the Answer Key. Score yourself by using this formula:

Number right
− Number wrong

YOUR SCORE

For example, if you completed 52 questions and got 8 wrong,

Number right	=	44
− Number wrong	=	− 8
Your score	=	36

Notice that you do *not* figure in the questions that you did not answer.

Guidelines

How good is the score you just made?

52 or higher . . . . Good
Between 32 and 52 . . . . . . Fair
Below 32 . . . . You need to improve.

These are commonly accepted figures. It is believed, however, that you should not be satisfied with anything *less* than 52. Experience in training many people to prepare for this test shows that most serious test candidates who use the preparation program described in this book (Chapter 3 covers Address Checking) will be able to raise their score to the upper sixties, seventies, or eighties.

Personal Progress Record

One of the most satisfying things that can happen while you are working toward a goal is to see signs of progress. The improvement you make on Address Checking can readily be seen by examining the scores you make on the practice tests and exercises in this book. Keeping track of your growing skill is important so a Personal Progress Record has been furnished for your use on page 430.

---

* Please note that the scores you obtain by following the computation instructions for the various parts of this test are "raw" scores. The Postal Service combines and converts the raw scores for the various parts of the test into a scaled score obtained by using special conversion formulas that are kept confidential. This scaled score (plus any veteran's credits to which you are entitled) forms the basis for your final rating and your standing on the list. This final rating will be sent to you after the tests have been marked.

Furthermore, even though you take one test, your final score will vary depending on the title. For example, your rating on the Mail Handler register may very well be different from your rating on the Postal Clerk-Carrier register. Apparently, the relative rating given to each part of the test varies according to title. This is another argument for taking as many tests in as many titles as possible, as suggested on page 3.

You are encouraged to calculate your raw scores because they furnish a realistic and convenient way for you to keep track of your relative performance and progress as you work your way through this book.

The following is a sample of this Personal Progress Record to familiarize you with it. The entries on this sample are based on the example above.

PERSONAL PROGRESS RECORD—SAMPLE

ADDRESS CHECKING												
Initial Tests								Repeated Tests			
Date	Test	Number Completed	Number Correct	–	Number Wrong	=	Score	Date	Score	Date	Score
5/15	Diagnostic Practice Test	52	44	–	8	=	36				
5/16	Practice Test 1	64	54	–	10	=	44				
5/18	Practice Test 2	66	57	–	9	=	48				
5/20	Practice Test 3	70	60	–	10	=	50				
	Practice Test 4			–		=					
	Practice Test 5			–		=					
	Practice Test 6			–		=					

Now turn to page 430. In the table entitled "Personal Progress Record—Address Checking," make the proper entries on the line for Practice Test 2, which you just took. Review the special techniques in Chapter 3: Address Checking—How to Improve Your Score, before taking Practice Test 3. After taking the additional practice tests, enter the results immediately. Keep this record. It will help you record your progress.

Part B—Memory for Addresses

Computing Your Score

Check the answers on your answer sheet against the Answer Key. Calculate your score by using these four steps:

1. Enter the number of answers you got right .... _______
2. Enter the number of answers you got wrong .... _______
3. Divide the number wrong by 4 (or multiply by ¼) .... – _______
4. Subtract Line 3 from Line 1 .... YOUR SCORE = _______

Follow this example to make sure that you have figured your score correctly. It will be assumed that you completed 32 questions, of which you got 24 right and 8 wrong.

Line 1....... Number right 24

Line 2....... Number wrong......... 8

Line 3....... ¼ of line 2 = ¼ × 8...... – 2

Line 4....... 24 – 2 .. YOUR SCORE = 22

Notice that, just as for Address Checking, questions that are not answered are *not* taken into account.

Guidelines

How good is the score you just made?

52 or higher . . . . Good
Between 32 and 52 . . . . . . Fair
Below 32 . . . . You need to improve.

If your score on this test was low, don't be discouraged. Nevertheless, you may wish to review Chapters 4 and 5, which offer special techniques for handling Part B—Memory for Addresses, before taking Practice Test 3.

Personal Progress Record

Turn to page 430. Use the table entitled "Personal Progress—Memory for Addresses" to keep a permanent record of your scores on List 3 of the practice tests. A sample is printed below to familiarize you with it. The first entry is based on the preceding example.

PERSONAL PROGRESS RECORD—SAMPLE

MEMORY FOR ADDRESSES											
Initial Tests								Repeated Tests			
Date	Test	Number Completed	Number Correct *A*	Number Wrong	× ¼ =	Points off *B*	Score (*A* − *B*)	Date	Score	Date	Score
5/15	Diagnostic Practice Test	32	24	8	× ¼ =	2	22				
5/16	Practice Test 1	46	38	8	× ¼ =	2	36				
5/18	Practice Test 2	58	52	6	× ¼ =	1½	50½				
5/20	Practice Test 3	64	60	4	× ¼ =	1	59				
	Practice Test 4				× ¼ =						
	Practice Test 5				× ¼ =						
	Practice Test 6				× ¼ =						

Part C—Number Series

Computing Your Score

Check the answers on your Answer Sheet against the Answer Key. Calculate your score by adding up the number of correct answers you have. You *do not* lose any credit for wrong answers or for questions you don't answer. For example, on a test having 24 questions, if you had 5 correct, 3 incorrect, and omitted 16, your score would be 5.

Guidelines

How good is the score you just made?

17 or higher . . . . Good
Between 12 and 16 . . . . . . Fair
Below 12 . . . . You need to improve.

Once you have mastered the techniques explained in this book, you should routinely be scoring 20 to 24 correct.

Personal Progress Record

The following is a sample of this Personal Progress Record to familiarize you with it. The entries on this sample are based on the example above.

PERSONAL PROGRESS RECORD—SAMPLE

NUMBER SERIES							
Initial Tests				Repeated Tests			
Date	Test	Number Completed	Number Correct (Your Score)	Date	Score	Date	Score
5/15	Diagnostic Practice Test	8	5				
5/16	Practice Test 1	15	11				
5/18	Practice Test 2	17	15				
5/20	Practice Test 3	20	19				
	Practice Test 4						
	Practice Test 5						
	Practice Test 6						

Now turn to page 431. Look at the table entitled "Personal Progress Record—Number Series." Make the proper entries on the line for the practice test you just took. This table will help you record your progress as you take additional practice tests.

Part D—Following Oral Directions

Computing Your Score

Check your answers against the Answer Key. Calculate your score by adding up the number of correct answers you have. You do *not* lost any credit for wrong answers or for questions you don't answer. For example, on a test having 30 questions, if you had 17 correct and 6 incorrect, and omitted 7, your score would be 17.

Guidelines

How good is the score you just made?

28 or higher . . . . Good
Between 24 and 27 . . . . . . Fair
Below 24 . . . . You need to improve.

Once you have mastered the techniques explained in this book (Chapter 7 covers Following Oral Directions), you should routinely score 28 to 30 correct.

Personal Progress Record

Now turn to page 431. In the table entitled "Personal Progress Record—Following Oral Directions," make the proper entries on the line for the practice test you just took. This table will help you record your progress as you take additional practice tests. A sample is printed below to familiarize you with it. The first entry is based on the preceding example.

PERSONAL PROGRESS RECORD—SAMPLE

FOLLOWING ORAL DIRECTIONS							
Initial Tests				Repeated Tests			
Date	Test	Number Completed	Number Correct (Your Score)	Date	Score	Date	Score
5/15	Diagnostic Practice Test	23	17				
5/16	Practice Test 1	23	19				
5/18	Practice Test 2	27	25				
5/20	Practice Test 3	29	28				
	Practice Test 4						
	Practice Test 5						
	Practice Test 6						

DIAGNOSTIC CHARTS

The following charts will help pinpoint your weaknesses by making it easy for you to determine what particular type of question in each part of the test is most difficult for you.

Part A—Address Checking

Type of Difference	"D" Questions	Number of "D" Questions Wrong		
		Trial 1	Trial 2	Trial 3
Numbers: transposed	1, 16, 17, 27, 33, 48, 60			
changed	5, 7, 22, 35, 69, 73, 89			
omitted				
Directions	3, 40, 71, 81, 91			
Abbreviations: streets, roads, avenues, etc.	8, 12, 45, 53, 61, 92 95			
states	10, 19, 29, 32, 54, 66			
Spelling: single letters	6, 11, 13, 28, 42, 47, 50 63			
groups of letters	34, 39, 58, 62, 77, 83, 88 93			
Total Number of All Types	48			
	Use the columns on the right to enter the question numbers of "A" items you marked "D."			

This chart will help you to pinpoint the kinds of errors you made on Practice Test 2. Use it as directed below after you have taken and marked the test.

The first column on the left, "Type of Difference," contains the categories whereby addresses may differ (see page 63). On the same line across, the second column gives the numbers of the questions that fall within each category. In the third column, you are to enter the numbers of any "A" questions you answered as "D." Do not include questions that you did not do. Checking the addresses you got wrong may reveal a problem on which you will want to work.

After you have made all the entries, you will be able to see the areas in which you need to improve. Then turn to the appropriate parts of Chapter 3: Address Checking—How to Improve Your Score, read them, and practice the drills that can help. For example, if you find you have been making too many errors picking out number differences, read page 88 and do Drills 18 through 21. If you have a problem with single letters because of reversals like *b* and *d*, or if you have been overlooking the differences between *a*, *e*, and *o*, read page 85. Examine the table and work on Drills 10 and 11 if the problem persists.

Remember that this chart is designed for diagnostic purposes and guidance on further practice. It has been drawn so that you can enter the results each time you retake a practice test. In this way you will be able to see how you are progressing. It is not necessary to record your scores here. That is best done by using the Personal Progress Record Card.

Part B—Memory for Addresses

Kind of Address	Number of Questions	Number Wrong		
		Trial 1	Trial 2	Trial 3
Direct:				
List 1	43			
List 2	41			
List 3	42			
Numbered:				
List 1	45			
List 2	47			
List 3	46			

The purpose of this chart is to help you evaluate your performance on the two kinds of memory questions that appear in these memory tests—the questions on the direct (name) addresses and the questions on the numbered addresses. Use the chart as directed below after you have taken and marked the entire test.

The first column on the left, "Kind of Address," is divided by category into "Direct Address" versus "Numbered Address." The second column gives the number of questions in each category on List 1, List 2, and List 3. Use the third column to enter the total number of questions in each category that you answered incorrectly. There is room for you to make additional entries if you take the practice test more than once.

At a glance, you will be able to see which area you need to concentrate on and how well you are progressing as you take repeat trials. Use Chapter 4 and the drills in it to improve your memory for the direct addresses. Use Chapter 5 for the numbered addresses.

Remember to use the Personal Progress Record Card (Memory for Addresses) on page 430 to keep track of your actual scores as you keep studying and practicing.

Part C—Number Series and Part D—Following Oral Directions

Because of the nature of the questions in these tests, Diagnostic Charts are not provided for them. If you find that you made many errors on these tests, study the techniques suggested in Chapters 6 and 7.

Answer Sheet—Practice Test 3

Part A—Address Checking

1 Ⓐ Ⓓ	25 Ⓐ Ⓓ	49 Ⓐ Ⓓ	73 Ⓐ Ⓓ
2 Ⓐ Ⓓ	26 Ⓐ Ⓓ	50 Ⓐ Ⓓ	74 Ⓐ Ⓓ
3 Ⓐ Ⓓ	27 Ⓐ Ⓓ	51 Ⓐ Ⓓ	75 Ⓐ Ⓓ
4 Ⓐ Ⓓ	28 Ⓐ Ⓓ	52 Ⓐ Ⓓ	76 Ⓐ Ⓓ
5 Ⓐ Ⓓ	29 Ⓐ Ⓓ	53 Ⓐ Ⓓ	77 Ⓐ Ⓓ
6 Ⓐ Ⓓ	30 Ⓐ Ⓓ	54 Ⓐ Ⓓ	78 Ⓐ Ⓓ
7 Ⓐ Ⓓ	31 Ⓐ Ⓓ	55 Ⓐ Ⓓ	79 Ⓐ Ⓓ
8 Ⓐ Ⓓ	32 Ⓐ Ⓓ	56 Ⓐ Ⓓ	80 Ⓐ Ⓓ
9 Ⓐ Ⓓ	33 Ⓐ Ⓓ	57 Ⓐ Ⓓ	81 Ⓐ Ⓓ
10 Ⓐ Ⓓ	34 Ⓐ Ⓓ	58 Ⓐ Ⓓ	82 Ⓐ Ⓓ
11 Ⓐ Ⓓ	35 Ⓐ Ⓓ	59 Ⓐ Ⓓ	83 Ⓐ Ⓓ
12 Ⓐ Ⓓ	36 Ⓐ Ⓓ	60 Ⓐ Ⓓ	84 Ⓐ Ⓓ
13 Ⓐ Ⓓ	37 Ⓐ Ⓓ	61 Ⓐ Ⓓ	85 Ⓐ Ⓓ
14 Ⓐ Ⓓ	38 Ⓐ Ⓓ	62 Ⓐ Ⓓ	86 Ⓐ Ⓓ
15 Ⓐ Ⓓ	39 Ⓐ Ⓓ	63 Ⓐ Ⓓ	87 Ⓐ Ⓓ
16 Ⓐ Ⓓ	40 Ⓐ Ⓓ	64 Ⓐ Ⓓ	88 Ⓐ Ⓓ
17 Ⓐ Ⓓ	41 Ⓐ Ⓓ	65 Ⓐ Ⓓ	89 Ⓐ Ⓓ
18 Ⓐ Ⓓ	42 Ⓐ Ⓓ	66 Ⓐ Ⓓ	90 Ⓐ Ⓓ
19 Ⓐ Ⓓ	43 Ⓐ Ⓓ	67 Ⓐ Ⓓ	91 Ⓐ Ⓓ
20 Ⓐ Ⓓ	44 Ⓐ Ⓓ	68 Ⓐ Ⓓ	92 Ⓐ Ⓓ
21 Ⓐ Ⓓ	45 Ⓐ Ⓓ	69 Ⓐ Ⓓ	93 Ⓐ Ⓓ
22 Ⓐ Ⓓ	46 Ⓐ Ⓓ	70 Ⓐ Ⓓ	94 Ⓐ Ⓓ
23 Ⓐ Ⓓ	47 Ⓐ Ⓓ	71 Ⓐ Ⓓ	95 Ⓐ Ⓓ
24 Ⓐ Ⓓ	48 Ⓐ Ⓓ	72 Ⓐ Ⓓ	

✂ Remove by cutting on dotted line.

Part B—Memory for Addresses—List 1

1	ⒶⒷⒸⒹⒺ	19	ⒶⒷⒸⒹⒺ	37	ⒶⒷⒸⒹⒺ	55	ⒶⒷⒸⒹⒺ	73	ⒶⒷⒸⒹⒺ
2	ⒶⒷⒸⒹⒺ	20	ⒶⒷⒸⒹⒺ	38	ⒶⒷⒸⒹⒺ	56	ⒶⒷⒸⒹⒺ	74	ⒶⒷⒸⒹⒺ
3	ⒶⒷⒸⒹⒺ	21	ⒶⒷⒸⒹⒺ	39	ⒶⒷⒸⒹⒺ	57	ⒶⒷⒸⒹⒺ	75	ⒶⒷⒸⒹⒺ
4	ⒶⒷⒸⒹⒺ	22	ⒶⒷⒸⒹⒺ	40	ⒶⒷⒸⒹⒺ	58	ⒶⒷⒸⒹⒺ	76	ⒶⒷⒸⒹⒺ
5	ⒶⒷⒸⒹⒺ	23	ⒶⒷⒸⒹⒺ	41	ⒶⒷⒸⒹⒺ	59	ⒶⒷⒸⒹⒺ	77	ⒶⒷⒸⒹⒺ
6	ⒶⒷⒸⒹⒺ	24	ⒶⒷⒸⒹⒺ	42	ⒶⒷⒸⒹⒺ	60	ⒶⒷⒸⒹⒺ	78	ⒶⒷⒸⒹⒺ
7	ⒶⒷⒸⒹⒺ	25	ⒶⒷⒸⒹⒺ	43	ⒶⒷⒸⒹⒺ	61	ⒶⒷⒸⒹⒺ	79	ⒶⒷⒸⒹⒺ
8	ⒶⒷⒸⒹⒺ	26	ⒶⒷⒸⒹⒺ	44	ⒶⒷⒸⒹⒺ	62	ⒶⒷⒸⒹⒺ	80	ⒶⒷⒸⒹⒺ
9	ⒶⒷⒸⒹⒺ	27	ⒶⒷⒸⒹⒺ	45	ⒶⒷⒸⒹⒺ	63	ⒶⒷⒸⒹⒺ	81	ⒶⒷⒸⒹⒺ
10	ⒶⒷⒸⒹⒺ	28	ⒶⒷⒸⒹⒺ	46	ⒶⒷⒸⒹⒺ	64	ⒶⒷⒸⒹⒺ	82	ⒶⒷⒸⒹⒺ
11	ⒶⒷⒸⒹⒺ	29	ⒶⒷⒸⒹⒺ	47	ⒶⒷⒸⒹⒺ	65	ⒶⒷⒸⒹⒺ	83	ⒶⒷⒸⒹⒺ
12	ⒶⒷⒸⒹⒺ	30	ⒶⒷⒸⒹⒺ	48	ⒶⒷⒸⒹⒺ	66	ⒶⒷⒸⒹⒺ	84	ⒶⒷⒸⒹⒺ
13	ⒶⒷⒸⒹⒺ	31	ⒶⒷⒸⒹⒺ	49	ⒶⒷⒸⒹⒺ	67	ⒶⒷⒸⒹⒺ	85	ⒶⒷⒸⒹⒺ
14	ⒶⒷⒸⒹⒺ	32	ⒶⒷⒸⒹⒺ	50	ⒶⒷⒸⒹⒺ	68	ⒶⒷⒸⒹⒺ	86	ⒶⒷⒸⒹⒺ
15	ⒶⒷⒸⒹⒺ	33	ⒶⒷⒸⒹⒺ	51	ⒶⒷⒸⒹⒺ	69	ⒶⒷⒸⒹⒺ	87	ⒶⒷⒸⒹⒺ
16	ⒶⒷⒸⒹⒺ	34	ⒶⒷⒸⒹⒺ	52	ⒶⒷⒸⒹⒺ	70	ⒶⒷⒸⒹⒺ	88	ⒶⒷⒸⒹⒺ
17	ⒶⒷⒸⒹⒺ	35	ⒶⒷⒸⒹⒺ	53	ⒶⒷⒸⒹⒺ	71	ⒶⒷⒸⒹⒺ		
18	ⒶⒷⒸⒹⒺ	36	ⒶⒷⒸⒹⒺ	54	ⒶⒷⒸⒹⒺ	72	ⒶⒷⒸⒹⒺ		

Part B—Memory for Addresses—List 2

1	ⒶⒷⒸⒹⒺ	19	ⒶⒷⒸⒹⒺ	37	ⒶⒷⒸⒹⒺ	55	ⒶⒷⒸⒹⒺ	73	ⒶⒷⒸⒹⒺ
2	ⒶⒷⒸⒹⒺ	20	ⒶⒷⒸⒹⒺ	38	ⒶⒷⒸⒹⒺ	56	ⒶⒷⒸⒹⒺ	74	ⒶⒷⒸⒹⒺ
3	ⒶⒷⒸⒹⒺ	21	ⒶⒷⒸⒹⒺ	39	ⒶⒷⒸⒹⒺ	57	ⒶⒷⒸⒹⒺ	75	ⒶⒷⒸⒹⒺ
4	ⒶⒷⒸⒹⒺ	22	ⒶⒷⒸⒹⒺ	40	ⒶⒷⒸⒹⒺ	58	ⒶⒷⒸⒹⒺ	76	ⒶⒷⒸⒹⒺ
5	ⒶⒷⒸⒹⒺ	23	ⒶⒷⒸⒹⒺ	41	ⒶⒷⒸⒹⒺ	59	ⒶⒷⒸⒹⒺ	77	ⒶⒷⒸⒹⒺ
6	ⒶⒷⒸⒹⒺ	24	ⒶⒷⒸⒹⒺ	42	ⒶⒷⒸⒹⒺ	60	ⒶⒷⒸⒹⒺ	78	ⒶⒷⒸⒹⒺ
7	ⒶⒷⒸⒹⒺ	25	ⒶⒷⒸⒹⒺ	43	ⒶⒷⒸⒹⒺ	61	ⒶⒷⒸⒹⒺ	79	ⒶⒷⒸⒹⒺ
8	ⒶⒷⒸⒹⒺ	26	ⒶⒷⒸⒹⒺ	44	ⒶⒷⒸⒹⒺ	62	ⒶⒷⒸⒹⒺ	80	ⒶⒷⒸⒹⒺ
9	ⒶⒷⒸⒹⒺ	27	ⒶⒷⒸⒹⒺ	45	ⒶⒷⒸⒹⒺ	63	ⒶⒷⒸⒹⒺ	81	ⒶⒷⒸⒹⒺ
10	ⒶⒷⒸⒹⒺ	28	ⒶⒷⒸⒹⒺ	46	ⒶⒷⒸⒹⒺ	64	ⒶⒷⒸⒹⒺ	82	ⒶⒷⒸⒹⒺ
11	ⒶⒷⒸⒹⒺ	29	ⒶⒷⒸⒹⒺ	47	ⒶⒷⒸⒹⒺ	65	ⒶⒷⒸⒹⒺ	83	ⒶⒷⒸⒹⒺ
12	ⒶⒷⒸⒹⒺ	30	ⒶⒷⒸⒹⒺ	48	ⒶⒷⒸⒹⒺ	66	ⒶⒷⒸⒹⒺ	84	ⒶⒷⒸⒹⒺ
13	ⒶⒷⒸⒹⒺ	31	ⒶⒷⒸⒹⒺ	49	ⒶⒷⒸⒹⒺ	67	ⒶⒷⒸⒹⒺ	85	ⒶⒷⒸⒹⒺ
14	ⒶⒷⒸⒹⒺ	32	ⒶⒷⒸⒹⒺ	50	ⒶⒷⒸⒹⒺ	68	ⒶⒷⒸⒹⒺ	86	ⒶⒷⒸⒹⒺ
15	ⒶⒷⒸⒹⒺ	33	ⒶⒷⒸⒹⒺ	51	ⒶⒷⒸⒹⒺ	69	ⒶⒷⒸⒹⒺ	87	ⒶⒷⒸⒹⒺ
16	ⒶⒷⒸⒹⒺ	34	ⒶⒷⒸⒹⒺ	52	ⒶⒷⒸⒹⒺ	70	ⒶⒷⒸⒹⒺ	88	ⒶⒷⒸⒹⒺ
17	ⒶⒷⒸⒹⒺ	35	ⒶⒷⒸⒹⒺ	53	ⒶⒷⒸⒹⒺ	71	ⒶⒷⒸⒹⒺ		
18	ⒶⒷⒸⒹⒺ	36	ⒶⒷⒸⒹⒺ	54	ⒶⒷⒸⒹⒺ	72	ⒶⒷⒸⒹⒺ		

✂ Remove by cutting on dotted line.

Part B—Memory for Addresses—List 3

1 ⒶⒷⒸⒹⒺ
2 ⒶⒷⒸⒹⒺ
3 ⒶⒷⒸⒹⒺ
4 ⒶⒷⒸⒹⒺ
5 ⒶⒷⒸⒹⒺ
6 ⒶⒷⒸⒹⒺ
7 ⒶⒷⒸⒹⒺ
8 ⒶⒷⒸⒹⒺ
9 ⒶⒷⒸⒹⒺ
10 ⒶⒷⒸⒹⒺ
11 ⒶⒷⒸⒹⒺ
12 ⒶⒷⒸⒹⒺ
13 ⒶⒷⒸⒹⒺ
14 ⒶⒷⒸⒹⒺ
15 ⒶⒷⒸⒹⒺ
16 ⒶⒷⒸⒹⒺ
17 ⒶⒷⒸⒹⒺ
18 ⒶⒷⒸⒹⒺ
19 ⒶⒷⒸⒹⒺ
20 ⒶⒷⒸⒹⒺ
21 ⒶⒷⒸⒹⒺ
22 ⒶⒷⒸⒹⒺ
23 ⒶⒷⒸⒹⒺ
24 ⒶⒷⒸⒹⒺ
25 ⒶⒷⒸⒹⒺ
26 ⒶⒷⒸⒹⒺ
27 ⒶⒷⒸⒹⒺ
28 ⒶⒷⒸⒹⒺ
29 ⒶⒷⒸⒹⒺ
30 ⒶⒷⒸⒹⒺ
31 ⒶⒷⒸⒹⒺ
32 ⒶⒷⒸⒹⒺ
33 ⒶⒷⒸⒹⒺ
34 ⒶⒷⒸⒹⒺ
35 ⒶⒷⒸⒹⒺ
36 ⒶⒷⒸⒹⒺ
37 ⒶⒷⒸⒹⒺ
38 ⒶⒷⒸⒹⒺ
39 ⒶⒷⒸⒹⒺ
40 ⒶⒷⒸⒹⒺ
41 ⒶⒷⒸⒹⒺ
42 ⒶⒷⒸⒹⒺ
43 ⒶⒷⒸⒹⒺ
44 ⒶⒷⒸⒹⒺ
45 ⒶⒷⒸⒹⒺ
46 ⒶⒷⒸⒹⒺ
47 ⒶⒷⒸⒹⒺ
48 ⒶⒷⒸⒹⒺ
49 ⒶⒷⒸⒹⒺ
50 ⒶⒷⒸⒹⒺ
51 ⒶⒷⒸⒹⒺ
52 ⒶⒷⒸⒹⒺ
53 ⒶⒷⒸⒹⒺ
54 ⒶⒷⒸⒹⒺ
55 ⒶⒷⒸⒹⒺ
56 ⒶⒷⒸⒹⒺ
57 ⒶⒷⒸⒹⒺ
58 ⒶⒷⒸⒹⒺ
59 ⒶⒷⒸⒹⒺ
60 ⒶⒷⒸⒹⒺ
61 ⒶⒷⒸⒹⒺ
62 ⒶⒷⒸⒹⒺ
63 ⒶⒷⒸⒹⒺ
64 ⒶⒷⒸⒹⒺ
65 ⒶⒷⒸⒹⒺ
66 ⒶⒷⒸⒹⒺ
67 ⒶⒷⒸⒹⒺ
68 ⒶⒷⒸⒹⒺ
69 ⒶⒷⒸⒹⒺ
70 ⒶⒷⒸⒹⒺ
71 ⒶⒷⒸⒹⒺ
72 ⒶⒷⒸⒹⒺ
73 ⒶⒷⒸⒹⒺ
74 ⒶⒷⒸⒹⒺ
75 ⒶⒷⒸⒹⒺ
76 ⒶⒷⒸⒹⒺ
77 ⒶⒷⒸⒹⒺ
78 ⒶⒷⒸⒹⒺ
79 ⒶⒷⒸⒹⒺ
80 ⒶⒷⒸⒹⒺ
81 ⒶⒷⒸⒹⒺ
82 ⒶⒷⒸⒹⒺ
83 ⒶⒷⒸⒹⒺ
84 ⒶⒷⒸⒹⒺ
85 ⒶⒷⒸⒹⒺ
86 ⒶⒷⒸⒹⒺ
87 ⒶⒷⒸⒹⒺ
88 ⒶⒷⒸⒹⒺ

Part C—Number Series

1 ⒶⒷⒸⒹⒺ
2 ⒶⒷⒸⒹⒺ
3 ⒶⒷⒸⒹⒺ
4 ⒶⒷⒸⒹⒺ
5 ⒶⒷⒸⒹⒺ
6 ⒶⒷⒸⒹⒺ
7 ⒶⒷⒸⒹⒺ
8 ⒶⒷⒸⒹⒺ
9 ⒶⒷⒸⒹⒺ
10 ⒶⒷⒸⒹⒺ
11 ⒶⒷⒸⒹⒺ
12 ⒶⒷⒸⒹⒺ
13 ⒶⒷⒸⒹⒺ
14 ⒶⒷⒸⒹⒺ
15 ⒶⒷⒸⒹⒺ
16 ⒶⒷⒸⒹⒺ
17 ⒶⒷⒸⒹⒺ
18 ⒶⒷⒸⒹⒺ
19 ⒶⒷⒸⒹⒺ
20 ⒶⒷⒸⒹⒺ
21 ⒶⒷⒸⒹⒺ
22 ⒶⒷⒸⒹⒺ
23 ⒶⒷⒸⒹⒺ
24 ⒶⒷⒸⒹⒺ

Part D—Following Oral Directions

1 ⒶⒷⒸⒹⒺ
2 ⒶⒷⒸⒹⒺ
3 ⒶⒷⒸⒹⒺ
4 ⒶⒷⒸⒹⒺ
5 ⒶⒷⒸⒹⒺ
6 ⒶⒷⒸⒹⒺ
7 ⒶⒷⒸⒹⒺ
8 ⒶⒷⒸⒹⒺ
9 ⒶⒷⒸⒹⒺ
10 ⒶⒷⒸⒹⒺ
11 ⒶⒷⒸⒹⒺ
12 ⒶⒷⒸⒹⒺ
13 ⒶⒷⒸⒹⒺ
14 ⒶⒷⒸⒹⒺ
15 ⒶⒷⒸⒹⒺ
16 ⒶⒷⒸⒹⒺ
17 ⒶⒷⒸⒹⒺ
18 ⒶⒷⒸⒹⒺ
19 ⒶⒷⒸⒹⒺ
20 ⒶⒷⒸⒹⒺ
21 ⒶⒷⒸⒹⒺ
22 ⒶⒷⒸⒹⒺ
23 ⒶⒷⒸⒹⒺ
24 ⒶⒷⒸⒹⒺ
25 ⒶⒷⒸⒹⒺ
26 ⒶⒷⒸⒹⒺ
27 ⒶⒷⒸⒹⒺ
28 ⒶⒷⒸⒹⒺ
29 ⒶⒷⒸⒹⒺ
30 ⒶⒷⒸⒹⒺ
31 ⒶⒷⒸⒹⒺ
32 ⒶⒷⒸⒹⒺ
33 ⒶⒷⒸⒹⒺ
34 ⒶⒷⒸⒹⒺ
35 ⒶⒷⒸⒹⒺ
36 ⒶⒷⒸⒹⒺ
37 ⒶⒷⒸⒹⒺ
38 ⒶⒷⒸⒹⒺ
39 ⒶⒷⒸⒹⒺ
40 ⒶⒷⒸⒹⒺ
41 ⒶⒷⒸⒹⒺ
42 ⒶⒷⒸⒹⒺ
43 ⒶⒷⒸⒹⒺ
44 ⒶⒷⒸⒹⒺ
45 ⒶⒷⒸⒹⒺ
46 ⒶⒷⒸⒹⒺ
47 ⒶⒷⒸⒹⒺ
48 ⒶⒷⒸⒹⒺ
49 ⒶⒷⒸⒹⒺ
50 ⒶⒷⒸⒹⒺ
51 ⒶⒷⒸⒹⒺ
52 ⒶⒷⒸⒹⒺ
53 ⒶⒷⒸⒹⒺ
54 ⒶⒷⒸⒹⒺ
55 ⒶⒷⒸⒹⒺ
56 ⒶⒷⒸⒹⒺ
57 ⒶⒷⒸⒹⒺ
58 ⒶⒷⒸⒹⒺ
59 ⒶⒷⒸⒹⒺ
60 ⒶⒷⒸⒹⒺ
61 ⒶⒷⒸⒹⒺ
62 ⒶⒷⒸⒹⒺ
63 ⒶⒷⒸⒹⒺ
64 ⒶⒷⒸⒹⒺ
65 ⒶⒷⒸⒹⒺ
66 ⒶⒷⒸⒹⒺ
67 ⒶⒷⒸⒹⒺ
68 ⒶⒷⒸⒹⒺ
69 ⒶⒷⒸⒹⒺ
70 ⒶⒷⒸⒹⒺ
71 ⒶⒷⒸⒹⒺ
72 ⒶⒷⒸⒹⒺ
73 ⒶⒷⒸⒹⒺ
74 ⒶⒷⒸⒹⒺ
75 ⒶⒷⒸⒹⒺ
76 ⒶⒷⒸⒹⒺ
77 ⒶⒷⒸⒹⒺ
78 ⒶⒷⒸⒹⒺ
79 ⒶⒷⒸⒹⒺ
80 ⒶⒷⒸⒹⒺ
81 ⒶⒷⒸⒹⒺ
82 ⒶⒷⒸⒹⒺ
83 ⒶⒷⒸⒹⒺ
84 ⒶⒷⒸⒹⒺ
85 ⒶⒷⒸⒹⒺ
86 ⒶⒷⒸⒹⒺ
87 ⒶⒷⒸⒹⒺ
88 ⒶⒷⒸⒹⒺ

Chapter 11

Practice Test 3

THE LAST WORD

You now know that score improvements are possible and that the means to attain them lie in your hands. The study techniques for all four parts of the test are yours. You know they work. You have completed drills and practice tests to sharpen your skills. You have also completed special drills and practice tests to help correct any areas of weakness, such as narrow eye span, regression, and perception problems. The strategies to use to make the most of your technique and skill have been prepared for you.

Also, by now you should be on your way to answering the test-taking questions posed in this book that are strictly personal:

- How fast should you go on the Address Checking questions to strike the balance between speed and accuracy that will yield the highest score?
- How should you divide your study time between the names and numbers on the Memory for Addresses questions?
- What method or combination of methods should you use to memorize the addresses in the boxes?
- How many addresses is it realistic for you to try to remember? Should you go for all 25, or are you better off concentrating on 16, 18, or 20?

As was noted before, it is important to come to the real test with your mind made up on these points.

There are four more full-scale practice tests to help you continue your exam preparation program. You may take them each more than once if you choose. Don't forget to make copies of the three blank Answer Sheets preceding each test chapter before you take the test itself. Remember that the keys to skills improvement are knowledge and practice. Use the tests in this book to forge ahead. There is a good Postal Service job waiting.

Practice Test 3

Part A — ADDRESS CHECKING

Work — 6 minutes

In this part of the test, you are to decide whether two addresses are alike or different. If the two addresses are *exactly alike in every way*, darken space Ⓐ. If they are *different in any way*, darken space Ⓓ.

Mark your answers on the Answer Sheet on page 297. Tear it out, put today's date on it, and place it next to the questions.

Allow yourself *exactly 6 minutes* to do as many of the 95 questions as you can. If you finish before the time is up, check your answers.

1.	Riverside CA	Riverside CO
2.	9006 Gage Center Cir	9060 Cage Center Cir
3.	3403 Lakeside Rd NW	3403 Lakeside Rd NW
4.	1734 E Alexandrine St	1734 E Alexandrine St
5.	2607 Maple Rd SE	2607 Mable Rd SE
6.	2323 18th St NE	2323 13th St NE
7.	7074 North Western Pky	7047 North Western Pky
8.	970 Harvard Sq	970 Harvard Ct
9.	6980 Montwood Ln	6890 Montwood Ln
10.	Sunflower MS 38778	Sunflower MS 38778
11.	515 Edmar Rd	515 Admar Rd
12.	3727 Imperial Woods Dr SW	3727 Imperial Woods Rd SW
13.	941 Rolf Ave	941 Rolf Ct
14.	3905 Renate Rd	3905 Renate Rd
15.	4600 Oak Lawn Rd	4600 Oak Lawn Rd
16.	Portland ME 04108	Portland ME 04018
17.	8612 Old Shepherdsville Rd	8612 Old Shepherdsville Rd
18.	95 Prentice St E	95 Prentice St E
19.	7432 Caffin Ave S	7432 Coffin Ave S
20.	2002 Grand Bayou Ln	2002 Grand Bayou Ln
21.	3715 Adams St SE	3715 Adams St NE
22.	6963 Fullerdale Ave	6963 Fullerdale Ave
23.	5837 White Oak Dr	5837 White Oak Dr
24.	10289 Hammond St	10289 Hammond St

25. Whitesboro OK	Whitesboro OH
26. 4883 Bloomsbury St	4883 Bloomsburg St
27. Wichita KS 67203	Wichita KS 67203
28. 57 Sheila Dr	57 Skeila Dr
29. 8409 Deckbar Ave NE	8409 Deckrab Ave NE
30. 4942 Woodward Hts E	4924 Woodward Hts E
31. 209 Valley Fair Way	209 Varley Fair Way
32. 7314 Edgewood Dr NE	7314 Edgeworth Dr NE
33. 3506 N Claireview St	3506 N Claireville St
34. Rushsylvania OH 43347	Rushsylvania OH 43847
35. 8023 Sea Cove Rd	8023 Sea Cove Rd
36. 948 Washington St SE	948 Washington St SE
37. 42 Maplebrook Pky N	42 Maplebrook Pky N
38. Saint Paul MN 55113	Saint Paul NM 55113
39. 5675 Zircon St	5765 Zircon St
40. 5998 Lakecrest Path N	5998 Lakecrest Path N
41. 8264 Queen Ct	8264 Queen St
42. 1412 Ingleside Ave SW	1412 Ingleside Ave SW
43. 7409 Parkdale Dr	7409 Parkdale Dr
44. 565 Zender Ln	565 Zender Ln
45. 3662 Westview St	3662 Westwood St
46. Baton Rouge LA 70807	Baton Rouge LA 70870
47. 2794 Beacon Hill Rd	2794 Beacon Hill Rd
48. 98 Wainwright Cir E	98 Wainwright Cir W
49. 5999 Nevada Ave N	5999 Nevada Ave N
50. Marquette NE	Marquette NH
51. 2401 Knollwood Dr NE	2401 Knollwood Dr NE
52. 174 W Lee St	174 W Lee Dr
53. 3019 Wentworth Dr	3109 Wentworth Dr
54. Louisville KY 40504	Louisville KY 40504
55. 3039 Kearney Rd W	3039 Kearney Rd W
56. 9038 N Kossuth St	9038 E Kossuth St
57. Forestdale PA	Forestdale PA
58. Champaign IL	Champaign IN
59. 4417 Daniels Ave	4417 Daniels Ave
60. 15299 Highway K4 SW	15299 Highway P4 SW

61. Litchfield Ct	Litchfield Ct
62. 7610 Russell St	7610 Russett St
63. 8768 E Ormond Ct	8768 E Ormont Ct
64. 5100 E Madeline St	5100 E Madeline St
65. Gathersburg MD 20879	Gathersburg MD 20879
66. 4001 Virginia Ave	4001 Virginia Ave
67. 2104 Illinois Ave	2014 Illinois Ave
68. 1899 7 Mile Rd W	1899 7 Mile Rd W
69. 5713 Eastlawn St	5713 Eastland St
70. 16473 Fiarfield St	16493 Fairfield St
71. 7465 Navarre Pl	7465 Navarro Pl
72. 4817 W Yupon St	4817 W Yupon St
73. 4010 Saint Charles Ln	4010 Saint Charles Rd
74. 2908 Jane Rd	2908 Janet Rd
75. 6453 Twin Hill Rd	6543 Twin Hill Rd
76. 642 Quebec Pl	642 Quebec Pl
77. 5927 Carnahan Pl	5927 Caravan Pl
78. 1447 James Ave S	1474 James Ave S
79. 6203 North Riverview Ln	6203 North Riverview Ln
80. 6686 Dancaster Rd SW	6686 Dancaster Rd SW
81. 4019 King Oak Ter	4019 King Oak Ter
82. 17046 U.S. Highway 60	17046 U.S. Highway 60
83. 9431 Elysian Fields Ave	9431 Elysian Fields Ave
84. 6213 E Barrington Dr	6213 W Barrington Dr
85. 3491 New Island Ave	3491 New Island Ave
86. 94 N 9th Ave W	94 N 9th Ave W
87. 1740 Gray Haven Ct	1749 Gray Haven Ct
88. 4427 Normandale Highlands Dr	4427 Normandale Highlands Dr
89. 8904 N Hampson St	8904 N Hampton St
90. 3008 S Catherine St	3080 S Catherine St
91. Venetia PA 15481	Vanetia PA 15481
92. Lowell MA 01850	Lowell MO 01850
93. 5294 Pamela Ter	5294 Pamela Trl
94. 3734 Upper Darby Rd	3734 Upper Darby Rd
95. 1043 N Abington Ave	1043 N Apington Ave

STOP.

If you finish before the time is up, go back and check the questions in this section of the test only.

PART B — MEMORY FOR ADDRESSES

In this part of the test, you will have five boxes labeled A, B, C, D, and E. Each box contains five addresses. Three of the five are groups of street addresses, such as 8000–8399 Orange, 8500–8899 Dellwood, and 6800–7599 Newman; and two are names of places. The addresses are different in each box.

There will be several opportunities to study the addresses and the boxes they are in. You will also be given three tests of 88 questions each, and the task of deciding where each address belongs. In some cases, you will have the list *and* the boxes in front of you at the same time; in others you will not. List 1 and List 2 are for warm-up practice. List 3 is the real one that will be scored.

Make sure you understand the format by examining the pretest samples below.

Pretest Samples

A	B	C	D	E
8900–9099 Orange	7400–7999 Orange	8000–8399 Orange	8400–8899 Orange	6900–7399 Orange
Tarmount	Railroad	Juniper	Alden	Sealey
8500–8899 Dellwood	8000–8499 Dellwood	8900–9499 Dellwood	7400–7999 Dellwood	7200–7399 Dellwood
Wheeling	Yule	Cantor	Hart	King
8400–8999 Newman	6800–7599 Newman	7600–7999 Newman	8000–8399 Newman	8900–9699 Newman

Questions 1 through 7 show the way the questions look. You have to decide in which lettered box (A, B, C, D, or E) the address belongs and then mark your answer by darkening the appropriate space in the answer grid.

1. Juniper — 1 Ⓐ Ⓑ Ⓒ Ⓓ Ⓔ
2. 7400–7999 Dellwood — 2 Ⓐ Ⓑ Ⓒ Ⓓ Ⓔ
3. 6900–7399 Orange — 3 Ⓐ Ⓑ Ⓒ Ⓓ Ⓔ
4. Yule — 4 Ⓐ Ⓑ Ⓒ Ⓓ Ⓔ
5. Sealey — 5 Ⓐ Ⓑ Ⓒ Ⓓ Ⓔ
6. 8400–8999 Newman — 6 Ⓐ Ⓑ Ⓒ Ⓓ Ⓔ
7. Cantor — 7 Ⓐ Ⓑ Ⓒ Ⓓ Ⓔ

Answers

1. **C** 2. **D** 3. **E** 4. **B** 5. **E** 6. **A** 7. **C**

Now that you know what to do, you may begin Part B of Practice Test 3. To get the most out of it and the remaining three practice tests in this book, follow the directions and timing *exactly*. Follow each phase of Part B of the test, page by page, until you've completed List 3. It is modeled on the way the Postal Service actually conducts its tests.

Turn to the next page to begin.

Study — 3 minutes

You will be given 3 minutes to spend memorizing the addresses in the boxes. *They are exactly the same ones that will be used for all three tests.* Try to memorize as many as you can. When the 3 minutes are up, turn to page 307 and read the instructions for *List 1*.

A	B	C	D	E
8900–9099 Orange	7400–7999 Orange	8000–8399 Orange	8400–8899 Orange	6900–7399 Orange
Tarmount	Railroad	Juniper	Alden	Sealey
8500–8899 Dellwood	8000–8499 Dellwood	8900–9499 Dellwood	7400–7999 Dellwood	7200–7399 Dellwood
Wheeling	Yule	Cantor	Hart	King
8400–8999 Newman	6800–7599 Newman	7600–7999 Newman	8000–8399 Newman	8900–9699 Newman

List 1

Work — 3 minutes

Tear out the Answer Sheet for List 1. For each question, mark the Answer Sheet on page 296 to show the letter of the box in which the address belongs. Try to remember the locations of as many addresses as you can. *You will now have 3 minutes to complete List 1.* If you are not sure of an answer, you should guess.

A	B	C	D	E
8900–9099 Orange	7400–7999 Orange	8000–8399 Orange	8400–8899 Orange	6900–7399 Orange
Tarmount	Railroad	Juniper	Alden	Sealey
8500–8899 Dellwood	8000–8499 Dellwood	8900–9499 Dellwood	7400–7999 Dellwood	7200–7399 Dellwood
Wheeling	Yule	Canter	Hart	King
8400–8999 Newman	6800–7599 Newman	7600–7999 Newman	8000–8399 Newman	8900–9699 Newman

1. Hart
2. 8400–8899 Orange
3. Tarmount
4. 7200–7399 Dellwood
5. Alden
6. 8000–8399 Orange
7. 8400–8999 Newman
8. Railroad
9. Hart
10. 7400–7999 Orange
11. 8500–8899 Dellwood
12. Cantor
13. 8900–9099 Orange
14. 6800–7599 Newman
15. Yule
16. 8900–9699 Newman
17. 6900–7399 Orange
18. King
19. 8900–9499 Dellwood
20. 8000–8399 Newman
21. Tarmount
22. 7400–7999 Dellwood
23. 7600–7999 Newman
24. Juniper
25. Railroad
26. 8000–8499 Dellwood
27. Wheeling
28. 8000–8399 Newman
29. 8400–8899 Orange
30. Railroad
31. 7400–7999 Dellwood
32. King
33. Tarmount
34. 8400–8999 Newman
35. 8000–8499 Dellwood
36. Wheeling
37. 8500–8899 Dellwood
38. Sealey
39. 7200–7399 Dellwood
40. Wheeling
41. 8900–9499 Dellwood
42. Yule
43. 8900–9099 Orange
44. 8000–8499 Dellwood

45. Alden
46. 8000–8399 Newman
47. Hart
48. Juniper
49. 6800–7599 Newman
50. Sealey
51. 6900–7399 Orange
52. 6800–7599 Newman
53. Juniper
54. 8000–8399 Orange
55. Tarmount

56. Juniper
57. 8900–9699 Newman
58. Wheeling
59. Cantor
60. 8500–8899 Dellwood
61. 7200–7399 Dellwood
62. Yule
63. King
64. 7400–7999 Orange
65. Tarmount
66. Alden
67. 7400–7999 Orange
68. 6900–7399 Orange
69. 7600–7999 Newman
70. Yule
71. 7400–7999 Dellwood
72. Cantor
73. 8900–9099 Orange
74. King
75. 8900–9699 Newman
76. Cantor
77. 8900–9499 Dellwood

78. Alden
79. Railroad
80. 8400–8899 Orange
81. Hart
82. Sealey
83. 8000–8399 Orange
84. 7600–7999 Newman
85. Hart
86. Sealey
87. 8400–8999 Newman
88. King

STOP.
If you finish before the time is up, go back and check the questions in this section of the test only.

List 2

Work — 3 minutes

Do these questions *without* looking back at the boxes. For each question, mark your answer on the Answer Sheet for List 2 on page 298. If you are not sure of an answer, you should guess.

1. 7400–7999 Orange
2. 7200–7399 Dellwood
3. 8000–8499 Dellwood
4. Alden
5. Sealey
6. 7200–7399 Dellwood
7. Juniper
8. 7400–7999 Dellwood
9. Alden
10. 7200–7399 Dellwood
11. 8900–9699 Newman
12. 6900–7399 Orange
13. 8500–8899 Dellwood
14. Alden
15. 8000–8399 Newman
16. Tarmount
17. 8000–8399 Newman
18. 6900–7399 Orange
19. Tarmount
20. Sealey
21. 8000–8399 Orange
22. King
23. Cantor
24. 7400–7999 Orange
25. 8000–8399 Orange
26. Wheeling
27. Hart
28. 8900–9499 Dellwood
29. King
30. 6800–7599 Newman
31. Railroad
32. Hart
33. 7600–7999 Newman
34. Wheeling
35. 8000–8399 Orange
36. Yule
37. 7400–7999 Dellwood
38. 6800–7599 Newman
39. 8900–9699 Newman
40. 8400–8899 Orange
41. Hart
42. Cantor
43. 8900–9499 Dellwood
44. Railroad

45. Juniper
46. Sealey
47. Wheeling
48. 7600–7999 Newman
49. 8900–9699 Newman
50. 8000–8499 Dellwood
51. King
52. 7400–7999 Orange
53. 8400–8999 Newman
54. Yule
55. 8900–9499 Dellwood
56. 8900–9099 Orange
57. Wheeling
58. 8400–8899 Orange
59. Tarmount
60. King
61. 8500–8899 Dellwood
62. Hart
63. Railroad
64. 6800–7599 Newman
65. 7600–7999 Newman
66. Tarmount
67. Hart
68. Cantor
69. Alden
70. 8900–9099 Orange
71. 8400–8999 Newman
72. Juniper
73. 8400–8899 Orange
74. 8000–8399 Newman
75. Railroad
76. Tarmount
77. Cantor
78. King
79. 8900–9699 Newman
80. Yule
81. 8400–8999 Newman
82. 6900–7399 Orange
83. 7400–7999 Dellwood
84. 8000–8499 Dellwood
85. Yule
86. 8500–8899 Dellwood
87. Juniper
88. 8900–9099 Orange

STOP.
If you finish before the time is up, go back and check the questions in this section of the test only.

List 3

Study — 5 minutes

You are now about to take the test using List 3. *(This is the test that counts!)*

Turn back to page 307 and study the boxes again. *You have 5 minutes to restudy the addresses.*

Work — 5 minutes

For each question, mark the Answer Sheet on page 299 to show the letter of the box in which the address belongs. You have *exactly 5 minutes* to do the test. During these 5 minutes, *do not* turn to any other page.

1. Railroad
2. 8900–9499 Dellwood
3. Cantor
4. Hart
5. 8400–8899 Cantor
6. 8900–9699 Newman
7. 6800–7599 Newman
8. 7400–7999 Dellwood
9. Yule
10. 8000–8399 Orange
11. Wheeling
12. 7600–7999 Newman
13. Hart
14. Railroad
15. 6800–7599 Newman
16. King
17. 8900–9499 Dellwood
18. Hart
19. Wheeling
20. 8000–8399 Orange
21. 7400–7999 Orange
22. Cantor
23. King
24. 8000–8399 Orange
25. Sealey
26. Tarmount
27. 6900–7399 Orange
28. 8000–8399 Newman
29. Tarmount
30. 8000–8399 Newman
31. Alden
32. 8500–8899 Dellwood
33. 6900–7399 Orange
34. 6800–7599 Newman
35. 7200–7399 Dellwood
36. Alden
37. 7400–7999 Dellwood
38. Juniper
39. 7200–7399 Dellwood
40. Sealey
41. Alden
42. 8000–8499 Dellwood
43. 7200–7399 Dellwood
44. 7400–7999 Orange

45. 8900–9099 Orange
46. Juniper
47. 8500–8899 Dellwood
48. Yule
49. 8000–8499 Dellwood
50. 7400–7999 Dellwood
51. 6900–7399 Orange
52. 8400–8999 Newman
53. Yule
54. 8900–9699 Newman
55. King
56. Cantor
57. Tarmount
58. Railroad
59. 8000–8399 Newman
60. 8400–8899 Orange
61. Juniper
62. 8400–8999 Newman
63. 8900–9099 Orange
64. Alden
65. Cantor
66. Hart
67. Tarmount
68. 7600–7999 Newman
69. 6800–7599 Newman
70. Railroad
71. Hart
72. 8500–8899 Dellwood
73. King
74. Tarmount
75. 8400–8899 Orange
76. Wheeling
77. 8900–9099 Orange
78. 8900–9499 Dellwood
79. Yule
80. 8400–8999 Newman
81. 7400–7999 Orange
82. King
83. 8000–8499 Dellwood
84. 8900–9699 Newman
85. 7600–7999 Newman
86. Wheeling
87. Sealey
88. 6900–7399 Orange

STOP.
If you finish before the time is up, go back and check the questions in this section of the test only.

PART C — NUMBER SERIES

Work — 20 minutes

For each Number Series question, there is a series of numbers that follow some definite order, and below each are five sets of two numbers each. You are to look at the numbers in the series and find out what order they follow. Then decide what the next two numbers in that series would be if the same order were continued. Mark your answers on the Answer Sheet on page 299.

You have 20 minutes to complete this part of the test. If you finish before the time is up, check your answers. The answers and explanations are on pages 321 to 323.

1. 17 41 13 17 41 13 17 __ __
   A) 13 41 B) 17 13 C) 41 13 D) 41 17 E) 17 41

2. 81 72 72 63 63 54 54 __ __
   A) 45 38 B) 54 45 C) 45 45 D) 46 46 E) 46 38

3. 5 4 6 6 7 8 8 __ __
   A) 9 8 B) 10 9 C) 8 9 D) 10 11 E) 9 10

4. 15 10 20 15 25 20 30 __ __
   A) 25 35 B) 30 25 C) 25 20 D) 35 20 E) 35 25

5. 18 16 14 19 17 15 20 __ __
   A) 17 18 B) 16 17 C) 18 17 D) 18 16 E) 19 17

6. 24 21 23 20 22 19 21 __ __
   A) 20 18 B) 19 21 C) 19 16 D) 18 20 E) 20 22

7. 29 26 32 23 20 26 17 __ __
   A) 14 20 B) 23 29 C) 20 11 D) 8 3 E) 8 14

8. 100 10 81 9 64 8 49 __ __
   A) 7 34 B) 34 8 C) 36 6 D) 7 25 E) 7 36

9. 36 33 43 30 27 40 24 21 37 __ __
   A) 34 31 B) 20 34 C) 18 34 D) 15 19 E) 18 15

10. 4 8 4 12 4 16 4 __ __
    A) 4 20 B) 18 4 C) 18 22 D) 14 20 E) 20 4

11. 128 2 64 4 32 8 16 __ __
    A) 32 10 B) 16 8 C) 12 8 D) 8 12 E) 12 16

12. 6 5 7 6 8 7 9 __ __
A) 8 10 B) 9 10 C) 7 9 D) 10 9 E) 8 9

13. 1 1 2 2 3 3 2 2 1 __ __
A) 2 3 B) 1 2 C) 1 1 D) 2 2 E) 2 3

14. 3 6 11 8 11 10 13 16 9 __ __
A) 19 17 B) 19 18 C) 18 20 D) 18 21 E) 17 20

15. 70 60 20 50 40 20 30 __ __
A) 20 10 B) 10 10 C) 20 30 D) 20 20 E) 10 0

16. 1 2 6 2 4 12 3 6 __ __
A) 7 18 B) 7 10 C) 4 18 D) 18 4 E) 8 10

17. 42 21 38 25 34 29 30 __ __
A) 31 35 B) 32 31 C) 33 26 D) 39 30 E) 28 35

18. +17 −18 +19 −20 +21 −22 +23 __ __
A) −25 +26 B) +24 +25 C) +24 −25 D) −24 −25 E) −24 +25

19. 6 6 6 7 8 8 8 10 10 9 __ __
A) 9 9 B) 11 12 C) 12 12 D) 10 11 E) 11 11

20. 16 15 14 12 11 10 8 __ __
A) 7 6 B) 6 7 C) 9 10 D) 9 11 E) 10 11

21. 0 1 1 2 4 7 13 24 __ __
A) 35 47 B) 44 81 C) 48 96 D) 54 83 E) 37 61

22. 24 25 26 12 27 28 29 13 30 31 __ __
A) 32 14 B) 15 33 C) 32 16 D) 14 32 E) 16 33

23. 8 6 4 12 10 8 24 22 __ __
A) 18 54 B) 22 20 C) 20 60 D) 18 36 E) 20 40

24. 16 18 22 21 20 20 22 19 __ __
A) 18 17 B) 19 21 C) 24 18 D) 22 24 E) 17 19

STOP.
If you finish before the time is up, go back and check the questions in this section of the test only.

PART D — FOLLOWING ORAL DIRECTIONS

This part of the test gauges your ability to understand and carry out spoken directions *exactly* as they are given to you.

In order to prepare to take Part D of the test, follow the steps below:

1. Enlist the help of a friend who will be the "reader." His or her job will be to read aloud a series of directions that you are to follow *exactly*. The reader will need a watch that displays seconds, because the directions must be read at the correct speed.
2. Tear out pages 319 and 320. These are the worksheets you should have in front of you as you listen to the directions given by the reader, who will tell you to do certain things with the items on each line on the worksheets.
3. Use the Answer Sheet for Following Oral Directions on page 299, and insert today's date. You will darken the appropriate spaces in accordance with the directions given by the reader.
4. *Now hand this entire book to the reader.* Ask him/her to review the section below headed "Instructions to the Reader." It explains exactly how the reader is to proceed.

When you and the reader are ready to start this part of Practice Test 3, he/she will begin reading to you the section marked "Directions." YOU ARE NOT TO READ THESE AT ANY TIME BEFORE OR DURING THE TEST. If you do, you will lose the benefit of this part of the practice test.

Instructions to the "Reader"

These instructions should be read at about 80 words per minute. You should practice reading the material in the box until you can do it in exactly 1 minute. This will give you a feel for the way you should read the test material.

1-MINUTE PRACTICE

> Look at line 20 on your worksheet. There are two circles and two boxes of different sizes with numbers in them. If 7 is less than 3 and if 2 is smaller than 4, write C in the larger circle. Otherwise write B as in *baker* in the smaller box. Now, on your answer sheet, darken the space for the number-letter combination in the box or circle.

You should read the entire test aloud before you read it to the person taking the test, in order to acquaint yourself with the procedure and the desired rate of reading.

Read slowly but at a natural pace. In other words, do not space the words so that there are unnaturally long pauses between them. The instruction "Pause slightly" indicates only enough time to take a breath. The other instructions for pauses give the recommended length for each. If possible, use a watch with a second hand.

All the material that follows, except the words in parentheses, is to be read aloud. Now start reading the directions. *Do not repeat any of the directions.*

Directions: In this test, I will read instructions to you. You are to mark your worksheets according to the instructions that I read to you. After each set of instructions, I'll give you time to record your answers on your answer sheet.

Try to understand the instructions as I read them; I cannot repeat them. Do not ask any questions from now on.

If, when you go to darken a space for a number, you find that you have already darkened another space for that number, either (1) erase the first mark and darken the space for your new choice, or (2) let the first mark stay and do not darken any other space. When you finish, you should have no more than one space darkened for each number.

Turn to Worksheet 1.

Look at line 1 on your worksheet. (Pause slightly.) Draw a line under the second letter in the line. (Pause 2 seconds.) Now, on your answer sheet, find number 16 and darken space E for the letter under which you drew a line. (Pause 5 seconds.)

Look at line 2 on your worksheet. (Pause slightly.) Draw a line under every "X" in the line. (Pause 5 seconds.) Count the number of lines you have drawn, add 4, and write that number at the end of the line. (Pause 5 seconds.) Now, on your answer sheet, find that number and darken space D as in *dog.* (Pause 5 seconds.)

Look at line 3 on your worksheet. (Pause slightly.) Write B as in *boy* in the last circle. (Pause 2 seconds.) Now, on your answer sheet, find the number in that circle and darken space B as in *boy* for that number. (Pause 5 seconds.)

Now, look at line 3 again. (Pause slightly.) Write a C in the third circle. (Pause 2 seconds.) Now, on your answer sheet, find the number in that circle and darken space C for that number. (Pause 5 seconds.)

Look at line 4 on your worksheet. (Pause slightly.) Draw a line under every number that is more than 15 but less than 30. (Pause 12 seconds.) Now, on your answer sheet, for each number that you drew a line under, darken space A. (Pause 25 seconds.)

Look at line 5 on your worksheet. (Pause slightly.) The four boxes are bins for storing mail. The bin with the lowest number is to be emptied last. Write a C on the line beside the lowest number. (Pause 2 seconds.) Now, on your answer sheet, darken the space for the number-letter combination that is in the bin you just wrote in. (Pause 5 seconds.)

Look at the five boxes in line 6 on your worksheet. (Pause slightly.) Write 74 on the blank in the middle box. (Pause 2 seconds.) Now, on your answer sheet, darken the space for the number-letter combination that is in the box you just wrote in. (Pause 5 seconds.)

Now look at line 6 again. (Pause slightly.) Write 31 on the blank in the fourth box. (Pause 2 seconds.) Now, on your answer sheet, darken the space for the number-letter combination that is in the box you just wrote in. (Pause 5 seconds.)

Look at the circle and words in line 7 on your worksheet. (Pause slightly.) Write the last letter of the first word in the last circle. (Pause 2 seconds.) Write the second letter of the last word in the second circle. (Pause 2 seconds.) Write the first letter of the second word in the first circle. (Pause 2 seconds.) Now, on your answer sheet, darken the spaces for the number-letter combinations that are in the three circles you just wrote in. (Pause 12 seconds.)

Look at the figures in line 8 on your worksheet. (Pause slightly.) In every figure that has more than four sides, write the letter A on the line in the figure. (Pause 5 seconds.) Now, on your answer sheet, darken the spaces for the number-letter combinations that are in the figures you just wrote in. (Pause 10 seconds.)

Look at line 9 on your worksheet. (Pause slightly.) Draw a line under every number that is more than 55 but less than 70. (Pause 12 seconds.) Now, on your answer sheet, for each number you drew a line under, darken space B as in *baker.* (Pause 25 seconds.)

Now look at line 10 on your worksheet. (Pause slightly.) There are five boxes on the line. Each box has a letter in it. (Pause slightly.) In the first box write the answer to this question: How many pennies are there in a half dollar? (Pause 2 seconds.) Now, on your answer sheet, darken the space for the number-letter combination that is in the box you just wrote in. (Pause 5 seconds.)

Look at line 10 again. In the second box write the number 87. (Pause 2 seconds.) Now, on your answer sheet, darken the space for the number-letter combination that is in the box you just wrote in. (Pause 5 seconds.) In the fourth box do nothing. In the last box write the answer to this question: Which of the following numbers is largest: 28, 56, 34, 52, 48? (Pause 2 seconds.) Now, on your answer sheet, darken the space for the number-letter combination that is in the box you just wrote in. (Pause 5 seconds.)

Look at line 11 on your worksheet. (Pause slightly.) In each circle there is a time when the mail is checked in. In the circle for the latest time, write on the line the last two figures of the time. (Pause 2 seconds.) Now, on your answer sheet, darken the space for the number-letter combination that is in the circle you just wrote in. (Pause 5 seconds.)

Now turn to Worksheet 2. (Pause 5 seconds.)

Look at the six boxes in line 12 on your worksheet. (Pause slightly.) If 6 is more than 7, write A in the fifth box. (Pause 2 seconds.) If 6 is not more than 7, write B as in *baker* in the second box. (Pause 2 seconds.) Now, on your answer sheet, darken the space for the number-letter combination that is in the box you just wrote in. (Pause 5 seconds.)

Look at line 13 on your worksheet. (Pause slightly.) Next to the left-hand number write the letter A. (Pause 2 seconds.) Now, on your answer sheet, find the number beside which you wrote and darken space E for that number. (Pause 5 seconds.)

Look at the letters in line 14 on your worksheet. (Pause slightly.) Draw a line under the fourth letter in the line. (Pause 2 seconds.) Now, on your answer sheet, find number 73 and darken the space for the letter under which you drew a line. (Pause 5 seconds.)

Look at line 14 again. Draw two lines under the second letter in the line. (Pause 2 seconds.) Now, on your answer sheet, find number 58 and darken the space for the letter under which you drew two lines. (Pause 5 seconds.)

Look at line 15 on your worksheet. There are two circles and two boxes of different sizes with numbers in them. (Pause slightly.) If 7 is more than 3 and if 5 is less than 4, write C in the larger circle. (Pause 2 seconds.) Otherwise, write E in the smaller box. (Pause 2 seconds.) Now, on your answer sheet, darken the space for the number-letter combination that is in the box or circle you just wrote in. (Pause 5 seconds.)

Look at line 16 on your worksheet. (Pause slightly.) If, in a year, August comes before July, write D as in *dog* in the box with the smallest number. (Pause 2 seconds.) If it does not, write A in the second box. (Pause 2 seconds.) Now, on your answer sheet, darken the space for the number-letter combination that is in the box you just wrote in. (Pause 5 seconds.)

Now look at line 17 on your worksheet. (Pause slightly.) Write the number 3 on the line next to the middle letter. (Pause 2 seconds.) Now, on your answer sheet, find the number that you just wrote and darken the space for the letter beside which you just wrote it. (Pause 5 seconds.)

Look at line 18 on your worksheet. (Pause slightly.) Mail for Coral Gables and Gainesville is to be put in box 64. Mail for Atlanta and Buford is to be put in box 84. (Pause slightly.) Write A on the line in the box in which you would put mail for Gainesville. (Pause 2 seconds.) Now, on your answer sheet, darken the space for the number-letter combination that is in the box you just wrote in. (Pause 5 seconds.)

Look at line 19 on your worksheet. (Pause slightly.) If the number in the left-hand box is smaller than the number in the right-hand circle, add 2 to the number in the left-hand box, and change the number in that box to this number. (Pause 2 seconds.) Then write D as in *dog* next to the new number. (Pause 2 seconds.) Otherwise, write E next to the number in the larger box. (Pause 2 seconds.) Now, on your answer sheet, darken the space for the number-letter combination in the box or circle you just wrote in. (Pause 5 seconds.)

END OF EXAMINATION.
If you finish before the time is up, go back and check the questions in this section of the test only.

Practice Test 3—Worksheet 1

Part D—Following Oral Directions

1. D E A C B

2. X O X O O X X X O O X X O O X

3. 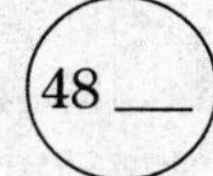

17 ___ 76 ___ 29 ___ 81 ___

4. 19 29 32 30 21 15 14

5. 82 ___ 40 ___ 38 ___ 59 ___

6. D ___ A ___ C ___ B ___ E ___

7. 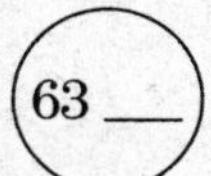

44 ___ 23 ___ REED AUNT BALL

8. 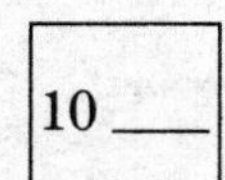

59 ___ 51 ___ 49 ___ 71 ___

9. 75 60 55 77 53 49 51 69 71

10. 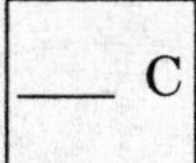

___ E ___ A ___ B ___ D

11. 3:45 ___ A 3:30 ___ D 3:09 ___ C 3:57 ___ E 3:54 ___ B

Remove by cutting on dotted line.

Practice Test 3—Worksheet 2

Part D—Following Oral Directions

12. 32 ___ 79 ___ 29 ___ 11 ___ 49 ___ 43 ___

13. 48 ___ 63 ___

14. C E D A E B C

15. 25 ___ 9 ___ 4 ___ 77 ___

16. 2 ___ 8 ___ 13 ___ 1 ___

17. ___ D ___ B ___ A

18. 64 CORAL GABLES GAINESVILLE ___ 84 ATLANTA BUFORD ___

19. 26 ___ 45 ___ 53 ___ 38 ___

ANSWER KEY

Part A—Address Checking

1. **D**	11. **D**	21. **D**	31. **D**	41. **D**	51. **A**	61. **A**	71. **D**	81. **A**	91. **D**
2. **D**	12. **D**	22. **A**	32. **D**	42. **A**	52. **D**	62. **D**	72. **A**	82. **A**	92. **D**
3. **A**	13. **D**	23. **A**	33. **D**	43. **A**	53. **D**	63. **D**	73. **D**	83. **A**	93. **D**
4. **A**	14. **A**	24. **A**	34. **D**	44. **A**	54. **A**	64. **A**	74. **D**	84. **D**	94. **A**
5. **D**	15. **A**	25. **D**	35. **A**	45. **D**	55. **A**	65. **A**	75. **D**	85. **A**	95. **D**
6. **D**	16. **D**	26. **D**	36. **A**	46. **D**	56. **D**	66. **A**	76. **A**	86. **A**	
7. **D**	17. **A**	27. **A**	37. **A**	47. **A**	57. **A**	67. **D**	77. **D**	87. **D**	
8. **D**	18. **A**	28. **D**	38. **D**	48. **D**	58. **D**	68. **A**	78. **D**	88. **A**	
9. **D**	19. **D**	29. **D**	39. **D**	49. **A**	59. **A**	69. **D**	79. **A**	89. **D**	
10. **A**	20. **A**	30. **D**	40. **A**	50. **D**	60. **D**	70. **D**	80. **A**	90. **D**	

Part B—Memory for Addresses

List 1

1. **D**	10. **B**	19. **C**	28. **D**	37. **A**	46. **D**	55. **A**	64. **B**	73. **A**	82. **E**
2. **D**	11. **A**	20. **D**	29. **D**	38. **E**	47. **D**	56. **C**	65. **A**	74. **E**	83. **C**
3. **A**	12. **C**	21. **A**	30. **B**	39. **E**	48. **C**	57. **E**	66. **D**	75. **E**	84. **C**
4. **E**	13. **A**	22. **D**	31. **D**	40. **A**	49. **B**	58. **A**	67. **B**	76. **C**	85. **D**
5. **D**	14. **B**	23. **C**	32. **E**	41. **C**	50. **E**	59. **C**	68. **E**	77. **C**	86. **E**
6. **C**	15. **B**	24. **C**	33. **A**	42. **B**	51. **E**	60. **A**	69. **C**	78. **D**	87. **A**
7. **A**	16. **E**	25. **B**	34. **A**	43. **A**	52. **B**	61. **E**	70. **B**	79. **B**	88. **E**
8. **B**	17. **E**	26. **B**	35. **B**	44. **B**	53. **C**	62. **B**	71. **D**	80. **D**	
9. **D**	18. **E**	27. **A**	36. **A**	45. **D**	54. **C**	63. **E**	72. **C**	81. **D**	

List 2

1. **B**	10. **E**	19. **A**	28. **C**	37. **D**	46. **E**	55. **C**	64. **B**	73. **D**	82. **E**
2. **E**	11. **E**	20. **E**	29. **E**	38. **B**	47. **A**	56. **A**	65. **C**	74. **D**	83. **D**
3. **B**	12. **E**	21. **C**	30. **B**	39. **E**	48. **C**	57. **A**	66. **A**	75. **B**	84. **B**
4. **D**	13. **A**	22. **E**	31. **B**	40. **D**	49. **E**	58. **D**	67. **D**	76. **A**	85. **B**
5. **E**	14. **D**	23. **C**	32. **D**	41. **D**	50. **B**	59. **A**	68. **C**	77. **C**	86. **A**
6. **E**	15. **D**	24. **B**	33. **C**	42. **C**	51. **E**	60. **E**	69. **D**	78. **E**	87. **C**
7. **C**	16. **A**	25. **C**	34. **A**	43. **C**	52. **B**	61. **A**	70. **A**	79. **E**	88. **A**
8. **D**	17. **D**	26. **A**	35. **C**	44. **B**	53. **A**	62. **D**	71. **A**	80. **B**	
9. **D**	18. **E**	27. **D**	36. **B**	45. **C**	54. **B**	63. **B**	72. **C**	81. **A**	

List 3

1. **B**	10. **C**	19. **A**	28. **D**	37. **D**	46. **C**	55. **E**	64. **D**	73. **E**	82. **E**
2. **C**	11. **A**	20. **C**	29. **A**	38. **C**	47. **A**	56. **C**	65. **C**	74. **A**	83. **B**
3. **C**	12. **C**	21. **B**	30. **D**	39. **E**	48. **B**	57. **A**	66. **D**	75. **D**	84. **E**
4. **D**	13. **D**	22. **C**	31. **D**	40. **E**	49. **B**	58. **B**	67. **A**	76. **A**	85. **C**
5. **D**	14. **B**	23. **E**	32. **A**	41. **D**	50. **D**	59. **D**	68. **C**	77. **A**	86. **A**
6. **E**	15. **B**	24. **C**	33. **E**	42. **D**	51. **E**	60. **D**	69. **B**	78. **C**	87. **E**
7. **B**	16. **E**	25. **E**	34. **B**	43. **E**	52. **A**	61. **C**	70. **B**	79. **B**	88. **E**
8. **D**	17. **C**	26. **A**	35. **E**	44. **B**	53. **B**	62. **A**	71. **D**	80. **A**	
9. **B**	18. **D**	27. **E**	36. **D**	45. **A**	54. **E**	63. **A**	72. **A**	81. **B**	

Part C—Number Series

1. C	4. A	7. A	10. E	13. B	16. D	19. C	22. A
2. C	5. D	8. E	11. B	14. D	17. C	20. A	23. C
3. B	6. D	9. E	12. A	15. D	18. E	21. B	24. A

Part D—Following Oral Directions

3. B	12. D	21. A	29. A	44. A	51. A	58. E	64. A	73. A	79. B
4. E	16. E	23. D	31. B	48. E	56. D	60. B	69. B	74. C	81. B
8. A	19. A	28. D	38. C	50. C	57. E	63. A	71. A	76. C	87. E

ANSWER EXPLANATIONS FOR PART C—NUMBER SERIES

1. **C** The three-number sequence, 17 41 13 keeps repeating.
2. **C** This series keeps decreasing by 9. Each number is repeated.
3. **B** Two alternating series make up this group of numbers. One, starting with 5, follows a + 1 rule; the other, starting with 4, a + 2 rule.
4. **A** You could progress from one number to the other by following a − 5, + 10, rule. Or you could see two alternating series here—each increasing by 5.
5. **D** Three-member mini-series make up this progression of numbers. Each series begins one number higher than the starting number of the preceding one. Within each series, a − 2 rule is used.
6. **D** The rule here is: −3, + 2; −3, + 2; and so on.
7. **A** A more complex pattern governs this series. It has three steps: − 3, + 6, − 9; which keep repeating.
8. **E** The first number in this series, 100, is the square of 10, which follows it. This pattern is used for each number descending from 10, i.e., 81 9; 64 8; and so on.
9. **E** Both of the two alternating series here follow a −3 rule. The first series continues for two numbers before it is interrupted by one number of the second series.
10. **E** The fixed number, 4, appears between each term in this simple + 4 series.
11. **B** Here you have an alternating series that uses *division* by 2 (128 ÷ 2, 64 ÷ 2, and so on), alternating with a series that uses *multiplication* by 2. (2 × 2, 4 × 2).
12. **A** You may view this either as a series following a −1, + 2; and so on rule, or as two alternating series each increasing by 1.
13. **B** This series follows an ascending-descending wave pattern. Each number is repeated after adding 1 to it. The series ascends from 1 1 until it reaches 3 3, after which it descends back to 1 1. This pattern keeps repeating.
14. **D** A series that follows a + 3, + 2; rule is interrupted after every two of its members by one member of a second series that keeps decreasing by 1.
15. **D** You have a −10 series here, with the number *20* appearing after every second term.
16. **D** You can view these numbers in two ways. Either as *three* alternating series or as a collection of mini-series. One alternating series begins with 1 and increases by 1; the second begins with 2 and increases by 2; the third begins with 6 and increases by 6. The diagram below shows how they may be viewed as "mini-series," each using a × 2, × 3; rule.

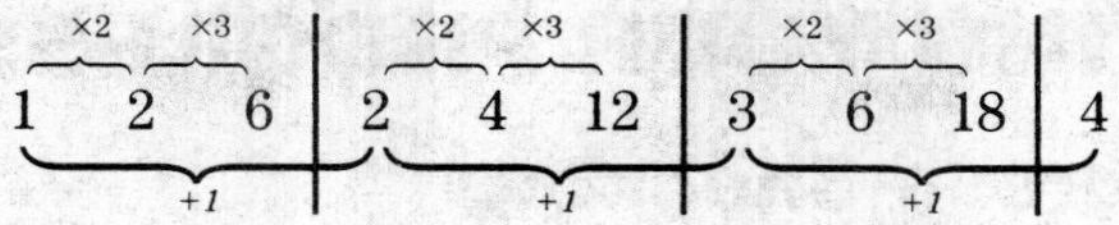

×2 ×3	×2 ×3	×2 ×3	
1 2 6	2 4 12	3 6 18	4
+1	+1	+1	

17. **C** A −4 series is alternating with a + 4 series.
18. **E** Even though these numbers follow a simple + 1 pattern, you must be careful to keep track of the alternating + and −*signs* that precede each number.
19. **C** Here again, are two alternating series. One follows a pattern of + 2, repeat the number; + 2, repeat the number; etc. After each repetition, it is interrupted by one member of a + 1 series. The proximity of the numbers makes this question quite tricky.
20. **A** You can see these numbers as following the complex rule: −1, −1, −2; −1, −1, −2; and so on. If you wish, you can consider them as three-member "mini-series." (For practice, see if you can diagram them this way.)
21. **B** The series progresses by *internal* addition of its members. Each number is obtained by adding the *three* preceding numbers together, e.g.; 0 + 1 + 1 = *2*; 1 + 1 + 2 = *4*; 1 + 2 + 4 = *7*; and so on.
22. **A** The first of the two alternating series begins with 24, increases by 1 and continues for *three* numbers before being interrupted by the second series. This series begins with the number 12 and keeps increasing by 1.
23. **C** The rule here uses subtraction *and* multiplication according to this complex rule: −2, −2, × 3; and so on.
24. **A** One series beginning with 16 increases by 2. It is interrupted after every two of its members by three members of a second series. This series beginning with 22 decreases by 1.

EVALUATING YOUR PROGRESS*

Part A—Address Checking

Computing Your Score

Check your answers against the Answer Key. Score yourself by using this formula:

Number right
− Number wrong
YOUR SCORE

For example, if you completed 52 questions and got 8 wrong,

Number right	=	44
− Number wrong	=	− 8
Your score	=	36

Notice that you do *not* figure in the questions that you did not answer.

Guidelines

How good is the score you just made?

52 or higher . . . . Good
Between 32 and 52 . . . . . . Fair
Below 32 . . . . You need to improve.

These are commonly accepted figures. It is believed, however, that you should not be satisfied with anything *less* than 52. Experience in training many people to prepare for this test shows that most serious test candidates who use the preparation program described in this book (Chapter 3 covers Address checking) will be able to raise their score to the upper sixties, seventies, or eighties.

Personal Progress Record

One of the most satisfying things that can happen while you are working toward a goal is to see signs of progress. The improvement you make on Address Checking can readily be seen by examining the scores you make on the practice tests and exercises in this book. Keeping track of your growing skill is important, so a Personal Progress Record has been furnished for your use on page 430.

---

* Please note that the scores you obtain by following the computation instructions for the various parts of this test are "raw" scores. The Postal Service combines and converts the raw scores for the various parts of the test into a scaled score obtained by using special conversion formulas that are kept confidential. This scaled score (plus any veteran's credits to which you are entitled) forms the basis for your final rating and your standing on the list. This final rating will be sent to you after the tests have been marked.

Furthermore, even though you take one test, your final score will vary depending on the title. For example, your rate on the Mail Handler register may very well be different from your rating on the Postal Clerk-Carrier register. Apparently, the relative rate given to each part of the test varies according to title. This is another argument for taking as many tests in as many titles as possible, as suggested on page 3.

You are encouraged to calculate your raw scores because they furnish a realistic and convenient way for you to keep track of your relative performance and progress as you work your way through this book.

The following is a sample of this Personal Progress Record to familiarize you with it. The entries on this sample are based on the preceding example.

PERSONAL PROGRESS RECORD—SAMPLE

ADDRESS CHECKING												
Initial Tests									Repeated Tests			
Date	Test	Number Completed	Number Correct	–	Number Wrong	=	Score		Date	Score	Date	Score
5/15	Diagnostic Practice Test	52	44	–	8	=	36					
5/16	Practice Test 1	64	54	–	10	=	44					
5/18	Practice Test 2	66	57	–	9	=	48					
5/20	Practice Test 3	70	60	–	10	=	50					
	Practice Test 4			–		=						
	Practice Test 5			–		=						
	Practice Test 6			–		=						

Now turn to page 430. In the table entitled "Personal Progress Record—Address Checking," make the proper entries on the line for Practice Test 3, which you just took. Review the special techniques in Chapter 3: Address Checking—How to Improve Your Score, before taking Practice Test 4. After taking the additional practice tests, enter the results immediately. Keep this record. It will help you record your progress.

Part B—Memory for Addresses

Computing Your Score

Check the answers on your answer sheet against the Answer Key. Calculate your score by using these four steps:

1. Enter the number of answers you got right .... ______

2. Enter the number of answers you got wrong .... ______

3. Divide the number wrong by 4 (or multiply by ¼)................. – ______

4. Subtract Line 3 from Line 1.. .... YOUR SCORE = ______

Follow this example to make sure that you have figured your score correctly. It will be assumed that you completed 32 questions, of which you got 24 right and 8 wrong.

Line 1....... Number right 24

Line 2....... Number wrong......... 8

Line 3....... ¼ of line 2 = ¼ × 8...... – 2

Line 4....... 24 – 2 .. YOUR SCORE = 22

Notice that, just as for Address Checking, questions that are not answered are *not* taken into account.

Guidelines

How good is the score you just made?

52 or higher . . . . Good
Between 32 and 52 . . . . . . Fair
Below 32 . . . . You need to improve.

If your score on this test was low, don't be discouraged. Nevertheless, you may wish to review Chapters 4 and 5, which offer special techniques for handling Part B—Memory for Addresses, before taking Practice Test 4.

Personal Progress Record

Turn to page 430. Use the table entitled "Personal Progress—Memory for Addresses" to keep a permanent record of your scores on List 3 of the practice tests. A sample is printed below to familiarize you with it. The first entry is based on the preceding example.

PERSONAL PROGRESS RECORD—SAMPLE

MEMORY FOR ADDRESSES											
Initial Tests								Repeated Tests			
Date	Test	Number Completed	Number Correct A	Number Wrong	× ¼ =	Points off B	Score (A − B)	Date	Score	Date	Score
5/15	Diagnostic Practice Test	32	24	8	× ¼ =	2	22				
5/16	Practice Test 1	46	38	8	× ¼ =	2	36				
5/18	Practice Test 2	58	52	6	× ¼ =	1½	50½				
5/20	Practice Test 3	64	60	4	× ¼ =	1	59				
	Practice Test 4				× ¼ =						
	Practice Test 5				× ¼ =						
	Practice Test 6				× ¼ =						

Part C—Number Series

Computing Your Score

Check the answers on your Answer Sheet against the Answer Key. Calculate your score by adding up the number of correct answers you have. You *do not* lose any credit for wrong answers or for questions you don't answer. For example, on a test having 24 questions, if you had 5 correct, 3 incorrect, and omitted 16, your score would be 5.

Guidelines

How good is the score you just made?

17 or higher . . . . Good
Between 12 and 16 . . . . . . Fair
Below 12 . . . . You need to improve.

Once you have mastered the techniques explained in this book, you should routinely be scoring 20 to 24 correct.

Personal Progress Record

The following is a sample of this Personal Progress Record to familiarize you with it. The entries on this sample are based on the example above.

PERSONAL PROGRESS RECORD—SAMPLE

NUMBER SERIES							
Initial Tests				Repeated Tests			
Date	Test	Number Completed	Number Correct (Your Score)	Date	Score	Date	Score
5/15	Diagnostic Practice Test	8	5				
5/16	Practice Test 1	15	11				
5/18	Practice Test 2	17	15				
5/20	Practice Test 3	20	19				
	Practice Test 4						
	Practice Test 5						
	Practice Test 6						

Now turn to page 431. Look at the table entitled "Personal Progress Record—Number Series." Make the proper entries on the line for the practice test you just took. This table will help you record your progress as you take additional practice tests.

Part D—Following Oral Directions

Computing Your Score

Check your answers against the Answer Key. Calculate your score by adding up the number of correct answers you have. You do *not* lose any credit for wrong answers or for questions you don't answer. For example, on a test having 30 questions, if you had 17 correct and 6 incorrect, and omitted 7, your score would be 17.

Guidelines

How good is the score you just made?

28 or higher . . . . Good
Between 24 and 27 . . . . . . Fair
Below 24 . . . . You need to improve.

Once you have mastered the techniques explained in this book (Chapter 7 covers Following Oral Directions), you should routinely score 28 to 30 correct.

Personal Progress Record

Now turn to page 431. In the table entitled "Personal Progress Record—Following Oral Directions," make the proper entries on the line for the practice test you just took. This table will help you record your progress as you take additional practice tests. A sample is printed below to familiarize you with it. The first entry is based on the preceding example.

PERSONAL PROGRESS RECORD—SAMPLE

FOLLOWING ORAL DIRECTIONS							
Initial Tests				Repeated Tests			
Date	Test	Number Completed	Number Correct (Your Score)	Date	Score	Date	Score
5/15	Diagnostic Practice Test	23	17				
5/16	Practice Test 1	23	19				
5/18	Practice Test 2	27	25				
5/20	Practice Test 3	29	28				
	Practice Test 4						
	Practice Test 5						
	Practice Test 6						

DIAGNOSTIC CHARTS

The following charts will help pinpoint your weaknesses by making it easy for you to determine what particular type of question in each part of the test is most difficult for you.

Part A—Address Checking

Type of Difference	"D" Questions	Number of "D" Questions Wrong		
		Trial 1	Trial 2	Trial 3
Numbers: transposed	7, 9, 16, 30, 39, 46, 53, 67, 75, 78, 90			
changed	6, 34, 70, 87			
omitted	2			
Directions	21, 48, 56, 84			
Abbreviations: streets, roads, avenues, etc.	8, 12, 13, 41, 52, 73 93			
states	1, 25, 38, 50, 58, 92			
Spelling: single letters	5, 11, 19, 28, 60, 63, 71, 74, 77, 89, 91, 95			
groups of letters	26, 29, 31, 32, 33, 45, 62, 69			
Total Number of All Types	53			
	Use the columns on the right to enter the question numbers of "A" items you marked "D."			

This chart will help you to pinpoint the kinds of errors you made on Practice Test 3. Use it as directed below after you have taken and marked the test.

The first column on the left, "Type of Difference," contains the categories whereby addresses may differ (see page 63). On the same line across, the second column gives the numbers of the questions that fall within each category. In the third column, you are to enter the numbers of any "A" questions you answered as "D." Do not include questions that you did not do. Checking the addresses you got wrong may reveal a problem on which you will want to work.

After you have made all the entries, you will be able to see the areas in which you need to improve. Then turn to the appropriate parts of Chapter 3: Address Checking—How to Improve Your Score, read them, and practice the drills that can help. For example, if you find you have been making too many errors picking out number differences, read page 88 and do Drills 18 through 21. If you have a problem with single letters because of reversals like *b* and *d*, or if you have been overlooking the differences between *a*, *e*, and *o*, read page 85. Examine the table and work on Drills 10 and 11 if the problem persists.

Remember that this chart is designed for diagnostic purposes and guidance on further practice. It has been drawn so that you can enter the results each time you retake a practice test. In this way you will be able to see how you are progressing. It is not necessary to record your scores here. That is best done by using the Personal Progress Record Card.

Part B—Memory for Addresses

Kind of Address		Number of Questions	Number Wrong		
			Trial 1	Trial 2	Trial 3
Direct:	List 1	43			
	List 2	42			
	List 3	41			
Numbered:	List 1	45			
	List 2	46			
	List 3	47			

The purpose of this chart is to help you evaluate your performance on the two kinds of memory questions that appear in these memory tests—the questions on the direct (name) addresses and the questions on the numbered addresses. Use the chart as directed below after you have taken and marked the entire test.

The first column on the left, "Kind of Address," is divided by category into "Direct Address" versus "Numbered Address." The second column gives the number of questions in each category on List 1, List 2, and List 3. Use the third column to enter the total number of questions in each category that you answered incorrectly. There is room for you to make additional entries if you take the practice test more than once.

At a glance, you will be able to see which area you need to concentrate on and how well you are progressing as you take repeat trials. Use Chapter 4 and the drills in it to improve your memory for the direct addresses. Use Chapter 5 for the numbered addresses.

Remember to use the Personal Progress Record Card (Memory for Addresses) on page 430 to keep track of your actual scores as you keep studying and practicing.

Part C—Number Series and Part D—Following Oral Directions

Because of the nature of the questions in these tests, Diagnostic Charts are not provided for them. If you find that you made many errors on these tests, study the techniques suggested in Chapters 6 and 7.

Answer Sheet—Practice Test 4

Part A—Address Checking

1 Ⓐ Ⓓ
2 Ⓐ Ⓓ
3 Ⓐ Ⓓ
4 Ⓐ Ⓓ
5 Ⓐ Ⓓ
6 Ⓐ Ⓓ
7 Ⓐ Ⓓ
8 Ⓐ Ⓓ
9 Ⓐ Ⓓ
10 Ⓐ Ⓓ
11 Ⓐ Ⓓ
12 Ⓐ Ⓓ
13 Ⓐ Ⓓ
14 Ⓐ Ⓓ
15 Ⓐ Ⓓ
16 Ⓐ Ⓓ
17 Ⓐ Ⓓ
18 Ⓐ Ⓓ
19 Ⓐ Ⓓ
20 Ⓐ Ⓓ
21 Ⓐ Ⓓ
22 Ⓐ Ⓓ
23 Ⓐ Ⓓ
24 Ⓐ Ⓓ
25 Ⓐ Ⓓ
26 Ⓐ Ⓓ
27 Ⓐ Ⓓ
28 Ⓐ Ⓓ
29 Ⓐ Ⓓ
30 Ⓐ Ⓓ
31 Ⓐ Ⓓ
32 Ⓐ Ⓓ
33 Ⓐ Ⓓ
34 Ⓐ Ⓓ
35 Ⓐ Ⓓ
36 Ⓐ Ⓓ
37 Ⓐ Ⓓ
38 Ⓐ Ⓓ
39 Ⓐ Ⓓ
40 Ⓐ Ⓓ
41 Ⓐ Ⓓ
42 Ⓐ Ⓓ
43 Ⓐ Ⓓ
44 Ⓐ Ⓓ
45 Ⓐ Ⓓ
46 Ⓐ Ⓓ
47 Ⓐ Ⓓ
48 Ⓐ Ⓓ
49 Ⓐ Ⓓ
50 Ⓐ Ⓓ
51 Ⓐ Ⓓ
52 Ⓐ Ⓓ
53 Ⓐ Ⓓ
54 Ⓐ Ⓓ
55 Ⓐ Ⓓ
56 Ⓐ Ⓓ
57 Ⓐ Ⓓ
58 Ⓐ Ⓓ
59 Ⓐ Ⓓ
60 Ⓐ Ⓓ
61 Ⓐ Ⓓ
62 Ⓐ Ⓓ
63 Ⓐ Ⓓ
64 Ⓐ Ⓓ
65 Ⓐ Ⓓ
66 Ⓐ Ⓓ
67 Ⓐ Ⓓ
68 Ⓐ Ⓓ
69 Ⓐ Ⓓ
70 Ⓐ Ⓓ
71 Ⓐ Ⓓ
72 Ⓐ Ⓓ
73 Ⓐ Ⓓ
74 Ⓐ Ⓓ
75 Ⓐ Ⓓ
76 Ⓐ Ⓓ
77 Ⓐ Ⓓ
78 Ⓐ Ⓓ
79 Ⓐ Ⓓ
80 Ⓐ Ⓓ
81 Ⓐ Ⓓ
82 Ⓐ Ⓓ
83 Ⓐ Ⓓ
84 Ⓐ Ⓓ
85 Ⓐ Ⓓ
86 Ⓐ Ⓓ
87 Ⓐ Ⓓ
88 Ⓐ Ⓓ
89 Ⓐ Ⓓ
90 Ⓐ Ⓓ
91 Ⓐ Ⓓ
92 Ⓐ Ⓓ
93 Ⓐ Ⓓ
94 Ⓐ Ⓓ
95 Ⓐ Ⓓ

✂ Remove by cutting on dotted line.

Part B—Memory for Addresses—List 1

1 ⒶⒷⒸⒹⒺ
2 ⒶⒷⒸⒹⒺ
3 ⒶⒷⒸⒹⒺ
4 ⒶⒷⒸⒹⒺ
5 ⒶⒷⒸⒹⒺ
6 ⒶⒷⒸⒹⒺ
7 ⒶⒷⒸⒹⒺ
8 ⒶⒷⒸⒹⒺ
9 ⒶⒷⒸⒹⒺ
10 ⒶⒷⒸⒹⒺ
11 ⒶⒷⒸⒹⒺ
12 ⒶⒷⒸⒹⒺ
13 ⒶⒷⒸⒹⒺ
14 ⒶⒷⒸⒹⒺ
15 ⒶⒷⒸⒹⒺ
16 ⒶⒷⒸⒹⒺ
17 ⒶⒷⒸⒹⒺ
18 ⒶⒷⒸⒹⒺ
19 ⒶⒷⒸⒹⒺ
20 ⒶⒷⒸⒹⒺ
21 ⒶⒷⒸⒹⒺ
22 ⒶⒷⒸⒹⒺ
23 ⒶⒷⒸⒹⒺ
24 ⒶⒷⒸⒹⒺ
25 ⒶⒷⒸⒹⒺ
26 ⒶⒷⒸⒹⒺ
27 ⒶⒷⒸⒹⒺ
28 ⒶⒷⒸⒹⒺ
29 ⒶⒷⒸⒹⒺ
30 ⒶⒷⒸⒹⒺ
31 ⒶⒷⒸⒹⒺ
32 ⒶⒷⒸⒹⒺ
33 ⒶⒷⒸⒹⒺ
34 ⒶⒷⒸⒹⒺ
35 ⒶⒷⒸⒹⒺ
36 ⒶⒷⒸⒹⒺ
37 ⒶⒷⒸⒹⒺ
38 ⒶⒷⒸⒹⒺ
39 ⒶⒷⒸⒹⒺ
40 ⒶⒷⒸⒹⒺ
41 ⒶⒷⒸⒹⒺ
42 ⒶⒷⒸⒹⒺ
43 ⒶⒷⒸⒹⒺ
44 ⒶⒷⒸⒹⒺ
45 ⒶⒷⒸⒹⒺ
46 ⒶⒷⒸⒹⒺ
47 ⒶⒷⒸⒹⒺ
48 ⒶⒷⒸⒹⒺ
49 ⒶⒷⒸⒹⒺ
50 ⒶⒷⒸⒹⒺ
51 ⒶⒷⒸⒹⒺ
52 ⒶⒷⒸⒹⒺ
53 ⒶⒷⒸⒹⒺ
54 ⒶⒷⒸⒹⒺ
55 ⒶⒷⒸⒹⒺ
56 ⒶⒷⒸⒹⒺ
57 ⒶⒷⒸⒹⒺ
58 ⒶⒷⒸⒹⒺ
59 ⒶⒷⒸⒹⒺ
60 ⒶⒷⒸⒹⒺ
61 ⒶⒷⒸⒹⒺ
62 ⒶⒷⒸⒹⒺ
63 ⒶⒷⒸⒹⒺ
64 ⒶⒷⒸⒹⒺ
65 ⒶⒷⒸⒹⒺ
66 ⒶⒷⒸⒹⒺ
67 ⒶⒷⒸⒹⒺ
68 ⒶⒷⒸⒹⒺ
69 ⒶⒷⒸⒹⒺ
70 ⒶⒷⒸⒹⒺ
71 ⒶⒷⒸⒹⒺ
72 ⒶⒷⒸⒹⒺ
73 ⒶⒷⒸⒹⒺ
74 ⒶⒷⒸⒹⒺ
75 ⒶⒷⒸⒹⒺ
76 ⒶⒷⒸⒹⒺ
77 ⒶⒷⒸⒹⒺ
78 ⒶⒷⒸⒹⒺ
79 ⒶⒷⒸⒹⒺ
80 ⒶⒷⒸⒹⒺ
81 ⒶⒷⒸⒹⒺ
82 ⒶⒷⒸⒹⒺ
83 ⒶⒷⒸⒹⒺ
84 ⒶⒷⒸⒹⒺ
85 ⒶⒷⒸⒹⒺ
86 ⒶⒷⒸⒹⒺ
87 ⒶⒷⒸⒹⒺ
88 ⒶⒷⒸⒹⒺ

Part B—Memory for Addresses—List 2

1 ⒶⒷⒸⒹⒺ
2 ⒶⒷⒸⒹⒺ
3 ⒶⒷⒸⒹⒺ
4 ⒶⒷⒸⒹⒺ
5 ⒶⒷⒸⒹⒺ
6 ⒶⒷⒸⒹⒺ
7 ⒶⒷⒸⒹⒺ
8 ⒶⒷⒸⒹⒺ
9 ⒶⒷⒸⒹⒺ
10 ⒶⒷⒸⒹⒺ
11 ⒶⒷⒸⒹⒺ
12 ⒶⒷⒸⒹⒺ
13 ⒶⒷⒸⒹⒺ
14 ⒶⒷⒸⒹⒺ
15 ⒶⒷⒸⒹⒺ
16 ⒶⒷⒸⒹⒺ
17 ⒶⒷⒸⒹⒺ
18 ⒶⒷⒸⒹⒺ
19 ⒶⒷⒸⒹⒺ
20 ⒶⒷⒸⒹⒺ
21 ⒶⒷⒸⒹⒺ
22 ⒶⒷⒸⒹⒺ
23 ⒶⒷⒸⒹⒺ
24 ⒶⒷⒸⒹⒺ
25 ⒶⒷⒸⒹⒺ
26 ⒶⒷⒸⒹⒺ
27 ⒶⒷⒸⒹⒺ
28 ⒶⒷⒸⒹⒺ
29 ⒶⒷⒸⒹⒺ
30 ⒶⒷⒸⒹⒺ
31 ⒶⒷⒸⒹⒺ
32 ⒶⒷⒸⒹⒺ
33 ⒶⒷⒸⒹⒺ
34 ⒶⒷⒸⒹⒺ
35 ⒶⒷⒸⒹⒺ
36 ⒶⒷⒸⒹⒺ
37 ⒶⒷⒸⒹⒺ
38 ⒶⒷⒸⒹⒺ
39 ⒶⒷⒸⒹⒺ
40 ⒶⒷⒸⒹⒺ
41 ⒶⒷⒸⒹⒺ
42 ⒶⒷⒸⒹⒺ
43 ⒶⒷⒸⒹⒺ
44 ⒶⒷⒸⒹⒺ
45 ⒶⒷⒸⒹⒺ
46 ⒶⒷⒸⒹⒺ
47 ⒶⒷⒸⒹⒺ
48 ⒶⒷⒸⒹⒺ
49 ⒶⒷⒸⒹⒺ
50 ⒶⒷⒸⒹⒺ
51 ⒶⒷⒸⒹⒺ
52 ⒶⒷⒸⒹⒺ
53 ⒶⒷⒸⒹⒺ
54 ⒶⒷⒸⒹⒺ
55 ⒶⒷⒸⒹⒺ
56 ⒶⒷⒸⒹⒺ
57 ⒶⒷⒸⒹⒺ
58 ⒶⒷⒸⒹⒺ
59 ⒶⒷⒸⒹⒺ
60 ⒶⒷⒸⒹⒺ
61 ⒶⒷⒸⒹⒺ
62 ⒶⒷⒸⒹⒺ
63 ⒶⒷⒸⒹⒺ
64 ⒶⒷⒸⒹⒺ
65 ⒶⒷⒸⒹⒺ
66 ⒶⒷⒸⒹⒺ
67 ⒶⒷⒸⒹⒺ
68 ⒶⒷⒸⒹⒺ
69 ⒶⒷⒸⒹⒺ
70 ⒶⒷⒸⒹⒺ
71 ⒶⒷⒸⒹⒺ
72 ⒶⒷⒸⒹⒺ
73 ⒶⒷⒸⒹⒺ
74 ⒶⒷⒸⒹⒺ
75 ⒶⒷⒸⒹⒺ
76 ⒶⒷⒸⒹⒺ
77 ⒶⒷⒸⒹⒺ
78 ⒶⒷⒸⒹⒺ
79 ⒶⒷⒸⒹⒺ
80 ⒶⒷⒸⒹⒺ
81 ⒶⒷⒸⒹⒺ
82 ⒶⒷⒸⒹⒺ
83 ⒶⒷⒸⒹⒺ
84 ⒶⒷⒸⒹⒺ
85 ⒶⒷⒸⒹⒺ
86 ⒶⒷⒸⒹⒺ
87 ⒶⒷⒸⒹⒺ
88 ⒶⒷⒸⒹⒺ

Remove by cutting on dotted line.

Part B—Memory for Addresses—List 3

1 ⒶⒷⒸⒹⒺ
2 ⒶⒷⒸⒹⒺ
3 ⒶⒷⒸⒹⒺ
4 ⒶⒷⒸⒹⒺ
5 ⒶⒷⒸⒹⒺ
6 ⒶⒷⒸⒹⒺ
7 ⒶⒷⒸⒹⒺ
8 ⒶⒷⒸⒹⒺ
9 ⒶⒷⒸⒹⒺ
10 ⒶⒷⒸⒹⒺ
11 ⒶⒷⒸⒹⒺ
12 ⒶⒷⒸⒹⒺ
13 ⒶⒷⒸⒹⒺ
14 ⒶⒷⒸⒹⒺ
15 ⒶⒷⒸⒹⒺ
16 ⒶⒷⒸⒹⒺ
17 ⒶⒷⒸⒹⒺ
18 ⒶⒷⒸⒹⒺ
19 ⒶⒷⒸⒹⒺ
20 ⒶⒷⒸⒹⒺ
21 ⒶⒷⒸⒹⒺ
22 ⒶⒷⒸⒹⒺ
23 ⒶⒷⒸⒹⒺ
24 ⒶⒷⒸⒹⒺ
25 ⒶⒷⒸⒹⒺ
26 ⒶⒷⒸⒹⒺ
27 ⒶⒷⒸⒹⒺ
28 ⒶⒷⒸⒹⒺ
29 ⒶⒷⒸⒹⒺ
30 ⒶⒷⒸⒹⒺ
31 ⒶⒷⒸⒹⒺ
32 ⒶⒷⒸⒹⒺ
33 ⒶⒷⒸⒹⒺ
34 ⒶⒷⒸⒹⒺ
35 ⒶⒷⒸⒹⒺ
36 ⒶⒷⒸⒹⒺ
37 ⒶⒷⒸⒹⒺ
38 ⒶⒷⒸⒹⒺ
39 ⒶⒷⒸⒹⒺ
40 ⒶⒷⒸⒹⒺ
41 ⒶⒷⒸⒹⒺ
42 ⒶⒷⒸⒹⒺ
43 ⒶⒷⒸⒹⒺ
44 ⒶⒷⒸⒹⒺ
45 ⒶⒷⒸⒹⒺ
46 ⒶⒷⒸⒹⒺ
47 ⒶⒷⒸⒹⒺ
48 ⒶⒷⒸⒹⒺ
49 ⒶⒷⒸⒹⒺ
50 ⒶⒷⒸⒹⒺ
51 ⒶⒷⒸⒹⒺ
52 ⒶⒷⒸⒹⒺ
53 ⒶⒷⒸⒹⒺ
54 ⒶⒷⒸⒹⒺ
55 ⒶⒷⒸⒹⒺ
56 ⒶⒷⒸⒹⒺ
57 ⒶⒷⒸⒹⒺ
58 ⒶⒷⒸⒹⒺ
59 ⒶⒷⒸⒹⒺ
60 ⒶⒷⒸⒹⒺ
61 ⒶⒷⒸⒹⒺ
62 ⒶⒷⒸⒹⒺ
63 ⒶⒷⒸⒹⒺ
64 ⒶⒷⒸⒹⒺ
65 ⒶⒷⒸⒹⒺ
66 ⒶⒷⒸⒹⒺ
67 ⒶⒷⒸⒹⒺ
68 ⒶⒷⒸⒹⒺ
69 ⒶⒷⒸⒹⒺ
70 ⒶⒷⒸⒹⒺ
71 ⒶⒷⒸⒹⒺ
72 ⒶⒷⒸⒹⒺ
73 ⒶⒷⒸⒹⒺ
74 ⒶⒷⒸⒹⒺ
75 ⒶⒷⒸⒹⒺ
76 ⒶⒷⒸⒹⒺ
77 ⒶⒷⒸⒹⒺ
78 ⒶⒷⒸⒹⒺ
79 ⒶⒷⒸⒹⒺ
80 ⒶⒷⒸⒹⒺ
81 ⒶⒷⒸⒹⒺ
82 ⒶⒷⒸⒹⒺ
83 ⒶⒷⒸⒹⒺ
84 ⒶⒷⒸⒹⒺ
85 ⒶⒷⒸⒹⒺ
86 ⒶⒷⒸⒹⒺ
87 ⒶⒷⒸⒹⒺ
88 ⒶⒷⒸⒹⒺ

Part C—Number Series

1 ⒶⒷⒸⒹⒺ
2 ⒶⒷⒸⒹⒺ
3 ⒶⒷⒸⒹⒺ
4 ⒶⒷⒸⒹⒺ
5 ⒶⒷⒸⒹⒺ
6 ⒶⒷⒸⒹⒺ
7 ⒶⒷⒸⒹⒺ
8 ⒶⒷⒸⒹⒺ
9 ⒶⒷⒸⒹⒺ
10 ⒶⒷⒸⒹⒺ
11 ⒶⒷⒸⒹⒺ
12 ⒶⒷⒸⒹⒺ
13 ⒶⒷⒸⒹⒺ
14 ⒶⒷⒸⒹⒺ
15 ⒶⒷⒸⒹⒺ
16 ⒶⒷⒸⒹⒺ
17 ⒶⒷⒸⒹⒺ
18 ⒶⒷⒸⒹⒺ
19 ⒶⒷⒸⒹⒺ
20 ⒶⒷⒸⒹⒺ
21 ⒶⒷⒸⒹⒺ
22 ⒶⒷⒸⒹⒺ
23 ⒶⒷⒸⒹⒺ
24 ⒶⒷⒸⒹⒺ

Part D—Following Oral Directions

1 ⒶⒷⒸⒹⒺ
2 ⒶⒷⒸⒹⒺ
3 ⒶⒷⒸⒹⒺ
4 ⒶⒷⒸⒹⒺ
5 ⒶⒷⒸⒹⒺ
6 ⒶⒷⒸⒹⒺ
7 ⒶⒷⒸⒹⒺ
8 ⒶⒷⒸⒹⒺ
9 ⒶⒷⒸⒹⒺ
10 ⒶⒷⒸⒹⒺ
11 ⒶⒷⒸⒹⒺ
12 ⒶⒷⒸⒹⒺ
13 ⒶⒷⒸⒹⒺ
14 ⒶⒷⒸⒹⒺ
15 ⒶⒷⒸⒹⒺ
16 ⒶⒷⒸⒹⒺ
17 ⒶⒷⒸⒹⒺ
18 ⒶⒷⒸⒹⒺ
19 ⒶⒷⒸⒹⒺ
20 ⒶⒷⒸⒹⒺ
21 ⒶⒷⒸⒹⒺ
22 ⒶⒷⒸⒹⒺ
23 ⒶⒷⒸⒹⒺ
24 ⒶⒷⒸⒹⒺ
25 ⒶⒷⒸⒹⒺ
26 ⒶⒷⒸⒹⒺ
27 ⒶⒷⒸⒹⒺ
28 ⒶⒷⒸⒹⒺ
29 ⒶⒷⒸⒹⒺ
30 ⒶⒷⒸⒹⒺ
31 ⒶⒷⒸⒹⒺ
32 ⒶⒷⒸⒹⒺ
33 ⒶⒷⒸⒹⒺ
34 ⒶⒷⒸⒹⒺ
35 ⒶⒷⒸⒹⒺ
36 ⒶⒷⒸⒹⒺ
37 ⒶⒷⒸⒹⒺ
38 ⒶⒷⒸⒹⒺ
39 ⒶⒷⒸⒹⒺ
40 ⒶⒷⒸⒹⒺ
41 ⒶⒷⒸⒹⒺ
42 ⒶⒷⒸⒹⒺ
43 ⒶⒷⒸⒹⒺ
44 ⒶⒷⒸⒹⒺ
45 ⒶⒷⒸⒹⒺ
46 ⒶⒷⒸⒹⒺ
47 ⒶⒷⒸⒹⒺ
48 ⒶⒷⒸⒹⒺ
49 ⒶⒷⒸⒹⒺ
50 ⒶⒷⒸⒹⒺ
51 ⒶⒷⒸⒹⒺ
52 ⒶⒷⒸⒹⒺ
53 ⒶⒷⒸⒹⒺ
54 ⒶⒷⒸⒹⒺ
55 ⒶⒷⒸⒹⒺ
56 ⒶⒷⒸⒹⒺ
57 ⒶⒷⒸⒹⒺ
58 ⒶⒷⒸⒹⒺ
59 ⒶⒷⒸⒹⒺ
60 ⒶⒷⒸⒹⒺ
61 ⒶⒷⒸⒹⒺ
62 ⒶⒷⒸⒹⒺ
63 ⒶⒷⒸⒹⒺ
64 ⒶⒷⒸⒹⒺ
65 ⒶⒷⒸⒹⒺ
66 ⒶⒷⒸⒹⒺ
67 ⒶⒷⒸⒹⒺ
68 ⒶⒷⒸⒹⒺ
69 ⒶⒷⒸⒹⒺ
70 ⒶⒷⒸⒹⒺ
71 ⒶⒷⒸⒹⒺ
72 ⒶⒷⒸⒹⒺ
73 ⒶⒷⒸⒹⒺ
74 ⒶⒷⒸⒹⒺ
75 ⒶⒷⒸⒹⒺ
76 ⒶⒷⒸⒹⒺ
77 ⒶⒷⒸⒹⒺ
78 ⒶⒷⒸⒹⒺ
79 ⒶⒷⒸⒹⒺ
80 ⒶⒷⒸⒹⒺ
81 ⒶⒷⒸⒹⒺ
82 ⒶⒷⒸⒹⒺ
83 ⒶⒷⒸⒹⒺ
84 ⒶⒷⒸⒹⒺ
85 ⒶⒷⒸⒹⒺ
86 ⒶⒷⒸⒹⒺ
87 ⒶⒷⒸⒹⒺ
88 ⒶⒷⒸⒹⒺ

Chapter 12

Practice Test 4

Part A — ADDRESS CHECKING

Work — 6 minutes

In this part of the test, you are to decide whether two addresses are alike or different. If the two addresses are *exactly alike in every way*, darken space Ⓐ. If they are *different in any way*, darken space Ⓓ.

Mark your answers on the Answer Sheet on page 331. Tear it out, put today's date on it, and place it next to the questions.

Allow yourself exactly 6 minutes to do as many of the 95 questions as you can. If you finish before the time is up, check your answers.

1. Columbine Hills CO 80123	Columbine Hills CO 80123
2. Ponce PR	Ponce PA
3. 492 Iolantha Lane	492 Iolantha Lane
4. 110 Hambiton Ave	110 Hamilton Ave
5. 53 S Dockerry Lane	53 S Bockerry Lane
6. 3776 E Yoakum St	3776 E Yoakum Sq
7. 910 Jumel Ter	10 Jumel Ter
8. 3992 Aristotle Dr	3992 Aristotel Dr
9. 4704 Clavier St	4740 Clavier St
10. 438 Hamakawai Court	438 Hamakawai Court
11. 3404 N Barrymore Ct	3404 N Barrymore Ct
12. 6381 W Blumberg Ave	6318 W Blumberg Ave
13. 58 SE Kramden Pl	58 SE Kramden Pl
14. 8940 N Dunkirk St	8940 N Dunkirk St
15. 9120 Martin Marietto Sq	9210 Martin Marietto Sq
16. 5038 Farley Granger Woods Walk	5038 Farley Granger Woods Walk
17. 3048 Damon Farms Ln	3048 Damon Farms Ln
18. 2401 Knight Blvd	2401 Knight Blvd
19. 8864 N Cheshire Pl	8864 S Cheshire Pl
20. 789 Iago Dr	789 Iaga Dr
21. 501 Wheelwood Blvd E	501 Wheelwood Blvd E
22. Denham Springs 71232	Denham Springs 72132
23. 683 N Quebec Tpke	683 N Quebec Tpke
24. Plainfield NH 03781	Plainfield NV 03781

25. 6234 S Drummond Dr	6234 W Drummond Dr
26. 7576 Goldwater Ter	7576 Goldwater Trl
27. 2341 Carmine Blvd	2341 Carmine Blvd
28. 49 Westlake Ave	49 Westlake Ave
29. 823 W Palmetto St	823 E Palmetto St
30. 119 Albermarle Rd N	119 Alpermarle Rd N
31. 959 NE Polakalua Pl	959 NE Polakalua Pl
32. 984 Classenfuls Ave NE	984 Clasenfuls Ave NE
33. 1382 Grindel Rock Blvd	1382 Glindel Rock Blvd
34. 2219 Altamount Canyon Tpke	2219 Altamount Canyon Tpke
35. 9412 Young Pl	9412 Youth Pl
36. 2800 Regalos el Modina	2800 Regaldos el Modina
37. 7383 Tremont West Dr	7383 Tremont East Dr
38. 2764 Partridge Ct	2764 Partridge Ct
39. 1005 W San Obispa Cir	1005 W San Obispa Cir
40. 1045 Chekea Ct SE	1045 Chekea Ct NE
41. 8000 Coronado de Bolivar Trail	8000 Coronado de Bolivar Trail
42. 3528 Virginia Park Pkwy	3528 Virginia Park Cswy
43. 6223 Farmingdale Park W	6223 Farmingdale Park W
44. 50 Iverness Pl	50 Iverness Pl
45. 1002 W 7 St	1002 W 7 St
46. Teton ID 83451	Teton DC 83451
47. 116 Evermonde Rd SW	116 Evermonde Dr SW
48. North Underwood City OH	North Underwood City OH
49. 1683 S Roanoke Ave	1685 S Roanoke Ave
50. 424 W Vernier Ave	424 W Vernier Ave
51. 308 Quentin Rd	308 Quentin Dr
52. 7721 Jerseyside Via	7721 Jerseyside Via
53. 875 Castle Hill Ave	875 Castel Hill Ave
54. 7904 Herricks Place	7904 Herricks Place
55. 1040 Davenport St	1040 Davenport Sq
56. Riverale MD 20737	Riverale MO 20737
57. 489 Esterwood Ln	489 Westerwood Ln
58. 5055 NW 264th Ave	5055 NW 26th Ave
59. 5005 Slatterside Loop E	5006 Slatterside Loop E
60. Bay City MI 48707	Boy City MI 48707

61. 3704 Eldano St	3704 Eldamo St
62. 4488 W Merryweather Ave	4488 W Merryweather Ave
63. North Attleboro MA	North Attleberg MA
64. 7803 S Uster Rd	7803 S Ulster Rd
65. East Meadow NY 11554	East Meadow NJ 11554
66. 707 E Wallington St	707 E Wallington St
67. 6016 Broadwatter Rd S	6016 Broadwatter Rd S
68. 8103 E. Shannon St	8103 E Shannon Ct
69. 1023 Fleissig St	1032 Fleissig St
70. 298 Hialeah St	298 Hialeah St
71. 9101 En Pacada Sq	9101 En Pacado Sq
72. 62 Old Woods Drive West	62 Old Woods Drive West
73. 2460 Nortondale Blvd	2460 Nortondell Blvd
74. 255 Ingersoll Pkwy NE	255 Ingersoll Pky SE
75. 31 E Greeley Sq	31 E Greeley Sq
76. 6515 Weathersfield Ct N	6515 Weathersford Ct N
77. 347 N 104th St	347 N 104th St
78. 15510 Jesper Blvd	15510 Jasper Blvd
79. 610 South Handy Ln NW	610 South Candy Ln NW
80. San Jose PR 00924	San Juan PR 00924
81. 403 Yuletide Tree Road	403 Yuletide Tree Road
82. 7704 NE 20th St	7704 NE 20th St
83. Glenham SD 57631	Glenham SD 57621
84. 2008 Steinway St	2008 Steinway St
85. 971 Larch Lake Road	917 Larch Lake Road
86. 6994 Kristofferson Blvd S	6994 Kristofferson Blvd S
87. Moorehead MN 56501	Moosehead MN 56501
88. 8138 S Ettiger Rd	8183 S Ettinger Rd
89. 88 E Garinow Dr	88 E Garinow Dr
90. 928 N 11th Rd	928 N 111th Rd
91. 43 Riverdale Cir S	43 Riverside Cir S
92. 846 Fremont Pl	846 Fremount Pl
93. 5912 E 213 St	5912 E 213 St
94. 1136 Simpson St	1136 Simpson St
95. 4106 East Country Hill Path	4106 East Country Hill Path

STOP.

If you finish before the time is up, go back and check the questions in this section of the test only.

PART B — MEMORY FOR ADDRESSES

In this part of the test, you will have five boxes labeled A, B, C, D, and E. Each box contains five addresses. Three of the five are groups of street addresses, such as 5400–5699 Garden, 6400–6699 Sunset, and 6000–6399 Ulster; and two are names of places. The addresses are different in each box.

There will be several opportunities to study the addresses and the boxes they are in. You will also be given three tests of 88 questions each, and the task of deciding where each address belongs. In some cases, you will have the list *and* the boxes in front of you at the same time; in others you will not. List 1 and List 2 are for warm-up practice. List 3 is the real one that will be scored.

Make sure you understand the format by examining the pretest samples below.

Pretest Samples

A	B	C	D	E
4100–4599 Garden	5400–5699 Garden	5700–6399 Garden	4600–5399 Garden	6400–6999 Garden
Raimes	Emory	Clarke	Sargeant	Violet
6400–6699 Sunset	5700–6399 Sunset	5400–5699 Sunset	4100–5399 Sunset	6700–7199 Sunset
Temple	Pearle	Atlantic	Bliss	Illinois
4600–5399 Ulster	6400–6899 Ulster	6000–6399 Ulster	5400–5999 Ulster	4100–4599 Ulster

Questions 1 through 7 show the way the questions look. You have to decide in which lettered box (A, B, C, D, or E) the address belongs and then mark your answer by darkening the appropriate space in the answer grid.

1. Sargeant — 1 Ⓐ Ⓑ Ⓒ Ⓓ Ⓔ
2. Pearle — 2 Ⓐ Ⓑ Ⓒ Ⓓ Ⓔ
3. Illinois — 3 Ⓐ Ⓑ Ⓒ Ⓓ Ⓔ
4. 4100–4599 Garden — 4 Ⓐ Ⓑ Ⓒ Ⓓ Ⓔ
5. Emory — 5 Ⓐ Ⓑ Ⓒ Ⓓ Ⓔ
6. 6400–6899 Ulster — 6 Ⓐ Ⓑ Ⓒ Ⓓ Ⓔ
7. 5700–6399 Sunset — 7 Ⓐ Ⓑ Ⓒ Ⓓ Ⓔ

Answers

1. **D** 2. **B** 3. **E** 4. **A** 5. **B** 6. **B** 7. **B**

Now that you know what to do, you may begin Part B of Practice Test 4. To get the most out of it and the remaining two practice tests in this book, follow the directions and timing *exactly*. Follow each phase of Part B of the test, page by page, until you've completed List 3. It is modeled on the way the Postal Service actually conducts its tests.

Turn to the next page to begin.

Study — 3 minutes

You will be given 3 minutes to spend memorizing the addresses in the boxes. *They are exactly the same ones that will be used for all three tests.* Try to memorize as many as you can. When the 3 minutes are up, turn to page 340 and read the instructions for *List 1*.

A	B	C	D	E
4100–4599 Garden	5400–5699 Garden	5700–6399 Garden	4600–5399 Garden	6400–6999 Garden
Raimes	Emory	Clarke	Sargeant	Violet
6400–6699 Sunset	5700–6399 Sunset	5400–5699 Sunset	4100–5399 Sunset	6700–7199 Sunset
Temple	Pearle	Atlantic	Bliss	Illinois
4600–5399 Ulster	6400–6899 Ulster	6000–6399 Ulster	5400–5999 Ulster	4100–4599 Ulster

List 1

Work — 3 minutes

For each question, mark the Answer Sheet on page 332 to show the letter of the box in which the address belongs. Try to remember the locations of as many addresses as you can. *You will now have 3 minutes to complete List 1.* If you are not sure of an answer, you should guess.

A	B	C	D	E
4100–4599 Garden Raimes 6400–6699 Sunset Temple 4600–5399 Ulster	5400–5699 Garden Emory 5700–6399 Sunset Pearle 6400–6899 Ulster	5700–6399 Garden Clarke 5400–5699 Sunset Atlantic 6000–6399 Ulster	4600–5399 Garden Sargeant 4100–5399 Sunset Bliss 5400–5999 Ulster	6400–6999 Garden Violet 6700–7199 Sunset Illinois 4100–4599 Ulster

1. Bliss
2. 5700–6399 Garden
3. Violet
4. Atlantic
5. 4100–5399 Sunset
6. Raines
7. 6700–7199 Sunset
8. 4600–5399 Ulster
9. 5400–5999 Ulster
10. Illinois
11. Temple
12. 4600–5399 Garden
13. 6000–6399 Ulster
14. Atlantic
15. Clarke
16. 6400–6899 Ulster
17. 5700–6399 Sunset
18. Raines
19. 5400–5699 Sunset
20. 5400–5999 Ulster
21. 5700–6399 Garden
22. Pearle
23. Emory
24. 6400–6999 Garden
25. Violet
26. 4100–4599 Ulster
27. 4100–4599 Garden
28. 5400–5699 Garden
29. Sargeant
30. 5700–6399 Sunset
31. 5400–5699 Sunset
32. Clarke
33. 6700–7199 Sunset
34. Sargeant
35. 5400–5699 Garden
36. Raines
37. 5400–5699 Sunset
38. Sargeant
39. 4600–5399 Ulster
40. Temple
41. 6400–6699 Sunset
42. Pearle
43. Violet
44. 4100–4599 Garden

45. 5400–5999 Ulster
46. 6000–6399 Ulster
47. 6400–6699 Sunset
48. 5700–6399 Garden
49. Emory
50. Temple
51. 6400–6699 Sunset
52. 5700–6399 Sunset
53. Atlantic
54. 4100–4599 Ulster
55. Pearle
56. 6000–6399 Ulster
57. 4600–5399 Garden
58. Emory
59. 4100–4599 Ulster
60. Bliss
61. Clarke
62. 4600–5399 Garden
63. Pearle
64. 6700–7199 Sunset
65. Violet
66. 4600–5399 Ulster
67. Temple
68. Atlantic
69. 4100–5399 Sunset
70. Bliss
71. Clarke
72. 6400–6999 Garden
73. Sargeant
74. Atlantic
75. Illinois
76. 6400–6899 Ulster
77. 4100–4599 Garden
78. 4100–5399 Sunset
79. 6400–6899 Ulster
80. Emory
81. 5400–5699 Garden
82. Bliss
83. Raines
84. 6400–6699 Sunset
85. Sargeant
86. Raines
87. 6400–6999 Garden
88. Illinois

STOP.
If you finish before the time is up, go back and check the questions in this section of the test only.

List 2

Work — 3 minutes

Do these questions *without* looking back at the boxes. For each question, mark your answer on the Answer Sheet for List 2 on page 332. If you are not sure of an answer, you should guess.

1. Atlantic
2. Sargeant
3. Violet
4. 5700–6399 Sunset
5. 6400–6699 Sunset
6. Emory
7. 4100–4599 Garden
8. Bliss
9. 4100–4599 Garden
10. 4600–5399 Ulster
11. 4100–5399 Sunset
12. 4100–4599 Garden
13. Illinois
14. 4600–5399 Garden
15. 5400–5699 Sunset
16. Temple
17. Atlantic
18. Emory
19. 5400–5699 Sunset
20. Sargeant
21. 4100–4599 Ulster
22. Raines
23. Temple
24. 6700–7199 Sunset
25. Raines
26. Atlantic
27. 5700–6399 Sunset
28. 5400–5999 Ulster
29. 4100–4599 Ulster
30. 5700–6399 Garden
31. Bliss
32. 6000–6399 Ulster
33. Sargeant
34. 5400–5999 Ulster
35. Emory
36. Bliss
37. 4600–5399 Ulster
38. Emory
39. Illinois
40. Temple
41. 4600–5399 Garden
42. 6400–6699 Sunset
43. 5700–6399 Sunset
44. 5400–5699 Garden

45. Clarke
46. Pearle
47. 4100–5399 Sunset
48. 5400–5699 Garden
49. 6400–6899 Ulster
50. Raines
51. Atlantic
52. Illinois
53. 6400–6699 Sunset
54. 6400–6999 Garden
55. Temple
56. 6400–6999 Garden
57. 4600–5399 Ulster
58. 5400–5699 Sunset
59. Pearle
60. 6000–6399 Ulster
61. Raines
62. Clarke
63. 4100–5399 Sunset
64. Raines
65. 5700–6399 Garden
66. 6000–6399 Ulster
67. 6400–6899 Ulster
68. Violet
69. Atlantic
70. 4100–4599 Ulster
71. Clarke
72. Violet
73. 6400–6999 Garden
74. 6700–7199 Sunset
75. Sargeant
76. Bliss
77. 6400–6899 Ulster
78. Violet
79. 4600–5399 Garden
80. 6700–7199 Sunset
81. 5400–5999 Ulster
82. 4100–4599 Ulster
83. Clarke
84. 5400–5699 Garden
85. 5700–6399 Garden
86. Pearle
87. Sargeant
88. 4600–5399 Ulster

STOP.
If you finish before the time is up, go back and check the questions in this section of the test only.

List 3

Study — 5 minutes

You are now about to take the test using List 3. *(This is the test that counts!)*

Turn back to page 340 and study the boxes again. *You have 5 minutes to restudy the addresses.*

Work — 5 minutes

For each question, mark the Answer Sheet on page 333 to show the letter of the box in which the address belongs. You have *exactly 5 minutes* to do the test. During these 5 minutes, *do not* turn to any other page.

1. 5400–5699 Garden
2. 5700–6399 Sunset
3. 6400–6699 Sunset
4. 4600–5399 Garden
5. Temple
6. Illinois
7. Emory
8. 4600–5399 Ulster
9. Bliss
10. Emory
11. 5400–5999 Ulster
12. Sargeant
13. 6000–6399 Ulster
14. Bliss
15. 5700–6399 Garden
16. 4100–4599 Ulster
17. 5400–5999 Ulster
18. 5700–6399 Sunset
19. Atlantic
20. Raines
21. 6700–7199 Sunset
22. Temple
23. 6400–6999 Garden
24. Pearle
25. Sargeant
26. 5400–5699 Sunset
27. Emory
28. Atlantic
29. Temple
30. 5400–5699 Sunset
31. 4600–5399 Garden
32. Illinois
33. 4100–4599 Garden
34. 4100–5399 Sunset
35. 4600–5399 Ulster
36. 4100–4599 Garden
37. Bliss
38. 4100–4599 Garden
39. Emory
40. 6400–6699 Sunset
41. 5700–6399 Sunset
42. Violet
43. Sargeant
44. Atlantic

45. Illinois
46. Sargeant
47. Pearle
48. 5700–6399 Garden
49. 5400–5699 Garden
50. Clarke
51. 4100–4599 Ulster
52. 5400–5999 Ulster
53. 6700–7199 Sunset
54. 4600–5399 Garden
55. Violet
56. 6400–6899 Ulster
57. Bliss
58. Sargeant
59. 6700–7199 Sunset
60. 6400–6999 Garden
61. Violet
62. Clarke
63. 4100–4599 Ulster
64. Atlantic
65. Violet
66. 6400–6899 Ulster
67. 6000–6399 Ulster
68. 5700–6399 Garden
69. Raines
70. 4100–5399 Sunset
71. 5700–6399 Sunset
72. Raines
73. 6000–6399 Ulster
74. Pearle
75. 5400–5699 Sunset
76. 4600–5399 Ulster
77. 6400–6999 Garden
78. Temple
79. 6400–6999 Garden
80. 6400–6699 Sunset
81. Illinois
82. 4600–5399 Ulster
83. Raines
84. 6400–6899 Ulster
85. 5400–5699 Garden
86. 4100–5399 Sunset
87. Pearle
88. Clarke

STOP.
If you finish before the time is up, go back and check the questions in this section of the test only.

PART C — NUMBER SERIES

Work — 20 minutes

For each Number Series question, there is a series of numbers that follow some definite order, and below each are five sets of two numbers each. You are to look at the numbers in the series and find out what order they follow. Then decide what the next two numbers in that series would be if the same order were continued. Mark your answers on the Answer Sheet for Number Series on page 333.

You have 20 minutes to complete this part of the test. If you finish before the time is up, check your answers. The answers and explanations are on pages 355 to 357.

1. 40 50 60 40 50 60 40 __ __

   A) 40 50 B) 50 60 C) 60 70 D) 50 40 E) 60 40

2. 31 40 28 37 25 34 22 __ __

   A) 18 21 B) 32 10 C) 19 31 D) 31 19 E) 30 18

3. 57 53 53 49 49 45 45 __ __

   A) 45 41 B) 41 37 C) 39 39 D) 41 41 E) 37 41

4. 16 21 19 18 23 21 20 __ __

   A) 24 22 B) 19 18 C) 18 17 D) 21 26 E) 25 23

5. 68 67 67 50 49 49 32 __ __

   A) 40 18 B) 32 15 C) 32 14 D) 29 19 E) 31 31

6. 36 30 30 32 23 23 28 16 __ __

   A) 24 24 B) 24 26 C) 16 24 D) 9 16 E) 21 24

7. 9 12 15 30 25 20 18 21 24 15 __ __

   A) 10 5 B) 18 21 C) 20 25 D) 18 10 E) 15 20

8. 15 35 20 28 25 21 30 __ __

   A) 14 35 B) 40 18 C) 14 40 D) 35 24 E) 23 24

9. 43 17 36 28 16 21 13 __ __

   A) 17 9 B) 5 17 C) 15 6 D) 12 14 E) 17 7

10. 32 30 38 28 26 36 24 __ __

    A) 22 32 B) 26 36 C) 22 34 D) 28 36 E) 24 34

11. 4 6 8 8 5 7 7 7 6 8 6 __ __

    A) 7 9 B) 8 9 C) 8 7 D) 7 8 E) 6 7

12. 1 2 4 5 7 8 10 __ __
A) 10 11 B) 11 13 C) 11 12 D) 9 10 E) 12 13

13. 5 7 10 10 12 15 10 __ __
A) 18 10 B) 10 10 C) 17 20 D) 10 13 E) 13 10

14. 4 10 8 14 12 18 16 __ __
A) 22 20 B) 14 20 C) 18 22 D) 22 26 E) 20 24

15. 3 6 2 5 10 6 9 __ __
A) 14 8 B) 10 12 C) 18 14 D) 12 24 E) 5 10

16. 27 72 62 26 16 61 51 __ __
A) 71 17 B) 16 6 C) 41 14 D) 17 71 E) 15 5

17. 1 13 8 8 13 15 15 13 __ __
A) 20 22 B) 22 25 C) 25 20 D) 22 22 E) 20 20

18. 56 56 48 48 41 41 35 __ __
A) 35 35 B) 35 30 C) 35 29 D) 29 29 E) 30 30

19. 16 17 18 12 14 19 20 21 16 18 22 __ __
A) 24 23 B) 19 23 C) 20 22 D) 23 24 E) 24 25

20. 26 24 16 23 21 17 20 18 18 17 __ __
A) 15 14 B) 17 19 C) 14 20 D) 15 19 E) 19 14

21. 31 32 33 32 33 34 33 __ __
A) 35 35 B) 32 33 C) 33 34 D) 33 33 E) 34 35

22. 1 20 2 18 4 16 8 __ __
A) 10 12 B) 12 10 C) 14 18 D) 32 10 E) 14 16

23. 5 10 11 6 12 13 7 __ __
A) 8 9 B) 14 8 C) 10 15 D) 14 15 E) 8 14

24. 2 3 5 9 17 33 65 __ __
A) 82 104 B) 120 162 C) 129 257 D) 165 330 E) 189 377

STOP.
If you finish before the time is up, go back and check the questions in this section of the test only.

Part D — FOLLOWING ORAL DIRECTIONS

This part of the test gauges your ability to understand and carry out spoken directions *exactly* as they are given to you.

In order to prepare to take Part D of the test, follow the steps below:

1. Enlist the help of a friend who will be the "reader." His or her job will be to read aloud a series of directions that you are to follow *exactly.* The reader will need a watch that displays seconds, because the directions must be read at the correct speed.
2. Tear out pages 353 and 354. These are the worksheets you should have in front of you as you listen to the directions given by the reader, who will tell you to do certain things with the items on each line on the worksheets.
3. Use the Answer Sheet for Following Oral Directions on page 333, and insert today's date. You will darken the appropriate spaces in accordance with the directions given by the reader.
4. *Now hand this entire book to the reader.* Ask him/her to review the section below headed "Instructions to the Reader." It explains exactly how the reader is to proceed.

When you and the reader are ready to start this part of Practice Test 4, he/she will begin reading to you the section marked "Directions." YOU ARE NOT TO READ THESE AT ANY TIME BEFORE OR DURING THE TEST. If you do, you will lose the benefit of this part of the practice test.

Instructions to the "Reader"

These instructions should be read at about 80 words per minute. You should practice reading the material in the box until you can do it in exactly 1 minute. This will give you a feel for the way you should read the test material.

1-MINUTE PRACTICE

Look at line 20 on your worksheet. There are two circles and two boxes of different sizes with numbers in them. If 7 is less than 3 and if 2 is smaller than 4, write C in the larger circle. Otherwise write B as in *baker* in the smaller box. Now, on your answer sheet, darken the space for the number-letter combination in the box or circle.

You should read the entire test aloud before you read it to the person taking the test, in order to acquaint yourself with the procedure and the desired rate of reading.

Read slowly but at a natural pace. In other words, do not space the words so that there are unnaturally long pauses between them. The instruction "Pause slightly" indicates only enough time to take a breath. The other instructions for pauses give the recommended length for each. If possible, use a watch with a second hand.

All the material that follows, except the words in parentheses, is to be read aloud. Now start reading the directions. *Do not repeat any of the directions.*

Directions: In this test, I will read instructions to you. You are to mark your worksheets according to the instructions that I read to you. After each set of instructions, I'll give you time to record your answers on your answer sheet.

Try to understand the instructions as I read them; I cannot repeat them. Do not ask any questions from now on.

If, when you go to darken a space for a number, you find that you have already darkened another space for that number, either (1) erase the first mark and darken the space for your new choice, or (2) let the first mark stay and do not darken any other space. When you finish, you should have no more than one space darkened for each number.

Turn to Worksheet 1.

Look at line 1 on your worksheet. (Pause slightly.) Write an E in the last box. (Pause 2 seconds.) Now, on your answer sheet, find the number in that box and darken space E for that number. (Pause 5 seconds.)

Now look at the numbers in line 2 on your worksheet. (Pause slightly.) Draw a line under the second number in the line. (Pause 2 seconds.) Now, on your answer sheet, find the number under which you drew a line and darken space C for that number. (Pause 5 seconds.)

Look at line 2 again. (Pause slightly.) Draw two lines under the first number in the line. (Pause 2 seconds.) Now, on your answer sheet, find the number under which you drew two lines and darken space D as in *dog.* (Pause 5 seconds.)

Look at the letters in line 3 on your worksheet. (Pause slightly.) Draw a circle around the fifth letter in the line. (Pause 2 seconds.) Now, on your answer sheet, find the number 19 and darken the space for the letter around which you drew a circle. (Pause 5 seconds.)

Look at line 3 again. (Pause slightly.) Draw a line under the middle letter in the line. (Pause 2 seconds.) Now, on your answer sheet, find the number 12 and darken the space for the letter under which you drew a line. (Pause 5 seconds.)

Look at the five circles in line 4 on your worksheet. (Pause slightly.) Each circle has a letter of the alphabet inside it. Write the number 2 in the circle that has the third letter of the alphabet inside it. (Pause 3 seconds.) Now, on your answer sheet, darken the space for the number-letter combination that is in the circle you just wrote in. (Pause 5 seconds.)

Look at line 5 on your worksheet. (Pause slightly.) Draw a line under every number that is more than 50 but less than 60. (Pause 10 seconds.) Now, on your answer sheet, for every number that you drew a line under, darken space A. (Pause 5 seconds.)

Look at the figures in line 6. (Pause slightly.) Each figure is made up of two triangles with a number or a letter in each triangle. (Pause slightly.) Add the number in the upper triangle of the first figure to the number in the lower triangle of the middle figure, and write that number in the upper triangle of the last figure. (Pause 5 seconds.) Now, on your answer sheet, darken the space for the number-letter combination that is in the triangle you just wrote in. (Pause 5 seconds.)

Look at line 7 on your worksheet. The number in each box is the number of customers visiting a certain post office in 1 hour. (Pause slightly.) In the box for the post office having the fewest number of visitors write on the line the first two figures of that number. (Pause 5 seconds.) Now, on your answer sheet, darken the space for the number-letter combination that is in the box you just wrote in. (Pause 5 seconds.)

Look at line 8 on your worksheet. (Pause slightly.) On the line next to the left-hand letter write the answer to this question: How many feet are there in 1 yard? (Pause 2 seconds.) Now, on your answer sheet, find the number you just wrote and darken space D as in *dog* for that number. (Pause 5 seconds.)

Look at the circles in line 9 on your worksheet. (Pause slightly.) Some circles on the line are fully shaded, some circles are partly shaded, and some circles have no shading. (Pause slightly.) Count the number of circles that have no shading, add 4, and write that number at the end of the line. (Pause 5 seconds.) Now, on your answer sheet, find the number you just wrote and darken space A for that number. (Pause 5 seconds.)

Look at line 9 again. (Pause slightly.) Count the number of circles that are fully or partly shaded, and put that number in the last circle. (Pause 4 seconds.) Now, on your answer sheet, find the number you just wrote and darken space D as in *dog* for that number. (Pause 5 seconds.)

Now look at line 10 on your worksheet. (Pause slightly.) There are two boxes and two circles of different sizes with numbers in them. (Pause slightly.) If 5 is smaller than 8 and 4 is larger than 6, write A in the smaller box. (Pause slightly.) Otherwise, write B as in *baker* in the larger circle. (Pause 2 seconds.) Now, on your answer sheet, darken the space for the number-letter combination in the box or circle you just wrote in. (Pause 5 seconds.)

Look at line 11 on your worksheet. (Pause slightly.) In each circle there is a time when a mail truck is dispatched. In the circle for the latest time, write on the line the last two figures of the time. (Pause 5 seconds.) Now, on your answer sheet, darken the space for the number-letter combination that is in the circle you just wrote in. (Pause 5 seconds.)

Now turn to Worksheet 2. (Pause 5 seconds.) Look at line 12 on your worksheet. (Pause slightly.) If, in a minute, there are 60 seconds, write the letter A in the box with the largest number. (Pause slightly.) Otherwise, write the letter C in the box with the smallest number. (Pause 2 seconds.) Now, on your answer sheet, darken the space for the number-letter combination that is in the box you just wrote in. (Pause 5 seconds.)

Look at line 13 on your worksheet. (Pause slightly.) There are three boxes and three words on the line. (Pause slightly.) Write the second letter of the third word in the first box. (Pause 2 seconds.) Write the first letter of the second word in the third box. (Pause 2 seconds.) Write the third letter of the first word in the second box. (Pause 2 seconds.) Now, on your answer sheet, darken the spaces for the number-letter combinations that are in the three boxes you just wrote in. (Pause 10 seconds.)

Look at line 14 on your worksheet. (Pause slightly.) Draw a line under every "X" in the line. (Pause 5 seconds.) Count the number of lines that you have drawn, and write that number at the end of the line. (Pause 5 seconds.) If the number you just wrote is an even number, write an A next to it. (Pause slightly.) Otherwise, write a B next to the number. (Pause slightly.) Now, on your answer sheet, darken the space for the number-letter combination you just wrote at the end of the line. (Pause 5 seconds.)

Now, look at line 15 on your worksheet. (Pause slightly.) There are five circles, each with a letter inside it. (Pause slightly.) In the fourth circle write the answer to this question: Which of the following numbers is largest: 28, 47, 36, 42, 39? (Pause 5 seconds.) In the first circle write 86. (Pause 2 seconds.) In the middle circle do nothing. In the last circle, write the answer to this question: How many hours are there in a day? (Pause 2 seconds.) Now, on your answer sheet, darken the spaces for the number-letter combinations that are in the circles you just wrote in. (Pause 10 seconds.)

Look at the numbers in line 16 on your worksheet. (Pause slightly.) Draw a line under every number that is more than 25 but less than 40. (Pause 10 seconds.) Now, on your answer sheet, darken space C for every number under which you drew a line. (Pause 20 seconds.)

Look at line 17 on your worksheet. (Pause slightly.) The number in each circle is the number of parcels in a mail sack. The three boxes with letters in them are bins to collect these parcels. (Pause slightly.) In the middle bin, write the number of parcels in the sack holding the smallest number of parcels. (Pause 2 seconds.) Now, on your answer sheet, darken the space for the number-letter combination that is in the bin you just wrote in. (Pause 5 seconds.)

Look at line 17 again. In the third bin, write the number of parcels in the sack holding the largest number of parcels. (Pause 2 seconds.) Now, on your answer sheet, darken the space for the number-letter combination that is in the bin you just wrote in. (Pause 5 seconds.)

Look at line 18 on your worksheet. (Pause slightly.) Mail for Nyack and Hudson is to be put in Box 40. Mail for Albany and Groton is to be put in box 79. (Pause slightly.) Write A on the line in the box in which you would put mail for Hudson. (Pause 2 seconds.) Now, on your answer sheet, darken the space for the number-letter combination that is in the box you just wrote in. (Pause 5 seconds.)

Now look at the letters and boxes in line 19 on your worksheet. (Pause slightly.) Write the right-hand letter below the number in the third box. (Pause 2 seconds.) Subtract 2 from the number in the box you just wrote in, and change the number in that box to this number. (Pause 3 seconds.) Now, on your answer sheet, darken the space for the number-letter combination that is in the box you just wrote in. (Pause 5 seconds.)

END OF EXAMINATION.
If you finish before the time is up, go back and check the questions in this section of the test only.

Practice Test 4—Worksheet 1

Part D—Following Oral Directions

1. 64 ___   15 ___   49 ___

2. 43   61   57   29

3. C   E   D   B   B   A   E

4. ___ C   ___ B   ___ A   ___ D   ___ E

5. 49   50   66   57   61   53   48   39

6. 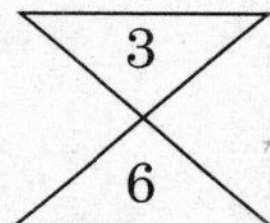

2 / 7
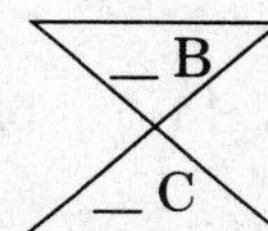

7. B ___ 151   E ___ 311   A ___ 298   C ___ 140   D ___ 532

8. ___ D   ___ B

9.  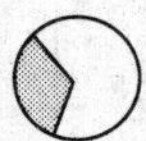 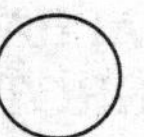 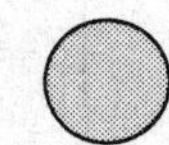   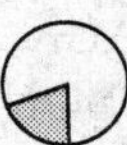 

10. 76 ___   69 ___   16 ___   84 ___

11. 12:51 ___ D   12:15 ___ E   12:41 ___ A   12:02 ___ C   12:34 ___ B

✂ Remove by cutting on dotted line.

Practice Test 4—Worksheet 2

Part D—Following Oral Directions

12. 43 ___ 19 ___ 36 ___ 68 ___

13. 75 ___ 62 ___ 27 ___ MICE ARM MEAT

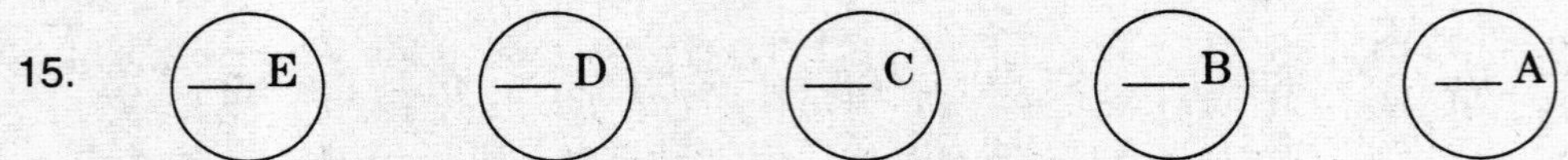

14. O X X X O O X O O O X O X O X X

15. ___ E ___ D ___ C ___ B ___ A

16. 25 15 39 14 32 55 40 28 35

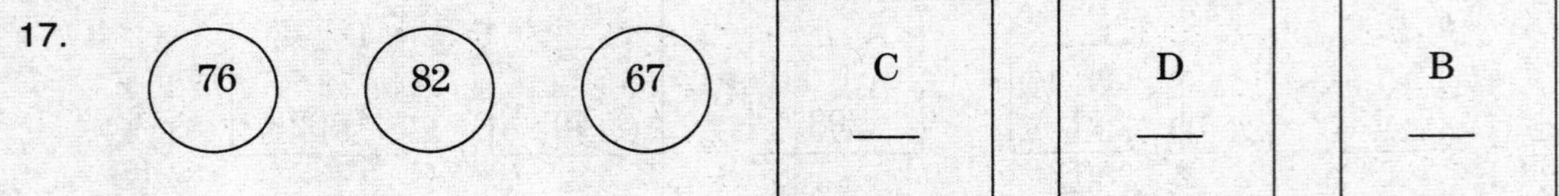

17. 76 82 67 C ___ D ___ B ___

18. 40 ___ NYACK HUDSON 79 ___ ALBANY GROTON

19. ___ E ___ C 37 ___ 76 ___ 83 ___

ANSWER KEY

Part A—Address Checking

1. **A**	11. **A**	21. **A**	31. **A**	41. **A**	51. **D**	61. **D**	71. **D**	81. **A**	91. **D**
2. **D**	12. **D**	22. **D**	32. **D**	42. **D**	52. **A**	62. **A**	72. **A**	82. **A**	92. **D**
3. **A**	13. **A**	23. **A**	33. **D**	43. **A**	53. **D**	63. **D**	73. **D**	83. **D**	93. **A**
4. **D**	14. **A**	24. **D**	34. **A**	44. **A**	54. **A**	64. **D**	74. **D**	84. **A**	94. **A**
5. **D**	15. **D**	25. **D**	35. **D**	45. **A**	55. **D**	65. **D**	75. **A**	85. **D**	95. **A**
6. **D**	16. **A**	26. **D**	36. **D**	46. **D**	56. **D**	66. **A**	76. **D**	86. **A**	
7. **A**	17. **A**	27. **A**	37. **D**	47. **D**	57. **D**	67. **A**	77. **A**	87. **D**	
8. **D**	18. **A**	28. **A**	38. **A**	48. **A**	58. **D**	68. **D**	78. **D**	88. **D**	
9. **D**	19. **D**	29. **D**	39. **A**	49. **D**	59. **A**	69. **D**	79. **D**	89. **A**	
10. **A**	20. **D**	30. **D**	40. **D**	50. **A**	60. **D**	70. **A**	80. **D**	90. **D**	

Part B—Memory for Addresses

List 1

1. **D**	10. **E**	19. **C**	28. **B**	37. **C**	46. **C**	55. **B**	64. **E**	73. **D**	82. **D**
2. **C**	11. **A**	20. **D**	29. **D**	38. **D**	47. **A**	56. **C**	65. **E**	74. **C**	83. **A**
3. **E**	12. **D**	21. **C**	30. **B**	39. **A**	48. **C**	57. **D**	66. **A**	75. **E**	84. **A**
4. **C**	13. **C**	22. **B**	31. **C**	40. **A**	49. **B**	58. **B**	67. **A**	76. **B**	85. **D**
5. **D**	14. **C**	23. **B**	32. **C**	41. **A**	50. **A**	59. **E**	68. **C**	77. **A**	86. **A**
6. **A**	15. **C**	24. **E**	33. **E**	42. **B**	51. **A**	60. **D**	69. **D**	78. **D**	87. **E**
7. **E**	16. **B**	25. **E**	34. **D**	43. **E**	52. **B**	61. **C**	70. **D**	79. **B**	88. **E**
8. **A**	17. **B**	26. **E**	35. **B**	44. **A**	53. **A**	62. **D**	71. **C**	80. **B**	
9. **D**	18. **A**	27. **A**	36. **A**	45. **D**	54. **E**	63. **B**	72. **E**	81. **B**	

List 2

1. **C**	10. **A**	19. **C**	28. **D**	37. **A**	46. **B**	55. **A**	64. **A**	73. **E**	82. **E**
2. **D**	11. **D**	20. **D**	29. **E**	38. **B**	47. **D**	56. **E**	65. **C**	74. **E**	83. **C**
3. **E**	12. **A**	21. **E**	30. **C**	39. **E**	48. **B**	57. **A**	66. **C**	75. **D**	84. **B**
4. **B**	13. **E**	22. **A**	31. **D**	40. **A**	49. **B**	58. **C**	67. **B**	76. **D**	85. **C**
5. **A**	14. **D**	23. **A**	32. **C**	41. **D**	50. **A**	59. **B**	68. **E**	77. **B**	86. **B**
6. **B**	15. **C**	24. **E**	33. **D**	42. **A**	51. **C**	60. **C**	69. **C**	78. **E**	87. **D**
7. **A**	16. **A**	25. **A**	34. **D**	43. **B**	52. **E**	61. **A**	70. **E**	79. **D**	88. **A**
8. **D**	17. **C**	26. **C**	35. **B**	44. **B**	53. **A**	62. **C**	71. **C**	80. **E**	
9. **A**	18. **B**	27. **B**	36. **D**	45. **C**	54. **E**	63. **D**	72. **E**	81. **D**	

List 3

1. **B**	10. **B**	19. **C**	28. **C**	37. **D**	46. **D**	55. **E**	64. **C**	73. **C**	82. **A**
2. **B**	11. **D**	20. **A**	29. **A**	38. **A**	47. **B**	56. **B**	65. **E**	74. **B**	83. **A**
3. **A**	12. **D**	21. **E**	30. **C**	39. **B**	48. **C**	57. **D**	66. **B**	75. **C**	84. **B**
4. **D**	13. **C**	22. **A**	31. **D**	40. **A**	49. **B**	58. **D**	67. **C**	76. **A**	85. **B**
5. **A**	14. **D**	23. **E**	32. **E**	41. **B**	50. **C**	59. **E**	68. **C**	77. **E**	86. **D**
6. **E**	15. **C**	24. **B**	33. **A**	42. **E**	51. **E**	60. **E**	69. **A**	78. **A**	87. **B**
7. **B**	16. **E**	25. **D**	34. **D**	43. **D**	52. **D**	61. **E**	70. **D**	79. **E**	88. **C**
8. **A**	17. **D**	26. **C**	35. **A**	44. **C**	53. **E**	62. **C**	71. **B**	80. **A**	
9. **D**	18. **B**	27. **B**	36. **A**	45. **E**	54. **D**	63. **E**	72. **A**	81. **E**	

Part C—Number Series

1. **B**	4. **E**	7. **A**	10. **C**	13. **C**	16. **E**	19. **D**	22. **E**
2. **D**	5. **E**	8. **A**	11. **E**	14. **A**	17. **D**	20. **D**	23. **D**
3. **D**	6. **C**	9. **C**	12. **B**	15. **C**	18. **B**	21. **E**	24. **C**

Part D—Following Oral Directions

2. **C**	7. **A**	12. **B**	24. **A**	32. **C**	43. **D**	51. **D**	61. **C**	68. **A**	81. **C**
3. **D**	8. **A**	14. **C**	27. **A**	39. **C**	47. **B**	53. **A**	62. **C**	69. **B**	82. **B**
6. **D**	10. **B**	19. **B**	28. **C**	40. **A**	49. **E**	57. **A**	67. **D**	75. **E**	86. **E**

ANSWER EXPLANATIONS FOR PART C—NUMBER SERIES

1. **B** The three numbers 40 50 60 keep repeating in the same sequence.
2. **D** Each of these two alternating series keeps decreasing by 3.
3. **D** The pattern is: – 4, repeat the number; – 4, repeat the number.
4. **E** This series follows the complex rule: + 5, – 2, – 1.
5. **E** The rule for this series is: – 1, repeat the number, – 17; and so on.
6. **C** There are two alternating series here. One decreases by 7 and repeats the number. The other decreases by 4 and appears after every second number of the first series.
7. **A** These two alternating series appear as triads. One increases by 3. The other, starting with 30, decreases by 5.
8. **A** Again, you have two alternating series but this time they appear in regular fashion, one number of each in turn. One ascends by 5; the other descends by 7.
9. **C** One of these two series follows the complex rule – 7, – 8; – 7, – 8; and so on. The other is a simple – 1 series. This pattern is very difficult to see unless you use a loop diagram (see below):

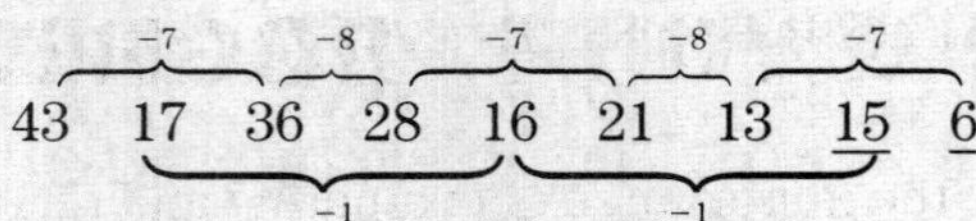

10. **C** Both series decrease by 2. One appears after every two numbers of the first.
11. **E** In effect, there are *three* alternating series here. The easiest way to visualize this most complex pattern is with a loop diagram:

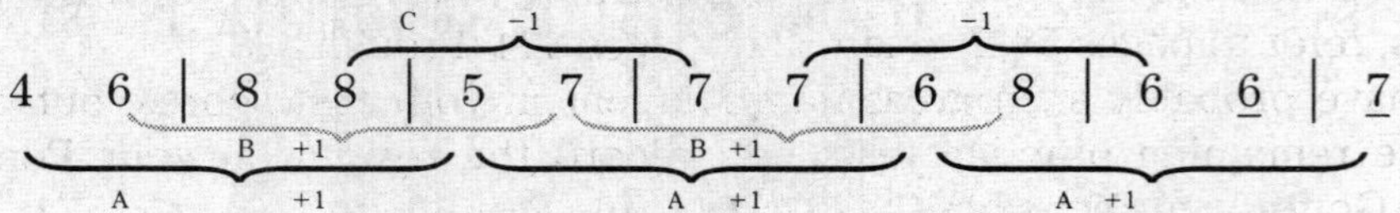

12. **B** The numbers in this series follow a + 1, + 2; + 1, + 2; and so on rule.
13. **C** The rule for this series is: + 2, + 3; + 2, + 3. The number 10 is inserted after every two numbers in the series.
14. **A** You may view this as a series that follows a + 6, – 2; + 6, – 2; rule or as two alternating series, each increasing by 4.
15. **C** Multiplication, subtraction, *and* addition are included in this rule: × 2, – 4, + 3; repeated.

16. **E** A key element in this pattern is *reversal.* A number reverses its digits to produce the next number, which is then reduced by 10. For example, 27 reversed is 72; 72 – 10 = 62, and so on.
17. **D** There is a + 7 series, which repeats each number. The arbitrary number 13 interrupts the series.
18. **B** The "subtractors" keep getting *smaller* as the series progresses. In addition, the numbers repeat. (See the diagram below.)

R –8 R –7 R –6 R –5

56 56 48 48 41 41 35 35 30

19. **D** There is a + 1 series here (16, 17, 18, 19, 20, and so on) that is interrupted after every *three* numbers by two members of a + 2 series (12 14 16 18, and so on).
20. **D** One of these two alternating series follows a – 2, – 1; rule. The other series increases by 1 and appears after every *two* numbers of the first. (If you tried to do this question without the aid of a loop diagram, you probably got the wrong answer. If so, do it over—this time, with a diagram.)
21. **E** You could see this as a + 1, + 1, – 1; series. You could also see the pattern by *chanting* the numbers in groups of three:

31 32 33 32 33 34 33 34 35

22. **E** One pair of these two alternating series *increases* by × 2; the other *decreases* by – 2.
23. **D** Both alternating series increase by 1. (One begins with 5; the other with 10.) One proceeds for two numbers before being interrupted by a member of the other series.
24. **C** The rule used to go from one number to the next involves *two* operations—multiplication by 2 and then subtraction by 1—in order to advance to the next number. For example, the first number in this series 2 × 2 = 4; 4 – 1 = 3. Similarly, to go from 3 to 5, you proceed as follows: 3 × 2 = 6; 6 – 1 = 5; and so on.

EVALUATING YOUR PROGRESS

Throughout this book, the importance of evaluating and recording your progress has been stressed, as you study and practice for the 460/470 Test Battery. At this point, if you have completed Practice Tests 1 through 3 and have made all the entries on your Personal Progress Record, you are quite familiar with the discussion on Computing Your Score, Guidelines, and the Personal Progress Record. If you wish to review the details of these subjects, refer to pages 58 through 62 or pages 324 through 328.

You have probably seen great improvement in your test scores, but don't stop now. Take the remaining practice tests and record the results on your Personal Progress Record. Go for a perfect score!

DIAGNOSTIC CHARTS

The following charts will help pinpoint your weaknesses by making it easy for you to determine what particular type of question in each part of the test is most difficult for you.

Part A—Address Checking

Type of Difference	"D" Questions	Number of "D" Questions Wrong		
		Trial 1	Trial 2	Trial 3
Numbers: transposed	9, 12, 15, 69, 85, 88			
changed	22, 49, 83			
omitted	58, 90			
Directions	19, 25, 29, 40, 74			
Abbreviations: streets, roads, avenues, etc.	6, 26, 42, 47, 51, 55, 68			
states	2, 24, 46, 56, 65			
Spelling: single letters	5, 8, 20, 30, 32, 33, 36, 53, 57, 60, 61, 64, 71, 78, 79, 87, 92			
groups of letters	4, 35, 37, 63, 73, 76, 80, 91			
Total Number of All Types	53			
	Use the columns on the right to enter the question numbers of "A" items you marked "D."			

This chart will help you to pinpoint the kinds of errors you made on Practice Test 4. Use it as directed below after you have taken and marked the test.

The first column on the left, "Type of Difference," contains the categories whereby addresses may differ (see page 63). On the same line across, the second column gives the numbers of the questions that fall within each category. In the third column, you are to enter the numbers of any "A" questions you answered as "D." Do not include questions that you did not do. Checking the addresses you got wrong may reveal a problem on which you will want to work.

After you have made all the entries, you will be able to see the areas in which you need to improve. Then turn to the appropriate parts of Chapter 3: Address Checking—How to Improve Your Score, read them, and practice the drills that can help. For example, if you find you have been making too many errors picking out number differences, read page 88 and do Drills 18 through 21. If you have a problem with single letters because of reversals like *b* and *d*, or if you have been overlooking the differences between *a*, *e*, and *o*, read page 85. Examine the table and work on Drills 10 and 11 if the problem persists.

Remember that this chart is designed for diagnostic purposes and guidance on further practice. It has been drawn so that you can enter the results each time you retake a practice test. In this way you will be able to see how you are progressing. It is not necessary to record your scores here. That is best done by using the Personal Progress Record Card.

Part B—Memory for Addresses

Kind of Address		Number of Questions	Number Wrong		
			Trial 1	Trial 2	Trial 3
Direct:					
	List 1	42			
	List 2	41			
	List 3	40			
Numbered:					
	List 1	46			
	List 2	47			
	List 3	48			

The purpose of this chart is to help you evaluate your performance on the two kinds of memory questions that appear in these memory tests—the questions on the direct (name) addresses and the questions on the numbered addresses. Use the chart as directed below after you have taken and marked the entire test.

The first column on the left, "Kind of Address," is divided by category into "Direct Address" versus "Numbered Address." The second column gives the number of questions in each category on List 1, List 2, and List 3. Use the third column to enter the total number of questions in each category that you answered incorrectly. There is room for you to make additional entries if you take the practice test more than once.

At a glance, you will be able to see which area you need to concentrate on and how well you are progressing as you take repeat trials. Use Chapter 4 and the drills in it to improve your memory for the direct addresses. Use Chapter 5 for the numbered addresses.

Remember to use the Personal Progress Record Card (Memory for Addresses) on page 430 to keep track of your actual scores as you keep studying and practicing.

Part C—Number Series and Part D—Following Oral Directions

Because of the nature of the questions in these tests, Diagnostic Charts are not provided for them. If you find that you made many errors on these tests, study the techniques suggested in Chapters 6 and 7.

Answer Sheet—Practice Test 5

Part A—Address Checking

1 Ⓐ Ⓓ
2 Ⓐ Ⓓ
3 Ⓐ Ⓓ
4 Ⓐ Ⓓ
5 Ⓐ Ⓓ
6 Ⓐ Ⓓ
7 Ⓐ Ⓓ
8 Ⓐ Ⓓ
9 Ⓐ Ⓓ
10 Ⓐ Ⓓ
11 Ⓐ Ⓓ
12 Ⓐ Ⓓ
13 Ⓐ Ⓓ
14 Ⓐ Ⓓ
15 Ⓐ Ⓓ
16 Ⓐ Ⓓ
17 Ⓐ Ⓓ
18 Ⓐ Ⓓ
19 Ⓐ Ⓓ
20 Ⓐ Ⓓ
21 Ⓐ Ⓓ
22 Ⓐ Ⓓ
23 Ⓐ Ⓓ
24 Ⓐ Ⓓ
25 Ⓐ Ⓓ
26 Ⓐ Ⓓ
27 Ⓐ Ⓓ
28 Ⓐ Ⓓ
29 Ⓐ Ⓓ
30 Ⓐ Ⓓ
31 Ⓐ Ⓓ
32 Ⓐ Ⓓ
33 Ⓐ Ⓓ
34 Ⓐ Ⓓ
35 Ⓐ Ⓓ
36 Ⓐ Ⓓ
37 Ⓐ Ⓓ
38 Ⓐ Ⓓ
39 Ⓐ Ⓓ
40 Ⓐ Ⓓ
41 Ⓐ Ⓓ
42 Ⓐ Ⓓ
43 Ⓐ Ⓓ
44 Ⓐ Ⓓ
45 Ⓐ Ⓓ
46 Ⓐ Ⓓ
47 Ⓐ Ⓓ
48 Ⓐ Ⓓ
49 Ⓐ Ⓓ
50 Ⓐ Ⓓ
51 Ⓐ Ⓓ
52 Ⓐ Ⓓ
53 Ⓐ Ⓓ
54 Ⓐ Ⓓ
55 Ⓐ Ⓓ
56 Ⓐ Ⓓ
57 Ⓐ Ⓓ
58 Ⓐ Ⓓ
59 Ⓐ Ⓓ
60 Ⓐ Ⓓ
61 Ⓐ Ⓓ
62 Ⓐ Ⓓ
63 Ⓐ Ⓓ
64 Ⓐ Ⓓ
65 Ⓐ Ⓓ
66 Ⓐ Ⓓ
67 Ⓐ Ⓓ
68 Ⓐ Ⓓ
69 Ⓐ Ⓓ
70 Ⓐ Ⓓ
71 Ⓐ Ⓓ
72 Ⓐ Ⓓ
73 Ⓐ Ⓓ
74 Ⓐ Ⓓ
75 Ⓐ Ⓓ
76 Ⓐ Ⓓ
77 Ⓐ Ⓓ
78 Ⓐ Ⓓ
79 Ⓐ Ⓓ
80 Ⓐ Ⓓ
81 Ⓐ Ⓓ
82 Ⓐ Ⓓ
83 Ⓐ Ⓓ
84 Ⓐ Ⓓ
85 Ⓐ Ⓓ
86 Ⓐ Ⓓ
87 Ⓐ Ⓓ
88 Ⓐ Ⓓ
89 Ⓐ Ⓓ
90 Ⓐ Ⓓ
91 Ⓐ Ⓓ
92 Ⓐ Ⓓ
93 Ⓐ Ⓓ
94 Ⓐ Ⓓ
95 Ⓐ Ⓓ

✂ Remove by cutting on dotted line.

Part B—Memory for Addresses—List 1

1 ⒶⒷⒸⒹⒺ
2 ⒶⒷⒸⒹⒺ
3 ⒶⒷⒸⒹⒺ
4 ⒶⒷⒸⒹⒺ
5 ⒶⒷⒸⒹⒺ
6 ⒶⒷⒸⒹⒺ
7 ⒶⒷⒸⒹⒺ
8 ⒶⒷⒸⒹⒺ
9 ⒶⒷⒸⒹⒺ
10 ⒶⒷⒸⒹⒺ
11 ⒶⒷⒸⒹⒺ
12 ⒶⒷⒸⒹⒺ
13 ⒶⒷⒸⒹⒺ
14 ⒶⒷⒸⒹⒺ
15 ⒶⒷⒸⒹⒺ
16 ⒶⒷⒸⒹⒺ
17 ⒶⒷⒸⒹⒺ
18 ⒶⒷⒸⒹⒺ
19 ⒶⒷⒸⒹⒺ
20 ⒶⒷⒸⒹⒺ
21 ⒶⒷⒸⒹⒺ
22 ⒶⒷⒸⒹⒺ
23 ⒶⒷⒸⒹⒺ
24 ⒶⒷⒸⒹⒺ
25 ⒶⒷⒸⒹⒺ
26 ⒶⒷⒸⒹⒺ
27 ⒶⒷⒸⒹⒺ
28 ⒶⒷⒸⒹⒺ
29 ⒶⒷⒸⒹⒺ
30 ⒶⒷⒸⒹⒺ
31 ⒶⒷⒸⒹⒺ
32 ⒶⒷⒸⒹⒺ
33 ⒶⒷⒸⒹⒺ
34 ⒶⒷⒸⒹⒺ
35 ⒶⒷⒸⒹⒺ
36 ⒶⒷⒸⒹⒺ
37 ⒶⒷⒸⒹⒺ
38 ⒶⒷⒸⒹⒺ
39 ⒶⒷⒸⒹⒺ
40 ⒶⒷⒸⒹⒺ
41 ⒶⒷⒸⒹⒺ
42 ⒶⒷⒸⒹⒺ
43 ⒶⒷⒸⒹⒺ
44 ⒶⒷⒸⒹⒺ
45 ⒶⒷⒸⒹⒺ
46 ⒶⒷⒸⒹⒺ
47 ⒶⒷⒸⒹⒺ
48 ⒶⒷⒸⒹⒺ
49 ⒶⒷⒸⒹⒺ
50 ⒶⒷⒸⒹⒺ
51 ⒶⒷⒸⒹⒺ
52 ⒶⒷⒸⒹⒺ
53 ⒶⒷⒸⒹⒺ
54 ⒶⒷⒸⒹⒺ
55 ⒶⒷⒸⒹⒺ
56 ⒶⒷⒸⒹⒺ
57 ⒶⒷⒸⒹⒺ
58 ⒶⒷⒸⒹⒺ
59 ⒶⒷⒸⒹⒺ
60 ⒶⒷⒸⒹⒺ
61 ⒶⒷⒸⒹⒺ
62 ⒶⒷⒸⒹⒺ
63 ⒶⒷⒸⒹⒺ
64 ⒶⒷⒸⒹⒺ
65 ⒶⒷⒸⒹⒺ
66 ⒶⒷⒸⒹⒺ
67 ⒶⒷⒸⒹⒺ
68 ⒶⒷⒸⒹⒺ
69 ⒶⒷⒸⒹⒺ
70 ⒶⒷⒸⒹⒺ
71 ⒶⒷⒸⒹⒺ
72 ⒶⒷⒸⒹⒺ
73 ⒶⒷⒸⒹⒺ
74 ⒶⒷⒸⒹⒺ
75 ⒶⒷⒸⒹⒺ
76 ⒶⒷⒸⒹⒺ
77 ⒶⒷⒸⒹⒺ
78 ⒶⒷⒸⒹⒺ
79 ⒶⒷⒸⒹⒺ
80 ⒶⒷⒸⒹⒺ
81 ⒶⒷⒸⒹⒺ
82 ⒶⒷⒸⒹⒺ
83 ⒶⒷⒸⒹⒺ
84 ⒶⒷⒸⒹⒺ
85 ⒶⒷⒸⒹⒺ
86 ⒶⒷⒸⒹⒺ
87 ⒶⒷⒸⒹⒺ
88 ⒶⒷⒸⒹⒺ

Part B—Memory for Addresses—List 2

1 ⒶⒷⒸⒹⒺ
2 ⒶⒷⒸⒹⒺ
3 ⒶⒷⒸⒹⒺ
4 ⒶⒷⒸⒹⒺ
5 ⒶⒷⒸⒹⒺ
6 ⒶⒷⒸⒹⒺ
7 ⒶⒷⒸⒹⒺ
8 ⒶⒷⒸⒹⒺ
9 ⒶⒷⒸⒹⒺ
10 ⒶⒷⒸⒹⒺ
11 ⒶⒷⒸⒹⒺ
12 ⒶⒷⒸⒹⒺ
13 ⒶⒷⒸⒹⒺ
14 ⒶⒷⒸⒹⒺ
15 ⒶⒷⒸⒹⒺ
16 ⒶⒷⒸⒹⒺ
17 ⒶⒷⒸⒹⒺ
18 ⒶⒷⒸⒹⒺ
19 ⒶⒷⒸⒹⒺ
20 ⒶⒷⒸⒹⒺ
21 ⒶⒷⒸⒹⒺ
22 ⒶⒷⒸⒹⒺ
23 ⒶⒷⒸⒹⒺ
24 ⒶⒷⒸⒹⒺ
25 ⒶⒷⒸⒹⒺ
26 ⒶⒷⒸⒹⒺ
27 ⒶⒷⒸⒹⒺ
28 ⒶⒷⒸⒹⒺ
29 ⒶⒷⒸⒹⒺ
30 ⒶⒷⒸⒹⒺ
31 ⒶⒷⒸⒹⒺ
32 ⒶⒷⒸⒹⒺ
33 ⒶⒷⒸⒹⒺ
34 ⒶⒷⒸⒹⒺ
35 ⒶⒷⒸⒹⒺ
36 ⒶⒷⒸⒹⒺ
37 ⒶⒷⒸⒹⒺ
38 ⒶⒷⒸⒹⒺ
39 ⒶⒷⒸⒹⒺ
40 ⒶⒷⒸⒹⒺ
41 ⒶⒷⒸⒹⒺ
42 ⒶⒷⒸⒹⒺ
43 ⒶⒷⒸⒹⒺ
44 ⒶⒷⒸⒹⒺ
45 ⒶⒷⒸⒹⒺ
46 ⒶⒷⒸⒹⒺ
47 ⒶⒷⒸⒹⒺ
48 ⒶⒷⒸⒹⒺ
49 ⒶⒷⒸⒹⒺ
50 ⒶⒷⒸⒹⒺ
51 ⒶⒷⒸⒹⒺ
52 ⒶⒷⒸⒹⒺ
53 ⒶⒷⒸⒹⒺ
54 ⒶⒷⒸⒹⒺ
55 ⒶⒷⒸⒹⒺ
56 ⒶⒷⒸⒹⒺ
57 ⒶⒷⒸⒹⒺ
58 ⒶⒷⒸⒹⒺ
59 ⒶⒷⒸⒹⒺ
60 ⒶⒷⒸⒹⒺ
61 ⒶⒷⒸⒹⒺ
62 ⒶⒷⒸⒹⒺ
63 ⒶⒷⒸⒹⒺ
64 ⒶⒷⒸⒹⒺ
65 ⒶⒷⒸⒹⒺ
66 ⒶⒷⒸⒹⒺ
67 ⒶⒷⒸⒹⒺ
68 ⒶⒷⒸⒹⒺ
69 ⒶⒷⒸⒹⒺ
70 ⒶⒷⒸⒹⒺ
71 ⒶⒷⒸⒹⒺ
72 ⒶⒷⒸⒹⒺ
73 ⒶⒷⒸⒹⒺ
74 ⒶⒷⒸⒹⒺ
75 ⒶⒷⒸⒹⒺ
76 ⒶⒷⒸⒹⒺ
77 ⒶⒷⒸⒹⒺ
78 ⒶⒷⒸⒹⒺ
79 ⒶⒷⒸⒹⒺ
80 ⒶⒷⒸⒹⒺ
81 ⒶⒷⒸⒹⒺ
82 ⒶⒷⒸⒹⒺ
83 ⒶⒷⒸⒹⒺ
84 ⒶⒷⒸⒹⒺ
85 ⒶⒷⒸⒹⒺ
86 ⒶⒷⒸⒹⒺ
87 ⒶⒷⒸⒹⒺ
88 ⒶⒷⒸⒹⒺ

Remove by cutting on dotted line.

Part B—Memory for Addresses—List 3

1 ⒶⒷⒸⒹⒺ
2 ⒶⒷⒸⒹⒺ
3 ⒶⒷⒸⒹⒺ
4 ⒶⒷⒸⒹⒺ
5 ⒶⒷⒸⒹⒺ
6 ⒶⒷⒸⒹⒺ
7 ⒶⒷⒸⒹⒺ
8 ⒶⒷⒸⒹⒺ
9 ⒶⒷⒸⒹⒺ
10 ⒶⒷⒸⒹⒺ
11 ⒶⒷⒸⒹⒺ
12 ⒶⒷⒸⒹⒺ
13 ⒶⒷⒸⒹⒺ
14 ⒶⒷⒸⒹⒺ
15 ⒶⒷⒸⒹⒺ
16 ⒶⒷⒸⒹⒺ
17 ⒶⒷⒸⒹⒺ
18 ⒶⒷⒸⒹⒺ
19 ⒶⒷⒸⒹⒺ
20 ⒶⒷⒸⒹⒺ
21 ⒶⒷⒸⒹⒺ
22 ⒶⒷⒸⒹⒺ
23 ⒶⒷⒸⒹⒺ
24 ⒶⒷⒸⒹⒺ
25 ⒶⒷⒸⒹⒺ
26 ⒶⒷⒸⒹⒺ
27 ⒶⒷⒸⒹⒺ
28 ⒶⒷⒸⒹⒺ
29 ⒶⒷⒸⒹⒺ
30 ⒶⒷⒸⒹⒺ
31 ⒶⒷⒸⒹⒺ
32 ⒶⒷⒸⒹⒺ
33 ⒶⒷⒸⒹⒺ
34 ⒶⒷⒸⒹⒺ
35 ⒶⒷⒸⒹⒺ
36 ⒶⒷⒸⒹⒺ
37 ⒶⒷⒸⒹⒺ
38 ⒶⒷⒸⒹⒺ
39 ⒶⒷⒸⒹⒺ
40 ⒶⒷⒸⒹⒺ
41 ⒶⒷⒸⒹⒺ
42 ⒶⒷⒸⒹⒺ
43 ⒶⒷⒸⒹⒺ
44 ⒶⒷⒸⒹⒺ
45 ⒶⒷⒸⒹⒺ
46 ⒶⒷⒸⒹⒺ
47 ⒶⒷⒸⒹⒺ
48 ⒶⒷⒸⒹⒺ
49 ⒶⒷⒸⒹⒺ
50 ⒶⒷⒸⒹⒺ
51 ⒶⒷⒸⒹⒺ
52 ⒶⒷⒸⒹⒺ
53 ⒶⒷⒸⒹⒺ
54 ⒶⒷⒸⒹⒺ
55 ⒶⒷⒸⒹⒺ
56 ⒶⒷⒸⒹⒺ
57 ⒶⒷⒸⒹⒺ
58 ⒶⒷⒸⒹⒺ
59 ⒶⒷⒸⒹⒺ
60 ⒶⒷⒸⒹⒺ
61 ⒶⒷⒸⒹⒺ
62 ⒶⒷⒸⒹⒺ
63 ⒶⒷⒸⒹⒺ
64 ⒶⒷⒸⒹⒺ
65 ⒶⒷⒸⒹⒺ
66 ⒶⒷⒸⒹⒺ
67 ⒶⒷⒸⒹⒺ
68 ⒶⒷⒸⒹⒺ
69 ⒶⒷⒸⒹⒺ
70 ⒶⒷⒸⒹⒺ
71 ⒶⒷⒸⒹⒺ
72 ⒶⒷⒸⒹⒺ
73 ⒶⒷⒸⒹⒺ
74 ⒶⒷⒸⒹⒺ
75 ⒶⒷⒸⒹⒺ
76 ⒶⒷⒸⒹⒺ
77 ⒶⒷⒸⒹⒺ
78 ⒶⒷⒸⒹⒺ
79 ⒶⒷⒸⒹⒺ
80 ⒶⒷⒸⒹⒺ
81 ⒶⒷⒸⒹⒺ
82 ⒶⒷⒸⒹⒺ
83 ⒶⒷⒸⒹⒺ
84 ⒶⒷⒸⒹⒺ
85 ⒶⒷⒸⒹⒺ
86 ⒶⒷⒸⒹⒺ
87 ⒶⒷⒸⒹⒺ
88 ⒶⒷⒸⒹⒺ

Part C—Number Series

1 ⒶⒷⒸⒹⒺ
2 ⒶⒷⒸⒹⒺ
3 ⒶⒷⒸⒹⒺ
4 ⒶⒷⒸⒹⒺ
5 ⒶⒷⒸⒹⒺ
6 ⒶⒷⒸⒹⒺ
7 ⒶⒷⒸⒹⒺ
8 ⒶⒷⒸⒹⒺ
9 ⒶⒷⒸⒹⒺ
10 ⒶⒷⒸⒹⒺ
11 ⒶⒷⒸⒹⒺ
12 ⒶⒷⒸⒹⒺ
13 ⒶⒷⒸⒹⒺ
14 ⒶⒷⒸⒹⒺ
15 ⒶⒷⒸⒹⒺ
16 ⒶⒷⒸⒹⒺ
17 ⒶⒷⒸⒹⒺ
18 ⒶⒷⒸⒹⒺ
19 ⒶⒷⒸⒹⒺ
20 ⒶⒷⒸⒹⒺ
21 ⒶⒷⒸⒹⒺ
22 ⒶⒷⒸⒹⒺ
23 ⒶⒷⒸⒹⒺ
24 ⒶⒷⒸⒹⒺ

Part D—Following Oral Directions

1 ⒶⒷⒸⒹⒺ
2 ⒶⒷⒸⒹⒺ
3 ⒶⒷⒸⒹⒺ
4 ⒶⒷⒸⒹⒺ
5 ⒶⒷⒸⒹⒺ
6 ⒶⒷⒸⒹⒺ
7 ⒶⒷⒸⒹⒺ
8 ⒶⒷⒸⒹⒺ
9 ⒶⒷⒸⒹⒺ
10 ⒶⒷⒸⒹⒺ
11 ⒶⒷⒸⒹⒺ
12 ⒶⒷⒸⒹⒺ
13 ⒶⒷⒸⒹⒺ
14 ⒶⒷⒸⒹⒺ
15 ⒶⒷⒸⒹⒺ
16 ⒶⒷⒸⒹⒺ
17 ⒶⒷⒸⒹⒺ
18 ⒶⒷⒸⒹⒺ
19 ⒶⒷⒸⒹⒺ
20 ⒶⒷⒸⒹⒺ
21 ⒶⒷⒸⒹⒺ
22 ⒶⒷⒸⒹⒺ
23 ⒶⒷⒸⒹⒺ
24 ⒶⒷⒸⒹⒺ
25 ⒶⒷⒸⒹⒺ
26 ⒶⒷⒸⒹⒺ
27 ⒶⒷⒸⒹⒺ
28 ⒶⒷⒸⒹⒺ
29 ⒶⒷⒸⒹⒺ
30 ⒶⒷⒸⒹⒺ
31 ⒶⒷⒸⒹⒺ
32 ⒶⒷⒸⒹⒺ
33 ⒶⒷⒸⒹⒺ
34 ⒶⒷⒸⒹⒺ
35 ⒶⒷⒸⒹⒺ
36 ⒶⒷⒸⒹⒺ
37 ⒶⒷⒸⒹⒺ
38 ⒶⒷⒸⒹⒺ
39 ⒶⒷⒸⒹⒺ
40 ⒶⒷⒸⒹⒺ
41 ⒶⒷⒸⒹⒺ
42 ⒶⒷⒸⒹⒺ
43 ⒶⒷⒸⒹⒺ
44 ⒶⒷⒸⒹⒺ
45 ⒶⒷⒸⒹⒺ
46 ⒶⒷⒸⒹⒺ
47 ⒶⒷⒸⒹⒺ
48 ⒶⒷⒸⒹⒺ
49 ⒶⒷⒸⒹⒺ
50 ⒶⒷⒸⒹⒺ
51 ⒶⒷⒸⒹⒺ
52 ⒶⒷⒸⒹⒺ
53 ⒶⒷⒸⒹⒺ
54 ⒶⒷⒸⒹⒺ
55 ⒶⒷⒸⒹⒺ
56 ⒶⒷⒸⒹⒺ
57 ⒶⒷⒸⒹⒺ
58 ⒶⒷⒸⒹⒺ
59 ⒶⒷⒸⒹⒺ
60 ⒶⒷⒸⒹⒺ
61 ⒶⒷⒸⒹⒺ
62 ⒶⒷⒸⒹⒺ
63 ⒶⒷⒸⒹⒺ
64 ⒶⒷⒸⒹⒺ
65 ⒶⒷⒸⒹⒺ
66 ⒶⒷⒸⒹⒺ
67 ⒶⒷⒸⒹⒺ
68 ⒶⒷⒸⒹⒺ
69 ⒶⒷⒸⒹⒺ
70 ⒶⒷⒸⒹⒺ
71 ⒶⒷⒸⒹⒺ
72 ⒶⒷⒸⒹⒺ
73 ⒶⒷⒸⒹⒺ
74 ⒶⒷⒸⒹⒺ
75 ⒶⒷⒸⒹⒺ
76 ⒶⒷⒸⒹⒺ
77 ⒶⒷⒸⒹⒺ
78 ⒶⒷⒸⒹⒺ
79 ⒶⒷⒸⒹⒺ
80 ⒶⒷⒸⒹⒺ
81 ⒶⒷⒸⒹⒺ
82 ⒶⒷⒸⒹⒺ
83 ⒶⒷⒸⒹⒺ
84 ⒶⒷⒸⒹⒺ
85 ⒶⒷⒸⒹⒺ
86 ⒶⒷⒸⒹⒺ
87 ⒶⒷⒸⒹⒺ
88 ⒶⒷⒸⒹⒺ

Chapter 13

Practice Test 5

PART A — ADDRESS CHECKING

Work — 6 minutes

In this part of the test, you are to decide whether two addresses are alike or different. If the two addresses are *exactly alike in every way,* darken space Ⓐ. If they are *different in any way,* darken space Ⓓ for the question.

Mark your answers on the Answer Sheet on page 361. Tear it out, put today's date on it, and place it next to the questions.

Allow yourself *exactly 6 minutes* to do as many of the 95 questions as you can. If you finish before the time is up, check your answers.

1.	8728 South Chelmsford Ave	8729 South Chelmsford Ave
2.	Wolcott IN 47995	Walcott IN 47995
3.	454 E Delgado Rd	454 E Delgado Rd
4.	4812 S Holmesburg Ave	4812 S Holmesbury Ave
5.	Colwich KS 67030	Colwich KS 67030
6.	4700 Mahopac Ln	4700 Mahopac Ln
7.	6304 Avalun Rd	6304 Avalun Rd
8.	5606 Quail Hollow Rd	5660 Quail Hollow Rd
9.	10472 Rolens Ave W	10472 Rolens Ave W
10.	8341 Quail Roost Rd N	8341 Quail Roost Rd N
11.	4811 E Yates St	4811 E Gates St
12.	5178 Indian Queen Ln	5178 Indian Queen Ln
13.	6118 Brushmore Ave NW	6118 Brushmore Ave NW
14.	3689 S Oxlow Ct	3689 S Oslow Ct
15.	2486 Zanfagna St NE	2486 Zanfagna St NE
16.	2001 Gorsten St	2001 Gorsten St
17.	362 Ortega Ct	362 Ortega Ct
18.	2037 Williamette Blvd	2037 Williamette Blvd
19.	Roselle IL 60172	Rosette IL 60172
20.	4401 Pickford Blvd N	4401 Pickford Ave N
21.	2140 S Magdalena Dr	1240 S Magdalena Dr
22.	4172 Ponagansett St	4172 Ponagansett St
23.	1012 Northwood Rd	1012 Northwalk Rd
24.	5116 Newell St	5116 Newall St

25. 2771 Onondago Trl	2771 Onondaga Trl
26. Independence MO	Independence MO
27. 1501 SW 2nd Ave	1501 SW 2nd Ave
28. 178 El Camino Way	178 El Camino Way
29. 4401 11th Ave E	4401 11th Ave W
30. Beaconsfield NY	Bakersfield NY
31. 4056 Yoncalla Ct	4056 Yoncalla Ct
32. 8630 Tim Dr	8630 Tin Dr
33. 290 Davisville River Rd	209 Davisville River Rd
34. 72 Peranna Path	72 Peranna Path
35. 3740 E Ellsworth Ave	3741 E Ellsworth Ave
36. Norfolk VA 23505	Norwalk VA 23505
37. 6198 Juniata Cir	6198 Juniata Cir
38. 3008 N Graham St	3008 N Graham Ct
39. 9134 McTaggard Dr	9134 McTaggard Dr
40. 3431 W 65th Cir	3431 W 64th Cir
41. 7260 Aldawood Hill Dr	7260 Aldawood Mill Dr
42. 5836 S Inverness Rd	5836 S Inverness Rd
43. 6405 Worcester Blvd N	6405 Worcester Blvd N
44. Medomak ME	Medomak MD
45. 923 Violet Memorial Pl	923 Violet Memorial Pl
46. 1045 East View Dr	1045 East View Dr
47. Rochester NY 14625	Rochester NY 14625
48. 913 Manayunk Hill St	913 Manayunk Hill Ct
49. 1908 West Van Cortland Ave	1908 East Van Cortland Ave
50. Tamassee SC 29686	Tamassee SC 29686
51. 1172 Jacobus St SE	1172 Jacobine St SE
52. 1137 N Woodstock Ave	1137 N Woodstock Ave
53. 14081 32 St NE	14081 32 St NE
54. 6962 Rolling Stone Rd	6632 Rolling Stone Rd
55. 1992 Verde Vista Ter NW	1992 Verde Vista Ter NW
56. Davanport IA 52807	Davanport LA 52807
57. 431 Coddington Ave	431 Coddingtown Ave
58. Kingshill VI	Kingshill VA
59. Bowlus MN	Bowlus MN
60. 1415 Ave X S	1415 Ave Y S

61.	2445 Nemesio Canales Rd	2444 Nemesio Canales Rd
62.	8232 La Burnum Dr	8232 La Barnum Dr
63.	3400 Aspen St	3400 Aspen St
64.	2976 Barrington Square Ext	2976 Barrington Square Ext
65.	8456 W Lancaster Pike	845 W Lancaster Pike
66.	7149 E Berghammer Ln	7149 E Bernhander Ln
67.	617 Owen Blvd	671 Owen Blvd
68.	7405 Kennebec Ln	7405 Kennebec Ln
69.	Salkum WA	Saltum WA
70.	4713 Hurlburt Ave	4713 Hurlburt Ave
71.	2638 Kingsbridge Ter W	2683 Kingsbridge Ter W
72.	1046 N Wynmill Rd	1046 N Windmill Rd
73.	7048 Kingsessing St	7048 Kingsessing St
74.	3810 University Commercial Place	3810 University Commercial Place
75.	398 N Laurel Ave	398 N Laurel St
76.	9081 Dogwood Ter	9181 Dogwood Ter
77.	1808 Armand Pl	1808 Armond Pl
78.	164 E Firestone Blvd	164 E Firestone Blvd
79.	619 Fairmount Pl S	619 Fairmount Pl N
80.	718 Schofield View Cir	718 Schofield View Ter
81.	5054 Digney Ln	5504 Digney Ln
82.	91 Whispering Oak Canyon Trl	91 Whispering Oak Canyon Trl
83.	5968 Ziggarut Cir	5968 Ziggarut Cir
84.	2066 Timrod St NE	2066 Timrod St SE
85.	9789 E Rhone Ct	9789 E Rhine Ct
86.	984 Derry Dell Ct	984 Derry Dell Ct
87.	Springfield MA 01104	Springfield MA 01104
88.	8560 Tanglewood St	8506 Tanglewood St
89.	6809 Jenkintown Rd	6809 Jenkintown Rd
90.	Frametown WV 26623	Frametown WV 26623
91.	Warwick RI	Warwick RI
92.	2803 Flowering Tree Cir	2803 Flowering Tree Cir
93.	2709 Bailey Ave	2709 Baisley Ave
94.	8452 Caroline Ct	8452 Caroline St
95.	5054 W Quapah Pl	5054 W Quapah Pl

STOP.

If you finish before the time is up, go back and check the questions in this section of the test only.

Part B — MEMORY FOR ADDRESSES

In this part of the test, you will have five boxes labeled A, B, C, D, and E. Each box contains five addresses. Three of the five are groups of street addresses, such as 5400–5699 Clocks, 3800–3999 Harmony, and 2600–3599 Parker; and two are names of places. The addresses are different in each box.

There will be several opportunities to study the addresses and the boxes they are in. You will also be given three tests of 88 questions each, and the task of deciding where each address belongs. In some cases, you will have the list *and* the boxes in front of you at the same time; in others you will not. List 1 and List 2 are for warm-up practice. List 3 is the real one that will be scored.

Make sure you understand the format by examining the pretest samples below.

Pretest Samples

A	B	C	D	E
4000–5099 Clocks	2600–3799 Clocks	5400–5699 Clocks	3800–3999 Clocks	5100–5399 Clocks
Hunt	Mason	Placid	Oakland	Carmel
5100–5399 Harmony	3800–3999 Harmony	2600–3799 Harmony	5400–6599 Harmony	4000–5099 Harmony
Victor	Wyatt	Dreier	Arkansas	McDonald
3600–3799 Parker	5400–6299 Parker	4000–5399 Parker	2600–3599 Parker	3800–3999 Parker

Questions 1 through 7 show the way the questions look. You have to decide in which lettered box (A, B, C, D, or E) the address belongs and then mark your answer by darkening the appropriate space in the answer grid.

1. Carmel — 1 Ⓐ Ⓑ Ⓒ Ⓓ Ⓔ
2. 4000–5399 Parker — 2 Ⓐ Ⓑ Ⓒ Ⓓ Ⓔ
3. 5100–5399 Clocks — 3 Ⓐ Ⓑ Ⓒ Ⓓ Ⓔ
4. Wyatt — 4 Ⓐ Ⓑ Ⓒ Ⓓ Ⓔ
5. Hunt — 5 Ⓐ Ⓑ Ⓒ Ⓓ Ⓔ
6. 5100–5399 Harmony — 6 Ⓐ Ⓑ Ⓒ Ⓓ Ⓔ
7. Placid — 7 Ⓐ Ⓑ Ⓒ Ⓓ Ⓔ

Answers

1. **E** 2. **C** 3. **E** 4. **B** 5. **A** 6. **A** 7. **C**

Now that you know what to do, you may begin Part B of Practice Test 5. To get the most out of it and the final practice test in this book, follow the directions and timing *exactly.* Follow each phase of Part B of the test, page by page, until you've completed List 3. It is modeled on the way the Postal Service actually conducts its tests.

Turn to the next page to begin.

Study — 3 minutes

You will be given 3 minutes to spend memorizing the addresses in the boxes. *They are exactly the same ones that will be used for all three tests.* Try to memorize as many as you can. When the 3 minutes are up, turn to page 370 and read the instructions for *List 1*.

A	B	C	D	E
4000–5099 Clocks	2600–3799 Clocks	5400–5699 Clocks	3800–3999 Clocks	5100–5399 Clocks
Hunt	Mason	Placid	Oakland	Carmel
5100–5399 Harmony	3800–3999 Harmony	2600–3799 Harmony	5400–6599 Harmony	4000–5099 Harmony
Victor	Wyatt	Dreier	Arkansas	McDonald
3600–3799 Parker	5400–6299 Parker	4000–5399 Parker	2600–3599 Parker	3800–3999 Parker

List 1

Work — 3 minutes

Tear out the Answer Sheet for List 1. For each question, mark the answer sheet on page 362 to show the letter of the box in which the address belongs. Try to remember the locations of as many addresses as you can. *You will now have 3 minutes to complete List 1.* If you are not sure of an answer, you should guess.

A	B	C	D	E
4000–5099 Clocks	2600–3799 Clocks	5400–5699 Clocks	3800–3999 Clocks	5100–5399 Clocks
Hunt	Mason	Placid	Oakland	Carmel
5100–5399 Harmony	3800–3999 Harmony	2600–3799 Harmony	5400–6599 Harmony	4000–5099 Harmony
Victor	Wyatt	Dreier	Arkansas	McDonald
3600–3799 Parker	5400–6299 Parker	4000–5399 Parker	2600–3599 Parker	3800–3999 Parker

1. 2600–3799 Clocks
2. 4000–5099 Clocks
3. Dreier
4. 5100–5399 Harmony
5. 3800–3999 Parker
6. 5400–5699 Clocks
7. Victor
8. Arkansas
9. 3600–3799 Parker
10. 4000–5099 Harmony
11. Mason
12. 3800–3900 Clocks
13. 3800–3999 Harmony
14. 2600–3599 Parker
15. Oakland
16. 5100–5399 Clocks
17. 2600–3799 Harmony
18. Carmel
19. 5400–6299 Parker
20. Hunt
21. Placid
22. McDonald
23. Wyatt
24. 4000–5399 Parker
25. 5400–6599 Harmony
26. Victor
27. 3600–3799 Parker
28. 2600–3599 Parker
29. McDonald
30. 5100–5399 Clocks
31. 4000–5099 Harmony
32. 3800–3999 Parker
33. Wyatt
34. Carmel
35. Dreier
36. 5400–5699 Clocks
37. Placid
38. 5400–6299 Parker
39. 5100–5399 Harmony
40. 5400–6299 Parker
41. Hunt
42. 4000–5399 Parker
43. Arkansas
44. 3800–3999 Harmony

45. Victor
46. 4000–5099 Clocks
47. Carmel
48. Dreier
49. McDonald
50. Placid
51. 5400–5699 Clocks
52. 2600–3799 Clocks
53. 4000–5099 Harmony
54. McDonald
55. Arkansas

56. Hunt
57. 5400–6599 Harmony
58. 2600–3599 Parker
59. Mason
60. 3600–3799 Parker
61. Oakland
62. Mason
63. 3800–3999 Clocks
64. Oakland
65. 4000–5399 Parker
66. 5100–5399 Clocks
67. 4000–5099 Clocks
68. Mason
69. 2600–3799 Clocks
70. 5400–6599 Harmony
71. 3800–3999 Harmony
72. Hunt
73. 2600–3799 Harmony
74. Arkansas
75. Oakland
76. Wyatt
77. Victor

78. 3800–3999 Parker
79. Dreier
80. Wyatt
81. 3800–3999 Clocks
82. 5100–5399 Harmony
83. 2600–3799 Harmony
84. Placid
85. Carmel
86. 2600–3599 Parker
87. McDonald
88. 4000–5099 Harmony

STOP.

If you finish before the time is up, go back and check the questions in this section of the test only.

List 2

Work — 3 minutes

Do these questions *without* looking back at the boxes. For each question, mark your answer on the Answer Sheet for List 2 on page 362. If you are not sure of an answer, you should guess.

1. Hunt
2. 4000–5099 Harmony
3. 3800–3999 Harmony
4. Arkansas
5. Dreier
6. Carmel
7. 3800–3999 Parker
8. Mason
9. 2600–3799 Harmony
10. 2600–3599 Parker
11. McDonald

12. 5400–5699 Clocks
13. 2600–3799 Clocks
14. Wyatt
15. Placid
16. 4000–5399 Parker
17. 4000–5099 Harmony
18. 5400–6599 Harmony
19. Carmel
20. 2600–3599 Parker
21. 5100–5399 Harmony
22. McDonald
23. 5100–5399 Harmony
24. Hunt
25. Arkansas
26. 3800–3999 Clocks
27. Arkansas
28. 4000–5099 Clocks
29. 4000–5099 Harmony
30. 3800–3999 Clocks
31. Dreier
32. 2600–3799 Harmony
33. Oakland

34. 5400–5699 Clocks
35. Victor
36. McDonald
37. 5100–5399 Clocks
38. 3800–3999 Parker
39. 3800–3999 Harmony
40. 4000–5099 Harmony
41. Oakland
42. 2600–3799 Clocks
43. 4000–5399 Parker
44. Wyatt

45. 5100–5399 Clocks
46. Placid
47. McDonald
48. 5400–5699 Clocks
49. 3600–3799 Parker
50. 5400–6299 Parker
51. 5100–5399 Clocks
52. 4000–5099 Clocks
53. Carmel
54. 5400–6599 Harmony
55. 3600–3799 Parker

56. Arkansas
57. 5100–5399 Harmony
58. Victor
59. 4000–5099 Clocks
60. 2600–3599 Parker
61. 3600–3799 Parker
62. Oakland
63. Victor
64. Hunt
65. Carmel
66. Mason
67. 3800–3999 Harmony
68. Oakland
69. Wyatt
70. Oakland
71. 2600–3799 Clocks
72. Dreier
73. Mason
74. McDonald
75. 2600–3799 Clocks
76. 3800–3999 Clocks
77. 3800–3999 Parker

78. Wyatt
79. 5400–6599 Harmony
80. 2600–3799 Harmony
81. Placid
82. 5400–5699 Clocks
83. Placid
84. Hunt
85. 4000–5399 Parker
86. 5400–6299 Parker
87. Mason
88. 5400–6299 Parker

STOP.
If you finish before the time is up, go back and check the questions in this section of the test only.

List 3

Study — 5 minutes

You are now about to take the test using List 3. *(This is the test that counts!)*

Turn back to page 370 and study the boxes again. *You have 5 minutes to restudy the addresses.*

Work — 5 minutes

For each question, mark the Answer Sheet on page 363 to show the letter of the box in which the address belongs. You have *exactly 5 minutes* to do the test. During these 5 minutes, *do not* turn to any other page.

1. Wyatt
2. 4000–5399 Parker
3. Victor
4. Oakland
5. 4000–5099 Harmony
6. 3800–3999 Harmony
7. 3800–3999 Harmony
8. 5100–5399 Clocks
9. McDonald
10. Victor
11. 5400–5699 Clocks
12. Oakland
13. 2600–3799 Harmony
14. Dreier
15. 3800–3999 Clocks
16. 4000–5099 Harmony
17. 4000–5099 Clocks
18. Arkansas
19. 3800–3999 Clocks
20. Hunt
21. 5100–5399 Harmony
22. McDonald
23. 5100–5399 Harmony
24. 2600–3599 Parker
25. Carmel
26. 5400–6599 Harmony
27. 4000–5099 Harmony
28. 4000–5399 Parker
29. Victor
30. Placid
31. Wyatt
32. 2600–3799 Clocks
33. 5400–5699 Clocks
34. McDonald
35. 2600–3599 Parker
36. 2600–3799 Harmony
37. Mason
38. 3800–3999 Parker
39. Carmel
40. Dreier
41. Arkansas
42. 3800–3999 Harmony
43. 4000–5099 Harmony
44. Hunt

45. 5400–6299 Parker
46. Mason
47. 5400–6299 Parker
48. 4000–5399 Parker
49. Hunt
50. Placid
51. Dreier
52. Placid
53. 2600–3799 Harmony
54. 5400–6599 Harmony
55. Wyatt
56. 3800–3999 Parker
57. 3800–3999 Clocks
58. 2600–3799 Clocks
59. McDonald
60. Mason
61. Dreier
62. 2600–3799 Clocks
63. Oakland
64. Wyatt
65. Oakland
66. 3800–3999 Harmony
67. 5100–5399 Clocks
68. Carmel
69. Hunt
70. Victor
71. Oakland
72. 3600–3799 Parker
73. 2600–3599 Parker
74. 4000–5099 Clocks
75. Victor
76. 5100–5399 Harmony
77. Arkansas
78. 3600–3799 Parker
79. 5400–6599 Harmony
80. Carmel
81. 4000–5099 Clocks
82. 5100–5399 Clocks
83. 5400–6299 Parker
84. 3600–3799 Parker
85. 5400–5699 Clocks
86. McDonald
87. Placid
88. 5100–5399 Clocks

STOP.
If you finish before the time is up, go back and check the questions in this section of the test only.

Part C — NUMBER SERIES

Work — 20 minutes

For each Number Series question, there is a series of numbers that follow some definite order, and below each are five sets of two numbers each. You are to look at the numbers in the series and find out what order they follow. Then decide what the next two numbers in that series would be if the same order were continued. Mark your answers on the Answer Sheet on page 363.

You have 20 minutes to complete this part of the test. If you finish before the time is up, check your answers. The answers and explanations are on pages 385 to 387.

1. 50 45 45 40 35 35 30 __ __

   A) 30 25 B) 25 25 C) 25 30 D) 30 30 E) 25 20

2. 4 6 6 6 7 7 8 8 __ __

   A) 8 10 B) 9 8 C) 9 9 D) 8 9 E) 9 10

3. 27 22 28 24 29 26 30 __ __

   A) 31 27 B) 28 31 C) 32 28 D) 28 30 E) 27 28

4. 10 1 15 20 10 1 15 20 __ __

   A) 15 1 B) 10 20 C) 10 15 D) 10 1 E) 20 15

5. 6 15 9 5 15 8 4 __ __

   A) 8 5 B) 5 11 C) 8 10 D) 3 9 E) 15 7

6. 18 22 17 21 16 20 15 __ __

   A) 17 18 B) 14 17 C) 18 19 D) 14 20 E) 19 14

7. $10\frac{3}{12}$ $11\frac{4}{11}$ $12\frac{5}{10}$ $13\frac{6}{9}$ $14\frac{7}{8}$ $15\frac{8}{7}$ $16\frac{9}{6}$ __ __

   A) $17\frac{9}{6}$ $18\frac{10}{7}$ B) $16\frac{10}{5}$ $16\frac{11}{6}$ C) $17\frac{10}{5}$ $18\frac{11}{4}$ D) $18\frac{9}{7}$ $19\frac{10}{6}$ E) $17\frac{8}{5}$ $18\frac{7}{6}$

8. 26 2 6 38 3 8 40 __ __

   A) 9 50 B) 4 9 C) 4 0 D) 40 10 E) 9 10

9. 9 2 8 14 14 20 19 __ __

   A) 15 18 B) 24 30 C) 25 31 D) 30 24 E) 26 32

10. 2 4 6 12 11 8 10 12 10 __ __

    A) 9 14 B) 14 16 C) 11 13 D) 14 15 E) 13 10

11. 2 3 2 3 3 2 4 3 __ __

    A) 3 4 B) 2 3 C) 2 5 D) 3 5 E) 3 3

12. 9 7 5 11 9 7 13 __ __
A) 11 9 B) 12 11 C) 14 8 D) 12 8 E) 10 12

13. 9 10 17 11 12 16 13 __ __
A) 15 16 B) 12 13 C) 14 15 D) 13 14 E) 12 15

14. 37 44 45 51 58 45 65 __ __
A) 75 45 B) 72 79 C) 65 45 D) 45 75 E) 72 45

15. 9 18 16 11 22 20 15 30 __ __
A) 25 23 B) 28 26 C) 60 58 D) 28 23 E) 23 25

16. 32 30 28 16 26 24 22 20 __ __
A) 18 20 B) 20 18 C) 16 18 D) 20 20 E) 18 16

17. 39 38 38 36 35 35 33 __ __
A) 31 31 B) 32 31 C) 32 32 D) 33 32 E) 31 30

18. 17 14 11 16 13 10 15 __ __
A) 20 17 B) 10 7 C) 12 9 D) 7 10 E) 13 10

19. 15 10 15 20 10 20 25 __ __
A) 20 25 B) 15 20 C) 20 20 D) 10 25 E) 25 25

20. 16 18 16 22 24 20 28 30 __ __
A) 32 18 B) 22 26 C) 30 32 D) 24 34 E) 32 38

21. 2 3 3 5 5 8 8 __ __
A) 12 12 B) 11 12 C) 8 11 D) 8 8 E) 11 11

22. 45 35 40 30 35 25 30 __ __
A) 25 35 B) 20 25 C) 40 45 D) 35 40 E) 35 30

23. 8 11 10 9 13 10 10 15 __ __
A) 16 10 B) 10 11 C) 12 14 D) 12 10 E) 11 10

24. 19 18 16 15 15 14 12 11 11 __ __
A) 10 9 B) 11 10 C) 10 10 D) 10 9 E) 10 8

STOP.
If you finish before the time is up, go back and check the questions in this section of the test only.

PART D — FOLLOWING ORAL DIRECTIONS

This part of the test gauges your ability to understand and carry out spoken directions *exactly* as they are given to you.

In order to prepare to take Part D of the test, follow the steps below:

1. Enlist the help of a friend who will be the "reader." His or her job will be to read aloud a series of directions that you are to follow *exactly.* The reader will need a watch that displays seconds, because the directions must be read at the correct speed.
2. Tear out pages 383 to 384. These are the worksheets you should have in front of you as you listen to the directions given by the reader, who will tell you to do certain things with the items on each line on the worksheets.
3. Use the Answer Sheet for Following Oral Directions on page 363, and insert today's date. You will darken the appropriate spaces in accordance with the directions given by the reader.
4. *Now hand this entire book to the reader.* Ask him/her to review the section below headed "Instructions to the Reader." It explains exactly how the reader is to proceed.

When you and the reader are ready to start this part of Practice Test 5, he/she will begin reading to you the section marked "Directions." YOU ARE NOT TO READ THESE AT ANY TIME BEFORE OR DURING THE TEST. If you do, you will lose the benefit of this part of the practice test.

Instructions to the "Reader"

These instructions should be read at about 80 words per minute. You should practice reading the material in the box until you can do it in exactly 1 minute. This will give you a feel for the way you should read the test material.

1-MINUTE PRACTICE

Look at line 20 in your worksheet. There are two circles and two boxes of different sizes with numbers in them. If 7 is less than 3 and if 2 is smaller than 4, write C in the larger circle. Otherwise write B as in *baker* in the smaller box. Now, on your answer sheet, darken the space for the number-letter combination in the box or circle.

You should read the entire test aloud before you read it to the person taking the test, in order to acquaint yourself with the procedure and the desired rate of reading.

Read slowly but at a natural pace. In other words, do not space the words so that there are unnaturally long pauses between them. The instruction "Pause slightly" indicates only enough time to take a breath. The other instructions for pauses give the recommended length for each. If possible, use a watch with a second hand.

All the material that follows, except the words in parentheses, is to be read aloud. Now start reading the directions. *Do not repeat any of the directions.*

Directions: In this test, I will read instructions to you.

You are to mark your worksheets according to the instructions that I read to you. After each set of instructions, I'll give you time to record your answers on your answer sheet.

Try to understand the instructions as I read them; I cannot repeat them. Do not ask any questions from now on.

If, when you go to darken a space for a number, you find that you have already darkened another space for that number, either (1) erase the first mark and darken the space for your new choice, or (2) let the first mark stay and do not darken any other space. When you finish, you should have no more than one space darkened for each number.

Turn to Worksheet 1.

Look at line 1 on your worksheet. (Pause slightly.) Draw a line under the first number in the line. (Pause 2 seconds.) Now, on your answer sheet, find the number under which you drew a line and darken space D as in *dog.* (Pause 5 seconds.)

Look at the circles in line 2 on your worksheet. (Pause slightly.) In the last circle, write the answer to this question: How many days are there in a week? (Pause 2 seconds.) Now, on your answer sheet, darken the space for the number-letter combination that is in the circle you just wrote in. (Pause 5 seconds.)

Look at line 2 again. In the third circle, write the number 18. (Pause 2 seconds.) Now, on your answer sheet, darken the space for the number-letter combination that is in the circle you just wrote in. (Pause 5 seconds.)

Look at the boxes in line 3 on your worksheet. (Pause slightly.) If the largest number is in the smallest box, write C on the line in the first box. (Pause slightly.) Otherwise, write D as in *dog* on the line in the largest box. (Pause 2 seconds.) Now, on your answer sheet, darken the space for the number-letter combination that is in the box you just wrote in. (Pause 5 seconds.)

Look at the letters in line 4 on your worksheet. (Pause slightly.) Draw a line under the letter that is the third letter in the alphabet. (Pause 2 seconds.) Now, on your answer sheet, find number 76 and darken the space for the letter under which you just drew a line. (Pause 5 seconds.)

Look at line 5 on your worksheet. (Pause slightly.) Mail for Liberty and Munsey is to be put in box 50. Mail for St. Clair and Reading is to be put in box 72. (Pause slightly.) Write A in the box in which you would put mail for Munsey. (Pause 2 seconds.) Now, on your answer sheet, darken the space for the number-letter combination that is in the box you just wrote in. (Pause 5 seconds.)

Look at the numbers in line 6 on your worksheet. (Pause slightly.) Draw a line under the fourth number in the line. (Pause 2 seconds.) Now, on your answer sheet, find the number under which you drew a line and darken space E for that number. (Pause 5 seconds.)

Look at line 6 again. Draw two lines under the second number in the line. (Pause 2 seconds.) Now, on your answer sheet, find the number under which you drew two lines and darken space B as in *baker.* (Pause 5 seconds.)

Now look at line 7 on your worksheet. (Pause slightly.) Each box has a number and a letter in it. In the box that has the highest number write on the line the middle figure of that number. (Pause 2 seconds.) Now, on your answer sheet, darken the space for the number-letter combination that is in the box you just wrote in. (Pause 5 seconds.)

Look at line 8 on your worksheet. (Pause slightly.) There are two boxes and two circles of different sizes with numbers in them. (Pause slightly.) If 4 is smaller than 6, and if 8 is less than 5, write E in the larger box. (Pause 2 seconds.) Otherwise, write A in the smaller circle. (Pause 2 seconds.) Now, on your answer sheet, darken the space for the number-letter combination that is in the box or circle you just wrote in. (Pause 5 seconds.)

Look at line 9 on your worksheet. (Pause slightly.) Draw a line under every "O" in the line. (Pause 5 seconds.) Count the number of lines you have drawn, subtract 3, and write that number at the end of the line. (Pause 5 seconds.) Now, on your answer sheet, find that number and darken space E. (Pause 5 seconds.)

Now look at line 10 on your worksheet. (Pause slightly.) Draw a line under every number in the line that is more than 50 but less than 65. (Pause 12 seconds.) Now, on your answer sheet, darken space B as in *baker* for every number under which you drew a line. (Pause 25 seconds.)

Look at line 11 on your worksheet. (Pause slightly.) There are 5 boxes, each with a letter in it. In the fifth box, write the answer to this question: Which of the following numbers is smallest: 28, 12, 23, 19, 14? (Pause 5 seconds.) Now, on your answer sheet, darken the space for the number-letter combination that is in the box you just wrote in. (Pause 5 seconds.)

In the middle box on line 11, write the number 35. (Pause 5 seconds.) Now, on your answer sheet, darken the space for the number-letter combination that is in the box you just wrote in. (Pause 5 seconds.) In the second box, do nothing. In the fourth box write the answer to this question: How many pennies are there in a dime? (Pause 2 seconds.) Now, on your answer sheet, darken the space for the number-letter combination that is in the box you just wrote in. (Pause 5 seconds.)

Now turn to Worksheet 2. (Pause 5 seconds.)

Look at line 12 on your worksheet. (Pause slightly.) There are two boxes and two circles of different sizes with numbers in them. If the number in the left-hand box is larger than the number in the right-hand box, subtract 3 from the number in the left-hand box and change the number in that box to this number. (Pause 6 seconds.) Then write D as in *dog* next to the new number. (Pause 2 seconds.) Otherwise, write C next to the number in the left-hand circle. (Pause 2 seconds.) Now, on your answer sheet, darken the space for the number-letter combination that is in the box or circle you just wrote in. (Pause 5 seconds.)

Look at the boxes and words in line 13 on your worksheet. (Pause slightly.) Write the fourth letter of the first word in the last box. (Pause 2 seconds.) Write the third letter of the second word in the first box. (Pause 2 seconds.) Write the second letter of the third word in the second box. (Pause 2 seconds.) Now, on your answer sheet, darken the spaces for the number-letter combinations that are in the boxes you just wrote in. (Pause 12 seconds.)

Look at line 14 on your answer sheet. (Pause slightly.) In each circle there is a time when the mail must leave. In the circle for the latest time, write on the line the last two figures of the time. (Pause 2 seconds.) Now, on your answer sheet, darken the space for the number-letter combination that is in the circle you just wrote in. (Pause 5 seconds.)

Now look at line 15 on your worksheet. (Pause slightly.) If, in a year, Independence Day comes after Labor Day, write the number 70 on the line next to the first letter. (Pause 2 seconds.) If it does not, write 40 on the line next to the last letter. (Pause 2 seconds.) Now, on your answer sheet, find the number you just wrote and darken the space for the letter next to which you wrote it. (Pause 5 seconds.)

Look at the numbers in line 16 on your worksheet. (Pause slightly.) Draw a line under every number that is more than 25 but less than 45. (Pause 12 seconds.) Now, on your answer sheet, for each number you drew a line under, darken space A. (Pause 25 seconds.)

Look at the circles in line 17 on your worksheet. (Pause slightly.) The number in each circle is the number of packages in a mail sack. In each of the circles holding an even number of packages write the letter C. (Pause 10 seconds.) Now, on your answer sheet, darken the spaces for the number-letter combinations in the circles you just wrote in. (Pause 25 seconds.)

Look at the boxes and circles in line 18 on your worksheet. (Pause slightly.) If the number in the first box is greater than the number in the last box, write B as in *baker* in the first circle. (Pause 2 seconds.) If it is not, write D as in *dog* in the last circle. (Pause 2 seconds.) Now, on your answer sheet, darken the space for the number-letter combination that is in the circle you just wrote in. (Pause 5 seconds.)

Look at the two rows of numbers and the single row of circles in line 19 on your worksheet. (Pause slightly.) Draw a line under the second number in the upper row of numbers. (Pause slightly.) Draw a line under the third number in the lower row of numbers. (Pause slightly.) Now, add up the numbers under which you have drawn lines and write the total in the last circle in the row. (Pause 5 seconds.) Now, on your answer sheet, darken the space for the number-letter combination that is in the circle you just wrote in. (Pause 5 seconds.)

END OF EXAMINATION.
If you finish before the time is up, go back and check the questions in this section of the test only.

Practice Test 5—Worksheet 1

Part D—Following Oral Directions

1. 84 57 16

2. (___ D) (___ E) (___ A) (___ C)

3. [64 ___] [39 ___] [72 ___]

4. B C E A D A B

5. [50 LIBERTY MUNSEY ___] [72 ST. CLAIR READING ___]

6. 13 29 27 23 9 38

7. [398 ___ B] [422 ___ D] [276 ___ A] [349 ___ C] [432 ___ E]

8. 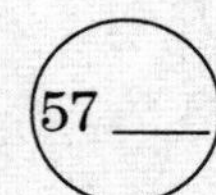 [79 ___] (33 ___) [19 ___]

9. O X O O X O X X O O O X O X

10. 67 45 49 51 72 58 43 50 64

11. [D ___] [A ___] [B ___] [C ___] [E ___]

Practice Test 5—Worksheet 2

Part D—Following Oral Directions

12. 64 ___ | 13 ___ | 51 ___ | 48 ___

13. JUNE | SCAR | ABOVE | 86 ___ | 17 ___ | 45 ___

14. 5:05 ___ D | 5:15 ___ E | 5:46 ___ C | 5:32 ___ B | 5:12 ___ A

15. ___ C | ___ A | ___ E

16. 47 25 43 22 15 48 27 50

17. 73 ___ | 68 ___ | 59 ___ | 81 ___ | 32 ___ | 80 ___

18. 11 ___ | 23 ___ | 61 ___ | 29 ___ | 77 ___

19.

2	4	8	6
1	3	2	5

___ D | ___ E | ___ A | ___ C

ANSWER KEY

Part A—Address Checking

1. D	11. D	21. D	31. A	41. D	51. D	61. D	71. D	81. D	91. A
2. D	12. A	22. A	32. D	42. A	52. A	62. D	72. D	82. A	92. A
3. A	13. A	23. D	33. D	43. A	53. A	63. A	73. A	83. A	93. D
4. D	14. D	24. D	34. A	44. D	54. D	64. A	74. A	84. D	94. D
5. A	15. A	25. D	35. D	45. A	55. A	65. D	75. D	85. D	95. A
6. A	16. A	26. A	36. D	46. A	56. D	66. D	76. D	86. A	
7. A	17. A	27. A	37. A	47. A	57. D	67. A	77. D	87. A	
8. D	18. A	28. A	38. D	48. D	58. D	68. A	78. A	88. D	
9. A	19. D	29. D	39. A	49. D	59. A	69. D	79. D	89. A	
10. A	20. D	30. D	40. D	50. A	60. D	70. A	80. D	90. A	

Part B—Memory for Addresses

List 1

1. B	10. E	19. B	28. D	37. C	46. A	55. D	64. D	73. C	82. A
2. A	11. B	20. A	29. E	38. B	47. E	56. A	65. C	74. D	83. C
3. C	12. D	21. C	30. E	39. A	48. C	57. D	66. E	75. D	84. C
4. A	13. B	22. E	31. E	40. B	49. E	58. D	67. A	76. B	85. E
5. E	14. D	23. B	32. E	41. A	50. C	59. B	68. B	77. A	86. D
6. C	15. D	24. C	33. B	42. C	51. C	60. A	69. B	78. E	87. E
7. A	16. E	25. D	34. E	43. D	52. B	61. D	70. D	79. C	88. E
8. D	17. C	26. A	35. C	44. B	53. E	62. B	71. B	80. B	
9. A	18. E	27. A	36. C	45. A	54. E	63. D	72. A	81. D	

List 2

1. A	10. D	19. E	28. A	37. E	46. C	55. A	64. A	73. B	82. C
2. E	11. E	20. D	29. E	38. E	47. E	56. D	65. E	74. E	83. C
3. B	12. C	21. A	30. D	39. B	48. C	57. A	66. B	75. B	84. A
4. D	13. B	22. E	31. C	40. E	49. A	58. A	67. B	76. D	85. C
5. C	14. B	23. A	32. C	41. D	50. B	59. A	68. D	77. E	86. B
6. E	15. C	24. A	33. D	42. B	51. E	60. D	69. B	78. B	87. B
7. E	16. C	25. D	34. C	43. C	52. A	61. A	70. D	79. D	88. B
8. B	17. E	26. D	35. A	44. B	53. E	62. D	71. B	80. C	
9. C	18. D	27. D	36. E	45. E	54. D	63. A	72. C	81. C	

List 3

1. B	10. A	19. D	28. C	37. B	46. B	55. B	64. B	73. D	82. E
2. C	11. C	20. A	29. A	38. E	47. B	56. E	65. D	74. A	83. B
3. A	12. D	21. A	30. C	39. E	48. C	57. D	66. B	75. A	84. A
4. D	13. C	22. E	31. B	40. C	49. A	58. B	67. E	76. A	85. C
5. E	14. C	23. A	32. B	41. D	50. C	59. E	68. E	77. D	86. E
6. B	15. D	24. D	33. C	42. B	51. C	60. B	69. A	78. A	87. C
7. E	16. E	25. E	34. E	43. E	52. C	61. C	70. A	79. D	88. E
8. E	17. A	26. D	35. D	44. A	53. C	62. B	71. D	80. E	
9. E	18. D	27. E	36. C	45. B	54. D	63. D	72. A	81. A	

Part C—Number Series

1. **B**	4. **D**	7. **C**	10. **A**	13. **C**	16. **B**	19. **D**	22. **B**
2. **A**	5. **E**	8. **C**	11. **C**	14. **E**	17. **C**	20. **D**	23. **B**
3. **B**	6. **E**	9. **E**	12. **A**	15. **D**	18. **C**	21. **A**	24. **E**

Part D—Following Oral Directions

3. **E**	7. **C**	17. **B**	27. **A**	35. **B**	45. **E**	51. **B**	61. **D**	72. **D**	80. **C**
5. **E**	10. **C**	18. **A**	29. **B**	40. **E**	46. **C**	57. **A**	64. **B**	76. **C**	84. **D**
6. **C**	12. **E**	23. **E**	32. **C**	43. **A**	50. **A**	58. **B**	68. **C**	77. **D**	86. **A**

ANSWER EXPLANATIONS FOR PART C—NUMBER SERIES

1. **B** This is a series that descends by 5. The new number is repeated after every second subtraction.
2. **A** The numbers of the two alternating series coincide in a way that makes the pattern in this question difficult to pick out. One series increases by 2. The other increases by 1 after repeating the number.
3. **B** There are two alternating series here, one increasing by 1; the other increasing by 2.
4. **D** The sequence 10 1 15 20 keeps recycling.
5. **E** The rule here is: + 3, − 4; with the arbitrary number 15 inserted after every second member of the series.
6. **E** You may consider these numbers as following the rule: + 4, − 5; or as belonging to two alternating series, each of which decreases by 1.
7. **C** There are *three* changes occurring among these fractions as they progress. The whole number at the beginning keeps increasing by 1. So does the numerator (top) of each fraction. The denominator (bottom) on the other hand keeps decreasing by 1. It's very easy to lose track of things unless you are really careful.
8. **C** Here is a series that uses *addition and position* to determine its pattern. Each two-digit number appears once and is followed by each of the *separate* digits that make it up. Thus, 26 leads to 2 and 6, 38 leads to 3 and 8, and so on. You must add 12 to go from one two-digit number to the next.
9. **E** Here are two series that alternate in a little more complex fashion than usual. The series that begins with the number 9 increases by 5 (9, 14, 19). It interrupts the + 6 series that starts with 2 after every second number.
10. **A** The two series in this question alternate in an even more complex manner than in question 9. As it progresses, every *three* members of the + 2 series (2, 4, 6) alternate with two members of the − 1 series, which begins with the number 12.
11. **C** This is merely a + 1 series made difficult because the arbitrary numbers *3* and *2* are periodically inserted.
12. **A** Here is a group of mini-series each of which descends by 2. Each three-member mini-series begins 2 higher than the one before. You could also see the numbers in this progression following a − 2, − 2, + 6; − 2, − 2, + 6; rule.

13. **C** One member of a −1 series (17, 16) appears after every two members of a + 1 series (9, 10, 11, 12, and so on)
14. **E** This is a + 7 series with the arbitrary number 45 appearing as every third number in the progression.
15. **D** There is a complex rule here using multiplication and subtraction: × 2, − 2, − 5; × 2, − 2, − 5; and so on.
16. **B** A descending series following a −2 rule is interrupted after every three members by one member of an ascending series starting with 16 and following a + 4 rule.
17. **C** The rule here is − 1, repeat the number, − 2; − 1, repeat the number, − 2; and so on.
18. **C** Here again we see a three-member mini-series. Each of these descends by 3. Each mini-series begins one number lower than the preceding series. You could also see a − 3, − 3, + 5 rule governing these numbers.
19. **D** There is a series here that follows the rule + 5, repeat the number; etc. The number 10 separates each repetition.
20. **D** Here the loop diagram is used to identify the complex pattern (three alternating series) for this series.

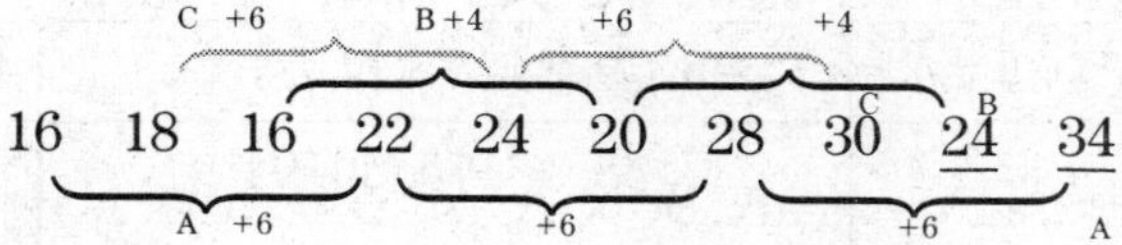

21. **A** This series uses a *variable* adder starting with + 1 and then repeats the number before going on.

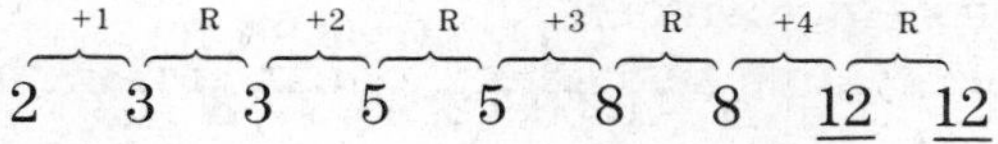

22. **B** You can see this as following a − 10, + 5; − 10, + 5; rule, or as two alternating series each decreasing by 5.
23. **B** There are two alternating series here, one (8, 9, and so on) increasing by a + 1 rule; the other by a + 2 rule (11, 3, and so on). The arbitrary number 10 appears as every third number in the series.
24. **E** The rule here is a complex one: − 1, − 2, − 1, repeat the number; − 1, − 2, − 1, repeat the number; and so on.

EVALUATING YOUR PROGRESS

Throughout this book, the importance of evaluating and recording your progress has been stressed, as you study and practice for the Test Battery 460/470. At this point, if you have completed Practice Tests 1 through 4 and have made all the entries on your Personal Progress Record, you are quite familiar with the discussion on Computing Your Score, Guidelines, and the Personal Progress Record. If you wish to review the details of these subjects, refer to pages 58 through 62 or pages 324 through 328.

You have probably seen great improvement in your test scores, but don't stop now. Take the remaining practice test and record the results on your Personal Progress Record. Go for a perfect score!

DIAGNOSTIC CHARTS

The following charts will help pinpoint your weaknesses by making it easy for you to determine what particular type of question in each part of the test is most difficult for you.

Part A—Address Checking

Type of Difference	"D" Questions	Number of "D" Questions Wrong		
		Trial 1	Trial 2	Trial 3
Numbers: transposed	8, 21, 33, 71, 78			
changed	1, 35, 40, 54, 61, 76, 81			
omitted	65			
Directions	29, 79, 84			
Abbreviations: streets, roads, avenues, etc.	20, 38, 48, 75, 80, 94			
states	44, 56, 58			
Spelling: single letters	2, 4, 11, 14, 24, 25, 32, 41, 60, 62, 69, 77, 85, 93			
groups of letters	19, 23, 30, 36, 49, 51, 57, 66, 72			
Total Number of All Types	48			
	Use the columns on the right to enter the question numbers of "A" items you marked "D."			

This chart will help you to pinpoint the kinds of errors you made on Practice Test 5. Use it as directed below after you have taken and marked the test.

The first column on the left, "Type of Difference," contains the categories whereby addresses may differ (see page 63). On the same line across, the second column gives the numbers of the questions that fall within each category. In the third column, you are to enter the numbers of any "A" questions you answered as "D." Do not include questions that you did not do. Checking the addresses you got wrong may reveal a problem on which you will want to work.

After you have made all the entries, you will be able to see the areas in which you need to improve. Then turn to the appropriate parts of Chapter 3: Address Checking—How to Improve Your Score, read them, and practice the drills that can help. For example, if you find you have been making too many errors picking out number differences, read page 88 and do Drills 18 through 21. If you have a problem with single letters because of reversals like *b* and *d*, or if you have been overlooking the differences between *a*, *e*, and *o*, read page 85. Examine the table and work on Drills 10 and 11 if the problem persists.

Remember that this chart is designed for diagnostic purposes and guidance on further practice. It has been drawn so that you can enter the results each time you retake a practice test. In this way you will be able to see how you are progressing. It is not necessary to record your scores here. That is best done by using the Personal Progress Record Card.

Part B—Memory for Addresses

Kind of Address		Number of Questions	Number Wrong		
			Trial 1	Trial 2	Trial 3
Direct:					
	List 1	41			
	List 2	40			
	List 3	41			
Numbered:					
	List 1	47			
	List 2	48			
	List 3	47			

The purpose of this chart is to help you evaluate your performance on the two kinds of memory questions that appear in these memory tests—the questions on the direct (name) addresses and the questions on the numbered addresses. Use the chart as directed below after you have taken and marked the entire test.

The first column on the left, "Kind of Address," is divided by category into "Direct Address" versus "Numbered Address." The second column gives the number of questions in each category on List 1, List 2, and List 3. Use the third column to enter the total number of questions in each category that you answered incorrectly. There is room for you to make additional entries if you take the practice tests more than once.

At a glance, you will be able to see which area you need to concentrate on and how well you are progressing as you take repeat trials. Use Chapter 4 and the drills in it to improve your memory for the direct addresses. Use Chapter 5 for the numbered addresses.

Remember to use the Personal Progress Record Card (Memory for Addresses) on page 430 to keep track of your actual scores as you keep studying and practicing.

Part C—Number Series and Part D—Following Oral Directions

Because of the nature of the questions in these tests, Diagnostic Charts are not provided for them. If you find that you made many errors on these tests, study the techniques suggested in Chapters 6 and 7.

Answer Sheet—Practice Test 6

Part A—Address Checking

1 ⒶⒹ
2 ⒶⒹ
3 ⒶⒹ
4 ⒶⒹ
5 ⒶⒹ
6 ⒶⒹ
7 ⒶⒹ
8 ⒶⒹ
9 ⒶⒹ
10 ⒶⒹ
11 ⒶⒹ
12 ⒶⒹ
13 ⒶⒹ
14 ⒶⒹ
15 ⒶⒹ
16 ⒶⒹ
17 ⒶⒹ
18 ⒶⒹ
19 ⒶⒹ
20 ⒶⒹ
21 ⒶⒹ
22 ⒶⒹ
23 ⒶⒹ
24 ⒶⒹ
25 ⒶⒹ
26 ⒶⒹ
27 ⒶⒹ
28 ⒶⒹ
29 ⒶⒹ
30 ⒶⒹ
31 ⒶⒹ
32 ⒶⒹ
33 ⒶⒹ
34 ⒶⒹ
35 ⒶⒹ
36 ⒶⒹ
37 ⒶⒹ
38 ⒶⒹ
39 ⒶⒹ
40 ⒶⒹ
41 ⒶⒹ
42 ⒶⒹ
43 ⒶⒹ
44 ⒶⒹ
45 ⒶⒹ
46 ⒶⒹ
47 ⒶⒹ
48 ⒶⒹ
49 ⒶⒹ
50 ⒶⒹ
51 ⒶⒹ
52 ⒶⒹ
53 ⒶⒹ
54 ⒶⒹ
55 ⒶⒹ
56 ⒶⒹ
57 ⒶⒹ
58 ⒶⒹ
59 ⒶⒹ
60 ⒶⒹ
61 ⒶⒹ
62 ⒶⒹ
63 ⒶⒹ
64 ⒶⒹ
65 ⒶⒹ
66 ⒶⒹ
67 ⒶⒹ
68 ⒶⒹ
69 ⒶⒹ
70 ⒶⒹ
71 ⒶⒹ
72 ⒶⒹ
73 ⒶⒹ
74 ⒶⒹ
75 ⒶⒹ
76 ⒶⒹ
77 ⒶⒹ
78 ⒶⒹ
79 ⒶⒹ
80 ⒶⒹ
81 ⒶⒹ
82 ⒶⒹ
83 ⒶⒹ
84 ⒶⒹ
85 ⒶⒹ
86 ⒶⒹ
87 ⒶⒹ
88 ⒶⒹ
89 ⒶⒹ
90 ⒶⒹ
91 ⒶⒹ
92 ⒶⒹ
93 ⒶⒹ
94 ⒶⒹ
95 ⒶⒹ

✂ Remove by cutting on dotted line.

Part B—Memory for Addresses—List 1

1 ⒶⒷⒸⒹⒺ
2 ⒶⒷⒸⒹⒺ
3 ⒶⒷⒸⒹⒺ
4 ⒶⒷⒸⒹⒺ
5 ⒶⒷⒸⒹⒺ
6 ⒶⒷⒸⒹⒺ
7 ⒶⒷⒸⒹⒺ
8 ⒶⒷⒸⒹⒺ
9 ⒶⒷⒸⒹⒺ
10 ⒶⒷⒸⒹⒺ
11 ⒶⒷⒸⒹⒺ
12 ⒶⒷⒸⒹⒺ
13 ⒶⒷⒸⒹⒺ
14 ⒶⒷⒸⒹⒺ
15 ⒶⒷⒸⒹⒺ
16 ⒶⒷⒸⒹⒺ
17 ⒶⒷⒸⒹⒺ
18 ⒶⒷⒸⒹⒺ
19 ⒶⒷⒸⒹⒺ
20 ⒶⒷⒸⒹⒺ
21 ⒶⒷⒸⒹⒺ
22 ⒶⒷⒸⒹⒺ
23 ⒶⒷⒸⒹⒺ
24 ⒶⒷⒸⒹⒺ
25 ⒶⒷⒸⒹⒺ
26 ⒶⒷⒸⒹⒺ
27 ⒶⒷⒸⒹⒺ
28 ⒶⒷⒸⒹⒺ
29 ⒶⒷⒸⒹⒺ
30 ⒶⒷⒸⒹⒺ
31 ⒶⒷⒸⒹⒺ
32 ⒶⒷⒸⒹⒺ
33 ⒶⒷⒸⒹⒺ
34 ⒶⒷⒸⒹⒺ
35 ⒶⒷⒸⒹⒺ
36 ⒶⒷⒸⒹⒺ
37 ⒶⒷⒸⒹⒺ
38 ⒶⒷⒸⒹⒺ
39 ⒶⒷⒸⒹⒺ
40 ⒶⒷⒸⒹⒺ
41 ⒶⒷⒸⒹⒺ
42 ⒶⒷⒸⒹⒺ
43 ⒶⒷⒸⒹⒺ
44 ⒶⒷⒸⒹⒺ
45 ⒶⒷⒸⒹⒺ
46 ⒶⒷⒸⒹⒺ
47 ⒶⒷⒸⒹⒺ
48 ⒶⒷⒸⒹⒺ
49 ⒶⒷⒸⒹⒺ
50 ⒶⒷⒸⒹⒺ
51 ⒶⒷⒸⒹⒺ
52 ⒶⒷⒸⒹⒺ
53 ⒶⒷⒸⒹⒺ
54 ⒶⒷⒸⒹⒺ
55 ⒶⒷⒸⒹⒺ
56 ⒶⒷⒸⒹⒺ
57 ⒶⒷⒸⒹⒺ
58 ⒶⒷⒸⒹⒺ
59 ⒶⒷⒸⒹⒺ
60 ⒶⒷⒸⒹⒺ
61 ⒶⒷⒸⒹⒺ
62 ⒶⒷⒸⒹⒺ
63 ⒶⒷⒸⒹⒺ
64 ⒶⒷⒸⒹⒺ
65 ⒶⒷⒸⒹⒺ
66 ⒶⒷⒸⒹⒺ
67 ⒶⒷⒸⒹⒺ
68 ⒶⒷⒸⒹⒺ
69 ⒶⒷⒸⒹⒺ
70 ⒶⒷⒸⒹⒺ
71 ⒶⒷⒸⒹⒺ
72 ⒶⒷⒸⒹⒺ
73 ⒶⒷⒸⒹⒺ
74 ⒶⒷⒸⒹⒺ
75 ⒶⒷⒸⒹⒺ
76 ⒶⒷⒸⒹⒺ
77 ⒶⒷⒸⒹⒺ
78 ⒶⒷⒸⒹⒺ
79 ⒶⒷⒸⒹⒺ
80 ⒶⒷⒸⒹⒺ
81 ⒶⒷⒸⒹⒺ
82 ⒶⒷⒸⒹⒺ
83 ⒶⒷⒸⒹⒺ
84 ⒶⒷⒸⒹⒺ
85 ⒶⒷⒸⒹⒺ
86 ⒶⒷⒸⒹⒺ
87 ⒶⒷⒸⒹⒺ
88 ⒶⒷⒸⒹⒺ

Part B—Memory for Addresses—List 2

1 ⒶⒷⒸⒹⒺ
2 ⒶⒷⒸⒹⒺ
3 ⒶⒷⒸⒹⒺ
4 ⒶⒷⒸⒹⒺ
5 ⒶⒷⒸⒹⒺ
6 ⒶⒷⒸⒹⒺ
7 ⒶⒷⒸⒹⒺ
8 ⒶⒷⒸⒹⒺ
9 ⒶⒷⒸⒹⒺ
10 ⒶⒷⒸⒹⒺ
11 ⒶⒷⒸⒹⒺ
12 ⒶⒷⒸⒹⒺ
13 ⒶⒷⒸⒹⒺ
14 ⒶⒷⒸⒹⒺ
15 ⒶⒷⒸⒹⒺ
16 ⒶⒷⒸⒹⒺ
17 ⒶⒷⒸⒹⒺ
18 ⒶⒷⒸⒹⒺ
19 ⒶⒷⒸⒹⒺ
20 ⒶⒷⒸⒹⒺ
21 ⒶⒷⒸⒹⒺ
22 ⒶⒷⒸⒹⒺ
23 ⒶⒷⒸⒹⒺ
24 ⒶⒷⒸⒹⒺ
25 ⒶⒷⒸⒹⒺ
26 ⒶⒷⒸⒹⒺ
27 ⒶⒷⒸⒹⒺ
28 ⒶⒷⒸⒹⒺ
29 ⒶⒷⒸⒹⒺ
30 ⒶⒷⒸⒹⒺ
31 ⒶⒷⒸⒹⒺ
32 ⒶⒷⒸⒹⒺ
33 ⒶⒷⒸⒹⒺ
34 ⒶⒷⒸⒹⒺ
35 ⒶⒷⒸⒹⒺ
36 ⒶⒷⒸⒹⒺ
37 ⒶⒷⒸⒹⒺ
38 ⒶⒷⒸⒹⒺ
39 ⒶⒷⒸⒹⒺ
40 ⒶⒷⒸⒹⒺ
41 ⒶⒷⒸⒹⒺ
42 ⒶⒷⒸⒹⒺ
43 ⒶⒷⒸⒹⒺ
44 ⒶⒷⒸⒹⒺ
45 ⒶⒷⒸⒹⒺ
46 ⒶⒷⒸⒹⒺ
47 ⒶⒷⒸⒹⒺ
48 ⒶⒷⒸⒹⒺ
49 ⒶⒷⒸⒹⒺ
50 ⒶⒷⒸⒹⒺ
51 ⒶⒷⒸⒹⒺ
52 ⒶⒷⒸⒹⒺ
53 ⒶⒷⒸⒹⒺ
54 ⒶⒷⒸⒹⒺ
55 ⒶⒷⒸⒹⒺ
56 ⒶⒷⒸⒹⒺ
57 ⒶⒷⒸⒹⒺ
58 ⒶⒷⒸⒹⒺ
59 ⒶⒷⒸⒹⒺ
60 ⒶⒷⒸⒹⒺ
61 ⒶⒷⒸⒹⒺ
62 ⒶⒷⒸⒹⒺ
63 ⒶⒷⒸⒹⒺ
64 ⒶⒷⒸⒹⒺ
65 ⒶⒷⒸⒹⒺ
66 ⒶⒷⒸⒹⒺ
67 ⒶⒷⒸⒹⒺ
68 ⒶⒷⒸⒹⒺ
69 ⒶⒷⒸⒹⒺ
70 ⒶⒷⒸⒹⒺ
71 ⒶⒷⒸⒹⒺ
72 ⒶⒷⒸⒹⒺ
73 ⒶⒷⒸⒹⒺ
74 ⒶⒷⒸⒹⒺ
75 ⒶⒷⒸⒹⒺ
76 ⒶⒷⒸⒹⒺ
77 ⒶⒷⒸⒹⒺ
78 ⒶⒷⒸⒹⒺ
79 ⒶⒷⒸⒹⒺ
80 ⒶⒷⒸⒹⒺ
81 ⒶⒷⒸⒹⒺ
82 ⒶⒷⒸⒹⒺ
83 ⒶⒷⒸⒹⒺ
84 ⒶⒷⒸⒹⒺ
85 ⒶⒷⒸⒹⒺ
86 ⒶⒷⒸⒹⒺ
87 ⒶⒷⒸⒹⒺ
88 ⒶⒷⒸⒹⒺ

✂ Remove by cutting on dotted line.

Part B—Memory for Addresses—List 3

1 ⒶⒷⒸⒹⒺ
2 ⒶⒷⒸⒹⒺ
3 ⒶⒷⒸⒹⒺ
4 ⒶⒷⒸⒹⒺ
5 ⒶⒷⒸⒹⒺ
6 ⒶⒷⒸⒹⒺ
7 ⒶⒷⒸⒹⒺ
8 ⒶⒷⒸⒹⒺ
9 ⒶⒷⒸⒹⒺ
10 ⒶⒷⒸⒹⒺ
11 ⒶⒷⒸⒹⒺ
12 ⒶⒷⒸⒹⒺ
13 ⒶⒷⒸⒹⒺ
14 ⒶⒷⒸⒹⒺ
15 ⒶⒷⒸⒹⒺ
16 ⒶⒷⒸⒹⒺ
17 ⒶⒷⒸⒹⒺ
18 ⒶⒷⒸⒹⒺ
19 ⒶⒷⒸⒹⒺ
20 ⒶⒷⒸⒹⒺ
21 ⒶⒷⒸⒹⒺ
22 ⒶⒷⒸⒹⒺ
23 ⒶⒷⒸⒹⒺ
24 ⒶⒷⒸⒹⒺ
25 ⒶⒷⒸⒹⒺ
26 ⒶⒷⒸⒹⒺ
27 ⒶⒷⒸⒹⒺ
28 ⒶⒷⒸⒹⒺ
29 ⒶⒷⒸⒹⒺ
30 ⒶⒷⒸⒹⒺ
31 ⒶⒷⒸⒹⒺ
32 ⒶⒷⒸⒹⒺ
33 ⒶⒷⒸⒹⒺ
34 ⒶⒷⒸⒹⒺ
35 ⒶⒷⒸⒹⒺ
36 ⒶⒷⒸⒹⒺ
37 ⒶⒷⒸⒹⒺ
38 ⒶⒷⒸⒹⒺ
39 ⒶⒷⒸⒹⒺ
40 ⒶⒷⒸⒹⒺ
41 ⒶⒷⒸⒹⒺ
42 ⒶⒷⒸⒹⒺ
43 ⒶⒷⒸⒹⒺ
44 ⒶⒷⒸⒹⒺ
45 ⒶⒷⒸⒹⒺ
46 ⒶⒷⒸⒹⒺ
47 ⒶⒷⒸⒹⒺ
48 ⒶⒷⒸⒹⒺ
49 ⒶⒷⒸⒹⒺ
50 ⒶⒷⒸⒹⒺ
51 ⒶⒷⒸⒹⒺ
52 ⒶⒷⒸⒹⒺ
53 ⒶⒷⒸⒹⒺ
54 ⒶⒷⒸⒹⒺ
55 ⒶⒷⒸⒹⒺ
56 ⒶⒷⒸⒹⒺ
57 ⒶⒷⒸⒹⒺ
58 ⒶⒷⒸⒹⒺ
59 ⒶⒷⒸⒹⒺ
60 ⒶⒷⒸⒹⒺ
61 ⒶⒷⒸⒹⒺ
62 ⒶⒷⒸⒹⒺ
63 ⒶⒷⒸⒹⒺ
64 ⒶⒷⒸⒹⒺ
65 ⒶⒷⒸⒹⒺ
66 ⒶⒷⒸⒹⒺ
67 ⒶⒷⒸⒹⒺ
68 ⒶⒷⒸⒹⒺ
69 ⒶⒷⒸⒹⒺ
70 ⒶⒷⒸⒹⒺ
71 ⒶⒷⒸⒹⒺ
72 ⒶⒷⒸⒹⒺ
73 ⒶⒷⒸⒹⒺ
74 ⒶⒷⒸⒹⒺ
75 ⒶⒷⒸⒹⒺ
76 ⒶⒷⒸⒹⒺ
77 ⒶⒷⒸⒹⒺ
78 ⒶⒷⒸⒹⒺ
79 ⒶⒷⒸⒹⒺ
80 ⒶⒷⒸⒹⒺ
81 ⒶⒷⒸⒹⒺ
82 ⒶⒷⒸⒹⒺ
83 ⒶⒷⒸⒹⒺ
84 ⒶⒷⒸⒹⒺ
85 ⒶⒷⒸⒹⒺ
86 ⒶⒷⒸⒹⒺ
87 ⒶⒷⒸⒹⒺ
88 ⒶⒷⒸⒹⒺ

Part C—Number Series

1 ⒶⒷⒸⒹⒺ
2 ⒶⒷⒸⒹⒺ
3 ⒶⒷⒸⒹⒺ
4 ⒶⒷⒸⒹⒺ
5 ⒶⒷⒸⒹⒺ
6 ⒶⒷⒸⒹⒺ
7 ⒶⒷⒸⒹⒺ
8 ⒶⒷⒸⒹⒺ
9 ⒶⒷⒸⒹⒺ
10 ⒶⒷⒸⒹⒺ
11 ⒶⒷⒸⒹⒺ
12 ⒶⒷⒸⒹⒺ
13 ⒶⒷⒸⒹⒺ
14 ⒶⒷⒸⒹⒺ
15 ⒶⒷⒸⒹⒺ
16 ⒶⒷⒸⒹⒺ
17 ⒶⒷⒸⒹⒺ
18 ⒶⒷⒸⒹⒺ
19 ⒶⒷⒸⒹⒺ
20 ⒶⒷⒸⒹⒺ
21 ⒶⒷⒸⒹⒺ
22 ⒶⒷⒸⒹⒺ
23 ⒶⒷⒸⒹⒺ
24 ⒶⒷⒸⒹⒺ

Part D—Following Oral Directions

1 ⒶⒷⒸⒹⒺ
2 ⒶⒷⒸⒹⒺ
3 ⒶⒷⒸⒹⒺ
4 ⒶⒷⒸⒹⒺ
5 ⒶⒷⒸⒹⒺ
6 ⒶⒷⒸⒹⒺ
7 ⒶⒷⒸⒹⒺ
8 ⒶⒷⒸⒹⒺ
9 ⒶⒷⒸⒹⒺ
10 ⒶⒷⒸⒹⒺ
11 ⒶⒷⒸⒹⒺ
12 ⒶⒷⒸⒹⒺ
13 ⒶⒷⒸⒹⒺ
14 ⒶⒷⒸⒹⒺ
15 ⒶⒷⒸⒹⒺ
16 ⒶⒷⒸⒹⒺ
17 ⒶⒷⒸⒹⒺ
18 ⒶⒷⒸⒹⒺ
19 ⒶⒷⒸⒹⒺ
20 ⒶⒷⒸⒹⒺ
21 ⒶⒷⒸⒹⒺ
22 ⒶⒷⒸⒹⒺ
23 ⒶⒷⒸⒹⒺ
24 ⒶⒷⒸⒹⒺ
25 ⒶⒷⒸⒹⒺ
26 ⒶⒷⒸⒹⒺ
27 ⒶⒷⒸⒹⒺ
28 ⒶⒷⒸⒹⒺ
29 ⒶⒷⒸⒹⒺ
30 ⒶⒷⒸⒹⒺ
31 ⒶⒷⒸⒹⒺ
32 ⒶⒷⒸⒹⒺ
33 ⒶⒷⒸⒹⒺ
34 ⒶⒷⒸⒹⒺ
35 ⒶⒷⒸⒹⒺ
36 ⒶⒷⒸⒹⒺ
37 ⒶⒷⒸⒹⒺ
38 ⒶⒷⒸⒹⒺ
39 ⒶⒷⒸⒹⒺ
40 ⒶⒷⒸⒹⒺ
41 ⒶⒷⒸⒹⒺ
42 ⒶⒷⒸⒹⒺ
43 ⒶⒷⒸⒹⒺ
44 ⒶⒷⒸⒹⒺ
45 ⒶⒷⒸⒹⒺ
46 ⒶⒷⒸⒹⒺ
47 ⒶⒷⒸⒹⒺ
48 ⒶⒷⒸⒹⒺ
49 ⒶⒷⒸⒹⒺ
50 ⒶⒷⒸⒹⒺ
51 ⒶⒷⒸⒹⒺ
52 ⒶⒷⒸⒹⒺ
53 ⒶⒷⒸⒹⒺ
54 ⒶⒷⒸⒹⒺ
55 ⒶⒷⒸⒹⒺ
56 ⒶⒷⒸⒹⒺ
57 ⒶⒷⒸⒹⒺ
58 ⒶⒷⒸⒹⒺ
59 ⒶⒷⒸⒹⒺ
60 ⒶⒷⒸⒹⒺ
61 ⒶⒷⒸⒹⒺ
62 ⒶⒷⒸⒹⒺ
63 ⒶⒷⒸⒹⒺ
64 ⒶⒷⒸⒹⒺ
65 ⒶⒷⒸⒹⒺ
66 ⒶⒷⒸⒹⒺ
67 ⒶⒷⒸⒹⒺ
68 ⒶⒷⒸⒹⒺ
69 ⒶⒷⒸⒹⒺ
70 ⒶⒷⒸⒹⒺ
71 ⒶⒷⒸⒹⒺ
72 ⒶⒷⒸⒹⒺ
73 ⒶⒷⒸⒹⒺ
74 ⒶⒷⒸⒹⒺ
75 ⒶⒷⒸⒹⒺ
76 ⒶⒷⒸⒹⒺ
77 ⒶⒷⒸⒹⒺ
78 ⒶⒷⒸⒹⒺ
79 ⒶⒷⒸⒹⒺ
80 ⒶⒷⒸⒹⒺ
81 ⒶⒷⒸⒹⒺ
82 ⒶⒷⒸⒹⒺ
83 ⒶⒷⒸⒹⒺ
84 ⒶⒷⒸⒹⒺ
85 ⒶⒷⒸⒹⒺ
86 ⒶⒷⒸⒹⒺ
87 ⒶⒷⒸⒹⒺ
88 ⒶⒷⒸⒹⒺ

Chapter 14

Practice Test 6

PART A — ADDRESS CHECKING

Work — 6 minutes

In this part of the test, you are to decide whether two addresses are alike or different. If the two addresses are *exactly alike* in every way, darken space Ⓐ. If they are *different in any way,* darken space Ⓓ.

Mark your answers on the Answer Sheet on page 391. Tear it out, put today's date on it, and place it next to the questions.

Allow yourself *exactly 6 minutes* to do as many of the 95 questions as you can. If you finish before the time is up, check your answers.

1.	1404 Irwin Cir	1404 Irvin Cir
2.	2209 W Sanders Ave	2209 W Sanders Ave
3.	704 E Malden Ave	704 E Malen Ave
4.	Dunstable MA 01827	Dunstable MA 01872
5.	807 Yorkshire Pl W	807 Yorkshire Pl W
6.	23 Fountain Spring Garden	23 Fountain Spring Garden
7.	635 S Quarries Ave	625 S Quarries Ave
8.	Fayetteville AR	Feyetteville AR
9.	7102 Henderson Pl NE	7102 Henderson Pl SE
10.	1107 N Rundell Ct	1107 W Rundell Ct
11.	204 Yates Blvd SE	204 Yates Blvd SE
12.	43 Heebe St	43 Heede St
13.	3840 Alston Ave	3840 Alston Ave
14.	Clermont FL 32711	Clarmont FL 32711
15.	1013 Jemina Ln	1013 Jamina Ln
16.	323 San Solcedo Ct	323 San Solcedo Ct
17.	287 Lytham Ct	287 Lytham Ct
18.	5161 Wayzata Blvd	5161 Wayzata Blvd
19.	8402 Yvonne Terr S	8401 Yvonne Terr S
20.	4162 Kingsborough 1st Walk	4162 Kingsborough 1st Walk
21.	2093 Urish Ln	2093 Irish Ln
22.	5604 N Bristowood Blvd	5604 N Bristolwood Blvd
23.	Kooskie ID 83539	Koskie IA 83539
24.	367 E Southern Blvd	367 E Southern Blvd

25.	101 Oak Leaf Trl	101 Oak Leaf Ter
26.	899 Upchurch Ter	899 Upchurch Ter
27.	9986 Timson Ct	9986 Timson Ct
28.	7071 Bensley Ave	7107 Bentley Ave
29.	1502 N Alcam Dr	1502 N Alcam Dr
30.	42 W Timbercove Ave	42 W Timbercove Ave
31.	Haleuva HI	Haleuva MI
32.	305 Foster Island Rd	305 Foster Island Rd
33.	567 Ulloa St NE	567 Ulloa Ave NE
34.	309 Prentice Ct E	309 Prentiss Ct E
35.	Hokes Bluff AL 39503	Hokes Bluff Al 39503
36.	5007 Urbana Path SE	5070 Urbana Path SE
37.	422 Montgomery Paper Mill St	422 Montgomery Paper Mill St
38.	200 Repondo Cir	200 Repondo Cir
39.	2002 N Kendall Rd	2002 N Kendall Rd
40.	12 Havasu Cir	12 Havasu Cir
41.	6820 Goley St SE	6820 Golly St SE
42.	10123 Ave N SW	10123 Ave N SW
43.	741 Zorich Dr NW	741 Zurich Dr NW
44.	4409 Lyman Pl W	4409 Lyman Pl W
45.	647 Rensu Dr	746 Rensu Dr
46.	902 E Olalie Cir	902 E Olalie Cir
47.	Bajadero PR 00616	Bajadero PR 00616
48.	Zwolle LA 71486	Swolle AL 71486
49.	7830 Sandhurst Ave	7830 Sandhurst Ave
50.	538 W Warrendale Rd	538 W Warendell Rd
51.	2 Olde Cape St E	2 Olde Cape St S
52.	972 Reedy Creek Ct	972 Reedy Creek Ct
53.	8749 Yeoman Ter	8749 Yeoman Ter
54.	3660 Alamedo Blvd S	3660 Alamedo Blvd S
55.	1326 Val De Via	1236 Val De Via
56.	Plummerville AR 72127	Plummetville AR 72127
57.	5166 Vreeland Ave	5166 Freeland Ave
58.	473 E Dawnview Way	473 W Dawnview Way
59.	Brevard NC	Brevard SC
60.	9604 W Unionport Rd	9604 W Unionport Dr

61.	15 Sue Ellen Snyder Dr	15 Sue Ellen Snyder Dr
62.	Everson WA	Everson WA
63.	893 32nd Pl NW	893 32nd Pl NW
64.	2634 SE Olney St	2634 SE Olney Ct
65.	125 Winding Valley Way Rd	125 Winding Valley Way Rd
66.	4002 Heatherhill Ave	4002 Heatherhill Ave
67.	704 2nd Ave	740 2nd Ave
68.	831 Lake Nokomis Pkwy	831 Lake Nokomis Path
69.	3128 Six Gables Rd	3123 Six Gables Rd
70.	4501 N 1st Ave	4501 S 1st Ave
71.	1400 Nandina Rd N	1400 Nandina St S
72.	4981 E Interstate 10	4981 E Interstate 10
73.	Paerdegat 7 St SW	Paerdegat 9 St SW
74.	51 Landov Way SW	51 Landov Way SW
75.	903 S La Playa St	903 S La Playa St
76.	Isabella MN 56607	Isabella MN 56607
77.	15 S Elbridge Dr	15 E Elbridge Dr
78.	3079 Davista Blvd	307 Davista Blvd
79.	Tiverton RI	Tiverton RI
80.	8256 Knolls Cres	8256 Knolls Cres
81.	3600 S Iva Ct	3600 S Ivy Ct
82.	Sioux City IA 50585	Sioux City IA 50585
83.	6464 SW Terrace Ln	6464 SW Terrace Ln
84.	809 Forestdale Rd	809 Fosterdale Rd
85.	971 New Napa Valley Plz	971 New Napa Valley Pkwy
86.	6734 Kerlerec St NW	6734 Kerlerec St NW
87.	790 Valley Belt Rd	790 Valley Belt Rd
88.	405 Palm Cir W	405 Palm Cir W
89.	412 Laclede Rd	412 Lacledo Rd
90.	5396 Inverness Ave	5396 Inverness Ave
91.	91 Fairhaven Pl	91 Fairhaven Pl
92.	1102 Campos Ct	1102 Campose Ct
93.	946 Axe Handle Dr	946 Axe Handle Dr
94.	639 Worchester Pl	639 Westchester Pl
95.	6918 Ridgemont Blvd	6918 Ridgemont Blvd

STOP.

If you finish before the time is up, go back and check the questions in this section of the test only.

Part B — MEMORY FOR ADDRESSES

In this part of the test, you will have five boxes labeled A, B, C, D, and E. Each box contains five addresses. Three of the five are groups of street addresses, such as 2000–2399 Drummond, 3900–4899 Landis, and 1300–1999 Marble; and two are names of places. The addresses are different in each box.

There will be several opportunities to study the addresses and the boxes they are in. You will also be given three tests of 88 questions each, and the task of deciding where each address belongs. In some cases, you will have the list *and* the boxes in front of you at the same time; in others you will not. List 1 and List 2 are for warm-up practice. List 3 is the real one that will be scored.

Make sure you understand the format by examining the pretest samples below.

Pretest Samples

A	B	C	D	E
2400–3199 Drummond	3200–3899 Drummond	3900–4699 Drummond	1300–1999 Drummond	2000–2399 Drummond
Green	Ocala	Fox	Union	Ritchie
3900–4399 Marble	2400–3199 Marble	3200–3899 Marble	2000–2399 Marble	1300–1999 Marble
Peale	Abbey	Marlboro	Presley	St. Peter
1300–1999 Landis	3200–3899 Landis	2000–2399 Landis	3900–4899 Landis	2400–3199 Landis

Questions 1 through 7 show the way the questions look. You have to decide in which lettered box (A, B, C, D, or E) the address belongs and then mark your answer by darkening the appropriate space in the answer grid.

1. Fox — 1 Ⓐ Ⓑ Ⓒ Ⓓ Ⓔ
2. 3200–3899 Marble — 2 Ⓐ Ⓑ Ⓒ Ⓓ Ⓔ
3. 2400–3199 Landis — 3 Ⓐ Ⓑ Ⓒ Ⓓ Ⓔ
4. Union — 4 Ⓐ Ⓑ Ⓒ Ⓓ Ⓔ
5. Ocala — 5 Ⓐ Ⓑ Ⓒ Ⓓ Ⓔ
6. 1300–1999 Drummond — 6 Ⓐ Ⓑ Ⓒ Ⓓ Ⓔ
7. St. Peter — 7 Ⓐ Ⓑ Ⓒ Ⓓ Ⓔ

Answers

1. **C** 2. **C** 3. **E** 4. **D** 5. **B** 6. **D** 7. **E**

Now that you know what to do, you may begin Part B of Practice Test 6. To get the most out of this test, follow the directions and timing *exactly*. Follow each phase of Part B of this test, page by page, until you've completed List 3. It is modeled on the way the Postal Service actually conducts its tests.

Turn to the next page to begin.

Study — 3 minutes

You will be given 3 minutes to spend memorizing the addresses in the boxes. *They are exactly the same ones that will be used for all three tests.* Try to memorize as many as you can. When the 3 minutes are up, turn to page 400 and read the instructions for *List 1*.

A	B	C	D	E
2400–3199 Drummond	3200–3899 Drummond	3900–4699 Drummond	1300–1999 Drummond	2000–2399 Drummond
Green	Ocala	Fox	Union	Ritchie
3900–4399 Marble	2400–3199 Marble	3200–3899 Marble	2000–2399 Marble	1300–1999 Marble
Peale	Abbey	Marlboro	Presley	St. Peter
1300–1999 Landis	3200–3899 Landis	2000–2399 Landis	3900–4899 Landis	2400–3199 Landis

List 1

Work — 3 minutes

Tear out the Answer Sheet for List 1. For each question, mark the answer sheet on page 392 to show the letter of the box in which the address belongs. Try to remember the locations of as many addresses as you can. *You will now have 3 minutes to complete List 1.* If you are not sure of an answer, you should guess.

A	B	C	D	E
2400–3199 Drummond	3200–3899 Drummond	3900–4699 Drummond	1300–1999 Drummond	2000–2399 Drummond
Green	Ocala	Fox	Union	Ritchie
3900–4399 Marble	2400–3199 Marble	3200–3899 Marble	2000–2399 Marble	1300–1999 Marble
Peale	Abbey	Marlboro	Presley	St. Peter
1300–1999 Landis	3200–3899 Landis	2000–2399 Landis	3900–4899 Landis	2400–3199 Landis

1. Ocala
2. Marlboro
3. 3900–4899 Landis
4. 2000–2399 Drummond
5. Presley
6. 3900–4699 Drummond
7. 2400–3199 Landis
8. Abbey
9. 1300–1999 Marble
10. Ritchie
11. 2000–2399 Drummond
12. Fox
13. 1300–1999 Landis
14. 2400–3199 Drummond
15. Peale
16. 2000–2399 Landis
17. Ritchie
18. 3200–3899 Landis
19. 1300–1999 Marble
20. 2000–2399 Marble
21. 2400–3199 Marble
22. Union
23. Green
24. 2400–3199 Landis
25. 3900–4399 Marble
26. 3200–3899 Drummond
27. 1300–1999 Drummond
28. St. Peter
29. 3200–3899 Marble
30. St. Peter
31. Presley
32. Abbey
33. 2400–3199 Marble
34. 2000–2399 Marble
35. Peale
36. 3900–4699 Drummond
37. Union
38. Peale
39. 3200–3899 Drummond
40. 3900–4899 Landis
41. 2000–2399 Landis
42. Union
43. 2000–2399 Drummond
44. Green

45. 2400–3199 Drummond
46. Union
47. 1300–1999 Landis
48. 1300–1999 Marble
49. 3900–4899 Landis
50. Marlboro
51. Peale
52. Ocala
53. Ritchie
54. 1300–1999 Drummond
55. 2000–2399 Landis
56. Marlboro
57. 2000–2399 Marble
58. Green
59. 2400–3199 Landis
60. Fox
61. 1300–1999 Drummond
62. Ritchie
63. St. Peter
64. 1300–1999 Landis
65. 3200–3899 Landis
66. Presley
67. 3200–3899 Drummond
68. 3900–4399 Marble
69. Presley
70. Fox
71. Abbey
72. 2400–3199 Drummond
73. Fox
74. Marlboro
75. Ocala
76. 2400–3199 Marble
77. 3900–4399 Marble
78. St. Peter
79. 3900–4699 Drummond
80. 3200–3899 Marble
81. Green
82. 2400–3199 Landis
83. 3200–3899 Drummond
84. Abbey
85. 3200–3899 Marble
86. Ocala
87. Green
88. 3200–3899 Landis

STOP.
If you finish before the time is up, go back and check the questions in this section of the test only.

List 2

Work — 3 minutes

Do these questions *without* looking back at the boxes. For each question, mark your answer on the Answer Sheet for List 2 on page 392. If you are not sure of an answer, you should guess.

1. Presley
2. Fox
3. 3200–3899 Drummond
4. 2400–3199 Marble
5. 2000–2399 Marble
6. 1300–1999 Drummond
7. Green
8. Fox
9. 3900–4699 Drummond
10. Peale
11. 3200–3899 Landis
12. Ocala
13. 2400–3199 Marble
14. 1300–1999 Landis
15. 3900–4699 Drummond
16. 2000–2399 Drummond
17. Marlboro
18. Presley
19. 2400–3199 Drummond
20. St. Peter
21. Presley
22. Abbey
23. 2000–2399 Drummond
24. 2400–3199 Drummond
25. Marlboro
26. 2400–3199 Marble
27. St. Peter
28. Green
29. 3900–4899 Landis
30. 3200–3899 Marble
31. Fox
32. 3900–4399 Marble
33. 3200–3899 Marble
34. 2000–2399 Landis
35. 3200–3899 Landis
36. 1300–1999 Drummond
37. 2400–3199 Landis
38. Union
39. 3200–3899 Drummond
40. Peale
41. Ritchie
42. Green
43. 1300–1999 Marble
44. Ocala

45. 2000–2399 Marble
46. Marlboro
47. 3200–3899 Drummond
48. St. Peter
49. 3200–3899 Marble
50. Ocala
51. 2000–2399 Landis
52. 3200–3899 Landis
53. Union
54. Abbey
55. 2000–2399 Marble
56. 3900–4399 Marble
57. Ritchie
58. 3900–4899 Landis
59. Ritchie
60. Fox
61. Green
62. 2400–3199 Drummond
63. Marlboro
64. Abbey
65. Union
66. 2400–3199 Landis
67. Presley
68. 3900–4899 Landis
69. 2400–3199 Drummond
70. Ocala
71. 3900–4699 Drummond
72. 1300–1999 Drummond
73. 1300–1999 Landis
74. Abbey
75. 1300–1999 Landis
76. 1300–1999 Marble
77. Union
78. Peale
79. Ritchie
80. 2000–2399 Landis
81. 3900–4399 Marble
82. 3200–3899 Drummond
83. 2400–3199 Landis
84. 2000–2399 Drummond
85. Green
86. 1300–1999 Marble
87. 2400–3199 Landis
88. St. Peter

STOP.

If you finish before the time is up, go back and check the questions in this section of the test only.

List 3

Study — 5 minutes

You are now about to take the test using List 3. *(This is the test that counts!)*

Turn back to page 400 and study the boxes again. *You have 5 minutes to restudy the addresses.*

Work — 5 minutes

For each question, mark the Answer Sheet on page 393 to show the letter of the box in which the address belongs. You have exactly 5 minutes to do the test. During these 5 minutes, *do not* turn to any other page.

1. Ocala
2. 1300–1999 Marble
3. Green
4. Ritchie
5. Peale
6. 3200–3899 Drummond
7. Union
8. 2400–3199 Landis
9. 1300–1999 Drummond
10. 3200–3899 Landis
11. 2000–2399 Landis
12. 3200–3899 Marble
13. 3900–4399 Marble
14. Fox
15. Presley
16. 3900–4899 Landis
17. Green
18. St. Peter
19. 2400–3199 Marble
20. Marlboro
21. 2400–3199 Drummond
22. 2000–2399 Drummond
23. Abbey
24. Presley
25. St. Peter
26. 2400–3199 Drummond
27. Presley
28. Marlboro
29. 2000–2399 Drummond
30. 3900–4699 Drummond
31. 1300–1999 Landis
32. 2400–3199 Marble
33. Ocala
34. 3200–3899 Landis
35. Peale
36. 3900–4699 Drummond
37. Fox
38. Green
39. 1300–1999 Drummond
40. 2000–2399 Marble
41. 2400–3199 Marble
42. 3200–3899 Drummond
43. Fox
44. Presley

45. St. Peter
46. 2400–3199 Landis
47. 1300–1999 Marble
48. Green
49. 2000–2399 Drummond
50. 2400–3199 Landis
51. 3200–3899 Drummond
52. 3900–4399 Marble
53. 2000–2399 Landis
54. Ritchie
55. Peale
56. Union
57. 1300–1999 Marble
58. 1300–1999 Landis
59. Abbey
60. 1300–1999 Landis
61. 1300–1999 Drummond
62. 3900–4699 Drummond
63. Ocala
64. 2400–3199 Drummond
65. 3900–4899 Landis
66. Presley
67. 2400–3199 Landis
68. Union
69. Abbey
70. Marlboro
71. Peale
72. Green
73. Fox
74. Ritchie
75. 3900–4899 Landis
76. Ritchie
77. 3900–4399 Marble
78. 2000–2399 Marble
79. Abbey
80. Union
81. 3200–3899 Landis
82. 2000–2399 Landis
83. Ocala
84. 3200–3899 Marble
85. St. Peter
86. 3200–3899 Drummond
87. Marlboro
88. 2000–2399 Marble

STOP.
If you finish before the time is up, go back and check the questions in this section of the test only.

PART C — NUMBER SERIES

Work — 20 minutes

For each Number Series question, there is a series of numbers that follow some definite order, and below each are five sets of two numbers each. You are to look at the numbers in the series and find out what order they follow. Then decide what the next two numbers in that series would be if the same order were continued. Mark your answers on the Answer Sheet for Number Series on page 393.

You have 20 minutes to complete this part of the test. If you finish before the time is up, check your answers. The answers and explanations are on pages 415 to 417.

1. 61 53 45 37 29 21 __ __
   A) 14 7 B) 13 5 C) 15 4 D) 13 7

2. 26 24 24 22 22 20 20 __ __
   A) 20 18 B) 18 20 C) 18 18 D) 16 18

3. 17 24 21 29 36 33 41 __ __
   A) 48 56 B) 45 48 C) 41 42 D) 48 45

4. 17 16 14 15 14 14 13 12 __ __
   A) 11 14 B) 13 14 C) 14 11 D) 11 10

5. 6 1 8 8 3 10 10 5 __ __
   A) 12 10 B) 12 8 C) 12 12 D) 5 12

6. 64 52 41 31 22 __ __
   A) 14 7 B) 14 8 C) 15 8 D) 15 7

7. 5 18 10 16 15 14 20 __ __
   A) 25 16 B) 12 25 C) 25 30 D) 25 13

8. 31 35 35 38 38 42 42 45 __ __
   A) 43 46 B) 44 45 C) 45 46 D) 45 49

9. 4 12 6 18 12 36 __ __
   A) 16 40 B) 24 42 C) 36 48 D) 30 90

10. 15 18 18 10 15 18 18 10 15 __ __
    A) 18 18 B) 15 15 C) 18 10 D) 15 18

11. 8 10 12 9 11 13 10 12 14 __ __
    A) 11 13 B) 15 16 C) 12 13 D) 15 12

12. 18 16 6 7 14 12 6 7 10 __ __
    A) 6 12 B) 8 9 C) 13 9 D) 8 6

13. 1 4 8 7 10 20 19 __ __
    A) 18 20 B) 28 22 C) 38 37 D) 22 44

14. 41 14 12 21 19 91 __ __
    A) 23 25 B) 100 25 C) 27 73 D) 89 98

15. 36 37 39 44 51 __ __
    A) 59 68 B) 58 67 C) 60 71 D) 61 74

16. 27 15 25 19 23 23 __ __
    A) 27 27 B) 27 29 C) 21 25 D) 21 27

17. 36 13 17 35 21 25 34 29 __ __
    A) 28 32 B) 35 30 C) 33 37 D) 33 33

18. 26 21 17 23 21 18 20 21 19 __ __
    A) 16 22 B) 21 22 C) 17 21 D) 17 23

19. 16 17 18 20 16 17 18 20 16 17 __ __
    A) 18 19 B) 17 18 C) 20 18 D) 18 20

20. 3 5 8 13 21 34 __ __
    A) 48 56 B) 55 89 C) 47 48 D) 57 91

21. 2 6 4 12 8 19 16 27 __ __
    A) 24 25 B) 36 32 C) 54 37 D) 32 36

22. 2 4 8 2 5 10 2 6 12 2 __ __
    A) 5 8 B) 6 12 C) 7 14 D) 3 14

23. 144 84 72 82 36 80 18 __ __
    A) 78 9 B) 16 40 C) 40 9 D) 38 9

24. 10 15 11 14 12 13 13 __ __
    A) 12 14 B) 14 16 C) 14 12 D) 13 15

STOP.

If you finish before the time is up, go back and check the questions in this section of the test only.

PART D — FOLLOWING ORAL DIRECTIONS

This part of the test gauges your ability to understand and carry out spoken directions *exactly* as they are given to you.

In order to prepare to take Part D of the test, follow the steps below:

1. Enlist the help of a friend who will be the "reader." It will be his or her job to read aloud a series of directions that you are to follow *exactly*. The reader will need a watch that displays seconds, because the directions must be read at the correct speed.
2. Tear out pages 413 and 414. These are the worksheets you should have in front of you as you listen to the directions given by the reader, who will tell you to do certain things with the items on each line on the worksheets.
3. Use the Answer Sheet for Following Oral Directions on page 393 and insert today's date. You will darken the appropriate spaces in accordance with the directions given by the reader.
4. *Now hand this entire book to the reader.* Ask him/her to review the section below headed "Instructions to the Reader." It explains exactly how the reader is to proceed.

When you and the reader are ready to start this part of Practice Test 1, he/she will begin reading to you the section marked "Directions." YOU ARE NOT TO READ THESE AT ANY TIME BEFORE OR DURING THE TEST. If you do, you will lose the benefit of this part of the practice test.

Instructions to the "Reader"

These instructions should be read at about 80 words per minute. You should practice reading the material in the box until you can do it in exactly 1 minute. This will give you a feel for the way you should read the test material.

1-MINUTE PRACTICE

Look at line 20 on your worksheet. There are two circles and two boxes of different sizes with numbers in them. If 7 is less than 3 and if 2 is smaller than 4, write C in the larger circle. Otherwise write B as in *baker* in the smaller box. Now, on your answer sheet, darken the space for the number-letter combination in the box or circle.

You should read the entire test aloud before you read it to the person taking the test, in order to acquaint yourself with the procedure and the desired rate of reading.

Read slowly but at a natural pace. In other words, do not space the words so that there are unnaturally long pauses between them. The instruction "Pause slightly" indicates only enough time to take a breath. The other instructions for pauses give the recommended length for each. If possible, use a watch with a second hand.

All the material that follows, except the words in parentheses, is to be read aloud. Now start reading the directions. *Do not repeat any of the directions.*

Directions: In this test, I will read instructions to you.

You are to mark your worksheets according to the instructions that I read to you. After each set of instructions, I'll give you time to record your answers on your answer sheet.

Try to understand the instructions as I read them; I cannot repeat them. Do not ask any questions from now on.

If, when you go to darken a space for a number, you find that you have already darkened another space for that number, either (1) erase the first mark and darken the space for your new choice, or (2) let the first mark stay and do not darken any other space. When you finish, you should have no more than one space darkened for each number.

Turn to Worksheet 1.

Look at the five boxes in line 1 on your worksheet. (Pause slightly.) Write the number 10 on the line in the middle box. (Pause 2 seconds.) Now, on your answer sheet, darken the space for the number-letter combination that is in the box you just wrote in. (Pause 5 seconds.)

Look at line 2 on your worksheet. (Pause slightly.) Draw a line under the smallest number in the line. (Pause 2 seconds.) Now, on your answer sheet, find the number you just drew a line under, and darken space B as in *baker.* (Pause 5 seconds.)

Look at line 2 again. (Pause slightly.) Draw a line under the highest number in the line. (Pause 2 seconds.) Now, on your answer sheet, find the number you just drew a line under and darken space A. (Pause 5 seconds.)

Look at the numbers in the circles in line 3 on your worksheet. (Pause slightly.) Write the letter C in each circle that has an *odd* number in it. (Pause 10 seconds.) Now, on your answer sheet, darken the spaces for the number-letter combinations that are in the circles you just wrote in. (Pause 25 seconds.)

Look at the letters in line 4 on your worksheet. (Pause slightly.) Draw a circle around the fifth letter in the line. (Pause 2 seconds.) Now, on your answer sheet, find the number 14 and darken the space for the letter around which you drew a circle. (Pause 5 seconds.)

Look at line 5 on your worksheet. (Pause slightly.) In each circle there is a time when a delivery is made. In the circle for the latest time, write on the line the last two figures of the time. (Pause 5 seconds.) Now, on your answer sheet, darken the space for the number-letter combination that is in the box you just wrote in. (Pause 5 seconds.)

Look at line 6 on your worksheet. (Pause slightly.) Draw a line under every number that is more than 45 but less than 55. (Pause 12 seconds.) Now, on your answer sheet, for every number that you drew a line under, darken space A. (Pause 25 seconds.)

Look at line 7 on your worksheet. (Pause slightly.) Draw a line under every "O" on the line. (Pause 5 seconds.) Count the number of lines you have drawn, add 6, and write that number at the end of the line. (Pause 8 seconds.) Now, on your answer sheet, find that number and darken space E. (Pause 5 seconds.)

Look at line 8 on your worksheet. (Pause slightly.) There are three words and three boxes on the line. (Pause slightly.) Write the second letter of the first word in the third box. (Pause 2 seconds.) Write the fourth letter of the second word in the first box. (Pause 2 seconds.) Write the first letter of the third word in the second box. (Pause 2 seconds.) Now, on your answer sheet, darken the spaces for the number-letter combinations that are in the boxes you just wrote in. (Pause 25 seconds.)

Look at line 9 on your worksheet. (Pause slightly.) Mail for Evans and Quincy is to be put in box 31. (Pause slightly.) Mail for Miller and Bolton is to be put in box 68. (Pause slightly.) Write A in the box in which you put mail for Evans. (Pause 2 seconds.) Now, on your answer sheet, darken the space for the number-letter combination that is in the box you just wrote in. (Pause 5 seconds.)

Look at line 10 on your worksheet. (Pause slightly.) On the line next to the left-hand letter, write the answer to this question: How many seconds are there in a minute? (Pause 2 seconds.) Now, on your answer sheet, darken the space for the number-letter combination you have just written. (Pause 5 seconds.)

Now turn to Worksheet 2. (Pause 5 seconds.)

Look at line 11 on your worksheet. (Pause slightly.) If the number in the larger box is smaller than the number in the smaller circle, write B as in *baker* in the large circle. (Pause 2 seconds.) Otherwise, write A in the smaller box. (Pause 2 seconds.) Now, on your answer sheet, darken the space for the number-letter combination you just wrote. (Pause 5 seconds.)

Look at line 12 on your worksheet. (Pause slightly.) There are five boxes. Each box has a letter in it. In the center box write the answer to this question: Which of the following numbers is the lowest: 27, 23, 72, 21, 30? (Pause 2 seconds.) Now, on your answer sheet, darken the space for the number-letter combination that is in the box you just wrote in. (Pause 5 seconds.) In the last box, do nothing. In the first box, write the answer to this question: How many seasons are there in a year? (Pause 2 seconds.) Now, on your answer sheet, darken the space for the number-letter combination you just wrote. (Pause 5 seconds.)

Look at the figures on line 13 on your worksheet. (Pause slightly.) In every figure that has more than five sides write the letter B as in *baker* on the line in that figure. (Pause 5 seconds). Now, on your answer sheet, darken the spaces for the number-letter combinations that are in the figures you just wrote in. (Pause 10 seconds.)

Look at line 13 again. (Pause slightly.) Count up the total number of sides that make up the first three figures, add 10, and write that number at the end of the line of boxes. (Pause 10 seconds.) Now, on your answer sheet, find the number you just wrote and darken space C. (Pause 5 seconds.)

Look at the numbers on line 14 on your worksheet. (Pause slightly.) Draw a line under the even numbers in the line. (Pause 5 seconds.) Now, on your answer sheet, darken space D as in *dog* for each number under which you drew a line. (Pause 2 seconds.)

Look at line 15 on your worksheet. (Pause slightly.) If, in a year, March comes after September, write the number 13 on the line next to the first letter. (Pause 2 seconds.) If it does not, write 30 on the line next to the last letter. (Pause 2 seconds.) Now, on your answer sheet, find the number you just wrote and darken the space for the letter next to which you wrote it. (Pause 5 seconds.)

Look at line 16 on your worksheet. (Pause slightly.) There are a number and a letter in each of four boxes. There is also a circle with 2 lines inside it. Select the smaller of the two numbers that are in the large boxes and write it on one of the lines inside the circle. (Pause 2 seconds.) Now, select the one of the letters in the small boxes that comes second in the alphabet and write it next to the number you have already written on the line in the circle. (Pause 2 seconds.) Now, on your answer sheet, darken the space for the number-letter combination in the circle. (Pause 5 seconds.)

Look at line 17 on your worksheet. (Pause slightly.) If the number in the right-hand circle is larger than the number in the left-hand box, add 2 to the number in the left-hand box and change the original number to this new number. (Pause 6 seconds.) Then write E next to this new number. (Pause 2 seconds.) Otherwise, write A next to the number in the left-hand circle. (Pause 2 seconds.) Now, on your answer sheet, darken the space for the number-letter combination in the box or circle you just wrote in. (Pause 5 seconds.)

Look at line 18 on your worksheet. (Pause slightly.) Count the number of letters, subtract 5, and enter the result on the first line on the right. Now, on your answer sheet, find that number and darken space C for that number. (Pause 5 seconds.)

Look at line 18 again. (Pause slightly.) Count the number of times the letter B as in *baker* appears, divide by 3, and enter the result on the second line at the right. Now, on your answer sheet, find that number and darken space A. (Pause 5 seconds.)

Look at line 19 on your worksheet. (Pause slightly.) If 8 is greater than 5 and 7 is less than 6, write the number 67 in the last box. (Pause 2 seconds.) Otherwise, write the number 80 in the middle box. (Pause 2 seconds.) Now, on your answer sheet darken the space for the number-letter combination you just wrote. (Pause 5 seconds.)

END OF EXAMINATION.
If you finish before the time is up, go back and check the questions in this section of the test only.

Practice Test 6—Worksheet 1

Part D–Following Oral Directions

1. C ___ | A ___ | D ___ | E ___ | B ___

2. 16 17 19 15 12 14

3. 10 ___ | 77 ___ | 24 ___ | 39 ___ | 18 ___

4. C D A B E D B C

5. 11:14 ___ E | 11:32 ___ A | 11:57 ___ C | 11:46 ___ D | 11:55 ___ B

6. 38 45 50 58 42 29 53 42

7. X O O O X X X X O X O

8. LEAD RICE BLUE | 41 ___ | 63 ___ | 24 ___

9. 31 EVANS QUINCY ___ | 68 MILLER BOLTON ___

10. ___ E ___ A

✂ Remove by cutting on dotted line.

Practice Test 6—Worksheet 2

Part D—Following Oral Directions

11.

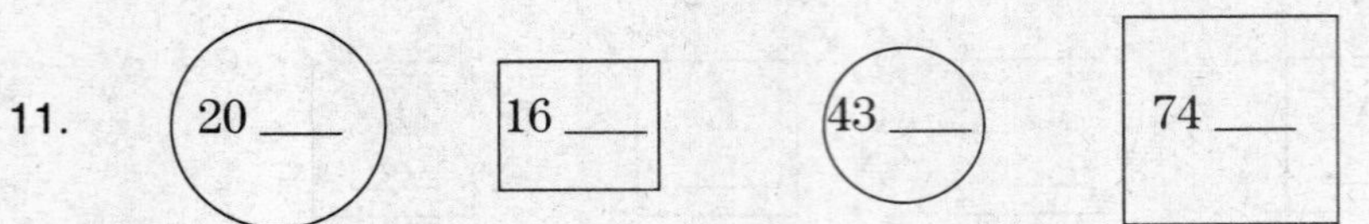

12. ___ D ___ B ___ A ___ E ___ C

13.

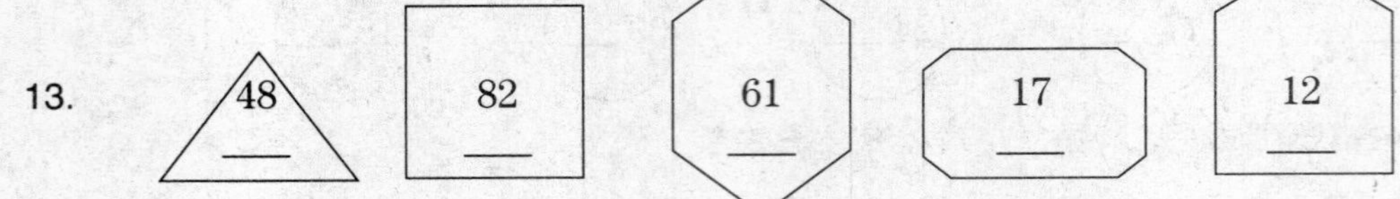

14. 29 32 41 54 68 77

15. ___ D ___ A ___ C

16. 3A 9C ___ ___ 6D 16B

17. 35 ___ 67 ___ 84 ___ 58 ___

18. B A B D A E C B ___ ___

19. ___ C ___ A ___ D

ANSWER KEY

Part A—Address Checking

1. **D**	11. **A**	21. **D**	31. **D**	41. **D**	51. **D**	61. **A**	71. **D**	81. **D**	91. **A**
2. **A**	12. **D**	22. **D**	32. **A**	42. **A**	52. **A**	62. **A**	72. **A**	82. **A**	92. **D**
3. **D**	13. **A**	23. **D**	33. **D**	43. **D**	53. **A**	63. **A**	73. **D**	83. **A**	93. **A**
4. **D**	14. **D**	24. **A**	34. **D**	44. **A**	54. **A**	64. **D**	74. **A**	84. **D**	94. **D**
5. **A**	15. **D**	25. **D**	35. **A**	45. **D**	55. **D**	65. **A**	75. **A**	85. **D**	95. **A**
6. **A**	16. **A**	26. **A**	36. **D**	46. **A**	56. **D**	66. **A**	76. **A**	86. **A**	
7. **D**	17. **A**	27. **A**	37. **A**	47. **A**	57. **D**	67. **D**	77. **D**	87. **A**	
8. **D**	18. **A**	28. **D**	38. **A**	48. **D**	58. **D**	68. **D**	78. **D**	88. **A**	
9. **D**	19. **D**	29. **A**	39. **A**	49. **A**	59. **D**	69. **D**	79. **A**	89. **D**	
10. **D**	20. **A**	30. **A**	40. **A**	50. **D**	60. **D**	70. **D**	80. **A**	90. **A**	

Part B—Memory for Addresses

List 1

1. **B**	10. **E**	19. **E**	28. **E**	37. **D**	46. **D**	55. **E**	64. **A**	73. **C**	82. **E**
2. **C**	11. **E**	20. **D**	29. **C**	38. **A**	47. **A**	56. **C**	65. **B**	74. **C**	83. **B**
3. **D**	12. **C**	21. **B**	30. **E**	39. **B**	48. **E**	57. **D**	66. **D**	75. **B**	84. **B**
4. **E**	13. **A**	22. **D**	31. **D**	40. **D**	49. **D**	58. **A**	67. **B**	76. **B**	85. **C**
5. **D**	14. **A**	23. **A**	32. **B**	41. **C**	50. **C**	59. **E**	68. **A**	77. **A**	86. **B**
6. **C**	15. **A**	24. **E**	33. **B**	42. **D**	51. **A**	60. **C**	69. **D**	78. **E**	87. **A**
7. **E**	16. **C**	25. **A**	34. **D**	43. **E**	52. **B**	61. **D**	70. **C**	79. **C**	88. **B**
8. **B**	17. **E**	26. **B**	35. **A**	44. **A**	53. **E**	62. **E**	71. **B**	80. **C**	
9. **E**	18. **B**	27. **D**	36. **C**	45. **A**	54. **D**	63. **E**	72. **A**	81. **A**	

List 2

1. **D**	10. **A**	19. **A**	28. **A**	37. **E**	46. **C**	55. **D**	64. **B**	73. **A**	82. **B**
2. **C**	11. **B**	20. **E**	29. **D**	38. **D**	47. **B**	56. **A**	65. **D**	74. **B**	83. **E**
3. **B**	12. **B**	21. **D**	30. **C**	39. **B**	48. **E**	57. **E**	66. **E**	75. **A**	84. **E**
4. **B**	13. **B**	22. **B**	31. **C**	40. **A**	49. **C**	58. **D**	67. **D**	76. **E**	85. **A**
5. **D**	14. **A**	23. **E**	32. **A**	41. **E**	50. **B**	59. **E**	68. **D**	77. **D**	86. **E**
6. **D**	15. **C**	24. **A**	33. **C**	42. **A**	51. **C**	60. **C**	69. **A**	78. **A**	87. **E**
7. **A**	16. **E**	25. **C**	34. **C**	43. **E**	52. **B**	61. **A**	70. **B**	79. **E**	88. **E**
8. **C**	17. **C**	26. **B**	35. **B**	44. **B**	53. **D**	62. **A**	71. **C**	80. **C**	
9. **C**	18. **D**	27. **E**	36. **D**	45. **D**	54. **B**	63. **C**	72. **D**	81. **A**	

List 3

1. **B**	10. **B**	19. **B**	28. **C**	37. **C**	46. **E**	55. **A**	64. **A**	73. **C**	82. **C**
2. **E**	11. **C**	20. **C**	29. **E**	38. **A**	47. **E**	56. **D**	65. **D**	74. **E**	83. **B**
3. **A**	12. **C**	21. **A**	30. **C**	39. **D**	48. **A**	57. **E**	66. **D**	75. **D**	84. **C**
4. **E**	13. **A**	22. **E**	31. **A**	40. **D**	49. **E**	58. **A**	67. **E**	76. **E**	85. **E**
5. **A**	14. **C**	23. **B**	32. **B**	41. **B**	50. **E**	59. **B**	68. **D**	77. **A**	86. **B**
6. **B**	15. **D**	24. **D**	33. **B**	42. **B**	51. **B**	60. **A**	69. **B**	78. **D**	87. **C**
7. **D**	16. **D**	25. **E**	34. **B**	43. **C**	52. **A**	61. **D**	70. **C**	79. **B**	88. **D**
8. **E**	17. **A**	26. **A**	35. **A**	44. **D**	53. **C**	62. **C**	71. **A**	80. **D**	
9. **D**	18. **E**	27. **D**	36. **C**	45. **E**	54. **E**	63. **B**	72. **A**	81. **B**	

Part C—Number Series

1. **B**	4. **C**	7. **B**	10. **A**	13. **D**	16. **D**	19. **D**	22. **C**
2. **C**	5. **C**	8. **D**	11. **A**	14. **D**	17. **D**	20. **B**	23. **A**
3. **D**	6. **A**	9. **D**	12. **D**	15. **C**	18. **C**	21. **D**	24. **A**

Part D—Following Oral Directions

1. **A**	6. **B**	12. **B**	17. **B**	23. **C**	31. **A**	39. **C**	53. **A**	60. **E**	68. **D**
3. **C**	10. **D**	14. **E**	19. **A**	24. **E**	32. **D**	41. **E**	54. **D**	61. **B**	77. **C**
4. **D**	11. **E**	16. **A**	21. **A**	30. **C**	37. **E**	50. **A**	57. **C**	63. **B**	80. **A**

ANSWER EXPLANATIONS FOR PART C—NUMBER SERIES

1. **B** Each number in this series descends by 8.
2. **C** This series follows a – 2 rule, with each new number being repeated once.
3. **D** A complex rule: + 7, – 3, + 8 determines the order of numbers.
4. **C** A loop diagram is useful in illustrating the rule governing this series:

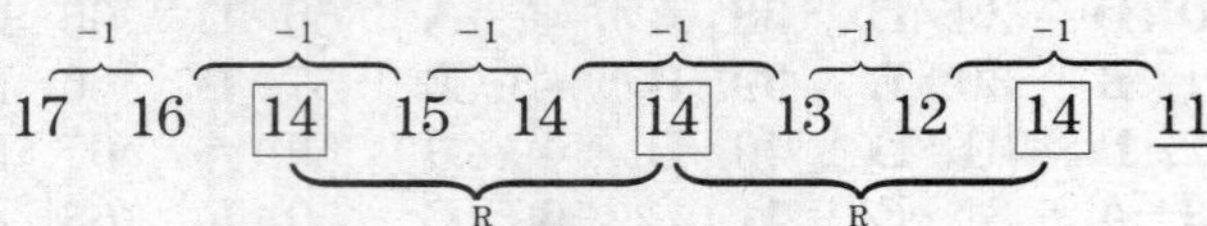

5. **C** Here again is a complex rule, but this time with a repetition: – 5, + 7, R

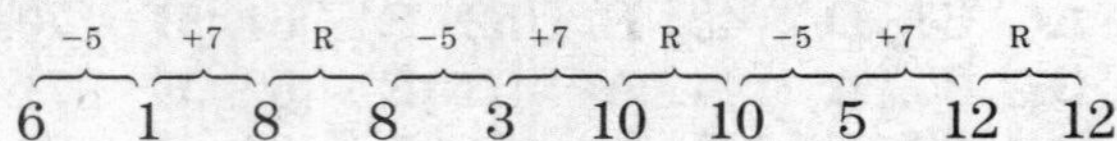

6. **A** This series employs a *variable* subtractor starting with – 12, – 11, – 10 . . . and so on.
7. **B** Here is an example of two alternating series, one increasing by 5; the other decreasing by 2.
8. **D** The rule for this series is + 4, R, + 3, R.
It seems complicated but when you use the loop diagram, it becomes perfectly clear.

+4 R +3 R +4 R +3 R +4
31 35 35 38 38 42 42 45 <u>45</u> <u>49</u>

9. **D** This series uses the guide rule × 3, – 6. If you had a problem with multiplication, you may review the Multiplication/Division Table in Chapter 3.
10. **A** This is an example of how an arbitrary sequence of four numbers (15, 18, 18, 10) keeps repeating.
11. **A** Here you have two alternating mini-series:

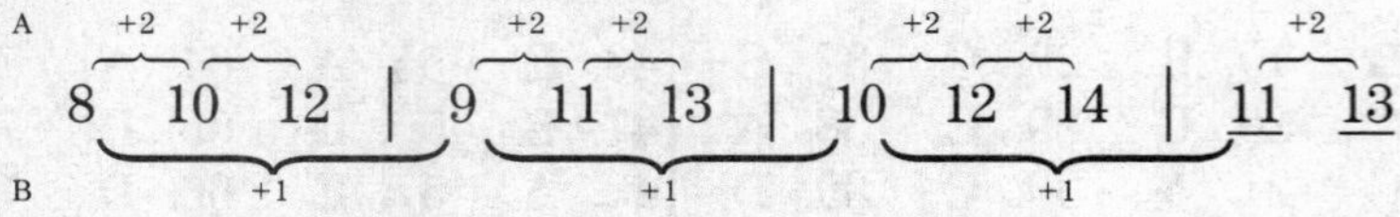

Both Series A and Series B follow a + 2 rule. Each series begins 1 higher than the other.

12. **D** This is a simple – 2 series that has been made difficult to see because of a pair of *arbitrarily* chosen numbers, 6 and 7 that appear after every second number in the series.

13. **D** The complex rule governing the series combines addition, multiplication, and subtraction.
It is + 3, × 2, – 1.
14. **D** To go from one number to the next, you have to recognize that a reversal of position has taken place and then apply a – 2 rule.

Reverse −2 Reverse −2 Reverse −2 Reverse

41 14 12 21 19 91 <u>89</u> <u>98</u>

15. **C** You use a *variable* adder as the rule here, starting with + 1, + 3, + 5. Notice that only *odd* numbers are used.
16. **D** Another example of alternating series. One decreases by 2; the other increases by 4.
17. **D** This is a very complex example of two alternating series that would be very difficult to follow without a loop diagram:

+4 +4 +4 +4 +4

36 13 17 35 21 25 34 29 <u>33</u> <u>33</u>

−1 −1 −1

18. **C** A series that follows a – 3 rule, alternates with one that follows a + 1 rule. The arbitrary number <u>21</u> is thrown in after every two numbers just to further test your ability to see patterns. This one would be almost impossible to see without using a loop diagram.

−3 −3 −3

26 [21] 17 23 [21] 18 20 [21] 19 17 [21]

+1 +1

19. **D** Here, a sequence of four numbers 16, 17, 18, 20 keeps repeating. It's easy unless you get careless and select choice A.
20. **B** Each number in this series beginning with 8, is obtained by adding together the two numbers preceding it: 3 + 5 = 8; 5 + 8 = 13; 8 + 13 = 24. In Chapter 3, it was demonstrated how to diagram it:

$$3 + 5 \overset{=}{+} 8 \overset{+}{=} 13 \overset{=}{+} 21 \overset{+}{=} 34 \overset{=}{+} \underline{55} = \underline{89}$$

21. **D** One of the alternating series here, follows a × 2 rule; the other, uses a variable adder, starting with + 7, + 8, and so on.
22. **C** You can analyze this series in different ways. One way is to see it as a succession of three numbers following a changing multiplier. Diagram it this way:

$$2 \times 4 = 8 \;\Big|\; 2 \times 5 = 10 \;\Big|\; 2 \times 6 = 12 \;\Big|\; 2 \times \underline{7} = \underline{14}$$

23. **A** A series following a – 2 alternates with a series following a ÷ 2 rule.
24. **A** This is an example of two alternating series, one using a + 1 rule, and the other a – 1 rule. But it is easy to pick the wrong answer because the numbers are so close.

EVALUATING YOUR PROGRESS

Throughout this book, the importance of evaluating and recording your progress has been stressed, as you study and practice for the Test Battery 460/470. At this point, if you have completed Practice Tests 1 through 5 and have made all the entries on your Personal Progress Record, you are quite familiar with the discussion on Computing Your Score, Guidelines, and the Personal Progress Record. If you wish to review the details of these subjects, refer to pages 58 through 62 or pages 324 through 328.

You have probably seen great improvement in your test scores as indicated on your Personal Progress Record. Are you pleased with your results? You can be certain that you are in a far, far better position than any of your competitors who have not prepared for this test. Good luck!

DIAGNOSTIC CHARTS

The following charts will help pinpoint your weaknesses by making it easy for you to determine what particular type of question in each part of the test is most difficult for you.

Part A—Address Checking

Type of Difference	"D" Questions	Number of "D" Questions Wrong		
		Trial 1	Trial 2	Trial 3
Numbers: transposed	4, 28, 36, 45, 67			
changed	7, 19, 55, 69, 73			
omitted	78			
Directions	9, 10, 51, 58, 70, 77			
Abbreviations: streets, roads, avenues, etc.	25, 33, 60, 64, 68, 71, 85			
states	31, 59			
Spelling: single letters	1, 3, 8, 12, 14, 15, 21, 22, 23, 41, 43, 48, 56, 57, 81, 89, 92			
groups of letters	34, 50, 84, 94			
Total Number of All Types	47			
	Use the columns on the right to enter the question numbers of "A" items you marked "D."			

This chart will help you to pinpoint the kinds of errors you made on Practice Test 6. Use it as directed below after you have taken and marked the test.

The first column on the left, "Type of Difference," contains the categories whereby addresses may differ (see page 63). On the same line across, the second column gives the numbers of the questions that fall within each category. In the third column, you are to enter the numbers of any "A" questions you answered as "D." Do not include questions that you did not do. Checking the addresses you got wrong may reveal a problem on which you will want to work.

After you have made all the entries, you will be able to see the areas in which you need to improve. Then turn to the appropriate parts of Chapter 3: Address Checking—How to Improve Your Score, read them, and practice the drills that can help. For example, if you find you have been making too many errors picking out number differences, read page 88 and do Drills 18 through 21. If you have a problem with single letters because of reversals like *b* and *d*, or if you have been overlooking the differences between *a*, *e*, and *o*, read page 85. Examine the table and work on Drills 10 and 11 if the problem persists.

Remember that this chart is designed for diagnostic purposes and guidance on further practice. It has been drawn so that you can enter the results each time you retake a practice test. In this way you will be able to see how you are progressing. It is not necessary to record your scores here. That is best done by using the Personal Progress Record Card.

Part B—Memory for Addresses

Kind of Address		Number of Questions	Number Wrong		
			Trial 1	Trial 2	Trial 3
Direct:					
	List 1	41			
	List 2	40			
	List 3	42			
Numbered:					
	List 1	47			
	List 2	48			
	List 3	46			

The purpose of this chart is to help you evaluate your performance on the two kinds of memory questions that appear in these memory tests—the questions on the direct (name) addresses and the questions on the numbered addresses. Use the chart as directed below after you have taken and marked the entire test.

The first column on the left, "Kind of Address," is divided by category into "Direct Address" versus "Numbered Address." The second column gives the number of questions in each category on List 1, List 2, and List 3. Use the third column to enter the total number of questions in each category that you answered incorrectly. There is room for you to make additional entries if you take the practice tests more than once.

At a glance, you will be able to see which area you need to concentrate on and how well you are progressing as you take repeat trials. Use Chapter 4 and the drills in it to improve your memory for the direct addresses. Use Chapter 5 for the numbered addresses.

Remember to use the Personal Progress Record Card (Memory for Addresses) on page 430 to keep track of your actual scores as you keep studying and practicing.

Part C—Number Series and Part D—Following Oral Directions

Because of the nature of the questions in these tests, Diagnostic Charts are not provided for them. If you find that you made many errors on these tests, study the techniques suggested in Chapters 6 and 7.

APPENDIX

STATE AND TERRITORY ABBREVIATIONS

Look over the list. It is not necessary to memorize it. Rather, practice your speed and accuracy of perception by looking at two or more adjoining abbreviations at a glance. Then, look away and jot down what you saw. Because many of the abbreviations begin with the same letter, you will be getting good practice in avoiding confusion should they appear on the test.

State	*Abbreviation*	*State*	*Abbreviation*
Alabama	AL	Nebraska	NE
Alaska	AK	Nevada	NV
Arizona	AZ	New Hampshire	NH
Arkansas	AR	New Jersey	NJ
American Samoa	AS	New Mexico	NM
California	CA	New York	NY
Colorado	CO	North Carolina	NC
Connecticut	CT	North Dakota	ND
Delaware	DE	Northern Mariana Islands	CM
District of Columbia	DC	Ohio	OH
Florida	FL	Oklahoma	OK
Georgia	GA	Oregon	OR
Guam	GU	Pennsylvania	PA
Hawaii	HI	Puerto Rico	PR
Idaho	ID	Rhode Island	RI
Illinois	IL	South Carolina	SC
Indiana	IN	South Dakota	SD
Iowa	IA	Tennessee	TN
Kansas	KS	Trust Territory	TT
Kentucky	KY	Texas	TX
Louisiana	LA	Utah	UT
Maine	ME	Vermont	VT
Maryland	MD	Virginia	VA
Massachusetts	MA	Virgin Islands	VI
Michigan	MI	Washington	WA
Minnesota	MN	West Virginia	WV
Mississippi	MS	Wisconsin	WI
Missouri	MO	Wyoming	WY
Montana	MT		

THOROUGHFARE ABBREVIATIONS*

Almost every street address appearing in Part A—Address Checking contains one of the kinds of thoroughfares in the following list. It has been included in this book just so that you may recognize these abbreviations more rapidly when taking the test; don't try to memorize them.

Familiarizing yourself with the abbreviations is especially worthwhile because some of them are quite similar. For example, it is easy to confuse "Rd" and "Dr," or "Ter" and "Trl." Many others begin with the same letter (see the "C's") or have the same number of characters (the "A's").

Merely look the abbreviations over from time to time. Practice your speed and accuracy of perception as suggested for States and Territory Abbreviations.

Thoroughfare	*Abbreviation*	*Thoroughfare*	*Abbreviation*
Alley	Aly	Loop	—
Arcade	Arc	Oval	—
Avenue	Ave	Parkway	Pkwy
Boulevard	Blvd	Pass	—
Branch	Br	Path	—
Bypass	Byp	Pike	—
Campus	—	Place	Pl
Causeway	Cswy	Plaza	Plz
Center	Ctr	Point	Pt
Chase	—	Road	Rd
Circle	Cir	Square	Sq
Concourse	—	Street	St
Court	Ct	Terrace	Ter
Crescent	Cres	Trail	Trl
Curve	—	Turnpike	Tpke
Drive	Dr	Viaduct	Via
Expressway	Expwy	Vista	Vis
Extension	Ext	Walk	—
Freeway	Fwy	Way	—
Highway	Hwy	Wharf	—
Lane	Ln		

* These abbreviations are approved by the U.S. Postal Service for use in addressing mail. That does not mean they are the only ones you will see on the job. People often invent their own versions, such as "Str" instead of "St." It really doesn't matter on the test as long as you can spot whether the abbreviations are "A" or "D" in any particular address line.

INSTRUCTIONS FOR COMPLETING PS FORM 2591, APPLICATION FOR EMPLOYMENT

Please read all the information on this page thoroughly. An incomplete application could have an adverse effect on your employment consideration. Bring the enclosed information including the completed application to the interview.

If your name has changed, please submit a copy of your legal paperwork, marriage license, or divorce papers.

Section A

Items 1 through 11 are self-explanatory.

Section B

ITEM 2 If you are a high school graduate, enter the graduation date. If you possess a high school equivalency diploma, enter the date you received it. If you did not graduate, enter the highest grade completed.

ITEM 5 List any additional training, for example, trade or vocational schools.

Section C

Start with your present employment/unemployment and recall back. Account for all periods in separate blocks. Go back as far as ten years or to your sixteenth birthday, whichever is later. Please given reasons for leaving, i.e., Resignation/Termination. List complete addresses, including zip code.

Section D

If you are claiming veteran preference, please submit a copy of your DD 214.

Sections E and F

These questions are self-explanatory and must be answered. If additional space is needed for your responses, please use the space provided in Section F.

Section G

Read, sign, and date.

Application for Employment

(Shaded Areas for Postal Service Use Only)

The US Postal Service is an Equal Opportunity Employer

Rated Application		Date Rcvd.	Veteran preference has been verified through proof that the separation was under honorable conditions, and other proof as required. (See Section D below.)	Check One:
Rated For	Rating	Time Rcvd.	Type of Proof Submitted & Date Issued	☐ 10 pts. CPS ☐ 10 pts. CP ☐ 10 pts. XP ☐ 5 pts. TP
Signature & Date			Verifier's Signature, Title & Date	

A. General Information

1. Name (First, MI, Last)		2. Social Security No. (SSN)	3. Home Telephone ( )
4. Mailing Address (No., Street, City, State, ZIP)		5. Date of Birth	6. Work Phone ( )
		7. Place of Birth (City & State or City & Country)	
8. Kind of Job Applied for and Postal Facility Name & Location (City & State)	9. Will You Accept: Temporary/Casual (Noncareer) Work ☐ Yes ☐ No	10. When Will You Be Available?	11. Are You Willing to Travel? (Complete only if you are applying for an executive or professional position.) ☐ Yes ☐ No

B. Educational History

1. Name and Location (City & State) of Last High School Attended	2. Are You a High School Graduate? Answer "Yes" if you expect to graduate within the next 9 months, or you have an official equivalency certificate of graduation. ☐ Yes - Month & Year: ☐ No - Highest Grade Completed:

3a. Name and Location of College or University (City, State, and ZIP Code if known. If you expect to graduate within 9 months, give month and year you expect degree.)	Dates Attended		No. of Credits Completed		Type Degree (BA, etc.)	Year of Degree
	From	To	Semester Hrs.	Quarter Hours		

b. Chief Undergraduate College Subjects	Semester Hrs. Completed	Quarter Hours Completed	c. Chief Graduate College Subjects	Semester Hrs. Completed	Quarter Hours Completed

4. Major Field of Study at Highest Level of College Work

5. Other Schools or Training (For example, trade, vocational, armed forces, or business. Give for each: name, city, state, & ZIP Code, if known, of school; dates attended; subjects studied; number of classroom hours of instruction per week; certificates; & any other pertinent information.)

6. Honors, Awards, & Fellowships Received

7. Special Qualifications & Skills (Licenses; skills with machines, patents or inventions; publications - do not submit copies unless requested; public speaking; memberships in professional or scientific societies; typing or shorthand speed, etc.)

Name (First, MI, Last)	Social Security No.	Date

C. Work History

(Start with your present position and go back for 10 years or to your 16th birthday, whichever is later. You may include volunteer work. Account for periods of unemployment in separate blocks in order. Include military service. Use blank sheets if you need more space. Include your name, SSN, and date on each sheet.)

May the US Postal Service ask your present employer about your character, qualifications, and employment record? A "No" will not affect your consideration for employment opportunities.

☐ Yes ☐ No

1. Dates of Employment (Month & Year) From To **Present**	Grade If Postal, Federal Service or Military	Starting Salary/Earnings $ per
Exact Position Title / Average Hours per Week	Number & Kind of Employees Supervised	Present Salary/Earnings $ per
Name of Employer and Complete Mailing Address	Kind of Business (Manufacturing, etc.)	Place of Employment (City & State)
	Name of Supervisor	Telephone No. (If Known) ( )
Reason for Wanting to Leave		
Description of Duties, Responsibilities, & Accomplishments		

2. Dates of Employment (Month & Year) From To	Grade If Postal, Federal Service or Military	Starting Salary/Earnings $ per
Exact Position Title / Average Hours per Week	Number & Kind of Employees Supervised	Present Salary/Earnings $ per
Name of Employer and Complete Mailing Address	Kind of Business (Manufacturing, etc.)	Place of Employment (City & State)
	Name of Supervisor	Telephone No. (If Known) ( )
Reason for Wanting to Leave		
Description of Duties, Responsibilities, & Accomplishments		

3. Dates of Employment (Month & Year) From To	Grade If Postal, Federal Service or Military	Starting Salary/Earnings $ per
Exact Position Title / Average Hours per Week	Number & Kind of Employees Supervised	Present Salary/Earnings $ per
Name of Employer and Complete Mailing Address	Kind of Business (Manufacturing, etc.)	Place of Employment (City & State)
	Name of Supervisor	Telephone No. (If Known) ( )
Reason for Wanting to Leave		
Description of Duties, Responsibilities, & Accomplishments		

Name (First, MI, Last)		Social Security No.	Date
4.	Dates of Employment (Month & Year) From To	Grade If Postal, Federal Service or Military	Starting Salary/Earnings $ per
	Exact Position Title Average Hours per Week	Number & Kind of Employees Supervised	Ending Salary/Earnings $ per
Name of Employer and Complete Mailing Address		Kind of Business (Manufacturing, etc.)	Place of Employment (City & State)
		Name of Supervisor	Telephone No. (If Known) ( )
Reason for Leaving			
Description of Duties, Responsibilities, & Accomplishments			

D. Veteran Preference

Answer all parts. If a part does not apply, answer "no".

	Yes	No
1. Have you ever served on active duty in the US military service? (Exclude tours of active duty for training as a reservist or guardsman.)		
2. Have you ever been discharged from the armed service under other than honorable conditions? You may omit any such discharge changed to honorable by a Discharge Review Board or similar authority. (If "Yes", give details in Section F.)		
3. Do you claim 5-point preference based on active duty in the armed forces? (If "Yes," you will be required to furnish records to support your claim.)		
4. Do you claim 10-point preference? If "Yes," check type of preference claimed and attach Standard Form 15, Claim for 10-Point Veteran Preference, together with proof called for in that form.		

☐ Compensable Disability (Less than 30%) ☐ Compensable Disability (30% or more) ☐ Non-compensable Disability (includes Receipt of the Purple Heart) ☐ Wife/Husband

☐ Widow/Widower ☐ Mother ☐ Other:

5. List for all military service: (Enter N/A if not applicable)

Dates (From - To)	Serial/Service Number	Branch of Service	Type of Discharge

THE LAW (39 U.S. CODE 1002) PROHIBITS POLITICAL AND CERTAIN OTHER RECOMMENDATIONS FOR APPOINTMENTS, PROMOTIONS, ASSIGNMENTS, TRANSFERS, OR DESIGNATIONS OF PERSONS IN THE POSTAL SERVICE. Statements relating solely to character and residence are permitted, but every other kind of statement or recommendation is prohibited unless it either is requested by the Postal Service and consists solely of an evaluation of the work performance, ability, aptitude, and general qualifications of an individual or is requested by a Government representative investigating the individual's loyalty, suitability, and character. Anyone who requests or solicits a prohibited statement or recommendation is subject to disqualification from the Postal Service and anyone in the Postal Service who accepts such a statement may be suspended or removed from office.

Privacy Act Statement: The collection of this information is authorized by 39 USC 401 and 1001. This information will be used to determine your qualifications and suitability for USPS employment. As a routine use, the information may be disclosed to an appropriate government agency, domestic or foreign, for law enforcement purposes; where pertinent, in a legal proceeding to which the USPS is a party or has an interest; to a government agency in order to obtain information relevant to a USPS decision concerning employment, security clearances, contracts, licenses, grants, permits or other benefits; to a government agency upon its request when relevant to its decision concerning employment, security clearances, security or suitability investigations, contracts, licenses, grants or other benefits; to a congressional office at your request; to an expert, consultant, or other person under contract with the USPS to fulfill an agency function; to the Federal Records Center for storage; to the Office of Management and Budget for review of private relief legislation; to an independent certified public accountant during an official audit of USPS finances; to an investigator, administrative judge or complaints examiner appointed by the Equal Employment Opportunity Commission for investigation of a formal EEO complaint under 29 CFR 1613; to the Merit Systems Protection Board or Office of Special Counsel for proceedings or investigations involving personnel practices and other matters within their jurisdiction; and to a labor organization as required by the National Labor Relations Act. Completion of this form is voluntary; however, if this information is not provided, you may not receive full consideration for a position

COMPUTER MATCHING: Limited information may be disclosed to a Federal, state, or local government administering benefits or other programs pursuant to statute for the purpose of conducting computer matching programs under the Act. These programs, include, but are not limited to, matches performed to verify an individual's initial or continuing eligibility for, indebtedness to, or compliance with requirements of a benefit program.

Name (First, MI, Last)	Social Security No.	Date

E. Other Information

	Yes	No
1. Are you a United States citizen?		
2. Are you a citizen of American Samoa or any other territory owing allegiance to the United States?		
3. Are you an alien with permanent residence status. If "yes," be prepared to show Form I-151 or I-551.		
If you answer "yes" to question 4 and/or 5, give details in Section F below. Give the name, address (including ZIP Code) of employer, approximate date, and reasons in each case. ▶ 4. Have you ever been fired from any job for any reason?		
5. Have you ever quit a job after being notified that you would be fired?		
6. Do you receive or have you applied for retirement pay, pension, or other compensation based upon military, postal, or federal civilian service? (If you answer "yes," give details in Section F.)		
7a. Have you ever been convicted of a crime or are you now under charges for any offense against the Law? You may omit: (1) any charges that were dismissed or resulted in acquittal; (2) any conviction that has been set aside, vacated, annulled, expunged, or sealed; (3) any offense that was finally adjudicated in a juvenile court or juvenile delinquency proceeding; and (4) any charges that resulted only in a conviction of a non-criminal offense. **All felony and misdemeanor convictions and all convictions in state and federal courts are criminal convictions and must be disclosed. Disclosure of such convictions are required even if you did not spend any time in jail and/or were not required to pay a fine.**		
7b. While in the military service were you ever convicted by special or general court martial?		
If you answer "Yes" to question 7a and/or 7b, give details in Section F. Show for each offense: (1) Date of conviction; (2) Charge convicted of; (3) Court and location; (4) Action taken. **Note: A conviction does not automatically mean that you cannot be appointed. What you were convicted of, and how long ago, are important. Give all of the facts so that a decision can be made.**		
8. Are you a former Postal Service or Federal Employee not now employed by the US Government? If you answer "Yes", give in Section F, name of employing agency(ies), position title(s), and date(s) employed.		
9. Does the US Postal Service employ any relative of yours by blood or marriage? Postal officials may not appoint any of their relatives or recommend them for appointment in the Postal Service. Any relative who is appointed in violation of this restriction can not be paid. Thus it is necessary to have information about your relatives who are working for the USPS. These include: mother, father, daughter, son, sister, brother, aunt, uncle, first cousin, niece, nephew, wife, husband, mother-in-law, father-in-law, daughter-in-law, sister-in-law, brother-in-law, stepfather, stepmother, stepdaughter, stepson, stepsister, stepbrother, half sister, and half brother. If you answer "Yes" to question 9, give in section F for such relatives: (1) Full name; (2) Present address and ZIP code; (3) Relationship; (4) Position title; (5) Name & location of postal installation where employed.		
10. Are you now dependent on or a user of ANY addictive or hallucinogenic drug, including amphetamines, barbiturates, heroin, morphine, cocaine, mescaline, LSD, STP, hashish, marijuana, or methadone, other than for medical treatment under the supervision of a doctor?		

F. Use This Space for Detailed Answers

(Use blank sheets if you need more space. Include your name, SSN, and date on each sheet.)

G. Certification

Enter number of additional sheets you have attached as part of this application:________ .

I certify that all of the statements made in this application are true, complete, and correct to the best of my knowledge and belief and are in good faith.	Signature of Applicant	Date Signed

Disclosure by you of your Social Security Number (SSN) is mandatory to obtain the services, benefits, or processes that you are seeking. Solicitation of the SSN by the USPS is authorized under provisions of Executive Order 9397, dated November 22, 1943. The information gathered through the use of the number will be used only as necessary in authorized personnel administration processes.

A false or dishonest answer to any question in this application may be grounds for not employing you or for dismissing you after you begin work, and may be punishable by fine or imprisonment. (US Code, Title 18, Sec. 1001). All the information you give will be considered in reviewing your application and is subject to investigation.

PS Form 2591, November 1993 (Page 4 of 4)

*U.S. Government Printing Office: 1993 — 342-723/83819

PERSONAL PROGRESS RECORD

Part A

ADDRESS CHECKING										
Initial Tests							Repeated Tests			
Date	Test	Number Completed	Number Correct –	Number Wrong =	Score	Date	Score	Date	Score
	Diagnostic Practice Test		–	=					
	Practice Test 1		–	=					
	Practice Test 2		–	=					
	Practice Test 3		–	=					
	Practice Test 4		–	=					
	Practice Test 5		–	=					
	Practice Test 6		–	=					

Part B

MEMORY FOR ADDRESSES										
Initial Tests							Repeated Tests			
Date	Test	Number Completed	Number Correct A	Number Wrong	× ¼ =	Points off B	Score (A – B)	Date	Score	Date	Score
	Diagnostic Practice Test				× ¼ =						
	Practice Test 1				× ¼ =						
	Practice Test 2				× ¼ =						
	Practice Test 3				× ¼ =						
	Practice Test 4				× ¼ =						
	Practice Test 5				× ¼ =						
	Practice Test 6				× ¼ =						

Part C

NUMBER SERIES							
Initial Tests				Repeated Tests			
Date	Test	Number Completed	Number Correct (Your Score)	Date	Score	Date	Score
	Diagnostic Practice Test						
	Practice Test 1						
	Practice Test 2						
	Practice Test 3						
	Practice Test 4						
	Practice Test 5						
	Practice Test 6						

Part D

FOLLOWING ORAL DIRECTIONS							
Initial Tests				Repeated Tests			
Date	Test	Number Completed	Number Correct (Your Score)	Date	Score	Date	Score
	Diagnostic Practice Test						
	Practice Test 1						
	Practice Test 2						
	Practice Test 3						
	Practice Test 4						
	Practice Test 5						
	Practice Test 6						

DRILL RECORD CHARTS*

Keeping a record of your drill scores is important. Below are guidelines, with examples, to help you enter and interpret your drill scores. Each example is also shown on the actual Drill Record Chart.

ADDRESS CHECKING												
Initial Drills									Repeated Drills			
Date	Drill Number	Number Done	Number Correct	Number Incorrect	Raw Score	Time Taken	Calculation	Final Score	Date	Score	Date	Score
	SAMPLE	—	80	—	—	—	—	80				
	Drill 1											
	Drill 2											
	Drill 3											
	Drill 4											
	Drill 5											
	Drill 6											
	Drill 7											
	Drill 8											
	Drill 9											
	SAMPLE	No entries needed										
	Drill 10											
	Drill 11											
	Drill 12											
	SAMPLE	10	8	—	—	30 sec.	$8 \times \frac{60}{30}$	= 16				
	Drill 13											
	Drill 14											
	Drill 15											
	Drill 16											
	Drill 17											
	Drill 18											
	Drill 19											
	Drill 20											
	Drill 21											
	SAMPLE	No entries needed										
	Drill 22											
	Drill 23											

* NOTE: If you do not wish to go through the arithmetic, you can get an approximate, but useful, idea of your progress as follows: Merely check the Drill Record Charts to see how many answers you finally get correct (Raw Score) against "Time Taken." If the number of correct answers increases (or even if it stays the same) while the time taken decreases, you know that you are making progress.

ADDRESS CHECKING												
Initial Drills									Repeated Drills			
Date	Drill Number	Number Done	Number Correct	Number Incorrect	Raw Score	Time Taken	Calcu-lation	Final Score	Date	Score	Date	Score
	SAMPLE	20	18	2	16	80 sec.	$16 \times \frac{60}{80}$	= 12				
	Drill 24											
	Drill 25											
	Drill 26											
	Drill 27											
	Drill 28											
	Drill 29											
	Drill 30											
	Drill 31											

MEMORY FOR *DIRECT* ADDRESSES												
Initial Drills									Repeated Drills			
Date	Drill Number	Number Done	Number Correct	Number Incorrect	Raw Score	Time Taken	Calcu-lation	Final Score	Date	Score	Date	Score
	SAMPLE	No entries needed										
	Drill 1											
	Drill 2											
	Drill 3											
	Drill 4											
	Drill 5											
	Drill 6											
	SAMPLE	40	28	12			$28 - \frac{1}{4}(12) = 25$					
	Drill 7											
	Drill 8											
	Drill 9											
	Drill 10											
	Drill 11											

MEMORY FOR *DIRECT* ADDRESSES

Initial Drills									Repeated Drills			
Date	Drill Number	Number Done	Number Correct	Number Incorrect	Raw Score	Time Taken	Calcu-lation	Final Score	Date	Score	Date	Score
	Drill 12											
	Drill 13											
	Drill 14											
	Drill 15											
	Drill 16											
	Drill 17											
	Drill 18											
	Drill 19											
	Drill 20											
	Drill 21											
	Drill 22											

MEMORY FOR *NUMBERED* ADDRESSES

Initial Drills									Repeated Drills			
Date	Drill Number	Number Done	Number Correct	Number Incorrect	Raw Score	Time Taken	Calcu-lation	Final Score	Date	Score	Date	Score
	SAMPLE	No entries needed										
	Drill 1											
	Drill 2											
	SAMPLE	44	35	9	—	—	$35 - \frac{1}{3} \times 9 = 32$					
	Drill 3											
	Drill 4											
	Drill 5											
	Drill 6											
	Drill 7											
	Drill 8											
	Drill 9											
	Drill 10											
	Drill 11											
	Drill 12											

MEMORY FOR *NUMBERED* ADDRESSES												
Initial Drills								Repeated Drills				
Date	Drill Number	Number Done	Number Correct	Number Incorrect	Raw Score	Time Taken	Calcu-lation	Final Score	Date	Score	Date	Score
	SAMPLE	44	36	8	—	—	$36 - \frac{1}{4} \times 8 = 34$					
	Drill 13											
	Drill 14											
	Drill 15											
	Drill 16											
	Drill 17											
	Drill 18											
	Drill 19											
	Drill 20											
	Drill 21											
	Drill 22											
	Drill 23											
	Drill 24											
	Drill 25											
	Drill 26											
	Drill 27											

Address Checking

The drills in Chapter 3 are designed to help you develop skills in different categories. Although all of them contribute to your progress and are relevant to how well you do on the address checking part of the exam, do not try to compare the results of one drill to another. That would be like judging a ballplayer's batting average by examining his fielding average. Both skills are important to his overall ability as a ballplayer, but they are, of course, entirely different. Rather, compare your results from one trial of a drill to another trial of the same drill.

Drills 1–9: Pencil Markings. Enter in the column marked Number Correct the number of satisfactory marks you make during 1 minute. Because the timing is constant (1 minute), your Final Score will be the same.

Sample: Assume that you made 80 satisfactory marks in 1 minute on Drill 1. Your score would be 80.

Drills 10–12: No entries are needed.

Drills 13–17: Word Differentiation. The time you need to complete each of these drills will keep decreasing as you build speed. Use the formula below to adjust your score so that it comes out in terms of correct answers per minute. In this way, the scores you make on Drills 13 to 17 can be compared with each other more accurately.

Formula: *Your Final Score*

$$= \text{Number of Correct Answers} \times \frac{60 \text{ (seconds)}}{\text{Time Taken (seconds)}}$$

Sample: On Drill 13, assume you had 8 correct answers in a 30-second trial test.

$$\textit{Your Final Score} = 8 \times \frac{60}{30} = 16$$

Drills 18–21: Number Differentiation. Use the same instructions as for Drills 13 to 17 above.

Drills 22 and 23. No entries are needed.

Drills 24–29: Eye Span. On these drills, you are checking complete addresses, the same as you do on the practice tests. They are rated like Drills 13 to 17 and Drills 18 to 21, but with one additional step:

Step 1: Number Right – Number Wrong = Raw Score

$$\text{Step 2: Raw Score} \times \frac{60 \text{ (seconds)}}{\text{Time Taken (seconds)}} = \text{Final Score}$$

Sample: Assume you had 18 correct answers and 2 wrong ones when you did Drill 24, and that it took you 80 seconds to do it.

Step 1: 18 − 2 = 16 (Raw Score)

$$\text{Step 2: } 16 \times \frac{60}{80} = 12 \text{ (Final Score)}$$

Drills 30 and 31: Regression. Use the same instructions as for Drills 24 to 29 above.

Memory for Addresses

Although the drills in Chapters 4 and 5 (like the address checking drills) are arranged by category, the results on most of them can be compared to each other.

Direct Name Addresses

Drills 1–6: Association. No entries are needed.

Drills 7–12: Association and Imagery, Loci, Reduction Coding.

Formula: *Your Final Score* = Number Correct − ¼ of the Number Wrong

Sample: Assume you got 28 questions correct and 12 incorrect. Take ¼ of the number incorrect, ¼ (12) = 3, and subtract this from the number correct, 28. The answer is 25.

Drills 13–22: Making Up Stories and Slogans. Use the same scoring method as for Drills 7 through 12, but make sure that only the letters that are placed in the *original* positions shown in the questions are counted as correct.

Numbered Addresses

Drills 1 and 2. No entries are needed.

Drills 3–12: Using Four-Digit Chunks. The ability to remember four-digit chunks is common to all categories of these drills. However, because the number of chunks and other conditions vary, compare your scores only within the *same* category: Drills 3 to 5, Drills 6 to 8, and so on.

The scoring formula is the same for all Drills 3 to 17. It reflects the fact that you have four choices instead of five. The formula to use is:

Formula: *Your Final Score* = Number Right − ⅓ of the Number Wrong

Sample: Assume that you answered 35 of the 44 questions in Drill 3 correctly. Your Score = 35 − ⅓ × 9 = 32

Drills 13–27: simulates all five boxes. These drills are designed to be answered using any or all of the memory techniques explained in Chapters 4 and 5, not just chunking. The regular formula for scoring is applied.

Formula: *Your Final Score* = Number Right − ¼ of the Number Wrong

Sample: Assume that you answered 36 of the 44 questions in Drill 23 correctly. Your Score = 36 − ¼ × 8 = 34

Checklist 1—Directions and Important Vocabulary

The following list includes directions that have appeared frequently on past Examinations, and also directions that may appear on future tests. The directions have been arranged according to type, together with the words that may appear in each. (Words separated by a dash are opposites; a word in parentheses has the same meaning as the one it follows.)

Type of Direction	*Words Used*
1. Position	up—down; above—below; inside—outside; left—right; beginning—end; before—after (following); first—last; right-hand—middle (center)—left-hand; low—high; next to (alongside) (beside) (adjoining); under—over; vertical—horizontal
2. Counting	first, second, third, fourth, fifth, sixth, seventh, eighth, ninth, tenth; few—many; more—less; highest—lowest
3. Shapes	□ ▭ △ ○ X — square (box); rectangle; triangle; circle; cross; dash; straight—curved; open—closed; thin—thick; figure
4. Size	small; medium; large
5. General comparison	same (identical)—different (opposite)
6. Arithmetic	add, subtract, multiply, divide; remainder (difference); total (sum); odd—even

Miscellaneous words (arranged alphabetically): blank, bracket, change, combination, draw, each, encircle, every, except, figure, indicated (shown), instruction, letter, locate (find), next, nothing, otherwise, package, parentheses, previous, represents, results, sample, space, underline, write.

Checklist 2—Knowledge of Common Measures

First of all, let us again make it clear that the test on Following Oral Directions does *not* require you to possess any *special* knowledge. Such a requirement would defeat the very purpose of this exam, which is to see how well you can follow orders that *most of us* should be able to understand. The persons preparing this test do not want to confuse the issue by making special knowledge a requirement. Nevertheless, the directions occasionally include a concrete fact you do have to know, for example, the number of feet in a yard or the sequence of months in a year (see the directions for line 18 of the Diagnostic Practice Test).

Even though you will probably know most of the "common knowledge" items that may come up on the test, this section has been prepared to give you some extra insurance for a perfect score. The checklist will allow you to quickly review some measures and other items we use continually in everyday life.

Time

60 seconds = 1 minute
60 minutes = 1 hour
24 hours = 1 day
A.M. is the period from 12 midnight to 12 noon.
P.M. is the period from 12 noon to 12 midnight.
7 days = 1 week
52 weeks = 1 year
12 months = 1 year

Distance

12 inches = 1 foot
3 feet = 1 yard
5,280 feet = 1 mile

Dry Weight

16 ounces = 1 pound
2,000 pounds = 1 ton

Liquid Measure

16 ounces = 1 pint
2 pints = 1 quart
4 quarts = 1 gallon

Checklist 3—Miscellaneous Facts

Important Holidays

New Year's Day—January
Martin Luther King Jr.'s Birthday—January
Lincoln's Birthday—February
Washington's Birthday—February
Presidents' Day—February
Memorial Day—May
Independence Day—July
Labor Day—September
Columbus Day—October
Election Day—November
Veterans' Day—November
Thanksgiving—November
Christmas—December

Facts About the United States

Has 50 states.
Declared independence from England in 1776.
Boundaries: North—Canada
South—Mexico
East—Atlantic Ocean
West—Pacific Ocean

NOTES

NOTES

NOTES

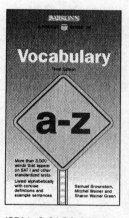

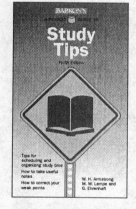